W9-DAS-060

THE
NEW AMERICAN NATION

1775–1820

*A Twelve-Volume
Collection of Articles
on the Development
of the Early American
Republic*

Edited by

PETER S. ONUF
UNIVERSITY OF VIRGINIA

A GARLAND SERIES

THE NEW AMERICAN NATION
1775–1820

Volume
3

★

THE
REVOLUTION
IN THE STATES

Edited with an
Introduction by

PETER S. ONUF

GARLAND PUBLISHING, INC.
NEW YORK & LONDON
1991

Library of Congress Cataloging-in-Publication Data

The Revolution in the states / edited with an introduction by Peter S. Onuf.
   p.   cm. — (New American nation, 1776–1815 ; v. 3)
   Includes bibliographical references.
   ISBN 0-8153-0438-2 (alk. paper) : $49.99
   1. United States—Politics and government—Revolution, 1775–1783. 2. United States—History—Revolution—1775–1783—Social aspects. I. Onuf, Peter S. II. Series.
   E. 164.N45   1991 vol. 3
   [E210]
   973s—dc20   91-14591
   [973.3]   CIP

Printed on acid-free, 250-year-life paper.
Manufactured in the United States of America

THE NEW AMERICAN NATION, 1775–1820

EDITOR'S INTRODUCTION

This series includes a representative selection of the most interesting and influential journal articles on revolutionary and early
national America. My goal is to introduce readers to the wide
range of topics that now engage scholarly attention. The essays in
these volumes show that the revolutionary era was an extraordi-
narily complex "moment" when the broad outlines of national
history first emerged. Yet if the "common cause" brought Americans together, it also drove them apart: the Revolution, historians
agree, was as much a civil war as a war of national liberation. And,
given the distinctive colonial histories of the original members of
the American Union, it is not surprising that the war had profoundly different effects in different parts of the country. This
series has been designed to reveal the multiplicity of these
experiences in a period of radical political and social change.

Most of the essays collected here were first published within
the last twenty years. This series therefore does *not* recapitulate
the development of the historiography of the Revolution. Many c
the questions asked by earlier generations of scholars now see
misconceived and simplistic. Constitutional historians wanted
know if the Patriots had legitimate grounds to revolt: was
Revolution "legal"? Economic historians sought to assess
costs of the navigation system for American farmers and
chants and to identify the interest groups that promoted
tance. Comparative historians wondered how "revolutiona'
Revolution really was. By and large, the best recent w(
ignored these classic questions. Contemporary scholar
stead draws its inspiration from other sources, most n
which is the far-ranging reconception and reconstr
prerevolutionary America by a brilliant generation (
historians.

Bernard Bailyn's *Ideological Origins of the Americai*
(1967) was a landmark in the new historical writin;
politics. As his title suggests, Bailyn was less '
constitutional and legal arguments as such than in '
or political language that shaped colonists' per(

responses to British imperial policy. Bailyn's great contribution was to focus attention on colonial political culture; disciples and critics alike followed his lead as they explored the impact—and limits—of "republicanism" in specific colonial settings. Meanwhile, the social historians who had played a leading role in the transformation of colonial historiography were extending their work into the late colonial period and were increasingly interested in the questions of value, meaning, and behavior that were raised by the new political history. The resulting convergence points to some of the unifying themes in recent work on the revolutionary period presented in this series.

A thorough grounding in the new scholarship on colonial British America is the best introduction to the history and historiography of the Revolution. These volumes therefore can be seen as a complement and extension of Peter Charles Hoffer's eighteen-volume set, *Early American History*, published by Garland in 1987. Hoffer's collection includes numerous important essays essential for understanding developments in independent America. Indeed, only a generation ago—when the Revolution generally was defined in terms of its colonial origins—it would have been hard to justify a separate series on the "new American nation." But exciting recent work—for instance, on wartime mobilization and social change, or on the Americanization of republican ideology during the great era of state making and constitution writing—has opened up new vistas. Historians now generally agree that the revolutionary period saw far-reaching and profound changes, that is, a "great transformation," toward a more recognizably modern America. If the connections between this transformation and the actual unfolding of events often remain elusive, the historiographical quest for the larger meaning of the war and its aftermath has yielded impressive results.

To an important extent, the revitalization of scholarship on revolutionary and early national America is a tribute to the efforts and expertise of scholars working in other professional disciplines. Students of early American literature have made key contributions to the history of rhetoric, ideology, and culture; political scientists and legal scholars have brought new clarity and sophistication to the study of political and constitutional thought and practice in the founding period. Kermit L. Hall's superb Garland series, *United States Constitutional and Legal History* (20 volumes, 1985), is another fine resource for students and scholars interested in the founding. The sampling of recent work in various disciplines offered in these volumes gives a sense of the interpretative possibilities of a crucial period in American history that is now getting the kind of attention it has long deserved.

Peter S. Onuf

INTRODUCTION

The movement for independence precipitated massive changes in the political life of the American states. As more and more Americans became active in public affairs, popular expectations and aspirations escalated. The exigencies of Patriot mobilization led to a proliferation of new forms of political organization and action. It was the radical expansion of the public realm, as Hannah Arendt emphasized in *On Revolution* (1963), that made the American Revolution truly revolutionary. Committees and conventions organized the war effort on a local and regional level, while newly constituted state governments made extraordinary new demands on taxpayers and conscripted citizens for the war effort. This politicization process, however, was not uniformly successful. In many areas, including Queens County, New York, the eastern shore of Maryland, and the lower South, Patriot mobilization efforts met stiff resistance from hostile local populations.

In his influential comparative study of late-eighteenth-century revolutions, R. R. Palmer argued that the Americans' most important contribution to political thought and practice was the constituent convention. Beginning with Massachusetts (1780), constitution writers developed a sequence of steps—the election of convention delegates, drafting, and popular ratification—that helped establish the legitimacy of the new state governments. Most studies of this process, including Willi Paul Adams's comprehensive *The First American Constitutions* (1980), emphasize the progressive development of more complex, less democratic charters, climaxing with the Pennsylvania Constitution of 1790. But what is most remarkable is the extraordinary outpouring of commentary and criticism inspired by the ongoing process of constitution making. These debates, reflecting and stimulating the spread of political participation, are brilliantly recapitulated in Gordon Wood's *Creation of the American Republic* (1969).

One revealing measure of mass politicization is the transformation of the social character of the legislatures, best chronicled in a series of important works by Jackson Turner Main. The exile or neutralization of Loyalists in the old colonial ruling classes opened up new opportunities for ambitious politicians, including a significant number of middling farmers, merchants, and mechanics who had been effectively excluded from provincial politics. In addition to sponsoring widespread participation in local resistance organizations, Patriot leaders sought greater constituency support by enlarging the state legislatures and making them more socially and geographically representative.

The new state legislatures hoped to strengthen their authority by extending the suffrage and making government more accessible and responsive, for instance, by electoral reapportionment or by relocating state capitals. During the war years, however, the goal of inclusiveness was balanced by the proscription and exclusion of Tories and other putative enemies of the Revolution. Redefining the limits of citizenship in the aftermath of the war as Loyalists sought to regain their civil rights under the terms of the Peace of Paris (1783) constituted one of the most controversial challenges to the state governments. The very policies that had sustained Revolutionary solidarity generated deep divisions in the postwar period. So too, popular demands for relief from widespread economic distress came into conflict with the high taxes and conservative fiscal policies recommended by creditors and overseas traders.

Despite the continuing process of constitutional reform, the effectiveness of the new state governments was limited by political cross-pressures and rising popular expectations. The most conspicuous failure of state authority was in frontier regions, where separatists sought to establish their own state governments. Vermont, the only durable new state movement, demonstrated the problematic character of old state jurisdictional pretensions. The renegade republic also showed how a responsive legal system, adapted to the needs of local farmers and speculators, could secure broad popular support.

The essays in this volume reveal the distinctive contexts of political experience from state to state as well as regions outside of Patriot control such as royal Georgia and independent Vermont. Whatever the local circumstances, however, all governments faced the common problems of securing their jurisdiction, mobilizing popular resources, and meeting external threats in a period of Revolutionary transformation. These studies suggest ways in which constitutional developments, political exigencies, and the experience of war converged.

Peter S. Onuf

ADDITIONAL READING

Willi Paul Adams. *The First American Constitutions: Republican Ideology and the Making of the State Constitutions in the Revolutionary Era.* Chapel Hill: University of North Carolina Press, 1980.

Hannah Arendt. *On Revolution.* New York: Viking, 1963.

Richard Buel, Jr. *Dear Liberty: Connecticut's Mobilization for the Revolutionary War.* Middletown, CT: Wesleyan University Press, 1980.

Edward Countryman. *A People in Revolution: The American Revolution and Political Society in New York, 1760–1790.* Baltimore: Johns Hopkins University Press, 1981.

Eric Foner. *Tom Paine and Revolutionary America.* New York: Oxford University Press, 1976.

Robert A. Gross. *The Minutemen and Their World.* New York: Hill & Wang, 1976.

Ronald Hoffman. *A Spirit of Dissension: Economics, Politics, and the Revolution in Maryland.* Baltimore: Johns Hopkins University Press, 1973.

―――― and Peter J. Albert, eds. *Sovereign States in an Age of Uncertainty.* Charlottesville: University Press of Virginia, 1981.

Jackson Turner Main. *Political Parties Before the Constitution.* Chapel Hill: University of North Carolina Press, 1973.

――――. *The Upper House in Revolutionary America, 1763–1788.* Madison: University of Wisconsin Press, 1967.

R. R. Palmer. *The Age of the Democratic Revolution: A Political History of Europe and America, 1760–1800.* 2 vols. Princeton, NJ: Princeton University Press, 1959–64.

J. R. Pole. *Political Representation in America and the Origins of the American Republic.* New York: St. Martin's Press, 1966.

Gordon S. Wood. *The Creation of the American Republic, 1776–1787.* Chapel Hill: University of North Carolina Press, 1969.

CONTENTS

Volume 3—The Revolution in the States

Joseph S. Tiedemann, "Patriots by Default: Queens County, New York, and the British Army, 1776–1783," *William and Mary Quarterly*, 1986, 43(1) (Third Series):135–63.

Mark Edward Lender, "The Conscripted Line: The Draft in Revolutionary New Jersey," *New Jersey History*, 1985, 103(1–2): 22–45.

J. R. Pole, "Suffrage Reform and the American Revolution in New Jersey," *Proceedings of the New Jersey Historical Society*, 1956, 74(3):173–194.

O. S. Ireland, "The Crux of Politics: Religion and Party in Pennsylvania, 1778–1789," *William and Mary Quarterly*, 1985, 42(4) (Third Series):453–475.

John K. Alexander, "The Fort Wilson Incident of 1779: A Case Study of the Revolutionary Crowd," *William and Mary Quarterly*, 1974, 31(4) (Third Series):589–612.

Emory G. Evans, "Private Indebtedness and the Revolution in Virginia, 1776 to 1796," *William and Mary Quarterly*, 1971, 28(3) (Third Series):349–374.

John R. Van Atta, "Conscription in Revolutionary Virginia: The Case of Culpepper County, 1780–1781," *Virginia Magazine of History and Biography*, 1984, 92(3):263–281.

Drew R. McCoy, "The Virginia Port Bill of 1784," *Virginia Magazine of History and Biography*, 1975, 83(3):288–303.

Patrick J. Furlong, "Civilian-Military Conflict and the Restoration of the Royal Province of Georgia, 1778–1782," *Journal of Southern History*, 1972, 38(3):415–442.

William W. Abbot, "The Structure of Politics in Georgia: 1782–1789," *William and Mary Quarterly*, 1957, 14(1)(Third Series):47–65.

ACKNOWLEDGMENTS

Volume 3—The Revolution in the States

Jackson Turner Main, "Government by the People: The American Revolution and the Democratization of the Legislatures," *William and Mary Quarterly*, 1966, 23(3) (Third Series):391–407. Originally appeared in the *William and Mary Quarterly*. Courtesy of Yale University Sterling Memorial Library.

Rosemarie Zagarri, "Representation and the Removal of State Capitals, 1776–1812," *Journal of American History*, 1988, 74(4):1239–1256. Reprinted with the permission of the *Journal of American History*. Courtesy of Yale University Sterling Memorial Library.

Peter S. Onuf, "State-Making in Revolutionary America: Independent Vermont as a Case Study," *Journal of American History*, 1981, 67(4):797–815. Reprinted with the permission of the *Journal of American History*. Courtesy of Yale University Sterling Memorial Library.

Michael A. Bellesiles, "The Establishment of Legal Structures on the Frontier: The Case of Revolutionary Vermont," *Journal of American History*, 1986–87, 73(4):895–915. Reprinted with the permission of the *Journal of American History*. Courtesy of Yale University Sterling Memorial Library.

Ronald Lettieri and Charles Wetherell, "The New Hampshire Committees of Safety and Revolutionary Republicanism, 1775–1784," *Historical New Hampshire*, 1980, 35(3):241–283. Reprinted with the permission of the New Hampshire Historical Society. Courtesy of the New Hampshire Historical Society.

Oscar Handlin and Mary F. Handlin, "Revolutionary Economic Policy in Massachusetts," *William and Mary Quarterly*, 1947, 4(1) (Third Series):3–26. Originally appeared in the *William and Mary Quarterly*. Courtesy of Yale University Sterling Memorial Library.

John L. Brooke, "To the Quiet of the People: Revolutionary Settlements and Civil Unrest in Western Massachusetts, 1774–1789," *William and Mary Quarterly*, 1989, 46(3): (Third Series):425–462. Originally appeared in the *William and Mary Quarterly*. Courtesy of the *William and Mary Quarterly*.

Oscar Zeichner, "The Rehabilitation of Loyalists in Connecticut," *New England Quarterly*, 1938, 11(2):308–330. Reprinted with the permission of the *New England Quarterly*. Courtesy of Yale University Sterling Memorial Library.

Edward Countryman, "Consolidating Power in Revolutionary America: The Case of New York, 1775–1783," *Journal of Interdisciplinary History*, 1976, 6(4):645–677. Reprinted with the permission of the Massachusetts Institute of Technology and the editors of the *Journal of Interdisciplinary History*. Courtesy of Yale University Sterling Memorial Library.

Bernard Friedman, "Hugh Hughes, a Study in Revolutionary Idealism," *New York History*, 1983, 64(3):228–259. Reprinted with the permission of the New York State Historical Association. Courtesy of Yale University Sterling Memorial Library.

Sung Bok Kim, "Impact of Class Relations and Warfare in the American Revolution: The New York Experience," *Journal of American History*, 1982, 69(2):326–346. Reprinted with the permission of the *Journal of American History*. Courtesy of Yale University Sterling Memorial Library.

Joseph S. Tiedemann, "Patriots by Default: Queens County, New York, and the British Army, 1776–1783," *William and Mary Quarterly*, 1986, 43(1) (Third Series):35–63. Originally appeared in the *William and Mary Quarterly*. Courtesy of Yale University Sterling Memorial Library.

Mark Edward Lender, "The Conscripted Line: The Draft in Revolutionary New Jersey," *New Jersey History*, 1985, 103(1-2):22–45. Reprinted with the permission of the New Jersey Historical Association. Courtesy of Yale University Sterling Memorial Library.

J. R. Pole, "Suffrage Reform and the American Revolution in New Jersey," *Proceedings of the New Jersey Historical Society*, 1956, 74(3):173–194. Reprinted with the permission of the New Jersey Historical Society. Courtesy of Yale University Sterling Memorial Library.

O. S. Ireland, "The Crux of Politics: Religion and Party in Pennsylvania, 1778–1789," *William and Mary Quarterly*, 1985, 42(2) (Third Series):453–475. Originally appeared in the *William and Mary Quarterly*. Courtesy of Yale University Sterling Memorial Library.

John K. Alexander, "The Fort Wilson Incident of 1779: A Case Study of the Revolutionary Crowd," *William and Mary Quarterly*, 1974, 31(4) (Third Series):589–612. Originally appeared in the *William and Mary Quarterly*. Courtesy of Yale University Sterling Memorial Library.

Emory G. Evans, "Private Indebtedness and the Revolution in Virginia, 1776 to 1796," *William and Mary Quarterly*, 1971, 28(3) (Third Series):349–374. Originally appeared in the *William and Mary Quarterly*. Courtesy of Yale University Sterling Memorial Library.

John R. Van Atta, "CONSCRIPTION IN REVOLUTIONARY VIRGINIA: The Case of Culpepper County, 1780–1781," *Virginia Magazine of History and Biography*, 1984, 92(3):263–281. Reprinted with the permission of the Virginia Historical Society. Courtesy of Yale University Sterling Memorial Library.

Drew R. McCoy, "The Virginia Port Bill of 1784," *Virginia Magazine of History and Biography*, 1975, 83(3):288–303. Reprinted with the permission of the Virginia Historical Society. Courtesy of Yale University Sterling Memorial Library.

Patrick J. Furlong, "Civilian-Military Conflict and the Restoration of the Royal Province of Georgia, 1778–1782," *Journal of Southern History*, 1972, 38(3):415–442. Reprinted with the permission of the Southern Historical Association. Courtesy of Yale University Sterling Memorial Library.

William W. Abbot, "The Structure of Politics in Georgia: 1782–1789," *William and Mary Quarterly*, 1957, 14(1) (Third Series):47–65. Originally appeared in the *William and Mary Quarterly*. Courtesy of Yale University Sterling Memorial Library.

Government by the People
The American Revolution and the Democratization of the Legislatures

Jackson Turner Main*

AN article with "democracy" in its title, these days, must account for itself. This essay holds that few colonials in British North America believed in a government by the people, and that they were content to be ruled by local elites; but that during the Revolution two interacting developments occurred simultaneously: ordinary citizens increasingly took part in politics, and American political theorists began to defend popular government. The ideological shift can be traced most easily in the newspapers, while evidence for the change in the structure of power will be found in the make-up of the lower houses during the revolutionary years.

Truly democratic ideas, defending a concentration of power in the hands of the people, are difficult to find prior to about 1774. Most articulate colonials accepted the Whig theory in which a modicum of democracy was balanced by equal parts of aristocracy and monarchy. An unchecked democracy was uniformly condemned.[1] For example, a contributor to the *Newport Mercury* in 1764 felt that when a state was in its infancy, "when its members are few and virtuous, and united together by some peculiar ideas of freedom or religion; the whole power may be lodged with the people, and the government be purely democratical"; but when the state had matured, power must be removed from popular control because history demonstrated that the people "have been incapable, collectively, of acting with any degree of moderation or wisdom."[2] There-

---

* Mr. Main, this year visiting in the University of Maryland, is a member of the Department of History, San Jose State College.

[1] See Richard Buel, Jr., "Democracy and the American Revolution: A Frame of Reference," *William and Mary Quarterly*, XXI (1964), 165-190.

[2] "Z. Y.," Apr. 23, 1764. Other characteristic newspaper articles praising a balanced government and disparaging a democratic one are, "A Son of Liberty," *Providence Gazette, and Country Journal*, Oct. 26, 1771; *Pennsylvania Chronicle, and Universal*

fore while colonial theorists recognized the need for some democratic element in the government, they did not intend that the ordinary people —the *demos*—should participate. The poorer men were not allowed to vote at all, and that part of the populace which did vote was expected to elect the better sort of people to represent them. "Fabricus" defended the "democratic principle," warned that "liberty, when once lost, is scarce ever recovered," and declared that laws were "made for the people, and not people for the laws." But he did not propose that ordinary citizens should govern. Rather, "it is right that men of *birth and fortune,* in every government that is free, should be invested with power, and enjoy higher honours than the people."[3] According to William Smith of New York, offices should be held by "the better Class of People" in order that they might introduce that "Spirit of Subordination essential to good Government."[4] A Marylander urged that members of the Assembly should be "ABLE in ESTATE, ABLE in KNOWLEDGE AND LEARNING," and mourned that so many "little upstart insignificant Pretenders" tried to obtain an office. "The *Creature* that is able to keep a little Shop, rate the Price of an Ell of Osnabrigs, or, at most, to judge of the Quality of a Leaf of Tobacco" was not a fit statesman, regardless of his own opinion.[5] So also in South Carolina, where William Henry Drayton warned the artisans that mechanical ability did not entitle them to hold office.[6] This conviction that most men were incompetent to rule, and that the elite should govern for them, proved a vital element in Whig thought and was its most antidemocratic quality. The assumption was almost never openly challenged during the colonial period.

Whether the majority whose capacity was thus maligned accepted the insulting assumption is another question. They were not asked, and as they were unable to speak or write on the subject, their opinions are uncertain. But the voters themselves seem to have adhered, in practice at least, to the traditional view, for when the people were asked to choose

---

Advertiser (Philadelphia), Aug. 29, Sept. 26, 1768, Aug. 14, 1769; *New-York Gazette: and the Weekly Mercury,* Apr. 23, May 14, 1770; Purdie and Dixon's *Virginia Gazette* (Williamsburg), Oct. 27, 1768; *Connecticut Journal* (New Haven), Mar. 17, 1769; *Newport Mercury,* Nov. 21, 1763.

[3] Rind's *Va. Gazette* (Williamsburg), June 9, 1768.

[4] Dec. 30, 1768, in *Journal of the Legislative Council of the Colony of New-York ... 1743 ... 1775* (Albany, 1861).

[5] *Maryland Gazette* (Annapolis), Dec. 3, 1767.

[6] *South Carolina Gazette* (Charleston), Sept. 21, 1769.

their representatives they seldom elected common farmers and artisans. Instead they put their trust in men of the upper class. In the colonies as a whole, about 30 per cent of the adult white men owned property worth £500 or more. About two thirds of these colonials of means had property worth £500 to £2,000; their economic status is here called *moderate*. The other third were worth over £2,000. Those worth £2,000 to £5,000 are called *well-to-do,* and those whose property was valued at more than £5,000 are called *wealthy.*[7] The overwhelming majority of the representatives belonged to that ten per cent who were well-to-do or wealthy. Government may have been for the people, but it was not administered by them. For evidence we turn to the legislatures of New Hampshire, New York, New Jersey, Maryland, Virginia, and South Carolina.

In 1765 New Hampshire elected thirty-four men to its House of Representatives.[8] Practically all of them lived within a few miles of the coast; the frontier settlements could not yet send deputies, and the Merrimack Valley towns in the south-central part of the colony, though populous, were allotted only seven. New Hampshire was not a rich colony. Most of its inhabitants were small farmers with property enough for an adequate living but no more. There were a few large agricultural estates, and the Portsmouth area had developed a prosperous commerce which supported some wealthy merchants and professional men; but judging from probate records not more than one man in forty was well-to-do, and true wealth was very rare. Merchants, professional men, and the like comprised about one tenth of the total population, though in Portsmouth, obviously, the proportion was much larger. Probably at least two thirds of the inhabitants were farmers or farm laborers and one in ten was an artisan. But New Hampshire voters did not call on farmers or men of average property to represent them. Only about one third of the representatives in the 1765 House were yeomen. Merchants and lawyers were just as numerous, and the rest followed a variety of occupations: there were four doctors and several millers and manufacturers. One third of the delegates were wealthy men and more than two thirds were at least well-to-do. The relatively small upper class of the colony, concen-

---

[7] A discussion of the distribution of property and income is contained in Jackson Turner Main, *The Social Structure of Revolutionary America* (Princeton, 1965).

[8] Biographical information is reasonably complete for 30 of the 34. Genealogies and town histories were the principal sources. The *New Hampshire Provincial and State Papers* contain much useful information, especially probate records, and the *New England Historical and Genealogical Register* is valuable.

3

trated in the southeast, furnished ten of the members. They did not, of course, constitute a majority, and the family background of most of the representatives, like that of most colonials, was undistinguished. Probably nearly one half had acquired more property and prestige than their parents. In another age New Hampshire's lower house would have been considered democratic—compared with England's House of Commons it certainly was—but this was a new society, and the voters preferred the prosperous urban upper class and the more substantial farmers.

New York was a much richer colony than New Hampshire. Although most of its population were small farmers and tenants, there were many large landed estates and New York City was incomparably wealthier than Portsmouth. In general the west bank of the Hudson and the northern frontier were usually controlled by the yeomanry, as was Suffolk County on Long Island, but the east bank from Albany to the City was dominated by great "manor lords" and merchants. The great landowners and the merchants held almost all of the twenty-eight seats in the Assembly.[9] In 1769 the voters elected only seven farmers. Five others including Frederick Philipse and Pierre Van Cortland, the wealthy manor lords from Westchester, were owners of large tenanted estates. But a majority of New York's legislators were townspeople. Merchants were almost as numerous as farmers, and together with lawyers they furnished one half of the membership. The legislators were no more representative in their property than in their occupation. At most, five men, and probably fewer, belonged to the middle class of moderate means. At least 43 per cent were wealthy and an equal number were well-to-do. The members' social background was also exceptional. Ten came from the colony's foremost families who had, for the times, a distinguished ancestry, and two thirds or more were born of well-to-do parents. Taken as a whole the legislators, far from reflecting New York's social structure, had either always belonged to or had successfully entered the colony's economic and social upper class.

New Jersey's Assembly was even smaller than that of New York. The body chosen in 1761, and which sat until 1769, contained but twenty men.[10] Half of these represented the East Jersey counties (near New

---

[9] Especially important for New York biographies are the volumes of wills included among the *Collections* of the New York Historical Society, and the *New York Biographical Record*.

[10] In 1769 four new members were added, and six more were chosen in 1772. The *New Jersey Archives* include several volumes of wills. Tax records, the earliest

York City) which were in general occupied by small farmers, but only three of the ten members came from that class. The others were merchants, lawyers, and large proprietors. Although several of these had started as yeomen they had all acquired large properties. West Jersey, which had a greater number of sizable landed estates, especially in the Delaware Valley region, sent the same sort of men as did East Jersey: three farmers, an equal number of large landowners, and an even larger number of prosperous townsmen, some of whom also owned valuable real estate. Merchants and lawyers made up one half of the membership. As usual, a considerable proportion—perhaps forty per cent—were self-made men, but the colony's prominent old families furnished at least 30 per cent of the representatives. Four out of five members were either well-to-do or wealthy.

In contrast to the legislatures of New Hampshire, New York, and New Jersey, Maryland's House of Delegates was a large body and one dominated by the agricultural interest. Like its northern equivalents, however, its members belonged to the upper class of the colony—in Maryland, the planter aristocracy. The 1765 House supposedly contained over sixty members, but only fifty-four appear in the records.[11] About one half of these came from the Eastern Shore, an almost entirely rural area. Except for Col. Thomas Cresap who lived on Maryland's small frontier, the remainder came from the Potomac River and western Chesapeake Bay counties, where agriculture was the principal occupation but where a number of towns also existed. About one sixth of the Delegates belonged to the yeoman farmer class. Most of these lived on the Eastern Shore. Incidentally they did not vote with the antiproprietary, or "popular," party, but rather followed some of the great planters in the conservative "court" party. As in the northern colonies, a number of the Delegates were *nouveaux riches,* but in Maryland's stable and primarily "Tidewater" society, fewer than one fifth had surpassed their parents in wealth. The overwhelming majority came from the lesser or the great planter class, and probably one third belonged to the colony's elite families. Four fifths were well-to-do or wealthy. Lawyers and merchants (among whom were

---

of which date from 1773, supply data on real estate but not on nonfarm property. They have been microfilmed from originals in the New Jersey State Library, Trenton.

[11] The *Maryland Historical Magazine* contains a great deal of biographical data. Essential are the unpublished tax lists in the Maryland State Archives, Annapolis, and the Maryland Historical Society, Baltimore.

several of the self-made men) furnished about one sixth of the principally rural membership.

Virginia's Burgesses resembled Maryland's Delegates, but they were even richer and of even more distinguished ancestry. The Old Dominion's much larger west helped to make the House of Burgesses twice as large a body, with 122 members in 1773.[12] Small property holders, though they formed a great majority of the voters, held only one out of six seats. Half of the Burgesses were wealthy and four fifths were at least well-to-do. Merchants and lawyers contributed one fifth of the members, much more than their proper share, but most of them were also large landholders and the legislature was firmly in control of the great planters. Indeed the median property owned was 1,800 acres and 40 slaves. Virginia's social structure was quite fluid, especially in the newly-settled areas, but between five sixths and seven eighths of the delegates had inherited their property. A roll call of the Burgesses would recite the names of most of the colony's elite families, who held nearly one half of the seats.

The planters of South Carolina, unlike the Virginians, were unwilling to grant representation to the upcountry, and its House of Commons was an exclusively eastern body.[13] The colony was newer and its society may have been more fluid, for in 1765 between 20 and 40 per cent of the representatives were self-made men. The legislature also differed from its southern equivalents in Maryland and Virginia in that nearly half of its members were merchants, lawyers, or doctors. But these figures are deceptive, for in reality most of these men were also great landowners, as were almost all of the representatives; and prominent old families contributed one half of the members of the House. All were at least well-to-do and over two thirds were wealthy. The rich planters of South Carolina's coastal parishes held a monopoly of power in the Assembly.

These six legislatures, from New Hampshire to South Carolina, shared the same qualities. Although farmers and artisans comprised probably between two thirds and three fourths of the voters in the six colonies,

---

[12] The 1773 legislature was chosen for study because the tax records of 1782, which are the earliest available, would be most nearly valid in determining the property of the members. The Virginia State Library, Richmond, contains the tax records as well as a remarkable collection of local records on microfilm. E. G. Swem, comp., *Virginia Historical Index* (Roanoke, 1934-36), I-II, is useful.

[13] The *South Carolina Historical Magazine* is essential, as is Emily Bellinger Reynolds and Joan Reynolds Faunt, eds., *Biographical Directory of the Senate of South Carolina 1776-1964* (Columbia, 1964). There are some quit rent and probate records in the State Archives building at Columbia.

they seldom selected men from their own ranks to represent them. Not more than one out of five representatives were of that class. Fully one third were merchants and lawyers or other professionals, and most of the rest were large landowners. Although only about 10 per cent of the colonials were well-to-do or wealthy, this economic elite furnished at least 85 per cent of the assemblymen. The mobile character of colonial society meant that perhaps 30 per cent had achieved their high status by their own efforts; but an even larger percentage were from prominent, long-established families.

Collectively these "representatives of the people" comprised not a cross section of the electorate but a segment of the upper class. Although the colonials cherished the democratic branch of their governments, and although a majority may have hoped to make the lower house all powerful, they did not yet conceive that the *demos* should actually govern. The idea of a government by as well as for the people was a product of the Revolution. It should be noted here that Rhode Island and Connecticut are exceptions to this general pattern, though the upper house of Connecticut was composed entirely of well-to-do men. As for Massachusetts, the number of representatives with moderate properties exceeded that in the royal and proprietary colonies; but the Massachusetts legislature was still controlled by the well-to-do. Of the 117 men in the House in 1765, at least fifty-six were not farmers and thirteen were large landowners; of the remaining forty-eight, thirty-seven were ordinary farmers and the occupations of eleven are unknown. Among those representatives whose economic status can be discovered (about nine tenths), well over one half were well-to-do or wealthy and two fifths of these had inherited their property.

Widespread popular participation in politics began during 1774 with the various provincial congresses and other extralegal organizations. Although the majority of these bodies seem to have been made up of men of standing, both artisans and farmers appeared in greater numbers than they had in the colonial legislatures. There were several reasons for this. Whereas heretofore the more recently settled areas of most colonies had been underrepresented—at times seriously so—the legal prohibitions on their sending representatives to the colonial assemblies did not apply to the extralegal congresses, and they chose delegates when they wished. Moreover the congresses were much larger than the colonial assemblies, and consequently the over-all number of men who could be elected was

7

greatly increased. For instance, South Carolina's House of Commons contained forty-eight men in 1772, but almost twice that number attended the first Provincial Congress in December 1774 and four times as many were present in January 1775. By 1775 the western districts were sending about one third of the members. Similarly, nothing now prevented New Hampshire's country villages from choosing representatives, and they seized the opportunity. By the time the fourth Provincial Congress met in New Hampshire, four times as many men attended as had been admitted to the 1773 legislature, and nearly one half of them came from the inland counties.

Perhaps an even more important reason for the greater participation in politics by men of moderate means than simply the enlarged and broadened membership of the Provincial Congresses was that the interior areas often contained no real upper class. They had no choice but to send men of moderate property. Furthermore, many men of the upper classes who had previously held political power were not sympathetic with the resistance movement and either withdrew from politics or did not participate in the extralegal Congresses. At the same time events thrust new men forward, as for example in Charleston where the artisans became increasingly active. As the Revolution ran its course, many new men came to fill the much larger number of civil offices, and new men won fame in battle. These developments were quickly reflected in the composition of the legislatures, and by the time the war ended the legislatures were far different bodies from what they had been in colonial days. At the same time democratic ideas spread rapidly, justifying and encouraging the new order.[14]

With the overthrow of royal government, the previously unrepresented New Hampshire villages hastened to choose representatives to the state legislature. The number of men present in the lower house varied considerably, for some smaller communities were too poor to send a man every year, while others combined to finance the sending of a single delegate; but during the 1780's between two and three times as many attended as before the war. The House chosen in 1786 had eighty-eight

[14] For the development of democratic ideas after 1774, see Merrill Jensen, "Democracy and the American Revolution," *Huntington Library Quarterly*, XX (1957), 321-341. The entrance of many new men into the upper house, and their transformation into more nearly democratic institutions, is emphasized in Main, "Social Origins of a Political Elite: The Upper House in the Revolutionary Era," *ibid.*, XXVII (1964), 147-158. The point will be elaborated in a forthcoming book.

members. The balance of power had shifted into the Merrimack Valley, for fewer than half of the delegates came from the two counties near the coast, and even these included frontier settlements.[15]

The socio-economic composition of the New Hampshire legislature also changed. All but four of the 1765 legislators can be identified, but more than one fifth of the post-war representatives are obscure, and the parentage of very few can be established despite the existence of many town histories, genealogies, and published records. Before the war fewer than one third were farmers, exclusive of large landowners but including the men whose occupation is doubtful; by 1786 at least 50 per cent were yeomen and if those whose occupations are unknown are added, as most of them should be, the proportion rises to over 70 per cent. Merchants and lawyers, who had furnished about one third of the members of the 1765 legislature, now comprised only one tenth of the membership. Similarly men of wealth totalled one third of the former legislature but less than one tenth of the latter. The well-to-do element who had dominated the prewar Assembly with 70 per cent of the seats were now reduced to a minority of about 30 per cent. Thus a very large majority of the new legislature consisted of ordinary farmers who had only moderate properties. Ten members of the prominent old families had seats in the 1765 house; by 1786 there were only four in a body two and one half times as large. Even if the newly-represented towns are eliminated, the trend toward the election of less wealthy and less distinguished representatives remains the same, though the degree of change was less. If only the towns which sent men to both legislatures are considered, one finds that whereas farmers formed between 20 and 30 per cent in 1765, they accounted for 55 to 67 per cent twenty years later. Similarly, in these towns the proportion of representatives having moderate properties rose from 30 per cent to more than twice that. Thus the economic and social character of the members in the lower house had been radically changed.

The pattern of change was much the same in other states. New York's society was fundamentally less egalitarian than that of New Hampshire, having more men with large estates and proportionately fewer areas dominated by small farmers. The agricultural upcountry had not yet extended much beyond Albany to the north and Schenectady to the west, so

[15] Strafford County, which contained the commercial center of Dover, extended north through what are now Belknap and Carroll Counties, then just under settlement.

that most New Yorkers still lived in the older counties. As might be expected the changes which occurred in New York were not as striking as in New Hampshire but they were still obvious. By 1785 the counties west of the Hudson, together with those north of Westchester, increased their representation from about one third to nearly two thirds of the total. That fact alone might not have guaranteed a social or economic change in the composition of the Assembly, for every county had its upper class, but the new legislature differed from the old in many respects. The voters selected far fewer townspeople. In the 1769 Assembly some 57 per cent of the members had been engaged primarily in a nonagricultural occupation; by 1785 the proportion had been halved. Farmers, exclusive of large landowners, had made up 25 per cent of the total in 1769; now they furnished about 42 per cent.[16] In contrast, one half of the 1769 legislators had been merchants and lawyers, but now such men held less than one third of the seats. Similarly the proportion of wealthy members dropped from 43 per cent to 15 per cent, whereas the ratio of men of moderate means increased from probably one seventh to nearly one half. New York's elite families, which had contributed ten out of twenty-eight Assemblymen in 1769, contributed the same number in 1785, but in a House twice as large. Meanwhile the number of men who had started without any local family background, newcomers to New York, increased from two to twenty-three. In general, the yeoman-artisan "middle class," which in colonial days had furnished a half-dozen members, now actually had a majority in the legislature. Under the leadership of George Clinton and others of higher economic and social rank, they controlled the state during the entire decade of the eighties.[17] In New York, as in New Hampshire, the trend was the same even within those counties which had been represented before the Revolution. If Washington and Montgomery counties are eliminated, the proportion of delegates who were well-to-do declines from 86 per cent to 60 per cent.

[16] So many men in the 1785 legislature are obscure that the figure cannot be exact, but it is a safe assumption that those who lived in the country and whose occupations are not given in local histories, genealogies, or other published sources, were farmers. Ordinarily men of importance, or business and professional men, are discussed in such sources, so that if one conscientiously searches the published materials, including of course the wills, most of those men who remain unidentified can be confidently termed farmers of moderate property.

[17] As far as the fathers of these legislators could be identified, 12 of the prewar 28 were merchants, lawyers, and large landowners, as were 12 or possibly 13 of the postwar 66.

New Jersey's lower house, the size of which had increased in stages from twenty members to thirty-nine after the Revolution, retained equal distribution of seats between East and West Jersey. As in New Hampshire and New York, the economic upper class of well-to-do men, which in New Jersey had held three fourths of the seats before the war, saw its control vanish; indeed two thirds of the states' representatives in 1785 had only moderate properties. The typical legislator before the war held at least 1,000 acres; in 1785 the median was about 300 acres. Merchants and lawyers were all but eliminated from the legislature, retaining only a half-dozen seats. The colonial elite, once controlling one third of the votes of the house, now had one eighth; the overwhelming majority of the new legislators were men who had been unknown before the war and whose ancestry, where ascertainable, was uniformly undistinguished. Fully two thirds of the representatives were ordinary farmers, presumably men of more than average ability and sometimes with military experience, but clearly part of the common people. Again these changes occurred not just because new areas were represented but because the counties which had sent delegates in the prewar years now chose different sort of men. In New Jersey, the counties of Cumberland, Salem, Hunterdon, Morris, and Sussex had previously been underrepresented. If these are eliminated, we find that the proportion of men of moderate property rose from 20 per cent to 73 per cent and of farmers (exclusive of large landowners) from 23.5 per cent to 60 per cent.[18]

Southern legislatures were also democratized. Maryland's House of Delegates expanded to seventy-four by 1785, with the addition of a few members from the western counties. As had been true before the war, most of the representatives were engaged in agriculture, the proportion of those with a nonfarm occupation remaining constant at about 20 per cent. The most obvious change in economic composition was the replacement of planters by farmers, of large property owners by men with moderate estates. If the planter is defined as one who held at least twenty slaves or 500 acres, then they formed 57 per cent of the House in 1765 and only 36.5 per cent in 1785, while the farmers increased from 18.5 to 28 per cent. Wealthy men occupied about two fifths of the seats in the pre-Revolutionary period, one sixth after the war, while delegates with moderate property, who had previously formed only one fifth of the total, now comprised one third. The yeoman farmer class, though still lacking a

[18] Those of unknown property or occupation are excluded.

majority, had doubled in numbers while members of the old ruling families, in turn, saw their strength halved.[19] By comparison with the northern states the shift of power was decidedly less radical, but the change was considerable. It was made more obvious, incidentally, by the great contrast between the postwar House of Delegates and the postwar Senate, for the large majority of the Senators were wealthy merchants, lawyers, and planters, who fought bitterly with the popular branch.

The planter class of Virginia, like that of Maryland, did not intend that the Revolution should encourage democracy, but it was unable to prevent some erosion of its power. The great landowners still controlled the lower house, though their strength was reduced from 60 per cent to 50 per cent, while that of ordinary farmers rose from perhaps 13 per cent in 1773 to 26 per cent in 1785. An important change was the decline in the number of wealthy members, who now held one quarter instead of one half of the seats. Power thus shifted into the hands of the lesser planters, the well-to-do rather than the wealthy. Meanwhile men with moderate properties doubled their share, almost equaling in number the wealthy Burgesses. Similarly the sons of the First Families lost their commanding position, while an even larger fraction of delegates were of humble origins. The general magnitude of the change is suggested by the decline in the median property held from 1,800 acres to about 1,100, and from forty slaves to twenty.[20]

Thus, although the planter class retained control of the Burgesses, the people were now sending well-to-do rather than wealthy men, and at least one out of four representatives was an ordinary citizen. A roll call of the House would still recite the familiar names of many elite families, but it would also pronounce some never heard before. The alteration in

[19] The proportion of self-made men in the House seems to have increased from one fifth to one fourth, but information on the delegates' fathers is too incomplete for precision. Material on land and slave ownership is drawn from manuscript census and tax records as well as from the usual secondary materials. The median acreage declined from 1,400 acres to 1,000 acres; the median number of slaves owned decreased from about 40 to 20. My figures are on two thirds of the men. Charles A. Barker gives 2,400 acres as the average for the 1771 legislature. *The Background of the Revolution in Maryland* (New Haven, 1940), 384.

[20] Data for land was obtained on 78 per cent of the 1773 Burgesses and 83 per cent of the delegates in the 1785 house. Percentages for slaves are 70 and 86 respectively. Tax lists beginning in 1782 were the most important source, supplemented by probate records and statements in secondary sources.

the composition of the Virginia legislature undoubtedly sprang in part from the growing influence of westerners, for counties beyond the Blue Ridge sent many more representatives in 1785 than before the war, while the representation from the Piedmont also increased in size. However, the same shift downward also occurred within the older counties, those which had been represented in 1773. If we eliminate from consideration all of the newly-formed counties, we find that delegates with moderate property increased from 13.5 per cent to 23 per cent, and that wealthy ones declined from 48 to 30 per cent, while the proportion of farmers rose from 13 to about 25 per cent.

The South Carolina constitution of 1778 is noted as an expression of conservatism. Its conservatism, however, was much more evident with respect to the Senate than to the House of Representatives, which was now nearly four times as large. Although the eastern upper class refused to grant westerners as many seats in the House as were warranted by their population, the upcountry did increase its share from not more than 6 or 8 per cent (depending on one's definition of where the upcountry started) to nearly 40 per cent. The urban upper class of merchants, lawyers, and doctors dropped to 20 per cent of the total membership in 1785, as compared to 36 per cent in 1765. The agricultural interest greatly increased its influence, the principal gain being made by farmers rather than by planters. A significant change was a reduction in the strength of wealthy representatives, who made up four fifths of those whose property is known in 1765 and but one third twenty years later. The pre-Revolutionary House of Commons seems to have contained not a single man of moderate property, but the postwar representatives included more than fifty such—probably over 30 per cent of the membership. The median acreage held by the 1765 members was certainly over 2,000 and probably a majority owned over 100 slaves each. The lack of tax records makes it impossible to determine what land the 1785 representatives held, but they obviously owned much less; while the median number of slaves was about twenty-five. The scarcity of such records as well as of genealogies and other historical materials also makes it exceedingly difficult to identify any but fairly prominent men. This situation in itself lends significance to the fact that whereas before the Revolution the desired information is available for seven out of eight representatives and even for over two thirds of their parents, data are incomplete concerning 30 per cent of the postwar delegates and most of their parents. Equally significant is the different social make-up of the two bodies. The long-established upper class of the province controlled half of the 1765 house, but less than one fourth of the 1785 legislature. Although most of the representatives were well-to-do, the house was no longer an exclusively aristocratic body, but contained a sizable element of democracy. It should be pointed out that South Carolina was peculiar in that the change in the House was due almost entirely to the admission of new delegates from the west. In those parishes which elected representatives both before and after the war, the proportion of wealthy delegates decreased very slightly, while that of men with moderate property rose from zero to between 7 and 14 per cent.

All of the six legislatures had been greatly changed as a result of the Revolution. The extent of that change varied from moderate in Virginia and Maryland to radical in New Hampshire and New Jersey, but everywhere the same process occurred. Voters were choosing many more representatives than before the war, and the newly settled areas gained considerably in representatives. The locus of power had shifted from the coast into the interior. Voters were ceasing to elect only men of wealth and family. The proportion of the wealthy in these legislatures dropped from 46 per cent to 22 per cent; members of the prominent old families declined from 40 per cent to 16 per cent. Most of these came from the long-established towns or commercial farm areas. Of course many men who were well-to-do or better continued to gain office, but their share decreased from four fifths to just one half. Even in Massachusetts the percentage of legislators who were wealthy or well-to-do dropped from 50 per cent in 1765 to 21.5 per cent in 1784.[21]

Significantly, the people more and more often chose ordinary yeomen or artisans. Before the Revolution fewer than one out of five legislators had been men of that sort; after independence they more than doubled their strength, achieving in fact a majority in the northern houses and

[21] *Economic status of Mass. Representatives (percentages)*

	1765	1784 duplicate towns	1784 total
wealthy	17	8	6.5
well-to-do	33	17	15
moderate	40	55	51.5
unknown	10	20	27

Probably most of those whose property is unknown had only moderate incomes. Similarly the proportion of men from prominent old families dropped from 22 per cent to 6 per cent, college educated delegates from 27 per cent to 9 per cent, and representatives whose fathers were well-to-do from 30 per cent to 10 per cent, the change being greatest in the new towns but occurring everywhere.

TABLE I

ECONOMIC STATUS OF THE REPRESENTATIVES[22]

	N.H., N.Y., and N.J.		Md., Va., and S.C.	
	Prewar (percentages)	Postwar (percentages)	Prewar (percentages)	Postwar (percentages)
Wealthy	36	12	52	28
Well-to-do	47	26	36	42
Moderate	17	62	12	30
Merchants & lawyers	43	18	22.5	17
Farmers	23	55	12	26

constituting over 40 per cent generally. The magnitude of the change is suggested by the fact that the legislators of the postwar South owned only about one half as much property as their predecessors. Also suggestive is the great increase in the proportion of men of humble origin, which seems to have more than doubled. Therefore men who were or had once been a part of the *demos* totalled about two thirds of the whole number of representatives. Clearly the voters had ceased to confine themselves to an elite, but were selecting instead men like themselves. The tendency to do so had started during the colonial period, especially in the North, and had now increased so dramatically as almost to revolutionize the legislatures. The process occurred also in those areas which were represented

[22] This table analyzes the property of about 900 representatives. The economic status of 85 per cent was discovered with reasonable certainty. Most of the rest were dealt with by informed guesswork. No one was admitted to the wealthy category unless their property was certainly known. Lawyers were assumed to be well-to-do, for almost all of them were. Merchants were also considered well-to-do if they lived in an important urban center, but inland shopkeepers were not. Doctors and judges were distributed on similar principles. Artisans were almost always of moderate property. Farmers and those whose occupation was unknown composed the two largest groups. Those who came from the inland, semi-subsistence communities were almost never well-to-do, the exceptions being conspicuous men, so that if nothing was discovered about them they were almost certainly of moderate means. On the other hand those who lived in the well-developed commercial farm areas were often well-to-do, so they were not assigned to any category unless other information was available. The basis for this procedure was derived from extensive study of property holdings as discussed in my *Social Structure of Revolutionary America*. By such an analysis the proportion of unknowns was reduced to 3 1/3 per cent, most of whom were probably of moderate property. They are eliminated in the table. Percentages for occupation are less accurate, especially those for the post-war South.

both before and after the Revolution, as compared with those which were allowed to choose delegates for the first time after the war.

TABLE II

ECONOMIC STATUS OF THE REPRESENTATIVES FROM PRE-REVOLUTIONARY DISTRICTS

	N.H., N.Y., and N.J.		Md., Va., and S.C.	
	Prewar	Postwar	Prewar	Postwar
Wealthy	35	18	50	38
Well-to-do	45	37	38	42
Moderate	20	45	12	20
Merchants & lawyers	41	24	22	18.5
Farmers	25	50	12	22

Although a similar change may not have taken place in Connecticut or Rhode Island, it surely did so in the states of Pennsylvania, Delaware, North Carolina, and Georgia, which have not been analyzed here.

The significance of the change may be more obvious to historians than it was to men of the Revolutionary era. Adherents of the Whig philosophy deplored the trend. They continued to demand a government run by the elite in which the democratic element, while admitted, was carefully checked. Such men were basically conservatives who conceived themselves as struggling for liberty against British tyranny, and who did not propose to substitute a democratical tyranny for a monarchical one.[23] The states, observed a philosophical New Englander in 1786, were "worse governed" than they had been because "men of sense and property have lost much of their influence by the popular spirit of the war." The people had once respected and obeyed their governors, senators, judges, and clergy. But "since the war, blustering ignorant men, who started into notice during the troubles and confusion of that critical period, have been attempting to push themselves into office."[24]

[23] Illustrations of this antidemocratic bias among Whig spokesmen are numerous, e.g., "A faithful Friend to his Country," *Independent Chronicle* (Boston), Aug. 7, 1777; "The Free Republican," *Boston Magazine*, Aug. 1784, pp. 420-423; "Constitutionalist," *Connecticut Courant* (Hartford), Apr. 10, 1786; "Honestus," *Vermont Gazette* (Bennington), Sept. 18, 1786; "Lycurgus," *Massachusetts Spy* (Worcester), July 12, 26, Aug. 2, 1775; Samuel Chase, *Md. Gazette*, Dec. 11, 1777; "Agricola," *Pennsylvania Packet* (Philadelphia), Feb. 6, 1779; "A Citizen of New Jersey," *New Jersey Gazette* (Trenton), Oct. 10, 1785; and *Falmouth Gazette*, Sept. 17, 1785.
[24] *American Herald* (Boston), Dec. 11, 1786.

16

On the other hand democratic spokesmen now rose to defend this new government by the people. A writer in a Georgia newspaper rejoiced in 1789 that the state's representatives were "taken from a class of citizens who hitherto have thought it more for their interest to be contented with a humbler walk in life," and hoped that men of large property would not enter the state, for Georgia had "perhaps the most *compleat* democracy in the known world," which could be preserved only by economic equality.[25] In Massachusetts as early as 1775 "Democritus" urged the voters to "choose men that have learnt to get their living by honest industry, and that will be content with as small an income as the generality of those who pay them for their service. If you would be well represented," he continued, "choose a man in middling circumstances as to worldly estate, if he has got it by his industry so much the better, he knows the wants of the poor, and can judge pretty well what the community can bear of public burdens, if he be a man of good common understanding."[26] "A Farmer" in Connecticut boldly declared it a maxim that the people usually judged rightly, insisted that politics was not so difficult but that common sense could comprehend it, and argued that every freeman could be a legislator.[27]

The change in men might be deprecated or applauded, but it could not be denied, and some found it good. To Jedidiah Morse the government of Virginia still seemed to be "oligarchical or aristocratical,"[28] but to a Virginian a revolution had taken place. The newly-chosen House of Burgesses, wrote Roger Atkinson in 1776, was admirable. It was "composed of men not quite so well dressed, nor so politely educated, nor so highly born as some Assemblies I have formerly seen," yet on the whole he liked it better. "They are the People's men (and the People in general are right). They are plain and of consequence less disguised, but I believe to the full as honest, less intriguing, more sincere. I wish the People may always have Virtue enough and Wisdom enough to chuse such plain men."[29] Democracy, for a moment at least, seemed to have come to Virginia.

[25] *Gazette of the State of Georgia* (Savannah), Jan. 1, 1789.
[26] *Mass. Spy*, July 5, 1775.
[27] *Weekly Monitor* (Litchfield), Aug. 6, 1787. For two more examples see "A Watchman," *Pa. Packet*, June 10, 17, 1776; and *Maryland Journal, and Baltimore Advertiser*, Feb. 18, 1777.
[28] Jedidiah Morse, *The American Geography* . . . (2d ed., London, 1792), 387.
[29] To Samuel Pleasants, Nov. 23, 1776, *Virginia Magazine of History and Biography*, XV (1908), 357.

Representation and the Removal of State Capitals, 1776–1812

Rosemarie Zagarri

Most Americans today assume that the only just form of representation is based on population. This idea has become so pervasive that numerical representation, as it is now called, has been attributed to the Founding Fathers and identified with the cause of republican government. In one of the apportionment cases of the early 1960s, *Reynolds v. Sims*, Chief Justice Earl Warren wrote that "the fundamental principle of representative government in this country is one of equal representation for equal numbers of people, without regard to race, sex, economic status, or place of residence within a State." In a 1983 case involving congressional districts in New Jersey, Justice William Brennan commented that "adopting any standard other than population equality, using the best census data available, would subtly erode the Constitution's ideal of equal representation."[1]

Yet the primacy of numerical representation (or proportional representation, as it was called at the time) in the American political system was by no means established or assured by the United States Constitution. States were represented equally, rather than proportionally, in the upper house of Congress. Furthermore, many states had successful republican governments without having numerical representation in either house of their legislatures. It took many decades before the system was fully accepted, either in principle or in practice.

To assume an anachronistic acceptance of numerical representation is to ignore the extent to which the years during and after the Revolution formed a period of experimentation in politics and governmental structure. At both the state and the national levels, Americans attempted to apply the lessons of the historical past and of their own experience to make government more just and equitable. Yet there were no clear answers, no easy solutions to the dilemmas they faced.

One of their most perplexing problems was in the realm of representation. Who would be represented and in what manner were questions that lay at the heart of republican government. Inequities in representation would reverberate through any

Rosemarie Zagarri is assistant professor of history at the Catholic University of America. The author would like to thank Jefferson Morley, Robert Blobaum, David Thelen, and Susan Armeny for their helpful comments and criticisms.

[1] *Reynolds v. Sims*, 377 U.S. 533 (1964); Stanley L. Kutler, ed., *The Supreme Court and the Constitution: Readings in American Constitutional History* (New York, 1977), 596. *New York Times*, June 23, 1983. Sec A, p. 3; sec. B, p. 10.

subsequent decisions a legislature made. Knowing that injustices had permeated colonial representation, Americans of the revolutionary era sought new means of equalizing representation.

The choice was not simply between the old system of corporate representation, in which a fixed number of legislators was assigned to a geographic unit without regard to the number of people in it, and the innovative notion of proportional representation. They experimented with a third, less well known method—moving a state's capital to a more central location. In the quarter century after the Revolution, capital removal emerged as a more common means of equalizing representation than reapportionment. While only six states of the original thirteen reapportioned their legislatures on the basis of population between 1776 and 1812, eleven moved their seats of government during that period. (See table 1.)

Americans had strong precedents to support their emphasis on centrality. Political philosophers with whom they were familiar had long advocated locating capital cities in the center of countries. Aristotle's *Politics*, for example, described the ideal seat of government as a "common centre, linked to the sea as well as land, and equally linked to the whole of the territory." Frenchman Alexandre Le Maître's 1682 tract, *La Metropolitée*, endorsed a capital fixed in the center of territory within a highly productive, easily defensible region. Central location was thus a highly valued attribute of capital cities.[2]

But Americans gave the concept a peculiarly American twist. James Madison and Thomas Jefferson, among other leading political thinkers, argued that centrality was the principle of equality expressed in geographic terms. Americans envisioned the republic as a circle in which the legislature's meeting place occupied the center. The notion was most explicitly stated by Thomas Paine, who wrote, "A nation is not . . . to be represented by the human body, but it is like the body contained within a circle, having a common centre, in which every radius meets; and that centre is formed by representation."[3] The natural limit of a republic, said Madison in *Federalist* No. 14, "is that distance from the center which will barely allow the representatives of the people to meet as often as may be necessary for the administration of public affairs." Extending the circle metaphor, and drawing on his experience of county-based politics in Virginia, Jefferson saw the center as the source of strength and life for the republic. In the margins of the bill to move Virginia's capital, Jefferson jotted:

> Central . . . Heart—Sun—Ch[ur]ch—C[our]thouse

Just as the heart sustained an individual's life, so the capital was the source of life in a republic. Similarly, just as Virginia's churches and county courthouses repre-

[2] Aristotle, *The Politics of Aristotle*, trans. Ernest Barker (London, 1974), 307; Alexandre Le Maître, *La metropolitée, ou de l'establissement des villes capitales, de leur utilité passive & active, de l'union de leurs parties & de leur anatomie, de leur commerce, &c.* (Amsterdam, 1682), 46.
[3] Thomas Paine, *The Rights of Man* (1791–1792; reprint, Harmondsworth, Eng., 1979), 203.

Table 1
Removal of State Capitals, 1776–1812

State	Date Removal Act Passed	Old Capital	New Capital
Delaware	May 12, 1777	Newcastle	Dover
Virginia	June 12, 1779	Williamsburg	Richmond
Georgia	January 26, 1786	Savannah	Louisville
	December 12, 1804	Louisville	Milledgeville
South Carolina	March 22, 1786	Charles Town	Columbia
North Carolina	August 4, 1788	New Bern	Raleigh
New Jersey	November 25, 1790	Burlington and Perth Amboy	Trenton
New York	March 10, 1797	New York City	Albany
Pennsylvania	March 30, 1799	Philadelphia	Lancaster
	February 21, 1810	Lancaster	Harrisburg
New Hampshire	1808 (de facto)	Portsmouth	Concord
Rhode Island	Rotated	Newport	Newport, Providence, East Greenwich, South Kingston, and Bristol
Connecticut	Rotated	New Haven	New Haven and Hartford

sented the focus of local public life, so the seat of government acted as the focus of public activities within the state.[4]

The demand for physical proximity to the seat of government also flowed naturally from the American concept of actual representation. During the revolutionary crisis, Americans had rejected the British notion of virtual representation—which prescribed that representatives speak for the general good of the community—and articulated their own understanding of the relationship between representatives and constituents. Legislators, they thought, should represent the particular interests of those who elected them; the assembly was to be a microcosm of the larger society. Unlike virtual representation, actual representation was inherently localistic. The people's confidence in their government rested on their ability to know and be known by their representatives. As a result, actual representation could not flourish in a large area.[5]

Furthermore, as inheritors of the Real Whig tradition deriving from John Locke, Viscount Bolingbroke, John Trenchard, and Thomas Gordon, Americans viewed their legislatures with suspicion. Only the people's vigilance could safeguard liberty.

[4] Alexander Hamilton, John Jay, and James Madison, *The Federalist*, ed. Jacob E. Cooke (Middletown, 1961), 85; "Notes concerning the Bill for the Removal of the Seat of Government of Virginia," November 11, 1776, *The Papers of Thomas Jefferson*, ed. Julian P. Boyd (22 vols., Princeton, 1951–), I, 602.
[5] Gordon S. Wood, *The Creation of the American Republic, 1776–1787* (New York, 1969), 162–96, 363–72.

1242   The Journal of American History

If residents did not supervise their representatives closely, their representatives might, as some Pennsylvanians put it in 1787, "pass laws . . . touching the life, liberty and property of the citizens before any steps could be taken to evade the evil."[6] Moving the capital would help preserve the intimacy between people and representatives required by actual representation and the Real Whig tradition.

The spate of removals originated in an impulse transcending state and sectional boundaries. Only the existence of a common set of assumptions about representation can adequately explain the pattern of removals. Yet, to the extent that historians have discussed capital removal at all, they have described it as a function of westward expansion: As more people moved west, they wanted easier access to the seat of government. Removal, historians argue, was just another chapter in the ongoing struggle between sections.[7]

Westward expansion may have been a necessary condition for the removal conflicts to occur, but it is not sufficient to explain the pervasiveness of the pattern. Even small states, such as Delaware and Rhode Island, which had no frontier areas, experienced removal controversies. In certain states, such as New York and North Carolina, the division over removal reflected north-south, much more than east-west, tensions.[8] Moreover, examination of the removal debates within the states reveals no single factor at work. While Antifederalists in Pennsylvania tended to support the idea of removal, those in North Carolina resisted it. While commercial interests in New Hampshire opposed removal, Maryland's merchants masterminded a removal campaign that, though ultimately unsuccessful, succeeded in splitting the state.[9]

Although unique factors in each state determined the outlines of its removal controversy, a shared cluster of assumptions about representation led to the widespread drive for removal. The principles of actual representation as well as the Real Whig tradition seemed to necessitate it. Even more important, it was assumed that placing the legislature in a more central location would promote better attendance by

---

[6] *Philadelphia Independent Gazetteer*, March 8, 1787.

[7] Frederick Jackson Turner, *The Frontier in American History* (New York, 1920), 121; Merrill Jensen, *The New Nation: A History of the United States during the Confederation, 1781–1789* (New York, 1950), 327–29; Jackson Turner Main, *Political Parties before the Constitution* (Chapel Hill, 1973), 355; Fletcher M. Green, *Constitutional Development in the South Atlantic States, 1776–1860: A Study in the Evolution of Democracy* (Chapel Hill, 1930), 164–66. For more general discussions of the function of capital cities, see O. H. K. Spate, "Factors in the Development of Capital Cities," *Geographical Review*, 32 (Oct. 1942), 622–31; James Bird, *Centrality and Cities* (London, 1977); David Lowenthal, "The West Indies Chooses a Capital," in *The Structure of Political Geography*, ed. Roger E. Kasperson and Julian V. Minghi (Chicago, 1969), 350–65; Dieter Prokop, *Urban Core and Inner City*, *Proceedings of the International Study Week, Amsterdam, 11–17 September 1966* (Leiden, 1967), 22–34; Raimondo Strassoldo, "Centre-Periphery and System-Boundary: Culturological Perspectives," in *Centre and Periphery: Spatial Variation in Politics*, ed. Jean Gottmann (Beverly Hills, 1980), 27–61.

[8] Jensen, *New Nation*, 329; Charles R. King, ed., *The Life and Correspondence of Rufus King* (2 vols., New York, 1894), I, 356–57.

[9] Callister Schawn, "William Findley in Pennsylvania Politics," *Western Pennsylvania Historical Magazine*, 20 (Oct. 1937), 37–40; Robert L. Brunhouse, *The Counter-Revolution in Pennsylvania, 1776–1790* (Harrisburg, 1942), 145–55; A Friend of the People, *Candid Appeal to the Freemen of Maryland on the Projected Removal of their Seat of Government* (n.p., 1817), 4–9; Aristides [A. C. Hanson], *Considerations on the Proposed Removal of the Seat of Government, Addressed to the Citizens of Maryland* (Annapolis, 1786); Edward C. Papenfuse, *In Pursuit of Profit: The Annapolis Merchants in the Era of the American Revolution* (Baltimore, 1975), 139, 179.

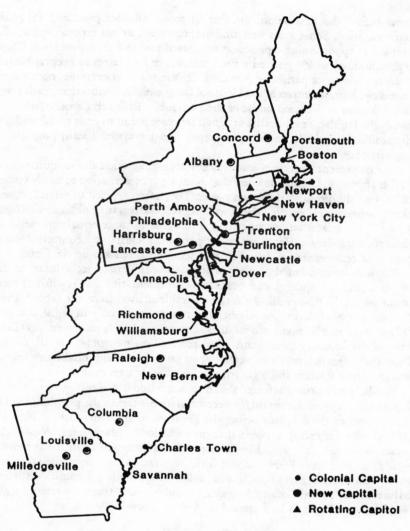

The state capital removal movement, 1776–1812.
Map by Alison Hanham.

representatives from all parts of the state and hence would guarantee more equitable representation. By 1812, however, those assumptions had changed, and the removal movement came to an end—opening the way for an increased acceptance of numerical representation.

Even before the Revolution, citizens in some colonies protested inequities in representation. Some areas were underrepresented, or not represented at all. The method of apportioning representatives caused many of these problems. Corporate representation, which granted a fixed number of legislators to geographic units— counties, towns, or parishes—prevailed. In Virginia, for example, each county received two representatives in the House of Burgesses. In Connecticut, each town sent two delegates to the lower house of their assembly. In South Carolina, on the other hand, the legislature arbitrarily assigned representation to each parish without any discernible formula. In no colony was representation systematically proportioned to population.[10]

The movement of settlers into western areas magnified the inequities inherent in this approach. Legislators knew that granting representation to newly settled territories would diminish their own power. They often refused to extend representation to westerners or granted them fewer representatives than older areas.[11] (See map 1.) By 1776, inland settlers had started to demand more equal representation in their state legislatures. Since the malapportioned legislatures controlled the distribution of representatives, however, the demands often fell on deaf ears.

Distance compounded the apportionment problem. Large distances directly affected the kind, quality, and quantity of representation an area had at meetings of the assembly. First of all, the farther a resident lived from the capital, the more limited was his information about government, especially in legislative matters. Whereas citizens living in or near urban centers could rely on newspapers for information, backcountry inhabitants often received no newspapers at all, or received them only after delays of two weeks to two months. Inland inhabitants feared that without their scrutiny the legislature might become tyrannical.

Similarly, some citizens feared that distance would breed corruption among legislators. State representatives might become as insensitive to the people as the English government to the colonists before the Revolution. A resident of the New Hampshire Grants, for example, noted that the inclusion of his region in New York State meant that "the state would be so large, that gentlemen from the extreme parts would not personally know but very little better the situation of the other extreme parts than a gentleman would from London." Expressing a common suspicion, inhabitants of Bedford County, Virginia, remarked that "from our remote situation, we are always liable to be imposed on by our assessors."[12]

[10] J. R. Pole, The Seventeenth Century: The Sources of Legislative Power (Charlottesville, 1969), 64–65; Michael Kammen, Deputyes and Libertyes: The Origins of Representative Government in Colonial America (New York, 1969), 13–68; Jack P. Greene, The Quest for Power: The Lower Houses of Assembly in the Southern Royal Colonies, 1689–1776 (Chapel Hill, 1963), 185; Raymond C. Bailey, Popular Influence upon Public Policy: Petitioning in Eighteenth-Century Virginia (Westport, 1979), 71–73; Joseph Alston, Speech of Joseph Alston, Member of the House of Representatives for Winyaw, in a Committee of the Whole. . . . (Georgetown, S. C., 1808), 21, 23.
[11] J. R. Pole, Political Representation in England and the Origins of the American Republic (New York, 1966), 63–64, 110, 173–74, 262–64.
[12] Ira Allen, Some Miscellaneous Remarks and Short Arguments on a Small Pamphlet . . . and Some Reasons given, why the District of the "New Hampshire Grants" had best be a State (Hartford, 1777), 25; Bedford County Petition, May 23, 1780, Petitions to the Virginia Assembly (Virginia State Library, Richmond, Va.).

Most importantly, distance determined attendance at meetings of the legislature. In a large state, such as New York or Pennsylvania, the most distant legislators had to journey hundreds of miles to reach the capital. Even in a small state, such as Delaware, they had to go fifty-five miles, the equivalent of a day's travel.[13]

Such journeys were difficult and expensive. By 1800, a light stagecoach could make the trip between New York and Philadelphia in two days; between New York and Boston in three days; and between New York and Baltimore in four to six days. Travel inland was even more time-consuming. "There are some of the western members," noted a North Carolinian in 1789, "who live near five hundred miles from the seat of government. When you consider the incidents that attend travelling across mountains in winter, and on bad roads, you must allow those members three or four weeks to come to the seat of government, or to return home."[14] To add to these difficulties, many states did not pay their legislators a salary; others did not even pay expenses, preferring to let each constituency support its own representatives.[15] Because the cost of supporting a legislator from a remote area might be substantial, many places chose to forgo representation altogether.

Eighteenth-century Americans routinely assumed that distant regions would not be represented as well as those nearer the capital — and they objected. In 1780, citizens of Springfield, Massachusetts, opposed their state constitution, commenting that, "It is probable, by Reason of their different situations, that many of the more distant Towns will generally omit the full Exercise of their Rights, and that those at or near the Center of Government will exercise them in their full Extent." Residents of Lenox objected to the Massachusetts Constitution of 1778 because "[it] has a tendency to induce the Remote parts of the State . . . to neglect keeping a Representative at the General Court. In a word it is making Representation unequal." Distance made the possibility of equal representation an illusion.[16]

In practice, a section's representation at the legislature was often inversely proportional to its distance from the seat of government. In 1788 North Carolina's far eastern counties were the least likely to send their full share of representatives to the assembly meeting in Fayetteville, in the south central portion of the state.[17] In New Hampshire too, distant inhabitants failed to send their full share of representa-

---

[13] *Journal of the House of Representatives of the State of Delaware* (Newcastle, 1797), 56; William A. Schaper, *Sectionalism and Representation in South Carolina* (1901; reprint, New York, 1968), 251; Allen, *Some Miscellaneous Remarks*, 8; *New York Daily Advertiser*, March 13, 1787; *Carlisle Gazette, & the Western Repository of Knowledge*, May 2, 1787.

[14] Henry Adams, *The United States in 1800* (1889; reprint, Ithaca, 1974), 8–10; C. U. Paullin, *Atlas of Historical Geography of the United States* (Baltimore, 1932), pl. 138a; Ralph H. Brown, *Mirror for Americans: Likeness of the Eastern Seaboard—1810* (New York, 1943), 43–54; "Extract of a Letter from Edenton, North Carolina," Jan. 28, 1789, *Providence Gazette, or Country Journal*, March 21, 1789.

[15] Allan Nevins, *The American States During and After the Revolution, 1775–1789* (New York, 1969), 182; Pole, *Political Representation in England and the Origins of the American Republic*, 285–86.

[16] Oscar Handlin and Mary Handlin, eds., *The Popular Sources of Political Authority: Documents on the Massachusetts Constitution of 1780* (Cambridge, Mass., 1966), 254, 607.

[17] The counties of Carteret, Dobbs, Duplin, Hawkins, Moore, Pasquotank, Tyrrel, and Wayne and the town of New Bern failed to send their full share of representatives. Conclusions are based on a comparison of representatives present at a vote on removal (November 20, 1788) with the list of counties deserving representation. See Walter Clark, ed., *The State Records of North Carolina 1776–1790* (22 vols., Goldsboro, 1903), XXI, 1–5, 73–74.

tives. Inhabitants of Portsmouth observed in 1790, "We neglect to improve the privilege to which by our constitution we are entitled, that of sending Representatives to the General Court. In the county of Rockingham, more than one half of the towns are unrepresented, whilst the representation from the upper counties [where the legislature was meeting] is very full." The underrepresentation of outlying areas persisted. In 1807, Stafford, the county most distant from the New Hampshire legislature's meeting place, sent the lowest percentage of representatives. Whereas counties near the capital sent over 90 percent of the permitted number of legislators, Stafford County sent only 79 percent.[18] When distant regions failed to send their assigned number of representatives, they aggravated the underrepresentation caused by malapportionment.

In the colonial period, legislatures met along the eastern seaboard in port towns such as Boston, New York City, Philadelphia, and Charles Town. (See table 1.) During the Revolution, the newly constituted state assemblies, as well as the Continental Congress, became peripatetic, shifting their meeting sites from place to place to avoid capture by the British.[19] Inland towns, which were much less vulnerable to surprise attack than coastal ones, became the representatives' favored sites. Although legislators probably regarded their moves as temporary wartime necessities, citizens soon became aware of the advantages of a centrally located seat of government. As more citizens moved farther from the coast, they began to call for a permanent relocation of capitals.

When Americans first began to think about the problems of equal representation, they focused on the issue of equal access to the seat of government. The other alternative — reapportionment on the basis of population — was a new, untried measure that required fundamental institutional change. If citizens were reluctant to tamper with corporate representation, legislators were even more resistant, since they had a direct stake in the old system. Physically removing the capital, however,

[18] *Osborne's New-Hampshire Spy* (Portsmouth), June 23, 1790. The New Hampshire legislature was meeting at Hopkinton in Hillsborough County. Conclusions are based on a comparison of the elected representatives with those in attendance on June 19, 1807, at a vote on removal. The attendance rates were: Hillsborough, 91%; Rockingham, 90.5%; Cheshire, 91%; Grafton, 93%; and Stafford, 79%. For the list of representatives, see *Concord Gazette*, June 16, 1807; for the vote, see *A Journal of the Proceedings of the House of Representatives of the State of New Hampshire* (Portsmouth, 1807), 95.

[19] See, for example, Edgar A. Werner, *Civil List and Constitutional History of the Colony and State of New York* (Albany, 1884), 313–21; Alonzo Thomas Dill, *Governor Tryon and His Palace* (Chapel Hill, 1955), 244–45; Samuel A. Ashe, *David Paton: Architect of the North Carolina State Capitol* (Raleigh, N.C., 1909), 3–4; George Barstow, *The History of New Hampshire: From Its Discovery in 1614 to the Passage of the Toleration Act in 1819* (Boston, 1853), 341; James O. Lyford, ed., *History of Concord, New Hampshire, from the Original Grant in Seventeen Hundred and Twenty-five to the Opening of the Twentieth Century* (2 vols., Concord, 1903), II, 1091. Two states established permanent new capitals during the war, Delaware and Virginia. *Laws of the State of Delaware* (New-Castle, 1777), II, 619–20; William Waller Hening, comp., *The Statutes at Large; Being a Collection of Laws of Virginia* (Richmond, 1822), X, 85–89. There were a few attempts to move capitals before the Revolution. In the seventeenth century, Virginia's capital was moved from Jamestown to Williamsburg and Maryland's from St. Mary's to Annapolis. Attempts in the early eighteenth century were less successful. Strong efforts were made in Virginia and North Carolina. See H. R. McIlwaine, ed., *Journals of the House of Burgesses of Virginia, 1742–1747, 1748–1749* (Richmond, 1909), 242, 244, 247, 283–84; Hugh Williamson, *The History of North-Carolina* (2 vols., Philadelphia, 1812), II, 58–59.

seemed an easier way for legislators to address the representation question while logically extending common assumptions about how representative government should work.

Petitions for removal often listed the time, expense, and difficulty of travel to the capital as reasons for shifting the seat of government. Over and over they mention the need for a more "conveniently" located capital. As South Carolina residents put it in a 1785 petition, "The Seat of Government is very inconvenient on account of loss of time and expence and also the hazard of Health to Inhabitants who are obliged to attend on public or private business. We would pray that it may be removed as near the Center of the State as the Legislature may see fit." "In a republic like this," asserted citizens from New Brunswick, New Jersey, in 1787, "it is not the interest or local situation of those who possess the honorable or lucrative offices of state but the convenience and advantages of the people at large which first bespeaks the attention of the legislature."[20]

Yet the demands for removal reflected more than a desire for easier journeys to the capital. If residents had merely objected to the difficulty of travel, then, as one Pennsylvania legislator proposed, "Good roads from one end of the state to the other, [would] be found a much better means of reducing the inconvenience of the distance of the seat of government" than physically relocating the capital.[21] But citizens wanted more than good roads.

Americans believed that it was a matter of right, not simply of personal comfort, to have a centrally located capital. Virginia's removal statute of 1779 stated that "the equal rights of all inhabitants require that such seat of government should be as nearly central [as possible]." During the debate over the national capital, Madison commented that "in every instance where the seat of Government has been placed in an uncentral position, we have seen the people struggling to place it where it *ought to be*." If distance alone had been the problem, residents of smaller states, who had relatively short distances to travel to their capitals, would not have demanded removal or would have demanded it less frequently. Yet citizens of small states as well as large clamored for the relocation of their capitals.[22]

When petitioners demanded a more conveniently located capital, they sought more than personal convenience. Certainly large distances inconvenienced individuals who had to attend court, pay taxes, or register land claims at the capital. Yet such concerns affected only a small minority. The common understanding of "convenience" had a public dimension as well. Outlying areas simply could not send their full share of representatives to meetings of the assembly, and therefore they were not fully represented. A more centrally located capital would help rectify that situation. A Maryland writer calling himself "Aristides" observed that Maryland's consti-

---

[20] Lark Emerson Adams, ed., *Journals of the [South Carolina] House of Representatives, 1785–1786* (Columbia, 1979), 195; Richard P. McCormick, *Experiment in Independence: New Jersey in the Critical Period, 1781–1789* (New Brunswick, 1950), 126.

[21] *Philadelphia Independent Gazetteer*, Aug. 15, 1787.

[22] Hening, comp., *Statutes at Large*, X, 85; *Annals of Congress*, 1 Cong., 1 sess., Sept. 4, 1789, p. 861–62 (emphasis added).

tution ordered "that the place for the meeting of the legislature must be the most convenient to the members." This clause, he argued, "means a place the most central, the most convenient for them to repair to, and best suited to them *in their public characters, as members of the legislature.*" For Americans living in the eighteenth century, the word "convenient" carried a much stronger connotation than it does today. The meaning was much closer to that of the word's Latin root, "coming together, uniting." Large distances in effect prevented the people's representatives from coming together to make laws for society. A more conveniently located capital meant one that would be more accessible to legislators from all parts of the state. That argument, then, had resonance in even the smallest state.[23]

In contrast to the agreement found among supporters of removal were the diverse reasons offered by opponents, even within a single state. In Pennsylvania in 1787, for example, Rep. William Findley proposed a motion to shift the capital from Philadelphia to Harrisburg. This action unleashed a torrent of abuse. Some accused Findley of seeking private gain through the bill. According to one critic, the people would have to bear additional taxes simply "in order that the member from Westmoreland may not have quite so many miles to ride!" More seriously, another author argued that Findley and his supporters "own all the property in the town and neighborhood of Harrisburg—the offices and influence of government of course would fall into their hands." Still others insisted that he had deliberately waited until the session's end, after many members had left, to raise the matter. Rather than present the issue to the whole assembly for debate, it had been "stolen through" without proper consideration.[24]

Other attacks focused on the larger public issues at stake. Moving the capital, some feared, would send the current capital into a precipitous economic decline. "Whatever tends to render Philadelphia flourishing and active," wrote Civis, "sheds a beneficial influence on the state at large. To withdraw the offices of government from the City may depress its trade and depopulate its streets." Another member, Hugh Henry Brackenridge, doubted that a removal undertaken at that time would be permanent. Another move would probably be necessary, causing the taxpayers extra expense and trouble. Still others believed that moving the legislature out of Philadelphia would give the people less, rather than more, control over their legislators. One member commented, "While the Assembly sits in this city, every individual in the state is informed of its proceedings, by the circulation of the newspapers which are published here, and in case of any attempt to abridge their privileges, have it in their power to shew their disapprobation, sooner than could be done if it was removed into the country." Despite their vehemence, the opponents of removal, like later opponents of the United States Constitution, had no

[23] [Hanson], *Considerations on the Proposed Removal of the Seat of Government*, 54 (emphasis added); *The Compact Edition of the Oxford English Dictionary* (1971; reprint U.S., 1980), 934–35; Garry Wills, *Confessions of a Conservative* (Middlesex, Eng., 1979), 57–58.

[24] *Philadelphia Independent Gazetteer*, March 8, March 9, 1787; *Carlisle Gazette*, March 28, 1787; *Philadelphia Independent Gazetteer*, March 8, March 9, 1787.

single rationale to unite them. The absence of an ideologically unified opposition may have contributed to the widespread success of the removal movement.[25]

Americans knew that some people would always have to travel farther than others to reach the seat of government. They realized, too, that those living near the capital would continue to have more direct influence on government than those living farther away, through their greater personal contact with legislators and their ability to form mobs. Yet in a political milieu where distance contributed so concretely to the kind, quality, and quantity of representation, relocating the seat of government seemed a logical method of equalizing representation. If the capital was moved to the state's center, no section would be able to exert a greater influence than any other. Contacts between representatives and constituents would remain frequent, meaningful, and financially feasible. For many eighteenth-century Americans, equal representation in the legislature meant equal access to the seat of government.

Legislators soon found, however, that locating the center was more complicated than they had at first believed. The concept of centrality was highly ambiguous. The "center" could refer to the center of population, wealth, or territory. In 1789, during the congressional debate over the national capital one congressman despaired: "The principles offered are vague, and lead to no certain conclusion. What is the centre of wealth, population, and territory? Is there a common centre? Territory has one centre, population another, and wealth a third. . . . This was not a practicable mode of settling the place [of government]."[26] As state legislators began to select precise locations for their new capitals, they too realized that they had to define centrality.

As the debates over capitals proceeded, the implications of different forms of centrality became apparent. Most legislators quickly rejected the notion of a capital in the center of wealth. Such a point would be difficult, if not impossible, to ascertain, and locating the capital there would not redress inequities in representation. The choice was basically between the centers of population and of territory. Each offered distinct benefits and drawbacks.

Legislators noted the ease with which geographic centers could be located. By consulting maps, geographies, and reports from surveying expeditions, representatives could pinpoint a state's territorial center with great precision. A legislative committee in South Carolina reported in 1786, for example, that it had "examined and Compared all the different Maps of the State which they could possess themselves of, and are of the Opinion that the Center of the State is included in a Circle whose Circumference strikes through the High Hills of Santee."[27] Given the paucity of detailed census data before 1790, the simplicity in determining the geographic center offered a substantial benefit.

A seat of government placed in the geographic center also offered the advantage of permanence. Provided a state's boundaries remained the same, the geographic

[25] *Carlisle Gazette*, March 28, 1787; *Philadelphia Independent Gazetteer*, March 8, Aug. 15, 1787.
[26] *Annals of Congress*, 1 Cong., 1 sess., Sept. 3, 1789, p. 841.
[27] Adams, ed., *Journals of the [South Carolina] House*, 533.

center would remain stationary. But as the population grew and settlers moved into new territory, the demographic center would shift. Population was growing so rapidly, a Pennsylvanian warned in 1787, that:

> To fix the seat [of government] at present, regarding only the peopled country, is making a garment for a youth fitted to his size, which he must outgrow in a short period. It is fixing the center of gravity of a machine while some of the parts of which it is to be composed are wanting.[28]

Some Americans believed, however, that people would eventually settle all parts of the state evenly, making the state's demographic center identical with its geographic center.[29] A geographically central capital, they suggested, would anticipate the future population distribution.

But permanence represented the territorial center's biggest handicap as well as its greatest advantage. Although geographic centers were fixed, they were not necessarily conveniently situated for most of the state's current population. They would often be located, as one South Carolina legislator put it, at "the centre of pine trees"—in other words, in the midst of an uninhabited wilderness. What demographic centers lacked in permanence, they gained, on the other hand, by being accessible to the greatest number of current residents. A Georgian commented that "the place most thickly settled [was] at the distance of nearly two hundred miles from Savannah," the current capital. Only moving the seat of government to the center of population would achieve a more equitable solution.[30]

Finding the demographic center was difficult, but it was by no means impossible. While Americans of the early national period did not have modern population distribution maps, they could and did consult tax rolls, voting records, and, as a Pennsylvania legislator put it in 1810, their own "knowledge of the country" to gauge population densities throughout the state.[31] After the first federal census in 1790, they had accurate population statistics to guide them.

States' geographic sizes influenced legislators' decisions as to where to place their new capitals. The smaller states tended to position their seats of government at sites determined by geographic considerations. Inhabitants defined centrality in terms of distance from state boundaries; the state was regarded strictly as a territorial unit. New Jersey and Delaware, for example, fixed their seats of government within twenty-five miles of the states' respective geographic centers.[32] In 1694 Maryland,

[28] *Philadelphia Independent Gazetteer*, Aug. 15, 1787.

[29] See, for example, "The People the Best Governors: Or a Plan of Government Founded on the Just Principles of Natural Freedom," in *American Political Writing during the Founding Era, 1760–1805*, ed. Charles S. Hyneman and Donald S. Lutz (2 vols., Indianapolis, 1983), I, 395; *Annals of Congress*, 1 Cong, 1 sess., Sept. 4, 1789, p. 865; Loammi Baldwin, *Thoughts on the Study of Political Economy as Connected with the Population, Industry, and Paper Currency of the United States* (1809; reprint, New York, 1968), 15.

[30] *Charleston Morning Post and Daily Advertiser*, March 15, 1786; Lucien F. Roberts, "Sectional Problems in Georgia during the Formative Period, 1776–1798," *Georgia Historical Quarterly*, 18 (Sept. 1934), 211.

[31] *Poulson's American Daily Advertiser* (Philadelphia), Feb. 2, 1810.

[32] William Paterson, comp., *Laws of the State of New-Jersey* (Newark, 1800), 104; McCormick, *Experiment in Independence*, 125–26; *Laws of the State of Delaware*, II, 619–20. For geographic centers, see Edward M. Douglas, *Boundaries, Areas, Geographic Centers and Altitudes of the United States and the Several States, with a Brief*

STATE CAPITOL OF NEW JERSEY AT TRENTON.
BUILT, 1794 — ALTERED & ENLARGED 1845 & 46.

In 1794 New Jersey's capital was removed to Trenton, closer to
the state's geographic center.
Courtesy Library of Congress.

another small state, had moved its capital to Annapolis, a site very near the state's geographic center. Two other small states, Rhode Island and Connecticut, alternated their legislatures' meeting places from site to site throughout the states. The Connecticut assembly met in Hartford and New Haven. The Rhode Island legislature moved from Newport to Providence to East Greenwich to South Kingston to Bristol.[33] By such rotation these states brought the capital to the people rather than forcing the people to go to the capital. In small states, both the geographically central capital and the rotating capital succeeded in giving all parts of the state equal access to the assembly. (See map 1.)

Record of Important Changes in Their Territory and Government (Washington, 1932), 254. South Carolina, a larger state, also placed its capital in the state's geographic center. See *Acts, Ordinances and Resolves of the General Assembly of the State of South-Carolina* (Charleston, 1786), 56–58; Francis N. Thorpe, comp., *The Federal and State Constitutions, Colonial Charters, and Other Organic Laws of the States, Territories, and Colonies Now or Heretofore Forming the United States of America* (7 vols., Washington, 1909), VI, 3260, 3265; David Duncan Wallace, *South Carolina: A Short History, 1520–1948* (Columbia, 1961), 342–43.

[33] An intense struggle developed in Maryland in the 1780s over whether the capital should be moved to Baltimore. See [Hanson], *Considerations on the Proposed Removal of the Seat of Government*, 37, 45. Forrest Morgan, *Connecticut as a Colony and as a State, or One of the Original Thirteen* (Hartford, 1904), 134–35; Edward Field, *State of Rhode Island and Providence Plantations at the End of the Century: A History* (2 vols., Boston, 1902), I, 390–91.

Delegates in larger states, on the other hand, tended to place their capitals at their states' current demographic centers. They realized that a capital located at the geographic center would not redress their constituents' grievances. Population in the large states was widely scattered. Not all regions had been settled. Geographically central capitals would be inconvenient to many of the states' residents and their representatives. In 1799, for example, legislators in Pennsylvania deliberately rejected Bellefonte, near the state's geographic center, in favor of Harrisburg, which seemed to be, in their words, "nearer the centre of population." In New York, representatives realized that the center of their territory lay in Madison County, a region virtually uninhabited in 1797. As a result, they placed their new seat of government at Albany, at the intersection of existing north-south and east-west settlement. New Hampshire, Virginia, North Carolina, and Georgia (in its first removal) also positioned their new seats of government at locations they deemed to be the centers of population. Legislators in Pennsylvania and Georgia moved their capitals more than once to keep them near their states' changing demographic centers.[34] (See map 1.)

The capital relocation process revealed that citizens in the larger states were beginning to see representation in terms of population rather than territory. Legislators in the large states regarded the state as a demographic unit whose seat of government should be located where the majority of people and their representatives could most easily reach it. Unlike legislators in the smaller states, they considered settlement patterns and population density rather than artificial boundary lines on a map. This demographic approach to capital removal signaled the beginning of a larger shift in Americans' assumptions about representation.

The use of then-current population estimates to situate capitals helps explain capital sites that may now appear irrational. Though subject to change, a demographic seat of government suited the needs of people living in the larger states at the time the capitals were moved. Residents in all inhabited parts of the state would

[34] *Journal of the First Session of the Ninth House of Representatives of Pennsylvania, 1798-1799* (Philadelphia, 1799), 127, 366-68, 378, 383, 391; *Journal of the Senate of the Commonwealth of Pennsylvania* (Philadelphia, 1798), IX, 232, 256-60; *Bache's Philadelphia Aurora*, April 1, 1799; *Journal of the Twentieth House of Representatives of the Commonwealth of Pennsylvania* (Lancaster, 1809), 351, 443, 445, 453-56, 472, 482-83, 491-92; *Journal of the Senate of the Commonwealth of Pennsylvania* (Lancaster, 1809), XX, 78, 121, 177, 188-89, 559. *Journal of the Assembly of the State of New-York* (Albany, 1797), 89-90, 108; *Laws of the State of New-York, Comprising the Constitution and Acts of Legislature, since the Revolution, from the First to the Twentieth Session, Inclusive* (New York, 1797), III, 391-93; *New York Diary*, Feb. 14, 1797. Hening, comp., *Virginia Statutes*, X, 85-89; Clark, ed., *State Records of North Carolina*, XXII, 28-29, 33; *State Gazette of North Carolina*, Sept. 8, 1788; *Journal of the House of Commons of North Carolina, 1792-3* (Edenton, 1793), 11, 14, 53, 59; *Laws of North Carolina, First Session, 1792* (n.p., 1792), 7-8; Eliphalet Merrill and Phinehas Merrill, *Gazetteer of the State of New-Hampshire* (Exeter, 1817), 102; Barstow, *History of New Hampshire*, 341; Lyford, ed., *History of Concord, New Hampshire*, II, 1091; *Laws of New Hampshire* (12 vols., Concord, 1920), VIII, 525; Allen D. Chandler, comp., *The Colonial Records of the State of Georgia* (3 vols., Atlanta, 1911), III, 466-68; Clark Howell, *History of Georgia* (2 vols., Chicago, 1926), I, 443-44; T. S. Arthur and W. H. Carpenter, *The History of Georgia, from its Earliest Settlement to the Present Time* (Philadelphia, 1853), 310-11; Augustin Smith Clayton, comp., *A Compilation of the Laws of the State of Georgia, passed by the Legislature since the Political Year 1800, to the Year 1810, Inclusive* (Augusta, 1812), 100-107, 209-10, 265-66. Although Pennsylvania voted in 1810 to shift its capital, that move from Lancaster to Harrisburg took place in 1812. Georgia voted in 1804 to move its capital a third time, from Louisville to Milledgeville.

have more equal access to—and presumably more equal representation in—the legislature.

The idea of centrality had to compete with another approach to representation that first gained prominence during the Revolution. Beginning in 1776, the same year that the removals began, a few states experimented with numerical representation. In their first constitutions, Massachusetts, New York, and Pennsylvania made representation proportional to population.[35] People, rather than territory, became the basis of apportionment.

However, politicians in many states seemed reluctant to implement the new system. Numerical representation seemed a radical, even a dangerous, innovation. It threatened the status quo. It changed the basis of representation from geographic units—counties, towns, or parishes—to the individual.' It gave more power to regions whose populations were increasing. And it undermined the authority of the established elite that had long dominated the assemblies. It is no surprise, then, that many states resisted the new system.

Some legislators promoted removal as a substitute for reapportionment. In eight of the original thirteen states, politicians agreed to shift their seats of government to new, more central locations but rejected the demands for reapportionment. Rhode Island, Connecticut, New Jersey, Delaware, Virginia, North Carolina, South Carolina, and Georgia staved off reapportionment for varying lengths of time, at least partly by moving their capitals. By 1812 only six states had reapportioned their assemblies, while eleven had moved their capitals. Only Maryland had neither relocated its capital nor reapportioned its legislature between the Revolution and the War of 1812.[36] (See table 1.)

The most explicit evidence of a trade-off between reapportionment and removal comes from South Carolina. Representation in the state favored the large planters of the Lowcountry and discriminated against the burgeoning western population. Although the Lowcountry had only one-fifth of the population, that area received 19 senators and 141 representatives to the Upcountry's 11 senators and 58 representatives. In 1778 South Carolinians wrote a new state constitution that promised the state would take a census of the people by 1785, to be followed by a reapportionment of the state's lower house. That year came and went, however, and the legislature ignored the constitution's mandate. Representation remained inequitable. At the same time, however, Upcountry citizens began to make another demand, calling for the removal of the state capital to a more central location. In 1786 the legislature

[35] Pole, *Political Representation in England and the Origins of the American Republic*, 200–204, 262–65, 274–75, 526–39; Willi Paul Adams, *The First American Constitutions: Republican Ideology and the Making of the State Constitutions in the Revolutionary Era* (Chapel Hill, 1980), 236–43.
[36] Malcolm E. Jewell and Samuel C. Patterson, *The Legislative Process in the United States* (New York, 1966), 50; Wilder Crane, Jr., and Meredith W. Watts, *State Legislative Systems* (Englewood Cliffs, 1968), 24–25; Gordon E. Baker, *The Reapportionment Revolution: Representation, Political Power, and the Supreme Court* (New York, 1966), 16–21.

made a concession to Upcountry wishes by agreeing to move the seat of government from Charleston, on the coast, to Columbia, near the state's geographic center.[37]

Lowcountry members viewed reapportionment with horror, as a threat to their interests and their power. Removal, while inconvenient, was more palatable and could be portrayed as a great concession to the Upcountry. Writing in the Lowcountry's defense, Henry De Saussure argued in 1790 that the removal was made with "the aid of some of the lower members who conceived the change just (though inconvenient to them) from the old spot. . . . This change was made entirely against the interests, and chiefly at the expense of the sea coast." De Saussure claimed that the current distribution of representatives, though inequitable, served the interests of both Lowcountry and Upcountry residents adequately.[38] He implied that in gratitude for removal, the Upcountry should relinquish its claims for greater representation in the legislature. After all, there had been a trade-off between two forms of representation—greater accessibility to the capital in return for preserving the status quo in apportionment.

By 1790 the compromise had broken down. Perhaps because Upcountry residents never fully accepted its terms, they felt no reluctance to continue insisting on greater representation in the legislature. At a constitutional convention in 1790, they tried once again to reapportion the legislature according to population. In retaliation, easterners attempted to return the seat of government to Charleston. Although they failed to move the legislature's meeting place, they did succeed in establishing dual capitals. The surveyor general and secretary of state would have offices in both Charleston and Columbia. The Court of Appeals was to hold sessions in both towns. The governor would not be required to live in Columbia, except during meetings of the legislature. The Lowcountry had reasserted its power and preserved its inequitable advantage in representation. The struggle continued for many years. South Carolinians had to wait until 1808 for the long-promised reapportionment of their lower house.[39]

Although the evidence for a trade-off between removal and reapportionment is not as direct in other states as in South Carolina, many states experienced intense controversies over the reapportionment issue. If removal was indeed regarded as a less radical substitute for reapportionment, then a long time between the two events suggests a connection between them. In Georgia, for example, the state with the

[37] Thorpe, comp., *Federal and State Constitutions*, VI, 3250–52; Alston, *Speech of Joseph Alston*, 18–19; Green, *Constitutional Development in the South Atlantic States*, 115, 119. Adams, ed., *Journals of the [South Carolina] House*, 573, 596; *Acts, Ordinances, and Resolves of the General Assembly of the State of South-Carolina. Passed in March, 1786* (Charleston, 1786), 56–58.

[38] Phocion [Henry W. De Saussure], *Letters on the Questions of the Justice and Expediency of Going into Alterations of the Representation in the Legislature of South Carolina, as Fixed by the Constitution* (Charleston, 1795), 25–27.

[39] Appius [Robert Goodloe Harper], *An Address to the People of South Carolina by the General Committee of the Representative Reform Association, at Columbia* (Charleston, 1794), 28; Green, *Constitutional Development in the South Atlantic States*, 121; Wallace, *South Carolina*, 342–43; Schaper, *Sectionalism and Representation in South Carolina*, 376–77; Thorpe, comp., *Federal and State Constitutions*, VI, 3260, 3265, 3266; Yates Snowden, ed., *History of South Carolina* (Chicago, 1920), 512–13.

shortest lapse between the two events, three years passed between removal and reapportionment. But in North Carolina, forty-seven years passed; in Virginia, fifty; in New Jersey, fifty-four; and similarly long periods in other states.[40] As resistant as many legislators were to removal, they may have seen it as the lesser of two evils, preferable to the more drastic alternative, a change in the basis of apportionment.

Even where there was no trade-off, explicit or implied, removal had a profound influence on ideas of representation—among the population at large, not just among legislators. As citizens shifted their capitals, they became increasingly aware of the limitations of that method of equalizing representation. The demands for removal were consistently blocked by legislatures in which the very people demanding removal were underrepresented. The problem was not simply an inability to send representatives to the assembly, but a skewed distribution of representatives that favored certain areas. Pennsylvanians, for example, did not succeed in moving their capital until 1799 when some disgruntled easterners joined with westerners to support the removal bill.[41]

The same was true in many other states. Remarking bitterly on the conflict in South Carolina, Robert Goodloe Harper said, "There can hardly be a question which will more deeply interest the upper country than the removal of the seat of government. But how was it carried: by their own strength? No, all their struggles for that purpose were ineffectual 'till they were joined by some members from below."[42] Supporters of removal could achieve victory only when those from sections with adequate representation came to their aid. On their own, they were essentially powerless.

As a part of the revolutionaries' restructuring of representative government, removal was an experiment that failed. Yet the movement still had significance. Americans tried many other such experiments during the revolutionary era. Pennsylvania's 1776 constitution, for example, established a Council of Censors, which would meet every seven years to judge the constitutionality of recently passed laws. The council, rather than the state's courts, would have the power later known as judicial review. In 1790, however, Pennsylvania scrapped the device and lodged this power in the state courts, where it has remained ever since.[43] Although a failure on its own terms, the Council of Censors represented a crucial stage in the evolution of judicial review, a means through which Americans articulated the concept and came to realize its full import.

---

[40] In Georgia the first removal took place in 1786, and reapportionment in 1789; in North Carolina removal in 1788 and reapportionment in 1835; in Virginia removal in 1779 and reapportionment in 1829; in New Jersey removal in 1790 and reapportionment in 1844; in Delaware removal in 1777 and reapportionment in 1831. Rhode Island and Connecticut began rotating their capitals during the revolutionary war. Rhode Island reapportioned its legislature in 1840, and Connecticut never did so before the Civil War. Thorpe, ed., *Federal and State Constitutions*, I, 536–48, 582–600, III, 1712–41, V, 2639–51, 2599–2614, 3104–17, VI, 3222–36, VII, 3819–28; Pole, *Political Representation*, 314–38; Green, *Constitutional Development in the South Atlantic States*, 146–47, 240.
[41] *Kline's Weekly Carlisle Gazette*, May 1, 1799; *Bache's Philadelphia Aurora*, April 5, 1799.
[42] [Harper], *Address to the People of South Carolina*, 35.
[43] Wood, *Creation of the American Republic*, 438–46.

In a similar fashion, removal helped clarify the importance of numerical representation. More clearly than before, people began to see that the real problem lay in the distribution of representatives in the legislature, not in people's distance from it. Even if the capital were relocated, even if all sections sent their allotted number of delegates to the assembly, each area would still not necessarily receive representation in proportion to its strength in numbers. Only a comprehensive reassignment of representatives could achieve that. Equal representation, Americans realized, should be defined in terms of numbers rather than distance, in terms of demography rather than geography.

By 1812 the era of removal had ended. In that year, Pennsylvanians moved their seat of government a second and last time, from Lancaster to Harrisburg. Among the original thirteen states, only Georgia altered its capital's location again — after, and as a direct result of, the Civil War.[44] Although settlers continued to move westward and demographic centers shifted, citizens no longer called for removal with the frequency or intensity that they once had. Other states besides the original thirteen subsequently moved their seats of government, but never again was there a wave of removals issuing from a common impulse. Although many new states chose to place their capitals near their centers, centrality no longer seemed a viable alternative to reapportionment on the basis of population. Americans had concluded that relocating their capitals was not the best means to achieve their ends.

Thereafter reapportionment superseded removal as the primary means of equalizing representation. Inhabitants turned their full attention to the issues of the legislature's size and the distribution of representatives. From the 1820s through the 1840s, states engaged in a new wave of constitution writing, in which reapportionment was a major concern. Three more of the original thirteen states adopted numerical representation; others seriously debated the issue. Most new states chose the method as well. All but two of the twenty states entering the Union between 1789 and 1860 provided for proportional representation in at least one house.[45] Despite some later deviations from the norm in the late nineteenth and twentieth centuries, the principle of numerical representation had become identified with republican government and entrenched in the American system.[46] So entrenched was it that by the mid-twentieth century it was hard for Americans to remember a time when equal representation meant anything other than population equality.

---

[44] In February 1869 a Georgia state constitutional convention voted to shift the capital from Milledgeville to Atlanta. See James C. Bonner, *Milledgeville: Georgia's Antebellum Capital* (Athens, 1978), 220.

[45] Sandra L. Myres, *One Man, One Vote: Gerrymandering v. Reapportionment* (Austin, 1970), 10; Jewell and Patterson, *Legislative Process in the United States*, 50; Crane and Watts, *State Legislative Systems*, 24–25; Baker, *Reapportionment Revolution*, 16–21.

[46] After the Civil War certain states, seeking to curb the influence of urban areas, passed amendments that modified the strict population basis of apportionment or refused to reapportion the legislature to keep pace with population. These changes and the opposition to them provoked the apportionment decisions of the 1960s. See Jewell and Patterson, *Legislative Process*, 48–49; Baker, *Reapportionment Revolution*, 24–31.

36

State-Making in Revolutionary America: Independent Vermont as a Case Study

Peter S. Onuf

Vermont was created in July 1777 when representatives of approximately twenty-eight towns in the New Hampshire Grants adopted their own constitution and declared their independence of the state of New York. New York and New Hampshire had contested for jurisdiction in the area until 1764 when the British Privy Council set New York's eastern boundary at the Connecticut River. The Vermont independence movement was the culmination of a subsequent series of challenges to the Privy Council's decision on behalf of settlers and speculators holding New Hampshire titles.[1] Vermont joined the American Revolution against British tyranny, but the revolutionary states did not embrace Vermont. Because the United States Congress would not sanction the involuntary division of one of its own members, Vermont was unable to gain recognition from neighboring states or protection from the British in Canada. When Vermont became independent, it became independent of all the world and remained so until 1791 when it was finally admitted to the union.

If the United States did not welcome Vermont into their ranks, neither were they willing to tolerate it as a neutral republic. The Americans were anxious to secure their northern flank from British attack; neighboring states sought to regain or extend their territorial jurisdiction; and New York speculators hoped to establish their land titles in the Grants. The impasse over Vermont statehood—which dragged through Congress for years—encouraged British overtures to the new state. The British hoped to disrupt the Revolutionary cause and gain a foothold in northern New England. The threat of invasion guaranteed that the Vermonters would give the British an attentive hearing.

In the first years of the war, Vermont participated actively in the American effort, capturing Ticonderoga (May 1775) and playing an important role in

Peter S. Onuf is a member of the department of history at Columbia University. Research for this essay was supported by a grant from Project '87.

[1] See Chilton Williamson, *Vermont in Quandary, 1763-1825* (Montpelier, Vt., 1949), and Matt Bushnell Jones, *Vermont in the Making, 1750-1777* (Cambridge, 1939).

37

thwarting Burgoyne's attack from the north (August-October 1777).[2] In recognition of these contributions, the new state's leaders expected to be welcomed into the American union. But New York insisted that the Grants remained a part of that state, and Congress could not afford to alienate one of its most important members. Nonrecognition by Congress left Vermont in a precarious position, exposing its tenuous hold on popular loyalties. Support for the new state was strongest on the west side of the Green Mountains. But several towns in the southeast had come to terms with New York before the Revolution and continued to favor New York's jurisdictional pretensions into the 1780s. Further up the Connecticut River, townsmen agitated for a union with their counterparts on the New Hampshire side—in either Vermont or New Hampshire, should the latter's colonial claim be revived.

Factional politics in Vermont as well as the state's vulnerable strategic situation provoked the adoption of aggressive policies toward its neighbors. In June 1778, sixteen New Hampshire towns were annexed in the first Eastern Union. The Vermont Assembly dissolved the union in October under heavy pressure from the American states and counting on the implicit suggestion that Congress would treat a statehood application favorably.[3] From this time on, New Hampshire entertained designs on the towns on the west bank of the Connecticut. Chilly responses from Congress and the threat of New Hampshire, as well as New York expansionism, led to new annexations: thirty-five New Hampshire towns were added in the second Eastern Union (April 1781) and twelve New York towns were added in the Western Union (June 1781).[4] Vermont's aggressive posture reflected a growing disregard for the power of the United States—particularly of New York, which Vermont routed in the border "war" of December 1781—and a willingness to enter into alliance with the former British enemy. Not coincidentally, the Haldimand negotiations (so-called after Frederick Haldimand, British commander at Quebec), beginning in May 1781, led to a cessation of hostilities in the north.[5] The talks were designed to secure Vermont's neutrality during the Revolution and its eventual readmission to the British Empire as a distinct colony, including the Eastern and Western unions. News of the prospective alliance prompted Congress to offer Vermont statehood in August 1781, if it would withdraw from New Hampshire and New York.[6] But when Vermont complied with the condition

[2] Page Smith, *A New Age Now Begins* (2 vols., New York, 1976), II, 891-947; Charles A. Jellison, *Ethan Allen: Frontier Rebel* (Syracuse, 1969), 102-20.

[3] *Journals and Proceedings of the General Assembly of the State of Vermont* (4 vols., Bellows Falls, Vt., 1924-1929), I, 24, 41-45. See also Ira Allen, *Address to the Inhabitants of Vermont* (Dresden, Vt., Nov. 27, 1778), and Josiah Bartlett to Meshech Weare, Sept. 26, 1778, Miscellaneous Manuscripts (Vermont Historical Society, Montpelier, Vt.).

[4] *Journals and Proceedings of the General Assembly*, I, 213-14, 242-44.

[5] For a good general treatment, see Williamson, *Vermont in Quandary*, 90-126. Documents relating to the talks may be found in *Collections of the Vermont Historical Society* (2 vols., Montpelier, Vt., 1870-1871), II.

[6] *Journals of the Continental Congress*, ed. Worthington C. Ford (34 vols., Washington, 1904-1937), XXI, 886-88, 892-93.

by dissolving the unions in February 1782, Congress recanted.[7] Meanwhile, with American victory assured, the British lost interest in Vermont.

Vermont's tortuous foreign policy succeeded in promoting havoc and confusion among its neighbors and in securing the state from invasion. But it did not establish the authority of the new state over its own citizens. Every foreign policy initiative provoked disgust and dissension in one part of the state or another. By all accounts, most Vermonters considered themselves loyal Americans, and they displayed little enthusiasm for returning to the empire when news of the Haldimand talks leaked. Westerners resented the domination of the Connecticut River towns resulting from the Eastern unions; at other times, easterners resented the domination of the west. Every faction in the state suspected the motives and loyalties of the other factions. This pervasive mistrust was symptomatic of the failure of the new state government to establish stable and legitimate authority.

The founders of Vermont had to create a state where no true community had existed. They could not command the communal loyalties of former colonies with distinctive institutions and political traditions. And even though the state constitution of 1777 incorporated many of the most advanced principles of popular republicanism, Vermont's leaders were hard pressed to convince the populace that it had a right to govern itself and that the constitution had any legal force.[8] They had to convince the rest of the world to recognize their claims, and they had to convince themselves that their self-constituted authority was legitimate. In the process, Vermonters explored and illuminated the ambiguous nature of statehood during the American Revolution.

American statehood claims rested on various, potentially contradictory premises. First, the prior status of the independent states as British colonies was invoked: new state governments simply succeeded old colony governments in political communities or "states" that long antedated the Revolution. But second, it was also argued that new communities came into being with the drafting of state constitutions: the sovereign people created new states. And finally, mutual recognition among the states through membership in the union and representation in Congress was a crucial component of American statehood claims. Indeed, "one of the great objects of the union" was "the protection and security" of state rights, as Congress resolved in September 1779.[9] Thus states as territorial communities were inherited from the colonial period; states as governments were created by the revolutionaries; and states in a community of states existed by virtue of the recognition of other states.

[7] The dissolution of the unions caught many Vermont leaders by surprise. *Journals and Proceedings of the General Assembly*, II, 60–65. A letter from George Washington to Governor Chittenden, Jan. 1, 1782, advising dissolution, apparently had a great impact on the assembly. *The Public Papers of Governor Thomas Chittenden*, ed. John A. Williams (Montpelier, Vt., 1969), 573–75. For congressional inaction on Vermont's renewed application in April 1782, see *Journals of the Continental Congress*, ed. Ford, XXII, 185–90.

[8] Vermonters' scruples about the legality of their constitution are discussed in Gordon S. Wood, *The Creation of the American Republic, 1776–1787* (Chapel Hill, 1969), 307–08.

[9] *Journals of the Continental Congress*, ed. Ford, XV, 1095–96.

Different definitions of statehood served different functions: to distinguish among state claims, to legitimize revolutionary governments, and to guarantee cooperation in the common cause. Ordinarily, they were compatible. The original thirteen states had all been colonies. Most adopted new state constitutions. In principle, they agreed to defend each other's claims. The American Revolutionary program combined the creation of a continental union with the reassertion of each colony-state's autonomy and territorial integrity.[10] Although the Continental Congress called for the constitution of new governments in the colonies as the necessary preliminary, if not the essence, of independence, it saw itself as the creature, not the creator, of existing polities. According to a report adopted in June 1777, Congress "is comprised of delegates chosen by, and representing the communities respectively inhabiting the territories" of the colony-states "as they respectively stood at the time of its first institution." Therefore, as Congress explained in 1780, "the lands contained within the limits of the United States are . . . under the jurisdiction of some one or other of the thirteen states."[11]

The unanimous, if belated, ratification of the Articles of Confederation in 1781 did not alter the supposition that the thirteen colony-states constituted the basic components of the American union. The Articles were supposed to guarantee the territorial integrity of the states, and they made the admission of new states exceedingly difficult, if not impossible. At the end of the Revolution, moreover, the Paris Treaty of 1783 listed each American state separately, giving international recognition to the exclusive claims of the thirteen states over all the territory in the "United States."[12]

It was one thing to insist on the exclusive claims of the original states in principle, but quite another to establish them in practice. Unfortunately, state claims based on colonial precedents overlapped. Furthermore, many Americans thought the larger states were too large. Maryland led a coalition of "landless" states in opposition to the extensive charter claims of Virginia and other "landed" states. Much was made of "the impracticality of governing the

---

[10] For recent discussion of this point, see Garry Wills, *Inventing America: Jefferson's Declaration of Independence* (Garden City, 1978), 44–48. See also Jack N. Rakove, *The Beginnings of National Politics: An Interpretive History of the Continental Congress* (New York, 1979), 164–76.

[11] Both resolutions were in response to the Vermont separation. *Journals of the Continental Congress*, ed. Ford, VIII, 491, 497, 508–13, XVII, 452.

[12] According to Article XI, Canada would be admitted into the union by "acceding to this confederation." Any other colony would be admitted by the vote of nine states; no mention was made of "states." James D. Richardson, ed., *A Compilation of the Messages and Papers of the Presidents* (11 vols., Washington, 1897–1911), I, 12. For examples of contemporary constitutional scruples, see James Madison to Edmund Pendleton, Jan. 22, 1782, *The Papers of James Madison*, ed. Robert A. Rutland et al. (12 vols., Chicago and Charlottesville, 1962–1979), IV, 38–39. Madison cites the opinion of several states that there was a "want of power" in Congress to admit new states. See also Ezra L'Hommedieu to George Clinton, Sept. 8, 1781, *Letters of the Members of the Continental Congress*, ed. Edmund Cody Burnett (8 vols., Washington, 1921–1936), VI, 212. L'Hommedieu wrote: "Many Gentlemen from the Southward are fully of opinion that Congress has no authority to admit those people [of Vermont] into the Federal Union as a separate State on the present principles." On the constitutional significance of the 1783 treaty, see C. C. Langdell, "The Status of Our New Territories," *Harvard Law Review*, XII (Jan. 25, 1899), 365–92.

extensive dominion claimed by that state."[13] That the new American republics would have to be small, perhaps in some cases smaller than the colonies they succeeded, was generally agreed, even, in candid moments, by large state politicians. According to a Virginian claims defense, it would not be "productive either of their or our happiness" for easterners and westerners to "remain under one government."[14] Reflecting on New York's unhappy experience in Vermont, John Jay conceded that "we have unquestionably more Territory than we can govern."[15]

Conflict over boundaries—in the West, or in settled areas like Pittsburgh (between Virginia and Pennsylvania) and the Wyoming Valley (between Connecticut and Pennsylvania), or in the New Hampshire Grants—undermined the basic premise of colony-state succession doctrine, that states as territorial communities were "given." Jurisdictional confusion encouraged separatists to advance their own claims. For, in the opinion of a sympathetic newspaper writer, "when it is for the interest and happiness of the people, for which all governments are, or ought to be formed or constituted, no good reason can be assigned why new states and empires should not arise and branch out from old ones."[16] And branch out they did, beginning with Vermont, the first and most successful new state movement.

Vermonters and other separatists set up one statehood claim—the right of revolutionary Americans to constitute themselves into a body politic—against another—the right of New York, for instance, to succeed to New York's colonial claims. But new state movements only strengthened the notion that old colony-state boundaries should be secured at all costs. "If every district so disposed, may for themselves determine that they are not within the claim of the thirteen states . . . we may soon have ten hundred states, all free and independent."[17] Where boundaries were uncertain, government was impossible. "Fix the boundaries," advised Joseph Jones of Virginia (referring to Vermont), and "let the people . . . know they are . . . Citizens and must submit to their Government."[18]

[13] Instructions to Maryland delegates, laid before Congress May 21, 1779, *Journals of the Continental Congress*, ed. Ford, XIV, 619–22. See Herbert B. Adams, *Maryland's Influence upon Land Cessions to the United States* (Baltimore, 1885), 1–54; Merrill Jensen, "The Creation of the National Domain, 1781-1784," *Mississippi Valley Historical Review*, XXVI (Dec. 1939), 323–42; Peter S. Onuf, "Sovereignty and Territory: Claims Conflict in the Old Northwest and the Origins of the American Federal Republic" (Ph.D. diss., Johns Hopkins University, 1973), 267–309.

[14] Thomas Jefferson [?], "Outline and Preamble of Argument on Virginia's Claim," 1782, *The Papers of Thomas Jefferson*, ed. Julian P. Boyd (19 vols., Princeton, 1950-1974), VI, 665.

[15] John Jay to George Clinton, Oct. 7, 1779, *The Public Papers of George Clinton, First Governor of New York*, ed. Hugh Hastings (10 vols., Albany, 1899-1914), V, 311-15.

[16] *Pennsylvania Herald*, June 11, 1785. See also the Petition of inhabitants on the West Side of Laurel Hill (Pennsylvania) to Congress, Jan. 27, 1783, Papers of the Continental Congress, vol. 48, p. 251 (National Archives). According to the petition: "the ease, happiness and convenience of the people ought to be the general rule of the limits, extent and government of human societies."

[17] Report of the Committee, Convention of towns in Cheshire County, New Hampshire, Nov. 15, 1780, Benjamin Bellows Papers (Force Transcripts, Library of Congress, Washington). See also Hugh Williamson to Alexander Martin, Nov. 18, 1782, *Letters of Members of the Continental Congress*, ed. Burnett, VI, 545.

[18] Joseph Jones to Madison, Oct. 2, 1780, *Papers of James Madison*, ed. Rutland et al., II, 106.

American revolutionaries were thus compelled to develop a counterrevolutionary argument against the independence of frontier regions from the original thirteen states. The colonies had not been in a "state of nature" in 1776; the right of revolution could only be exercised by governments which could claim to be legitimate successors to British colonial governments. In its most naked form, when applied to separatist movements, this doctrine sanctioned the exercise of state authority with the same supposedly arbitrary rationale that the British invoked against the states themselves.

Territorial controversies illuminated the difficulties that the American states faced in establishing effective authority throughout their claims. Controversial claims—and contradictory notions of statehood—encouraged separatists to set up new states. But these new states also faced serious obstacles, and most could not surmount them. The creators of Vermont, for instance, could not appeal to a colonial past (although, as we shall see, they attempted to invent one). Nor could Vermont benefit from the recognition of the other states, as could the United States in Congress. It was not enough for the new state's leaders simply to claim the people's right to self-government, particularly when the people were so deeply divided on so many issues—including Vermont's independence. Thomas Chittenden, Vermont's first governor, admitted that many Vermonters were under the misapprehension "that a public acknowledgement of the powers of the earth is essential to the existence of a distinct separate state."[19] Indeed, few Vermonters thought Vermont could survive indefinitely without the recognition and protection of a higher authority, American or English. Thus the new state's leaders had to convince not only the "powers of the earth," but also the people of Vermont and themselves, that they were entitled to statehood.

The defense of the Vermont claims was eclectic. It drew together apparently contradictory arguments premised on the people's natural rights, the absolute authority of the British king in crown lands before the Revolution, and the rights of a community derived from a spurious colonial charter. These divergent strands were synthesized in a concept of statehood that called for independence of the other American states and recognition by, and some kind of dependence on, a higher authority.

The "Vermont doctrine" that the people had a natural right to establish new states as well as new governments was widely perceived as the basic premise of Vermont's pretensions to independent statehood.[20] Certainly that right was routinely invoked. But Vermont propagandists, conscious of a skeptical audience in Vermont as well as elsewhere, did not dilate on natural law claims. Instead, they attempted to show that Vermont had existed as a political community long before the Revolution and so had earned a prescriptive right to self-government within determinate territorial limits. Because the other American states would not recognize these claims, Vermonters could not make the conventional argument that a colony became a state by virtue of par-

[19] Governor Chittenden's proclamation, June 3, 1779, *Public Papers of Governor Thomas Chittenden*, ed. Williams, 458–59.
[20] Thomas Jefferson to Edmund Randolph, Feb. 15, 1783, *Papers of Thomas Jefferson*, ed. Boyd, VI, 247–48.

ticipation in the common cause and membership in Congress. They had to demonstrate that Vermont's independence was not essentially linked with the independence of the United States.

According to Governor Chittenden, Vermont dated its political existence "from the royal adjudication of the boundary line between New York and New Hampshire the 20th July 1764"; therefore, they were "now [in 1783] in the eighteenth year of . . . independence [of the other states] and cannot submit to be resolved out of it" by Congress.[21] As Chittenden explained on an earlier occasion, "this important controversy" between the Vermonters and New York "subsisted many years before the [American] revolution took place."[22] Ethan Allen, a central figure in the state's ruling group, asserted that New York forfeited its jurisdiction after 1764 by its "illegal measures" and "oppressive acts." At the same time, New Hampshire forfeited its claims (which Vermonters holding New Hampshire land titles of course considered legitimate) by acquiescing in the boundary settlement. Thus, "from the commencement of their controversy with the government of New York," Ethan Allen reported, "the inhabitants of these contested lands governed themselves, and managed their internal police under the direction of committees and conventions," just as the colonies had when hostilities with Britain began.[23]

The people of the New Hampshire Grants participated in two revolutions. As good American patriots, they embraced the struggle against British tyranny and broke with the empire. But, beginning in 1764, they also conducted a revolution against New York (or so it was claimed), a revolution that was designed to alter, though not necessarily to renounce, the colonial status of the Grants. The goals of these two revolutions were not always compatible. Freedom from New York's jurisdiction and security of New Hampshire's and later the new state's own land grants were most important for most Vermonters. But what if the United States ultimately upheld New York's claims? Of course, Vermont polemicists strove mightily to associate the two sources of tyranny and oppression: Congress could not support the Yorkers without betraying its fundamental ideals. New York's tyranny represented in microcosm the tyranny of the crown. "The hatred subsisting between us, is equivalent to that which subsists between the independent States of America and Great Britain."[24] New York had been Britain's "favourite government."

[21] Thomas Chittenden to the President of Congress, Jan. 9, 1783, *Public Papers of Governor Thomas Chittenden*; ed. Williams, 593–606.

[22] Chittenden to Jay, Aug. 5, 1779, *ibid.*, 470–72. Roger Sherman of Connecticut, a warm supporter of the Vermont cause, argued that Vermonters "never were subjects of New York with their own consent." Gouverneur Morris's notes on Congressional debates, May 29, 1779, Gouverneur Morris Collection (Columbia University Library, New York, N.Y.).

[23] Ethan Allen, *A Vindication of the Opposition of the Inhabitants of Vermont to the Government of New York* (Dresden, Vt., 1779), 47–48, 12–13.

[24] Ethan Allen, *An Animadversary Address to the Inhabitants of the State of Vermont* (Hartford, 1778), 4. For a colorful account of the struggle between Yankees and Yorkers, see Jellison, *Ethan Allen*, 18–101; and on the origins of this enmity, see particularly Edward Countryman, "'Out of the Bounds of the Law': Northern Land Rioters in the Eighteenth Century," in *The American Revolution: Explorations in the History of American Radicalism*, ed. Alfred F. Young (DeKalb, Ill., 1976), 37–69.

Yorker partisans in Vermont were all Tories; they were in league with the "avaricious monopolizers" to reduce us to "tenants."[25] Anti-Yorker rhetoric served the interests of claimants under New Hampshire titles; it also fit perfectly with popular concepts of why the American Revolution itself was being fought. The "monopoly" that New York jurisdiction would secure to a few powerful landlords would "enslave" the people. Indeed, Ethan Allen wrote in 1779, it would be idle for Vermonters "to dispute any more about liberty, for a sovereign nod of their landlord, cannot fail to overawe them."[26] In other words, why should Vermonters be obliged to "defend the independence of the United Claiming States," Ethan Allen asked Congress in 1781, "and they at the same time [be] at full liberty to overturn and ruin the independence of Vermont?"[27]

When Congress seemed inclined to defend New York's claims and Vermont's two revolutions appeared to be working at cross purposes, manipulation of anti-Yorker sentiment made rapprochement with the British crown less unthinkable. Furthermore, in seeking to define Vermont before the American Revolution as neither part of New York nor part of New Hampshire, Vermont propagandists argued that the crown's jurisdiction had not been mediated by intervening colonial jurisdictions. After 1764, the area was "extra-provincial," "derelict" with respect to the neighboring colonies. Significantly, however, this did not mean that the New Hampshire Grants were in a state of nature; they were still "crown lands" and "the King's authority . . . was therefore absolute."[28]

The argument for British imperial claims followed logically from the attempt to discredit the pretensions of the claiming states in Vermont. It also reflected the popular belief in the years before the Revolution that the British government would eventually rescind the 1764 boundary and vindicate the claims of settlers and grantees under New Hampshire against later, conflicting grants under New York. The apparent contradiction between pleas for the "absolute authority" of the crown and the notorious "Vermont doctrine" which held that the people had a natural right to set up their own government was resolved in their common rejection of the claims of British colonies in the region. Indeed, because Vermont was unconnected with New York or New Hampshire, "the people of Vermont legally speaking, remained under the British Government . . . from the 4th day of July 1776, to the 15th day of January next" when in convention they solemnly "disavowed the British Government."[29] A "people's declaration of independence" drafted at this

[25] Allen, *Animadversary Address*, 16; Aaron Hutchinson, *A Well-Tempered Self-Love a Rule of Conduct toward Others* (Dresden, Vt., 1777), as reprinted in *Collections of the Vermont Historical Society*, I, 67-101, 85; Ira Allen, *Miscellaneous Remarks on the Proceedings of the State of New York against the State of Vermont* (Hartford, 1777), as reprinted in *ibid.*, 135-44.

[26] Allen, *Vindication*, 52.

[27] Ethan Allen to Samuel Huntington, March 9, 1781, *Public Papers of Governor Thomas Chittenden*, ed. Williams, 345-47.

[28] Ethan Allen and Jonas Fay, *A Concise Refutation of the Claim of New Hampshire and Massachusetts-Bay to the Territory of Vermont* (Hartford, 1780), 10-14.

[29] *Ibid.*, 14.

session in Westminster laid the groundwork for adoption of a new constitution in July.

The attack on neighboring state claims enhanced Britain's authority in the Grants. It also encouraged Vermonters to trace their right to independent existence to authoritative British acts. This was at once reflected in the invention of a colonial charter as the putative basis of Vermont's status as a distinct community and later in the eagerness of the Vermont leadership to obtain a new colonial charter in the Haldimand negotiations.

The British government was supposed to have set up a new colony in the Grants just before the American Revolution began, with Philip Skene commissioned as its first governor. (In fact, Skene was to command a garrison at Lake Champlain.) Vermonters apparently believed that a charter for the new colony actually existed. They asked Congress to postpone deliberations on the claims controversy until it could be located, and in later negotiations with the British they solicited a copy of the charter in order to support the state's claims up to the Hudson River.[30]

The Vermonters' reliance on the Skene charter was a tribute to the enormous prestige of charters in defining rights during the Revolutionary era. Even when making the most radical claims to self-government, Vermonters spoke of their "charter of liberty from Heaven."[31] In the Haldimand negotiations, Vermont sought to obtain a new charter under the British crown, modeled on Connecticut's colonial charter (still in force there as that state's "constitution"). The emphasis on charters revealed a deep-seated uneasiness about the legitimacy of a self-constituted state. With the invention of a charter, Vermont's claims became congruent with those of other American states. Paradoxically, assertions of equality with the other states were premised not on the sovereign right of the people to make themselves independent of all the world, but rather on spurious claims to have enjoyed a similar independent status within the empire.

Throughout the war, military insecurity and the tenuous loyalties of its own citizens compelled the Vermont leadership to seek admission to the American union or reunion with the British crown. Notwithstanding the brave talk of the state's propagandists, few Vermonters were ready to believe that a state could exist—in practice or in theory—without the recognition and protection of a higher authority. If neutrality became a necessity as the war progressed, when it was over Vermont "must . . . be subject to the then ruling power."[32]

One of Vermont's leading men (probably Ethan Allen) claimed in June 1782 that Vermont was a "neutral republic," but the foreign policy of the new state pointed to either incorporation into the United States or a return to the empire.[33] According to Ethan's brother Ira Allen, "there was a north

---

[30] Ira Allen to Frederick Haldimand, July 11, 1782, *Collections of the Vermont Historical Society,* II, 283–86. For a brief discussion on the supposed charter, see Hiland Hall, *The History of Vermont, from Its Discovery to Its Admission into the Union in 1791* (Albany, 1868), 195–96.

[31] Allen and Fay, *Concise Refutation,* 27.

[32] Speech of Ira Allen at negotiations with British agents at Isle au Noix, May 8–25, 1781, *Collections of the Vermont Historical Society,* II, 110.

[33] "C" (Ethan Allen?) to Haldimand, June 16, 1782, *ibid.,* 275–76.

pole"—the British in Canada—"and a south pole"—the Americans: "should a thunder gust come from the south, they would shut the door opposite that point and open the door facing the north."[34] This ambivalent policy did not simply reflect the state's precarious situation; the vindication of Vermont independence required the sanction of higher authority. Daniel of St. Thomas Jenifer, Maryland delegate to the Congress, recognized this fundamental point: "if we do not make them independent" of New York and New Hampshire, "the British will endeavour to do it."[35].

International recognition was a practical necessity. It would also help Vermonters overcome their misgivings about their right to set up a new government. Ironically, a misrepresentation of congressional sentiment facilitated the original break from New York. According to Thomas Young's public letter to the "People of the Grants," Congress would be receptive to the formation of a new state. The congressional call for new governments in the colonies in May 1776 applied to all "such bodies of men as looked upon themselves [as] returned to a state of nature."[36] It was necessary, then, for the people of the Grants to take the initiative, draft a plan of government and "become a body politic." According to Young, "you have as good a right to chose how you will be governed and by whom" as the thirteen states already in Congress.

It did not take long for Vermont's leading men to learn from firsthand experience that little could be expected from Congress. Yet it was necessary to convince the people that the new government was committed to the American Revolution and that Congress, once it saw through the schemes of the claiming states, was bound to recognize Vermont. The state was "virtually in alliance with the States of America already," Governor Chittenden claimed in 1779.[37] In the same year, Ethan Allen asserted that a "mere formal declaration" would transform the virtual union into full confederation.[38] The popular conviction that Vermont was really part of the United States and devoted to its cause was reflected in an assembly resolution of October 1780 that it would "not consider any person born in the United States of America to be a foreigner."[39] While Vermont could not concede to Congress the right to determine whether or not it would exist (as it "does not belong to some one of the United States"), the new state's leaders repeatedly proclaimed Vermont's fidelity to the Revolution. If interested parties in Congress prevented its ad-

[34] Report of Dr. George Smith, enclosed in Philip Schuyler to Washington, May 24, 1781, *ibid.*, 132.

[35] Daniel of St. Thomas Jenifer to John Hall, July 24, 1781, *Letters of Members of the Continental Congress*, ed. Burnett, VI, 155.

[36] "Thomas Young to the People of the Grants" (Philadelphia, April 11, 1777), as reprinted in *The Documentary History of the State of New York*, ed. E. B. O'Callaghan (4 vols., Albany, 1849-1851), IV, 934-36. The congressional resolution was addressed only to "the respective assemblies and conventions of the United Colonies," May 10, 1776, and May 15, 1776, *Journals of the Continental Congress*, ed. Ford, IV, 342, 357-58.

[37] Chittenden to Jay, Aug. 5, 1779, *Public Papers of Governor Thomas Chittenden*, ed. Williams, 470-72.

[38] Allen, *Vindication*, 55.

[39] *Journals and Proceedings of the General Assembly*, I, 127.

mission to the Union, Governor Chittenden was prepared to propose separate alliances with neighboring states.[40]

Popular attachment to the Revolution constituted a major limitation to Vermont's claims to independent statehood. It also severely limited the freedom of Vermont agents in negotiations with the British (the Haldimand negotiations), which began in earnest in May 1781. These talks revolved around the possibility of Vermont's returning to the British empire as a distinct colony, with its independence of its neighbors finally guaranteed and the land claims of its citizens confirmed. But "nothing will induce the bulk of the people to defect from the common cause," Philip Schuyler confidently predicted in November 1780.[41] At the outset of the war, Ira Allen told the British, many Vermonters thought "Congress was next to God almighty, both in power and perfections." "It has been with great difficulty that the idea is so far erased and is at present [May 1781] in such a decline."[42] The political education of the common people thus presented the major challenge to the new state leadership. It was as necessary that "the people should be prepossessed against the proceedings of Congress" before they join Great Britain "as it is for a Christian new light to be damned before he can become a true convert."[43]

Popular patriotism notwithstanding, the Vermont leadership became convinced that Great Britain would emerge victorious. Stephen R. Bradley believed that "American independency must fall through" and that "no solid agreement can therefore be made by Vermont except with [Britain]."[44] Neutrality was a temporary expedient; it protected Vermont from attack and gave the new state leaders time to prepare the common folk for a second revolution that would return Vermont to the British empire. Indeed, as long as Congress refused to recognize Vermont, political logic strongly suggested reunion with the crown. The British had no designs on Vermont lands. Without their protection, Vermont faced the "great probability" of "being ruined by . . . haughty neighbors" at the end of the war.[45] The Haldimand negotiators assured their Vermont counterparts that the crown intended to "make you a happy and free government." A proclamation was drafted, though held in reserve, announcing that Britain would consider Vermont "as a separate province, independent of, and unconnected with every government in America." This independence would be secured through a new charter,

[40] Chittenden to Huntington, July 25, 1780, *Public Papers of Governor Thomas Chittenden*, ed. Williams, 326–30; Chittenden to Weare, Dec. 12, 1780, *ibid.*, 335–37; Chittenden to Clinton, Nov. 22, 1780, *Public Papers of George Clinton*, ed. Hastings, VI, 430–31; Chittenden to Jonathan Trumbull, Dec. 12, 1780, Vermont Council of Safety Papers (Force Transcripts); Chittenden to John Hancock, Dec. 12, 1780, *ibid.*

[41] Schuyler to Washington, Nov. 12, 1780, George Washington Papers (Library of Congress), microfilm edition, ser. 4, reel 72.

[42] Ira Allen's information, May 11, 1781, *Collections of the Vermont Historical Society*, II, 122.

[43] Report of negotiations at Isle au Noix, May 8–25, 1781, *ibid.*, 112.

[44] Micah Townshend's abstract of intelligence from Col. Samuel Wells to Henry Clinton, April 10, 1781, Public Record Office of Great Britain, Colonial Office, 5/158.

[45] One of the British agents to Ira Allen (?), Feb. 28, 1782, *Collections of the Vermont Historical Society*, II, 250–51.

identical with Connecticut's, except that the governor would be a crown appointee. Not only would the crown guarantee Vermont against New York and New Hampshire, it also promised to recognize the new state's claims up to the Hudson River and across the Connecticut.[46]

Declining congressional prestige and the possibility of a British alliance on generous terms helped clarify the loyalties of many Vermonters. Isaac Tichenor, a Vermont councillor who was known to be hostile to the Allens and well disposed to New York in 1780, was prepared in late 1781 to lay down "his Life and Fortune" to defend Vermont and its unions.[47] The patriotic Colonel Benjamin Fletcher was reluctantly willing to align with the crown if "the existence of Vermont, as a separate political body, depends on it."[48] By June 1782, the usually skeptical General Haldimand thought it "probable" that the Vermonters will "close with [the British] Government, knowing how little they have to expect from Congress and their neighboring provinces if left to their mercy."[49] Vermonters were well aware of British forbearance on the northern frontier during the course of the Haldimand negotiations, and the promise of military support against Congress and the claiming states now took on an added urgency.

Ironically, the rumored progress of the Haldimand talks prompted Congress to make its only statehood offer to the Vermont separatists in August 1781. But Vermont's imperialist adventures in New York and New Hampshire prevented immediate acceptance; by February 1782, when Vermont renounced its Eastern and Western unions, the military situation was no longer critical and Congress withdrew its offer. As a result, popular support for Congress rapidly diminished. It became clear that the United States were determined to uphold the interests of New York and New Yorkers with title to Vermont lands. This identification of New York and Congress undermined congressional prestige in Vermont and strengthened the tenuous hold of the new state on popular support.

Significantly, growing popular dissatisfaction with Congress was matched by increasingly open advocacy of the British cause. One belligerent Vermonter was supposed to have sworn that "By God as long as the King and Parliament of Great Britain approved of and maintained the State of Vermont he was determined to drive it and so was its leaders."[50] It was said that Vermonters would have nothing to do with Congress, "for they had strength enough to defend their state." They "damned the Congress" and "drank their con-

[46] For the proposed proclamation, ca. Oct. 1, 1781, see *ibid.*, 181–82.

[47] Affidavits of Dirck Swart and Major Daniel Dickenson, Dec. 20, 1781, *Public Papers of George Clinton*, ed. Hastings, VII, 613–14. On Isaac Tichenor's earlier attitude, see John Lansing, Jr., to Schuyler, July 26, 1780, Philip Schuyler Papers, Bancroft Collection (New York Public Library, New York). According to this source: "he admires the State of New York, and I believe, cordially wishes that the Grants may remain under New York."

[48] Answers of Vermont loyalists to queries concerning the Haldimand negotiations, Aug. 18, 1781, photocopy, Ira Allen Papers (University of Vermont, Burlington).

[49] Haldimand to Sir Guy Carleton, June 22, 1782, *Collections of the Vermont Historical Society*, II, 280–81.

[50] Benjamin Baker's declaration, Jan. 10, 1782, reporting statement of Josiah Arms of Brattleborough, Dec. 3 or 4, 1781, Vermont Council of Safety Papers.

fusion"—they drank to the health of George III.[51] Vermonters believed that the common folk of neighboring states would come to their aid against the Continental army. After New Hampshire attempted to collect taxes at Walpole, "the populace went to their Liberty pole . . . and cryed aloud Liberty is gone." They cut the pole "down and at the fall Huzza'd aloud for King George and his Laws."[52]

If Vermont's foreign policy reflected a consensus that statehood required recognition and protection, the implementation of that policy undermined those premises. The loss of legitimacy in higher authorities subverted their ability to legitimize—or destroy—the new state. Early in the war, for instance, the people of Vermont seemed "disposed to acquiesce in the decision of Congress," whatever that might be. As late as 1780, "there are very few but will readily acquiesce."[53] Thereafter, however, calls for congressional decision were joined by calls for armed intervention: the people of Vermont were no longer expected to submit to the will of Congress, unless it was supported by force. The amount of force thought necessary was a good measure of declining congressional prestige. "One year ago," Jacob Bayley wrote in 1781, "ten men would have subdued all that would oppose" Congress, but now "two thousand will not [do] and I am afraid they will still increase."[54] Now, Vermonters would "join the enemy on a mere suspicion that Congress would judge against them." If Congress were to find for New York, "the continent must be involved in a war to enforce" its determination.[55]

Hostility to Congress encouraged a revival of pro-British sentiment; yet this was a highly interested and calculated species of "loyalism," as the Haldimand negotiators were quick to recognize. After all, Vermonters had participated actively in the American war effort. They grew disenchanted with Congress as it became apparent that it would not guarantee the new state's existence or secure Vermonter land claims. They now turned to Britain in order to achieve these goals, not because they suddenly recognized the legitimacy of British authority. At the end of the war, the British lost what little interest they had had in enlisting Vermont's support. Meanwhile, as congressional prestige plummeted to new lows throughout the United States,

[51] Thomas Baker and David Lamb affidavit, sworn before Samuel Bixby at Halifax, Sept. 9, 1782, *Records of the Council of Safety and Governor and Council of the State of Vermont*, ed. E. P. Walton (8 vols., Montpelier, Vt., 1873), III, 240. For a collection of such sentiments, see Benjamin H. Hall, *History of Eastern Vermont from Its Earliest Settlement to the Close of the Eighteenth Century* (2 vols., Albany, 1865), II, 478–79.

[52] Luke Knowlton to Haldimand, Jan. 10, 1783 (Vermont Historical Society).

[53] Egbert Benson to Jay, July 6, 1779, *Public Papers of George Clinton*, ed. Hastings, V, 113–16; Bezaleel Woodward to the President of Congress, Aug. 31, 1781, *State Papers of New Hampshire* (40 vols., Concord, N.H., 1867–1943), X, 374–75.

[54] Jacob Bayley to Washington, Feb. 26, 1781, Washington Papers, ser. 4, reel 75.

[55] Jacob Bayley so suspected the loyalty of Vermonters, but John Sullivan thought his "reasoning . . . ridiculous." John Sullivan to Weare, Dec. 11, 1780, *Letters of Members of the Continental Congress*, ed. Burnett, V, 481. But it was Sullivan who thought a "war" would be necessary. Sullivan to Weare, Sept. 16, 1780, *The Letters and Papers of Major General John Sullivan*, ed. Otis G. Hammond (3 vols., Concord, N.H., 1930–39), III, 187–90.

Vermonters were assured that "no coercive measures will be pursued."[56] Vermont appeared more likely to survive than Congress itself.

The end of the American Revolution left a power vacuum in the Vermont region which the new state was prepared to fill. The ineffectiveness of both Congress and the crown and the very fact that the state's allegiance to one or the other came to be seen as negotiable and contingent helped minimize the political liabilities of nonrecognition. At the same time, volatile loyalties and constantly changing boundaries subverted the authority of state governments in the region. The process of drafting the first state constitutions led to disputes over the basic organization of power in the revolutionary states and appeared to make their territorial limits negotiable as well. In the subsequent confusion, Vermont often enjoyed a relative advantage over its competitors, offering favorable terms of union or backing its claims with superior force. But the popular perception of the "tyranny" of New Hampshire and New York did not mean that Vermont's authority would be seen as legitimate. Rather, the skill with which Vermonters combined appeals to interest and threats of reprisal served to emphasize the expediency of submitting to Vermont rather than to emphasize its right to govern. In fact, the loss of legitimacy in state governments throughout greater Vermont was mutually exacerbating. The Connecticut Valley towns grew accustomed to "anarchy" as they were "deserted by the states."[57] "What can we expect but to see our states crumble to pieces?" asked Jacob Bayley of Newbury.[58]

The American states sought to secure their interests and gain recognition of their jurisdictional claims through membership in Congress. But Vermont was not recognized by the United States and therefore was not bound by the same formal and informal conventions that normalized interstate relations. Because its neighbors would not even recognize its right to exist, there was no reason for Vermont to respect their territorial rights. As a result, the jurisdiction and claims of the new state were in a constant state of flux, causing considerable instability in Vermont as well as in New York and New Hampshire. As George Washington warned President Meshech Weare of New Hampshire, "so long as this Dispute of Territory subsists, the parties, divisions and Troubles, both external and internal, will . . . encrease."[59] With uncertain boundaries, domestic factionalism in Vermont shaded imperceptibly into schemes to annex frontier areas of adjacent states or to establish the claims of those states in Vermont.

[56] On the "collapse" of Congress at this time, see Merrill Jensen, *The New Nation: A History of the United States during the Confederation, 1781-1789* (New York, 1950), 67-84. For the failure to use force against Vermont, see George Clinton to William Floyd, Feb. 6, 1783, *Public Papers of George Clinton*, ed. Hastings, VIII, 64. George Washington was particularly reluctant to send his forces against Vermont. See Washington to Jones, Feb. 11, 1783, *Public Papers of Governor Thomas Chittenden*, ed. Williams, 608-10.

[57] Silvanus Ripley to John Phillips, Dec. 6, 1780, Eleazer Wheelock Papers (New Hampshire Historical Society, Concord).

[58] Bayley to Washington, Feb. 26, 1781, Washington Papers, ser. 4, reel 75.

[59] Washington to Weare, July 31, 1782, *The Writings of George Washington from the Original Manuscript Sources: 1745-1799*, ed. John C. Fitzpatrick (39 vols., Washington, 1931-1944), XXIV, 449-50.

Individual towns and groups of towns meeting in convention undertook negotiations with the contending states; sometimes they appealed directly to Congress or General Washington for resolution of the claims controversy and protection from the enemy. Towns strung along the Connecticut River refused to join New Hampshire without adequate representation in its legislature.[60] Virtually every town in Cheshire and Grafton counties rejected the proposed constitution of 1779 and declined to sit in subsequent conventions and assemblies. Some towns collected New Hampshire taxes but impounded them in town treasuries "to be disposed of hereafter as the town shall judge proper." These towns were also interested, with their counterparts on the west bank, in securing the "union of the [New Hampshire] Grants on both sides of Connecticut River."[61] Moretown, on the west side, proclaimed it "our desire to be a new state," but, if Congress would not approve, was willing to join New Hampshire. Thetford also voted to be part of Vermont, but Newbury, another west bank town, voted to be under New Hampshire.[62]

To the south, adjacent towns in Cumberland/Windham County (New York/Vermont) pledged allegiance to different states. Even Yorker partisans asserted their "full liberty" to look elsewhere for protection if New York could not establish effective jurisdiction. The county convention told New York in 1776 that it would also consider an alliance with Massachusetts.[63] Nor did the Yorkers hesitate to register serious misgivings about the New York constitution. In 1778, another Yorker convention acknowledged "ourselves bound by the most sacred of human ties" to New York; nonetheless, their opposition to Vermont was premised on the "inexpedience" of a separate government "in the present time," the "poverty" of the people, and the lack of local legal talent to draft a "new and equitable system of laws."[64] In 1779, the Cumberland Yorkers warned that they would submit to Vermont if New York did not govern effectively. The threat was made good two years later when many Yorkers participated in negotiations with the new state leaders resulting in the second Vermont union with towns on the east bank of the

[60] In general see Jackson Turner Main, *The Sovereign States, 1775-1783* (New York, 1973), 214-17, 354-56; and Jere R. Daniell, *Experiment in Republicanism: New Hampshire Politics and the American Revolution, 1741-1794* (Cambridge, 1970), 164-79. For details see microfilm copies of town records (New Hampshire State Library). For an early statement of the idea that "every body politic" (that is, town) "whether large or small are legally the same," see *An Address of the Inhabitants of Plainfield* (Norwich, Conn., 1776), as reprinted in *State Papers of New Hampshire*, X, 229-35.

[61] Cornish town meeting, June 28, 1778 (New Hampshire State Library); Charlestown town meeting, April 2, 1781, *ibid.*

[62] Moretown town meeting, May 25, 1779, *State Papers of New Hampshire*, X, 340; Thetford town meeting, June 11, 1782, *Records of the Council of Safety and Governor*, ed. Walton, III, 283; Memorial to New Hampshire General Court by convention of town committees from Newbury, Bradford, Norwich, and Hartford, May 31, 1782, *ibid.*, 281-82; Newbury town meeting, May 31, 1782, Vermont Council of Safety Papers.

[63] Instructions to delegates to New York Provincial Congress, June 11-21, 1776, and Cumberland Committees to Provincial Congress, June 21, 1776, in Hall, *History of Eastern Vermont*, I, 258-61.

[64] Protest of the Inhabitants of Guilford, Brattleboro, Putney, New Fane, Hinsdale, Rockingham, Westminster, and Weathersfield to the Vermont General Assembly, June 4, 1778, photocopy, Ira Allen Papers.

Connecticut.[65] Of course, this submission to Vermont was also contingent. The "unconstitutional" dissolution of the Eastern Union in February 1782 set "the subjects of New York State . . . free from Vermont."[66] Ironically, the Yorkers were now assuming the doctrinal stance of the Vermonters themselves: they were under no authority at all, though "at least three quarters of the people east of the Green Mountains *want* to return to New York." But they would only do so if civil government were established and military protection were extended.

Popular hostility to state authorities on New Hampshire's western frontier and on New York's northeastern frontier paved the way for Vermont's expansion east and west. "The idea of the tyranny of New Hampshire is immovably fixed" in the river towns; "the General Assembly, the compilers of the Constitution, and the executive authority have combined together to enslave the people."[67] New York had been "remiss" in not protecting its citizens against the British. The state's staunchest supporters were exasperated by its failure to do anything. According to a Cumberland County petition, "we esteem" New York's help "not one farthing's better than what Congress" has done—that is, nothing.[68]

Yet Vermont's grasp on popular loyalty was also weak. Before the annexations of 1781, support for the new state had declined precipitously.[69] The eastern counties enthusiastically supported the Eastern Union with New Hampshire towns, but the western counties, fearing a radical shift in power within the state, were considerably less enthusiastic. Expansion in the west reestablished the balance, but these new Vermonters—known as "Cattermounters"—were extremely unpopular in the east. "Great division" was reported in Vermont in the wake of the unions. The Cattermounters "are supported only by the Governor, Council and a few hot-headed people"; many Vermonters were "daily falling off from their new state."[70] Disenchantment reached new depths when the Haldimand negotiations were widely publicized

[65] Petition of Cumberland Committees, May 4, 1779, *Documentary History of the State of New York*, ed. O'Callaghan, IV, 957–60; Cumberland Convention, Oct. 31, 1780, meeting with New Hampshire towns at Charlestown, Nov. 8, 1780, and at Walpole, Nov. 15, 1780, in Hall, *History of Eastern Vermont*, II, 401. On the wavering loyalties of Yorkers, see Townshend to George Clinton, April 12, 1780, *Public Papers of George Clinton*, ed. Hastings, V, 616–17.

[66] Guilford Address to Congress, George Clinton, and New York General Assembly, Jan. 8, 1782, in Hall, *History of Eastern Vermont*, II, 415; manuscript address, n.d. (early 1782?), James H. Phelps Collection (Vermont Historical Society).

[67] Thomas Sparhawk and Benjamin Bellows to Committee of Safety, July 30, 1782, *State Papers of New Hampshire*, X, 491–93.

[68] Solomon Pendleton to George Clinton, Dec. 7, 1781, *Public Papers of George Clinton*, ed. Hastings, VII, 556–59; Brinton Paine to George Clinton, April 16, 1781, *ibid.*, VI, 775–77; petition to Clinton, June 3, 1783, James Phelps Scrapbook (Vermont Historical Society).

[69] The majority of the population was said to be "under very little, if any, subjection to their nominal leaders." See extracts of letters from agents for negotiating with the people of Vermont, Aug. 2–18, 1781, *Collections of the Vermont Historical Society*, II, 148–50.

[70] Beverley Robinson to Haldimand, May 8, 1781, *ibid.*, 119–20; New York delegates to George Clinton, Sept. 9, 1781, *Letters of Members of the Continental Congress*, ed. Burnett, VI, 213; John Younglove to George Clinton, June 20, 1781, *Public Papers of George Clinton*, ed. Hastings, VII, 34–36; petition to Clinton, June 3, 1783, Phelps Scrapbook.

in early 1782. Yorkers reported that their Vermont tormentors were now "heartsick of Vermont."[71]

In the long run, however, Vermont stood to gain most by the delegitimation of state authority and the related collapse of congressional prestige. What was being destroyed, after all, was the notion that political community was a given and that states had legitimate claims to obedience under all circumstances. Lacking recognition and a given status as a state, Vermont was forced to rely entirely on popular consent. And nowhere in America did local communities become so thoroughly accustomed to such a high degree of political self-determination. At the same time, political imperatives were clarified to an unusual degree. Americans in the greater Vermont region needed to secure a modicum of law and order; they needed to be protected from foreign invaders and, most of all, from each other.

The solution to ineffective state government was to adapt revolutionary infrastructure—county militia, committees of safety, and county conventions—to fill the jurisdictional vacuum. The new state of Vermont itself came into being after a series of such conventions which were superseded by general assemblies beginning in 1778.[72] But in the Connecticut Valley, particularly in Cheshire and Grafton counties (New Hampshire) and Windham/Cumberland (Vermont/New York), conventions continued to sit throughout the war. Conventions derived their sanction from the interruption of legitimate authority and, at least inferentially, from the sovereignty of the people. As intermediaries between towns and the contending states or Congress, the conventions were supposed to facilitate the transition to legitimate authority. Yet one of the hallmarks of American constitutional development, reflecting the crisis of legitimacy in the new state governments, was to identify legitimate, constituent authority with the conventions themselves and to grant constitutional as well as temporal priority to these extralegal, supralegal, and temporary organizations.

In greater Vermont, the convention movement had a continuing vitality throughout the war precisely because of the low repute of state governments, including Vermont's. But the claims of the new state were inextricably linked with the convention movement (through sheer lack of any other justification for its existence), and as conventions acquired prestige and legitimacy, other kinds of claims to state jurisdiction identified with the pretensions of the "claiming states" suffered corresponding losses. According to the emerging standards of American constitutionalism, Vermont's claims to self-

[71] Petition and remonstrance, March 23, 1782, ibid.; petition of May 17, 1782, ibid.; Charles Phelps to Clinton, April 27, 1782, ibid. See also Hall, History of Eastern Vermont, II, 421. Resolutions of Brattleboro, March 12, 1782, and Guilford, March 13, 1782, publicizing the negotiations, were printed and distributed by the Yorkers. See Phelps Scrapbook.

[72] Records of the early conventions, July 24, 1776 (Dorset; Sept. 25, 1776 (adjourned session, Dorset), Oct. 30, 1776 (adjourned session, Westminster), Jan. 15, 1777 (adjourned session, Westminster), June 4, 1777 (adjourned session, Windsor), July 2, 1777 (Windsor), are collected in Public Papers of Governor Thomas Chittenden, ed. Williams, 5–54. In general see, R. R. Palmer, "The American Revolution: The People as Constituent Power," in The Reinterpretation of the American Revolution, 1763–1789, ed. Jack P. Greene (New York, 1968), 338–61.

government became increasingly credible. The "right" was not derived from history or from higher authority: it came from its own constitution.

Vermont became a state because the people "consented" to its creation, even when that consent was coerced by force. Indeed, consent implied coercion: effective authority depended on a monopoly of power. Vermont propagandists recognized this in their enthusiasm for the classic natural law doctrine that "allegiance must be founded on a reciprocal protection."[73] During the course of the war, all parties in the Vermont controversy came to identify jurisdiction with the exercise of force. The Vermont leadership had to proceed cautiously at the outset because of widespread doubts about the legitimacy and durability of the state and the dubious loyalty, if not outright hostility, of the eastern counties. But it was apparent to Yorkers as early as 1779 that "they will establish their State by the sword."[74] With typical bravado, Ethan Allen made the same point. If the United States withheld recognition from Vermont, it would be compelled to support its claims "by right of Conquest."[75] Still, no definitive move was made against the Yorker towns until 1782 and 1783 when Ethan Allen led punitive expeditions across the Green Mountains. The display of force was followed by vigorous prosecution of Yorkers in the Vermont courts, leading to the imprisonment or exile of several key leaders and the political conversion of many others. Ethan Allen was supposed to have agreed that "it was a savage way to support government as he did, but they could not carry the point without it."[76] Jailed Yorkers suffered loss of property and threats to their lives; they also had to submit to the taunts and boasts of their captors. Ethan Allen would "march into Albany with the Green Mountain Boys, and set up and be absolute monarch of all America," according to one reported harangue—obviously intended for the edification of New York Governor George Clinton.[77]

The expeditions against Windham County Yorkers represented a definitive contribution to the sustained debate over the nature of legitimate authority: what was a state supposed to be? The attack on the Yorkers was also, of course, an attack on New York State. The vindication of New York's claims had long ceased to be one of legal right to Yorkers—though for their part, the state's politicians continued to devote an inordinate amount of energy to proving the validity of its pretensions to Congress. Yorker partisans in Vermont knew that

[73] Governor Chittenden's Annexation Proclamation, July 18, 1781, *Public Papers of Governor Thomas Chittenden*, ed. Williams, 541–43.

[74] Samuel Minott to George Clinton, May 25, 1779, *Documentary History of the State of New York*, ed. O'Callaghan, IV, 965–66.

[75] For report of a conversation between Ethan Allen and Robert R. Livingston, see James Duane to Jay, Aug. 22–24, 1778, *John Jay: The Making of a Revolutionary. Unpublished Papers. 1745–1780*, ed. Richard B. Morris (New York, 1975), 494. See also George Clinton's sarcastic comments on the "conquest" right, George Clinton to Duane, Sept. 18, 1778, *Public Papers of George Clinton*, ed. Hastings, IV, 46.

[76] Samuel Bixby and other Cumberland County Yorkers to George Clinton, Sept. 22, 1782, Vermont Council of Safety Papers. "I yield to brute force," Timothy Phelps announced to the Vermont Court at Marlborough, February 4–11, 1783. See Hall, *History of Eastern Vermont*, II, 492–94.

[77] Timothy Phelps to George Clinton (May–June?) 1783, in Hall, *History of Eastern Vermont*, II, 496–98.

only a show of force would be effective against the separatists. This realistic appraisal, combined with their own predisposition, apparent since 1776, to treat statehood as a negotiable issue, in which rights necessarily gave way to more expedient calculations, meant that Yorkers and Vermonters saw their respective problems in similar terms, equally remote from, if not hostile to, New York's assertions of territorial right or the similarly theoretical claims of New York City speculators to Vermont lands. The Vermonters' violent language—and the language of their violence—struck even the most sympathetic congressmen (attuned to the pretense that the controversy was among title claims which Congress would adjudicate) as a brazen admission of the moral bankruptcy of the Vermonters, tantamount to treason to the common cause.[78] Certainly, Vermonters had learned not to take Congress very seriously, but Yorkers had learned the same lesson. They had warned that without adequate support they would come to terms with Vermont, that their loyalty to New York was contingent. The Allen expeditions were shaped by these expectations; their violence was not gratuitous or unexpected. If they convinced many Congressmen that Vermont should not be a state, they convinced the Yorkers that it was one.

Vermont's survival as a state was made possible by the inability of the claiming states to enforce their jurisdictional claims. As a result, the kinds of claims made by those states—based on "legal" precedent—were radically devalued. Similarly, the impotence of Congress helped delegitimize congressional authority. The Vermont leadership could not easily overcome the pervasive conviction that the security and legitimacy of the new regime rested on the recognition and protection of higher authority. But playing one side against the other taught the leaders of the new state as well as the people in general to look on loyalty as a contingent matter.[79] And, in the aftermath of the war, only Vermont could govern Vermonters. Only Vermont could provide institutions responsive to local self-determination and coercive force sufficient to establish and maintain law, order, and land titles.

Outside the union, Vermont could not make the kinds of claims to statehood so essential to the pretensions of the United States. Only in Vermont was the concept of a state as a self-constituted political community fully and radically tested against, rather than in tandem with, orthodox notions of legitimate state authority, premised on succession to the claims of colonial communities and recognized and guaranteed by other states in Congress. In this sense, Vermont was the only true American republic, for it alone had truly created itself.

[78] See, for instance, Connecticut delegates to Trumbull, Jan. 21, 1782, *Letters of Members of the Continental Congress*, ed. Burnett, VI, 294–95.

[79] James H. Kettner, *The Development of American Citizenship, 1608–1870* (Chapel Hill, 1978), 173–209.

The Establishment of Legal Structures on the Frontier: The Case of Revolutionary Vermont

Michael A. Bellesiles

Inside the small wooden jailhouse in Bennington, Vermont, David Redding waited for frontier justice to exact its price. A Vermont court had found Redding, a New York Tory, guilty of fighting with the British against his fellow Americans and of stealing horses for Gen. John Burgoyne's recently defeated army. But on that very morning, June 4, 1778, John Burnham, the only person in that part of Vermont who could make any claim to knowledge of the law, had pointed out to the governor and his council that a jury of only six men had passed judgment on Redding, whereas English common law required twelve. The embarrassed council ordered a stay of execution. The crowd of angry Vermonters gathered outside the jail, denied the spectacle of a public execution, was calling for vengeance; they had come to hang Redding, not to protect his inalienable rights as a freeborn Englishman.

Just as the sheriff was getting nervous and had sent a call for reinforcements, a long-absent but familiar voice was heard clearly shouting above the crowd's din, "Attention the whole!" After two years as a prisoner of the British, Ethan Allen made his dramatic reentry to Vermont politics, leaping onto a tree stump and immediately obtaining the attention of the crowd in his usual flamboyant fashion. Witnesses reported that Allen made a colorful and amusing speech, quieting the crowd's disappointment and calling on them not to besmirch the fair name of Vermont with any hint of injustice. He closed with the peculiar and unlikely reassurance that by the next day someone would be hanged, if not Redding, then Allen himself. The crowd roared with approval and dispersed to the taverns to toast Ethan Allen.

To ensure that his promise to the crowd was fulfilled, Allen had his old friend Gov. Thomas Chittenden appoint him state prosecutor. The fact that Redding's crimes had occurred in New York, which had requested his extradition, was overcome by appointing Allen, in effect, a United States attorney. The proclamation naming him prosecutor read that "Colonel Ethan Allen . . . is hereby chosen to act in the Capacity & to do the duty of State Attorney in the cause depending Be-

Michael Bellesiles recently received a Ph.D. in history from the University of California, Irvine. This essay received the Louis Pelzer Memorial Award for 1986. The author wishes to acknowledge the generous assistance and advice of Christine Heyrman, Michael Johnson, James Kettner, Peter Onuf, and the staff of the American Antiquarian Society.

ALLEN AT TICONDEROGA.

Ethan Allen as a revolutionary war hero.
Reproduced from *Harper's New Monthly Magazine*, 17 (1858), 730.

tween this & the United States of America & David Redding."[1] That Redding had committed no crime in Vermont other than escaping from its officers, that Vermont was not then part of the United States, and that Vermont had no authority to appoint attorneys to act in the interests of the United States were all ignored. But then such technicalities hardly mattered to the Vermonters. As Allen persuaded Governor Chittenden and his council, the appearance of legality and legitimacy was all-important. Vermont gained an aura of power and comradeship with the United States, while thumbing its nose at the authority of New York.

[1] E. P. Walton, comp., *Records of the Council of Safety and Governor and Council of the State of Vermont* (8 vols., Montpelier, 1873–1880), I, 120, 261, 263–64; Walter H. Crockett, comp., *Journals and Proceedings of the General Assembly of the State of Vermont* (4 vols., Bellows Falls, Vt., 1924), III, pt. 1, 22–23. Governor Chittenden wrote that "This Council do not Doubt in the Least but sd Redding will have Justice done with to the satisfaction of the public." Walton, *Records*, I, 261.

Redding's new trial was brief and effective. Defense counsel John Burnham's knowledge of correct legal procedures proved no match for Allen's rhetoric, and the properly constituted twelve-man jury duly found Redding guilty. He was hanged to great public approval the same afternoon. The presence of the entire General Assembly at Redding's hanging on June 6, 1778, just two days after Burnham had won his stay of execution, suggests the importance attached to this execution by the state of Vermont.[2]

Redding's trial represented a crucial moment in Vermont's thirty-year struggle with New York. The main battlefield of that conflict was the courtroom. Essential to the process of revolution and state formation in Vermont was the efficacy of the legal system sponsored by the new state contending for legitimacy. Inability to triumph in the courthouse translated into a failure to win the consent of the governed. Thus, the Vermont government's prosecution of Redding, despite New York's request for his transportation to its jurisdiction, served to emphasize the independence of the new state. Allen's quick actions demonstrated that the power of Vermont and its courts was at least equal to that of New York, and obviously superior within the contested jurisdiction of the former New Hampshire Grants. In the process Allen prevented a lynching, an act of lawlessness that would have been a black mark against the state—though Allen's intervention hardly made a difference to David Redding.[3]

Traditionally historians have seen law and order as generated principally from above. More recently, some have written of the direct transportation of common law to the American frontier as though every settler carried a copy of Blackstone in his luggage.[4] The case of New York's northeastern counties, which eventually became the state of Vermont, indicates that legal structures are generated from below and are representative of a broadly felt desire for consistent standards and comprehensible notions of justice. New York's efforts to impose law from above were reluctantly undertaken and an abysmal failure. As a consequence, the inhabitants of the Green Mountains acted in concert to create and operate a court system that would protect their land titles and serve the needs of their fragile frontier economy. The settlers of the northern frontier did not feel that they were violating the law in resisting and overthrowing the repressive government of New York. They felt that the New

[2] For the first full account of the Redding case, based on the testimony of eyewitnesses, see William Slade, *Vermont State Papers* (Middlebury, Vt., 1823), 269. See also Hiland Hall's version in Abbey Hemenway, ed., *Vermont Historical Gazeteer* (5 vols., Burlington, Vt., 1865–1891), I, 161–62; John Pell, *Ethan Allen* (Lake George, N.Y., 1929), 139–41; Isaac Jennings, *Memorials of a Century* (Boston, 1869), 222; and, esp., John Spargo, *The Story of David Redding Who Was Hanged* (Bennington, Vt., 1945).

[3] Victor H. Paltsits, comp., *Minutes of the Commissioners for Detecting and Defeating Conspiracies in the State of New York: Albany County Sessions, 1778–1781* (3 vols., Albany, 1909–1910), I, 92, 97–98.

[4] See, for instance, Lord Cross and G. J. Hand, *The English Legal System* (London, 1971); Karl N. Llewellyn, *The Common Law Tradition: Deciding Appeals* (Boston, 1960); Joseph Smith, "New Light on the Doctrine of Judicial Precedent in Early America: 1607–1776," in *Legal Thought in the United States of America under Contemporary Pressures*, ed. John N. Hazard and Wenceslas J. Wagner (Brussels, 1970), 9–39; David Grayson Allen, *In English Ways: The Movement of Societies and the Transferral of English Local Law and Custom to Massachusetts Bay in the Seventeenth Century* (Chapel Hill, 1981); John P. Reid, *Law for the Elephant: Property and Social Behavior on the Overland Trail* (San Marino, Ca., 1980). One exception is Robert Dykstra, *Cattle Towns* (New York, 1965).

York government was itself illegitimate because it employed the law to impede the region's stable development. The perception and operation of legal institutions would thus prove important in shaping the society of revolutionary Vermont.

It is a misuse of Ockham's Razor to simplify the conflict in the Green Mountains to a struggle of Yorker versus Yankee culture. It is unlikely that people would spend thirty years resisting the authority of established government just because their conceptions of proper social organization did not match. A conflict of political forms and personal characteristics does not make a revolution. While some have seen the struggle as cultural, others have seen class as the primary determinant. Edward Countryman, for instance, declares that the Green Mountain rioters knew that they were "committing treason when they took over government's tasks," making it "plain enough that they thought of what they were doing in class terms." True, the settlers described themselves as poor: "a poor people . . . fatigued in settling a wilderness country." Is *poor* a class label? If so, it is far too inclusive to be of much explanatory use. When everyone in a region is poor, the difference tends to be between inhabitants and outsiders. That Ethan Allen occasionally called himself a peasant did not make him one; his use of the term certainly does not mean that the frontier farmers were fighting a "peasant revolution." To clarify the nature of the conflict, this article will look at the practical effects of New York's attempts to establish its dominance, rather than at historical theories that draw selected facts to them or at the justifications the two sides offered for their actions.[5]

The confused structure of British colonial North America, which accounts for so many features of the American Revolution, helps explain why and how a group of disaffected frontier farmers was able to resist and then to topple the authority of one of the most powerful and centralized American states, to establish a competing state government without any outside support, to survive independently for fourteen years despite the hostile efforts of Britain, New York, and the Continental Congress to eliminate it, and, finally, to enter the United States entirely on its own terms. Or, put another way, how, and why, did a group of frontier settlers become lawmakers and state builders?

In 1741 George II made the mistake of appointing an American, Benning Went-

---

[5] Dixon R. Fox, *Yankees and Yorkers* (Port Washington, N.Y., 1963); Chilton Williamson, *Vermont in Quandary: 1763–1825* (Montpelier, 1949). Countryman supports his notion that the Vermonters were peasant rebels by quoting Samuel Huntington, *Political Order in Changing Societies* (New Haven, 1968), 298–99. Countryman's definition of peasants is illusory. As the Vermonters already owned their land—bought and sold it without hindrance, paid no quitrents, and had no landlords above them—they could easily be taken for yeoman farmers. But by calling the settlers peasants, Countryman is able to construe their struggle as a peasant revolution aimed at the expropriation of property. Edward Countryman, "'Out of the Bounds of the Law': Northern Land Rioters in the Eighteenth Century," in *The American Revolution: Explorations in the History of American Radicalism*, ed. Alfred F. Young (DeKalb, 1976), 37–69, see 48–49; see also Edward Countryman, "Consolidating Power in Revolutionary America: The Case of New York, 1775–1783," *Journal of Interdisciplinary History*, 6 (Spring 1976), 645–77; Eric R. Wolf, *Peasants* (Englewood Cliffs, N.J., 1966), 1–4, 12–17, 91–109; Barrington Moore, Jr., *Social Origins of Dictatorship and Democracy: Lord and Peasant in the Making of the Modern World* (Boston, 1966); Robert Redfield, *Peasant Society and Culture: An Anthropological Approach to Civilization* (Chicago, 1956); E. J. Hobsbawm, *Primitive Rebels: Studies in Archaic Forms of Social Movement in the 19th and 20th Centuries* (Manchester, Eng., 1959), 4–5, 23–28; and Huntington, *Political Order*, 291–300, 374–80.

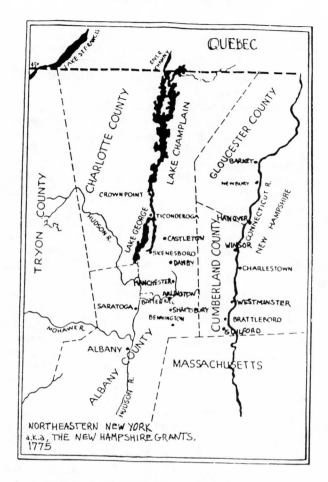

QUEBEC

CHARLOTTE COUNTY

TRYON COUNTY

LAKE CHAMPLAIN

GLOUCESTER COUNTY

BARNET

NEWBURY

CROWN POINT

HUDSON R.

LAKE GEORGE

TICONDEROGA

HANOVER

WINSOR

NEW HAMPSHIRE

CONNECTICUT R.

CASTLETON

SKENESBORO

DANBY

CHARLESTOWN

MANCHESTER

ARLINGTON

SARATOGA

BUTTENKILL

CUMBERLAND COUNTY

WESTMINSTER

SHAFTSBURY

BENNINGTON

BRATTLEBORO

GUILFORD

MOHAWK R.

ALBANY

ALBANY COUNTY

MASSACHUSETTS

HUDSON R.

NORTHEASTERN NEW YORK
a.k.a., THE NEW HAMPSHIRE GRANTS,
1775

Adapted by Kate Dornhuber from Matthew A. Lotter,
A Map of the Provinces of New-York and New-Jersey (Augsburg, Ger., 1777).

worth, governor of New Hampshire. The Harvard-educated Wentworth was wealthy, ambitious, pompous, and as crafty a manipulator of vague charter rights as ever disrupted the British Empire. He possessed that most notorious American characteristic, an eye for the main chance. An examination of the various colonial charters convinced Wentworth that there were opportunities in the West. Jurisdiction over the area between the Connecticut and Hudson rivers was claimed by New York, New Hampshire, and Massachusetts. Wentworth lost no time in exploiting this haziness, making a fortune selling the rights to 129 townships totaling three million acres. New York complained, and fifteen years later, in 1764, the Privy Council declared all of Wentworth's New Hampshire Grants to be illegal.

Meanwhile several thousand people, mostly from Massachusetts and Connecticut, had settled in the area. They refused either to leave or to pay New York for lands they already owned by deeds under the king's name. The settlers were also repelled by New York's higher quitrents and more centralized political structure. They were accustomed to New England ways and were intent on reestablishing them in the Green Mountains. But what truly threatened them was the plan of New York's largest speculators to *replace* the settlers on the west side of the Green Mountains with more pliant foreign tenants. Faced with the threat from New York, the settlers also appealed to the king. The ponderous weight of the British Empire collapsed into inaction, the Privy Council ordering in 1765 that no party should issue any more grants or attempt to enforce its authority until his majesty made his desires known. The king was still trying to make up his mind eleven years later when the whole issue became irrelevant.[6]

In this intervening decade, New York moved ineptly to confirm its jurisdiction over the region that had become known as the New Hampshire Grants. Many inhabitants of the eastern Grants—who were not threatened with complete dispossession—overcame their objections to the laws and ways of New York and welcomed the prospect of being part of any province, if it would insure "that offenders may be brought to Justice, and Creditors may Recover their Just Dues." But they could not understand why New York refused to act to assert its own jurisdiction. On numerous occasions in the late 1760s, the leading inhabitants of Connecticut River towns petitioned Lt. Gov. Cadwallader Colden of New York for the creation of a county and the establishment of courts. The petitioners, all New Englanders holding New Hampshire title to their lands, stated that they had too long been "without Law, Notwithstanding we have made application to be protected, but as yet are not answered."[7]

The petitions were denied despite the support of New York's governor, Sir Henry Moore. Some large landowners in Albany County, which was adjacent to the contested region, felt threatened by the possibility of Grants settlers suing them, even in a New York court. Since their own titles to land in the area were of dubious origin, these influential proprietors, led by the Livingston family, sought to avoid the courts as long as possible, especially as their continued control of the New York judiciary was under attack by Colden. When the internal power struggle was decided in favor of the De Lancey faction in 1769, the legislature responded to the appeals of the Grants settlers and created courts. The New York legislature went further than the

---

[6] Lord Dartmouth, secretary of state for the colonies, to Gov. William Tryon of New York, June 2, 1773, E. B. O'Callaghan, comp., *Documentary History of New York* (4 vols., Albany, 1850–1851), IV, 856–59; Earl Hillsborough, secretary of state for the colonies, to Tryon, April 18, 1772, J. R. Brodhead and E. B. O'Callaghan, comps., *Documents Relating to the Colonial History of New-York* (11 vols., Albany, 1856–1861), VIII, 294; Rowland Berthoff and John M. Murrin, "Feudalism, Communalism, and the Yeoman Freeholder: The American Revolution Considered as a Social Accident," in *Essays on the American Revolution*, ed. Stephen G. Kurtz and James H. Hutson (Chapel Hill, 1973), 256–88. For the best short study of the New York/New Hampshire controversy, see Peter Onuf, "State-Making in Revolutionary America: Independent Vermont as a Case Study," *Journal of American History*, 67 (March 1981), 797–815. For conflicting views, see Matt Jones, *Vermont in the Making, 1750–1777* (n.p., 1939); Williamson, *Vermont in Quandary*; and Frederic Van DeWater, *The Reluctant Republic: Vermont, 1724–1791* (Taftsville, Vt., 1974).

[7] O'Callaghan, comp., *Documentary History*, IV, 578–83. See also Frank L. Fish, "The Vermont Bench and Bar," in Walter Crockett, ed., *Vermont, the Green Mountain State* (5 vols., New York, 1923), V.

petitioners desired, though, imposing officers on all the Grants settlements and thus bypassing the traditional New England town's right to elect its own. In the process, New York also violated Privy Council instructions to take no further action in the "New Hampshire District" until the king had determined its fate. Further violating the king's orders, the government of New York issued an additional 180,000 acres in land grants, though most of them were on the west side of the Green Mountains. After more debates, setbacks, vetoes by the Privy Council, and the appointment of officers who did not reside in the Grants, the east side of the Green Mountains finally obtained a court system in mid-1770, after more than four years of effort.[8]

From the point of view of the east side settlers, those courts were inefficient and insufficient.[9] The Gloucester County courts, for example, were established by New York in March 1770, but judges were not appointed until the end of May. The courts were to be held in the county seat, the uninhabited town of Kingsland, whose chief virtue was its name. The first session of the court adjourned without transacting any business; the second session, in August, appointed four constables and then adjourned. The third session, in November, exemplified the major fault of the New York judiciary in the Grants by continuing all eight cases that it heard. The fourth session was worthy of a Jacques Tati comedy. Scheduled for February, the court was to meet in a town with no year-round inhabitants, no buildings, and no roads leading there. The chief judge and his two main officers struggled through the snow for two days without being able to find any surveyors' markings or other indications that they were anywhere near the shire town of Kingsland. Finally they resolved to hold the court in the woods, continued all the cases on their agenda, and adjourned the court. And so it went through the next year, most sessions being adjourned without actually hearing any cases. It was not until 1772, after the New York officials had wised up and moved the shire to Newbury, which was inhabited, that any cases were resolved before this court. Even then, their record was dismal.[10]

In the four-year history of the Gloucester County courts, a total of 121 cases were heard. Of them, 103 (85 percent) were continued, some several times, and only 5 of the continued cases were ever resolved. In only 18 cases (15 percent), was some definite judgment reached. It is significant that in 11 of the 18 cases the plaintiff won his case because the defendant refused to appear. And in only *one* of the resolved cases is it certain that the plaintiff actually received satisfaction.[11]

A similar story is evident in the Cumberland County courts, a far busier and more successful bench. In the last two sessions of 1774 there were 152 cases, of which 95, or just short of two-thirds, were continued. As with the Gloucester courts, almost

---

[8] New York granted a total of 2.1 million acres in the Grants region. Hiland Hall, "New York Land Grants in Vermont, 1765–1776," *Collections of the Vermont Historical Society* (12 vols., Montpelier, 1870–1946), I, 145–51; William Smith, *Historical Memoirs*, ed. William Sabine (New York, 1956), 185–89; O'Callaghan, comp., *Documentary History*, IV, 577–78, 583–84, 586–88, 609–11; Lords of Trade to the King, [April 1767], Brodhead and O'Callaghan, comps., *Documents*, VII, 918–19; and Fish, "Vermont Bench and Bar," 326–27.

[9] Ira Allen, *The Natural and Political History of the State of Vermont* (London, 1798), 21–24.

[10] Gloucester County Court Records (Orange County Clerk's Office, Chelsea); Fish, "Vermont Bench and Bar," 327–28.

[11] Gloucester County Court Records.

all of the cases involved debts. Only 2 of the 57 resolved cases were decided in the defendant's favor. The officers of the Cumberland County courts were not quite so scrupulous as their Gloucester peers. After a certain point, if the defendant failed to show, he was guilty. One-third of the cases decided for the plaintiff have the notation that the defendant did not appear. The court also decided on many occasions that the defendant's plea was "not agreeable," and therefore voided it; whereupon the court ordered judgment for the plaintiff "for want of a plea."[12]

The history of New York's courts in Gloucester and Cumberland counties is a study of inaction. The records are full of statements such as "Neither appearing, Nothing done," of bonds forfeited, summonses ignored, and clumsy attorneys, of "capi corpus" (the sheriff being unable to locate the defendant), and of jurisdiction denied. A grand jury would be sworn in, only to be dismissed because there were no cases to hear. It was little wonder that the judges had trouble getting people to serve and tended to rely on their immediate neighbors, family, and political allies. Doing so proved helpful, as one of the jurors or the judge himself might be subject to a suit. In one curious instance Judge Samuel Sleeper was the defendant in a case and, though present at the beginning of the session, was declared "not appearing," and the case was continued as a consequence. One cannot be certain if he stepped outside for a few minutes, ducked under the table, or simply created a legal fiction on paper. In any event, it was a poor example, though a valuable lesson, to any other defendants who might have been waiting their turn to appear before the vanishing judge.[13]

Such corruption did the court party no good though, as their sessions started playing to empty houses and the judges found it impossible to get even their constables to attend. The nonappearance of so many of those ordered to appear was a reflection of the attitude of the settlers along the Connecticut River toward the New York courts, one of denial and contempt. It appears that the courts were unable even to collect costs from the losing party, thus bearing some fairly hefty expenses with nothing to show for their money but ill will.[14]

[12] Cumberland County Court Records, bound in with Windham County Court Records, II (Windham County Courthouse, Newfane, Vt.).

[13] Ibid., 8, for example; and Gloucester County Court Records. For an indication of the New York council's awareness of this corruption, see Smith, Historical Memoirs, ed. Sabine, 22, 188–89.

[14] The legitimacy of New York's judges was often denied in the courtroom itself, for instance, in the cases of Elisha Hawley, Ebenezer Hoisington, Sr., Ebenezer Hoisington, Jr., Andrew Norton, and Elnathan Strong in Cumberland County; and the cases of John White and Azariah Wright in Gloucester County. All denied the right of New York's courts to pass judgment on them. See Cumberland and Gloucester County Court Records; Allen, History, 31–35; Slade, Vermont State Papers, 22–33; O'Callaghan, comp., Documentary History, IV, 778, 792–93, 824–27, 871–73; Vermont Historical Society Collections, I, 6; "The Vision of Junus the Benningtonite," Hartford Connecticut Courant, Sept. 22, 1772; Ira Allen, Some Miscellaneous Remarks on the Proceedings of the State of New York against the State of Vermont (Hartford, Ct., 1777), 141–42; William Smith Manuscript Diary, June 15, Oct. 21, 1772 (New York Public Library); Hillsborough to Tryon, April 18, 1772, Brodhead and O'Callaghan, comps., Documents, VIII, 294; Ethan Allen, A Brief Narrative of the Proceedings of the Government of New York Relative to Their Obtaining the Jurisdiction of That Large District of Land Westward from Connecticut River (Hartford, 1774), 14–23, 36–48, 51–65, 67–68, 72; Hartford Connecticut Courant, July 14, Sept. 22, 1772, June 8, June 21, 1774; Hemenway, ed., Vermont Historical Gazeteer, I, 77–80; Slade, Vermont State Papers, 38–39, 49–54; Dummerston Town Records, I, 19–20 (Town Clerk's Office, Dummerston); Chester Town Meeting Records, Oct. 10, 1774 (Town Clerk's Office, Chester); Records of the first Cumberland County Convention, Oct. 19, 1774, Reuben Jones, "A Relation of the Proceedings of the People of the County of Cumberland," March 23, 1775, Noah Sabin, et al., "State of the Facts," March 14, 1775, in Walton, comp., Records, I, 317–19, 334, 337–38.

Despite these difficulties, New York insisted on rigorous adherence to the rules.[15] What ensued was a string of technically minded decisions that disgusted most of those who came before New York's courts and reflected a basic inability to conduct business efficiently. The mass of people on both sides of the Green Mountains desired a court system that would work, but they found New York's system worthless, its decisions unenforceable, and its proceedings dominated by a clique of New York attorneys and their patrons.[16] Lieutenant Governor Colden, who often attempted to use the courts for his personal advantage, found the entire New York judiciary dominated by the province's largest landowners. Colden condemned the "dilatory Proceedings in the Courts of Law" and "the heavy Expence in obtaining Justice," and demanded that the legislature investigate, something that self-interested party would not do. At best the courts in the Grants region were as corrupt and alienating as those of the rest of New York; the evidence indicates that they were even worse. Those who associated with New York's courts in any capacity, whether as defendants, plaintiffs, officials, or jury members, found their time wasted and unproductive.[17]

If, as David Konig has insisted was the case in seventeenth-century Essex County, Massachusetts, the courts served as an active socializing institution, maintaining and enforcing certain moral and political behavioral patterns for and on the majority of citizens, then New York failed miserably. New York's courts were unable to enforce any aspect of that province's culture or social system in the Grants region. In short, the New York government proved incapable of making use of its own legal system.[18]

But worse lay ahead for New York, in the shape of Allen and the Green Mountain Boys. Historians have gotten and given the impression that the Green Mountain Boys were some sort of mountain Mafia, the muscle for their land speculating godfather, Ethan Allen. In fact, they formed a broadly based popular movement. Records indicate that several hundred men, a sizeable proportion of the total adult male population, served at one time or another in local ad hoc militia companies

[15] O'Callaghan, comp., *Documentary History*, IV, 526, 748–55, 786–96.

[16] On the corruption of the New York Courts, see Julius Goebel, Jr., "The Courts and the Law in Colonial New York," in *Essays in the History of Early American Law*, ed. David Flaherty (Chapel Hill, 1969), 245–77; Smith, *Historical Memoirs*, ed. Sabine, 22; Henry S. Wardner, *The Birthplace of Vermont: A History of Windsor to 1781* (New York, 1927), 142–58; O'Callaghan, comp., *Documentary History*, IV, 636–40, 645–7; Benjamin Hall, *History of Eastern Vermont* (New York, 1858), 146–58; New York Land Papers, XXVII, 132 (New York State Library, Albany); and New York Council Minutes, XXIX, 447, April 22, 1771, *ibid.*

[17] Gloucester County Court Records; Colden quote from *Journal of the Votes and Proceedings of the General Assembly of the Colony of New York* (New York, 1764–1766), II, 669. See also the Cumberland County Court Records; O'Callaghan, comp., *Documentary History*, IV, 759, 777; Fish, "Vermont Bench and Bar," 8–9; *New York Historical Society Collections*, IV, V: William Smith, Jr., *The History of the Late Province of New York* (New York, 1829), IV, 247–48; *ibid.*, IX, X: *The Colden Letter Books, 1760–1775* (2 vols., New York, 1876–1877), IX, 149–50, 157, 191, 231; *The Letters and Papers of Cadwallader Colden* (9 vols., New York, 1917–1923, 1934–1935), V, 283–95, 310–319; Milton Klein, "Prelude to Revolution in New York: Jury Trials and Judicial Tenure," *William and Mary Quarterly*, 27 (Oct. 1960), 439–63, see 446–47.

[18] David T. Konig, *Law and Society in Puritan Massachusetts: Essex County, 1629–1692* (Chapel Hill, 1979); Hiland Hall, *The History of Vermont From Its Discovery to Its Admission into the Union* (Albany, N.Y., 1868), 134; Jones, *Vermont in the Making*, 291; O'Callaghan, comp., *Documentary History*, IV, 747, 776–78, 796–98, 800–801, 956–57; Ira Allen, *History*, 348; New York Land Papers, XXXI, 73, April 1, 1772; New York Land Patents, XVII, 5; Zadock Thompson, *History of Vermont* (Burlington, Vt., 1833), pt. 3, 55; Slade, *Vermont State Papers*, 500; Hall, *History of Eastern Vermont*, 237–38.

THE GREEN MOUNTAIN BOYS IN COUNCIL.

Reproduced from *Harper's New Monthly Magazine*, 17 (1858), 725.

operating under the appellation of Green Mountain Boys. Those units looked entirely to themselves for authorization and Allen certainly had no complaints if
anyone called himself a Green Mountain Boy, just so he supported the cause of resistance to New York's rule. There was a rough hierarchy, with Allen or his cousin Seth
Warner as commander, but even the roster of officers changed constantly, and no
town ever asked for approval to form a company.[19]

This informal structure made the Green Mountain Boys both attractive and effective. Almost any male above the age of fourteen could join for almost any duration,
take part in the fun of a military outing, share in the reflected glory of the heroic
and victorious Ethan Allen and his Green Mountain Boys, and then return to the
farm without any further responsibilities. As a consequence, Allen could ride into
an area, quickly collect a company of men, and march to meet some crisis. Allen's
ability to draw anyone into the unit without ceremony allowed him to build up a
vast reservoir of potential troops and sympathetic supporters, a force that he used
with increasing effectiveness to battle New York's courts and later to support
Vermont's.[20]

By the summer of 1772, the Green Mountain Boys had taken to harrassing any
New York courts that attempted to meet within what they were coming to see as
their own jurisdiction. All officials of those courts, in Cumberland County and
eastern Albany County, found themselves the target of constant abuse, both in the
courtroom and out. In the courtrooms the Green Mountain Boys protected defen-

[19] Records of the Second Cumberland County Convention, Nov. 30, 1774, in Walton, comp., *Records*, I,
320–22; and Dummerston Town Records, I, 28, 37–40.
[20] Ethan Allen, *Brief Narrative*, 8.

ALLEN DISPOSSESSING THE NEW YORK SETTLERS.

Reproduced from *Harper's New Monthly Magazine*, 17 (1858), 727.

dants, intimidated plaintiffs and witnesses, and sought to disrupt the sessions to the extent that the judges themselves would be compelled to adjourn. Outside the courthouse they tore down the fences of New York officials, trampled crops, threatened, bullied, slandered, and generally made life miserable for anyone who dared to conduct any business with the "land-jobbers" who ran New York's courts.[21]

The decisive step came in 1774, when the Green Mountain Boys and their allies moved to close down the New York courts permanently. They were entirely suc-

[21] O'Callaghan, comp., *Documentary History*, IV, 486, 529–30, 637–72, 685–91, 710–12, 720, 723–24, 732–47, 757–63, 770–71, 799–800, 842–43, 846–54, 891; Wardner, *Birthplace of Vermont*, 154–65; Brodhead and O'Callaghan, comps., *Documents*, VIII, 252; Cumberland County Court Records; Jones, *Vermont in the Making*, 175–76, 284–89, 304–7; Abraham Yates to James Duane and John Tabor Kempe, July 20, 1771, William Cockburn to Duane, Sept. 10, 1771, James Duane Papers (New-York Historical Society, New York); Ira Allen, *History*, 345–48, 356–57; Hall, *History*, 124–30, 139; New York Land Papers, XVIII: 160; *Hartford Connecticut Courant*, April 28, June 2, 9, 1772; Ethan Allen, *Brief Narrative*, 71, 152–55; [James Duane], *A Narrative of the Proceedings Subsequent to the Royal Adjudication* (New York, 1773), 22; affidavit of Colonel John Reid, Colonial Office Papers 5/1103, 759–62 (British Public Record Office, London); Hemenway, ed., *Vermont Historical Gazetteer*, I, 79; Ira Allen's autobiography in James B. Wilbur, *Ira Allen, Founder of Vermont* (2 vols., Boston, 1928), I, 16–18.

cessful.[22] Having triumphed, the anti-Yorkers found it necessary to establish something to replace the New York courts. Initially they relied on drumhead courts and local committees of safety. But in 1777 the northeastern counties of New York declared their independence not only from Britain, but also from the province of New York. The creation of the state of Vermont made it necessary for Allen and his clique to establish their legitimacy, and creating a legal system seemed a logical and useful route. In Allen's view the state served only two functions beyond his personal aggrandizement: to protect the frontiers and to maintain economic order and social stability through the courts.[23]

Few of us today, except lawyers, view our court system as central to our lives. But to settlers on the frontier of New England in the eighteenth century, the court system was essential to their economic survival and the security of their communities. Their economy worked by the exchange of notes of hand and book accounts, debts that represented commitments rather than exact monetary values. There was almost no currency on the frontier; such notes functioned in its place. When an agreement foundered, filing a lawsuit was a way to push the defendant to take responsibility for the debt. The defendant was usually willing to do so, if some extension or arrangement could be reached. The paucity of jury trials; the symbolic attachments of some piece of the defendant's personal property, such as a book or piece of furniture; and the great number of guilty pleas—nearly 70 percent a year in Vermont's first decade—indicate the willingness of creditors and debtors to reach a speedy resolution. Likewise, the absence of primary litigants, creditors who prosecuted more than two or three cases a year, indicates an economy in which nearly everyone wrote and held notes. In the Windham County Court records, for instance, only one person, a lawyer, brought more than three suits in any one year, while the extant justice-of-the-peace records contain no such individual. The same lawyers worked for both plaintiffs and defendants, as creditors and debtors were one and the same. In the Bennington records, where the lawyers in each case are noted, the same attorney often defended the individual he had just prosecuted. Historians have long noted the extreme litigiousness of New England society and have taken it as a sign of barely suppressed conflict. Yet the opposite conclusion seems equally valid; remove the debt cases and the people of Vermont almost never went to court. Indiscriminate violence was not a disease to which they were subject.[24]

[22] Cumberland County Court Records; John Gale and Harriet Thompson, comps., *Official History of Guilford, Vermont* (Brattleborough, Vt., 1961), 26; Dummerston Town Records, I, 18–20; Hall, *History of Eastern Vermont*, 218, 222, 232–33, 236, 746–55; O'Callaghan, comp., *Documentary History*, IV, 905–6, 912–14; Jones, *Vermont in the Making*, 270; *New York Journal*, March 23, 1775; Walton, comp., *Records*, I, 332–38; Stephen R. Bradley, *Vermont's Appeal to the Candid and Impartial World* (Hartford, Ct., 1780).

[23] Ethan Allen, *A Vindication of the Opposition of the Inhabitants of Vermont to the Government of New-York* (1779), in Walton, comp., *Records*, I, 444–517, see 479, 515–17, 338–39, 356; *Vermont Historical Society Collections*, I, 5–6; Ira Allen, *History*, 345–47; Hall, *History*, 127, 130; O'Callaghan, comp., *Documentary History*, IV, 523, 712, 762, 764, 848–54, 859–69, 893–903, 914–16; Pell, *Ethan Allen*, 35, 65; Ethan Allen to the town of Durham, [Nov. 1773], Emmett Collection (New York Public Library).

[24] Bennington County Court Records (Bennington County Courthouse, Bennington); Windham County Court Files (abandoned jailhouse, Newfane, Vt.); Justice Strong's Records, Wilbur Collection (University of Vermont, Burlington). In contrast, see Jessica Kross, *The Evolution of an American Town: Newtown, New York, 1642–1775* (Philadelphia, 1983); Christine L. Heyrman, *Commerce and Culture: The Maritime Communities of Colonial Mas-

The courts were important precisely because of their influence on the mundane details of daily life. They were at the center of most people's understanding and acceptance of any government. When the people of the Green Mountains rejected New York's courts as inadequate, as the empty shells Allen insisted they were, they rejected all aspects of that province's rule. When they created their own state, its courts stood at the core of its legitimation, its reason for being. The judiciary had to be run as the people desired, for these transplanted New Englanders had experience in eliminating systems of which they disapproved, as they had demonstrated to New York.[25]

The timing of Vermont's effort to establish its own judiciary was perfect. In 1777 and 1778 the New York legal system was in confusion, and much of the state, including New York City, was occupied by the British. The New York Constitution of 1777 made the common law and statutes of Great Britain the operative laws of New York, unless the legislature chose to change them. The court records of New York demonstrate the uncertainty of the period—transcripts break off, old forms bear new names, and new forms are printed in old styles. Court clerks wrote to the busy Provincial Congress of New York seeking instructions on a steady stream of cases, the mass of cases being postponed indefinitely. There was one type of justice for Tories and another for patriots, and apparently one legal system for large landowners and another for tenants and small freeholders.[26] In contrast, the assurance and briskness of Vermont's judiciary seemed an anchor, a sign of self-confident and effective authority. The irony is that the frontier attained quick stability, the older established communities being chaotic and unformed. But then Vermont did not carry the burden of an imperial heritage.

Historians of Vermont have long insisted that the Allen/Chittenden government lacked popular support and thus turned to coercion and deception to maintain its power.[27] Yet the enormous number of people who made use of Vermont's courts

---

sachusetts, 1690-1750 (New York, 1984); Stephen Innes, Labor in a New Land: Economy and Society in Seventeenth-Century Springfield (Princeton, 1983); John Demos, A Little Commonwealth: Family Life in Plymouth Colony (New York, 1970), esp. 46-51. In more commercial communities, there was a definite creditor class and individuals who appeared in court a dozen times a year and more.

[25] Ethan Allen, Vindication, 512-17; O'Callaghan, comp., Documentary History, IV, 861; John P. Reid, In a Defiant Stance: The Conditions of Law in Massachusetts Bay, the Irish Comparison, and the Coming of the American Revolution (University Park, 1977); John P. Reid, "The Irrelevance of the Declaration," in Law in the American Revolution and the Revolution in the Law, ed. Hendrik Hartog (New York, 1981), 46-89; John P. Reid, "In a Defensive Rage: The Uses of the Mob, the Justification in Law, and the Coming of the American Revolution," New York University Law Review, 49 (Dec. 1974), 1043-91; Garry Wills, Inventing America: Jefferson's Declaration of Independence (New York, 1978); Robert Gross, The Minutemen and Their World (New York, 1976); William Nelson, The Americanization of the Common Law: The Impact of Legal Changes on Massachusetts Society, 1780-1830 (Cambridge, Mass., 1975); Morton Horowitz, The Transformation of American Law, 1780-1860 (Cambridge, Mass., 1977); Robert Hine, Community on the American Frontier (Norman, 1980), 88-89; and Williamson, Vermont in Quandary, 1-23.

[26] New York Constitution of 1777, Article 35. Julius Goebel, Jr., and T. Raymond Naughton, Law Enforcement in Colonial New York: A Study in Criminal Procedure, 1664-1776 (New York, 1944); Edward Countryman, A People in Revolution: The American Revolution and Political Society in New York, 1760-1790 (Baltimore, 1981); Patricia Bonomi, A Factious People: Politics and Society in Colonial New York (New York, 1971); Michael Kammen, Colonial New York: A History (New York, 1975).

[27] Williamson set the tone for this view, which has been supported by the vast majority of his successors. See Williamson, Vermont in Quandary, 68-164.

is striking. In the single critical year of 1781 there were 176 cases brought before the Bennington and Windham county courts alone; the next year there were 250. At that time the population of the two counties was around ten thousand. If one-fourth of this population consisted of males over sixteen—the overwhelming majority of those appearing in court—almost one-tenth of the adult males living in those countries appeared before a Vermont county court in the single year of 1782.[28] Such a figure does not even include the justice courts. John Strong, justice of the peace for Dorset, heard 30 cases in 1781 and 59 in 1782, in a town with an estimated population of four hundred.[29] Perhaps the upstart Vermont government was unpopular, but if so, it is difficult to explain why so many relied on its structures—went to its courts to resolve conflicts, respected court decisions, and paid as ordered. There is an important distinction to be made between the leadership of Ethan Allen, which was resented by some of the more conservative inhabitants of the Connecticut River towns, and the institutions he helped to create and nurture. Even the conservative opposition did not hesitate to make use of Vermont's courts while they worked to overturn Allen's dominance in Vermont's legislature.

Why did the inhabitants of the scattered frontier communities lying on either side of the Green Mountains turn to Vermont's courts with such enthusiasm? What did Vermont offer in place of New York's discredited structures? First, a court system that worked, one that could reach and enforce decisions. Vermont's court records are not crowded with the endless stream of continuations that filled New York's dockets; nor was there the long line of frustrated constables reporting that defendants, witnesses, and even jurors refused to appear and complaining that they lacked power to collect the ordered fines. The bulk of Vermont's cases in the years from 1777 to 1790 were decided within two hearings, the majority being executed within a few months of the court's decision. Under New York's courts the only conflicts that were quickly resolved were those involving the lands of wealthy New York speculators. Under Vermont's courts even the smallest debt was quickly ordered paid and was collected.

Second, Vermont had a court system that addressed the needs of its clientele, meeting public requirements for flexibility and the regulation of a fragile frontier economy. More than 90 percent of all cases heard by Vermont's new courts prior to 1790 were debt litigations. While a large minority of the disputes involved debts as much as ten years overdue, the vast majority were brought to trial within six months of the date on which payment was due, demonstrating that creditors had substantial confidence in the efficacy of the courts. Coming to trial was *not* the last and usually useless resort of the creditor, as had been the case under New York authority, and as many historians have implied was the general case in New England. As they were intended to, the courts replaced violence. Rather than seize the debtor's goods by brute force to reclaim unpaid debts, creditors could turn to the

---

[28] Windham County Court Records, II; Windham County Court Files, 1782; Bennington County Court Records, 1782; Jay Mack Holbrook, *Vermont 1771 Census* (Oxford, Ma., 1982), xii–xxiii.

[29] See Justice Strong's Records, the only known justice-of-the-peace book from this period. Holbrook, *Vermont 1771 Census*.

courts with the expectation of some peaceful satisfaction. Seizure was now the last resort, used only when a debtor refused to pay court-ordered damages, and almost always undertaken by officials of the state rather than by the claimant and a few burly friends.

Third, Vermont's court system fulfilled the expectations of the Grants settlers, performing only those functions that the New Englanders felt a court should undertake. New York had used its courts as instruments of the central state government and the interests that ran it. New York's judiciary blatantly served the needs of the ruling class and its supporters. For example, in the ejectment case that first brought Ethan Allen to the Grants, both judges (Robert Livingston and George Duncan Ludlow), the prosecutor (James Duane), the attorney general (John Tabor Kempe), and even the lieutenant governor (Colden), were all major speculators in the contested area under New York patents. While Vermonters generally conceived of courts as a means of social control, their conception was based on the well-being of the immediate community rather than the success of a distant elite. To New Englanders, with their heightened sensitivity to encroachments upon local autonomy and stability, the exercise of such unrestrained outside authority was intolerable.

And fourth, Vermont's court system could punish its enemies and reward its friends. Behind all other justifications, whether intellectual or economic, stood the power of the military. As noted, the informal nature of the Green Mountain Boys, which allowed companies to form and disband on short notice, was the source of its strength. Along with the courts, they constituted the one agency encountered by the average settler that surpassed local authority. As such this "posse comitatus" was vital as both a theoretical and practical prop of Vermont's stability. Serving for even a short time made the resident of a farming community into a Vermonter.

The merging of state interest with local town structure proved particularly effective. A violator of state decrees took immense chances of alienating himself from his community.[30] It was almost an abstract act to resist the distant and impotent authority of New York. It was quite another matter to contest the legitimacy of Vermont. To do so would be to risk calling down the wrath of Ethan Allen, who could raise up the resister's neighbors against him. Not only were the courts' decisions usually complied with, but any further acts of resistance were avoided. By 1780 most, though not all, Yorkers had been recruited to the Vermont cause or had withdrawn to the quiet contemplation of their grievances.[31]

[30] Crockett, comp., *Journals of the General Assembly*, III, pt. 1, 91; Ian C. B. Pemberton, "Justus Sherwood, Vermont Loyalist, 1747-1798" (Ph.D. diss., University of West Ontario, 1972), 313-14; Walton, comp., *Records*, I, 15-30; Sarah Kalinoski, "Sequestration, Confiscation, and the 'Tory' in the Vermont Revolution," *Vermont History*, 45 (Fall 1977), 237; Samuel Williams, *The Natural and Civil History of Vermont* (Walpole, N.H., 1794), 210-310; Lyman Hayes, *History of the Town of Rockingham, Vermont* (Bellows Falls, 1907), 205; Wardner, *Birthplace of Vermont*, 242, 445; Frederic Wells, *History of Newbury, Vermont* (St. Johnsbury, Vt., 1902), 79, 86, 657.

[31] Walton, comp., *Records*, I, 61, 134-36, 283, 287, 518-25, II, 62-63; *Journal of the Provincial Congress of the State of New York, 1775-77* (Albany, 1842), I, 826; Mary G. Nye, comp., *Sequestration, Confiscation, and Sale of Estates* (Montpelier, 1941), 15-17, 37-39, 54; John A. Williams, comp., *The Public Papers of Governor Thomas Chittenden, 1778-97* (Montpelier, 1969), 162-65, 177, 196; Williamson, *Vermont in Quandary*, 79-84; Slade, *Vermont State Papers*, 272, 305-12; Crockett, comp., *Journals and Proceedings of the General Assembly*, III, pt. 1, 127-28.

Nowhere was the willingness of the state to enforce its will more evident than in that peculiar combination of military intimidation, legal retribution, and political absolution that made up Allen's coup d'etat of May 1779. On that occasion, Allen and his Green Mountain Boys moved with stunning speed to arrest on a single day all but one of the New York officials remaining in the area claimed by Vermont. Allen did not act quietly, making sure that everyone, especially New York's governor, George Clinton, knew that forty-one New York officials were sitting in Vermont's jails. The prisoners were even encouraged to write a petition to Clinton begging him to send immediate relief, preferably military. While Clinton simply repeated his assertion of authority over the state, Vermont held a giant show trial, found thirty-six of the miscreants guilty of impersonating officers, and fined the lot of them. Allen then turned around and not only forgave all their fines and court costs, but also offered these former enemies positions in the new state government.[32] Although many did leave in bitterness, some never to return to Vermont, others seized the chance to work for the winning side and quickly rose to positions of prominence in Vermont.[33] For instance, all of Cumberland County's representatives in the New York assembly—Micah Townshend, John Sessions, and Elkanah Day—all of whom were arrested and convicted in Allen's coup, were Vermont officials by 1783.[34]

"After so open a challenge," Micah Townshend bluntly warned Governor Clinton, if New York did not immediately move to protect its subjects, "it cannot be thought strange if they should in a body join the only government under which they can be secure. Who will dare resist the execution of the laws of Vermont? . . . For New York to delay taking arms, however specious the reasons, is the same as to yield the point."[35] This analysis was both astute and accurate, and goes a long way toward explaining the willingness of so many Yorkers, including Townshend, to join their old enemy Allen. Years later Ira Allen explained his brother's actions by noting that "the object was to shew power and leinty at once, as the most effectual mode of uniting the inhabitants of Vermont in the cause of their own Government."[36]

The New England settlers of the Grants sought and attained an informal and flexible legal structure. Points of law had their place, but justice came first. Lawyers, every one of whom had been a supporter of New York, were popularly perceived as vultures, or as creeping parasites creating litigation where none had previously existed, and as agents of oppression. Several times in the 1780s the Vermont General Assembly considered limiting the number of attorneys and their fees. And in one

[32] Ira Allen, *History*, 400–403; Walton, comp., *Records*, I, 298–300, 302–3, 307–9, 402–3, 442–43, 518–25; Eleazar Patterson to George Clinton, May 5, 1779, Clinton to Samuel Minot, May 14, 1779, in O'Callaghan, comp., *Documentary History*, IV, 957–66; Ethan Allen Papers, 289–90 (Secretary of State's Office, Montpelier); Windham County Court Records, 1779; Supreme Court Records (Rutland Court House); Gale and Thompson, *Official History of Guilford*, 45–50; Hall, *History of Eastern Vermont*, 332–45, 362–63; Slade, *Vermont State Papers*, 305–12; Hall, *Early Vermont*, 284–88.
[33] Allen Soule, comp., *Laws of Vermont, 1777–1780* (Montpelier, 1964), June 2, 1779; Records of General Assembly, June 2–3, 1779, in Walton, comp., *Records*, I, 302–3.
[34] Ethan Allen, *Vindication*, 462.
[35] Micah Townshend to Governor Clinton, June 9, 1779, George Clinton Papers, VIII, document 2397 (New York State Library, Albany).
[36] Ira Allen, *History*, 401.

memorable election speech in 1786 Governor Chittenden rejected the suggestion that lawyers and deputy sheriffs be put to death, offering instead to tax lawsuits and regulate legal fees. Since judges were elected in Vermont, it is not too surprising that only one lawyer was elevated to that office in Vermont's first fifteen years.[37]

A key element in Vermont's success was the paucity of lawyers; especially on the bench. Vermont's citizens felt closer to and more confident of their court system knowing that their judge might choose to overlook a point of law if it seemed a hindrance. To Vermont judges, justice seemed something that anyone could understand; it was an element of human nature. In one case, two lawyers were embroiled in a technical debate over a point of law. The judge picked up one of the documents and asked the defendant's attorney what it was. "It is a demurrer, Yr Honor." The judge considered and said, "I do not know what a demurrer is, but I know what justice is, and this plaintiff is entitled to a judgment." In another instance a runaway slave appeared in court demanding recognition of his right to stay in Vermont. His master responded by producing the bill of sale from the previous owner. The judge demanded a bill of sale from "God Almighty" as original proprietor before he would recognize the title within the territory of Vermont. The former slave stayed. It was exactly such creative interpretation of the law that allowed Vermont to maintain its jurisdiction in the face of hostile superior authority, including the Continental Congress. Just as in the Redding case, Vermont's judges did not hesitate to extend their jurisdiction into whatever areas they deemed necessary for the security of the state.[38]

In the view of most Vermonters the technical manipulation of justice represented by New York's courts had bogged down the Grants; hindering the area's growth, disrupting its economy, and passing power into the hands of a few. Such justice, Allen pointed out, could "conceive it to be just to inslave negroes."[39]

In many ways Vermonters were on the cutting edge in their rejection of legal formalism. William Nelson has demonstrated that after the Revolution Massachusetts's courts acted to eliminate pleadings based on excessive technicality from common

[37] Leonard Deming, *Catalogue of the Principal Officers of Vermont* (Middlebury, Vt., 1851); A. M. Gaverly, *History of the Town of Pittsford, Vermont* (Middlebury, Vt., 1872), 602–3; Fish, "Vermont Bench and Bar," 59; *Bennington Vermont Gazette,* Aug. 28, 1786; *Bennington Gazette,* Feb. 7, 1784; Manuscript State Papers, XVII, 169 (Secretary of State's Office, Montpelier); Bennington County Court Dockets, I, 2 (Bennington County Courthouse). On the New England tradition of lay judges and the lack of concern for the separation of the branches of government, see George L. Haskins, "Lay Judges: Magistrates and Justices in Early Massachusetts," *Publications of the Colonial Society of Massachusetts,* 62 (1984), 39–55. Vermont politician Matthew Lyon felt that lawyers should not be allowed to hold public office; see Lyon, "Twelve Reasons," *Rutland Farmer's Library,* Aug. 19, 1794.

[38] Fish, "Vermont Bench and Bar," 77–78, 364; Spargo, *Redding*; Old Superior Court Files, II, n.p., Sept. 1784 (Rutland County Courthouse). On the continuing American suspicion of lawyers, see Perry Miller, *The Life of the Mind in America* (New York, 1965), 99–116; Maxwell Bloomfield, *American Lawyers in a Changing Society, 1776–1876* (Cambridge, Mass., 1976), 32–58.

[39] Ethan Allen, *Vindication,* 459–60. See also George L. Haskins, "Reception of the Common Law in Seventeenth-Century Massachusetts: A Case Study," in *Law and Authority in Colonial America,* ed. George Billias (Barre, Mass., 1965), 17–31; Max Radin, "The Rivalry of Common-Law and Civil Law Ideas in the American Colonies," in *Law, A Century of Progress* (3 vols., New York, 1937), II, 427. Vermonters often regarded the common law as the enemy of democracy, and their legislature worked to bring it under their control. John A. Williams, comp., *Laws of Vermont, 1785–1791* (Montpelier, 1966), 17–20, 110–13, 143–45, 168, 238–39. One act declared that the common law was "manifestly repugnant to that spirit which should ever distinguish a free, civilized and Christian People."

73

law hearings.[40] Legal procedures became separated from the substance of a case, allowing Massachusetts's judges to develop the law, gaining independence from British formalism. The Vermont courts anticipated Massachusetts's developments in their reaction to the excessive formalism, the "Anglicization," of the New York courts. Vermont's courts were less technical tribunals, where the abstract goal of justice was sought even if the wrong writ had been filed or some other pleading error made. Their innovations grew from past experiences in New England and, except for the absence of lawyers from the bench, formed the pattern followed elsewhere in the last two decades of the eighteenth century. Vermont's courts were more flexible, more responsive to growth and change, and more democratic than any of their predecessors or competitors.[41] The quality of their justice was questioned by many local conservatives and by outside observers shocked by what they deemed an anarchic and archaic approach to the law, an approach unsuited to the complex economy and society of the new nation.[42] Yet it is doubtful that a state as isolated and economically underdeveloped as Vermont truly required the predictability and regularity of a professional legal system. The local orientation of Vermont's lay courts served the overwhelmingly rural state and its primitive trade networks well.[43]

In sum, a court system was created in Vermont that could ensure the survival of its authorizing state by actively involving citizens in its legal proceedings. What New York would not do was enforce its will. The leaders of New York were not inclined to expend the funds necessary to send their own forces into the Grants region, preferring to rely at first on the British, their troops and their authority, and later on the American Congress and its army. The government of New York had not looked to its own strength to assert and maintain its legitimacy, but to the power of higher governmental levels, perhaps in reflection of its leaders' hierarchical view of the world.[44] The failure of New York to respond more forcefully to the rebellion in its

[40] Nelson, *Americanization of the Common Law*, 77–88. See also William Nelson, "The American Revolution and the Emergence of Modern Doctrines of Federalism and Conflict of Laws," *Publications of the Colonial Society of Massachusetts*, 62 (1984), 419–67. Even Nelson's critics agree with him on this point. See Reid, "Irrevelance of the Declaration."

[41] Daniel Chipman, *Reports of Cases Argued and Determined in the Supreme Court of the State of Vermont* (Middlebury, Vt., 1824); Horowitz, *Transformation of American Law*.

[42] In the political conflicts of the late eighteenth and early nineteenth centuries, support for an independent judiciary was seen as a Federalist expression of distrust of democracy and popular rule. An independent judiciary would operate as a "guardian class," to employ the Federalist phrase. Richard Ellis, *The Jeffersonian Crisis: Courts and Politics in the Young Republic* (New York, 1971), esp. 111–22; Miller, *Life of the Mind*, 105–16, 239–54; Brook Thomas, "*The Pioneers*, or the Sources of American Legal History: A Critical Tale," *American Quarterly*, 36 (Spring 1984), 86–111; Shaw Livermore, Jr., *The Twilight of Federalism* (Princeton, 1962); John T. Horton, *James Kent: A Study in Conservatism* (New York, 1939).

[43] Williams, comp., *Public Papers of Governor Chittenden*, 162, 177–79, 186; Nye, *Sequestration*; Hall, *History of Eastern Vermont*, 720; Audit Office Transcripts, 12.24.305 (Public Archives of Canada, Ottawa); Windham County Court Records; Kalinoski, "Sequestration," 241; Lewis Aldrich and Frank R. Holmes, *History of Windsor County, Vermont* (Syracuse, N.Y., 1891), 367; Crockett, comp., *Journals and Proceedings of the General Assembly*, III, pt. 1, 99.

[44] New York's Governor Clinton made an effort to get first troops and then artillery from Washington. O'Callaghan, comp., *Documentary History*, IV, 975–76. As Allen noted, New York was trying to "procure a sufficient force from the united states to carry into execution the reduction of Vermont; an enterprise which their own militia seem not inclined to undertake." Ethan Allen, *Vindication*, 462. See also Cumberland County Committee to Gov. Clinton, June 8, 1779, George Clinton Papers, VIII, document 2394. For similar plaints, see O'Callaghan, comp., *Documentary History*, IV, 957–60, 964–67, 981–95, 1010–14.

northeastern counties in the seven years after 1776 is understandable. In those years New York was a state under siege, with a British army to the north and another in New York City, tenant uprisings on the estates of several patriot leaders, a large Loyalist population, and substantial political divisions in its ruling revolutionary councils.[45] These were divisions which Allen and the Vermonters constantly played on, appealing for support on different occasions to factions as diverse as New York's tenant farmers and the British army. By 1783, when New York was again able to press its jurisdiction over the region, Vermont was already well established, the Allens having bought valuable time through their not-always-secret negotiations with the English and having tied the interests of the vast majority in the new state to its continued stability.[46]

In contrast to New York, Vermont looked entirely to itself and its people for validation. It was Vermont's military, the Green Mountain Boys, which enforced the decisions of its executive, legislature, and judiciary. Allen was not above sending a company of troops to a farm to guarantee adherence to a court decision or to a town with Yorker officials to enforce the laws of Vermont. To justify such actions, Allen did not turn to the superior legitimacy of the American struggle or nation, but to the will of the Vermonters as a self-realized and self-reliant people.[47] In the most liberal definition of citizenship then existing, Vermont required only that an individual acknowledge the right of Vermont to exist and state his willingness to be part of it. Vermont's Declaration of Rights made very clear who was subject to the state's protection; the fourth article stated that "the sole, exclusive, and inherent right of governing and regulating" Vermont was vested in all those who acknowledged its jurisdiction.[48]

In the same fashion, those who made use of Vermont's courts recognized the legitimacy of Vermont and had a stake in preserving its stability and success. This was true not just of the plaintiffs, but also of all who used the courts. For in the same day a single person might appear as plaintiff, defendant, and juror. There was as yet no creditor or debtor class; in the economy of frontier Vermont almost everyone was both. A particular defendant might have no reason for wishing the continued existence of a state whose courts had just ordered him or her to make good on a note of hand, but most defendants understood that the next day might bring a reversal of roles; the defendant would become a plaintiff. Courts were needed to keep the economy functioning and to protect the land and land transfers. In establishing courts, the people of the Green Mountains had employed what they saw as extralegal, not illegal, methods. The result was a potentially inclusive and

[45] *Colden Papers*, VII, 280–81; Countryman, *A People in Revolution*; Smith, *Historical Memoirs*; Peter Onuf, *The Origins of the Federal Republic: Jurisdictional Controversies in the United States, 1775–1787* (Philadelphia, 1983), 103–25.

[46] Countryman, *A People in Revolution*; Fox, *Yankees and Yorkers*; O'Callaghan, comp., *Documentary History*, IV, 875–77; Wilbur, *Ira Allen*; Williamson, *Vermont in Quandary*; John B. Brebner, *North Atlantic Triangle* (New York, 1945); Pemberton, "Justus Sherwood"; Van DeWater, *Reluctant Republic*, 221–339.

[47] Ira Allen, *History*, 405; Ethan Allen, *Vindication*, 459; Walton, comp., *Records*, I, 442–43, 528, II, 169–92; Slade, *State Papers*, 556–57.

[48] Walton comp., *Records*, I, 94; James Kettner, *The Development of American Citizenship, 1608–1870* (Chapel Hill, 1978).

democratic legal system, recognizing the rights of any who would in turn acknowledge the legitimacy of Vermont.

The trial and execution of David Redding presented Vermont with its first opportunity to exercise jurisdiction in direct defiance of New York. Few incidents in Vermont's early history were as well known and attracted as much attention. Redding's execution occasioned "tremendous public excitement," calling forth "enormous crowds," perhaps the largest in Bennington's history to that point, who were drawn by "the spectacular role of Ethan Allen in that drama."[49] More than just a remarkable story, the Redding trial revealed several key concerns of the new government of Vermont and its citizens. It was imperative to this government, half a year old and still experimenting with forms and standards of conduct, to make evident its authority and back up its pretensions to legitimacy with tangible judicial action, thus refuting the accusations of frontier lawlessness made by New York. The state of Vermont was saved from the failure of the new court system and the humiliation of a lynch mob by Allen's fortuitous intervention. Allen presented Vermonters with a careful navigation between their inexperience with the laws they were trying to implement and their distrust of legal systems. Since law emerged from the needs of the people, it could be redefined to serve their concerns. The Redding case was just the first of many such alterations in the legal lexicon of Vermont.

The conflict between the New Hampshire Grants and New York has long fascinated American historians. Some have seen the struggle in rational economic terms, New England land speculators competing with New York land speculators for the right to exploit the Green Mountains for their individual profit. Others have argued that the controversy was a jurisdictional dispute fought to determine the political nature and future development of the frontier, while others have seen frontier peasants engaged in class struggle. These interpretations beg the more fundamental question of basic human motivation. Why was land so important? Why were the frontiersmen willing to risk so much in order to control the political organization of the Grants region?

There were more powerful human concerns at work here than political perceptions or the desire for a quick, private profit. Courts were integral to the process of revolution and state formation because they were necessary to the daily life of the frontier family, adjudicating social and, primarily, economic disputes. Family and community were the twin poles in New Englanders' conception of social existence. Security of land ownership was essential to a family's continued well-being. The New York court system presented the Grants settlers with a crisis—its inefficiency and corruption endangered their land titles and economic stability.[50] At the same time, New York's jurisdiction, which sought to bring local structures under centralizing state control, was seen by the settlers as a threat to their communities.[51] Looking to their poorer New York neighbors, the Vermonters were con-

[49] Spargo, *Redding*, 1, 16, 45.
[50] Ethan Allen, *Brief Narrative*, 79–84, 125–28, 157–60; Milton Klein, *The Politics of Diversity: Essays in the History of Colonial New York* (Port Washington, N.Y., 1974), 156–61, 166–72.
[51] Joseph H. Smith, *Appeals to the Privy Council from the American Plantations* (New York, 1965) 390–412;

vinced that the choice was clear; they could either give in and see themselves reduced to the status of landless tenants dominated by a distant oligarchy, or they could resist. Eventually the majority chose the latter course.[32]

In writing of the broader jurisdictional disputes in America at this time, Peter Onuf observed that "the problem with American governments, on all levels, was that they did not inspire confidence or loyalty. The states were not effective polities."[33] Such was the case with New York. In the Green Mountains, the efforts of the settlers to preserve their traditional way of life led them first to oppose New York's courts and then to establish their own. The need for local structures transformed these frontier "outlaws" into revolutionaries, state builders, and constitution writers. The result was the state of Vermont, an effective political unit.

Colden Papers, VII, 1–7, 9, 205–6; Colden Letter Books, I, 421–25, 444–45, 455, 462, II, 70–71; Klein, Politics of Diversity, 166–72; Helen Miller, The Case for Liberty (Chapel Hill, 1965), 185–202; The Report of an Action of Assault (New York, 1764); "Sentinel" series, New York Gazette, Feb. 28–July 18, 1765; Goebel, "Courts and the Law."

[32] Ethan Allen, Vindication, 466. As Peter Teachout has said, "the colonists perceived law, not simply as an inheritance 'mystically regarded,' but as a creative force in the struggle against a repressive established order." See Teachout, "Light in Ashes: The Problem of 'Respect for the Rule of Law' in American Legal History," in Law in the American Revolution, ed. Hartog, 167–225, see 197–98.

[33] Onuf, Origins, xvi.

The New Hampshire Committees of Safety and Revolutionary Republicanism, 1775-1784

Ronald Lettieri and
Charles Wetherell

When New Hampshire's Fourth Provincial Congress created a state Committee of Safety on May 26, 1775, a new stage in the Revolutionary struggle was reached. Although the province had been governed by four such extra-legal congresses since July 1774, the Committee provided the Revolutionary movement with the institutional continuity and the effective leadership that it lacked. As functioning governmental bodies, both the state and local committees of safety reveal a dimension of Revolutionary republicanism that, for the most part, lies outside the realm of ideology.[1] And while historians of the state's Revolutionary political system from Jeremy Belknap to Jere Daniell

Ronald Lettieri and Charles Wetherell have recently received Ph.D. degrees in early American History from the University of New Hampshire. Mr. Wetherell is Assistant Professor of History at the University of California, Riverside. An earlier version of this paper was presented before the New England Historical Association, April 1979. The authors would like to thank Richard Ryerson, Charles Clark, Jere Daniell, and Frank Mevers for their comments, and Karen Andresen for providing wealth data on Committee members. The study was funded in part by a grant from the University of New Hampshire's Central University Research Fund.

1. Few terms in the lexicon of Revolutionary historians have been as evasive of precise definition as republicanism. Since Bernard Bailyn's *The Ideological Origins of the American Revolution* (Cambridge, Mass., 1968), the prevailing trend has been to define republicanism as a pervasive political ideology encompassing such diverse ideas as the proper institutional frame-

have recognized the Committee as an important, if not the dominant, political force during the Revolution, the Committee and its local counterparts have not been subjected to an institutional analysis nor placed within the context of Revolutionary political thought.[2]

Our analysis of the Committees of Safety allows an institutional dimension of Revolutionary government to be seen. The State Committee functioned for nine years and during its

work of government, a code of individual conduct, an ideal vision of the relationship between social groups, and the way of electing governmental officials. For a treatment of the variety of definitions of republicanism, see Robert E. Shallope, "Toward a Republican Synthesis: The Emergence of an Understanding of Republicanism in American Historiography," *The William and Mary Quarterly*, 3rd Ser., 29 (1972), 49-80. Essential to an understanding of the subject is Gordon Wood, *The Creation of the American Republic, 1776-1787* (Chapel Hill, N.C., 1969), esp., 46-124, 430-68, 593-615. See also, Pauline Maier, *From Resistence to Revolution: Colonial Radicals and the Development of American Opposition to Britain, 1765-1776* (New York, 1972), 287-96.

2. See, for example, Jeremy Belknap, *History of New Hampshire*, 3 vols. (Dover, 1812-1832), 2:395; Nathaniel Bouton, "New Hampshire Committee of Safety," New Hampshire Historical Society, *Collections*, 7 (1863), v; Richard F. Upton, *Revolutionary New Hampshire: An Account of the Social and Political Forces Underlying the Transition from Royal Province to American Commonwealth* (Hanover, N.H., 1936); Jackson Turner Main, *The Sovereign States, 1775-1783* (New York, 1973), 350-51; and Jere R. Daniell, *Experiment in Republicanism: New Hampshire Politics and the American Revolution, 1741-1794* (Cambridge, Mass., 1970), 128. The absence of an institutional analysis of the Committee is not peculiar to New Hampshire. In his recent study of Pennsylvania politics, Richard Ryerson noted that "almost nothing" is known about the Committees of Safety in the thirteen colonies even though at the outbreak of the war they "became the primary vehicle for providing necessary leadership, building community solidarity, and translating abstract concepts and beliefs into daily policy and practice." Richard Ryerson, *The Revolution is Now Begun: The Radical Committees of Philadelphia, 1765-1776* (Philadelphia, 1978), 2. The only full scale study of the committees is Agnes Hunt, *Provincial Committees of Safety of the American Revolution* (Cleveland, 1904), which does not make much use of the available material.

tenure ran the state's Revolutionary government nearly two thirds of the time. Local committees of safety mirrored the State Committee in both form and function, but lasted only about three years. The membership of the State Committee reflected general trends in Revolutionary leadership in that it was composed of men of local prominence and political experience but who for the most part were new to provincial politics. Committee membership also reflected the changing social reality of New Hampshire. The men who served on the State Committee came overwhelmingly from inland areas which provides a social explanation for the dramatic locational shift in power that occurred during the Revolution. On a day-to-day basis the State Committee exercised a wide range of executive, legislative, and judicial functions — far greater than historians have supposed. Local committees functioned in the same capacities as well, but traditional local constraints worked to moderate the effects. The State Committee by contrast operated within an atmosphere of few formal restraints. Only factional politics, which became increasingly intense as the war progressed, served to harness the Committee. And it was factional politics rather than ideological concerns that brought the Committee's history to an end.

The newly created Committee displayed its value as a functioning arm of the State's Revolutionary government by the wide array of immediate and pressing tasks it handled in the summer of 1775.[3] Indeed, throughout the course of the Revolution, the Committee exercised power in virtually every area

---

3. Unlike those of other states, New Hampshire's Committee of Safety maintained detailed records of its transactions which have survived. In addition to its daily journal, the Committee collected the bulk of its official correspondence during the period from 1779 to 1784 in a letterbook. The journal provides brief accounts of the Committee's meetings as well as attendence records for the years from 1775 to 1784. Both the journal and letterbook are at the New Hampshire State Archives in Concord (hereafter cited as NHSA). In addition, there is a Miscellaneous File of Committee material at the NHSA relating primarily to the judicial activities of the

of government. If performance was truly the acid test of eighteenth century governmental institutions, then the Committee, acting as the most energetic arm of New Hampshire's Revolutionary government, was, as Richard Upton maintains, the state's "real revolutionary government."[4] The Committee exercised its authority from May 23, 1775, until May 29, 1784, when a new state constitution replaced it with a permanent executive. Save on four occassions, the Committee sat only during legislative recesses and literally held absolute control over the state government during the frequent and lengthy legislative adjournments.[5]

From 1775 to 1784 there were nineteen separate state Committees. Table 1 summarizes the statistics of each. Individual Committee sessions ranged in duration from 66 to 345 days, with an average of 168 days. Because the Committee shared power with the legislature, meeting when the Assembly did not, and because sessions varied so much in length, the time the Committee actually met provides a better measure of their activity. During its nine year existence the Committee actually met on 960 days, an average of 51 days for each and roughly 30 percent of the days they were actually in session. Forty-

---

Committee. The journal is printed in Henry Harrison Metcalf, ed., *The Laws of New Hampshire*, 9 vols (Bristol, N.H., 1912-1922), 4:575-883 (hereafter cited as Metcalf, *Laws of New Hampshire*), New Hampshire Historical Society, *Collections*, 7 (1863), 1-340 (hereafter cited as NHHS, *Colls.*). The Committee's letterbook is printed in Nathaniel Bouton, et al., eds., *Documents and Records Relating to New Hampshire*, 40 vols. (Concord and Manchester, 1867-1943), 7:501-620 (hereafter cited as *NHSP* for New Hampshire State Papers). Other supplementary material can be found in *NHSP*, 7-21.

4. Upton, *Revolutionary New Hampshire*, 45. On performance being the "acid test" of government, see Pauline Maier, "The Beginnings of American Republicanism," in *The Development of A Revolutionary Mentality* (Washington, 1972), 104.

5. The four overlapping sessions occurred on Oct. 10 and 11, 1779; June 29, 1780; and Dec. 19, 1781.

Table 1
New Hampshire State Committee of Safety:
Duration, Size, Turnover, and Attendance,
By Session, 1775-1784

Ses No.	Session Dates	Ses Dur	Days Met	Pct Met	No. App	Act Size	No. New	Turn (%)	Att. (%)
1	5 / 23 / 1775- 1 / 19 / 1776	242	106	43.8	10	10	10	—	58.3
2	1 / 20 / 1776- 4 / 1 / 1776	73	22	30.1	6	6	2	33.3	65.2
3	4 / 2 / 1776- 7 / 4 / 1776	94	17	18.1	9	9	3	33.3	73.2
4	7 / 5 / 1776- 9 / 18 / 1776	76	26	34.2	15	15	8	53.3	60.0
5	9 / 19 / 1776- 1 / 19 / 1777	123	25	20.3	11	11	1	9.1	69.8
6	1 / 20 / 1777- 4 / 14 / 1777	85	21	24.7	12	12	8	66.7	67.1
7	4 / 15 / 1777- 6 / 19 / 1777	66	20	30.3	12	12	3	25.0	90.0
8	6 / 20 / 1777-12 / 19 / 1777	183	27	14.8	13	13	3	23.1	59.8
9	12 / 20 / 1777- 8 / 19 / 1778	243	76	31.3	18	13	6	33.3	62.1
10	8 / 20 / 1778-12 / 22 / 1778	125	34	27.2	13	13	1	7.7	68.3
11	12 / 23 / 1778- 3 / 30 / 1779	98	30	30.6	12	12	4	33.3	78.9
12	4 / 1 / 1779-12 / 31 / 1779	275	77	28.0	9	9	1	11.1	72.4
13	1 / 1 / 1780- 3 / 17 / 1780	77	4	5.2	5	5	0	0.0	85.0
14	3 / 18 / 1780- 6 / 28 / 1780	103	23	22.3	7	7	2	28.6	72.7
15	6 / 29 / 1780-12 / 16 / 1780	171	75	43.9	7	7	0	0.0	78.9
16	1 / 31 / 1781-12 / 19 / 1781	323	114	35.3	7	7	3	42.9	78.0
17	1 / 17 / 1782-12 / 27 / 1782	345	127	36.8	9	7	3	33.3	76.1
18	12 / 28 / 1782-12 / 6 / 1783	344	89	25.9	5	5	1	20.0	80.7
19	1 / 8 / 1784- 5 / 29 / 1784	143	47	32.9	5	5	1	20.0	71.5
	Mean	168	51	28.2	9.7	9.4	3.2	26.3	72.0
	Std. Dev.	97.5	37.7	9.3	3.6	3.2	2.9	17.5	8.8
	C Mean	—	—	—	—	10.4	5.6	—	—

Notes and Sources: Ses No. = Committee session, Ses Dur = duration or length of session in days, Days Met = number of days the Committee actually met within the session, Pct Met = percentage of all possible days the Committee met, No. App = number of men appointed to the Committee in the session, Act Size = the actual size of the sitting Committee in the session (reflects departures and new appointments within the session), No. New = number of men appointed to the Committee who were not members of the previous Committee, Turn = percentage of new men appointed to the Committee session, Att. = mean percentage of days attended of all days the Committee actually met. C Mean is a measure of central tendency for the individuals within the units being described. Thus the C Mean of 5.6 for the number of new men indicates that, on the average, when new men were appointed to the Committee, they could expect to be in a group of between 5 and 6 other new men. See Daniel Scott Smith, "Averages for Units and Averages for Individuals Within Units: A Note," *Journal of Family History*, 4 (1979), 84-86. For sources see note 3.

three men served on the Committee. The vast majority, 67.5 percent, served on fewer than three Committees, and only one person served on all nineteen. The size of the Committee ranged from 5 to 15 members, with an average of between 9 and 10. Evidently the legislature deliberately limited membership to permit the Committee to act swiftly. In addition to its small size, attendence at Committee meetings averaged only 72 percent, further reducing the actual size of each Committee at any given time to an average of 7 men. Turnover on the Committee averaged 26.3 percent, which meant that each Committee included 2 to 3 persons who had not sat on the previous Committee.

The fact that turnover was moderately high, particularly in the Committee's initial years, and that most Committeemen served on less than three Committees meant that only a handful of men did the bulk of work. The five most active members of the Committee — John Dudley, Meshech Weare, Josiah Bartlett, Josiah Moulton, and John Calfe — accounted for 49.2 percent of all man-days of service on the Committee. These five men, moreover, have been recognized as the core of the state's Revolutionary leadership, and it would appear that they perceived service on the Committee as a vital means of exercising political power in the newly proclaimed state.[6]

The membership of the State Committee reflects some general trends in revolutionary executive leadership. According to James Kirby Martin, executive positions throughout the colonies at the start of the Revolution were being filled by men who prior to 1775 had enjoyed local positions of power but who, because they lacked imperial connections, had been barred from higher provincial office and the avenues of greater wealth which this often brought. These "lesser officials" were men of comfortable means and local political authority

---

6. Main, *Sovereign States*, 350.

who were frustrated by their inability to achieve provincial power.[7]

The forty-three members of the New Hampshire State Committee seem to be of a similar mold.[8] At first appointment, Committee members ranged in age from the 62 year old

---

7. James Kirby Martin, *Men in Rebellion: Higher Governmental Leaders and the Coming of the American Revolution* (New Brunswick, N.J., 1973).

8. The forty-three members of the State Committee were: Samuel Ashley (1720-92) of Winchester; Otis Baker (1727-1801) of Dover; Benjamin Barker (1729-1801) of Stratham; Josiah Bartlett (1729-95) of Kingston; Thomas Bartlett (b. 1745) of Nottingham; Jonathan Blanchard (1738-88) of Dunstable; John Calfe (1741-1808) of Hampstead; Wyseman Claggett (1721-84) of Litchfield; Samuel Cutts (1726-1801) of Portsmouth; Levi Dearborn (1730-92) of North Hampton; John Dudley (1725-1805) of Raymond; Stephen Evans (1724-1808) of Dover; Nathaniel Folsom (1726-90) of Exeter; George Gaines (1736-1809) of Portsmouth; Benjamin Giles (1717-87) of Newport; John T. Gilman (1753-1828) of Exeter; Joseph Gilman (1738-1806) of Exeter; Nicholas Gilman (1731-83) of Exeter; Samuel Gilman (1732-99) of Newmarket; Samuel Hobart (1734-98) of Exeter; Pierse Long, Jr. (1739-89) of Portsmouth; Jonathan Lovewell (1713-92) of Dunstable; John McClary (1720-1801) of Epsom; Hercules Mooney (1710-1800) of Durham; Israel Morey (1735-1809) of Orford; Josiah Moulton (1720-84) of Hampton; Thomas Odiorne (1733-1819) of Exeter; Matthew Patten (1719-95) of Bedford; Nathaniel Peabody (1745-1823) of Atkinson; Samuel Philbrick (1734-1806) of Weare; Ebenezer Potter (1745-1822) of Kensington; Nathaniel Prentice (1735-1815) of Alstead; Ephraim Robinson (1744-1809) of Exeter; John Smith, III (1737-91) of Durham; Ebenezer Thompson (1737-1802) of Durham; Matthew Thornton (1714-1803) of Londonderry; Timothy Walker, Jr. (1737-1822) of Concord; Meshech Weare (1713-86) of Hampton Falls; Samuel Webster (1743-77) of Temple; John Wentworth, Jr. (1745-87) of Dover; William Whipple (1730-85) of Portsmouth; Phillips White (1729-1811) of South Hampton; Robert Wilson (1744-91) of Chester. Biographical data on the forty-three members of the State Committee was compiled from a variety of sources, the principal one being John A. Morahan, "A Prosopographical Study of the New Hampshire Committee of Safety," (M.A. thesis, University of New Hampshire, 1977). Supplementing Morahan were the genealogical holdings of the New Hampshire Historical Society (hereafter cited as NHHS), and town histories.

Meshech Weare to the 27 year old John T. Gilman, with an average age of 45.4. The religious composition of the Committee reflected the overall configuration of the state, heavily Congregational with Presbyterians and Baptists a distant second and third respectively.[9] Twenty-four (77.4 percent) of the 31 members with known religious affiliation were Congregationalist; the rest (22.6 percent) were Presbyterians, Baptists, Unitarians, and splinter sects. Occupationally, the Committee favored merchants and large farmers. And of the thirteen members whose wealth can be estimated, eleven (84.6 percent) can be placed in the top 20 percent of their town's economic strata on the eve of the war. The composite picture of the Committee suggests that its members were drawn, not surprisingly, from a middle-aged, Congregational, economic elite of farmers and merchants.

The vast majority of Committee members had local political experience. In fact, only three did not. Of these, one was only 27 when he was first appointed to the Committee in 1781, one was a minister, and another, Wyseman Claggett, had been the King's Attorney. Of the 40 who had held local political office, 35 (87.5 percent) had served as selectmen, and 9 (22.5 percent) were local justices of the peace. Fifteen (34.8 percent) of the 43 had severed in the Provincial Assembly in the Wentworth years, but 19 (44.2 percent) gained their first provincial experience as delegates to one of the unauthorized Provincial Congresses that met in 1774 and 1775. For a majority, the war and the Committee provided the initial exposure to political power on the provincial level.

The Committee's membership also reflected the changing demographic composition of the state, and with it a changing political complexion. In 1775 the Assembly selected the first

9. Upton, *Revolutionary New Hampshire*, 208, gives the following rough estimation of religious affiliation based on the number of churches: Congregational (71.8%), Presbyterian (12.8%), Baptist (9.4%), Others (6.0%).

Committee on the basis of county residence in an attempt to have the Committee represent the five county interests in the state.[10] The Assembly's scheme, however, provided both the most populous county, Rockingham, and the least populous county, Grafton, with disproportionate — although not statistically disproportionate — representation. Rockingham County had roughly 50 percent of the population and 60 percent of the Committee's seats. Grafton held less than 5 percent of the state's population and 10 percent of the initial Committee's slots.[11] The Assembly discarded the method of selecting committee members by county with the second Committee it formed in January 1776. After this, the Committee was chosen proportionally from the two houses of the legislature.[12]

10. On May 24, 1775, the Provincial Congress ordered "that there be added to the Committee of Safety one [member] from the County of Hillsboro, one from Chesire, and one from Grafton." The two other counties, Rockingham and Strafford already were represented. It should be noted that the creation of the State Committee proceeded the general call of the Continental Congress on July 18, 1775, for such bodies by two months. *NHSP*, 7:483; Worthington C. Ford, ed., *Journals of the Continental Congress*, 2 (Washington, 1907), 189.

11. A breakdown by county of the Committee's membership as a reflection of the state's population in 1773 is as follows:

County	% Pop. 1773	% COS Membership
Rockingham	49.3	62.8
Stafford	13.4	14.0
Hillsborough	18.6	14.0
Cheshire	13.8	6.9
Grafton	4.9	2.3
Totals	100.0	100.0

The proportions of Committee appointments and population are not statistically different (Chisquare = 6.16, $df = 4$). "Census of 1773," *NHSP*, 10:623-35.

12. *NHSP*, 8:111. The selection process of the committee was as follows. Under general orders of the Assembly, a committee of both houses was created to designate candidates for the Committee of Safety. Nominations

County divisions, however, are fundamentally arbitrary units, the social, economic, and political complexion if which can change. Indeed, the battle over drawing county lines in the late 1760's focused on precisely these issues.[13] To view the Committee as a reflection of county interests hides the essential social foundations of the political divisions within the Committee and within the state. The factionalism of the Committee is best depicted as emerging from three distinct geopolitical areas: the Connecticut River Valley, Portsmouth and its satellite towns, and the Merrimack Valley inland agricultural and commercial towns. These three areas reflect both the political divisions within the Committee and the social and demographic complexion of the state at the outset of the war.

The first of these areas, the Connecticut River Valley, was comprised of towns lying along the Connecticut River on the western boundary of the state. Held together by their common origins and farming interests, settlers of such towns as Orford, Hanover, Plainfield, and Alstead, never truly conceived of themselves as full participants in the state's political system. Constantly complaining of their lack of political power under the Revolutionary Constitution of 1776 and the monopoly of power enjoyed by the eastern seaboard, the Connecticut River Valley towns had emerged as a distinct geopolitical area by 1777.[14] When the state's eastern dominated leadership refused

---

were then submitted to the Assembly for an election, those receiving the most votes were appointed. Obviously the number chosen varied, but whether candidates nominated were not appointed or whether the nominating committee itself effectively set the size of the Committee of Safety cannot be said. Only one list of nominees survives. It includes fourteen names but only five are ranked. Committee of Safety, Miscellaneous File, undated, NHSA; *NHSP*, 8:192, 195, 340, 548.

13. See John Durel, "Dividing the Province of New Hampshire into Counties," *Historical New Hampshire*, 32 (1977), 28-41.

14. Daniell, *Experiment in Republicanism*, 145-47, 152-62.

to grant the area greater representation, the westerners attempted to secede. Although the secession movement ultimately failed, the actions of the Connecticut River Valley towns clearly point to their identity as a separate and distinct political area.

The second area, Portsmouth and its satellite towns of Dover and Durham, was the pre-Revolutionary power base of the state. Prior to the war men from this area had enjoyed a monopoly of political power rivaled in few of the American colonies. The pre-Revolutionary Portsmouth elite was an extremely close-knit body, sharing kinship ties with the Wentworths, imperial trading interests, and a conscious identity as a religious minority of Anglicans.[15] With the outbreak of the war, however, this area's source of power — the royal governor — vanished, and with him their monopoly of colonial government. Beginning in 1775, the area found itself in the unfamiliar position of being a political minority among the state's new ruling elite, an elite drawn not from the seacoast but from the inland towns.[16]

The third geopolitical area of the new state, one that provided the majority of revolutionary leaders, was comprised of agricultural and inland commercial towns of the Merrimack Valley.[17] Men from this area by and large had been denied access to high political office by the Wentworths. Its political leaders shared a sense of alienation from imperial politics (and a distrust of Portsmouth political figures), the common experience of being a local economic and political elite, provincial as opposed to imperial economic interests, and a fear of social and political disorder which the Revolution might

15. James Kirby Martin, "A Model for the Coming American Revolution: The Birth and Death of the Wentworth Oligarchy in New Hampshire, 1741-1776," *Journal of Social History*, 4 (1970), 41-60.

16. Daniell, *Experiment in Republicanism*, 141-45.

17. Main, *The Sovereign States*, 350-51.

bring.[18] The Revolution provided an opportunity for leaders of this area to participate — and eventually to control — the province's affairs. Once men from this area achieved political control, they held it for the duration of the war.

These three areas also reflected very real demographic differences within the state which lend a social underpinning to the dramatic shift in political power during the Revolution.[19] In essence, the Portsmouth area was an old, high population density region, one which grew slowly, and which relied on specialized economic opportunity such as trading rather than agriculture. The Merrimack Valley-Inland Commercial area was comprised of towns which had only recently achieved what can be termed "demographic maturity": a position where a town was still growing, where population density was at or below its optimum level, and where the business of settling the town was over.[20] By contrast, the Connecticut River Valley

---

18. Daniell, *Experiment in Republicanism*, 119-22.

19. Daniell, *Experiment in Republicanism*, 135-36; Martin, *Men in Rebellion*, 110; Main, *Sovereign States*, 350, 354-56.

20. The idea of demographic maturity is taken from Darrett B. Rutman, "People in Process: The New Hampshire Towns of the Eighteenth Century," *Journal of Urban History* 1 (1975), 268-92; and Charles Wetherell, "A Note on Hierarchial Clustering," *Historical Methods Newsletter*, 10 (1977), 109-16. The essential model of demographic growth developed in these essays is that town growth is a process keyed to population density. In this scheme, when a town is initially settled it grows rapidly through the in-migration of young men up to a density of roughly ten persons per square mile. After reaching this threshold density, the town continues to grow (although not as rapidly) through in-migration and natural growth until an optimum density is reached. At this point the town starts losing population through out-migration. Normally the town recovers to its optimum density, which for eighteenth-century agricultural towns was centered on a mean of forty-four persons per square mile. Towns could and did grow beyond this level but needed specialized economic opportunities to sustain a significantly higher population density. See, Wetherell, "Clustering," 113.

towns were young and not yet demographically mature. Population density was low, in-migration high, and the business of settling was still incomplete.

In these terms, the shift in political leadership away from Portsmouth to the Merrimack Valley and Inland Commercial towns, and with the virtual exclusion of the Connecticut River Valley, reflects the changing social reality of the state. The Connecticut River Valley towns were not truly settled and local needs predominated. The Portsmouth area, numerically outnumbered but politically experienced, participated in provincial affairs as a minority. The Merrimack Valley-Inland Commercial towns, numerically superior to either of the other areas, demographically mature yet not economically specialized, developed a provincial outlook based upon common interests and a shared political experience.[21]

As a reflection of the three geopolitical areas, the State Committee was clearly dominated by the Merrimack Valley-Inland Commercial towns. Of the forty-three Committeemen, thirty (69.8 percent) were from the Merrimack area, 10 (23.2 percent) were from Portsmouth, Dover, or Durham, and only three men (6.9 percent) came from Connecticut River Valley towns. Numerical superiority clearly accounts for the fundamental imbalance among the areas, for the Merrimack Valley

---

21. Using the town of residence of Committee members as a reflection of the three geopolitical areas, a breakdown by mean density, age, and population in 1773 is as follows:

Mean Density, Town Age, and Population,
By Geopolitical Area, 1773

	Connecticut River Valley (N = 3)	Portsmouth Area (N = 3)	Merrimack Valley Area (N = 22)
Density	7.5	141.8	41.2
Age	13.3	141.7	71.3
Population	343.3	2395.3	885.4

While the numbers involved are too small for any definitive conclusions to be drawn, they indicate very fundamental demographic differences.

simply had more towns. Yet attendance at the Committee's meetings is instructive as well, as Table 2 suggests.

Table 2
New Hampshire State Committee of Safety: Membership and Attendance by Geopolitical Area, 1775-1784

	Connecticut River Valley				Portsmouth and Satellites				Merrimack Valley Inland Commercial			
Ses No.	No. App	Pct Mem	Tot Ser	Att. (%)	No. App	Pct Mem	Tot Ser	Att. (%)	No. App	Pct Mem	Tot Ser	Att. (%)
1	1	10.0	37	34.9	2	20.0	191	90.1	7	70.0	376	52.5
2	—	—	—	—	2	33.3	38	86.4	4	66.7	48	54.6
3	—	—	—	—	3	33.3	45	88.2	6	66.7	67	65.7
4	1	6.7	0	0.0	4	26.7	78	75.0	10	66.7	156	60.0
5	—	—	—	—	4	36.4	84	84.0	7	63.6	108	61.7
6	—	—	—	—	3	25.0	42	66.7	9	75.0	127	67.2
7	—	—	—	—	3	25.0	54	90.0	9	75.0	162	90.0
8	1	7.7	0	0.0	3	23.1	37	45.7	9	69.2	173	71.2
9	1	5.6	0	0.0	4	22.2	96	45.8	13	72.2	524	72.0
10	—	—	—	—	2	15.4	20	29.4	11	84.6	282	75.4
11	—	—	—	—	3	25.0	71	78.9	9	75.0	213	78.9
12	—	—	—	—	2	22.2	80	51.9	7	77.8	422	78.3
13	—	—	—	—	2	40.0	5	62.5	3	60.0	12	100.0
14	—	—	—	—	2	28.6	21	45.7	5	71.4	96	83.5
15	—	—	—	—	2	28.6	98	65.3	5	71.4	316	84.3
16	—	—	—	—	1	14.3	63	55.3	6	85.7	559	81.8
17	—	—	—	—	1	11.1	4	66.7	8	88.9	669	77.3
18	—	—	—	—	—	—	—	—	5	100.0	359	80.7
19	—	—	—	—	—	—	—	—	5	100.0	168	71.5
Mean	1	7.5	—	8.7	2.5	23.3	—	66.3	7.3	75.8	—	74.0
Std. Dev.	—	1.9	—	17.5	.9	7.8	—	18.6	2.6	11.3	—	12.0
C Mean	1	—	—	2.9	—	—	—	—	7.1	—	—	—

Notes and Sources: Ses No. = Committee session, No. App = number of men appointed to the Committee in the session, Pct Mem = percent of Committee appointments, Tot Ser = total days of actual service amassed by Committee members, Att. = mean percentage of days attended of all days the Committee actually met. Means were computed using the number of sessions in which men from each area were appointed, that is 4, 17, and 19, respectively. The differences between the rates of attendance of Committee members from the three areas are significantly at the .01 level (F = 11.9, N = 185, *df* = 2). For sources see note 3.

The Connecticut River Valley simply did not participate. Men from this area were appointed to four Committees yet in three instances failed to attend any meetings. While the Connecticut River Valley is some distance from Exeter, the site of the Committee's meetings, distance does not appear to be the exclusive cause. Portsmouth, Durham, and Dover are closer to Exeter than Dunstable or Hillsborough are, yet attendance of members of the Portsmouth group was on the average lower (66.3 percent) than it was for the Merrimack Valley-Inland Commercial group (74 percent). In the first few years of the Committee's existence, members from the Portsmouth area attended at a higher rate than the Merrimack Valley majority. And as we shall see, the Merrimack Valley faction reversed the situation as it closed out the Committee to its political opponents after 1778.

The Committee's very existence altered the institutional structure of the state. The legislature, despite its status as the only constitutionally recognized institution in the state, was an extremely inefficient political body.[22] Judging from contemporary views, the Assembly's problems stemmed primarily from the low quality of its members.[23] The exclusionary policies of the Wentworths and the exodus of loyalist officials in 1775 had left the colony without the seasoned politicians

---

22. Daniell, *Experiment in Republicanism*, 125-27; John K. Gemmill, "The Problems of Power: New Hampshire Government During the Revolution," *Historical New Hampshire*, 22 (1967), 34-35; Main, *The Sovereign States*, 349-50; Upton, *Revolutionary New Hampshire*, 43.

23. In a letter to Ebenezer Hazard, Jeremy Belknap recounted a tale of a legislator who had stolen a hammer to buy "a jill of rum." Belknap drew the following conclusion from the episode: "This is a specimen of the little villainy of the cattle by whom we are . . . governed." After receiving a second letter from Belknap regarding the poor quality of the state's legislators, Hazard concurred and observed "it is a great pity that an institution which, in proper hands, might be useful, should be so scandalously prostituted." John Langdon likened the Assembly's members to "dogs." And General John Sullivan shared a low opinion of the legislature: "Our General Assembly is dissolved after getting over the Publick Business in our usual way. Lord help us." Belknap to Ebenezer Hazard, Dec. 28, 1779 and

needed to run an Assembly.[24] As a result, the inexperienced, locally-oriented, essentially leaderless legislators, often engaged in frequent and bitter debates over what William Whipple termed "triffles."[25]

Given this state of affairs, legislative sessions were characterized by their short duration, high absenteeism, and an annual turnover rate of roughly 50 percent. From May 1775 to June 1783, the legislature met an average of 64 days a year, a figure all the more significant when compared to the State Committee's 100 days.[26] After 1778, the Committee met twice as much as the legislature, averaging 65.6 percent of the days

Mar. 13, 1780, and Hazard to Belknap, Apr. 1, 1780, *Belknap Papers*, 3 vols. (Boston, 1877-91 [published as Massachusetts Historical Society, *Collections*, Ser. 5, Vols. 2 and 3, Ser. 6, Vol. 4]), 1:27, 43-44, 47; John Langdon to Josiah Bartlett, Jun. 3, 1776, Bartlett Papers (microfilm), Reel 1, NHHS; John Sullivan to ?, Nov. 13, 1780, Otis G. Hammond, ed., *The Letters and Papers of Major-General John Sullivan*, 3 vols. (Concord, 1930-34), 3:199 (hereafter cited as *Sullivan Papers*).

24. Main, *Sovereign States*, 350. On the existence of "professional" politicians in the colonial period, men similar to Wentworth's legislative leaders, see Robert Zemsky, *Merchants, Farmers, and River Gods: An Essay on Eighteenth-Century American Politics* (Boston, 1971), 39-74.

25. William Whipple to Josiah Bartlett, Sep. 10, 1776, Bartlett Papers, Reel 1. Edward Parry made the observation in April 1777 that the legislators were "in a very ill humor . . . quarrelling with one another." Edward Parry, *Journal, March 28, 1775 to August 23, 1777*, in James H. Maguire, "A Critical Edition of Edward Parry's *Journal*" (Ph.D. diss., Indiana Univ., 1970), 104 (hereafter cited as Parry, *Journal*).

26. The number of days the legislature and the Committee met from May 1775 to June 1783, by year, is as follows:

Year	Committee of Safety		Legislature	
	No.	Pct.	No.	Pct.
1775	106	65.0	57	35.0
1776	90	48.1	97	51.9
1777	68	43.3	89	56.7
1778	100	59.2	69	40.8
1779	107	67.3	52	32.7

both Committee and legislature sat. Based on days of service alone, the Committee appears to have been the true political force behind New Hampshire's successful revolution.

The relationship between the Committee and legislature was close and for the most part harmonious. The Committee was, after all, drawn from the legislature, thus enhancing a unified policy between the two. Assembly committees often provided agendas for the Committee of Safety. In addition, the Assembly reserved the right to review the Committee's records, but the fact that it exercised this right on only three occasions suggests a high degree of approval of the Committee's work.[27]

Yet there were nonetheless indications that the Committee was reluctant to share authority with the Assembly. Less than two months after its creation the Committee displayed doubts about the legislature's ability to deal effectively with pressing matters. Writing to the state's delegation at the Continental Congress in July 1775, the Committee noted that, despite having met twice, the Assembly had not and would not "proceed to the public business."[28] The Committee's distrust of the legislature most clearly appears in its reluctance to call the

1780	102	61.1	65	38.9
1781	114	62.0	70	38.0
1782	127	62.8	55	38.2
1783	89	80.9	21	19.1
Mean	100.3	61.1	63.9	37.2
Std. Dev.	16.8	10.8	22.1	9.7

No. = number of days met, Pct. = percentage of total days both bodies met. The differences between the days of governmental activity are significantly different at the .01 level (Chisquare = 62.0, df = 8). Legislative days taken from Gemmill, "Problems of Power," 35, notes 30-31.

27. Examples of the agendas provided the Committee can be found for Mar. 21, 1776, and Mar. 25, 1782. *NHSP*, 8:109; and Metcalf, *Laws of New Hampshire*, 4:465. Reviews were ordered by the Assembly on Mar. 22, 1776, Jun. 4, 1777, and Feb. 13, 1778. *NHSP*, 8:111-12, 573, 768.

28. Committee of Safety to N.H. Delegates at Continental Congress, Jul. 8, 1775. *NHSP*, 7:560.

legislature into special session. In its nine-year existence the Committee exercised this power only four times, and as early as July 1775 the Assembly reminded the Committee that it had this power.[29] Thus the willingness of the Committee of Safety to serve the state nearly twice as much as the legislature appears to be a result of conscious design.

Of all aspects of the Committee's history the one most studied by historians has been its exercise of political power. Yet from Belknap on, most scholars have contended that the Committee served exclusively as the executive that was lacking in the government created by the 1776 state constitution.[30] Pointing to its compact size, frequent meetings, and low turnover, these historians have concluded that the Committee fulfilled its executive responsibilities efficiently and thus provided the state with the strong executive it needed during the war. Yet in 1783 a New Hampshire resident observed that the Committee had done much more than act as

---

29. Emergency sessions were called on Oct. 16, 1776, Jul. 17, 1777, and Apr. 19, 1780. The 1776 session was called to raise troops requested by the Continental Congress; the 1777 session after the fall of Fort Ticonderoga; and the 1780 session to consider a request from the Continental Congress for provisions and to consider the depreciation of currency. *NHSP*, 8:348, 629, 855. See also Josiah Bartlett to Nathaniel Folsom, May 13, 1780, Bartlett Papers, Reel 3, for reasons surrounding the call for the 1780 session.

30. Belknap, *History of New Hampshire*, 2:62; Joseph B. Walker, *New Hampshire's Five Provincial Congresses, July 21, 1774 - January 5, 1776* (Concord, 1905), 44; Bouton, "Committee of Safety," NHHS, *Colls.*, 7:v; Hunt, *Provincial Committees of Safety*, 20; Upton, *Revolutionary New Hampshire*, 42-43; Daniell, "The Revolutionary Government," in Peter E. Randall, ed., *New Hampshire, Years of Revolution: 1774-1783* (Hanover, N.H., 1976), 18; Main, *The Sovereign States*, 351; Avery J. Butters, "New Hampshire History and the Public Career of Meshech Weare," (Ph.D. diss., Fordham Univ., 1961), 175; Charles G. Douglas, III, "Judicial Review and the Separation of Powers under the New Hampshire Constitutions of 1776 and 1784," *Historical New Hampshire*, 31 (1976), 178.

an executive, that it had in fact been "cloathed with all the legislative, executive, and judicial powers of government."[31]

The dominant characteristics of the Committee's exercise of power was its repeated violation of the doctrine of mixed government which recent scholarship has established as the core idea of eighteenth-century American political theory.[32] Although the Committee acted only during legislative capacity, the Committee frequently utilized its power of the purse to appropriate money from the State Treasury for any purpose it deemed necessary.[33] The Committee also administered the col-

---

31. *New Hampshire Gazette*, March 1, 1783.

32. For discussions of the theory of mixed government, including the idea of the separation and balance of powers, in eighteenth-century American political thought, see Bailyn, *The Ideological Origins of the American Revolution*, 66-86; Wood, *The Creation of the American Republic*, 197-222; Paul Conkin, *Self-Evident Truths: Being a Discourse on the Origins and Development of the First Principles of American Government . . .* (Bloomington, Ind., 1974), 143-84; Henry Steele Commager, *The Empire of Reason* (New York, 1977), 206-55; Paul Eidelberg, *The Philosophy of the American Constitution* (New York, 1968), 3-35; and Martin Diamond, "The Separation of Powers and the Mixed Regime," *Publius*, 7 (1978), 35-43.

33. Hunt, *Provincial Committees of Safety*, 24-26; Committee of Safety to Haverhill Committee of Safety, May 27, 1780; Committee of Safety to Nathaniel Peabody and Nathaniel Folsom, May 27, 1780; Committee of Safety to ? , Jul. 15, 1780; Committee of Safety to Capt. Samuel Gilman, Sep. 8, 1780; Committee of Safety to Maj. Jonathan Child, Sep. 6, 1780; Committee of Safety to Charles Johnston and James Woodward, Apr. 7, 1781; Committee of Safety to Eliphalet Hale and George Davie, Apr. 12, 1781; Committee of Safety to Samuel Chase, Apr. 12, 1781; Meshech Weare to Capt. Titus Salter, May 16, 1783; Meshech Weare to Eleazer Russel, May 23, 1783; Meshech Weare to John Pierce, Jun. 6, 1783; NHHS, *Colls.*, 7:18, 73, 140, 143, 148, 151, 163, 165, 169, 176, 182-83, 186-87, 203, 252, 260, 267, 313-314, 333-39; *NHSP*, 7:516, 559, 609, 618-19, 647, 685; 8:71-72, 204-05, 558, 815; 10:509-11, 529, 537-38, 610, 595-97; 11:98-100; Committee of Safety, Mar. 27, 1778, Misc. File, NHSA; *New Hampshire Gazette*, Jun. 23, 1778, Oct. 5, 1782.

lection of taxes, settled all fiscal claims against the state, passed measures regulating imports, exports, and maritime traffic, and controlled the purse of the state's military units. On one occasion the Committee even forwarded to the Assembly a package of bills it had drawn up during a legislative recess.[34]

The Committee also acted in a judicial capacity.[35] As a tribunal, the Committee was especially concerned with cases of counterfeiting and suspected treason, and in many instances acted as "prosecutor, judge, and executor of the sentence."[36] Its trials lacked juries and resulted in immediate action which was often based more on suspicion than on actual evidence.[37] The Committee also sat as a military tribunal and took under its special purview cases of desertion. In addition to its own original sphere of jurisdiction, the Committee acted as an

---

34. In 1779, the Committee of Safety submitted a report to the Assembly outlining the business it planned to undertake during its forthcoming session. "Report to the New Hampshire Assembly, 1779," Committee of Safety, Misc. File, NHSA.

35. Committee of Safety to Cheshire County, Jun. 30, 1777; Committee of Safety to Brig. Gen. Prescott, Apr. 23, 1777; Committee of Safety to Moses Kelly, Jul. 23, 1779; Committee of Safety to Sheriff of Salem, Nov. 2, 1782; Committee of Safety, Warrant, Mar. 27, 1779; Committee of Safety, Misc. File, NHSA; "Records of the Committee of Safety," Nov. 23, 1775; Sept. 24, 1776; Jan. 31, 1777; Jun. 5, 1778; Nov. 2, 1778; Feb. 20, 1784. NHHS, *Colls.*, 7:25, 59, 74, 155-56, 170; Meshech Weare to Joseph Huntoon, Jul. 5, 1781; Weare to Charles Johnston, Weare to Sheriff of Rockingham County, Nov. 1, 1781; Weare to Simeon Ladd, Dec. 5, 1782; *NHSP*, 7:549, 572-73, 603. "Journal of the House," Apr.-May, 1777; Jun. 14, 1777; Jun. 30, 1777; Jan. 1, 1780. *NHSP*, 8:545-54, 585-86, 597-98, 845-46. The Committee's judicial powers were greatly enhanced after Jun. 19, 1777 when the legislature granted the Committee the power to hear treason cases without juries and to confine and restrain suspects who were denied bail. Metcalf, *Laws of New Hampshire*, 4:97-98.

36. Hunt, *Provincial Committees of Safety*, 27.

37. Upton, *Revolutionary New Hampshire*, 121; Otis G. Hammond, "The Tories of New Hampshire," NHHS, *Proceedings*, 5 (1917), 284-85.

appellate court for local committees of safety and on several occasions reversed decisions reached by the lesser ad hoc tribunals.

It was in its executive capacity that the Committee undertook most of its work.[38] The most common duties performed were the appointment of military officers and the deployment of the state's military units. During the abortive secession movement of the Connecticut River Valley towns, the Committee, acting on its own accord as military commander-in-chief, ordered that troops be raised and an assault launched. And while the Committee's actions followed other efforts which had failed and were not carried out as a settlement was reached, the lengths to which it would go illustrate the range of executive functions performed. The Committee also granted pardons, appointed delegates to a variety of regional conventions,

---

38. Hunt, *Provincial Committees of Safety*, 154; Upton, *Revolutionary New Hampshire*, 43-44, 96; "Records of the Committee of Safety," May 23 and 24, 1775; Jun. 1, 3, 5, 6, 8-15, 18-20, 22-30, 1775; Jul. 6, 13-Sep. 18, 1775; Apr.-Jul. 5, 1776; Jan. 31, 1777; Feb. 14, 1777; May 17, 1777; Apr. 3, 1778; Aug. 25, 1779; Oct. 8, 1779; Jul. 29, 1780; Aug. 18, 1781. NHHS, *Colls.*, 7:1, 3-4, 6-7, 8-18, 43, 45-46, 74, 79-80, 98, 146, 201, 206, 229, 265. *NHSP*, 7:480-81, 483-84, 487, 492-93, 497-98, 503, 505, 518-23, 527-31, 535, 544-46, 548, 555-58, 569-574, 578, 582-83, 610-637; 8:46, 297-318, 640-50, 785, 930, 962. "Letters of the Committee of Safety," Committee of Safety to Dr. Peter Warren, Jul. 18, 1780; Committee of Safety to Capt. Eliphalet Giddings, Jul. 18, 1780; Committee of Safety to Capt. Samuel Reynolds, Jul. 18, 1780; Committee of Safety to Col. Stephen Evans, Jul. 20, 1780; Committee of Safety to John Langdon, Jul. 29, 1780; Committee of Safety to Samuel Livermore, Aug. 5, 1780; Committee of Safety to Capt. Shubael Geer, Aug. 10, 1780; Committee of Safety to Jonathan Martin, Aug. 10, 1780; Committee of Safety to Maj. Elisha Whitcomb, Aug. 12, 1780; Committee of Safety to Jedidiah Jewett, Aug. 19, 1780; Committee of Safety to Capt. Josiah Moulton and Col. Samuel Folsom, Aug. 19, 1780; Committee of Safety to N.H. Board of War, Aug. 19, 1780; Committee of Safety to Capt. Eliphalet Giddings, Aug. 23, 1780; Committee of Safety to John Langdon, Jul. 26, 1783; *NHSP*, 10:519-28, 613; *New Hampshire Gazette*, Feb. 18, 1777; Jul. 13, 1782.

and established embargos. Because the Committee disregarded the Whig doctrine of mixed government, it was able to expand its already broad range of political powers. Judged by their performance on the Committee, New Hampshire's revolutionary leaders appeared to be motivated more by the practical necessities of war than by abstract Whig ideology.

Although the collapse of royal government resulted in a dramatic shift in leadership and institutions at the provincial level, there was little change at the local level. For the most part towns relied upon the traditional institutions of the town meeting and selectmen to withstand the crisis. As the struggle between Britain and the colonies intensified during the summer of 1774, however, towns began to create local committees of safety to meet the additional demands and responsibilities thrust upon them by the collapse of royal authority. To some extent the creation of these local committees can be viewed as a traditional response of New England towns to an unforseen crisis: the appointment of a special committee by the town, gathered in Town Meeting, to deal with a specific matter at hand.[39] But local committees of safety were short-lived and restricted in power by the presence of the established local officials who continued — committee or not — to handle the majority of the town's day-to-day affairs throughout the war.[40]

The state's revolutionary leaders desired to minimize the dislocation of local government brought on by the organized

---

39. Edward R. Cook, *The Fathers of the Towns: Leadership and Community Structure in Eighteenth-Century New England* (Baltimore, 1976), 191. According to Cook, the increased reliance upon committees by town government was due in large part to the accelerating process of formalization of local government during the eighteenth century.

40. An examination of the town records of thirty towns from 1773 to 1784 revealed no evidence of any committee wielding authority on a par with the State Committee. Instead, traditional town officers were assigned the bulk of the responsibilities for the towns' affairs with the local committees of safety *supplementing* existing institutions.

resistance to British rule, and with some success. Prior to the creation of town committees of safety, local action against British officials often took on the appearance of direct democratic action. On September 20, 1774, a crowd estimated at three hundred assembled at Amherst in response to Joshua Atherton's efforts to thwart the election of delegates to the First Provincial Congress. Matthew Patten, sent as a delegate from the Bedford Town Meeting to question Atherton, watched helplessly as the crowd took matters into its own hands. Completely ignoring the officially sanctioned Bedford delegate, the assembled throng selected a committee and, acting as the official representatives of the town, this ad hoc committee questioned Atherton and forced him to sign a public recantation.[41]

In the wake of similar incidents throughout the province in the fall of 1774, and motivated by the Whig disdain for mob action, towns began creating local committees of safety early in 1775 to supervise interrogations of suspected loyalists, a move which can be viewed as an effort by New Hampshire's Revolutionary leaders to maintain control over local affairs, protect property, and channel anti-imperial sentiment through established town government.[42] The Assembly gave its sanction to these actions on June 2, 1775, when it issued an address urging citizens to cease acting as roaming bands of vigilantees and ordered "that there . . . be no movements of this nature, but by the direction of the Committees of the Respective Towns or Counties."[43]

---

41. Daniell, *Experiment in Republicanism*, 82. *The Diary of Matthew Patten . . ., 1754-1798* (Bedford, N.H., 1903), Sep. 19, 1774, 329-30 (hereafter cited as Patten, *Diary*).

42. On the Whig disdain for mob action, see Dirk Hoeder, *Crowd Action in Revolutionary Massachusetts, 1765-1780* (New York, 1977), 97-118, esp. 117-18.

43. Matthew Thornton to the "Inhabitants of New Hampshire," Jun. 2, 1775, *NHSP*, 8:497.

Based on a random sample of New Hampshire towns, some form of committee of safety existed in every town by 1779.[44] Towns themselves determined the membership of these committees in town meetings. The minutes of town meetings suggest, moreover, that the voting for committee membership was conducted by an open show of hands, a procedure which would only serve to enhance deferential tendencies, a proclivity attested to by the petition of eighteen Dover residents to change the procedure from a "Hands-vote" to a written, secret ballot.[45]

The successful effort to moderate local revolutionary behavior by town and state alike is clear from an examination of the members selected to town committees. Following their New England counterparts, members of a majority of New Hampshire's town committees were drawn from the ranks of the existing town leadership.[46] According to Governor Wentworth, the Portsmouth committee was composed of "the principal freeholders" of the town.[47] In Francestown and Keene the Town Meetings simply voted that the towns' selectmen serve as committees of safety. In other towns, such as Concord and Rye, the selectmen shared committee membership with lesser officials. Local militia officers held seats on the committees to

---

44. Town records for the period from 1773 to 1784 were examined for Portsmouth, Epping, Deerfield, Chester, Hampton, Concord, Rye, Pembroke, Brentwood, Candia, Keene, Winchester, Richmond, Chesterfield, Hinsdale, Amherst, Hillsborough, Mason, Bedford, New Ipswich, Francestown, Hanover, Orford, Lebanon, Dover, Northumberland, Barrington, Lee, Madbury, and Gilmanton.

45. Of the thirty towns examined, only Dover used a written ballot. Dover Town Recs., Jun. 10, 1777, NHHS. See also, "Selectmen's Precepts," Oct. 15, 1775, New Ipswich Town Recs., NHHS.

46. Cook, *Fathers of the Towns*, 186-87.

47. Governor John Wentworth to the Earl of Dartmouth, May 17, 1775, in G.K. Davies, ed., *Documents of the American Revolution, 1770-1783*, 21 vols. (Shannon, Ireland, 1972-78), 9:135.

supervise military affairs.[48] Local committees of safety were thus placed under the control of established community leaders.

Local committees were compelled to operate under a variety of other controls as well. For one, many committees were delegated only very specific and limited authority. In Rye the Town Meeting ordered its committee to oversee the militia and never assigned it another task. For the committees of safety in Keene, Chesterfield, Francestown, and Candia, the task delegated by the town meetings was to see that the towns' "inhabitants complied with the resolves of the Continental Congress." The most extreme example of control over a committee existed in Dover where the committee's powers were enumerated in writing and its members required to swear an oath to maintain their office. Finally, committees were subjected to inquiries from the Town Meeting, and the practice of appointing men for specified terms allowed it to remove any troublesome member.[49] In sum, local constraints worked to moderate both the authority and action of local committees of safety.

Perhaps the single greatest restraint on the local committees came from the State Committee and the legislature. Evidently unwilling to deposit sole authority with the local committees in the towns, these provincial bodies maintained

---

48. Francestown Town Recs., Mar. 18, 1777, NHHS; Keene Town Recs., Mar. 8, 1778, NHHS; Concord Town Recs., Mar. 2, 1776, Mar. 4, 1777, Mar. 2, 1778, NHHS; Rye Town Recs., Mar. 27, 1776, Mar. 21, 1777, NHHS; Portsmouth Town Recs., Vol. 2, Apr. 22, 1775, New Hampshire State Library, Concord (hereafter cited as NHSL); Rye Town Recs., Mar. 17, 1779, NHHS.

49. Rye Town Recs., May 16, 1775, NHHS; Keene Town Recs., Dec. 7, 1775, NHHS; Chesterfield Town Recs., Mar. 1, 1775, NHHS; "Selectmen's Precepts," Jun. 10, 1775, Francestown Town Recs., NHHS; Candia Town Recs., Jan. 3, 1775, NHHS; Dover Town Recs., Jun. 10, 1777, NHHS; New Ipswich Town Recs., Aug. 19, 1775, NHHS. The New Ipswich town meeting was acting upon the recommendation of its selectmen. See, *ibid.*, Aug. 14, 1775.

close surveillance over local committees.[50] Because the Assembly and the State Committee met at different times, they shared responsibility for overseeing local committees. Both bodies maintained an extensive correspondence with the local committees and frequently relied on them to enforce state requisitions and laws. As an additional measure of control, the Assembly and the State Committee held the authority to grant emergency provisions, military aid, and tax exemptions to local committees.

Although the State Committee was compelled at times to castigate a local committee for delays in collecting taxes or raising troops, the arrangement between the state and local units, according to Jere Daniell, "worked smoothly and to the satisfaction of those involved."[51] Rarely did a local committee challenge a provincial decree. In most cases the town committees willingly accepted their subservient role.[52] The close cooperation that existed between the state and local committees was also recognized on the state level. On March 14, 1776, the Assembly issued a general proclamation that gave that body's stamp of approval to the local committees by decreeing that the constitution of 1776 did not "Interfere with the Power of the Necessary Committees of Safety chosen in the several towns."[53]

Despite the efficient system that existed between the local committees and the state government, there was an effort in Hillsborough County in the spring of 1775 to establish a county committee of safety.[54] On May 13, 1775, Daniel Campbell and

---

50. See, for example, the actions of the Assembly during January and March 1776 dealing with the committees in Portsmouth, Exeter, Londonderry, and Newmarket, *NHSP*, 8:33, 43, 52-53, 57, 109.

51. Daniell, *Experiment in Republicanism*, 105.

52. See, for example, Portsmouth committee of safety to the New Hampshire Assembly, Jun. 2, 1775. *NHSP*, 7:502.

53. New Hampshire Assembly, "General Proclamation," Mar. 14, 1776. *NHSP*, 8:103.

54. Daniell, "Revolutionary Government," 18; Edward D. Boylston, *The Hillsborough County Congresses, 1774 and 1775* (Amherst, N.H., 1884).

Jonathan Martin sent a letter to all Hillsborough county towns advising them to select delegates to a County Congress that would improve the security of the county and "prevent declining into a state of nature." The convention subsequently met and on May 24 established a fifteen member committee of safety that was granted the broad power "to act in any affairs that may come before them."[55] Yet the Hillsborough Committee encountered such intense opposition from the county's towns that it ceased to function by August 1775.

The most serious opposition came from the town of Hollis. Early in July the County Committee tried and convicted Hollis' Benjamin Whiting of disloyalty. Less than four days after rendering its verdict, the County Committee received a stinging rebuke from the Hollis committee of safety which charged the County Committee with usurping authority granted to the local committee, and labeled the County Committee's action as "mistaken," "of Dangerous Consequence," and harmful to "the Common Cause." More significantly, the Hollis Committee charged that by acting arbitrarily, the County Committee had violated the guidelines provided by the Assembly and the Continental Congress, and so concluded that the members of the County Committee had become "Enemies to their Country."[56]

As news of the Whiting affair spread, confusion emerged over the exact relationship between the Hillsborough Committee and its town counterparts. As late as September 1776, the New Ipswich committee asked General John Sullivan "Wheather a Countys Committy has a Rite to Restore Ane one when a Townes Committy Has upon good Evidence Published him and Wheather a Voyolator of the Association has a

55. Daniel Campbell and Jonathan Martin, Circular Letter, May 3, 1775; Hillsborough County Congress Minutes, May 24, 1775; quoted in Boylston, *Hillsborough County Congresses*, 18-19.

56. Boylston, *Hillsborough County Congresses*, 22; Hollis Committee of Safety to Hillsborough Committee of Safety, Jul. 17, 1775, quoted in *ibid.*, 20-21.

write to an apeal from the Judgment of one Committy to any other Committy."[57] Before the matter reached crisis proportions, however, the experiment in provincial federalism died. The Hollis charge of disloyalty evidently had done the job, for when Chairman Matthew Patten called for another tribunal only one member of the County Committee attended.[58] After the quiet dissolution of the Hillsborough County Committee of Safety in August 1775, the situation returned to the status quo of state and local committees.

Despite efforts to minimize institutional dislocation, local committees of safety did change New Hampshire's political system. Like their provincial counterpart, local committees were institutional expressions of rebellion. As such, the appointment of these town committees can be used as a crude barometer by which to gauge the diffusion of revolutionary sentiment. Twenty-nine of the thirty sample towns incorporated prior to 1776, and twenty-four had created committees of safety before the Declaration of Independence was signed in July 1776.[59] Portsmouth was the first, appointing a committee as early as November 1774. Six other towns formed committees in January 1775. The latest creation of any committee was May 17, 1777, when Lee organized one.[60] Thus the vast majority of New

---

57. Josiah Brown to Gen. John Sullivan, Sep. 16, 1775. *Sullivan Papers* 1:88-89.

58. Patten, *Diary*, Aug. 1, 1775, 346.

59. The one sample town not incorporated before 1776 was Northumberland, but at its first town meeting after incorporation in 1779 it selected a three-member committee of safety as its fifth order of business. Northumberland Town Recs., Apr. 18, 1780, NHHS. The twenty-four towns which had established committees by July 1776 were Portsmouth, Rye, Dover, New Ipswich, Concord, Hillsborough, Gilmanton, Bedford, Chesterfield, Candia, Hanover, Chester, Amherst, Hampton, Epping, Brentwood, Keene, Richmond, Winchester, Lebanon, Canaan, Exeter, Londonderry, and Newmarket.

60. Lee Town Recs., May 17, 1777, NHHS.

Hampshire towns had declared themselves willing partners with their provincial government in escalating rebellion well before July 4, 1776.

The implications of these developments for the state's political system did not escape the notice of seasoned political figures. In May 1775 Governor Wentworth, reflecting upon the Portsmouth committee, observed that while the form of the New Hampshire policy had not been greatly altered, the reality of political power had undergone a massive transformation.[61] Less than two months later the ever-cautious Meshech Weare notified the Continental Congress that the colony was "wholly governed by this [Provincial] congress and the committees of the respective towns."[62]

It is impossible to offer a definitive assessment of how the local committees utilized their newly acquired power for no records of local committees have survived, if indeed they ever existed. While helpful in tracing specific incidents, town meeting records provide only scattered clues as to the functions of the committees. Yet some general observations are possible based upon the personal memoirs of committee members and scattered official records.

Although individual differences exist, there are some general patterns to the action of local committees of safety. The primary function of many committees at the outset of the imperial conflict seems to have been the maintenance of the peace.[63] Although a general order to keep the peace might include a multiplicity of tasks, most early committees defined their own

---

61. Governor John Wentworth to the Earl of Dartmouth, May 17, 1775, in Davies, ed., *Documents of the American Revolution*, 9:135.

62. Meshech Weare to the Continental Congress, Jul. 8, 1775. *NHSP*, 7:561.

63. Belknap, *History of New Hampshire*, 2:361; Daniell, *Experiment in Republicanism*, 99; Portsmouth Town Recs., May 15, 1775, Vol. 2, NHSL; Gilmanton Town Recs., Jul. 17, 1775, NHHS; Rye Town Recs., May 10, 1775, NHHS.

responsibilities as restoring harmony and the rule of law in their communities. Whether it was by the dispersal of local bands of vigilantes or by the arrest of suspected loyalists, the committees allowed a smooth transition from royal to state government on the local level.

Of necessity, a large number of committees became involved in the economic affairs of their towns. In New Ipswich the committee punished all violators of the Continental Congress' resolves regarding British imports. On February 18, 1777, the Portsmouth committee placed a notice in the *New Hampshire Gazette* declaring that it would embargo designated items. The most widespread of all economic functions, however, involved the confiscation of property. During 1775 the Portsmouth committee oversaw confiscated gunpowder and foodstuffs. It also appears that many committees later held the authority to manage the confiscated estates of loyalists.[64]

In many locales the committees oversaw military affairs. The Pelham committee twice conducted recruitment drives for the state's militia units. To the indefatigable Portsmouth committee was granted the sole authority to command the town's minutemen. On May 10, 1777, the closely regulated Dover committee was empowered to take all necessary action to prepare for a British invasion. The most ambitious military action taken by any local committee occurred in August 1776 when all Cheshire County committees gathered to plan for the mutual defense of the area.[65]

---

64. New Ipswich Town Recs., Feb. 4, 1775, Mar. 3, 1775, NHHS; Portsmouth committee of safety, *New Hampshire Gazette*, Feb. 18, 1777; Portsmouth committee of safety to New Hampshire Committee of Safety, Oct. 7 and 11, 1775, *NHSP*, 7:618-21. See especially the act passed by the legislature Mar. 18, 1780, regarding confiscated estates. Metcalf, *Laws of New Hampshire*, 4:286. See also, Patten, *Diary*, 350-51.

65. Pelham Inhabitants, Petition to the Assembly, Apr. 21, 1777 and Jul. 10, 1777, *NHSP*, 8:146-148; Portsmouth Town Recs., Vol. 2, Apr. 22, 1775, NHSL; Dover Town Recs., May 10, 1777, NHHS; "Selectmen's Precepts," Keene Town Recs., Aug. 8, 1776, NHHS.

Although the local committees served in a variety of other minor capacities, their exercise of judicial powers drew the most attention from contemporaries, as it has from historians. According to General Burgoyne, the committees acted in a despotic manner unmatched by even "the inquisitions of the Romish Church" and freely relied upon "arbitrary imprisonment," "persecution," and "torture."[66] Burgoyne's assessment has been repeated by a number of modern scholars, one of whom described the Portsmouth committee's decision in the case of loyalist Edward Parry as "little more than a swindle upheld by a kangaroo court."[67] For Otis G. Hammond, the local committees acting as courts never conducted themselves in a judicial manner: "The judges in these cases were not versed in the law, and there were no rules of evidence. Witnesses were allowed to say what they pleased, and hearsay evidence was fully admitted. . . . Commitments to prison were made oftener on reasonable suspicion than on proven charges."[68]

While for the most part these ad hoc courts limited themselves to cases of suspected disloyalty, they did render judgements in a wide variety of other legal matters.[69] In September

---

66. "General Burgoyne's Proclamation to the Americas," Jun. 29, 1777, *NHSP*, 8:661.

67. James H. Maguire, "Introduction," in "A Critical Edition of Edward Parry's *Journal*," xvii. Edward Parry was the Royal Mast Agent for New Hampshire and what is now Maine. He resided in Portsmouth and was placed under house arrest by the Portsmouth committee until 1777 when he was returned to England.

68. Hammond, "Tories of New Hampshire," 284.

69. Daniell, *Experiment in Republicanism*, 136-37. Carried under the umbrella of "disloyalty" were such crimes as counterfeiting, trading with the enemy, unsanctioned travel, hoarding, criticizing the patriot cause, and other sundry things. In addition, local committees held the power to place any person they deemed suspicious under house arrest. For an excellent description of a trial before a committee of safety, see Parry, *Journal*, 106-08.

1775, the Londonderry committee ruled on a case of property damage and even charged the guilty party for court costs. In the same year the Portsmouth committee assumed original jurisdiction in cases involving the deportation of refugees. The Hanover committee twice acted as a court and rendered verdicts on a suspected counterfeiter and later on an unlicensed tavern owner. And in Lebanon, the chairman of the local committee was ordered by the town to act as a court of deeds.[70]

In cases of suspected treason it is not surprising that opinions of the committees' judicial capacities varied with their verdicts. In January 1776 Eleazar Wheelock, the founder of Dartmouth College, was brought before a committee on charges of disloyalty, stemming from Wheelock's refusal to repeat a Thanksgiving sermon as ordered by the Assembly. According to Wheelock, the charges were "horrid lies and Slanders," yet he could only hope the committee would "search out the Bottom of the Evil" through its "painful and unvaried Endeavors."[71] After hearing of his friend's subsequent acquittal, John Phillips categorized the committee's conduct as one of "sense and discernment" that "baffl[ed] . . . the designs of the malicious" and corrected the "mistakes of ignorant persons." Wheelock, understandably in accord with Phillips, had the committee's ruling published.[72] Less than nine months later, however, when

---

70. Londonderry Committee of Inspection records, Bell Papers, Miscellaneous, Box 3, NHHS; Portsmouth Town Recs., May 15, 1775, Vol. 2, NHSL; Hanover committee of safety to New Hampshire Committee of Safety, Mar. 25, 1776. *NHSP*, 8:115-17; Hanover Town Recs., Mar. 20, 1777, NHHS; Lebanon Town Recs., Mar. 11, 1777, NHSL.

71. Eleazar Wheelock to John Phillips, Dec. 18, 1775, NHHS, *Colls.*, 9 (1889), 75-76. According to the records of the committees of Hanover and Lebanon, Wheelock was the victim of John Pain's slander. Report of committees of safety of Hanover and Lebanon, Jan. 2 and 6, 1776. Wheelock Papers (microfilm), Reel 11, Dartmouth College Archives, Hanover.

72. John Phillips to Eleazar Wheelock, Dec. 25, 1775. Wheelock Papers, Reel 10. The day after receiving his acquital, and on the recommendation

Wheelock and his students were forced to evacuate the college because of a smallpox epidemic, he raised this question of Hanover's committee: "whether such [a] Committee can be rightfully authorized and impowered by the town of Hanover to come authoritatively, and with all the airs and language of authority assume the form of a Judicatory, call before them who they please, order, direct, and determine in all things and put their decrees in execution . . . without advising with . . . any others but themselves."[73]

Unlike Wheelock's political response, many other defendants before committee tribunals assigned base, personal motives to their judges. According to Edward Parry, a leading business competitor used his authority as a committee member to ruin Parry. For persecuted Claremont Anglicans, their trial before a local committee was due to the efforts of Congregationalists to stamp out the Society for the Propagation of the Gospel. Justice Ephraim Baldwin observed that suspected loyalists in Chesterfield "were fined and confined to their farms" only "for the sake of the Rabble." Yet when brought before the same Chesterfield committee for making these statements, Baldwin thanked the committee for "their great tenderness" and acknowledged that the committee was "obligated in their office" to take such action "for the safety of the state."[74]

---

of the committees of Hanover, Lebanon, Plainfield, and Cornish, Wheelock wrote to Ebenezer Watson, a printer in Hartford, Connecticut, and ordered three hundred copies published along with a sermon. Hanover and Lebanon committee of safety records, Jan. 6, 1776, and Wheelock to Ebenezer Watson, Jan. 7, 1776. Wheelock Papers, Reel 11.

73. Eleazar Wheelock to John Phillips, Oct. 14, 1777. NHHS, *Colls.*, 9 (1889), 102. According to David MacClure, Wheelock's later problem stemmed from Wheelock's correspondence with British officers. MacClure to Wheelock, May 8, 1777, Wheelock Papers, Reel 11.

74. Parry, *Journal*, 45; Col. John Peters to Rev. Samuel Peters, Jul. 20, 1778, and Rev. Rauna Cassitt to S.P.G., Jun. 6, 1779, in Hammond, "Tories of New Hampshire," 307-08; Chesterfield committee of safety to Meshech Weare, Nov. 3, 1777. *NHSP*, 11:333; Ephraim Baldwin, "Confession," Sep. 25, 1777, *NHSP*, 11:337.

It is difficult to draw a completely accurate portrait of the committees as courts based on such subjective evidence. Yet some characteristics of the ad hoc courts do emerge. Many local committees abstained from ruling in cases involving their fellow townsmen.[75] When faced with the prospect, they would request committees from two or three neighboring towns to undertake the trial in an apparent effort to achieve some semblence of impartiality. The committees did not, however, follow traditional common law procedure. There were no juries; the accused was expected to answer all questions; and in at least one case, the defendant was denied the right to know his accusers.[76] The committees also reserved the sole right to levy punishments, the most common being house arrest and its attendant social isolation.[77]

Yet the local committee courts cannot be considered an American version of England's Star Chamber. They did not function as a court of last resort, for appeals were made to the State Committee or the Assembly. Furthermore, many of the accused openly and defiantly refused to obey the orders and judgements of the local committee. In the case of Oliver Parker, the Stoddard committee reported that not only did the accused have "no regard at all to the Summons" presented to him, but five other summoned witnesses also denied "the authority of

---

75. According to Matthew Patten, in July 1775 the Bedford committee called in committee members from Goffstown, Merrimack, and Derryfield to try a suspected loyalist from Bedford. Patten, *Diary*, Jul. 17, 1775, 345; Stoddard committee of safety to New Hampshire Committee of Safety, Jun. 5, 1776. *NHSP*, 13:458; committee of safety of Hanover, Lebanon, Plainfield and Cornish, "Report on Eleazar Wheelock," Jan. 2 and 6, 1776. Wheelock Papers, Reel 11. In this regard, see the concern expressed by the Hanover committee to the Assembly over its own legal jurisdiction, Mar. 25, 1776. *NHSP*, 8:115-16.

76. Parry, *Journal*, 106-08.

77. See, for example, the ruling of the Hillsborough County Committee of Safety in the case of Benjamin Whiting of Hollis, Jul. 13, 1775, in Boylston, *Hillsborough County Congresses*, 22.

the Committee" and treated the body "with Scurrilous Language." After being ordered to house arrest by the Claremont committee in 1776, Captain Benjamin Sumner completely ignored the sentence and travelled freely about the state. The most blatant disregard for the authority of the local committees occurred in November 1777, when Justice Baldwin, after signing a confession, took the document in full view of the Chesterfield committee and began "eras[ing] out some words and . . . Putting in others."[78]

Despite the valuable services provided by the local committees of safety, none of these revolutionary bodies survived the war. Of the thirty towns examined, only six had committees functioning after 1779.[79] In six others, the committees disappeared within a year of their creation.[80] The last reference to a local committee occurred in March 1781, when the town of Orford selected a three man committee for the ensuing year.[81] Local committees proved to be short-lived, indeed.

There are few indications to explain why local committees

---

78. Committee of Safety to Cheshire County, Jun. 30, 1777, Committee of Safety, Misc. File, NHSA; Stoddard committee of safety to New Hampshire Committee of Safety, Jun. 5 and 18, 1777; Ruling of the Provincial Congress on the Windham committee of safety, Nov. 15, 1775; Stoddard committee of safety to N.H. General Court, May 22, 1776; Claremont committee of safety to N.H. General Court, Dec. 9, 1776; Chesterfield committee of safety to Meshech Weare, Nov. 3, 1777. *NHSP*, 8:458-60; 7:661; 13:459-60; 11:365-66, 333-38.

79. Amherst Town Recs., Mar. 11, 1780 and Mar. 13, 1781, NHHS; New Ipswich Town Recs., Mar. 13, 1780, NHHS; Orford Town Recs., Mar. 16, 1781, NHHS; Hanover Town Recs., Mar. 8, 1781, NHHS; Lebanon Town Recs., Mar. 14, 1780, NHHS; Northumberland Town Recs., Apr. 18, 1780, NHHS.

80. Madbury Town Recs., Mar. 14, 1780, NHHS; Barrington Town Recs., Jul. 10, 1775, NHHS; Pembroke Town Recs., Mar. 31, 1776, NHHS; Hampton Town Recs., Sep. 4, 1775, NHHS; Northumberland Town Recs., Apr. 18, 1780, NHHS.

81. Orford Town Recs., Mar. 6, 1781, NHHS.

failed to survive longer. The committees always functioned within the broader sphere of traditional town government and it may well have been that the state's town leaders no longer saw the need for these political units after the major campaigns of the war shifted to the southern states. Furthermore, by 1781 political attention in the state had itself shifted from issues of military security to those surrounding a new state constitution. Thus, when "A Farmer," writing in the *New Hampshire Gazette* of August 12, 1780, called for a return of the local committees of safety, he was greeted with silence by his fellow citizens.[82]

The single best explanation for the local committees' sudden disappearance may lie in a petition directed to the Assembly by John Goffe in 1779. Goffe, a Bedford selectman and former member of the town's committee of safety, began his petition by reviewing the contributions made by the town committees in the early stages of the war. Yet Goffe recounted how in 1779 the Assembly, in an attempt to restore "the Original Laws of this Land," had made "these former Committees . . . Liable to be tryed by a course of Law, and some are actually engaged and many others Exposed to be brought in Question for their former Complying with those Resolves of the Congress and acts of this State." That Goffe spoke from direct experience is evident from a later petition he submitted to the Assembly, informing it that he had been successfully sued by Michael Dalton for £888 for seizing Dalton's cattle and grain.[83] Although Goffe argued that he had confiscated the goods under direct orders from the Assembly, he still lost his case. Clearly rulings of this sort would serve as stern warning to other local committee members who, like Goffe, faced similar charges. It is small wonder that the New Hampshire local committees slipped from view in such a sudden yet silent fashion.

---

82. "A Farmer," *New Hampshire Gazette*, Aug. 12, 1780.

83. John Goffe, Petitions to N.H. Assembly, Mar. 8, 1779, and Mar. 14, 1782, *NHSP*, 11:181-82.

As local committees of safety disappeared, the State Committee began to show signs of increased institutional hardening. Prior to 1778 committee membership was relatively fluid; but after August 1778 turnover declined. In the ten separate committees appointed from August 1778 to May 1784, new members accounted for only 19.7 percent of all committeemen as compared to 34.6 percent in the previous eight Committees. The Committee continued to meet roughly 30 percent of the days within each session, and the hardening of the institution can be seen more directly in the share of governmental activity the Committee began to assume. Prior to 1778 the Committee divided its terms of service almost equally with the legislature. From May 1775 to January 1777 the committee met 264 days to the legislature's 243 days. From August 1778 to its expiration in 1784, however, the Committee sat as the sole governing body of the state for almost twice as long as the legislature. In other words, the State Committee of Safety sat as New Hampshire's only government nearly two-thirds of the last six years of the Revolution.

The State Committee's position as the major arm of government did not come by default but rather by conscious action, action which did not go unnoticed. Indeed, the major factional disputes within the state centered on the Committee, and hence bear directly on its institutional history. Beginning in December 1779 the state's political out-groups began to challenge the Committee's domination of the government, initiating a four-year power struggle between the Committee and the Portsmouth faction led by Speaker John Langdon. Thus, the institutional hardening of the Committee in the last four years of the Revolution can be seen as both a symptom and a source of the intense factionalism that would ultimately reshape the state's political system.

The first blatant factional dispute over the Committee emerged during the December session of the 1779 legislature and rapidly developed into an open and ruthless contest between Langdon and the Committee for political control of the state. Langdon's attack on the Committee stemmed in part from his earlier clashes with that body over the confiscation of loyalist estates and the political career of his brother Woodbury.[84] At the December session, Langdon unleashed a direct assault on the Committee as an institution and its power.[85] With the aid of a large number of freshman legislators, Langdon initially worked to weaken the Committee through its membership. He first reduced the size of the Committee from nine to five and saw to it that two of the five were Portsmouth merchants. Yet failing to remove Dudley and Weare from their entrenched positions on the Committee, Langdon concocted another scheme. Believing the Committee's political power an extension of its financial authority, Langdon sponsored a measure that stripped the Committee of all independent fiscal power. During the legislature's January recess, the Committee sat for only three days, but by choice.

The Committee's reluctance to act — on any matter — proved to be a successful gambit. According to Josiah Bartlett, when town officials began to pour into Exeter during the January recess to settle financial accounts with the Committee only to discover that they had made a trip in vain, they began to raise "a great Clamour against the [General] Court."[86] The Assembly responded at its next session by refusing to enforce the Langdon-inspired restrictions on the Committee. From this point on, Langdon's power began to decline.

---

84. For a general discussion of the Langdon-Committee clash, see Daniell, *Experiment in Republicanism*, 139-45. See also, NHHS, *Colls.*, 7:117; Woodbury Langdon to Nathaniel Peabody, Dec. 5, 1779. Langdon Papers, Box 2, Folder 13, NHHS; Woodbury Langdon to Nathaniel Peabody, Dec. 14, 1779. Peabody Papers, NHHS.

85. Josiah Bartlett to Nathaniel Peabody, Dec. 18, 1779. Bartlett Papers, Reel 3; John Langdon to Nathaniel Peabody, Dec. 6, 1779, Langdon Papers, Box 2, Folder 9.

86. Josiah Bartlett to Nathaniel Folsom, Mar. 11, 1780. Bartlett Papers, Reel 3.

The Committee was not content, however, with merely regaining its former powers. Apparently believing that Langdon's assault was sponsored by the Portsmouth faction, the Committee began to close it ranks in March 1780, reducing its reliance on the Portsmouth group and increasing the influence of the Merrimack Valley and Inland Commercial group. No representative of the Portsmouth faction was appointed to the Committee in its last two sessions, and even before that the attendence of the Portsmouth delegates was less than that of the majority. From August 1778 until December 1782, Portsmouth area delegates attended Committee meetings at rate of 57 percent, as opposed to 82.4 percent for the Merrimack Valley-Inland Commercial group. Numerically outnumbered, the Portsmouth Committeemen seemed to view their attendence almost as futile.

Faced with this turn of events, the already politically weakened Portsmouth faction realized its entire political future was at stake. In April 1781, however, the Assembly, seeking to replace the temporary 1776 Constitution with a more permanent plan of government, called for a state constitutional convention. All factions viewed a new constitution favorably, for the 1776 plan was clearly temporary, but the Portsmouth faction seized the opportunity to renew its struggle with the Committee. After managing to have its delegates appointed to all the key positions at the convention, the faction forced through a plan of government that was nothing short of an open attempt to dismantle the Committee, for the proposed constitution called for an annually elected executive to replace the Committee.[87] Furthermore, the faction attempted to curb the Committee members' political influence outside the Committee itself by establishing elaborate restrictions on plural-office-holding. Only in such a way could the anti-Committee faction protect itself from retribution from the politically powerful Committee.

---

87. *NHSP*, 8:894-97; Daniell, *Experiment in Republicanism*, 171-73.

That the Portsmouth-led delegates intended these measures to dismantle the Committee was made clear by an address prefixed to the constitution, written by three Portsmouth delegates. According to the address, one of the major flaws of the government was the "sad experience" of uniting separate judicial, executive, and legislative powers in a single body, which led to "the total abolition of justice" and "a complete system of tyranny." Given the Committee's repeated practice of functioning in all three capacities, such an assessment — in the context of the very real political situation of the state — seems clearly meant as a condemnation of the Committee. The address, moreover, offered an even more pointed and direct criticism when it claimed the Committee was arbitrarily created by the Assembly "without any new authority derived from the people, or without consulting them."[88]

Once again, however, the anit-Committee faction suffered a defeat as the proposed constitution was overwhelmingly rejected by the towns. With Langdon's political fortunes steadily declining, the Portsmouth faction enjoyed few avenues of attack and thus in 1782, sought to use the Assembly's call for a fourth constitutional convention as an opportunity to break the Committee's hold on political power. As with the earlier plan of government, the 1782 constitution contained proposals for an independent executive and an exclusion bill against plural officeholding. The 1782 constitution's preamble took aim at the Committee. But rather than implicitly attacking the Committee, the preamble's author, George Atkinson, explicitly directed charges against the Committee. While admitting that the Committee was a creature of wartime necessity, the war was over, and the Portsmouth merchant now accused the Committee of incurring "great expense by frequent meetings" and causing dangerous delays in executing its responsibilities because of its large membership.[89]

---

88. George Atkinson, "Address of the Constitutional Convention of 1781." *NHSP*, 9:845-52.

89. Daniell, *Experiment in Republicanism*, 175; George Atkinson, "Address of the Constitutional Convention of 1782," *NHSP*, 9:878-82.

Much to the convention's dismay, the proposed constitution met widespread apathy and disapproval.[90] Apparently considering that this constitution was the only option left to them, the Portsmouth-led delegates resubmitted the plan to the towns and mounted an impressive campaign to win adoption. "The Examiner" touched off the drive in the *New Hampshire Gazette* by accusing the Committee members of being "servants" to a despotic government.[91] In particular, "The Examiner" focused on the Committee's power to arrest arbitrarily. As further evidence, "The Examiner" pointed out that the Committee's members held "all the legislative, executive, and judicial powers of government," had "unlimited influence," and were "arrayed with power to create others to join them in sentiment." The public assault was continued by "Quibus" in September 1783, the message being much the same. Fearing that the Committee was capable of usurping the "rights of the people," "Quibus" concluded that it was "time that the powers of the Committee were exactly ascertained or totally annihilated, for at present, both the people and the laws, seem to be the sport of their will."[92]

After four years of bitter and intense struggle the anti-Committee forces finally achieved victory on October 31, 1783, when the resubmitted and much ammended constitution was ratified. Between its passage and its implimentation in June, the Committee continued to function, yet without the energy and vitality that had characterized its earlier years. It was a lame duck institution, to be sure. No longer did it rule during wartime, rejecting the niceties of republican ideology in favor of the necessities of war. Now, the Committee spent its last year adjusting war claims and overseeing the disbandment of

---

90. Daniell, *Experiment in Republicanism*, 176; *New Hampshire Gazette*, Feb. 8, 1783.

91. "The Examiner," *New Hampshire Gazette*, Mar. 1, 1783.

92. *New Hampshire Gazette*, Sep. 20, 1783.

the state's military. When the Committee died its official death on May 29, 1784, it was but a shadow of its former self.[93]

The State Committee of Safety was the major arm of New Hampshire's government during the Revolution. For nine years it served the state, and for six it met and served nearly twice as much as did the legislature. The Committee provided New Hampshire not only with an agency which could act swiftly in wartime emergencies, but also an arena in which political battles could be fought. As a governing body it functioned consistently in executive, legislative, and judicial capacities, much like the governor's councils of the pre-war years. Its members reflected the changing social complexion of the state and the attendant shift in political power which this brought. The local committees of safety, for their part, were short-lived, lasting a little more than three years. Like their provincial counterpart, local committees functioned in executive and judicial capacities. Yet local committees operated within an institutional environment which did not lend itself to their assumption of governmental tasks on a large scale. No effective institutional constraints existed at the state level. Only practical, factional politics limited the Committee's actions, and then only toward the end.

The relationship between the committees of safety and Revolutionary political thought is problematic at best. As a functioning governmental body the Committee defies precise definition within the confines of Revolutionary republican thought. As an appointed body that consistently exercised executive, legislative, and judicial powers, the Committee cannot be characterized as either an institutional embodiment of the three orders or estates within society, characteristic of the doctrine of mixed government, or a political construct ad-

---

93. Hunt, *Provincial Committees of Safety*, 21; Upton, *Revolutionary New Hampshire*, 45. The last entry made in the Committee's Record Books was on May 29, 1784. No mention of the Committee found its way into the records of the next legislative assembly. *NHSP*, 20:39-53, 62-89.

hering to some functional separation of powers. Instead, the Committee existed throughout the war in a theoretical limbo, justified only by its ability to meet wartime needs. Only when this condition disappeared in 1783 did the Committee fall prey to its factional opponent's belated appeal to republican principles.

Similarly, although the composition of the State Committee clearly points to a sudden alteration in the social location of political power, that shift was ruled more by the dictates of factional politics than by any concerted effort to reflect a republican mode of representation. Yet because this locational shift actually extended power to most of the state, the Committee reflected, however inadvertently, a harmony between the social reality of the state and its political institutions. Finally, the increasing reliance upon constitutional conventions in New Hampshire resulted from the limited options available to the opponents of the state's ruling elite rather than a linear progression in the development of political thought. Thus the portrait of the Committee of Safety is one composed more from the haphazard brush strokes of wartime exegency and political infighting than from the canvas of Revolutionary republican thought.

Revolutionary Economic Policy
in Massachusetts*

Oscar and Mary F. Handlin[1]

T HE revolution was America's time of troubles. A period which
raised the most fundamental questions as to the nature of the
state stripped away the conventional patterns which cloaked the
exercise of political power. The luminous objectives of the struggle
fired imaginations and by contrast threw a shadow over the desperate
quest for gain that marked the actual conduct of the enterprise. The government faced new, unprecedented problems, as the war touched deeply
the welfare of all people. Its policy was vitally and directly significant
to citizens who yet lacked the familiar guides to action of more tranquil
years. Expediency and principle both operated in politics. Men thought
in terms of the immediate effects of specific measures, but they nevertheless faced the compulsion of discovering bases for cooperation with
each other and of defending their interests in terms of a larger patriotic
purpose.[2]

In Massachusetts these characteristics came into the open as a succession of insurrectionary governments struggled with the complex questions
of the interregnum between the open break with England and the establishment of constitutional government in 1780.

---

*The materials for this paper were gathered in the course of a study of the role
of government in the economy of Massachusetts sponsored by the Committee on Research in Economic History of the Social Science Research Council. We found
helpful the following secondary sources: Allan Nevins, *American States during and
after the Revolution 1775-1789* (New York, 1927) ; A. B. Hart, ed., *Commonwealth
History of Massachusetts* (New York, 1929), III; J. T. Adams, *New England in
the Republic* . . . (Boston, 1926), 5-67; R. V. Harlow, "Aspects of Revolutionary
Finance, 1775-1783," *American Historical Review*, XXXV (1929) ; J. B. Felt,
Historical Account of Massachusetts Currency (Boston, 1839) ; H. H. Burbank,
"General Property Tax in Massachusetts 1775 to 1792 with Some Consideration of
Colonial and Provincial Legislation and Practices" (MS, 1915, Harvard University
Archives) ; A. M. Davis, "Limitation of Prices in Massachusetts, 1776-1779,"
Colonial Society of Massachusetts Publications, X (1907).

[1] Mr. Handlin is a member of the History Department of Harvard University.
He and Mrs. Handlin are the authors of *Commonwealth: a Study of the Role of
Government in the American Economy: Massachusetts, 1774-1861.*

[2] We have discussed the political and constitutional aspects of the question in
Chapter I of our *Commonwealth* . . . (New York, 1946).

The Revolution, moving swiftly onward, had not immediately revolutionized the small important matters of daily living. Central government or no, the people in their towns concerned themselves with everyday affairs much as they had for almost a century and a half. They voted to build and repair roads and bridges; they appointed committees to supervise the taking of fish; they argued as to whether pigs should go at large, and whether to fence in common fields. They chose the usual officers—selectmen, surveyors of highways, hogreeves, preservers of deer, cullers of fish, guagers of casks, sealers of leather, viewers of fences, and inspectors of beef, lumber, grain, markets, and pearl ash. Such affairs, petty in the total picture, loomed large in immediate interest and consumed much of the energy of local government.[3] In the fields of "ordinary legislation" the state, too, continued long-standing practices, granting lotteries, licensing innholders, and regulating fences, beef, grain, usury, pearl ash, roads, and ferries. Blanket measures simply extended the duration of old laws. The very pressure of war precluded much discussion; these issues had to be disposed of in a cursory fashion.[4]

Statutes directly and obviously essential to the prosecution of the war were also enacted with dispatch. Particularly in the first flush of excitement, only those foolhardy enough to risk the dire Tory label would openly deny the need for men and supplies to carry on the conflict with Britain. In regard to these measures the government could chance no dissension; those opposed, it excluded from the polity. Though policy found few direct precedents, the absence or elimination of contending interests facilitated decisive action.[5]

Massachusetts, the first scene of combat, immediately faced the problem of raising men. The Provincial Congress urged recruitment and

[3] See, for example, *Old Records of the Town of Fitchburgh, Massachusetts, 1764-1796* (Fitchburg, 1898-99), I, 147 ff., 168 ff.; *Weston, Records of the First Precinct, 1746-1754 and of the Town, 1754-1803* (Boston, 1893), 210, 214, 217; *Watertown Records . . . 1769 to 1792 . . .* (Newton, 1928), VI, 113, 124; S. A. Bates, ed., *Records of the Town of Braintree, 1640 to 1793* (Randolph, 1886), 454-56; J. H. Temple, *History of North Brookfield, Massachusetts . . .* (North Brookfield, 1887), 226.

[4] Provincial Congress to Continental Congress, June 20, 1775, *Journals of Each Provincial Congress of Massachusetts in 1774 and 1775 . . .* (Boston, 1838), 365. Also, st. 1775-6, ch. 8; st. 1776-7, ch. 42; st. 1777-8, ch. 8; st. 1778-9, ch. 32; st. 1779-80, chs. 4, 18; st. 1780, ch. 1.

[5] F. T. Bowles, "The Loyalty of Barnstable in the Revolution," *Colonial Society of Massachusetts Publications*, XXV (1923), 265 ff.

gathered and organized an army; by the summer of 1775 some nine thousand soldiers were in regular service. Subsequent events dramatized the valor, but also the inadequacy, of minutemen who divided their time between battlefield and wheat field. Long-term replaced short-term enlistments; finally a draft of three-year men called for one out of seven eligibles, a substantial percentage of the state's males. Through the war, Massachusetts put a larger proportion of her population under arms on land and sea than any other state.[6]

These measures reduced productive capacity and bore heavily upon those left behind who had to pay for the high bounties and the tax-exemption granted the soldiers.[7] By the middle of 1776, the Council complained that the state was "so greatly thinned . . . of men that it has become extreamly difficult if not impracticable to raise any more, or even to carry on our Necessary Husbandry Business."[8] In the next year there were grumblings that "you may as well fish for pearls in Oyster River . . . as seek for such creatures in Boston as a taylor or shoemaker."[9] Scarcity affected the price of labor; in Leicester, for instance, a day's work on the highways fixed at 3s. in 1774 had risen to £6 by 1780, a sharp rise, even considering the embellishments of paper money. The poor rural communities, unable to raise the bounties to hire substitutes, suffered disproportionately. Thus Malden gave 231 men to the army of a total population of 1,030 in 1776 and Leicester by 1781 had given 102 of a total little over 800.[10]

These harsh and unequally distributed burdens occasioned some requests for special dispensations in the light of peculiar circumstances. But there was no challenge of the policy itself. Compulsory service followed the tradition of government calls upon manpower. Permitting the well-to-do to escape by payments in money only extended to a new

[6] *Massachusetts Soldiers and Sailors of the Revolutionary War . . . Published by the Secretary of the Commonwealth. . . .* (Boston, 1896-1908), I, ix-xxxix; Frederick Freeman, *History of Cape Cod: Annals of the Thirteen Towns of Barnstable County* (Boston, 1869), I, 543.

[7] Temple, *North Brookfield*, 237.

[8] Council to Hancock, July 19, 1776, Massachusetts Archives [Hereafter M.A.], CXCV, 425, 426.

[9] Eliot to Belknap, Jan. 12, 1777, *Massachusetts Historical Society Collections,* Sixth Series (Boston, 1886-98), IV, 103.

[10] Emory Washburn, "Topographical and Historical Sketches of the Town of Leicester," *Worcester Magazine and Historical Journal*, II (1826), 72, 114; D. P. Corey, *History of Malden, Massachusetts, 1633-1785* (Malden, 1899), 761.

area the customary techniques of road building, for instance, where taxes fell unequally upon the muscles of the poor and the purses of the wealthy. While the consequences of drafting so many men emerged soon enough, the exigencies of war left no room for alternatives.

Recruitment was the first essential but inevitably it unlocked a Pandora's box from which flew forth a host of corollary problems. An empty treasury and an economy geared to limited production and extensive imports somehow had to yield supplies for a fighting army. The aspiration for ever-increasing, self-sufficient war production consistently animated the Provincial Congress and its successor the General Court. These bodies urged local activity "to preclude as far as Possible, any dependence upon foreign States for any Necessary Article," while constant pressure from the Continental Congress underlined the significance of encouraging "agriculture, manufactures, and aeconomy."[11]

Unceasingly the state went about the business of harnessing available supplies for the war effort. Hortatory proclamations were the earliest recourse; every shortage occasioned a wishful appeal to the public. Lest lack of information stand in the way of popular cooperation, the government garnered data on such diverse subjects as the availability and methods of extracting sulphur, the making of salt, and the smelting and refining of lead.[12] The legislature even appointed a committee to manufacture saltpetre experimentally for three months at its own expense, and to communicate the resultant knowledge to ambitious enterprisers.[13] As further encouragement, towns from time to time set up special premiums and the state offered a wide range of bounties together with a guarantee to purchase many items at specified prices.[14] Upon another occasion the state assumed the lead when it lost patience with private initiative, acquir-

[11] Res. 1777-8, ch. 142; *Massachusetts Spy*, Dec. 22, 1774; J. Adams to Warren, Oct. 20, 1775, E. C. Burnett, ed., *Letters of Members of the Continental Congress* (Washington, 1921-36), I, 239. For the activities of the Provincial Congress, see *Boston Gazette*, Dec. 19, 1774; for local action, see *Records of Braintree*, 458 *ff.*; *Journals of Each Provincial Congress*, 601 *ff.*

[12] M.A., CXXXVII, 63, 86, 104 *ff.*; res. 1775-6, chs. 148, 929; res. 1776-7, ch. 172.

[13] For a pamphlet on methods forwarded by the Continental Congress to be reprinted and sent to the seacoast towns, see res. 1775-6, ch. 162.

[14] Temple, *North Brookfield*, 234; res. 1775-6, chs. 162, 319, 343, 481, 810, 873; res. 1776-7, ch. 358; res. 1777-8, chs. 142, 171; res. 1778-9, ch. 69; res. 1779-80, ch. 698; M.A., CXXXVII, 110, 111, 114. For claims, see M.A., CLXXXVII, 12. For other material on the manufacture of iron, see M.A., CXCV, 230.

ing and operating for a time two powder mills at Stoughton and Sutton.[15]

These activities and the war effort in general brought enormous demands for money into a community which had perennially complained about the costs of government. Taxation seemed no solution. The legislature had the power but not the courage to impose new burdens upon those who had so recently grumbled about the old. In any case it felt its influence not strong enough to exact levies from towns already weighed down by the extraordinary local expenditures involved in raising soldiers, arms, and munitions. Voluntary loans, tried early, proved unsuccessful. The search for specie to support the expedition to Canada in the summer of 1776 vividly illustrated the elusiveness of hard money.[16]

Thus the Provincial Congress and the General Court resorted to the same desperate expedient. Between August 23, 1775, and December 7, 1776, seven measures emitted £470,000 in Bills of Credit in denominations of from 2d. to 48s. With continental and other state currency, these were to be legal tender in payment of all debts, public and private.

The legislature by no means designed to introduce a soft-money policy. Memories of disastrous colonial experiments in paper and of the suffering occasioned by the losses of the land bank in 1741 were still fresh in the minds of many. The government perforce resorted to these emissions, which represented the capitalization of its "single available asset: the hope of winning the war." But it attempted to guard against depreciation. Each act provided heavy penalties for passing bills at discount and specifically set up future taxes for redemption.[17]

But the remoteness of victory and the uncertainty of eventual payment almost immediately left their mark. In addition, even cheaper currencies from the Continental Congress, from Connecticut, and from Rhode Island soon entered into competition, compounding the confusion. All paper fell into a steady decline that did not halt for a decade. By the end of 1775 the failure of bills to circulate at par excited committees of safety; and in the next year accusations were rampant against "Evil minded

[15] For gunpower policy, see res. 1775-6, chs. 495, 502, 535, 579, 647, 799, 960. For later premiums, see res. 1776-7, ch. 593. On the state mills, see res. 1775-6, ch. 1046; res. 1777-8, ch. 1061; res. 1778-9, ch. 606. For some light on the later history of the state furnaces, see M.A. CXXXVII, 397.

[16] See res. 1775-6, chs. 658, 698; res. 1776-7, chs. 96, 192, 698; Morris to Gates, Apr. 6, 1776, Burnett, Letters, I, 416; Paine to Gerry, Apr. 12, 1777, James T. Austin, Life of Elbridge Gerry ... (Boston, 1828-29), I, 219 ff.

[17] Harlow, "Aspects of Revolutionary Finances," Am. Hist. Rev., XXXV, 48; st. 1775-6, chs. 2, 9, 18; st. 1776-7, chs. 1, 10, 16, 26, 28.

persons" who injured credit. Early in 1777 the value of the emissions had fallen almost one-third and there was acute danger that paper might become "as plenty and of Course as cheap as Oak leaves."[18]

The spectre of depreciation began to haunt the state. Had not experience proved the ineffectiveness of such policies? The old despotic rulers had been unable to give currency to their paper; could a fledgling republic, beset by the harrowing problems of war and revolution do so? And if it failed would that not weaken the confidence of an uncertain public in the whole structure of government? Aside from these considerations was the stark fact that depreciation directly threatened the financing of the war. Harassed by the problems of raising large sums, of getting its bills accepted for supplies, and of satisfying soldiers with their wages, the state favored measures that would keep its money and credit at as high a level as possible.

The simplest way to achieve that objective was to pass laws exorcising any decline. Successive acts declared Massachusetts and United States bills legal tender, set up heavy penalties for altering, counterfeiting, or passing them at less than face value, forbade the sale of goods at lower prices in specie than in paper, excluded offenders from civil and military office, and finally imposed heavy fines and prison sentences on those who did anything to hurt the credit of the currency.[19]

These punitive techniques quickly became ancillary. The General Court turned to more orthodox methods for giving substance to its emissions as soon as it felt secure enough to borrow or to tax. By the end of 1776 it issued successfully two series of treasury notes for a total of more than £400,000 at 6 per cent.[20] Like the notes of the Provincial Congress and those issued in subsequent loans, these undoubtedly had some circulation, but they lacked the essential character of legal tender. Indeed, the bills issued by the Act of December 7, 1776, proved the last emission of state money that was legal tender.[21]

[18] See res. 1775-6, ch. 587; Adams to Warren, Apr. 3, 1777, Burnett, *Letters*, II, 354.

[19] St. 1775-6, ch. 18; st. 1776-7, chs. 37, 44; st. 1779-80, ch. 7, sec. 2; *Acts and Resolves, Public and Private of the Province of the Massachusetts Bay . . ., Vol. V, Acts Passed 1769-80* (Boston, 1886) [Hereafter: *Province Acts*], 1452.

[20] St. 1776-7, chs. 24, 27. For other loans, see st. 1776-7, chs. 4, 43; st. 1777-8, chs. 12, 19. For the policies of the Provincial Congress, see *Journals of Each Provincial Congress*, 185-87, 246, 464-65; Jackson to Wendell, Apr. 27, 1775, K. W. Porter, *Jacksons and the Lees . . .* (Cambridge, 1937), I, 298 ff.

[21] Harlow, "Aspects of Revolutionary Finance," *Am. Hist. Rev.*, XXXV, 49,

With the shift to loans came also a revival of taxation by Massachusetts. In 1775 levies had been light; in 1776, there were none at all; and even the next year, S. A. Otis was still apprehensive that taxation "will make our people look about them."[22] Yet the state lacked an alternative source of income to maintain lenders' confidence. It did not profit as much as others from confiscated Tory property.[23] A lottery in 1778 raised almost £2,000,000 but many objected to that painless method on moral grounds and, in any case, it was hardly dependable for larger sums.[24] Taking the cost of war out of taxpayers' pocketbooks could not long be evaded. In 1777, John Adams thundered, "Taxation, My dear Sir, Taxation, and Oeconomy, are our only effectual Resources."[25] Reverberations in the General Court resolved the question. Levies that year were heavier than in any other state and soared spectacularly thereafter.[26]

Meanwhile local rates rose rapidly. The task of raising soldiers and war materials, and of paying directly therefor, often delegated to the towns, complicated their once simple finances.[27] The exigencies of war perversely created new expenses which could not be anticipated. Moreover soldiers sent to the battlefields contributed "but Little to Support thir families" which frequently became a further charge upon the

---

minimizes the difference between bills of credit and treasury notes. But the absence of legal tender character and the payment of interest seem more important than the fact that both circulated and both depreciated. Above all the motives behind their issue were significantly different.

[22] Otis to Gerry, Austin, *Gerry*, I, 266.

[23] For a plan to use loyalist estates to support the currency, see *Independent Chronicle*, Apr. 27, 1780. For Massachusetts scruples and the development of the policy in general, see st. 1783, ch. 69; Pickering Papers (MSS, Massachusetts Historical Society), V, 316; A. M. Davis, "The Confiscation Laws of Massachusetts," *Colonial Society of Massachusetts Publications*, VIII (1906), 50 *ff.* Confiscation was complicated by such problems as the standing of mortgages and debts on Tory estates (see st. 1780, chs. 52, 53; st. 1781, ch. 42; st. 1782, ch. 69).

[24] See res. 1777-8, ch. 1079; st. 1778-9, ch. 42; st. 1779-80, ch. 45; Charles H. J. Douglas, *Financial History of Massachusetts . . . to the American Revolution* (New York, 1892), 107 *ff.*; J. Adams to Palmer, May 6, 1777, Burnett, *Letters*, II, 356.

[25] J. Adams to Warren and A. Adams, Aug. 18, Oct. 15, 1777, Burnett, *Letters*, II, 455; C. F. Adams, ed., John and Abigail Adams, *Familiar Letters . . . during the Revolution . . .* (New York, 1876), 316 *ff.*

[26] St. 1776-7, ch. 13; st. 1777-8, chs. 13, 26; st. 1778-9, chs. 12, 39; st. 1779-80, chs. 12, 30, 44, 49; st. 1780, chs. 9, 16; *Province Acts*, 668; H. A. Cushing, ed., Samuel Adams, *Writings . . .* (New York, 1908), IV, 19 *ff.*; Paine to Gerry, Apr. 12, 1777, Austin, *Gerry*, I, 220; "Squaretoes," *Independent Chronicle*, Nov. 2, 1780. See also res. 1778-9, chs. 405, 406, 444; res. 1779-80, ch. 302.

[27] St. 1776-7, ch. 41; st. 1777-8, ch. 20; *Weston Records*, 243.

towns.[28] Thus, Braintree's taxes, only £150 in 1774 and 1775, climbed to £1,500 in 1777, while, by 1778, the community had a debt of £4,000 "occasioned by the war." In the three years, 1778-1780, the Second Parish of Brookfield alone had to raise £4,264.6.6, much of it in specie and in kind, for military purposes. Depreciation accounted only partially for these increases. Throughout the period, local taxes were so large "as to equal their proportion of the public tax."[29] Despite a steady stream of petitions for abatements, the new exactions continued. Massachusetts taxpayers, formerly resentful of the mild Provincial levies, found themselves yoked to the high costs of independence.[30]

Wartime difficulties in the distribution of commodities confronted the government with another set of ineluctable problems, the ramifications of which affected the entire economy. Disruption of normal channels of trade, diversion of manpower from civilian pursuits, and extraordinary activity by the state as a large-scale purchaser, all contributed to a fabulous increase in costs and to inability to procure even the essentials of life. The emergency almost immediately fostered a scarcity and dearness of "every article . . . in the West India way" and created an unimaginable want of "many . . . small articles, which are not manufactured amongst ourselves," while a drought in the summer of 1775, the worst in many decades, foreshadowed the constriction of agricultural supplies.[31]

[28] See, for example, Corey, *Malden*, 778, 779; *Records of Braintree*, 511; also M.A., CLXXXI, 32. For action on support of soldiers' families, see *Records of Braintree*, 484, 511.

[29] *Records of Braintree*, 448, 463, 467, 485, 493, 512; Temple, *North Brookfield*, 237-41, 243; S. C. Damon, *History of Holden* . . . (Worcester, 1841), 47, 74; Paine to Gerry, Apr. 12, 1777, Austin, *Gerry*, I, 219 ff.; J. G. Holland, *History of Western Massachusetts* . . . (Springfield, 1855), II, 593.

[30] In 1774, the total province tax was only £12,960 (*Massachusetts Spy*, Jan. 27, 1774).

Average Annual Tax, 1692-1769

1692-9	£12,000	1730-9	£25,000
1700-9	£18,000	1740-9	£39,000
1710-9	£15,000	1750-9	£48,000
1720-9	£16,000	1760-9	£53,000

(Hart, *Commonwealth History*, II, 215, III, 341, 342). See also C. J. Bullock, *Historical Sketch of the Finances and Financial Policy of Massachusetts from 1780 to 1905* (New York, 1907), 5; Enoch Pratt, *Comprehensive History, Ecclesiastical and Civil, of Eastham, Wellfleet and Orleans* . . . (Yarmouth, 1844), 129, 130.

[31] Abigail to J. Adams, July 16, 1775, C. F. Adams, ed., *Letters of Mrs. Adams, the Wife of John Adams* . . . (Boston, 1840), I, 56; Eliot to Belknap, Nov. 8, 1774,

Time did not abate the shortages, attended by an unrelenting rise in prices. By June, 1776, it was said, "living is double what it was one year ago."[82] Depreciation and speculation—"a corrupt, avaricious, unnatural, infectious Disease"—certainly contributed to, but did not cause high prices.[83] Even in 1778, with the fall of money accentuated, "the necessaries of life and labour" were "rising more than the proportion of the declension of the currency." Paine noted, "Many that are supposed good judges in the mercantile way tell you, that if silver and gold were passing instead of paper, the prices of goods would be as high"; and John Adams, who was not always consistent on the subject, agreed that "the high prices of many Articles arises from their scarcity." The roots of the question lay in the supply of goods rather than in the worth of the currency.[84]

As the largest consumer, plagued by the quest for funds, the state wanted assurance against an interruption of supplies. While it objected to rising prices that compounded its monetary difficulties, the disappointing response to requisitions repeatedly compelled it to raise the amount it was willing to offer in payment for the desired commodities.[85] Yet mounting costs, for which the government's own purchases often set the pace, lowered the morale of soldiers who had enlisted at fixed rates of pay now insufficient to maintain themselves or their families. Those "too much exposed to the Oppressions of Harpys who for Triffles have stript them of their Wages" were not likely to re-enlist.[86] Even supplies for the helpless private citizen became a matter of concern to the legislature anxious to retain his loyalty and maintain his efficiency.

As the self-regulating free market failed to produce low prices and

---

Massachusetts Historical Society Collections, Sixth Series, IV, 61; W. P. and J. P. Cutler, *Life, Journals and Correspondence of Rev. Manasseh Cutler, LL.D.* (Cincinnati, 1888), I, 52.

[82] A. to J. Adams, June 3, 1776, J. and A. Adams, *Familiar Letters*, 183. See also the petitions, *Province Acts*, 669.

[83] Dyer to Trumbull, Mar. 12, 1778, Burnett, *Letters*, III, 125.

[84] Paine to Gerry, Apr. 12, 1777, Austin, *Gerry*, I, 219 ff.; Burnett, *Letters*, II, 252. R. V. Harlow, "Aspects of Revolutionary Finance," *Am. Hist. Rev.*, XXXV, 58, thinks of the rise in prices purely in terms of depreciation and sees in price fixing only an "effort to fix the value of paper in terms of commodities," disregarding the real shortages and the absolute rise in prices.

[85] Res. 1775-6, ch. 517.

[86] Wolcott to Griswold, Nov. 18, 1776, Lee to S. Adams, Nov. 23, 1777, and Burke to Caswell, Mar. 12, 1778, Burnett, *Letters*, II, 158, 568, III, 128; Austin, *Gerry*, I, 250 ff.

smoothly flowing supplies, Massachusetts began to wrestle with questions of where and how goods were to be sold, of the profit margins at various levels of distribution, and of the adjustment of the flow of commodities from producer to consumer. At the very beginning, the framers of the continental association had foreseen that non-importation would produce rising prices, and had inserted a provision against profiteering. Efforts of towns like Braintree to enforce that clause proved futile.[37] A petition to the General Court in November, 1776, complained that

some Persons have been so lost to all Virtue, and the Love of their Country, as to engross the most Necessary, and saleable Articles, purchasing them at retail Price, & immediately advancing upon that retail Price, at least Cent for Cent . . . . the soldiers and others not concerned in this unrighteous Commerce, are groaning under their Burdens, & we fear cannot endure them much longer . . . . we are greatly alarmed lest Tumults, Disorders, and even a Disunion and Backwardness in, or Defection from the common Cause of America will appear in many Places, and great Difficulties [will] arise in recruiting and supporting the american *Army* . . . unless some Method can be found out, & speedily applied, to relieve the oppressed, and remedy those Evils.[38]

To appeals in the name of the soldiers, the war effort, the poor, the honest trader, the drive against counterfeiters, the censure of depreciators, the need of action against the Tories, the legislature responded by appointing a committee to meet in conference with representatives from the other New England states and to consider among other things a regulating act to "give value to the soldiers' wages and stability to . . . currency."[39]

Following the recommendations of the conference, the Act of January 25, 1777, "to Prevent Monopoly and Oppression" set up a long series of specific rates for wages and for domestic commodities in Boston which were to serve as a standard for the prices set by the selectmen in each town. Imported merchandise was to sell at wholesale at an advance of no more than 175 per cent over cost at point of origin, and, at retail, at not more than 20 per cent. Strict penalties dealt with violators who

[37] W. C. Ford, ed., *Journals of the Continental Congress 1774-1789* . . . (Washington, 1904 ff.), I, 78, 79; *Records of Braintree*, 459 ff.

[38] M.A., CLXXXI, 351.

[39] For these complaints, see *Massachusetts Spy*, Dec. 11, 1776; M.A., CLXXXI, 351; General Court Address, Jan. 26, 1777, Thomas C. Amory, *Life of James Sullivan* . . . (Boston, 1859), I, 87-90.

could be forced to sell not only to the army but also to the necessitous at the legal rates.[40] An amending act in May acknowledged that the prices originally set appeared "not adequate to the expence which will hereafter probably be incurred in procuring such articles," raised some, and provided that the selectmen could periodically make revisions for certain others. The new law took further steps to regulate the forced sale of hoarded goods and to forestall violations.[41]

Measures to keep the stock of commodities within the state supplemented these regulations. Control of trade was by then a familiar weapon. Non-importation and the boycott proclaimed in 1775 by a Continental Congress beguiled by the ephemeral prospect of commercial coercion had lapsed as independence became a reality and did away with "unmanageable plans and chimeras of non-importation agreements." For many had asked with Major Hawley, how "can we subsist and support our trading people without trade?"[42] But in the winter of 1776-77 commercial regulation was revived with the dual purpose of conserving precious resources within the state and of keeping them out of the hands of the enemy. A series of laws closed the state's borders to the export of scarce goods and placed an embargo on almost all shipping. Finally, the stringent "Land Embargo" of February 7, 1777, forbade entirely the transportation, even to other states, of rum, molasses, cocoa, linen, wool, provisions, and some other articles. Together these steps looked forward to a self-contained and regulated system of distribution.[43]

By the spring of 1777, Massachusetts had defined its position on currency and commodities. But in these matters, policy could not develop merely with reference to the needs of the state as such, as it could in the levy of men. Action on money and prices impinged immediately, directly, and vitally upon people's fortunes. Soon enough each edict of the government became more than an effervescent expedient clothed in traditional forms; it was a real matter affecting the entire society. Once the momentum of the initial insurrection had subsided, various groups could

[40] St. 1776-7, ch. 14.
[41] St. 1776-7, ch. 46. See also the clarifying res. 1776-7, ch. 928. For local action, see Freeman, *Cape Cod*, II, 121; C. F. Swift, *History of Old Yarmouth* . . . (Yarmouth Port, 1884), 157.
[42] To Gerry, Feb. 20, May 1, 1776, Austin, *Gerry*, I, 164, 176. See also, S. Adams to Warren, Nov. 4, 1775, Burnett, *Letters*, I, 248; *Records of Braintree*, 456 ff.
[43] St. 1776-7, chs. 9, 15; st. 1778-9, ch. 36; st. 1780, ch. 7; res. 1776-7, chs. 653, 877.

speak their pieces, disavowing criticism of the war the more freely to indulge in criticism of wartime policies. The government, dubious as to the security of such distinctions, responded to pressures lest it alienate important elements in the population and lose support for the objectives for which it fought. As policy evolved, it thus affected and was affected by the interests of many citizens.

Few could find a clear and consistent picture of the line of legislation that would be to their advantage. All sought what was to their own benefit. Yet the conditions of the quest put obstacles in the way of attaining the goal. Rapid economic changes constantly altered status and fortunes and each alteration brought confusing shifts in perspective. Above all, how could people foretell the probable consequences of unfamiliar measures when turbulent and uncertain conditions made laws in practice radically different from laws in the intent of legislators? Men sharpened and defined their attitudes only under the impact upon their unfolding interests of policy in operation.[44]

Thus, the first effect of the rise in prices had been a well-nigh universal demand for some sort of stabilization. Suspicious of the profiteering of those from whom they were accustomed to purchase, everyone had righteously demanded regulation to level the exploiters. As Abigail Adams noted, "The merchant complains of the farmer and the farmer of the merchant—both are extravagant," condemning, from the viewpoint of the consumer, all who had anything to do with supply.[45]

A few months were enough, however, to show the weakness of the program. Despite the popularity of price control in Congress, John Adams expected "only a partial and temporary relief from it."[46] "Though called for by almost every body," and passed "almost unanimously," the Act against Monopoly and Oppression was soon "reprobated by many and obeyed by few." By April, it was "no more heeded than if it had never been made."[47] Everywhere compliance was desultory. In the capital a town meeting complained that the law failed to work. Vigilante efforts cropped up here and there; "Joyce, Junior" warned against withholding goods

---

[44] See Oscar and Mary F. Handlin, "Radicals and Conservatives in Massachusetts after Independence," *New England Quarterly*, XVII (1944), 350 *ff*.

[45] A. to J. Adams, June 3, 1776, J. and A. Adams, *Familiar Letters*, 183.

[46] J. to A. Adams, Feb. 7, 1777, *ibid.*, 239; Burnett, *Letters*, II, 250 *ff*.

[47] Paine to Gerry, Apr. 12, 1777, Otis to Gerry, Mar. 17, 1777, Austin, *Gerry*, I, 219 *ff*., 264; A. to J. Adams, Apr. 20, 1777, J. and A. Adams, *Familiar Letters*, 261 *ff*.

and refusing to take paper currency, and "Tories" who offered to sell more cheaply in exchange for silver were carted from Boston. Elsewhere many towns failed to elect enforcement committees, and even those which did, found it possible to exercise wide discretion in enforcing the provisions of the statute, so that the maxima set in Boston were seldom adhered to.[48]

In the long run, the law effected little that was hoped of it.[49] If anything, the breakdown of distribution became more pronounced. Frightened farmers refused to bring provisions to the cities where it became increasingly difficult to procure food and fuel. Petitioners begged the General Court for salt, flour, and bread for civilian use, and in at least one case, the State released corn from the Board of War to the poor of a town. The War Office itself had trouble and on one occasion ordered the Suffolk County sheriff to seize molasses withheld from army use at the legal rate.[50] Where enforcement threatened to be efficient, indignant citizens clamored for increases in ceilings, on the ground that the mounting costs of labor and raw materials deprived them of a "reasonable & moderite Profit upon their Work, Labour & Business."[51] No one was pleased; the merchant scolded, the farmer growled, "and every one seems wroth that he cannot grind his neighbor."[52]

By September, 1777, the General Court, in accordance with a recommendation of a conference of New England states in Springfield, repealed both the embargo and the Act against Monopoly and Oppression because they were "far from answering the salutary purposes for which they were intended."[53] The only carry overs were measures directing the towns to supply soldiers' families with the necessities of life at fixed prices, prohibit-

---

[48] M.A. CLXXXII, 246; *Old Records of Fitchburgh*, I, 157; Damon, *Holden*, 50; Washburn, "Town of Leicester," *Worc. Mag. and Hist. Jour.*, II, 98; Pratt, *Eastham, Wellfleet and Orleans*, 130; Aaron Hobart, *Historical Sketch of Abington* . . . (Boston, 1839), 136; Walter S. Hayward, "Paul Revere and the American Revolution, 1765-1783," (MS, Harvard University Archives), I, 414.

[49] Hayward, "Paul Revere," I, 418; A. to J. Adams, Apr. 20, 1777, J. and A. Adams, *Familiar Letters*, 261 *ff*.; Corey, *Malden*, 769, 770, 773.

[50] See, for example, M.A. CLXXXIII, 4, 106, 125, 131, CXLII, 46; Eliot to Belknap, June 17, 1777, *Massachusetts Historical Society Collections*, Sixth Series, IV, 124; C. R. King, *Life and Correspondence of Rufus King* . . . (New York, 1894 *ff*.), I, 25.

[51] See petitions by owners of a forge in Middlesex County and by the tanners of Boston, M.A., CLXXXII, 147, 161 *ff*.

[52] A. to J. Adams, Feb. 8, 1777, J. and A. Adams, *Familiar Letters*, 243.

[53] Res. 1777-8, chs. 117, 274; st. 1777-8, ch. 6; *Province Acts*, 811, 1012.

ing the distillation of spirits to conserve grain, and forbidding all sales at auction save those growing out of sheriffs' executions.[54] Even when the army was "frequently near to starving" that winter, and when the central government found itself "on the Brink of a Precipice" because of fabulous costs, the state opposed new movements to return to price fixing.[55]

The convention of northern states called by the Continental Congress in New Haven in January, 1778, urged the states to fix the charges for labor, transportation, and key commodities, all of which were still rising inexorably.[56] But the Massachusetts legislature was unable to agree, and finally addressed Congress, laying down the reasons—"not built on mere Speculation but upon unfortunate experiment." Opinion was so divided, the General Court wrote, that enforcement was impracticable. In addition, it pointed out, all the states could simplify the problem by reducing their circulating medium as Massachusetts had done and as Congress had recommended. With the currency stabilized, prices would fall naturally. In the face of similar intransigence from other quarters, Congress recognized the futility of piecemeal legislation and recommended that summer that existent price control laws be repealed everywhere.[57]

These months of trial, by defining attitudes in the light of consequences, were enough to transform the initial universal approval of price fixing as a war measure into a tohu-bohu of discordant voices muttering about their own advantage. The farmers close to market benefitted not only from ever-increasing demands for food and fuel that raised prices in specie to three times the pre-war level, but also from the flourishing conditions of household industries. Many a husbandman accumulated enough surpluses from his loom and last as well as from his fields to invest in public securities, make loans, and become a large-scale creditor.[58]

[54] The Act against Monopoly and Oppression had previously imposed some limits upon auctions. See st. 1776-7, ch. 14, sec. 8; also st. 1777-8, chs. 2, 3, 9, 22; st. 1778-9, chs. 29, 45; st. 1779-80, ch. 26; M.A., CLXXXIII, 93; *Province Acts*, 809, 811 *ff.*, 1012; Committee of Congress to the States, Nov. 11, 1778, Burnett, *Letters*, III, 492; Freeman, *Cape Cod*, II, 122.

[55] Lee to S. Adams, Nov. 23, 1777, Witherspoon to Houston, Jan. 27, 1778, Dyer to Trumbull, Mar. 12, 1778, Burnett, *Letters*, II, 568, III, 57, 125.

[56] By 1778, teaming cost almost £1.10 per mile in western Massachusetts (Temple, *North Brookfield*, 240). See also T. to J. Pickering, Apr. 24, 1777, Pickering Papers, V, 44; *Province Acts*, 1012 *ff.*

[57] *Province Acts*, 1017 *ff.*, 1255 *ff.*

[58] For the connection of industry and agriculture and the effect of the war, see J. Adams to Calkoen, Oct. 27, 1780, C. F. Adams, ed., John Adams, *Works . . .*

The agrarian middlemen, provision dealers who were often army contractors, shared the good fortune of the farmers whose livestock they drove to metropolitan markets. All these people early saw that no margin of profit set by law was high enough so long as prices would shortly be even higher. They had almost immediately demanded an end to "the inverted and perverted opperation of the monopoly act," and had campaigned for repeal so that it would not "continue any longer the mere sport of mercantile avarice, and a burlesque upon authority." That attained, they consistently opposed all efforts at restoration and flouted any measure that might stand in the way of the search for the best buyer.[59]

By contrast, the urban mechanics and laborers whose wages did not keep up with expenses favored commodity regulation. The fishing communities, denied access to their livelihood from the sea by the threat of British cruisers, also pressed for state action that would assure a flow of the ordinary necessities of life. Ultimately, the resentment of these people found its mark in the selfish farmers, the hoarders who failed to feed them at reasonable prices because higher profits could be gotten elsewhere.[60]

Other city people shared the same attitude with greater or lesser degrees of intensity.[61] Professional men, those on fixed incomes, smarting from the effects of rising agricultural prices, saw in regulation a safeguard against ruinous costs.[62] And even the well-to-do merchants who had, with John Adams, feared the effect of the Act against Monopoly and Oppression soon found the legal markup on foreign goods high

---

(Boston, 1850-56), VII, 310 ff.; also J. F. Jameson, *American Revolution Considered as a Social Movement* (Princeton, 1940), 70; W. B. Weeden, *Economic and Social History of New England 1620-1789* (Boston, 1891), II, 779; R. A. East, *Business Enterprise in the American Revolutionary Era* (New York, 1938), 21, 54.

[59] Worcester town meeting, *Massachusetts Spy*, May 29, 1777. See also East, *Business Enterprise*, 54.

[60] See Truro, Marblehead, Edgartown, and Salem petitions, M.A., CXXIV, 141 ff., CLXXX, 33, 53, 275, 373, CLXXXI, 32, CLXXXV, 118, CLXXXVI, 370; also East, *Business Enterprise*, 216; Pratt, *Eastham, Wellfleet and Orleans*, 79; *Records of the Town of Plymouth, 1636-1783* (Plymouth, 1889-1903), III, 383; Austin, *Gerry*, I, 221.

[61] See in this respect, John Adams' definition of the "merchantile interest." Burnett, *Letters*, I, 240; also Adams to Palmer, Feb. 20, 1777, *ibid.*, II, 268; S. Adams, *Writings*, IV, 19 ff.

[62] Fixed incomes were also hit by the relatively high tax on money at interest ("O.P.Q.," *Massachusetts Spy*, May 18, 1776). See also Ezra Ripley, *Half Century Discourse* . . . (Concord, 1829), 8; J. Adams to Van der Capellen, Jan. 21, 1781, Adams, *Works*, VII, 357 ff.; C. F. Swift, *History of Old Yarmouth* . . . (Yarmouth Port, 1884), 163.

enough to protect their profits.[63] For the shortage of imports ended early and the prices of some, like West India merchandise, began to drop.[64]

But wartime developments rendered this question unimportant for those prepared to grasp opportunities when they saw them. No price law could diminish the spoils of enterprisers who made capital of unusual opportunities for trade, legal and illegal, who had the proper patriotic connections to gain entrée to profitable government contracts, and who speculated in privateering and in the confiscated estates of loyalists. Having found adequate consolation for the inconveniences of higher living costs they were primarily interested in the monetary problem. With a growing proportion of their property tied up in government paper and in securities fluctuating in value, and with extensive interests as creditors, they were far more agitated over the worth of the currency than over the rise in prices.

As the first phase of commodity control petered out, they were able to win over to a hard money policy the artisans and fisher folk by the argument, sedulously propagated, that only the "Radical cure" of putting finances on a sound basis would halt the debilitating rise of prices. And in furthering a creditor policy, which incidentally deflected public interest from price control, they found themselves in the enviable position of being able to cooperate as well with the yeomen farmers. Despite differences of status and interest, these groups discovered in the question of money a common basis of action for the indirect attainment of disparate objectives.[65]

Isolated in the face of this emerging alignment were farmers in areas only recently settled, where subsistence agriculture still prevailed. The prosperity of the yeomen did not comfort these people; small holdings or lack of access to markets deprived them of the saleable surplus. In the

---

[63] Burnett, *Letters*, II, 252; see also the profit rates in East, *Business Enterprise*, 50. The fact that maxima on imported goods were set in terms of percentages rather than in terms of fixed sums as for domestic goods further protected merchants' profits.

[64] East, *Business Enterprise*, 51. Shortly thereafter Boston was overstocked with such goods as velvets (see Jarvis and Russell to Lopez, Mar. 3, 1779, "Letters of Boston Merchants, 1763-1790" [MSS, Harvard Business School], II, 92). See also Otis to Gerry, Mar. 17, 1777, Austin, *Gerry*, I, 264.

[65] J. Adams to Palmer, Feb. 20, 1777, Burnett, *Letters*, II, 268; S. Adams, *Writings*, IV, 19 ff. See also R. H. Lee to S. Adams, Nov. 23, 1777, Oct. 5, 1778, Burnett, *Letters*, II, 568, III, 438; *ibid.*, II, 250 ff.; J. to A. Adams, Feb. 7, 1777, J. and A. Adams, *Familiar Letters*, 240.

outskirts of Middlesex, Worcester, Hampshire, Berkshire, and Bristol counties where cash was rare, the weight of taxes was ruinous. Many towns failed to meet their levies or had to borrow to do so, accumulating in either case obligations, the repayment of which became increasingly difficult under the weight of deflationary state action.[66] Debt, direct or indirect, was an ever-impending threat, menacing the husbandman's land, the source of his livelihood, the guarantee of his independence, and the mark of his status in the community. The prospect of foreclosure, and of working for others was unenviable. And unlike the impecunious in fishing or trading communities, these, once landless, could expect little relief from the end of the war.[67]

Resumption of taxation and widespread delinquency in payment had increased the number of these debtors. But the consequences, though disturbing, were not oppressive until the end of 1777. To sink more deeply into the bog was hardly inconvenient so long as the government was impotent to collect taxes, so long as courts were closed, and so long as ever-cheaper paper could be tendered in satisfaction. Such loopholes vanished when yeomen farmers, merchants, and other urban elements, influenced by varying motives, united on a program to further a hard money policy.

In the absence of a rigorous system of collection, higher taxes had not halted depreciation, nor could state loans without taxes do so. In fact, putting new obligations into circulation had further injured the outstanding currency. The legal tender qualities of the old Bills of Credit had already become purely fictional. Their only claim to public confidence lay in the state's promise to redeem. But the new paper offered better guarantees of redemption, and interest to boot. Their emission brought home to many the realization that "nothing but reducing the glut of paper . . . will save the credit of it."[68] That Massachusetts had already stopped printing was not enough unless the amount in circulation was reduced, unless other states adopted the same policy, and unless the tide of continentals flowing from Philadelphia receded.

Following the recommendations of conferences of the New England

[66] See, for example, M.A., CLXXX, 275, CLXXXI, 42 ff.; G. W. Chase, History of Haverhill . . . (Haverhill, 1861), 407, 414. For the place of the town in the state tax system, see Douglas, Financial History, 17 ff.

[67] See the petitions, M.A., CLXXX, 13, 14, 15, 21, 287, 315, 315b, CLXXXI, 14, 16, 100 ff., CLXXXV, 56, 63, 65, 111, CLXXXVI, 26, 43.

[68] Paine to Gerry, Apr. 12, 1777, Austin, Gerry, I, 219 ff.

states in Providence and Springfield, an act of October 13, 1777, required the conversion, no later than January, 1778, of all bills into treasury notes of £10 or more at 6 per cent, to be redeemed out of taxes by 1782. Bills of credit were deprived of their character as legal tender and were not even to be received for taxes after December 1, 1777.[69] Complaints secured some mitigation of this drastic action but did not change the basic policy. By June, 1779, £337,249 had been turned in, and the compulsory exchange continued. Meanwhile, persistence of heavy taxes and short loans at 6 per cent drained away paper. Three loans between June, 1778, and January, 1780, alone raised £470,000.[70]

The positive step of drawing back currency, unlike the ineffective measures which preceded it, ended the apathy of debtor farmers who began to feel the sting of state financial policy. Now government threatened to take the gains from depreciation away from those who owed. Rare concessions were meaningless to the poor.[71] They could look forward only to mounting taxes—one-third of the total on polls—to collectors at their heels, and to loss of their land.[72]

Impassioned protests bore little weight against the influence of those who pressed for a continuation of the hard money policy. The General Court defended itself in an address to the inhabitants of Massachusetts, acknowledging that public creditors would profit, but pointing out that only this step could prevent the continued rise in prices the government paid for the prosecution of the war, and effect a saving which would shortly amount to "more than the whole principle."[73]

Withdrawal of Massachusetts paper hurt debtors but failed to give

[69] M.A., CXLII, 89; *Province Acts*, 815; st. 1777-8, ch. 7. See also res. 1776-7, ch. 531; res. 1777-8, ch. 346; M.A., CXLIV, 13, CXCV, 379, 380; *Province Acts*, 813. Harlow, "Aspects of Revolutionary Finance," *Am. Hist. Rev.*, XXXV, 60, believes this "was a measure of evasion rather than contraction" because he fails to recognize the difference between bills and notes, for which see *supra*, note 21.

[70] St. 1777-8, chs. 14, 27; st. 1778-9, chs. 4, 11, 46; st. 1779-80, ch. 31; res. 1777-8, chs. 615, 617; res. 1778-9, chs. 358, 477; res. 1779-80, chs. 3, 450, 757; M.A., CXXXVII, 192, CLXXXIII, 239, 240.

[71] J. Adams to Gerry, Dec. 6, 1777, Adams, *Works*, IX, 470 *ff.*; st. 1777-8, ch. 16; M.A., CXXXVII, 192; *Old Records of Fitchburgh*, I, 165, 166; Freeman, *Cape Cod*, II, 122.

[72] See Paine to Gerry, Apr. 12, 1777, Austin, *Gerry*, I, 221; Billerica petition, M.A., CLXXXIII, 292 *ff.* Petitions to alter the proportion on polls had no effect (see, for example, Lanesborough petition, M.A., CLXXXIV, 129).

[73] *Province Acts*, 817 *ff.* For the hostile reception accorded this address, see, for example, *Weston Records*, 243 *ff.* See also Belcherstown, Billerica remonstrances, M.A., CLXXXIII, 292 *ff.*, 307.

creditors the security they sought. The step raised by almost 15 per cent the value of the continental currency which remained in the state.[74] But before long, the hard-worked printers in Philadelphia more than com- pensated for the recall of the local bills. By the end of 1779 Congress had issued $241,500,000, a large share of which had found its way to Massachusetts. The state struggled to strengthen the continentals and to reduce the volume of their circulation, but in vain. The decline in value, fairly gradual until then, was precipitous after the opening of 1779; in 1778 paper stood to specie in the ratio of 4:1, by January, 1779, it was 8:1, during that year it fell to 40:1, and in 1780, it was almost out of sight.[75] By now it was clear to many that no Massachusetts action alone would uphold the value of the bills and that only "the Stopping the press," would "restore money & effects to an equilibrium."[76] The most earnest measures seemed to have meagre results. Jarvis and Russell, for instance, had expected much from "the taking so much money out of circulation" in 1779, but had been disappointed by the failure of notes to rise.[77]

Ineffective financial policies raised again the problem of commodity control. The suffering urban population threatened to disrupt the political balance by putting pressure on the merchants for the rigorous commodity control resented by the yeomen farmers. The Boston Committee of Cor- respondence proscribed the auction of prize goods, and the Town peti- tioned for an act against forestallers to alleviate distress caused by high prices. Fishing communities accused the agrarian towns, on which they were dependent, of withholding supplies "without what they call hard money." In Beverly, riotous women forced merchants to sell sugar for paper. And the hard-hit commercial community of Salem, complaining

[74] Witherspoon to Houston, Jan. 27, 1778, Burnett, *Letters*, III, 57.
[75] See res. 1778-9, ch. 628; st. 1779-80, ch. 40; res. 1779-80, chs. 134, 156, 230, 234, 994; *Province Acts*, 1034, 1338-40; William Abbatt, ed., William Heath, *Memoirs* . . . (New York, 1901), 216; Adams to Palmer, June 20, 1775, Burnett, *Letters*, I, 140; *Independent Chronicle*, Apr. 27, May 11, 1780; Nevins, *American States*, 471; Bullock, *Historical Sketch of the Finances of Massachusetts*, 7. For Congressional action, see Burnett, *Letters*, V, ix, 85; Felt, *Massachusetts Currency*, 187 ff.; Harlow, "Aspects of Revolutionary Finance," *Am. Hist. Rev.*, XXXV, 61; Hart, *Commonwealth History*, III, 344. For a justification of policy, see J. Adams to de Vergennes, June 22, 1780, Adams, *Works*, VII, 195 ff. Incidentally, the in- flationary tendencies were heightened by the hard cash which the French fleet brought into the state.
[76] T. to J. Pickering, Dec. 13, 1779, Pickering Papers, V, 132; S. Adams to Winthrop, Feb. 6, 1779, S. Adams, *Writings*, IV, 121 ff.
[77] Jarvis and Russell to Lopez, "Letters of Boston Merchants," II, 92.

against the farmers, "cruel as death," pointed out, "We see the produce of land increased not less than six-fold by means of the war, and the land itself more than doubled in value, while the proprietors suffer no losses, and daily exhaust our interest, for the necessaries of life, which are purchased by us at a most exhorbitant price." [78]

Complainants could also draw ammunition from the arsenal of patriotism; by 1778 the situation had deteriorated to a point that seriously endangered military operations. The general government warned the states that it would be "almost impossible to supply the army and French fleet with bread, unless it can be taken out of the hands of Engrossers and Monopolizers." [79]

The agrarian interest had been able to stand in the way of a new price-fixing law, but with reference to the evils of hoarding few dared dissent, particularly in view of the insistent Congressional appeals for action. The proponents of regulation accepted the compromise to make more goods available by proscribing hoarding. The Massachusetts act against monopoly and forestalling (February, 1779), following a plan devised in Philadelphia, prohibited any person from keeping on hand or buying more grain or meat than necessary to support his family for a specified period, and imposed heavy penalties for forestalling and for speculative sales that involved no service. A complementary law in June allowed selectmen to seize hoarded goods with payment in "the common currency of this state." But unlike the Congressional plan, the statute included no price-fixing provisions. [80]

Neither these acts nor tinkering with the currency affected prices. Instead, the situation became more acute. Boston felt "the miseries of famine" and a general scarcity of food in the seaports precipitated riots. [81]

[78] M.A., CLXXXIII, 93, CLXXXIV, 39, 125, 143; Edwin M. Stone, *History of Beverly, Civil and Ecclesiastical* . . . (Boston, 1843), 83 ff.; *Journals of the Continental Congress*, IX, 1071.
[79] See Lovell to Gates, June 9, 1778, Burnett, *Letters*, III, 285; also *ibid.*, III, 437, 438, 480, IV, 179 ff.; V. L. Johnson, *Administration of the American Commissariat during the Revolutionary War* (Philadelphia, 1941), 104 ff.; *Province Acts*, 1019-20.
[80] St. 1778-9, ch. 31. For the Congressional plan, see Burnett, *Letters*, III, 490 ff.; also st. 1779-80, ch. 7. These acts were temporary, but were extended until 1781 by st. 1779-80, ch. 16 and st. 1780, ch. 7.
[81] Eliot to Belknap, Mar. 17, Oct. 20, 1779, *Massachusetts Historical Society Collections*, Sixth Series, IV, 138, 152; Burnett, *Letters*, IV, 232 ff.; T. to J. Pickering, Sept. 24, 1779, Pickering Papers, V, 125; King, *King*, I, 30; Bradford Kingman, *History of North Bridgewater* . . . (Boston, 1866), 359.

To make matters worse, paper by now was so completely divorced from the ordinary processes of trade and the position of sellers was so secure that they could refuse to take anything but specie. The feebleness of the sickly currency gave another string to the arguments of those who wanted price fixing; a handbill called for a meeting against those who "are reducing the currency to waste paper, by refusing to take it for many articles."[82] By the middle of 1779, the urban communfties were ready to take voluntary action to halt the spiral. The merchants and traders of the capital determined to raise no prices, and announced self-imposed ceilings conditioned on the acquiescence of other towns. To implement their resolution, the Boston Committee of Correspondence called a meeting of towns to consider remedies for the "excessive high prices of every article of consumptio:."[83]

The proponents of price fixing dominated the convention in Concord, because many farming districts failed to send delegates.[84] But to push recommendations through the General Court, in which agrarian interests were strong, was impossible. Some towns, particularly the fishing and trading towns like Eastham, Plymouth, Braintree, and Sandwich, took the matter into their own hands, setting up local committees to fix prices. Boston went even further; officials placed at the ferries and at the Neck saw to the equitable distribution of incoming goods.[85] But on a state-wide basis, those who sought compulsory regulation had to be content with embargoes.[86]

The interdiction of export, easily circumvented in practice, failed to satisfy the advocates of price fixing. On recommendation of the Concord Convention, an assembly of all the New England states met in Hartford, proposed a national meeting, asked for legislation by the states, for

[82] See Albert S. Bolles, *Financial History of the United States, from 1774 to 1789* (New York, 1896), 163.

[83] *Province Acts*, 1254-56.

[84] John H. Lockwood, *Westfield and Its Historic Influences, 1669-1919* . . . (Springfield, 1922), II, 47 ff.; John H. Lockwood, *Western Massachusetts a History, 1636-1926* (New York, 1926), I, 114, 115; *Province Acts*, 1254; Henry Cabot Lodge, *Life and Letters of George Cabot* (Boston, 1877), 15.

[85] *Records of the Town of Plymouth*, III, 382; *Records of the Town of Braintree*, 502-504; Freeman, *Cape Cod*, II, 126; Pratt, *Eastham, Wellfleet and Orleans*, 79; *Weston Records*, 274; Shebnah Rich, *Truro—Cape Cod* . . . (Boston, 1883), 281; D. H. Hurd, *History of Bristol County* . . . (Philadelphia, 1883), 540; Chase, *Haverhill*, 415; Hobart, *Abington*, 136.

[86] *Province Acts*, 1255 ff.; st. 1779-80, chs. 13, 15. These measures were not repealed until June, 1780 (st. 1780, ch. 4).

the levy of supplies by taxation rather than by purchase, and for the repeal of the embargo.[87] The sympathetic Continental Congress approved, and called the convention to gather in Philadelphia in January, 1780, suggesting that this body set the rates for articles of domestic produce, farming, and common labor, the wages of tradesmen and mechanics, and the charges of water and land carriage, none to be over twenty times the prices current in 1774, with imports in due proportion.[88]

Massachusetts appointed commissioners to the Philadelphia convention, but their instructions stressed the difficulty of enforcement, the possible effect on the currency, the relative advantages to the mercantile and disadvantages to the agrarian interests, and indicated clearly that no salutary results were expected.[89] Ultimately the legislature refused to act on any of the recommendations on the subject. After five years of debate, the question remained as chaotic as ever.[90]

The Philadelphia convention met as the problem of currency also approached a decisive crisis. Despite occasional prosecutions by zealous local authorities, the continentals rapidly lost the power to circulate.[91] Even creditors abandoned the straight path of sound money. They wanted bills to pass current to keep up values; but in everyday dealings they were reluctant to accept the depreciated issue. Those who found paper useless in the West Indies and foreign trade had an additional motive for disregarding laws which, in the abstract, they approved.[92]

In 1780, creditors began to perceive that only a complete reversal in legislation would rescue them. As affairs had developed, no measure could maintain the value of the currency. Salvation was possible only by recognizing depreciation and by readjusting all obligations to it. Revaluation was the last refuge from the merciless borrowers who pursued lenders with payment in worthless bills. Those who were being sacrificed "to the Desires of these fraudulent Debtors, who are supported in their Iniquity (as they say) by the laws of this State" earnestly fought for a law to

[87] *Province Acts,* 1254-60.

[88] *Ibid.,* 1019, 1262; Burnett, *Letters,* IV, 514, 523, 526, 528, 537, V, vi, 98; Bolles, *Financial History,* 168.

[89] Res. 1779-80, ch. 659.

[90] *Province Acts,* 1262; also Sewall to Jackson, Jan. 27, 1780, *Essex Institute Historical Collections,* VII (1865), 195 *ff.*

[91] M.A., CLXXX, 378-81, 384; *Province Acts,* 1254, 1256 *ff.; Records of the Town of Plymouth,* III, 381.

[92] See complaint of Amos Knowles, M.A., CLXXX, 384; *ibid.,* CLXXXIII, 367, 368.

"enable them to recover their righteous and just Demands from their remorseless Debtors."[93]

A tentative step in the direction of aligning bills with real values by recognizing legally the fact of depreciation came in the act of January 13, 1780, for paying the arrears of the Continental army. The result of pressure from soldiers whose three-year enlistments were about to expire, the measure provided for the settlement of accounts in notes carrying 6 per cent interest and payable in four installments between 1781 and 1788 in the money current at the time of payment "in a greater or less sum, according as five bushels of corn, sixty-eight pounds and four-sevenths parts of a pound of beef, ten pounds of sheepswool and sixteen pounds of sole-leather shall then cost, more or less, than one hundred and thirty pounds current money, at the then current prices of said articles; this sum being thirty-two times and a-half what the same quantities of the same articles would cost" in 1777. The justices of the Supreme Judicial Court were to compute the rate annually on the basis of monthly reports from the selectmen of each town.[94]

Through the winter various committees worked on a broader plan to cover all obligations, public and private, but the House resisted the Council's efforts to enact any such scheme, and, in December, flatly refused to consider a bill by a vote of thirty-one to twenty-eight. But its advocates were persistent; the bill finally passed in September at the end of the session by a vote of fifty-two to thirty-six.[95] It repealed all penalties for abatement on bills of credit and set up a monthly scale of depreciation beginning in January, 1777, and ending in April, 1780, when the value of bills was brought down to forty to one, in terms of which all contracts and debts were to be executed.[96]

Financial policy in this period was inconsistent as to methods but not as to objectives. Invariably it favored the interests of creditors against

[93] See petition of Desire Bangs, widow of Harwich, M.A., CLXXXVI, 148.

[94] St. 1779-80, ch. 29; *Province Acts*, 1133 *ff.*, 1397. See also st. 1780, ch. 6; res. 1779-80, ch. 765; *Independent Chronicle*, May 11, 1780. The story of the negotiations between the officers and the legislature that led to the enactment of this law may be traced in the papers of Judge Benjamin Heywood, printed in the *Worc. Mag. and Hist. Jour.*, I (1825-26), 134 *ff.*, 165 *ff.*, 198 *ff.*, 232 *ff.*, 267 *ff.*, 310 *ff.*, 356 *ff.* See also Heath, *Memoirs*, 208; W. C. Fisher, "Tabular Standard in Massachusetts History," *Quarterly Journal of Economics*, XXVII (1913), 427 *ff.*

[95] A long note summarizes the legislative history of the act, *Province Acts*, 1340, 1452-55. See also Burnett, *Letters*, IV, 524, V, 85.

[96] St. 1780, ch. 12; *Independent Chronicle*, Oct. 2, 1780.

those of debtors for the former could draw to their support a combination of groups united in a common program by the impact of revolutionary economy.[97] That decisiveness was absent in the evolution of state action on commodities. In that field, the artisans and fishermen, the only ones who had strong feelings on the subject, could not attract enough support from other people to hold the legislature to a steady line.

The establishment of constitutional government and the shift of the seat of the war to the South after 1780 fundamentally transformed the nature of the problems of both money and prices. But wartime economic policy between 1774 and 1780 was immensely significant for the future of Massachusetts.

In a period of flux in which control was still fluid and still contingent, men confronted the task of answering vital questions, often still unformulated. When they turned for aid to the state, embodiment of so many other hopes, they uncovered a maze of frustrating relationships that consistently led to unexpected ends. Hardly a measure achieved the results its proponents expected of it, for the recourse to political power invariably had unforeseen corollary consequences, larger in importance than the intentions of lawmakers. Under these circumstances those favored by the forces of a turbulent economy found most room for manoeuvre. Yeomen farmers and merchants, riding the crest of the economic wave, had the resilience to avoid the ill effects of unfavorable laws, and the resources to take advantage of the favorable ones. The new conditions of life and labor thus acquired inordinate importance from the immediacy of issues in a time of crisis and left a permanent imprint upon the subsequent character of politics in Massachusetts and upon the relations of government to the economy of the state.

[97] See J. Adams to Warren, Feb. 12, 1777, Burnett, *Letters*, II, 246 *ff.*; Adams, *Works*, IX, 452 *ff.*

To the Quiet of the People:
Revolutionary Settlements and
Civil Unrest in Western Massachusetts,
1774-1789

John L. Brooke

ON January 5, 1782, Samuel Ely, formerly a minister of the gospel, urged a gathering at Sunderland, by the Connecticut River in troubled Hampshire County, Massachusetts, to "throw up our Constitution." Not two years since its ratification, the Massachusetts constitution of 1780 was "broke[n] already," and Ely claimed to have "a Constitution in his pocket that the angel Gabriel could not find fault with." He enumerated a series of violations of the 1780 constitution: the salaries paid the governor and the Supreme Court justices were excessive, some men were holding two offices, and the Supreme Court justices had "gone beyond their power" in recently assuming the authority to assign new value to the old bills of credit. The justices therefore "should not sit," nor should the General Court: the people "should pay no more regard to them than to puppies." Ely asked the selectmen of Sunderland to draw up a warrant for a meeting of the town to vote to close the Court of Common Pleas, and to give him such a warrant to carry to the nearby hilltown of Conway, where he had been living for the last five years. In a final flourish he declared that "the Courts ought not to sit, and that the Attornies [sic], Sheriffs, & all Officers should be sacrificed." In particular, John Chester Williams of Hadley, justice of the peace and register of probate for Hampshire County, "should be made a sacrifice of, his Body should be given to the Fowls of the Air and to the Beasts of the Field."[1]

With the ratification of the state constitution in 1780, revolutionary

Mr. Brooke is a member of the Department of History at Tufts University. This essay was originally presented at "Shays's Rebellion and the Constitution: A Bicentennial Conference," sponsored by Historical Deerfield, Inc., and Amherst College, Nov. 13-14, 1986. The author would like to thank Van Beck Hall for sharing aggregate data from his research on Massachusetts in the 1780s, and Joyce Appleby, Joseph Ernst, Van Beck Hall, John Murrin, Gregory H. Nobles, and William Pencak for useful comments on successive drafts.

[1] Massachusetts Supreme Judicial Court Docket Book, 1781-1782 (formerly at the Suffolk County Court House, presently at the Massachusetts Archives at Columbia Point), 179-180.

drama should have given way to institutional routine in Massachusetts. But the public response to Samuel Ely's exhortation indicates that the institutional routines of the court system were not easily reestablished in Hampshire County. If Ely's sentiments were "depraved" and "Seditious"—as they were to the justices of the Supreme Judicial Court sitting in Northampton later that year—so, too, were those of many throughout Hampshire County, men who rose to march with Ely against the courts that April. Ely's focus on institutional structure among the various problems besetting the county and the commonwealth was widely shared. As even the conservative people of Belchertown had written in their return ratifying the 1780 state constitution, a restructuring and decentralizing of county institutions would "greatly Tend to the Quiet of the People."[2]

The twin problems of public debt and a North Atlantic credit crisis made civil unrest inevitable throughout the Confederation. The stringent measures adopted by the Massachusetts General Court, at the insistence of creditor-merchant interests, made it likely that such unrest would be particularly intense in Massachusetts.[3] However, while people throughout the commonwealth were concerned about the pressure of public and private debt, open rebellion against public institutions broke out only in certain places, most especially in Hampshire County. This article proposes that it was the collapse of institutional legitimacy, rather than simply high levels of economic distress, that provided the context for rebellion against the courts in that county in the 1780s. In turn, Hampshire's experience with conventions and armed insurgency in 1782 and 1783, rooted in prior revolutionary experience, established the precedent for the greater uprising against constitutional government in 1786. In short, the roots of Shays's Rebellion lay in great part in a failure of a revolutionary settlement of civil institutions unique to Hampshire County.

Most fundamentally, a revolution involves the transformation of governing regimes; the stable structure of constitutional framework and civil institutions that is the outcome of such a transformation may be termed a revolutionary settlement. To endure, such a settlement must be accepted as legitimate and noncontroversial. In the American Revolutionary experience, the appeal to popular sovereignty in the constitution-making process, building on political traditions that had developed over the colonial era, required that this legitimacy rest, not in raw power, but in a

[2] *Ibid.*, 179; Oscar and Mary Handlin, eds., *The Popular Sources of Political Authority: Documents on the Massachusetts Constitution of 1780* (Cambridge, Mass., 1966), 541.

[3] E. James Ferguson, *The Power of the Purse: A History of American Public Finance, 1776-1790* (Chapel Hill, N.C., 1961), 179-286; Van Beck Hall, *Politics without Parties: Massachusetts, 1780-1791* (Pittsburgh, Pa., 1972), 104-110, 194-203; Joseph A. Ernst, "The Political Economy of Shays's Rebellion in Long Perspective: The Merchants and the Money Question," in Robert A. Gross, ed., *In Debt to Shays: The Legacy of an Agrarian Rebellion* (Charlottesville, Va., forthcoming).

broad consensus concerning the authority of institutions. The concept of a revolutionary settlement shaped contemporary views and historical interpretations of the entire period between 1776 and 1789 and into the early republic. Most obviously, the dissatisfaction with the Articles of Confederation among a broad coalition fueled demands for an overarching national revolutionary settlement, resulting in the Constitutional Convention of 1787. Despite widespread suspicions of the convention and its product, the federal Constitution rapidly became the ground for the national revolutionary settlement that endured for seven decades before it collapsed under the contradictions posed by the existence of chattel slavery.[4]

But in 1782 there was no such national framework; revolutionary settlements resided in the various state constitutions and governments, most dramatically manifested in the states' separate responsibilities for the war debt. And as the events of the 1780s in Hampshire County clearly suggest, revolutionary settlements also depended on more local circumstances. The conclusion of the revolutionary process, and the restoration of the routine operation of institutions, also required the minimal fulfillment of popular expectations regarding the transformation of local structures of power and authority.

Such expectations were deeply rooted in the provincial experience of Massachusetts. The men who marched with Samuel Ely and Daniel Shays were acting out a conflict of institutions that had lurked just below the surface of Massachusetts politics since the establishment of the 1691 charter. As Richard L. Bushman has recently argued, the royally chartered courts were the pivotal institutions in a "sociology of corruption"; judicial determinations of debt obligations perpetually threatened to reduce households to poverty and dependence—"enslavement," in the language of the Country tradition. In both 1782 and 1786, insurgents drew upon

[4] The theme of an American Revolutionary settlement has been developed to different degrees by Staughton Lynd, *Class Conflict. Slavery. and the United States Constitution: Ten Essays* (New York, 1967), 25-63, 109-132; Gordon S. Wood, *The Creation of the American Republic. 1776-1787* (Chapel Hill, N.C., 1972), 567-615; Lance Banning, "Republican Ideology and the Triumph of the Constitution, 1789 to 1793," *William and Mary Quarterly.* 3d Ser., XXXI (1974), 167-188; John M. Murrin, "The Great Inversion, or Court versus Country: A Comparison of the Revolution Settlements in England (1688-1721) and America (1776-1816)," in J.G.A. Pocock, ed., *Three British Revolutions: 1641. 1688. 1776* (Princeton, N.J., 1980), 368-453; Edward Countryman, *A People in Revolution: The American Revolution and Political Society in New York. 1760-1790* (Baltimore, 1981), 283-296; Rhys Isaac, *The Transformation of Virginia. 1740-1790* (Chapel Hill, N.C., 1982), 273-295, and Robert H. Wiebe, *The Opening of American Society: From the Adoption of the Constitution to the Eve of Disunion* (New York, 1984). Thomas Bender, "Wholes and Parts: The Need for Synthesis in American History," *Journal of American History.* LXXIII (1986), 120-136, and the "Roundtable" essays *ibid..* LXXIV (1987), 107-130, provide useful perspectives on the problem of the "public culture" of which a "revolutionary settlement" is a central component.

the example of the formative events of the Revolutionary crisis of 1774, when the demands of county conventions that the royal courts be closed were executed by militias throughout the province. During the crises of the 1780s the configuration of economy, civil institutions, and ideology that had shaped Revolutionary beginnings was still very much in place. People in Massachusetts towns wanted justice from local, rather than distant, courts; neighbors holding state commissions could act in judicial capacities at far less cost than county magnates. Corruption and ruin had been feared in 1774; in 1782 and 1786 they seemed a reality. Anxieties about "slavery" and "lordships" that had been so powerful in 1774 reappeared in the language of the Regulators. In 1774, 1782, and 1786 there was the same fear that an unaccountable provincial bureaucracy reaching down into the county courts would be the agent of impoverishment, stratification, and a progressive erosion of household independence, the social basis of the republican experiment.[5]

In many places the events of the 1770s reshaped and relegitimized the institutional fabric of the county courts. But these years brought no viable countywide revolutionary settlement to the broad valley and hills of Hampshire, and progress toward such a settlement was only halting and selective during the 1780s. The failure of such a settlement was a primary cause of the civil unrest that culminated in Shays's Rebellion. To the west and east, Berkshire and Worcester counties achieved settlements that deflected popular unease under proportionately greater burdens of public or private debt, and mitigated the confrontation of men and institutions in Shays's Rebellion, when armed uprisings spread far beyond the bounds of Hampshire County. Furthermore, these distinct revolutionary histories and settlements of county institutions played a central role in the politics of the federal constitutional ratifying convention and the first elections for federal representatives. Paradoxically, the partial resolution of Hampshire County's institutional problems in a section of the western hill towns ensured the critical margin for ratification at the Massachusetts constitutional convention in 1788; here the uneven progress of a county revolutionary settlement played a pivotal role in the broader national settlement. In examining the local circumstances of political mobilization in these three counties from the 1760s through 1789, this article may

[5] Bushman, "Massachusetts Farmers and the Revolution," in Richard M. Jellison, ed., *Society. Freedom. and Conscience: The American Revolution in Virginia. Massachusetts. and New York* (New York, 1976), 77-124, and *King and People in Provincial Massachusetts* (Chapel Hill, N.C., 1985), 176-210, esp. 190-206; Robert Gross, *The Minutemen and Their World* (New York, 1976), 68-108; Michael Zuckerman, *Peaceable Kingdoms: New England Towns in the Eighteenth Century* (New York, 1970), 220-258. Examples of Regulator language can be found in Shays's Rebellion Collection, Folder 5, American Antiquarian Society, Worcester, Mass., and Robert Treat Paine Papers, Box 23, Massachusetts Historical Society, Boston.

encourage historians to temper their use of broad, regional categories with some attention to the specific local arenas, compounded of class, institutions, and political tradition, which shaped the civil life of the young republic.

The first obvious signs of Hampshire County's controversy with the commonwealth were two county conventions in the spring of 1782, soon after Samuel Ely's exhortation of the people of Sunderland. The convention that met in Hadley on February 11, 1782, echoed Ely's concerns, complaining of the governor's salary and the cost of the courts. Articulating Ely's visceral sense of a profound conflict between town and county institutions, the convention advocated the transferal of a host of administrative functions from the county courts to the towns. The convention's final resolve was its most controversial: it requested that "the laws in civil matters," with the exception of those relating to taxation, be suspended until the people were "redressed relative to the foregoing grievances." A more moderate convention of thirty-seven towns meeting in Hatfield on the following April 9 rejected this resolve, voting twenty-one to fifteen against the suspension of civil actions. But this convention nonetheless voted that the Court of General Sessions was a wasteful expense and should be dissolved. Beyond its charge of hearing minor criminal cases, the General Sessions acted as an unelected county government, regulating the towns, assessing taxes, licensing taverns, and determining the location of county roads and bridges; it was widely viewed as an arbitrary relic of royal government that should be eliminated. The votes against the courts by the Hadley and Hatfield conventions provided the authority for Ely's insurrection against the Court of Common Pleas at Northampton. On April 4, 1782, Ely sent a circular letter through the Hampshire towns declaring that "the court was going contrary to the mind of the convention" and summoning the people to action. Eight days later, he led a crowd against the court, with threats to knock off the justices' gray wigs and "send them out of the World in an instant."[6]

For the next two months Hampshire County endured civil war, as bodies of militia and Regulators parried, hostages were exchanged, and court and jail at Northampton were besieged. A complex political choreography of competing institutions and sovereign authorities unfolded across the county in the spring and summer of 1782. While the courts attempted to meet under the constitution, conventions of town committees criticized the courts' procedures and their very existence. On the authority of those conventions, towns raised militias to regulate the

[6] Hadley Convention Petition, Feb. 11, 1782, House Documents (Unpassed) 1133A, Massachusetts Archives, Boston. The proceedings and resolves of Hatfield Convention, Apr. 9, 1782, are detailed in George Sheldon, *A History of Deerfield. Massachusetts* . . . (Deerfield, Mass., 1896), II, 751, and in John H. Lockwood, *Westfield and Its Historic Influences. 1669-1919* . . . (Westfield, Mass., 1922), II, 48. Details on Ely are from Supreme Judicial Court Docket Book, 1781-1782, 180.

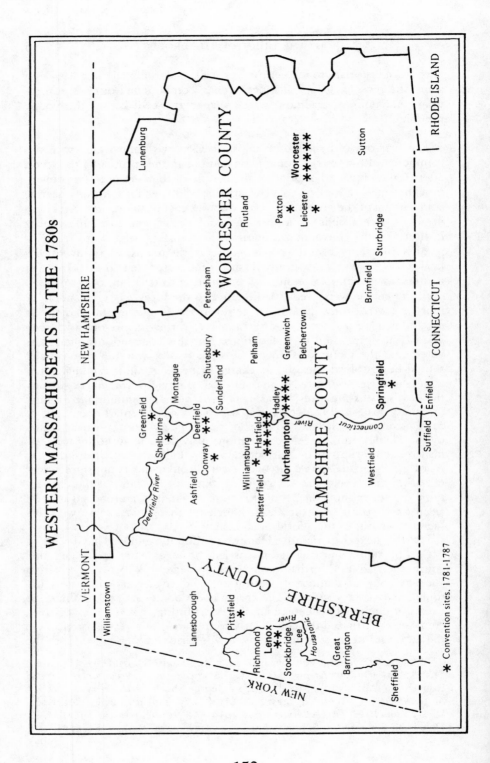

WESTERN MASSACHUSETTS IN THE 1780s

VERMONT

NEW HAMPSHIRE

RHODE ISLAND

CONNECTICUT

NEW YORK

WORCESTER COUNTY

Lunenburg

Rutland

Worcester ✴✴✴✴✴

Paxton ✴

Leicester ✴

Sutton

Petersham

Brimfield

Sturbridge

HAMPSHIRE COUNTY

Montague

Shutesbury ✴

Sunderland

Pelham

Greenwich

Belchertown

Springfield ✴

Greenfield ✴

Shelburne ✴

Deerfield ✴✴

Conway ✴

Hadley ✴✴✴✴

Hatfield ✴✴✴✴

Northampton

Williamsburg

Chesterfield

Ashfield

Westfield

Suffield

Enfield

Connecticut River

Deerfield River

BERKSHIRE COUNTY

Williamstown

Lanesborough

Pittsfield ✴

Richmond

Lenox ✴✴

Stockbridge

Lee

Great Barrington

Sheffield

Housatonic River

✴ Convention sites, 1781-1787

152

courts. The direct action of the people out-of-doors, in conventions and armed assemblies led by local notables, was substituted for an unresponsive legislative process. Representing an alternative sovereignty to the constituted government of Massachusetts, the conventions and assemblies gave evidence that the Revolution was not over in Hampshire County. Four years later, Ely's Rebellion would be replicated on a grander scale in Shays's Rebellion, when, across the three counties of western Massachusetts, as well as Middlesex and Bristol to the east, conventions would draw up petitions that set the stage for Regulators to close the courts as a means of forcing a legislative redress of grievances. In both episodes, the institutions of constituted government clashed with the institutions of a corporate politics of "the body of the people."[7]

The disturbances in Hampshire County in 1782 and the years following were not paralleled in the other two western Massachusetts counties. To the west, in Berkshire, where the Constitutionalists had defied the state government for four years, the courts were closed only once after 1780, and the few conventions that met actually supported the government.[8] To the east, in Worcester, conventions met to consider public affairs on a regular basis, and a flurry of small riots aimed at specific sheriffs' sales disrupted some towns in 1782 and 1783. But the county courts went unchallenged until September 1786, and even then the Regulators politely listened to a two-hour exhortation against their proceedings by Justice Artemas Ward of Shrewsbury before they stopped the court.[9] Events in Hampshire County stood in sharp contrast: Ely's challenge to the Northampton courts in 1782 was repeated in Springfield in 1783, and the arrests stemming from these disturbances provoked further rioting as crowds attempted to rescue men from jail. Conventions of towns met in Hampshire on at least twenty occasions between 1781 and 1786, and Shays's Rebellion began in Northampton, when 1,500 men closed the Court of Common Pleas on August 29. It was on Hampshire's model of the preceding four years that Regulators in Berkshire, Worcester, Middlesex, and Bristol challenged their county courts. The following January, Hampshire County was the scene of the most dramatic moments of the rebellion, as state troops at the Springfield arsenal fired on the Regulators

---

[7] Ely's Rebellion is described in Robert J. Taylor, *Western Massachusetts in the Revolution* (Providence, R.I., 1954), 112-121; Robert E. Moody, "Samuel Ely: Forerunner of Shays," *New England Quarterly*. V (1932), 105-117; and Hall, *Politics without Parties*. 187-189. The concept of a corporate politics has been developed by, among others, Wood, *Creation of the American Republic*. 181-196, and Countryman, *People in Revolution*. 55-58, 180-181.

[8] Taylor, *Western Massachusetts*. 111-115, 120-121, 141; George R. Minot, *The History of the Insurrections in Massachusetts*. 2d ed. (Boston, 1810), 43.

[9] Hall, *Politics without Parties*. 185-189, distinguishes between rioting against sheriffs' sales and court closings. On Ward's speech to the Regulators see William Lincoln, *History of Worcester. Massachusetts . . .* (Worcester, Mass., 1837), 135-137.

led by Daniel Shays and pursued them through the snowy Quabbin hilltowns to Petersham.[10]

However, with regard to the critical issues of public and private debt, the circumstances of unrest and rebellion in Hampshire County seem curious on close examination, at least by comparison with some of the other counties. Van Beck Hall's analysis of the recognizances filed with the Supreme Judicial Court—cases of debt appealed from the common pleas where the debtor failed to appear—suggests that the level of private debt in Hampshire County was only half that of either Worcester or Middlesex in 1782, and the pattern grew stronger over the following years. (See Table I.) To a degree, this difference may have reflected the marginally greater average wealth of the people of Worcester and Middlesex counties, which would have made it easier to advance the costs of the appeal. But David P. Szatmary's figures for the cases prosecuted in the Court of Common Pleas between 1784 and 1786 similarly suggest that the burden of debt was far heavier in Worcester than in Hampshire. Similarly, Hall's analysis of taxes owed and on execution in 1786 indicates that Worcester County towns delinquent in their tax returns owed significantly higher amounts than towns in Hampshire County. None of this economic evidence provides obvious reasons for Hampshire County's role in the civil disturbances leading up to the Regulation of 1786.[11]

Thus debt alone cannot account for the particular intensity of unrest in Hampshire County between 1782 and 1786 or for the local patterns of mobilization in the western counties.[12] The level of debt was a primary grievance, but it was not the sole factor in mobilizing men against the courts. Another deeper source of the persistent civil unrest in Hampshire was the absence of a satisfactory and legitimate revolutionary restructuring of the civil institutions that impinged directly on local economic transactions. The failure to arrive at an acceptable reconfiguration of town and county authority, in combination with the crisis of the post-Revolutionary

[10] Taylor, *Western Massachusetts,* 111-127, 137-144, 159-162; David P. Szatmary, *Shays' Rebellion: The Making of an Agrarian Insurrection* (Amherst, Mass., 1980), 68, 98-105.

[11]

	Debt Cases Prosecuted in Common Pleas Aug.'84-Aug.'86	Polls in 1790	Cases per 1,000 Polls
Worcester	4,789	14,615	327.7
Hampshire	2,977	15,119	196.9

Debt cases from Szatmary, *Shays' Rebellion.* 29; polls from 1790 census; Szatmary reaches somewhat different conclusions from these data.

[12] In a parallel essay I present evidence indicating that the mobilization of debtors in Shays's Rebellion followed very different patterns in gentry-dominated towns, small orthodox towns, and among dissenters ("A Deacon's Orthodoxy: Religion, Class, and the Moral Economy of Shays's Rebellion," in Gross, ed., *In Debt to Shays*).

TABLE I
LEVELS OF PUBLIC AND PRIVATE DEBT BY COUNTY, 1782-1787

	Berkshire	Hampshire	Worcester	Middlesex	State
Percentage of Towns with Executions Pending for Overdue Taxes. 1787					
Over £1 due per poll	16	56	57	n.c.	n.c.
Over £3.4 due per poll	4	29	52	3	22
Recognizances for Cases of Debt Filed at the Supreme Judicial Court. 1782-1786. per 1,000 Polls					
1782	1	8	17	18	10
1783	4	5	16	21	11
1784	15	8	34	17	15
1785	13	6	32	20	14
1786	15	2	30	17	12

Source: Van Beck Hall, *Politics without Parties: Massachusetts. 1780-1791* (Pittsburgh, Pa., 1972), Table 47, page 195, and data supplied from Hall's records.
Note: n.c. indicates that these were not calculated.

economy, set the stage for armed uprisings against the constitutional order. As much as the pervasive pressure of public and private debt, the failure to achieve an acceptable revolutionary settlement of county institutions in Hampshire played a critical role in shaping the tumultuous politics of the 1780s in western Massachusetts.

Before we can consider revolutionary settlements, we must look to revolutionary beginnings, and before that to provincial political traditions. If revolutionary settlements shaped the response to the economic crisis, they in turn were shaped by very different political traditions developed long before the Revolution, and by the very different ways in which these Massachusetts counties moved from royal to popular authority in and after 1774.

Two provincial political cultures cast long shadows over the Revolutionary struggle in western Massachusetts. The Popular party had a powerful presence in the Worcester countryside, but it was virtually absent to the west, where the old Court-faction elite dominated the courts, legislative politics, and the mercantile economy. The Popular tradition provided the ground for a smooth transition from royal to popular sovereignty in Worcester County and facilitated a satisfactory revolutionary settlement of county institutions. Things were very different in Hampshire and Berkshire.[13]

[13] The political traditions of 18th-century Massachusetts are ably described in Robert Zemsky, *Merchants. Farmers. and River Gods: An Essay on Eighteenth-Century American Politics* (Boston, 1971); Stephen E. Patterson, *Political Parties in Revolutionary Massachusetts* (Madison, Wis., 1973), 33-62; William Pencak, *War. Politics. and Revolution in Provincial Massachusetts* (Boston, 1981); and most recently in Bushman, *King and People*.

To be sure, the pinnacle of institutional power in provincial Worcester County was monopolized by Court party notables—the Chandlers, the Willards, Timothy Ruggles, and John Murray—who were tied by numerous obligations to the governor's interest.[14] But Popular or Country party principles were deeply rooted in a broad stratum of leading men across the county. When the crisis struck, these men led the county into the Revolution and very rapidly reestablished county institutions as accepted and legitimate.

The roots of Worcester Popular tradition lay in the currency disputes of the 1730s, manifested most concretely in the Land Bank of 1740-1741. A scheme advanced by the Popular leadership in Boston to base an issue of private bank notes on mortgaged lands, the Land Bank was enthusiastically supported in agricultural towns of Popular inclinations, most especially in Worcester County. The county had led the province in Land Bank mortgages in 1740 and had voted almost unanimously for the Land Bank in the General Court. Having staunchly opposed Gov. Jonathan Belcher on the Land Bank, the majority of the county's representatives in the General Court moved to support Gov. William Shirley in the late 1740s and early 1750s, only to rejoin the Popular opposition in the late 1750s. Popular party men outnumbered Court adherents by twenty-two to nine among the thirty-one Worcester deputies who either voted on partisan issues in the General Court in the 1760s or were among the Rescinders or delegates to the 1768 convention of towns.[15] In 1763, the government revived the bitter politics of currency by publishing a list of delinquent Land Bank mortgagees; Worcester had three times as many per population as the rest of the province. At least three of the Popular party men of the 1760s had been Land Bank investors—two of them ranked first and third on the county list of delinquents—and the sons and nephews of Land Bankers served in the county conventions and provincial congresses in 1774 and 1775 and in the minute companies in April 1775.[16]

Thus the Popular politics of currency shaped the patterns of Revolu-

[14] This elite Court party group is central to Kevin Joseph MacWade's, "Worcester County, 1750-1774: A Study of a Provincial Patronage Elite" (Ph.D. diss., Boston University, 1974).

[15] Based on an analysis of votes on roll calls in the General Court between 1726 and 1765, recorded in *Journals of the House of Representatives of Massachusetts* (Boston, 1919-   ). The votes of the 1760s are *ibid.*. XXXVIII, 224-225, 319-320, XL, 256-257. The rescinders of the Circular Letter and the delegates to the 1768 convention are listed in Richard D. Brown, "The Massachusetts Convention of Towns, 1768," *WMQ*. 3d Ser., XXVI (1969), 101-104.

[16] For the original Land Bankers see Andrew McFarland Davis, *Currency and Banking in the Province of the Massachusetts Bay* (New York [1901]), II, 295-313. In the June 1740 roll call the Worcester Co. representatives supported the Land Bank 11-1 (92%), as against the rest of the province, which favored the Land Bank 48-36 (57%). See *Journals of the House*. XVIII, 47-48. Kathy Mitten, "The New England Paper Money Tradition and the Massachusetts Land Bank of 1740" (M.A. thesis, Columbia University, 1979), 88-93, lists the 1763 delinquents.

tionary mobilization in Worcester County. But when the crisis came to an end, the county courts were reestablished with little trouble by a block of experienced men. Of the twenty-two Popular partisans of the 1760s, seven were appointed to the reconstituted county court system in the winter of 1775. Four of these new justices drawn from the old Popular men, including Artemas Ward, had served as royal justices; few in number, they were symptomatic of broader patterns, and they provided a key element of institutional and political continuity across the Revolutionary transition.[17]

Such a group was utterly missing west of the present Quabbin Reservoir, in old Hampshire and Berkshire counties. The Connecticut Valley had long been under the political and economic domination of an intermarried cluster of great families known as the River Gods, closely tied to the Court interest, who began to extend their power into the upcountry hinterland of the Housatonic Valley in the 1730s in what in 1761 became Berkshire County. In the partisan sparring of the 1760s, four Popular men were outnumbered by nineteen Court adherents among the representatives serving from Hampshire and Berkshire. In the 1740s the only Land Bank sentiment in Hampshire County lay in the outlying towns of Brimfield, Enfield, and Suffield. These were the only towns to elect dissenters to the General Court; they were also the towns with the lowest level of representation by county officers and their close relations. Brimfield was one of only three Hampshire or Berkshire towns to send a delegate to the 1768 convention of towns, while seventeen Worcester County towns were represented. Two Country partisans from Brimfield and Montague, in Hampshire County, played a role in the establishment of Revolutionary government, serving in the 1774 house and the provincial congresses, and receiving appointments to the judiciary in the winter of 1775-1776. But neither of these men had served among the royal justices, and they were counterbalanced among the Revolutionary placeholders by two royal justices who had stood with the Court in the 1760s.[18] A noted Revolutionary leader, Joseph Hawley of Northampton, might have played a dominant role, but his decline into melancholic depression in 1776 left the leadership of Hampshire County to the decidedly

[17] Royal judicial appointments for all three counties are listed in William H. Whitmore, ed., *The Massachusetts Civil List for the Colonial and Provincial Periods. 1630-1774* . . . (Albany, N.Y., 1870); Revolutionary appointments are listed in "List of Justices, December 23, 1775," Folder 6, Box 23, Worcester County, Massachusetts Papers, Am. Antiq. Soc., and in Council Records, 17: 64, 67-68, 84-85, 95, 106, 109, 114, 125, 147, 152, 156, Mass. Archs.

[18] On partisanship, the Land Bank, and placeholding see material in notes 16-17 above; on representation see Ronald K. Snell, " 'Ambitious of Honor and Places': The Magistracy of Hampshire County, Massachusetts, 1692-1760," in Bruce C. Daniels, ed., *Power and Status: Officeholding in Colonial America* (Middletown, Conn., 1986), 20, 22. Enfield and Suffield were set off to Connecticut in 1749. See also George Billias, *The Massachusetts Land Bankers of 1740* (Orono, Maine, 1959), 49-53, and Taylor, *Western Massachusetts.* 52-54.

conservative Caleb Strong, who had signed a loyalist declaration before siding with the Revolution.[19] The absence of a group of leaders with experience in the Popular tradition in Berkshire and Hampshire would have profound consequences.

The key to the local power of the Court party gentry of provincial Hampshire lay in their monopoly of judicial placeholding "in the form of a close corporation," as Robert J. Taylor put it thirty years ago, a theme recently reinforced by the work of Gregory H. Nobles and Ronald K. Snell. Snell has demonstrated that almost three-quarters of the county officials serving in Hampshire between 1731 and 1760 were close relations of one of a half dozen River God families.[20] Equally important, the placeholders were highly concentrated along the Connecticut River and in the Housatonic Valley, severely limiting access to relatively cheap local justice for the people of the outlying towns. In 1774, roughly 65 percent of the people of Hampshire County and 45 percent of Berkshire County lived in towns without a resident justice of the peace. In sharp contrast, even though Worcester County had a roughly similar ratio of justices to population, its placeholders were far more widely distributed; in 1774 only 25 percent of the county's people lived in towns without a local justice. (See Table II.)

Here, then, lay the makings of an early and satisfactory revolutionary settlement in Worcester County and the failure of such a settlement in Hampshire and Berkshire. Except for the removal of the small group of elite tory placeholders, Worcester moved through the Revolutionary transition with remarkable stability. By contrast, neither Hampshire nor Berkshire experienced such continuity. Instead, they entered the Revolutionary era with disrupted elites and discredited political traditions.

The county conventions of 1774 and 1775 were critical in shaping Revolutionary beginnings and settlements across western Massachusetts. The political and institutional stability evident in Worcester County was reinforced by aggressive, popular actions taken by the county convention in the summer and fall of 1774. First meeting on August 9, the convention condemned the county justices who had written a loyal address to Gen. Thomas Gage. Reconvening on August 30 in the courthouse itself, the convention unanimously resolved "to prevent the sitting of the respective courts" and asked "the inhabitants of the county, to attend, in person," the court sessions that were to be held a week following. After acting to limit both the ritual debasement of the justices and the more radical proposals

[19] On Hawley see E. Francis Brown, *Joseph Hawley: Colonial Radical* (New York, 1931), 94-95, 146-148, 170-173, and Taylor, *Western Massachusetts.* 69-71.

[20] Taylor, *Western Massachusetts.* 24-26; Zemsky, *Merchants. Farmers. and River Gods.* 32-33, 55-56; Nobles, *Divisions throughout the Whole: Politics and Society in Hampshire County. Massachusetts. 1740-1775* (New York, 1983), 12-35; Snell, "'Ambitious of Honor and Places'," in Daniels, ed., *Power and Status.* 17-36. See also Kevin M. Sweeney, "Mansion People: Kinship, Class, and Architecture in Western Massachusetts in the Mid-Eighteenth Century," *Winterthur Portfolio.* XIX (1984), 231-255.

TABLE II
JUSTICES AND POPULATION IN THE THREE WESTERN COUNTIES, 1774-1796

	No. of Justices	Population per Justice[a]	Towns and Districts without Local Justice		Population without Local Justice[b]	
Worcester						
1774	50	859	16/42	38%	11,793/45,031	26%
1782	61	825	6/45	13%	7,552/56,807	13%
1786	70	765	10/49	20%	8,675/56,807	15%
1796	84	708				
Hampshire						
1774	32	948	31/44	70%	21,276/32,701	65%
1782	41	1,048	27/50	54%	29,234/59,681	49%
1786	51	1,020	23/60	39%	19,134/59,681	32%
1796	97	694	11/60	18%	6,735/59,681	11%
Berkshire						
1774	18	869	6/16	37%	8,185/17,952	45%
1782	37	631	6/23	26%	4,188/30,291	14%
1786	40	671	4/24	17%	2,603/30,291	9%
1796	52	624				

[a] Ratio of county population estimates, based on a simple extrapolation between census figures for 1764, 1776, 1790, and 1800, and the number of justices in a given year.

[b] Total population in 1776 and 1790 of towns without a resident justice.

Residences are unknown for three J.P.s in Worcester in 1774 and one J.P. in Hampshire in 1774. I am obliged to James Parish for the identification of the residences of several Berkshire J.P.s.

Sources: *Fleming's Register* (Boston, 1773); William H. Whitmore, ed., *The Massachusetts Civil List for the Colonial and Provincial Periods, 1630-1774* . . . (Albany, N.Y., 1870); Evarts B. Greene and Virginia D. Harrington, *American Population before the Federal Census of 1790* (New York, 1932), 26-29, 33-39; U.S. Censuses for 1790 and 1800.

from "the body of the people" assembled on Worcester common, the convention delegates proceeded to govern the county in the place of the courts, dealing with tories, organizing the militia, advising the towns on administrative matters, and pressing them to set up courts to adjudicate cases of debt. Isaiah Thomas's *Massachusetts Spy*, established in Worcester in May 1775, helped make the convention's influence felt throughout the county.[21]

Worcester was not the first of the western counties to call a convention in 1774, but neither of the conventions sitting earlier in Berkshire and Hampshire so effectively led the people against the royal courts. The first

[21] "Convention of Worcester County," in William Lincoln, ed., *The Journals of Each Provincial Congress of Massachusetts in 1774 and 1775. . . . containing the Proceedings of the County Conventions* (Boston, 1838), 621-652; L. Kinvin Wroth et al., eds., *Province in Rebellion: A Documentary History of the Founding of the Commonwealth of Massachusetts, 1774-1775* (Cambridge, Mass., 1975), 59-67, 96-97; Lincoln, *History of Worcester*, 290-292, 316-317.

convention in Massachusetts met at Stockbridge in Berkshire County on July 6. Chaired by Rescinder John Ashley, it protested royal infringements upon the charter and enjoined the people to observe the nonconsumption covenant as well as to avoid "licentiousness" and unnecessary lawsuits. Nowhere in the convention's resolves were the courts mentioned. When a crowd of 1,500 closed the Great Barrington courts on August 18, it was acting on the recommendation of the town of Pittsfield, which had voted three days before that "the Courts of Justice [should] immediately seace, and the People of this Province fall into a State of nature."[22]

Things were even more haphazard in Hampshire. The county convention held at Hadley on August 26, 1774, was deeply divided on the issue of closing the royal courts. After voting that the courts might lawfully sit, the convention sent a committee to question the Court of Common Pleas as to the authority under which the court acted. A crowd assembled at Springfield cut short the legal niceties first by voting that the courts should not sit and then by forcing the justices to renounce their commissions. Similarly, the county conventions in Hampshire and Berkshire never achieved the quasi-governmental status that their counterparts did in Worcester. The Hampshire convention met sporadically over the next several years, but its influence was severely curtailed by the lack of a local press. Except for the *Massachusetts Gazette,* published for a short time in Springfield in 1782, there was no local newspaper in Hampshire until the *Hampshire Gazette* was established. Its first issue appeared a week after the August 1786 court closing in Northampton.[23]

In short, the Revolution came to Worcester County in an orderly fashion, led by old Popular party men and by the county convention. To the west the Revolution brought chaos; with the old Court elite splintered and broken, no effective group of leaders emerged from the conventions of 1774 and 1775. These histories diverged still more sharply and strikingly in 1775 and 1776, when county courts were reestablished by the General Court.

In Worcester County the process was again a smooth one; fifteen of the thirty-one new justices had served under royal commissions, and eighteen had served in the county convention or the provincial congresses. The

[22] See Taylor, *Western Massachusetts.* 75-76; Lincoln, ed., *Journals of Each Provincial Congress.* 652-655. Wroth *et al.,* eds., *Province in Rebellion.* 58, argues differently that the Berkshire convention first suggested action against the courts, citing a letter from a "Berkshire Committee" to the Boston Committee, dated July 25, 1774. This letter, signed by John Brown of Pittsfield, refers to "the proceedings of this Town" as quite distinct from "the Result of a County Congress." It appears to have been written by a committee from Pittsfield and perhaps other central Berkshire towns, not by the county convention that met in Stockbridge on July 6. See *ibid..* Docs. 213 (n. 79), 229, and 243.

[23] Wroth *et al.,* eds., *Province in Rebellion.* Doc. 314; James Russell Trumbull, *History of Northampton. Massachusetts. from Its Settlement in 1654* (Northampton, Mass., 1902) II, 345-346, 479-483; Taylor, *Western Massachusetts.* 64-65.

TABLE III

TOWNS REPRESENTED BY JUSTICES OR "ESQUIRES," 1760-1788 (IN PERCENTAGES)

	Berkshire		Hampshire		Worcester	
1760-1764			71	(48/68)	55	(46/84)
1765	40	(2/5)	62	(8/13)	62	(13/21)
1768	100	(3/3)	36	(4/11)	62	(13/21)
1770	67	(4/6)	16	(3/19)	54	(14/26)
1774	33	(4/12)	25	(6/24)	37	(10/27)
Provincial Congress	28	(7/25)	7	(6/90)	10	(11/114)
1775-1779	18	(9/49)	26	(32/122)	20	(33/162)
State Constitutional Convention, 1779	35	(7/20)	14	(5/35)	29	(12/41)
1780-1786	41	(42/103)	19	(38/200)	34	(68/199)
1787	33	(7/21)	17	(7/42)	17	(8/47)
1788	42	(8/19)	18	(6/34)	20	(7/35)
Federal Constitutional Convention, 1788	32	(7/22)	16	(8/49)	17	(8/46)

Sources: *Journals of the House of Representatives of Massachusetts* (Boston, 1919-   );
Massachusetts Register, 1778-1788; William Lincoln, ed., *The Journals of Each Provincial Congress of Massachusetts in 1774 and 1775. . . . containing the Proceedings of the County Conventions* (Boston, 1838); Everett, *Journal of the Convention* (1770); Bradford K. Peirce et al.. eds., *Debates and Proceedings in the Convention of the Commonwealth of Massachusetts. Held in the Year 1788 . . .* (Boston, 1856) (1788).

sitting of the Worcester courts was adjourned by the legislature in 1778 but otherwise never challenged until September 1786. After the ratification of the constitution in 1780, justices were elected to represent the county's towns in increasing numbers, suggesting popular acceptance of the new judiciary.[24] (See Table III.)

In Berkshire County, events followed a strikingly different path toward a roughly similar outcome. The story of the Berkshire Constitutionalists has been ably told by Taylor, Stephen E. Patterson, and Theodore M. Hammett. The Constitutionalists were immediately concerned with the appointment of judges and militia officers; this institutional focus developed into a broader demand that the royal charter be abandoned and a new constitution drawn up. Inspired by a Lockean natural rights rhetoric drawn from the writings of Thomas Paine and Richard Price, and articulated by the Reverend Thomas Allen of Pittsfield, the people of central Berkshire rose to stop the Court of Quarter Sessions in February 1776. The 1778 plan for the legislature to write a constitution further fueled the Constitutionalist cause. Berkshire voted in convention to keep the courts closed and to demand a constitutional convention. In 1779 a

[24] On the adjournment of the Worcester Co. courts in 1778 see Patterson, *Political Parties*. 203; John M. Murrin, "Review Essay," *History and Theory*. IX (1972), 269-270, discusses the significance of the election of justices to the House.

161

crowd acting on the authority of another county convention stopped the
Superior Court session planned for Great Barrington. In all, four conventions met in Berkshire between December 1775 and May 1779 to ratify
popular opposition to the courts and demands for a popular constitution.[25]

The Lockean politics of Constitutionalism was rooted in Berkshire's
relative lack of history and tradition. Berkshire was a new frontier; its
people were for the most part indifferent to the established traditions of
provincial Massachusetts. Sparsely populated by the 1760s along the
Housatonic River, the county grew by 500 percent between 1765 and
1776. The old placeholding elite was located in southern towns settled
before the French and Indian War; the Constitutionalists dominated in the
newly settled but very fertile towns of the upper valley. As Hammett has
demonstrated, the leading Constitutionalists were not poor, struggling
debtors.[26] Rather, they were an emergent elite for whom the Revolution
was an opportunity to destroy the power of the Court party gentry of the
south county towns. Many of Berkshire's people were recent arrivals from
Connecticut and Rhode Island who had no particular allegiance to the
Massachusetts charter; they were often inclined toward religious dissent
rather than the Stoddardean orthodoxy of the older towns with links to the
Connecticut Valley. Thomas Allen himself came from a New Light family
in Northampton that had stood among the supporters of Jonathan
Edwards. Constitutionalism in Berkshire sprang from conscious hostility
to ancient ways in Massachusetts.[27]

The Berkshire Constitutionalists were successful in keeping the courts
closed until 1780. With the establishment of a new framework of
authority, their leadership moved to gain control of the court system.
Seven signers of a 1778 Constitutionalist petition served in the judicial
system in the 1780s; staunch Constitutionalists from Lenox—Caleb Hyde
and William Walker—replaced south county conservatives as sheriff and
register of probate. And in a dramatic move, unique in confederation-era
Massachusetts, the Constitutionalists managed to have the town of Lenox

[25] Taylor, *Western Massachusetts*, 81-100; Patterson, *Political Parties*, 204-208,
235; J.E.A. Smith, *The History of Pittsfield, Massachusetts* (Boston, 1869), 356-365;
Theodore M. Hammett, "Revolutionary Ideology in Massachusetts: Thomas
Allen's 'Vindication' of the Berkshire Constitutionalists, 1778," *WMQ*. 3d Ser.,
XXXIII (1976), 514-527. Constitutionalist Berkshire came into direct conflict
with Popular Worcester in the fall of 1778. See Handlin and Handlin, eds., *Popular
Sources of Political Authority*. 366-379.

[26] Theodore Marriner Hammett, "The Revolutionary Ideology in Its Social
Context: Berkshire County, Massachusetts, 1725-1785" (Ph.D. diss., Brandeis
University, 1976).

[27] See David Dudley Field, *A History of the County of Berkshire, Massachusetts*
(Pittsfield, Mass., 1829), *passim*. for dissenting churches and the Connecticut and
Rhode Island origins of Berkshire Co. population. On Thomas Allen see Trum-
bull, *Northampton*. II, 234, 608, and Clifford K. Shipton, ed., *Sibley's Harvard
Graduates: Biographical Sketches of Those Who Attended Harvard College* (Boston,
1933-   ), XV, 153-165.

established as the county seat, superseding the older south county towns of Stockbridge and Great Barrington. With this coup, the Constitutionalists moved to reshape the county's institutional geography and to establish the symbolic basis of a new political order.[28]

As in Worcester County, the number of justices elected to the legislature in the 1780s indicates the success of Berkshire's revolutionary settlement and an acceptance of the newly legitimized county institutions. Between 1775 and 1777, roughly a quarter of Berkshire towns were represented by justices; in the crisis years of 1778 and 1779 not one justice was elected. Then in April 1780, a month after the state convention submitted the constitution to the towns for ratification, fully half of the towns sent justices to the legislature, and during the better part of the 1780s, as the economic crisis heated up, Berkshire sent the highest proportion of justices of all three western counties. (See Table III.) In this electoral endorsement of the county's justices, Berkshire County arrived at a revolutionary settlement on the surface not unlike that of Worcester.

Things were significantly different in Hampshire. That county's towns had normally elected justices as representatives to the General Court during the provincial era. Again, they sent the highest proportion of justices in 1776 and 1777, but fewer, rather than more, in the 1780s. The share of Hampshire justices in town representation was the lowest of the three western counties, and roughly half that of Berkshire, an indication that they had not achieved the public acceptance that their counterparts enjoyed in the other two counties.

The dwindling role of Hampshire's placeholders as representatives was an important symptom of a public crisis specific to that county. In both Worcester and Berkshire the action of conventions, articulating the priorities of Popular and Constitutionalist politics, brought accommodation between elites and broad segments of the county electorate. But no such accommodation was reached in Hampshire. With the same vacuum of legitimacy that Berkshire experienced, Hampshire attempted to muddle through, rather than to cut loose from the past.

Efforts to build a new consensus in Hampshire failed to gain sufficient support. Thomas Allen of Pittsfield had some influence in the western hill towns, particularly Chesterfield, where he had preached to families clearing farms in 1763. At Allen's urging, Chesterfield and three neighboring towns called for a convention to consider the courts. Twenty-eight towns, meeting in Northampton in March 1776, voted unanimously that the quarter sessions courts be suspended temporarily, but only narrowly agreed that the justices could not act under the commissions granted in the name of the king. By 1778, the full court system had been reestablished, without any public meetings on the subject, at the same time that the Berkshire Constitutionalists were stiffening their resistance. Even when the Constitutionalists in Chesterfield engineered another convention in

[28] Smith, *Pittsfield*. 360-361, 427-433; judicial appointment from the *Massachusetts Register*.

March 1779, a conservative majority voted that the General Court could call a constitutional convention without consulting the towns.[29]

Discontent with the court system was expressed throughout the returns of the Hampshire towns to the proposed state constitutions of 1778 and 1780. In particular, the towns wanted local control of the justices of the peace. Chesterfield proposed in 1778 that J.P.s be nominated by the assembly, rather than appointed by the governor, while Greenwich suggested the annual election of justices in each town, with town recording of probates and deeds. Ashfield in 1780 held that local election of justices was "the Natural Right of the Commonwealth." In 1778 Belchertown argued that such local control of the justices was "agreeable to the spirit of Liberty"; two years later the town suggested that justices be distributed according to the number of representatives each town could send to the General Court.[30]

Belchertown's formula reflected a widespread concern with the continuing inaccessibility of justice in the Hampshire court system. Provincial practice had persisted through the Revolution. By the mid-1780s the ratio of justices to population in Hampshire County had risen only slightly and placeholders were still strikingly concentrated: just under 50 percent of the people lived in towns without resident justices, especially in the towns of the eastern hills. In sharp contrast, the judicial system was becoming more accessible in Berkshire and Worcester. (See Table II.) The population per justice ratio in these two counties was dropping, quite dramatically in Berkshire, and only 13 percent of each county's population lived in towns lacking resident justices. These circumstances were reflected in the returns on the constitution in 1780, where 25 percent of the Hampshire towns proposed local election of justices of the peace, as against 15 percent of the Berkshire and Worcester towns.[31] In 1786, after what was clearly a concerted effort to expand access to justice, one-third of Hampshire's people were still unable to go to a neighbor to have routine legal business transacted. Ten years later the problem would be

[29] Taylor, *Western Massachusetts.* 85, 92, 98; Trumbull, *Northampton.* II, 389-390; Shipton, ed., *Sibley's Harvard Graduates.* XV, 153-165.

[30] Handlin and Handlin, eds., *Popular Sources of Political Authority.* 213, 219, 536, 540.

[31] Responses to Ch. 2, Sect. 1, Art. 9 of the 1780 constitution (justices to be nominated and appointed by the governor with the advice and consent of the Council):

	Berkshire	Hampshire	Worcester
Total returns:	17 (100%)	39 (100%)	43 (100%)
Proposed that J.P.s be			
elected by towns:	3 (17%)	10 (26%)	6* (14%)
be nominated by county			
or by representatives:	3 (17%)	3 (8%)	5 (12%)

Source: Handlin and Handlin, eds., *Popular Sources of Political Authority.* 459, 475-506, 532-626, 807-901. *These six returns were from towns in the northwest corner of the county, adjacent to Hampshire Co.

alleviated; the number of justices in Hampshire County doubled and the proportion of the population living in towns with justices rose to the same level as in the two other counties. But in the 1780s Hampshire saw nothing like the accommodation of people and institutions evident in Worcester and Berkshire.

The economic crisis that preceded Shays's Rebellion was rooted in a disordered revolutionary economy. War generated price inflation as manufactured goods disappeared and agricultural commodities were bid up by military demand; it also led to the depreciation of currency, as bills of credit, issued for the first time since Shirley's redemption of 1749, rapidly lost value. Inflation was combatted by legislation empowering town committees to fix prices and by the resolves of provincial and county conventions meeting in 1779. Efforts to slow depreciation of bills of credit and Continental notes focused on returning the state to a specie currency, by legislation in 1777 that converted the bills into redeemable treasury notes and by the 1781 "Consolidation Act." Passed immediately after the ratification of the constitution, this act comprised a series of measures that effectively lowered the value of the Continental notes of 1780 and converted the state war debt into securities not subject to depreciation, which would be repaid in specie with interest by 1788, based on a high rate of taxation.[32]

The people of western Massachusetts responded to this economic pressure in very different ways. Rather than expressing the sentiments of a single, coherent region, the local initiatives, convention politics, and legislative voting of the late 1770s and early 1780s all reflected the sharply divergent provincial traditions and Revolutionary histories of the western counties. Worcester County stood out in its consistent and sophisticated attention to the complex fiscal affairs that dominated the state's politics. Rooted in a Popular tradition running back to the 1730s, Worcester's united opposition to the creditor interests in convention and legislature built a consensus between leadership and electorate that survived the turmoil of the rebellion of 1786. In Berkshire, the workings of Lockean Constitutionalism militated against a corporate politics of conventions, and the county's representatives sided not with the opposition but with the creditor forces in the General Court. The result was a growing division within the county and a particularly bitter confrontation in 1786. In Hampshire, a proliferation of conventions focused on the problems of local institutions, in some cases directly challenging the courts, in others seeking reform. Here a paradox developed. As demands for reform were gradually met, the cadre of pro-government notables spread selectively beyond its traditional confines in the valley towns. Nonetheless, the

---

[32] Ferguson, *Power of the Purse*. 245-250; Patterson, *Political Parties*. 168-169, 177-180; Hall, *Politics without Parties*. 100-114; Ernst, "The Political Economy of Shays's Rebellion," in Gross, ed., *In Debt to Shays*.

cumulative mobilization for protest established the political model for rebellion in 1786.

These different county politics were expressed most vividly in January 1781 in the final vote on the Consolidation Act, the measure that fundamentally shaped the economic crisis over the next five years. Berkshire supported the bill, eleven to four, while Hampshire was narrowly opposed, ten to eleven; the delegation from Worcester County cast an overwhelming five to twenty vote to lead the opposition. This pattern would typify the voting of these delegations until 1786. On nineteen key votes on fiscal affairs, the national impost, the tories, and the Confederation Congress's request for a supplemental fund, the representatives from Berkshire consistently leaned toward the creditor interests and the Worcester delegation typically voted in a block with the opposition, with Hampshire following.[33]

Worcester's legislative opposition to plans to consolidate and retire both paper currency and the debt in the 1780s had been anticipated by the county's actions in the late 1770s. In 1777, after the first legislation retiring paper currency, thirty-two towns had sent letters of protest to the General Court. Seventeen were Worcester towns, followed by a block of seven from Bristol and Plymouth; only two towns in Hampshire County wrote in protest, and none in Berkshire. Six of the nine old Land Bank strongholds in Worcester County were among the protesting towns.[34] Similarly, despite the apparent benefits of price inflation to the farming economy, Worcester joined the eastern counties in vigorously supporting the price-fixing movement. With only one exception, every town in that county sent at least one delegate to the provincial convention that met in Concord in July and October 1779 to set prices of commodities. In sharp contrast, only a fifth of the towns in Hampshire and Berkshire counties

[33] Overall, on these 19 votes, Berkshire representatives voted 47% (83-94) with the opposition, Hampshire representatives voted 68% (231-108) with the opposition, and Worcester representatives voted 73% (264-98) with the opposition. The overall Worcester record of voting with the opposition was tempered by its 67% vote (29-14) in favor of the 1781 federal impost, and by its 52% vote (10-9) to reconsider the 1782 direct tax. This analysis is based on a transcript of roll-call voting by county supplied by Van Beck Hall, from his notes on the manuscript House Journal, 1: 246-247, 2: 67-68, 306-308, 432-433, 507, 568, 715-716, 3: 140-141, 150-151, 4: 121-123, 259-261, 433-434, 5: 177-178, 338-339, 6: 467-468, 519-520, 7: 69-70, 152-155. The near unanimous opposition of the Worcester Co. representatives to the merchant-sponsored legislation is noted in Robert A. East, "The Massachusetts Conservatives in the Critical Period," in Richard B. Morris, ed., *The Era of the American Revolution: Studies Inscribed to Evarts Boutell Greene* (New York, 1939), 351, 364-365, and Stephen E. Patterson, "After Newburgh: The Struggle for the Impost in Massachusetts," in James Kirby Martin, ed., *The Human Dimensions of Nation Making: Essays on Colonial and Revolutionary America* (Madison, Wis., 1976), 218-242.

[34] The 1777 letters of protest are listed in *The Acts and Resolves. Public and Private. of the Province of the Massachusetts Bay* (Boston, 1869-1922), V, 516-518; for a discussion see Patterson, *Political Parties.* 180-181.

sent delegates, and Northampton and other Hampshire towns refused to participate in a county convention on prices. In Worcester, an apparently well-attended county price convention adopted the Concord resolves, setting prices and recommending that towns establish "large committees" to ensure compliance. Approaches to the intricacies of state fiscal policy differed sharply in these western counties, reflecting local experience with the provincial Court and Popular traditions.[35]

The recommendations of the Concord convention articulated a compromise between the advocates of paper money and of specie. The delegates stated unequivocally that demands for hard currency were the root cause of inflation, as they set up a spiraling differential between paper and metal. "[T]he buying and selling Silver and Gold, and the demanding or receiving *either of them, . . .* has been one great Cause of our *present Evils.*" The inhabitants of the state were enjoined against *"such wicked and pernicious Practices."* But the convention also argued that *"loaning and taxing"* would be "the most effectual Methods" of restoring value to the paper currency and urged that the people pay their taxes promptly.[36]

This compromise also characterized the voting of Worcester County's delegation to the General Court. The county's representatives were united against the retirement of paper money, but on several occasions they lent judicious support to certain tax bills. Unlike Hampshire's delegation, Worcester's supported the 1781 impost and excise proposals, and in 1782 narrowly supported the direct tax.[37]

Worcester County's stance was expressed most strikingly in the three county conventions that met in 1781, 1782, and 1784. These conventions were centrally concerned with currency, fiscal accountability, and expenditures, and only secondarily with the level of taxation and the structure of county institutions. Meeting in April after the passage of consolidation, the 1781 convention had "reason to believe" that, except for the consolidation measures, the old currency would have appreciated "so rapidly that in a short time the difference between paper and silver currency would have been very inconsiderate." The convention scoffed at the idea of justices of the Supreme Judicial Court assigning value to the bills of credit: it was common knowledge that the value was "not settled by them, but by Money-Jobbers & those who have it in their power to make specie either scarce or plenty at their pleasure." Nothing was said about taxes or county

[35] *Proceedings of the Convention Begun and Held at Concord . . . on the 14th Day of July. 1779 . . .* (Boston [1779]); *Proceedings of the Convention Begun and Held at Concord . . . on the Sixth Day of October. A.D. 1779 . . .* (Boston [1779]); *Proceeding of the Convention. Began and Held at Worcester. in and for the County of Worcester. on the 3d Day of August. 1779* ([Worcester, 1779]); Trumbull, *Northampton.* II, 429-430; Lockwood, *Westfield.* II, 47-48; [Nathaniel B. Sylvester, ed.], *History of the Connecticut Valley in Massachusetts . . .* (Philadelphia, 1879), 690.

[36] *Proceedings of the Convention . . . 14th Day of July.* Resolves 6 and 7.

[37] Manuscript House Journal, 1: 246-247, 2: 67-68, Mass. Archs. See Van Beck Hall, *Politics without Parties.* 100-110 (votes 7 and 8).

courts.[38] The next convention, meeting in April 1782, did discuss court reforms, but these were subordinated to an interest in public expenditure. This convention was "not satisfied in what manner the IMMENSE SUMS of PUBLICK MONEY" recently assessed had "been DISPOSED OF." The question involved taxation, but the convention resolves said nothing about the levying of taxes other than to ask that supplies for the army be raised in beef rather than currency. The central concern was "EXPENDITURE": the state of treasury accounts, the settlement of accounts between the commonwealth and the Confederation Congress, and the control of the impost bill. Two years later another convention voiced similar concerns. It demanded repeal of the legislation assigning revenue from the impost to the Continental debt and protested state expenditures for "days of public rejoicing." It also complained about grants to Continental officers, arguing that they were no more binding than "the redemption of the Old Money" and that "the good People of this State are greatly oppressed & Distressed for the want of a balance of a Circulating medium." Again, there was nothing in the convention's resolves regarding the structure of the county courts.[39] Even at the conventions of the summer and fall of 1786 at Leicester and Paxton—the prelude to the court closings in Worcester— the proceedings were dominated by this politics of money and public credit. The Paxton convention introduced new grievances about the expenses of the disastrous 1779 Penobscot expedition, the new Supplementary Fund request, and the interests of security holders. In total, the Worcester conventions meeting between 1781 and 1784 passed ten resolutions regarding fiscal policy and only two regarding the county courts.[40] (See Table IV.)

The language of these conventions was strikingly similar to that of the price-fixing conventions of 1779. Equally important, the same men occasionally served in both sets of conventions, and they were often drawn from the same Land Bank background, as were many of the delegates to the Worcester convention of 1774.[41] It may seem paradoxical that these

[38] Worcester County Convention Petition, 142: 333-335, Mass. Archs.

[39] Lincoln, *History of Worcester.* 130-133; *Worcester County Convention* (Worcester, Mass., 1782), Apr. 9 and May 14, 1782; Worcester County Convention Petition, Apr. 22, 1784 [approval voted in Worcester town meeting, May 14, 1784] House Doc. Unpassed 1320, Mass. Archs.

[40] *Massachusetts Gazette* (Boston), Aug. 25, 1786; *Worcester Magazine.* Sept. 1786, 334-335. Other sources for the Worcester conventions include *Massachusetts Spy* (Worcester), Sept. 12, 1782; Petition of a meeting of towns and committees in Worcester, Dec. 1786, 190: 301-303, Mass. Archs. William A. Benedict and Hiram A. Tracy, *History of the Town of Sutton. Massachusetts. from 1704 to 1876* . . . (Worcester, Mass., 1878), 127; and *Worcester Mag..* Mar. 1787, 628-629.

[41] Among 62 price convention delegates, at least 12 (19%) were related to Land Bankers. Among 25 known delegates to the 1781-1784 conventions, 4 had served in the 1779 price convention, and 7 (29%) were related to Land Bankers. Sources:

TABLE IV
SUMMARY OF RESOLVES VOTED AND ISSUES DISCUSSED IN COUNTY
CONVENTIONS

County	Conventions Meetings and Adjournments	Issues Discussed or Resolves Voted		
		Fiscal Policy	Taxes and Debt	County Institutions
Worcester, 1781-1784	5	10	4	2
Worcester, August 1786-1787	5	12	4	6
Hampshire, 1781-May 1786	17	8	12	15
Hampshire, August 1786-1787	4	7	3	5
Berkshire, 1782	2	2	3	7

This count includes the actual resolves voted by conventions, when available, and the references to issues being discussed, even if there is no evidence on resolves being voted.

Note: to conserve space on the map, meetings of a county convention in a single town in a given year are indicated with one star. Thus the map does not indicate three convention adjournments that met in Worcester, and four adjournments that met in Hadley or Hatfield.

Sources: see notes 6, 38-40, and 42-45.

two convention movements were so complementary, because those of 1781-1784 have always been seen as inflationary, the antithesis of price-fixing corporatism. But it should be recognized that both movements were concerned with maintaining the value of paper money and held in common a long tradition favoring a corporately regulated paper currency—a tradition with direct, living roots in the Land Bank of 1740.

The point should be plain: the smooth continuity of Worcester County's early Revolutionary settlement carried with it a deeply rooted county tradition of support for paper money, economic regulation, and public accountability. This was a tradition nurtured among a broad stratum of county leaders in the Popular faction in the decade before the Revolution. Far from being backward-looking subsistence farmers, they were men with an eye to commercial possibilities. But neither were they rural embodiments of Adam Smith; they would have utterly rejected a vision of an economy of dissassociated private interests. Their world view was structured by traditional expectations of corporate mutuality and obligation. Both the Land Bank and the convention represented an experimental groping toward a system that would mediate between corporatism and commerce. Both occupied a poorly defined position between public and private institutional forms; both were condemned as irregular and illegal by establishment voices. This Popular tradition of public meetings, fiscal oversight, and paper money provided a common ground for public debate and discourse in Worcester that was utterly absent in the counties to the

Davis, *Currency and Banking*, II, 295-313; convention proceedings, and town histories and records.

west. The action in this common political arena, combined with a relatively acceptable court system, worked to contain civil unrest in the county with the highest rate of public and private debt in the entire commonwealth.

The convention politics in Hampshire County had a drastically different character. Rather than the issues of currency and expenditure that dominated the agenda in Worcester County, the Hampshire conventions were overwhelmingly concerned with the structure of county institutions. These themes were enumerated in detail by the February 11, 1782, Hadley convention. The convention was concerned about the salaries of the governor and "all other salary men in the civil department," the costs of the quarter sessions court, and the fees required by attorneys and by clerks of the civil courts. But more important, it recommended a wholesale decentralization of county responsibilities. It resolved that deeds should be registered in the towns rather than by a county register and complained that having but one probate judge in "this larg County" was a "general and Capital grievance," costing "the Publick great expense in Probate matters." The convention wanted town constables to assume the responsibilities of the county deputy sheriffs, and selectmen to assume full authority to license innkeepers and retailers, eliminating the review by the county Court of Quarter Sessions. It petitioned for the restoration of the Confession Act of 1777, giving local justices of the peace the authority to take written statements of debt, and urged that the justices be granted the power to decide debt cases of up to twenty pounds rather than the traditional forty shillings.[42] While high taxation, the excise, fiscal accountability, and the nature of legal tender were all under debate in the spring of 1782, this Hampshire County convention subordinated these issues to grievances about institutional form and structure. Seen through the lens of both Samuel Ely's passionate rhetoric and the more prosaic language of the Hadley convention, the pivotal issue in 1782 was not the press of private debts or the controversial plan to retire the public debt, but the administration of economic relationships and transactions by county institutions.

Time and again, subsequent Hampshire conventions complained about the jurisdiction of the Court of General Sessions and the operation of the registry of deeds and the probate court. A movement with wide support advocated a division of the county, which resulted in two petitions to the General Court in 1784, a county convention at Hatfield in May 1786, where a division was rejected twenty-two to nineteen, and a series of smaller conventions between 1783 and 1787. At the August 22, 1786, convention at Hatfield that immediately preceded the Northampton court closings, county issues were obscured by a host of fiscal and political concerns. They reappeared at the November 1786 Hadley convention, where, at the height of the rebellion, the delegates could only agree that the registry of deeds and the probate court were grievances. Overall, before the August 1786 convention at Hatfield, which may well have been

[42] Hadley Convention Petition, Feb. 11, 1782, House Documents (Unpassed) 1133A.

influenced by the attention to fiscal matters so prominent in Worcester, the Hampshire conventions voted roughly twice as many resolves regarding county institutions as fiscal issues.[43] (See Table IV.)

Berkshire County had significantly higher levels of actions for personal debt, and discontent was brewing below the surface, as indicated in the bitter language of Robert Karson, a Richmond yeoman convicted in 1782 for cursing the court as a "damned pack of rascals" and swearing that he wanted "to kill a Judge or a Lawyer." Yet neither legislative nor convention politics provided any outlet for rising tensions. Between 1781 and 1785, Berkshire representatives cast almost 60 percent of their votes on key roll calls with the creditor interests, and in 1786 over a third supported the supplemental fund for the Confederation government. Similarly—and particularly striking in a county where conventions had acted throughout the 1770s on the Constitutionalist agenda—very few conventions met in Berkshire in the 1780s. A small "rump" convention assembled in Pittsfield in February 1782 and with a show of numbers stopped the sitting of the Court of Common Pleas. In response, a larger convention, meeting a month later, stated flatly that "in a Commonwealth to suspend the Laws and to Stop the Courts of justice is of the most fatal Tendency to that Community." This convention then passed resolves quite similar in tone to those of the Hadley convention. But these were the only conventions to meet in Berkshire County before the late summer of 1786, except for the one where the former Constitutionalists engineered the transfer of the courts to Lenox. Similarly, other than scuffles in Lanesborough and Pittsfield in 1782, there was relatively little civil violence in Berkshire County before the fall of 1786.[44] The county's leading men took seriously the contractual theory of society and government. In their thinking, the county had acted legitimately in convention during the state of nature lasting from the Declaration of Independence in 1776 to the ratification of the state constitution in 1780. But now that the constitution had restored a state of society, the Constitutionalists' Lockean

[43] In addition to those cited above, the sources for the conventions in Hampshire Co. include Taylor, *Western Massachusetts.* 107, 121, and *passim;* Carpenter and Morehouse, *The History of the Town of Amherst. Massachusetts* (Amherst, Mass., 1896), pt. I, 121; Sheldon, *Deerfield.* 671, 751, 762; Lockwood, *Westfield.* II, 48, 53-55; Trumbull, *Northampton.* II, 466, 469, 477-478; James M. Crafts, *History of the Town of Whately. Mass....* (Orange, Mass., 1899), 235; Hatfield Convention Petition, Aug. 10, 1782, 237: 380; Supreme Judicial Court Docket Book, 1785, 181-184, 1786, 204-205; and the *Hampshire Gazette* (Northampton, Mass.), Nov. 15, 1786, Jan. 10, 1787.

[44] For Karson, see Supreme Judicial Court Docket Book, 1781-1782, 291-292; for the conventions and riots in Berkshire Co. see Taylor, *Western Massachusetts.* 111; Berkshire Convention Resolves, Mar. 26, 1782, Local History Collections, Berkshire Athenaeum, Pittsfield, Mass.; Testimony vs. James Harris, 156: 356-379, Mass. Archs.; typescript of account of "Battle in Berkshire" [Pittsfield Riot] for *Mass. Gaz..* Local History Collections, Lenox Library, Lenox, Mass.

political culture worked to discourage traditional meetings of the people in their corporate capacity.

When rebellion erupted in the fall of 1786, triggered by a new round of taxes, it was shaped and conditioned by these three county histories, these very different movements through the Revolutionary experience. Suppressing any corporate politics, liberal Berkshire County was a powder keg waiting to explode; here the Regulation was a desperate class war between haves and have nots. In Hampshire, divisions between the county elite and the discontented were rooted in the proliferation of conventions rather than their absence, and reflected the overarching problem of a failed revolutionary settlement. Here a continuing interaction between conventions and Regulators between 1782 and 1786 structured the core of the county's opposition. In Worcester, the Popular tradition fed both moderation and mediation when rebellion finally broke out in the most heavily burdened county in the commonwealth.

With few conventions meeting, and the county's representatives voting as often as not with the creditor forces in the legislature, Berkshire had few public outlets for political opposition during the 1780s. Similarly, when a convention did meet in Lenox in August 1786 to consider the impending crisis, it voiced decidedly pro-government opinions, supporting the current tax system and the grants made to the Congress, opposing any paper money proposal, and pledging to support the courts. With the friends of government firmly in control of public forums, Berkshire's Regulators were politically isolated: the rebellion there took on an especially violent, polarized character. As David Szatmary has emphasized, it resembled an extended guerrilla war, particularly in the Regulators' winter march from New Lebanon, New York, through Stockbridge, sacking the mansions of the old Court party gentry, to the final skirmish in Sheffield. Even after this showdown, insurgents staged hit-and-run raids on the property of county notables—real social banditry—and as late as October 1787 a crowd ran through Great Barrington cheering for Shays.[45]

Court records indicate that the Berkshire insurgents lacked support among men of local standing and that the courts hounded them unmercifully. Among men listed in state warrants, imprisoned, or formally indicated for insurrection by the Supreme Judicial Court, fewer than 20 percent in Berkshire County were gentlemen or militia officers, as compared to 60 percent in subsequently Antifederalist Worcester towns and more than 90 percent in Antifederalist Hampshire towns.[46] (See

[45] Minot, *History of Insurrections in Massachusetts*. 43; Smith, *Pittsfield*. 400-401, 414; Szatmary, *Shays' Rebellion*. 109-115; Taylor, *Western Massachusetts*. 162-163; Anson Ely Morse, *The Federalist Party in Massachusetts to the Year 1800* (Princeton, N.J., 1909) 209, 211.

[46] I have used lists of individuals singled out for arrest and prosecution to establish patterns of leadership for the Regulation in the fall and winter of 1786-1787. I avoided using the oaths of allegiance signed in spring 1787 as an index of Regulator support, as these oaths were somewhat erratically administered

TABLE V

POLITICAL EXPERIENCE OF COUNTY CONVENTION DELEGATES AND ACCUSED
REGULATORS FROM ANTIFEDERALIST TOWNS

	Berkshire	Hampshire	Worcester
A: Delegates to County Conventions, 1781-1784			
Total Known	na	29	25
Any service as representative to the General Court	na	9 31.0%	16 64%
Supported the Regulation	na	11 37.9%	5 20%
B: Regulators Identified by the Courts, 1787			
Total	94	35	71
Any service as representative to the General Court	3 3.1%	3 8.6%	3 4.2%
Regulators whose social status is identified	62	24	51
Regulators of gentry status*	11 17.7%	22 91.6%	33 64.7%

* Identified in state records as a "gentleman," "esquire," "physician," or militia officer.

Note: This table includes only those delegates and Regulators who were inhabitants of towns that voted against the Federal Constitution in Feb. 1788.

Sources: delegates: from a range of town records and histories; representatives: see Table III; Regulators: see n. 46.

Table V.) While the courts in Hampshire and Worcester aimed at men of some local stature, the Berkshire courts indicted large numbers of laborers and yeomen; among these indicted yeomen were Regulator leaders such as Aaron Knapp of West Stockbridge and Perez Hamlin of Lenox. It is telling that the only executions in the wake of the rebellion—the hangings of John Bly and Charles Rose for burglary at Lenox in December 1787—took place in Berkshire. Witnessed by hundreds of assembled militiamen, including some from Regulator hilltowns, these executions were a means by which a shaken Berkshire elite attempted to reassert its newly established—and violently challenged—public authority.[47]

and were aimed at the rank and file, not the Regulator leadership. Sources include warrants, indictments, and imprisonments listed in the following: 189: 75-76, 81-84, 100-102, 135, 210, Mass. Archs.; Supreme Judicial Court File #155325 (initial list of 21 indictments); Supreme Judicial Court Docket Book, 1787, 58-60, 63, 77-80, 101-102 (and September Session, Worcester County, np); Jail Register, Folder 1, Box 2, Worcester County, Mass., Papers, Am. Antiq. Soc.; Supreme Judicial Court File #155296-7; Prison Lists in Original Papers of Shays's Rebellion, Berkshire Athenaeum, and in Box 23, Robert Treat Paine Papers.

[47] Militia Muster Rolls, 192: 21-22, 24, 29, 49, 122, 227-230, Mass. Archs. Szatmary, *Shays' Rebellion*. 115.

By contrast, conventions and Regulation were fundamentally linked in Hampshire County. Attending a convention on taxes at Hatfield in 1783 with Justice Joseph Hawley of Northampton, Jonathan Judd noted that though "we were very good Natured," the delegates "wanted to get rid of Major Hawley and myself. Near night we set off leaving all the rest."[48] Judd's comments provide a striking vignette of the growing divide between county notables and town leaders in Hampshire. Conventions there were increasingly the domain of men of local experience and the vehicle of protest against a highly self-conscious valley elite. They were intertwined with Regulator mobilization, first with the Hadley and Hatfield conventions of 1782, second in the Springfield court closing of 1783, and most dramatically in the events of August 1786. Almost 40 percent of the convention delegates from Antifederalist towns can be identified as supporting the Regulation, most notably Daniel Shays, Henry McCullock, and Thomas Johnson, all of Pelham, who had represented their town in the Hadley conventions of 1782, where they voted to stop civil proceedings.[49] There was also a continuity between the crowd actions of 1782-1783 and participation in Shays's Rebellion. At least a third of the men indicted for rioting against the courts in Hampshire in 1782-1783 later were to be found among the Shaysite ranks.[50]

In Worcester County there was a different line of demarcation, expressed most succinctly by Josiah Walker of Sturbridge when he refused his election as captain of the Regulators in 1786 because "he was a Convention man." There appears to have been a distinct division between two levels of leadership in Worcester—a county gentry who served in the legislature and the conventions, and a group of town leaders who would lead the Regulators. The delegates to the conventions of 1781-1784 at Worcester typically had experience in the legislature but were far less likely to be drawn into the Regulation. As in Hampshire, the Regulator leaders in Worcester were men of more local experience; they were often

---

[48] Trumbull, *Northampton*. II, 469; Morse, *Federalist Party*. 207.

[49] [Sylvester, ed.], *Connecticut Valley in Massachusetts*. 496-497; Charles Oscar Parmenter, *History of Pelham. Mass.. from 1738 to 1898 . . .* (Amherst, Mass., 1898), 144, 150, 151.

[50] Thirty-three percent of those involved in the Hampshire disturbances of 1782-1783 (20/60) were later implicated in the Regulation in 1786-1787, as against only 7% (5/66) of a sample of those involved in the Worcester Co. rioting of 1782-1783. The Worcester figure is only for men from towns for which extensive lists of Regulators are available. The Hampshire figure is a minimum, because it includes men from towns where I have not made an exhaustive search for Regulator names. There very well may have been far more Regulators among those involved in the Hampshire disturbances of 1782-1783. One hundred fifteen rioters were indicted in Worcester Co. courts in the early 1780s; 17 of these were from Gloucester, R.I. For Worcester men involved in riots against sheriffs' sales see Supreme Judicial Court Docket Book, 1783, 212-220, 239-241, 1784, 265, 1785, 177; for Hampshire "rioters," primarily involved in efforts to close the courts, see *ibid.*. 1783, 99, 232, 1784, 144-145, 1785, 181, 1786, 204-205.

selectmen or militia officers but few had served as representatives. The Worcester Regulator leadership was thus broadly similar to its counterparts in Hampshire and seems to have followed their example. While the Hampshire Regulators had participated in the court closings of 1782-1783, the Worcester Regulators of 1786 had stood back from small-scale rioting against sheriffs' sales in those years; some even gave evidence against the rioters. There is reason to believe that Regulator leaders in the two counties were in communication, as men from Pelham were reported to have attended the Worcester County convention in Leicester on August 15. It was through such connections that the idea of closing the courts was developed in Worcester County.[51]

While civil violence did break out in Worcester County, it was at least mitigated by the Popular tradition and the county's revolutionary settlement. This county political culture was manifested in the Regulators' tolerance of Artemas Ward's speech at the Worcester court closing in September and again in the Regulators' restraint in Worcester that December, when, in sharp contrast to the "plundering insurgents" of Berkshire, they strictly avoided commandeering supplies while occupying the court town. At the same time, county gentry of Popular and convention experience made strenuous efforts to mediate between the Regulators and the government force commanded by Gen. Benjamin Lincoln.[52]

Worcester's Popular tradition and revolutionary settlement may have softened the confrontation of 1786, but that confrontation did take place, and it requires explanation. Regulator mobilization to close the courts was the strongest in those places in western Massachusetts where the Popular tradition had been the weakest or where revolutionary settlements were fragile or nonexistent. Worcester County was no exception.

The geography of the Regulation can be mapped across the three western counties by charting the distribution of Regulators singled out for arrest and prosecution and of captains who raised militia companies for the government. Both groups comprised notable men with influence among neighbors and townsmen, able to mobilize recruits for the government or the insurgency.[53] By this measure the towns of the western counties can

[51] Trumbull, *Northampton*. II, 485-486; see above, n. 50. The local priorities of the Regulator leaders resembled those of the militia officers described in Fred Anderson, *A People's Army: Massachusetts Soldiers and Society in the Seven Years' War* (Chapel Hill, N.C., 1984).

[52] Lincoln, *History of Worcester*. 147; Hall, *Politics without Parties*. 224-225; Benedict and Tracy, *Sutton*. 125-127; Petitions for Henry Gale, 189: 401-402, Mass. Archs.

[53] I have used lists of captains who raised companies for government service and of individuals singled out for arrest and prosecution after the Regulation (see above, n. 46) to establish the distribution of support for the government and the Regulation in the fall and winter of 1786-1787. Militia captains were recorded from Mass. Archs. 191 and 192, *passim*. and were associated with towns using the 1790 census, as listed in *Heads of Families at the First Census of the United States*

be divided into four categories: pro-government, Regulator, conflicted, and neutral. Overall, militia towns had distinctly lower levels of overdue taxes, but there was little difference between the conflicted and Regulator towns on this key measure of economic stress.[54] (See Table VI.) Particularly in Hampshire and Worcester, the core Regulator towns were not raw frontier settlements but places established during the three decades before the Revolution. They were also towns that had never been represented in the provincial General Court, usually because they had been incorporated as districts without the rights of representation. They were overwhelmingly located in the upland areas of regions that had been dominated by Court party men before the Revolution.

This circumstance, by default, characterized Hampshire and Berkshire, but it was also the case in Worcester County. There, seven of the nine Regulator towns were situated in the county's northwest, within or immediately adjacent to the original grant of Rutland, dominated before the Revolution by Court man and loyalist John Murray. These northwest uplands had formed a Court party bastion within an otherwise Popular county. Similarly, these Regulator towns were not places that had experience in the Land Bank or had protested the hard-money legislation of 1777, both closely linked with Popular politics. Such circumstances characterized the pockets of Regulator sentiment to the east. In Middlesex County, the six men singled out for arrest by the government were from Shirley, Groton, and Chelmsford, towns that had had few Land Bankers, whose representatives had voted solidly with the governor before the Revolution, and where there had been sentiment for the establishment of a new county. In all these points these Middlesex towns were very much like Hampshire County. In Bristol County, Regulators were arrested in Easton, Freetown, Rehoboth, Dartmouth, Mansfield, and Swansey. None of these towns was noted for Court party voting, but none had had large numbers of Land Bankers.[55]

Taken in the Year 1790: Massachusetts (Washington, D.C., 1908). Sources for the presence of Regulator leadership are listed in note 46, with the addition of the "Hampshire County Black List," Box 23, Robert Treat Paine Papers. This list allows more of Hampshire's 60 towns and districts to be classified, adding four towns to the "Regulator" category and shifting three towns from the "Militia" to the "Conflicted" category. The numbers of militia captains and Regulator "leaders" in each of the 134 towns in the three western counties are listed in the appendix to Brooke, "A Deacon's Orthodoxy." For suggestive discussions of the importance of such local "notables" and of politics as a form of militia muster, see Hall, *Politics without Parties*. 207-208, and Wiebe, *Opening of American Society*. 37-38.

[54] This calculation of the distribution of back taxes (summarized in Table VI) is based on data provided by Van Beck Hall enumerating the taxes per poll in each town out on execution at the death of Treasurer Ivers (*Politics without Parties*. 195).

[55] Arrests in Middlesex and Bristol from 189: 83-84, 210, 127, 136, 211, Mass. Archs. For provincial voting records and Land Bank investors see Pencak, *War. Politics. and Revolution*. 244-245, 248, and Patterson, *Political Parties*. 258-265.

TABLE VI

AGGREGATE ANALYSIS OF MILITIA AND REGULATOR SUPPORT

	Total Towns and Districts in 1786		Militia		Conflicted		Regulator		Other	
	N	%	N	%	N	%	N	%	N	%
All Three Counties	134	100.0	31	100.0	45	100.0	32	100.0	26	100.0
Town status by 1774	41	30.6	16	51.6	19	42.2	3	9.4	3	11.5
District status to 1774	63	47.0	6	19.4	24	53.3	22	68.8	11	42.3
Incorporated post-1774	30	22.4	9	29.0	2	4.4	7	21.9	12	46.2
J.P. present in 1774	48	35.8	15	48.4	22	48.8	7	21.9	4	15.4
J.P. present in 1782	83	61.9	21	67.7	36	80.0	17	53.1	9	34.6
J.P. present in 1786	92	68.7	22	71.0	41	91.1	19	59.4	12	46.2
Overdue taxes >£1/poll	66	49.3	11	35.5	23	51.1	18	56.3	14	53.8
Nay on Federal Constitution	87	64.9	15	48.4	32	71.1	28	87.5	12	46.2
Yea on Federal Constitution	31	23.1	13	41.9	12	26.7	0	0	6	23.1
Upland Regions in Hampshire County										
Western Hills	27	100.0	6	100.0	11	100.0	4	100.0	6	100.0
J.P. present in 1774	2	7.4	0	0	2	33.3	0	0	0	0
J.P. present in 1782	10	37.0	1	16.7	7	63.6	2	50.0	0	0
J.P. present in 1786	12	44.4	2	33.3	7	63.6	2	50.0	1	16.7
Overdue taxes >£1/poll	12	44.4	1	16.7	7	63.6	2	50.0	2	33.3
Nay on Federal Constitution	9	33.3	1	16.7	4	36.4	3	75.0	1	16.7
Yea on Federal Constitution	11	40.7	3	50.0	6	54.5	0	0	2	33.3
Eastern Hills	19	100.0	3	100.0	5	100.0	8	100.0	3	100.0
J.P. present in 1774	1	5.3	1	33.3	0	0	0	0	0	0
J.P. present in 1782	5	26.3	2	66.7	3	60.0	0	0	0	0
J.P. present in 1786	8	42.1	2	66.7	3	60.0	2	25.0	1	33.3
Overdue taxes >£1/poll	11	57.9	0	0	2	40.0	7	87.5	2	66.7
Nay on Federal Constitution	16	84.2	1	33.3	5	100.0	8	100.0	2	66.7
Yea on Federal Constitution	1	5.3	1	33.3	0	0	0	0	0	0

Sources: see Tables I and III, and notes 46, 53, 54, and 57.

Levels of public and private debt certainly played a role in the mobilization of 1786, but political contexts were equally important. The Regulation gained the strongest support in places, particularly in Hampshire County, where there were few local justices and, more generally, where the population had been effectively disfranchised in the late provincial period. Lacking the right of direct representation, the people of these towns had to defer to the authority of the Court faction placeholders in the dominant towns in their region; their political experience above the level of the town was truncated and stifled. In Hampshire County, their Revolutionary experience had been one of continuing struggle with an unresponsive court system and of resort to the direct action of convention and riot for political expression. This political mode was well established in Pelham, the town that gained the reputation of being the center of the Regulation. As Gregory H. Nobles has noted, Pelham had a long history of civil violence against the county elite, rioting against a sheriff in 1762, marching on Hatfield in February 1775 to smoke Justice Israel Williams into submission, and the next day threatening to give the same treatment to Solomon Stoddard of Northampton, son of Justice John Stoddard and a leading creditor in the county.[56] Action against the courts in 1786 was thus part of a continuous tradition of direct action among a people for whom the provincial public culture manifested in placeholding and representation had been alien and inaccessible.

Within the broader pattern of Regulator mobilization in outlying districts in old Court party regions, the revolutionary settlement in the west Hampshire hills provides the exception that proves the rule. Here the expansion of the judicial system seems to have turned a region that might well have been a Regulator stronghold decisively toward the government. In Hampshire County, Regulator towns were concentrated in the eastern hills and in towns where justices had not been appointed by 1786. But in the western hills there were a surprising number of towns where militia captains were able to raise small companies to defend the courts. In 1786, these conflicted western towns differed from the Regulator towns of the eastern hills less in their level of overdue taxes (64 percent vs. 87 percent) than in the presence of local justices (64 percent vs. 25 percent). (See Table VI.) In 1776 many of these western hilltowns had voted to keep the courts closed, acting on the encouragement of Constitutionalist Thomas Allen. But by 1782 almost two-thirds of these towns had been granted local justices, and their delegates voted in the Hatfield convention of April 1782 against closing the courts. It was in these same towns that militia captains were able to raise companies for the

---

The Nashua Valley county secession effort is mentioned in Barbara Karsky, "Profiles of Protest: Regulators and Their Families in Shays's Rebellion" (paper presented at "Shays's Rebellion and the Constitution: A Bicentennial Conference," Deerfield, Mass., 1986).

[56] Nobles, *Divisions throughout the Whole.* 122, 169.

government in 1786-1787. By contrast, in eight of the older hilltowns to the east where no resident justices had been appointed by 1782, no such pro-government notables emerged; including Shays's hometown of Pelham, these towns composed the epicenter of the Regulation. The progress toward a revolutionary settlement in the west Hampshire hilltowns would have even more dramatic results over the next two years.

The final episodes in this political drama were acted out in the state convention called to ratify the federal Constitution in January 1788 and in the first election of federal representatives, which began the following December. These events brought the closure of the national revolutionary settlement and the beginning of a routine national politics. Once again, the pattern of sentiment expressed in this convention and this election reflected the distinct political histories of the three counties and was decisively conditioned by local revolutionary outcomes.

Worcester's Popular consensus reemerged after Shays's Rebellion and left its permanent record at the ratifying convention. The county's delegates cast an overwhelming 86 percent vote (forty-three to seven) against ratification, the strongest Antifederalist vote in the commonwealth. Men of the Revolutionary generation and of countywide stature led this majority, in sharp contrast to the still-divided counties to the west. Seven of the eight Worcester delegates who had served in the Provincial Congress of 1774-1775 voted against ratification, the exact opposite of Hampshire delegates. Justices and "esquires" from Worcester County opposed the Constitution, six to two; those from the west favored it, twelve to three. All three state senators from Worcester opposed ratification; every senator from Berkshire and Hampshire voted for it.[57] One of the Worcester senators at the convention was Amos Singletary of Sutton, long a leading figure in a town where the Popular tradition was deeply rooted, a Land Bank stronghold, and the storm center of convention politics from 1777 through 1786. Warning the convention that "moneyed men" intended "to be managers of this Constitution" and "swallow up all us little folks, like the great leviathan," Singletary's speech against federal powers of taxation has survived as the essential voice of grass-roots Antifederalism. Another convention man and state senator voting against the Constitution, Jonathan Grout of Petersham, was elected to Congress in 1789. In making this choice the county was reaching deep into the Popular tradition, for Grout's father, a small-time lawyer in Lunenburg, had been a Land Banker, had voted for the bank in the 1740 house, and was still listed among the delinquents in 1763.[58]

[57] The delegates and votes on ratification are listed in Bradford K. Peirce et al., eds., *Debates and Proceedings in the Convention of the Commonwealth of Massachusetts, Held in the Year 1788...* (Boston, 1856), 31-43, 87-92; representatives to provincial congresses from Lincoln, ed., *Journals of Each Provincial Congress;* state senators from the *Mass. Register.*

[58] On Singletary see Peirce et al., eds., *Debates and Proceedings,* 202-203; Benedict and Tracy, *Sutton,* 106-128, 727; and Lincoln, *History of Worcester.*

To the west, roughly two-thirds of the towns in Berkshire and Hampshire opposed the Constitution. Berkshire's vote apparently hinged on a reaction to the efforts to suppress the Regulation, because its 68 percent Antifederalist vote (fifteen to seven) was a significant departure from its legislative voting record of most of the preceding decade.[59] Very obscure men were elected delegates in a number of important towns, and the protests from Williamstown, Great Barrington, and Sheffield against the procedures by which Federalist delegates were elected may have turned men against ratification. Such was the case in Hampshire County, where the delegates from Deerfield and Conway announced after the convention that they had planned to vote in favor of the Constitution but had voted with the opposition to protest "insults" to Antifederalist delegates. Nonetheless, the 63 percent vote for the Constitution by Hampshire delegates (thirty-three to nineteen) was decisive to its passage.[60]

Delegates from the older Hampshire towns along the river voted predictably for ratification, but the critical margin came from the western hilltowns. To a startling degree, Massachusetts's ratification of the Constitution depended on the gradual progress of a revolutionary settlement of county institutions in these hinterland localities. This story centered in the town of Chesterfield, which had taken the lead in the Constitutionalist initiatives of 1776, voting with a narrow majority against the justices acting under a commission in the king's name. Among the men active on committees in the years following, Benjamin Mills was appointed justice of the peace by 1778, Luke Bonney, a Baptist and the town's delegate to the constitutional convention of 1779, raised a government company in January 1787, and his brother Benjamin, another committeeman, drew pay as a colonel. Benjamin Bonney chaired the August 1786 Hatfield convention and issued the call for the convention that met that November in Hadley—a convention that, among all the problems confronting the state, resolved only that the location of the probate courts was a grievance. This complaint had been voiced by Samuel Ely, by the 1782 Hadley convention, and by numerous town resolves, and it finally received attention. It was addressed the following March, when the General Court

---

133-134; on Grout see Abner Morse, *The Genealogy of the Descendants of Capt. John Grout* (Boston, 1857), 8-10, 41-47, and Merrill Jensen and Robert A. Becker, eds., *The Documentary History of the First Federal Elections. 1788-1790* (Madison, Wis., 1976-   ), 619, 665-667, 682-683.

[59] Richard D. Brown, "Shays's Rebellion and the Ratification of the Federal Constitution in Massachusetts," in Richard Beeman, Stephen Botein, and Edward C. Carter II, eds., *Beyond Confederation: Origins of the Constitution and American National Identity* (Chapel Hill, N.C., 1987), 113-127; see also Richard D. Brown, "Shays's Rebellion and Its Aftermath: A View from Springfield, Massachusetts," *WMQ*, 3d Ser., XL (1983), 598-615.

[60] Peirce et al.. eds., *Debates and Proceedings*. 51-55; Samuel B. Harding, *The Contest over the Ratification of the Federal Constitution in the State of Massachusetts* (New York, 1896), 103-104.

established four registries of deeds and four sittings of the probate court at Deerfield, Northampton, Hadley, and Springfield. Ten months later, Benjamin Bonney and nine other delegates from small towns in the west Hampshire hills voted to ratify the Constitution.[61]

If these towns had followed the example of their neighbors in Deerfield and Conway, of the east Hampshire hill towns, or of Worcester County, the Constitution might well not have been ratified in Massachusetts. As it was, the Federalists won by a margin of only nineteen votes, 187 to 168. If the ten Federalist delegates from the west Hampshire hills had turned against the Constitution, the vote would have stood at 177 to 178. Given the crucial position of the Massachusetts vote in the entire ratification process, it may fairly be said that the selective settlement of county institutions in Hampshire County played a decisive role in the far grander national revolutionary settlement. The pace of this settlement of county institutions meant that Massachusetts stood poised between two very different outcomes. On the one hand, a more rapid appointment of local justices in the 1770s and early 1780s might well have diffused some of the discontent among local notables that resulted in conventions and regulation. On the other, a slower process might have meant that fewer pro-government leaders would have emerged in the west Hampshire hills, that the Regulation would have been less contested in this region, and that the vote on the Constitution would have been far closer, perhaps even reversed.

In the first Federal election the old Court tradition reemerged in the west. Combined into one enormous district, Berkshire and Hampshire produced such an excess of candidates that it took five polls to achieve a result. In the end, Theodore Sedgewick of Stockbridge, heir to the Berkshire Court tradition, emerged the winner in an election that turned on two basic factors. First, Sedgewick outlasted his two competitors in Berkshire County, William Whiting of Great Barrington and Thompson Skinner of Williamstown, and gradually attracted a growing proportion of votes in Constitutionalist towns in central and north Berkshire, towns that would be staunchly Republican in the years to come. Second, old Hampshire County, with its long history and double Berkshire's population, failed to produce a viable candidate. Sedgewick won most of Hampshire's old valley towns, but once again the Constitutionalist towns of the western hills provided the critical edge in a very tight election. William Lyman of Springfield, a colonel in the government forces in 1787, was the improbable favorite of the Regulator upcountry. The result was

---

[61] [Sylvester, ed.], *Connecticut Valley in Massachusetts.* 496-497, 501, 505; *Hampshire Gaz.*. Nov. 15, 1786; Judd MSS, Misc., 8: 71, Forbes Library, Northampton; *The Laws of the Commonwealth of Massachusetts. Passed from the Year 1780 to the End of the Year 1800 . . .* (Boston, 1801), I, 383-385; *History and Genealogy of the Families of Chesterfield. Massachusetts. 1762-1962* (Chesterfield, Mass. [1962]), 56-57. The 11th Federalist town in the "western hills," Westfield, is not included in this discussion because, even though it was not adjacent to the river, it was an old town, settled in the 1660s.

the supreme irony of an arch-Federalist representing the two most turbulent counties in Revolutionary America.[62]

But it was an irony shaped by the two counties' revolutionary settlements. There was no Popular tradition in the western counties, and thus no Jonathan Grout could emerge to dominate the field. Both counties had entered the Revolutionary era saddled with an entrenched Court party elite, but Berkshire had gone through a dramatic and traumatic transformation. The Constitutionalist gentry had defeated the old Court party elite from which Sedgewick emerged; they had then closed ranks to stand against the threat of anarchy from below. Sedgewick provided a useful haven for Berkshire's friends of order, but the future would lie with the liberalism that flowed from the Constitutionalists' settlement of the revolution—a Jeffersonian and Jacksonian Democracy that ultimately would absorb even Sedgewick's son.[63] Old Hampshire's failure to produce a viable candidate points again to the faltering revolutionary settlement in that county. Attempting to rule in the style of the River Gods, the county leaders had alienated wide stretches of the upland countryside. Hampshire was still a "valley of discord," still racked by "divisions throughout the whole."[64]

The interweaving of local circumstance and national revolutionary process outlined here was by no means unique to western Massachusetts. The history of the confederated states in the 1770s and 1780s was a compound of hundreds of such dramas, as the workings of revolutionary settlements in neighborhoods, towns, and counties established the ground for a decision on the final national settlement of 1787-1788. Some of the more critical of these local dramas are well known. As Staughton Lynd outlined a generation ago, four critical votes for the razor-thin (thirty to twenty-seven) ratification of the federal Constitution in New York State were cast by delegates from the freeholding sections of Dutchess County, popular whig leaders who had played a mediating role between the opposing coalitions of a conservative Livingston faction and the former tenants of dispossessed tory landlords.[65] In Virginia, Baptist insurgency against the establishment, culminating in the disestablishment of the Anglican church in 1785 and a powerful revival in 1787-1789, decisively

[62] Analysis of election returns in Jensen and Becker, eds., *First Federal Elections*. 620-623, 673-675, 691-694, 705-707, 732-735.

[63] Thomas Lawrence Davis, "Aristocrats and Jacobins in Country Towns: Party Formation in Berkshire County, Massachusetts (1775-1816)" (Ph.D. diss., Boston University, 1975); Marvin Meyers, *The Jacksonian Persuasion: Politics and Belief* (Stanford, Calif., 1957), 163-184. Berkshire Co. Jeffersonianism epitomized that described in Joyce Appleby, *Capitalism and a New Social Order: The Republican Vision of the 1790s* (New York, 1984).

[64] Paul R. Lucas, *Valley of Discord: Church and Society along the Connecticut River. 1636-1725* (Hanover, N.H., 1976); Nobles, *Divisions throughout the Whole*.

[65] Staughton Lynd, "Who Should Rule at Home? Dutchess County, New York, in the American Revolution," *WMQ*. 3d Ser., XVIII (1961), 330-359.

shaped the call for a federal Bill of Rights. In the same years the county courts in Virginia, long a bastion of traditional gentry authority, were reformed by the legislature under the leadership of James Madison. In Orange County, Madison's long-term support of dissenters' rights must have played an important role in his election to the ratifying convention; it certainly was critical to his election to the first United States Congress.[66] If Virginia saw a negotiated revolutionary settlement and relatively little civil violence in the 1780s, Pennsylvania's oddly convulsive constitutional history contributed to its western counties' challenge to the national constitutional settlement in the Whiskey Rebellion of 1793-1794. The rapidity with which the Federalists moved on the Constitution sparked a riot in Carlisle and provoked western Antifederalists to meet in convention in Harrisburg to protest the powers of new federal inferior courts. In Westmoreland County a committee of correspondence mobilized sentiment against the Constitution; five years later, men throughout Westmoreland and neighboring Washington counties rose against the new government's excise and the authority of its distant courts.[67]

The unique element in western Massachusetts's passage through the revolutionary process was the degree to which the settlement of state and county institutions was challenged by civil disorder in the 1780s. Certainly, economic conflict shaped this political crisis. But mobilization in legislature, convention, regulation, and election was powerfully conditioned by the specific political and institutional histories of the western counties. These histories, compounded of provincial traditions, Revolutionary beginnings, and revolutionary settlements, shaped the public arenas in which people engaged in political discourse and action. These public arenas, which determined the circumstances of everyday economic life, were contested territories, but contested in very different ways. In each county a different history shaped a different mosaic of relations among placeholders, legislators, convention delegates, local notables of town and neighborhood, and ordinary householders—a mosaic that responded in quite different ways to the growing pressure of public and private debt. In Berkshire, a fragile settlement based on liberal Lockean

[66] Isaac, *Transformation of Virginia*. 273-295; A. G. Roeber, *Faithful Magistrates and Republican Lawyers. Creators of Virginia Legal Culture. 1680-1810* (Chapel Hill, N.C., 1981), 182-202; Wesley M. Gewehr, *The Great Awakening in Virginia. 1740-1790* (Durham, N.C., 1930), 173-177, 189, 194, 203-209; Richard R. Beeman, *The Old Dominion and the New Nation. 1788-1801* (Lexington, Ky., 1972), 65-66; Robert Allen Rutland, *James Madison: The Founding Father* (New York, 1987), 34-35, 47-48.

[67] Jackson Turner Main, *The Antifederalists: Critics of the Constitution. 1781-1788* (Chapel Hill, N.C., 1961), 188-189; Thomas P. Slaughter, *The Whiskey Rebellion: Frontier Epilogue to the American Revolution* (New York, 1986), 72-74, 169-171, 187; Richard A. Ifft, "Treason in the Early Republic: The Federal Courts, Popular Protest, and Federalism during the Whiskey Insurrection," in Steven R. Boyd, ed., *The Whiskey Rebellion: Past and Present Perspectives* (Westport, Conn., 1985), 165-182.

principles was shattered; in Worcester, an ongoing process of communication within a well-established political tradition mitigated the crisis; in
Hampshire, the failure of elites to accommodate popular expectations for
revolutionary change brought a collapse of institutional legitimacy. Local
men, responding to popular grievances, mobilized in a manner that
challenged the sovereign power of the new state. As nowhere else in the
newly sovereign states in the 1780s, revolutionary expectations in Hampshire County clashed with persistent elite formations. But everywhere in
these newly sovereign states, local histories of conflict and accommodation, flowing from varying compounds of political culture and structural
circumstance, linked locality to the national revolutionary settlement.

THE REHABILITATION OF LOYALISTS
IN CONNECTICUT

OSCAR ZEICHNER

THE social composition of the loyalist class in Connecticut during the Revolution was in general similar to that in the other colonies. Many of its members were Anglicans who during the war suffered because of their religious allegiance. The correspondence of Episcopalian ministers in Connecticut with their friends in England contains numerous indications of their active sympathy with and support of the royal government, combined with severe indictments of the motives that allegedly inspired the American cause. They charged that they were persecuted merely because "of their attachment to their Church and King," as a result of which many of them were forced to take refuge at New York or in Canada, while others entered the army "that they might contribute their aid for the recovery of the King's rights."[1] The loyalist clergy, fully realizing the influence of the pulpit in molding opinion, urged upon their parishioners the necessity of maintaining peaceful relations with the mother country and remaining faithful subjects of the sovereign. All the evidence, in fact, tends to support the assertion of Ezra Stiles that the New England Episcopalians were among the most zealous defenders of the Crown.[2]

It should also be recognized that the conservative and prosperous elements in the province responded to the forces that led the same groups elsewhere to uphold the British cause. Conservatism characterized the sections dominated by the successful in politics, business, and religion, while radi-

---

[1] F. L. Hawks and W. S. Perry, *Documentary History of the Protestant Episcopal Church in the United States* (New York, 1864), II, 198–205.

[2] *The Literary Diary of Ezra Stiles*, F. B. Dexter, editor (New York, 1901), III, 151; Beardsley, E. E., *History of the Episcopal Church in Connecticut* (New York, 1869), I, 301, and Chapters 23 and 24.

308

calism developed mostly in those areas where economic and social unrest prevailed. Gipson, in his study of Jared Ingersoll, has observed that in most communities there was, in the fifteen years preceding the outbreak of the Revolution, a very close relationship between the existence of large debtor classes and the development of radical sentiment.[3] It was natural, on the other hand, for the conservatives, whose high rank in society had already been secured, to denounce and oppose those movements that seemed to be directed against the social order, and thus at their own privileged position in it.[4] The wealthy and established elements in the community became loyalists because they feared the unsettling influence of a resort to arms upon the political and social order. The native aristocracy of culture, wealth, religion, and politics was naturally Tory.

All estimates of the number of loyalists in Connecticut agree that in 1774 it comprised about 2,000 out of a male population of 25,000. A large number of these lived in the western towns, which had on many other issues taken a more conservative stand than the eastern half. During the war, many sought safety within the British lines, and after its conclusion others left their homes for England or the British provinces. Exact information on the number of those who fled has never been secured, but estimates based on scanty evidence place the total number who remained in the State at 1,000, and of those who fled, at the same figure.[5]

---

[3] L. H. Gipson, *Jared Ingersoll, A Study in American Loyalism in Relation to British Colonial Government* (New Haven, 1920), 252, Note 4.

[4] E. A. Bailey, *Influences toward Radicalism in Connecticut, 1754-1775* (Northampton, 1920), 242-243; see also F. B. Dexter, "Notes on Some of the New Haven Loyalists," in *Miscellaneous Historical Papers*, 335; and E. B. Huntington, *History of Stamford* (Stamford, 1868), 220-221.

[5] For information on the number of loyalists in Connecticut and their geographical distribution, see G. A. Gilbert, "The Connecticut Loyalists," in the *American Historical Review*, IV (1899), 278; Bailey, *Influences toward Radicalism in Connecticut*, 244-246; W. H. Siebert, "Refugee Loyalists of Connecticut," in *Transactions of the Royal Society of Canada*, Series III, x,

During the course of the war, the attitude of the state legislature toward the Tories changed from time to time, with the varying fortunes of the opposing forces. When prospects of military success appeared dim, and the activities of the loyalists took on a serious character, legislation to restrict or prohibit these activities was enacted; but when the danger from such sources lessened, the policy of restriction was relaxed and the loyalists were offered the opportunity to escape punishment by joining the American ranks and taking the oath of allegiance. No loyalist was at any time attainted or proscribed, although general confiscation measures were passed. In general the policy of the State was characterized by a willingness to forgive and forget.[6]

As a result of these changing attitudes and the opportunities they afforded to those who might benefit by a politic reversal of standards, many persons shifted from one side to the other during the course of the war. As early as 1774, for example, and during the next few years, numerous cases of political conversion occurred. In 1777 many acknowledged

Section II, 92; and Lorenzo Sabine, *Biographical Sketches of Loyalists in the American Revolution* (Boston, 1864), I, 27.

  [6] *The Public Records of the State of Connecticut with the Journal of the Council of Safety, 1776–1781,* C. J. Hoadly, editor (Hartford, 1894–1922), I, 8, 27–28, 228–229, and 412–413; II, 9, 280, and 386–387; III, 234–235, and 307–309.

  There is no comprehensive treatment of the loyalists who remained in the United States after the establishment of American independence. Whatever analyses exist are sketchy and lack insight. In the conclusion of his volume *The Colonial Merchants and the American Revolution* (New York, 1918), A. M. Schlesinger seemed to touch upon the problem when he wrote, "In the troubled years that followed 1783 the merchants of the country regardless of their antecedents drew together in an effort to found a government which would safeguard the interests of their class." Although this statement literally refers to the role played by the merchants in framing the Constitution, it also reveals the fundamental economic and political unity of the merchants, whether formerly loyalist or Whig, as opposed to the radicals, in the period 1783–1789. J. B. McMaster, in his first volume of the *History of the People of the United States* (New York, 1931), 108–123, discusses the loyalist question, but his treatment is incomplete and seriously underestimates the efforts made by conservative Whigs on behalf of the Tories. Connecticut is mentioned only twice, once in reference to Stamford (Page 116), and once to New Haven (Page 118).

and suspected Tories took advantage of a liberal statute to renounce allegiance to the British crown and declare their support of the American cause. Although this liberality was not constantly maintained after 1777, it was not uncommon for loyalists to repent their past and regain the good graces of the Whigs.[7] This practice became more frequent when the success of the American armies made it appear certain that the states would win the war.

The middle-of-the-road course followed by Connecticut during the war and its willingness to pardon those who had adhered to the royal cause foreshadowed the future. Once independence had been secured, the fundamental differences between conservative and radical Whigs divided them just as they had in the period before the outbreak of the Revolution. The conservative Whigs were not natural allies of the people who had composed the Sons of Liberty or who had pressed the formation of the revolutionary committees; they had been temporarily forced into the ranks of the radicals by British imperial policy; but conservative "families ... who joined the patriot cause abandoned none of their conservative principles."[8] With the end of the war in 1783, these principles reasserted themselves in a split between moderate and radical Whigs over the policy to be followed towards the loyalists. The conservative Whigs, in general, urged a speedy reconciliation; the radicals strongly protested against the return of the Tories and sought to prevent those who had fled to or remained within the British lines from re-entering the State.

The spark that set the fire raging was struck even before the war had ended. In the January, 1783, session of the legis-

---

[7] E. Peck, "The Loyalists of Connecticut," in *Publications of the Tercentenary Commission of the State of Connecticut* (New Haven, 1934), 21–22; Gilbert, "The Connecticut Loyalists," 288–290; J. Shepard, "The Tories of Connecticut," in *The Connecticut Quarterly*, IV, 146.

[8] S. E. Morison, *Life and Letters of Harrison Gray Otis* (Boston, 1913), I, 49.

lature, the petition of Richard Smith praying for permission to reside in Connecticut was considered, and after it had listened to "the Sentiments of Several Gentlemen, pro and con," the General Assembly voted in the affirmative to allow Smith to reside and bring his goods into Connecticut.[9] Smith was a merchant, a former resident of Massachusetts, and had been proscribed as a loyalist by the latter state. Immediately a heated controversy developed. Protests against the action of the legislature poured in from residents in Connecticut and from radicals in other parts of New England. At the end of January some New London citizens set forth the reasons for their disapproval, but the House of Representatives refused to reconsider the matter.[10] Letters of criticism and protest were also received from Rhode Island and Massachusetts, and the volume of dissent became so loud that a committee was recommended to answer these letters.[11]

The matter was made more complicated by the capture of Smith's goods by an American privateer. The proscribed Massachusetts loyalist had placed his effects upon the sloop *Polly*, which had then proceeded to sail for Connecticut. While it was cruising on Long Island Sound, six miles from the shores of that state, according to the affidavit of the outfitters of the privateer, the *Polly* was captured, on February 1, 1783, by the *Hampton Packet*, a ship commissioned by

---

[9] *Journal of the Connecticut House of Representatives*, January 14 and 15, 1783.

[10] It is interesting to notice that the objections of the New Londoners were especially directed against the admission of Smith's goods into the town. *Journal of the Connecticut House of Representatives*, February 3, 1783.

[11] *Connecticut Archives*, XXIV, Item Number 240b. All citations from the *Connecticut Archives* in this paper refer to the Revolutionary Series. At a town meeting held on March 3, 1783, the residents of Cheshire strongly criticized the action of the General Assembly. Their resolution noted for especial censure that the former refugee would be allowed to collect his debts due before the war, and in effect, to import British goods into the State. The citizens of the town thereupon agreed to have no relations with Smith and voted to continue to regard him as "an enemy to the Rights of American Freedom," despite the action of the legislature. *Boston Gazette and Country Journal*, March 31, 1783.

Congress. Since the capture had taken place outside the jurisdiction of Connecticut, the law of that state protecting Smith's property was ignored, and the vessel taken to Rhode Island. Smith, however, did not acquiesce complacently in the capture of his property. A brigantine was fitted out, and after a series of minor adventures the sloop was recaptured by Smith, who succeeded in getting his goods into New London. But this did not end the controversy. The backers of the privateer applied to the governor of Rhode Island, who in turn asked Governor Trumbull, of Connecticut, to have the *Polly* and its cargo returned to the former state, where the capture might undergo a trial. This request was refused, as was a later petition to Governor Trumbull for permission to examine the cargo of the sloop.[12] The publication of the complaint of the privateer's outfitters, which charged that Governor Trumbull was using the authority of his position to protect Smith, an "open enemy of the State of Massachusetts Bay," was the starting point of a series of arguments on the Tory problem.[13] Sides were taken, pens were inked, and for the next few months the loyalist question was intimately bound up with the Smith case.

At first the dispute was conducted on the narrow legal principles involved, namely whether the jurisdiction of the laws of Connecticut applied to those of its citizens who were outside the boundaries of the State, and if so, whether it conflicted with the broader jurisdiction of the Congress, which was still at war, and which had commissioned the privateer.[14] But the debates were not long confined to an interpretation of the law. On April 25, there appeared in the *Connecticut Gazette* the argument of a "Constitutional Whig," who defended the seizure of Smith's goods upon the broader grounds of his political sympathies and affiliations. The Massachusetts

---

[12] It was also charged that the *Polly* had on board a cargo of British goods.
[13] *Connecticut Gazette*, March 28, 1783.
[14] *Connecticut Gazette*, April 4, 1783; April 18, 1783.

law of proscription under which Smith had been banished was quoted, and then a direct appeal was made to anti-loyalist sentiment in Connecticut. The writer declared,

Here you see the light in which Mr. Smith was viewed in the State where he had been an inhabitant, and where his character must be supposed to be better known than it could be in this State. And here you also see the spirit of that State respecting the admission of our absentees into that State, and consequently what they have a right to expect from us with regard to theirs.[15]

Once the loyalist controversy escaped the legal issues arising from the Smith incident, it for the most part remained clear of them.[16] Broader principles were invoked, and the scope of the dispute was widened to embrace the whole Tory problem in Connecticut. A frank plea to the citizens of the State to forget past differences was combined with a bitter attack upon radical sentiment, in the contentions of "A Spectator," who described the Massachusetts act of proscription and banishment as "impolitic, unjust, and cruel." His argument tended to ignore the political reasons for the law and dwelt at length upon the fact that many "good" inhabitants had been included in its provisions of exclusion. It also charged that a large number of banished Tories had not deserved the harsh punishment that they had suffered, and warned that an adoption of the policy of the radicals would result in sacrificing the public welfare to satisfy the selfish interests of merely a few. In order to forestall any future criticism of his reasoning as unjust or selfish, "Spectator" modestly identified his motives and objectives with "that of the wise and good in all ages."[17]

---

[15] *Connecticut Gazette*, April 25, 1783. All participants in the newspaper debate were careful to conceal their real identity under pseudonyms.

[16] See, however, the argument of "A Constitutional Whig" in the *Connecticut Gazette*, May 9, 1783, which attempts to analyze the legal aspects of the question.

[17] *Connecticut Gazette*, May 9, 1783.

The debate took on added virulence from the fact that at the very same time the state legislature was considering what position it should adopt towards those loyalists who, now that the war was over, were returning to Connecticut. On January 15, 1783, the town of Norwalk had protested against the return of the loyalists and had petitioned the General Assembly to take all effective measures to prevent such a return.[18] The legislature was forced to act, and in the same report that recommended the establishment of a committee to consider the letters of protest from Massachusetts and Rhode Island respecting Richard Smith, it advised the appointment of another to consider what measures should be adopted to prohibit the return and residence within Connecticut of all those who had voluntarily remained with the British during the late war.[19] The radicals apparently controlled the committee, for no recommendation was made to consider whether former loyalists should be allowed to return or not. It seemed to be agreed that they were to be excluded; the question was how this objective could best be achieved.

As a result of the recommendation, a committee was set up which reported back to the House at the end of January. This report marks the high point of anti-loyalist sentiment in the legislature. The committee declared that all inhabitants of the United States who had joined or assisted the British or who had voluntarily remained under their jurisdiction during the war had thereby lost all their rights to the privileges of the State and therefore should not be allowed to return and reside in it. In order to make this prohibition effective, the committee report provided that those loyalists who returned to the State should be sent back to areas under the control of

---

[18] *Connecticut Archives*, XXVI, Item Number 247, a, b, c, and d.

[19] *Connecticut Archives*, XXIV, Item Number 240b. Those loyalists who were able to secure the approval of the state to which they had originally belonged were to be excepted from these measures.

Great Britain. Those who returned after they had thus been sent back were to be liable to be whipped with not less than ten nor more than twenty strokes, this punishment to be repeated once a month as long as they remained in the State. Former Tories who were able to secure the permission of the civil authority and to provide satisfactory assurance of their good behavior were to be allowed to stay in the State until the General Assembly had judged their case. But the committee intended to go no further in restoring the privileges of citizenship to the loyalists than to permit their return under these conditions, for it urged that all Tories who succeeded in securing the right to remain in Connecticut be prohibited from voting or holding any public office for a period of seven years. Nor were they to be allowed to secure these rights even after seven years had passed, without the consent of three-fourths of the inhabitants of the town in which they resided.[20]

Although this report was made in January, no action was taken, and consideration of it was deferred to the May session of the legislature.[21] In the meantime the controversy in the Smith case had placed the loyalist issue before those people of the State who read the *Connecticut Gazette*.[22] The dissatisfaction caused by his admission to citizenship, and the fear that returning loyalists might secure important political positions led a Whig writer to caution voters eager to remove legislators who had favored him against electing others who might admit all loyalists. He advised the citizens to consider carefully the political character of every candidate, and to elect none but real Whigs, since it seemed that the combined forces of the Tories and their allies were mak-

---

[20] The last few provisions were not to apply to those who had been or might be enfranchised by special act of the legislature.

[21] *Connecticut Archives*, XXVI, Item Number 248.

[22] It is interesting to note that the other Connecticut newspapers devoted practically no space to the Smith incident.

ing strenuous efforts to control the next General Assembly.[23] A similar warning appeared in the *Gazette* three days later, which advised the voters to beware of the "insidious designs" of the Tories, who, now that they had failed to win the war, were endeavoring to secure control of the political machinery of the State.[24]

The most important arguments, so far as they were intended to influence the legislature, were presented in May, when the General Assembly met to consider, among other matters, what action it would take with respect to the loyalists.[25] On May 16, 1783, there appeared in the New London paper under the pseudonym "Anonymous" an ironic analysis of the reasons advanced by those who urged that the loyalists should be readmitted. The article embodied the ideas and sympathies of a large number of the radical farmers in all the states in its distrust of commercial wealth and its amenities, and the firm feeling that former loyalists did not belong in a political democracy. Those who advocated a general admission of the Tories were criticized for placing the welfare of Connecticut, assuming that the Tories would become an asset to the State, above that of the general welfare of the United States, and were warned that their policy ran directly counter to the "Laws and Interests of all the confederate States." The article was concluded with a thinly veiled invitation to the legislature to ignore the expected recommendation of Congress in behalf of the loyalists.[26]

This was answered two weeks later by "A Friend to Prudence," who defended an admission of the Tories in the same ironic style that his radical opponent had used to condemn it. Whereas the Whig argument had been based upon fear of

---

[23] *Connecticut Courant*, April 1, 1783, argument of "A Freeman."
[24] "Philanthropus" in the *Connecticut Gazette*, April 4, 1783.
[25] The position of "A Spectator" has already been discussed. See above, Page 314.
[26] *Connecticut Gazette*, May 16, 1783.

and hostility to wealthy loyalist merchants, the argument
of the conservatives stressed the economic benefits to be derived from admitting prosperous Tories into the State. The
reasons specifically advanced to support the pro-loyalist position were that Connecticut needed more inhabitants, and
that it would be advantageous to admit the loyalists, who by
their European connections could increase the trading importance of the State.[27] Nor would an increase in the number
of merchants endanger the economic prosperity of the Whig
traders; in fact, it would add to the wealth of the community,
and since the Connecticut farmer would be assured of a ready
and accessible market, the rural areas would benefit by the
higher prices that would be commanded for their produce.
Thus Connecticut would draw the trade of her country towns
to her own ports, which would become thriving and prosperous communities, while at the same time the farmer would
profit from an enlarged market and improved transportation
facilities.[28]

In the following week this argument was repeated in greater detail by the same correspondent, who emphasized again
the economic benefits that a large and wealthy merchant class
would bring to the State.[29] He minimized the fears of those

---

[27] At this point the writer accused those who were hostile to the loyalists
of being motivated in their attitude by the desire to possess and ensure their
possession of confiscated loyalist estates.

[28] "A Friend to Prudence," *Connecticut Gazette*, May 30, 1783.

[29] The following excerpt from the writer's ironic argument indicates
clearly the economic conditions which, it was maintained, an admission of
the loyalists would remove: "This State will never have much to export—we
have more vessels and money than we want—one merchant in each sea-port
town with a few under-strappers and shop keepers under his sovereign command is more than sufficient to engross all the trade of Connecticut together
with that of all the inland parts of the neighboring States—we have no fondness for the customs or manufactures of any other country, for we always
manufacture more of every kind of goods than we consume—corn stalks afford
us more rum and molasses than we use, we have therefore no occasion to
trade to the West Indies. . . . This State needs no capital; we should be much
more wealthy if Boston, New York, Newport, and Providence had all our
trade. Who does not know that it is much easier and cheaper to carry our
produce 100 or 200 miles, and to fetch what we want from thence, than to be

who held that if the loyalists were readmitted they might capture political control, but expounded on the dangerous repercussions a harsh anti-loyalist program would have on the attitude of foreign powers, especially Great Britain, toward this country.[30] On the same day there appeared an even more outspoken defense of the economic motives involved in the loyalist issue than had been presented by other pro-loyalist sympathizers. In very direct language the writer declared that if "the Massachusetts State have a sovereign right to proscribe for disobedience or dislike 1,000 of their most opulent inhabitants, Connecticut has the same sovereign right to declare the same persons free citizens of this State. . . ."[31]

By this time, however, the policy of Connecticut had already been decided. The radical recommendations of the committee that had advised enactment of a severe anti-loyalist law have been described above.[32] The bill also empowered town authorities to take all necessary measures to carry these provisions into execution.[33] Although this bill was much more moderate than that which had been proposed in January, 1783, it was defeated when it reached the lower house in May. Taking advantage of the failure of the radicals to have their program adopted, the legislature, apparently in the control of the conservatives, approved the report of a committee that had been set up to consider what laws ought to be changed or repealed. This report recommended the abrogation of most of the wartime loyalist legislation.[34] Both houses of the General

---

put to the intolerable hardship of going 10 or 20 miles with our produce . . . our legislature ought to discourage trade as much as possible."

[30] Another war with Great Britain was also held forth as a possibility. *Connecticut Gazette*, June 6, 1783.

[31] *Connecticut Gazette*, June 6, 1783.

[32] See above, Pages 315–316.

[33] *Connecticut Archives*, XXVI, Item Number 291. The archives, unfortunately, do not specify the dates of submission and rejection, nor do they indicate how the votes were given on the measure.

[34] *Connecticut Archives*, XXIV, Item Number 258. In all probability most

Court asked that a committee be established to draw up the bill or bills necessary to effect the recommendations, and in the same month that the radicals lost, the conservatives won. The most important acts that had been directed against the Tories during the war with Great Britain were now repealed, and no other discriminatory legislation was enacted in their stead.[36] Final state action on the loyalist question was taken in 1787, when the legislature, although recognizing that the problem had long been solved, passed an act, in accordance with a recommendation of Congress, repealing all legislation repugnant to the peace treaty of 1783.[37]

Another example of the unwillingness of the State to adopt a hostile position toward the former Tories may be seen in the very sympathetic attitude taken by the General Assembly toward those loyalists who were members of the Anglican Church. Although the followers of the latter institution had played a very active role in furthering the British cause in Connecticut during the war, once the conflict was ended, the

---

of the substantial men in Connecticut were in favor of admitting the loyalists under no disabilities. For example, on April 23, 1783, Jonathan Trumbull, Jr., wrote to his father, the governor of Connecticut: "Our country will want inhabitants; the refugees, a few characters excepted, might perhaps with proper policy become very good citizens of the United States when forsaken by their British friends." *Collections*, Massachusetts Historical Society, Seventh Series, "The Trumbull Papers" (New Haven, 1902), III, 414. Benjamin Tallmadge expressed the same opinions in a letter to Barnabas Deane, dated May 13, 1783. *Collections*, Connecticut Historical Society, XXII, "The Deane Papers" (Hartford, 1930), 178.

[36] It should be noticed, however, that the severe confiscation acts of 1778 and 1781 were not recommended for repeal, nor were they abrogated until 1787. Moreover, the legislature did not see fit to rescind the moderate act of October, 1777, despite the recommendation of the committee to do so. *Acts and Laws of Connecticut*, May, 1783. In an effort to placate those who would now be forced to pay back debts due to loyalists, the state government passed a law allowing debtors to plead any special matter that might help abate either the principal or interest of their debt. The courts were required to decide cases according to the rules of equity, and to consider the special matter pleaded by defendants in making their decisions. *Acts and Laws of Connecticut*, May, 1784.

[37] *Acts and Laws of Connecticut*, 1787.

past seemed to have been forgotten.[38] When Dr. Samuel Seabury, who had very definitely placed himself on the loyalist side during the Revolution, was attempting to secure consecration as Bishop of Connecticut from the English bishops, the latter objected that Connecticut might consider it an improper interference and refuse to accept him. Seabury thereupon advised the Connecticut clergy to approach the legislature and sound out the members on the matter. Many of the more important members of both branches of the General Assembly were consulted for their opinions, which were given "with a degree of attention and candour beyond ... expectation." To the further surprise of the clergymen, it was found that these opinions apparently coincided with their own with respect to "the need, the propriety, or the impropriety of [applying] for the admission of a Bishop into the State."[39]

The attitude of some of the Connecticut towns, however, differed greatly from that assumed by the state government. In the local communities the radicals were able to make their influence felt, and it is by the town resolutions that one can estimate the strength of anti-loyalist sentiment.[40] Refusing to wait for the State to define its position on the Tory question, many of the towns drew up regulations and set up committees to keep loyalists without their limits and to expel those who returned despite the law that banned them. On April 10, 1783, the town meeting of Fairfield decided to prohibit all

[38] Those loyalists of Anglican persuasion who were forced to leave Connecticut after 1783 did not do so because of state action, but because of hostile local action.

[39] Perry and Hawks, *Documentary History of the Episcopal Church*, II, 224–225.

[40] A complete discussion of this subject would necessitate a thorough analysis of the local town records during the years 1783–1789. Unfortunately, the records have not been collected, but remain in the files of the town halls, if they have not in the meantime been destroyed. The writer intends to consult these records in a larger work on the post-war loyalist problem in the United States.

those who had gone over to the British from returning to and residing in the town, and set up a committee to remove all such persons who were already in Fairfield or might enter it in the future.[41] A month and a half earlier the town meeting at Norwalk had adopted a similar resolution, and a committee of eight had been created to assist the selectmen and other authorities in seeing that the law was properly carried into effect, and to inform the town officials of the return of former loyalists.[42] When the Boston *Continental Journal* complained that a proscribed loyalist clergyman had taken refuge in Middletown, Connecticut, the Committee of Inspection of the town reassured the printer of the paper that the "Committee have been very vigilant in taking up that class of gentry."[43] While the state legislature was refusing to take action against the loyalists, the Committee of Safety and Inspection of Norwich warned all those who had voluntarily left Connecticut or any of the United States during the war to remain clear of the town. The loyalists were also warned that if they were found inside the town limits they would immediately be deported to some region under the jurisdiction of Great Britain. This restriction was to remain in effect until such time as Congress or the legislatures of the several states decided upon a policy with respect to the loyalists.[44] In town meeting held on April 4, 1783, the residents of Stratford expressed their disgust and alarm at seeing "whole shoals" of Tories crossing the Sound from Long Island to reside in the towns of Connecticut, and pledged themselves to "drive off and expel all such persons who shall make the attempt" to return to Stratford. A loyalist who had dared to resettle in that town was placed under guard to be expelled

---

[41] The records of the town meeting are quoted in E. H. Schenck, *The History of Fairfield County, 1700–1800* (New York, 1905), II, 423–424.

[42] *The Ancient Historical Records of Norwalk, Connecticut*, E. Hall, compiler (Norwalk, 1847), 144–145.

[43] *Connecticut Courant*, February 4, 1783.

[44] *Connecticut Gazette*, June 6, 1783.

immediately, and a committee was appointed to prevent the return of other Tories. On April 7, several loyalists who had ventured to come back were cited to appear before the town meeting, which, after having heard each case, ordered all of them to return to British territory.[45] After issuing a declaration similar to the one adopted by Norwich, Windham set up a Committee of Safety and Inspection on June 9, 1783, to carry out a resolution prohibiting loyalists who had left the State from returning to the town.[46] In December, 1783, the selectmen of Stamford were directed by the town meeting to enforce rigorously the law prohibiting all loyalists and all those who during the war had placed themselves under British protection from remaining in or entering the town of Stamford.[47]

But even the radicalism that succeeded in forcing the towns to adopt anti-loyalist resolutions seemed, after a while, to relax of its own volition, or to have been curbed by the more moderate elements. The Norwalk town meeting, held on the last Monday in December, 1783, decided to allow the selectmen and committee of loyalist inspection to act at their discretion in all cases concerning the loyalists, notwithstanding any former votes or resolutions.[48] In Fairfield, opposition sentiment gradually dissipated, and, according to the town historian, many former Tories returned to become citizens of the town and state.[49] Similar developments took place in Stamford, while in Guilford it was voted on April 12, 1790, to strike from the records the story of all activities directed against the Tories.[50] In Windham, however, the spirit of an-

---

[45] *Connecticut Journal*, April 17, 1783; *The Freeman's Journal*, April 30, 1783.

[46] *Connecticut Gazette*, June 20, 1783; E. D. Larned, *History of Windham* (Worcester, 1880), II, 205–206.

[47] E. B. Huntington, *History of Stamford*, 231.

[48] Hall, *Ancient Historical Records of Norwalk*, 145.

[49] Schenck, *History of Fairfield County*, II, 424.

[50] Huntington, *History of Stamford*, 259; B. C. Steiner, *A History of the Original Town of Guilford* (Baltimore, 1897), 442–443.

tagonism and enmity toward the former loyalists continued to prevail, and, as late as 1785, the town resolved that a committee of inspection be appointed to see that all loyalists and those who had left the town since the outbreak of the war be prohibited from re-entering it.[51]

Although in the absence of definite information the motives that influenced these towns to change their policies have to be guessed at, it can be shown definitely that in New Haven economic considerations were the chief factors that determined the shift with respect to the loyalists. In March, 1783, a town meeting instructed its representatives in the legislature to prevent the return of all those who had deserted the patriot cause and joined the British.[52] Immediately, however, a movement began in the town, led by those who desired to see New Haven become a powerful commercial city, to raise the ban on the loyalists, especially on those who were wealthy enough to be considered commercial assets. On May 1, 1783, Ezra Stiles recorded in his diary that he had on that day been offered "a subscription Paper to invite about 120 Tory Families of the City of New York, of which 40 are Merchants of Property, to come and settle in New Haven." The President of Yale further stated that the Tory merchants offered to "bring Two-Thirds of the Mercantile property of the whole City" into New Haven, and that General Parsons was supposed to have "carried a like subscribed Invitation from the Town of New London."[53]

---

[51] Larned, *History of Windham County*, II, 206.

[52] F. B. Dexter, "New Haven in 1784," in *Miscellaneous Historical Papers*, 131; *Pennsylvania Gazette*, April 23, 1783.

[53] Dexter, *The Literary Diary of Ezra Stiles*, III, 70. The argument heard frequently in New York, that restrictive legislation against the loyalists in that State would drive wealthy merchants from its towns, was answered in an anti-loyalist article written by "Brutus." In it he scoffed at the fear that the State would be depopulated or would lose its most prosperous citizens should it be urged that the rich Tories be banished. "Brutus" did not attach much credence to the argument of those who maintained that wealthy loyalists were being asked to settle in Connecticut and other states. *Connecticut Courant*, May 27, 1783. As late as 1784 those residents of New York City

For a long time the position of Connecticut as a mercantile power had been considered of little significance. Situated between important natural harbors, it had been forced to see its trade flow through the ports of New York, Boston, and Newport. In the 1760's the merchants formed only a small percentage of the total population of the State. Trade was carried on in a narrow area, and New London, which had the best harbor, was but a small town. In 1768 an observer in Connecticut who had been questioned by a London friend as to the possibilities of establishing business relations with the colony replied that "he would not give £800 for the whole Province." After investigating conditions in New Haven and New London, he reported that practically all goods for these towns were received through Boston and New York traders, that there were very few merchants in New Haven and New London, and that almost everybody there was mortgaged to the Boston and New York business men.[54]

With the end of the Revolutionary War, however, Connecticut proposed to end her economic dependence upon other cities and to develop her own seaports into important trading communities.[55] Although Ezra Stiles distrusted the

who feared that wealthy loyalists were being driven out of the State by its anti-Tory policy pointed, as proof of their fears, to a resolution adopted by a group of New Jersey inhabitants, promising that its subscribers would use all their "influence and endeavors to secure peaceable settlements and trade to any merchant or body of merchants, who will retire from New York or any other place and settle in the Jersies." Among the eight reasons offered to justify this invitation, it included the statement that two states, New Hampshire and Connecticut, being in a position similar to New Jersey, had already attempted to profit by inviting wealthy Tories from other states to settle within their areas. *Connecticut Courant*, April 20, 1784.

[54] Quoted in Gipson, *Jared Ingersoll*, 254. The commercial position of New London had been just as bad in 1774. The value of British manufactures, imported chiefly through New York and Boston, was between £150,000 and £160,000 sterling, while the total value of New London's foreign and coastal trade was only £70,000 sterling. As a result many merchants failed and much of their landed property was taken over in payments by New Yorkers. J. W. Barber, *Connecticut Historical Collections* (New Haven, 1849), 285.

[55] When in January, 1784, Hartford, New Haven, New London, Norwich, Wethersfield, and Middletown petitioned the State legislature to be incor-

Tories even though they bore gifts,[56] others did not hesitate to use wealthy loyalists banished or forced to flee from other states as a means of attaining this objective. In order to convince those who might not realize the benefits to be derived from inviting prosperous, conservative Tory merchants to Connecticut, and to New Haven in particular, a campaign was carried on in the press of the State to show the injustice of a policy that would operate against the former Tories, and to expose the base motives that prompted other states to adopt such an unjust policy. It was expected, and correctly, as later events were to prove, that the righteous people of Connecticut would in due time learn the soundness of this policy and adjust their attitude accordingly.

In July, 1783, the *Connecticut Gazette* printed an article by an anonymous contributor which quoted an excerpt from the writings of Abbé Fénélon, entitled "A Mandate ... for Ordaining Prayers for a Peace." Although written seventy-

---

porated with the privileges of cities, the *Norwich Packet* of January 29, 1784, expressed the hope that "at last ... some attention will be paid by the Legislature to the commercial interest of the State." Correspondence from New Haven noted that the citizens of that town were "Determined to depend no longer on other States for the exportation of their staples ... and to strain every nerve and exert every laudable industry to render their new city happy, free, and commercial." *Pennsylvania Gazette*, February 18, 1784. The petitions of New London and New Haven were successful, and an act of the legislature made them free cities and ports for seven years from June 1, 1784. The cities were given the right to regulate the admission of foreigners and citizens of other states, and state citizenship was accorded those who were admitted and who took the oath of allegiance to the State. This provision was apparently intended to include former Tories, since a later clause excluded from the benefits of the act those loyalists who had "been guilty of lawless and unauthorized plundering or murder or who had waged War against the United States of America contrary to the Laws and Usages of civilized nations." The qualifying phrases in this definition of obnoxious Tories could have excluded only a very small number of loyalists from the privileges of the act, as seemed to have been the intention of its framers. These privileges allowed merchants in either city who imported £3,000 in goods or £2,000 in money to be exempt from the taxes on the profits arising from such importation for a period of seven years, and exempted ships used in the European, Asiatic, or African trade four months in one year, from taxes for those years in which they were thus employed. *Connecticut Journal*, June 9, 1784.

[56] *Diary of Ezra Stiles*, III, 70.

five years before and under different circumstances, the excerpt was appropriate to the situation, since it strongly advised its readers not to destroy their former enemies, but to become reconciled with them by a just peace.[57] In the following month the same paper published a criticism of the manner in which the loyalists were treated in New York. This article attributed the rabid anti-loyalist spirit of the Whigs in that state to their mean desire to profit from the confiscaion of Tory estates.[58] In September, 1783, the *Connecticut Journal*, a New Haven paper, described the attitude of the radical Whigs in Dutchess County, New York, as a manifestation of persecution that could be expected only of barbarians. The paper elaborately narrated an incident in that county in which it was alleged that a loyalist had been harshly mishandled.[59] Letters supposedly received from Europe were printed to give semi-official approval of this condemnation of anti-loyalism. On January 7, 1784, for example, an extract of a letter signed by John Adams, Benjamin Franklin, and John Jay, dated September 10, 1783, was given to the New Haven public by the *Journal*. The letter severely criticized the manner in which many of the towns had dealt with the Tories and declared that this unfair treatment had placed the United States in a bad light. It recommended that the article in the peace treaty concerning the Tories be scrupulously performed and fulfilled in good faith, and condemned the radical resolutions of the towns on the subject, the banishment of Tories, and the open hostility displayed in the newspapers and pamphlets as harmful to the best interests of the country and undeserving of the "approbation of disinterested and dispassionate posterity."[60]

---

[57] *Connecticut Gazette*, July 11, 1783.
[58] *Connecticut Gazette*, August 8, 1783.
[59] *Connecticut Journal*, September 24, 1783.
[60] Dexter, "New Haven in 1784." 131; *Connecticut Journal*, January 7, 1784. The letter also appeared in the *Connecticut Gazette*, April 2, 1784.

This skilful propaganda soon brought about the desired results. On March 8, 1784, a New Haven town meeting set up a committee to consider the propriety of admitting former loyalists who were of fair character and would be desirable additions to the community. The committee reported back with extraordinary speed on the same day, and recommended the admission of those Tories who fulfilled the above requirements and who had not "committed unauthorized and lawless plundering and murder."[61] To justify its position, the committee resorted to legal considerations and the ideals of mercy and justice, but it buttressed its defense with the solid opinion that "as this town is most advantageously situated for commerce, having a spacious harbour, surrounded by extensive and fertile country, which is inhabited by an industrious and enterprizing people fully sensible of the advantage of trade, and as the relative and essential importance and consequence of this State depend on the prosperity and extent of its agriculture and commerce . . . in point of real honor and permanent utility the measure proposed will be highly expedient."[62] The other voters at the town meeting approved the committee's recommendation and on that day New Haven allowed the Tories to return to and become residents of the town.[63]

---

[61] This is the same language that was used in the act making New Haven and New London free ports. See above, Note 55.

[62] Dexter, "New Haven in 1784," 130–131. The proceedings of the town meeting are printed in the Connecticut Courant, April 6, 1784, Supplement.

[63] Although Ezra Stiles could not become enthusiastic over the event (Diary, III, 116), the press used it to further its pro-loyalist propaganda. On August 17, 1784, the Connecticut Courant published a letter from a "gentleman in Londonderry" in which the Irishman allegedly wrote to his New Haven friend that he was very much pleased at the admission of the loyalists by that city and that all persons of liberal sentiment were joining with him in applauding the action that it had taken. Noah Webster described the New York loyalists as being persecuted and subjected to wanton insults, and declared that the anti-Tory mob constituted the greatest danger to the State in that it was usurping the authority to administer justice from the hands of the legal magistrates by taking independent action against the loyalists. The leaders of the radical Whigs were dismissed as mere "Fools or Knaves."

Already by February, 1784, the city elections in New Haven had presaged the future influence of the loyalists. The Whig candidate for mayor, Roger Sherman, received 125 votes; the candidate of the conservative Whigs, Thomas Howel, 102; and Thomas Darling, the aspirant supported by allegedly Tory elements, 22. Thus the combined strength of the conservative Whig and loyalist forces was but two votes short of a majority. Stiles also asserted that two of the Aldermen and eight members of the Common Council were former Tories. From these facts the head of Yale College sadly concluded that "The City Politics are founded in an endeavor silently to bring the Tories into an equality and Supremacy among the Whigs."[64]

It may be concluded, therefore, that in Connecticut the problem of the loyalists after 1783 was resolved in their favor shortly after the War of Independence ended. Although the treatment of individual Tories varied, in no case did the state government punish a former loyalist with the same severity that characterized the radical position taken by some of the Connecticut towns.[65] Those loyalists who were forced to leave the State in the early months after the war did not do so because of State action, but because individual towns, of-

---

Connecticut Courant, May 4, 1784. In June, 1784, the South Carolina Whigs were accused of defying the laws and violating the terms of the peace treaty rather than to cease their persecution of the Tories. *Connecticut Courant*, June 8, 1784.

[64] *Diary*, III, 109–112; L. H. Boutell, *The Life of Roger Sherman* (Chicago, 1896), 43.

[65] The case of Andrew Fowler was exceptional. In 1784 the legislature refused to release him from prison until he should have time to move to British territory. *Connecticut Archives*, XXVII, Items Numbers 247–250. At the end of the year, however, Fowler was released and the fines he had paid were remitted to him. Steiner, *History of Guilford*, 443. This instance may be contrasted with the case of George Ross, an avowed New York loyalist, whose petition to remove to and become a citizen of New Haven was approved in October, 1783, by the state legislature. Ross incidentally included in his petition the desirable fact that he possessed a "competent share of property to enable him to be useful to a Commercial People." *Connecticut Archives*, XXVI, Items Number 133 and 134a.

ficially or through the hostility of their inhabitants, refused to allow the Tories to remain and reside in the community.[66] But even the radical temper of the towns subsided or was curbed by the more moderate elements. The natural conservatism of the substantial Whigs, combined with their desire to increase the commercial importance of the State, led them to advocate the repeal of anti-loyalist legislation and uphold the wisdom and expediency of admitting the former Tories. Their policy was quickly accepted. Months before news of the signing of the definitive peace treaty reached the United States, Connecticut removed from the statute books all laws against the loyalists excepting the confiscation measures that had been enacted during the war with England; and in 1787 whatever discriminatory legislation still remained was annulled. Those towns that had adopted resolutions banning the Tories gradually relaxed their restrictions, and soon the loyalists were granted permission to return. In Connecticut the victory of the conservatives over the radicals was complete on the first issue which divided them after independence had been secured.

---

[66] *Norwich Packet,* February 12, 1784; Sabine, *Loyalists in the American Revolution,* I, 224, 255, and 572.

Journal of Interdisciplinary History VI:4 (Spring 1976), 645–677.

Edward Countryman

Consolidating Power in Revolutionary America: The Case of New York, 1775-1783

Between October 2, 1777 and February 7, 1778 the newly founded state assembly of New York took votes on the state supreme court, on prohibiting the sale of scarce grain to customers out of the state, and on an extra-constitutional convention that had seized power in the face of a military crisis in the late autumn of 1777 and that held it until the legislature could reassemble.[1] There is no reason, on the face of it, to expect any relationship among these divisions; none of them was a party issue and none of them was identified with the governor, George Clinton. Yet these votes—there were five in all—formed a single Guttman scale.[2] In other words, voting patterns showed that the votes turned on a single basic issue: the existence and powers of the extra-legal convention and other bodies like it. The problem with the court was the refusal of its judges, named to their posts by an earlier extra-legal convention, to carry out their duties until reappointed constitutionally. The debate over the embargo bill asked whether the assembly should merely continue a prohibition already imposed by the convention or whether it should impose a new one, without mentioning the convention at all. The issue, in short, was legitimacy: should New York's constitutional republican institutions recognize the power that revolutionary bodies had exercised in the state since the collapse of the colonial government? And if they did, would that betoken an abandonment of their own claim to be the sole legitimate political power in the state?

Conventional wisdom says that such a problem should not have existed in revolutionary America. Ever since its French counterpart provided a first basis for comparison, students of the American Revolution have remarked on the ease and smoothness with which that event

Edward Countryman is Lecturer in American History at the University of Warwick, England.

The author would like to thank the following people for aid, encouragement, and criticism: Oskar Anweiler, Hannah Arendt, Rhys Isaac, Michael Kammen, Richard Ryerson, Luke Trainor, Gordon Wood, and Alfred Young. Part of the research for this article was done under a grant from the University of Canterbury, New Zealand.

1 *Journal of the Assembly of the State of New York*, microfilm ed., *Records of the States of the United States*, William Sumner Jenkins (ed.) (Washington, 1949) [hereafter *RSUS*], N.Y. A.1b., Reel 4, Unit 1, 2 October, 1777–7 February, 1778.
2 For the scale see Edward Francis Countryman, "Legislative Government in Revolutionary New York, 1777–1788," Ph.D. diss. (Cornell University, 1971), 257–258.

209

was accomplished. Not for Americans the years or even decades of disorder; not for them the succession of constitutions and provisional governments, the Bonapartes of right and left, the terror and counter-terror that have plagued others seeking to emerge from revolution. On the contrary, effective state governments went into operation at the very moment of independence and, following the current para-digm, when these proved themselves inadequate, a suitable remedy for their ills was found in the Federal Constitution, the unprecedented authority created by that document being built on the solid founda-tion of a desire for authority and order at the state and local levels. Or so it seems from both old and new accounts.[3]

From a theoretical and comparative point of view this would demand explanation, but from the point of view of those five votes it seems that it may not be wholly accurate. In any case, much of the interesting work on revolution in general and on the American Revolution in particular has been concerned with disintegration rather than with re-integration. A decade ago Eckstein could observe that "almost nothing careful and systematic" has been written about "how political legitimacy and social harmony may be restored after violent disruption." Huntington's powerful book has gone a long way toward filling that gap, but the problem of the re-establishment of order is still less thoroughly explored than that of breakdown. The popular nature of the American Revolution, which recent studies have emphasized, makes the problem all the more pressing. As Amann has argued, "If an established government is overthrown by a massive popular uprising, the chances of a revolutionary situation prevailing long after the actual overthrow of the established government are much greater. . . . Mass insurrection shatters the habit of obedience on a large scale and therefore tends to perpetuate revolution after it is 'officially' over." Among the great popular revolutions, only the Russian offers a comparable spectacle of power swiftly being con-solidated and a new order quickly taking hold, and it differed from the American in nearly every other respect.[4]

3 For the most recent statements of this position see Gordon S. Wood, *The Creation of the American Republic, 1776–1787* (Chapel Hill, 1969); Richard D. Brown, *Revolutionary Politics in Massachusetts: The Boston Committee of Correspondence and the Towns, 1772–1774* (Cambridge, Mass., 1970); Pauline Maier, *From Resistance to Revolution: Colonial Radicals and the Development of American Opposition to Britain* (New York, 1972).

4 Harry Eckstein, "On the Etiology of Internal Wars," *History and Theory*, IV (1965), 136; Samuel P. Huntington, *Political Order in Changing Societies* (New Haven, 1968). See also Gordon Wood, "A Note on Mobs in the American Revolution," *William and Mary*

Revolution is perhaps the most complicated concept in the modern historian's vocabulary, and its usage in this article is intentionally limited.[5] The article's concern is with the process of a political revolution, and the most sophisticated thought on how that happens in Western society has come from Lenin and from Huntington and Amann. Lenin argued in *State and Revolution* that the task of the people whom his Bolsheviks sought to lead in 1917 was to smash the institutions and apparatus of the old order, not merely to capture them, and to create something new in their place.[6] Amann and, especially, Huntington have built on that point, both of them seeing as revolutionary a situation in which there is no accepted claimant to political power. One might use the modern metaphor of the "political system" operating, in normal times, on its "environment" and suggest that revolution, by destroying the system, forces the environment itself to make the public decisions and take the public actions that would normally be the task of the system.[7] Actual study of such a case—as in this essay—demonstrates the limitations of the metaphor, for both the "system" and the "environment" are made up of people whose real worldly interests are difficult to accommodate in systemic theory. The difference is more than semantic if we substitute "ruling class" or even "elite" for "system" in our vocabulary. Yet the point will be allowed that there is a difference between non-revolutionary

Quarterly, XXIII (1966), 635–642; Jesse Lemisch, "The American Revolution Seen from the Bottom Up," in Barton J. Bernstein, (ed.), *Towards a New Past: Dissenting Essays in American History* (New York, 1968), 3–45; "Jack Tar in the Street: Merchant Seamen in the Politics of Revolutionary America," *William and Mary Quarterly*, XXV (1968), 371–407; "Listening to the 'Inarticulate': William Widger's Dream and the Loyalties of American Revolutionary Seamen in British Prisons," *Journal of Social History*, III (1969), 1–29; Staughton Lynd, *Anti-Federalism in Dutchess County, New York: A Study of Democracy and Class Conflict in the Revolutionary Era* (Chicago, 1962), and *Class Conflict, Slavery and the United States Constitution, Ten Essays* (Indianapolis, 1967); Peter Amann, "Revolution: A Redefinition," *Political Science Quarterly* LXXVII (1962), 40.

5 For discussions of the concept see Eugene Kamenka, "Revolution—The History of an Idea," in Eugene Kamenka (ed.), *A World in Revolution?* (Canberra, 1970); Isaac Kramnick, "Reflections on Revolution: Definition and Explanation in Recent Scholarship," *History and Theory*, XI (1972), 26–63; Perez Zagorin, "Theories of Revolution in Contemporary Historiography," *Political Science Quarterly*, LXXXVIII (1973), 23–52.

6 V. I. Lenin, *State and Revolution* (Moscow, 1972, orig. ed. 1917); see also notes 5 and 7 above.

7 See David Easton, *A Systems Analysis of Political Life* (New York, 1956); Robert A. Dahl, *Modern Political Analysis* (Englewood Cliffs, 1970). But was not Trotsky speaking of the same thing when he said that "The most indubitable feature of a revolution is the direct interference of the masses in historical events"? Leon Trotsky (trans. Max Eastman), *The History of the Russian Revolution* (London, 1934), 17.

and revolutionary forms of popular political life, between activity in which "the environment" puts pressure on "the system" to act and activity in which "the environment" either opposes the system directly or takes over functions that it would normally exercise. Arendt, one of the most penetrating thinkers of our time, has described the latter situation as one in which public liberty (the "*right* to a *share* in the government*," in Hamilton's phrase) is real and meaningful for vast numbers of people, not simply for the few.[8] It may be because such public liberty is both enjoyable in its own right and an effective means for remedying real social grievances that the consolidation of the power of a post-revolutionary régime is no simple task.

Some studies have directly confronted the problem of how that task was accomplished in the American Revolution. Maier has suggested that in South Carolina debate over direct action by crowds was transmuted into debate over the right of the people to organize politically and participate in governmental decision-making. The Handlins have analyzed the troubled 1780s in Massachusetts in terms of consolidating power, and Daniell's book on New Hampshire, although it stresses internal consensus and suggests an immediate legitimization of the new order, shows in detail the difficulty of achieving stabilization.[9] In both Massachusetts and New Hampshire there was dramatic popular action in the 1780s to draw the historian's attention. In New York, the subject of this essay, the 1780s were relatively tranquil; the years immediately following independence were critical in that state, because the independence crisis brought severe disintegration and internal conflict. The new government had to prove itself even to the patriot population. This essay will show that New York met some of these difficulties with a subtle combination of the carrot and the stick, and that it failed to solve others. Most importantly, it will show that it required a strong demonstration by men in power that they could use their power creatively and positively to curtail

8 Alexander Hamilton, "A Second Letter from Phocion to the Considerate Citizens of New York. Containing Remarks on Mentor's Reply" [1784], *The Papers of Alexander Hamilton*, Harold C. Syrett *et al.* (eds.) (New York, 1962), III, 545; Hannah Arendt, *On Revolution* (London, 1963), *passim*.
9 Pauline Maier, "The Charleston Mob and the Evolution of Popular Politics in Revolutionary South Carolina, 1765–1784," *Perspectives in American History*, IV (1970), 173–196. Oscar Handlin and Mary Flug Handlin, *Commonwealth, A Study of the Role of Government in the American Economy: Massachusetts, 1774–1861* (Cambridge, Mass., 1969, rev. ed.), Chs. 1–2. Jere R. Daniell, *Experiment in Republicanism, New Hampshire Politics and the American Revolution, 1741–1794* (Cambridge, Mass., 1970).

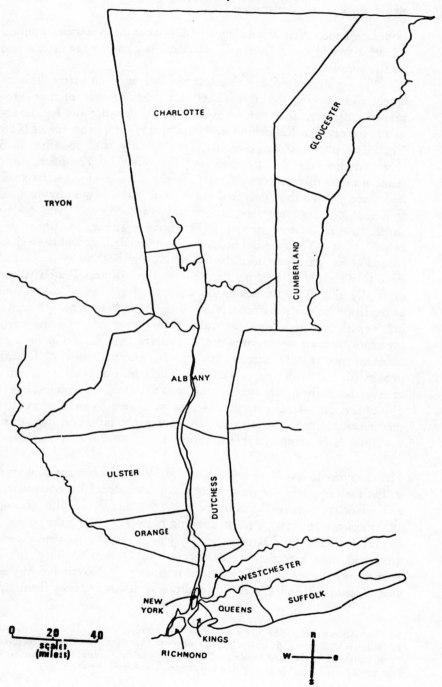

CHARLOTTE

GLOUCESTER

TRYON

CUMBERLAND

ALBANY

ULSTER

DUTCHESS

ORANGE

WESTCHESTER

NEW YORK

SUFFOLK

QUEENS

KINGS

RICHMOND

0   20   40
scale
(miles)

N
W   E
S

213

popular direct action and bring about what most American political scientists would call a "normal" relationship between the system and its environment.

The legitimacy of an order can be challenged on many different levels, and denying the rightfulness of a ruler, or even of a governmental structure, does not necessarily mean denying the legitimacy of the society that lies behind it.[10] But by 1775 the province of New York was under stress politically, ideologically, and socially. Two recent studies, one by Bonomi and the other by Friedman, have demonstrated that in New York City the decade of imperial strife had made politics the "universal topic" and that a new individualistic frame of political reference, a "radical consciousness," was taking shape. British imperialism was, as Friedman suggests, "deeply implicated" in New York's social order and that social order had been challenged in the ten years since the Stamp Act by both urban strife and rural land riots.[11] The events that followed the Boston Tea Party and especially the news of Lexington completed the mobilization and polarization of the province's population. In such an atmosphere the break with Britain meant far more than the eviction of the royal governor and a few customs men. It meant that the declaration of independence would inspire widespread internal dissent, forcing provincial authorities to contend with loyalism as well as internal secessionists in the northeastern counties of the state, and with local, revolutionary extra-legal committees that continued to exist even after the reinstitution of constitutional government. Stabilization demanded widespread, fundamental internal change.

The motives of New York loyalists varied. What is important, however, is that they opposed the movement for independence by both words and collective action. Perhaps the most thoroughly loyalist area in all America was the region surrounding New York City: the counties of Queens, Kings, and Richmond. By June, 1775, the provincial congress had been forced to recognize that in Queens County public opinion was overwhelmingly against resistance. In November of that year Richmond and Queens formally severed themselves from the

10 Ted Robert Gurr, *Why Men Rebel* (Princeton, 1970), Ch. 6.
11 Patricia U. Bonomi, *A Factious People, Politics and Society in Colonial New York* (New York, 1971), Ch. 7. Bernard Friedman, "The Shaping of the Radical Consciousness in Provincial New York," *Journal of American History*, LVI (1970), 781–801, 799.

rest of the province by voting against sending delegates to the congress. In Queens voters rejected that step by more than three to one. They also publicly declared their intention to resist being disarmed by the whigs. Military operations eventually brought the county under revolutionary control but its people, like those of Kings and Richmond, were more than ready to receive the British forces that occupied New York's southern district in the late summer of 1776.[12]

In those counties the problem was one not of internal division but of overwhelmingly tory sentiment; it was the whigs who were reduced to impotent gestures and who braved the disapproval of the vast majority of their neighbors. Elsewhere, in Westchester, Dutchess, Albany, and Tryon Counties, the two sides were more evenly matched and, as a result, the Hudson and Mohawk Valleys were beset with angry and increasingly violent conflict. In Westchester a battle of signatures took place in April, 1775, over the formation of a county committee, with opponents apparently outnumbering supporters. Observers in Connecticut reported late in the year that in southern Westchester (the present Bronx) the whigs were vastly outnumbered and loyalists were supplying the British fleet with impunity; at the same time the provincial congress was told that groups of armed loyalists were marauding in Mamaroneck. The situation remained unstable until the British occupation of the southern district; thereafter whigs and loyalists harassed one another across the lines.[13]

Dutchess, just to the north of Westchester, was equally divided, but the loyalists there never achieved a secure territorial base. As a result their agitation remained, in Gurr's terms, at the level of turmoil.[14] Surviving records of those who signed and refused the association in the summer of 1775 suggest that whigs outnumbered loyalists

12 Minutes of New York Provincial Congress, June 22, June 28, 1775, Peter Force (comp.), *American Archives*, 4th Ser., II, 1312, 1328; Queens County Poll List, Nov. 7, 1775, *ibid.*, III, 1389–1392; Paul Micheau to New York Provincial Congress, Dec. 1, 1775, *ibid.*, IV, 149; Queens County Declaration, Dec. 6, 1775, *ibid.*, 203–204.

13 Protest of Westchester County Freeholders and Residents, April 13, 1775, *ibid.*, II, 321–323; "To the Publick," May 7, 1775, *ibid.*, 323–324; Report from Greenwich Connecticut, Dec. 26, 1775, *ibid.*, IV, 590–591; Examination of Col. Gilbert Budd, New York Provincial Congress Minutes, Nov. 3, 1775, *ibid.*, III, 1321–1322.

14 In analyzing forms of rebellion Gurr distinguishes *turmoil* ("relatively spontaneous, unstructured mass strife, including demonstrations, political strikes, riots, political clashes, and localized rebellions"), *conspiracy* ("intensively organized, relatively small-scale civil strife, including political assassinations, small-scale terrorism, small-scale guerrilla wars, coups, mutinies, and plots and purges . . ."), and *internal war* ("large-scale, organized, focused civil strife, almost always accompanied by extensive violence, including large scale revolts"). Gurr, "A Causal Model of Civil Strife: A Comparative Analysis Using

in the county as a whole by about two to one, but the 907 non-signers and their families and sympathizers represented, nonetheless, a considerable force. Recruiting for the British service went on apace among them. By the middle of 1776 the chairman of the county committee reported that it was necessary to keep a garrison on full-time anti-loyalist duty. Privates and even officers regularly refused to serve when the militia was called out. Just after independence was declared 150 loyalists in the eastern part of the county disarmed the local whigs and took possession of the revolutionary committee's meeting room: only the intervention of a massive force from Connecticut defeated them. The loyalist historian William Smith, observing northern Dutchess from his house arrest in neighboring Livingston Manor, reported instance after instance of covert or open resistance to the movement in 1777 and 1778, including militia disobedience, pressure on clergymen not to pray for the Continental Congress, and mass departures for regions under royal control.[15]

The situation was much the same in Albany County. People in the City of Albany were drinking the King's health as late as 1779 and one evening in 1777, as Burgoyne's army was approaching, 300 loyalists gathered in the town of Schenectady. Patriots disarmed them, but the local committee ordered that a heavy watch patrol the town day and night. Large numbers in the northern part of the county joined Burgoyne and some attempted to collect supplies for him.[16]

New Indices," in Ivo K. Feierabend, Rosalind L. Feierabend, and Ted Robert Gurr (eds.), *Anger, Violence, and Politics, Theories and Research* (Englewood Cliffs, 1972), 188. One factor determining which form will occur is "the coercive balance," with internal war being most likely when opposing forces are evenly balanced, turmoil when the dissident side is significant but overmatched, and conspiracy when one side is heavily over-balanced by the other. See Gurr, *Why Men Rebel*, Ch. 8.

15 Signers and non-signers of the association in New York, Force, *American Archives*, 4th Ser., III, 581–620; Minutes of New York Provincial Congress, November 2, 1775, ibid., 1312–1314; Dutchess County Committee to New York Provincial Congress, Dec. 5, 1775, ibid., IV, 187–188; Minutes of New York Provincial Congress, ibid., VI, 1415–1416; Colonel John Fields to New York Provincial Congress, June 5, 1776, ibid., 1429; Report from Hartford, Connecticut, July 15, 1776, ibid., 5th Ser., I, 360; William Smith, *Historical Memoirs From 16 March, 1763, to 25 July, 1778 of William Smith*, William H. W. Sabine (ed.) (New York, 1969), Jan. 7, 1777, II, 61–62, Feb. 21, 1777, II, 84, Apr. 15–17, 1777, II, 113–114, Apr. 21–23, 1777, II, 118–119, Feb. 23, 1778, II, 309.

16 Victor Hugo Paltsits (ed.), *Minutes of the Commissioners for Detecting and Defeating Conspiracies in the State of New York, Albany County Sessions, 1778–1781* (Albany, 1909), Apr. 1, 1779, 325, June 9, 1779, 357; James Sullivan (ed.), *Minutes of the Albany Committee of Correspondence, 1775–1778* (Albany, 1923–1925), Schenectady Committee Minutes, Aug. 10, 1777, II, 1114–1115.

The centers of militant loyalism, however, lay in the manors of Rensselaerwyck and Livingston. Loyalist activity there manifests again the close connection between insurrection and crime that both Hobsbawm and Johnson, Marxist and non-Marxist, have discussed.[17] The rugged "Helleberg" at the western end of Rensselaerwyck became a haven for persons avoiding military duty as early as 1776, and the lack of attachment to the cause on the part of the manor tenants needs no fresh demonstration.[18] In 1778 and 1779, however, loyalists and deserters from the armies of both sides began to operate in large bands in these districts. The whigs called them robbers, but their motivations were more political than pecuniary. The Helleberg band forced militiamen whom it captured to take an oath of neutrality for the duration of the conflict, imitating the practice of the whig authorities toward tories. It even proposed negotiations to the Albany leadership, offering to cease its activities if loyalist exiles were allowed to return to their homes. The band that operated on the east bank of the Hudson, in Rensselaerwyck, Livingston, and northern Dutchess, afflicted only prominent whigs, but the group publicly advertised its intention of bringing "murder and fire to all rebels." Captured members of the band declared that they were fighting for the king. Another loyalist band operating across the river demanded that one of its victims return fines exacted by his son, a Continental captain. This was little short of guerrilla warfare and it was made possible not only by the existence of a mountain refuge, but also by the presence of a population that would support and hide the guerrillas, that would serve as a sea to their fish.[19]

But the problem was most serious on the western frontier, in Tryon County, where the whig-loyalist confrontation turned into a vicious and protracted internal war. That the sides were evenly matched was demonstrated by an initial confrontation, in July, 1775, which developed when a crowd of about one hundred freed a whig who had been arrested by the loyalist county sheriff. The sheriff and the crowd

---

17 E. J. Hobsbawn, *Primitive Rebels: Studies in Archaic Forms of Social Movement in the Nineteenth and Twentieth Centuries* (Manchester, 1959), esp. Chs. 2, 3; Chalmers Johnson, *Revolutionary Change* (Boston, 1966), Ch. 6.

18 See Lynd, *Anti-Federalism in Dutchess County* and *Class Conflict, Slavery and the Constitution*, both *passim*.

19 *Conspiracies Commissioners Minutes, Albany County Sessions*, Sept. 5, 1778, 233, Sept. 15, 1778, 243, Sept. 30, 1778, 246–247, Oct. 3, 1778, 252, Oct. 16, 1778, 259, Apr. 25, 1779, 331–332, May 11, 1779, 341, June 7, 1779, 354–355, June 18, 1779, 364–365, July 19, 1779, 388–389; Smith, *Historical Memoirs*, May 6, 1778, II, 370, June 25, 1778, II, 404.

exchanged fire and the crowd swelled to a size of more than 500. The sheriff found protection at the fortified house of the county's leading figure, Sir John Johnson, who immediately mobilized his own force of some 400 persons. Whig leaders from outside the county arranged a truce but not before the whig crowd had tried to obtain cannon to break Sir John's defences. During the next year the loyalists were driven westward to the Iroquois country and five years of fighting followed. By the time it was over, according to one estimate, 700 buildings had been burned, 12,000 farms abandoned, hundreds of thousands of bushels of grain destroyed, nearly 400 women widowed, and some 2,000 children orphaned. The totals are small compared to the deeds of modern military technology, but for an eighteenth-century farming community the price was frightful.[20] As Mackesy suggests, the fiercest fighting in the war was between American and American.[21]

For the moment no attention has been paid to the social roots of loyalism in New York; these have been examined elsewhere, and their importance will be considered again below.[22] The main immediate point is that loyalism was a very serious problem throughout much of the state. It meant that significant numbers of New Yorkers denied the legitimacy of the Revolution. Resistance to revolutionary authority varied with the percentage of loyalists, with geography, and with the military situation more generally. As Fig. 1 suggests the forms it took can be arranged according to Gurr's schema of rebellion, the object of rebellion being not George III but the revolutionary movement.

The final crisis brought a second major challenge to New York's revolutionary authority: the movement for the creation of Vermont. This took place in the counties of Gloucester, Cumberland, and Charlotte, New York's northeastern corner. New York's title to the region had long been in dispute. Not until 1764 was it finally confirmed by the Privy Council, which disallowed the claims of Massachusetts and New Hampshire. But New Englanders who had settled under New Hampshire auspices and New Yorkers who had fled the Hudson Valley after the tenant rising of 1766 resisted the imposition of New York authority. Their resistance culminated in the "rent wars" of

20 J. Howard Hanson and Samuel Ludlow Frey (eds.), *The Minute Book of the Committee of Safety of Tryon County* (New York, 1905), Aug. 25, 1775, 49–51; *Albany Committee Minutes*, July 22–29, 1775, I, 165–172; Alexander C. Flick, *The American Revolution in New York* (Albany, 1926), 173.
21 Piers Mackesy, *The War for America, 1775–1783* (London, 1964), 343–344.
22 See Alexander Clarence Flick, *Loyalism in New York During the American Revolution* (New York, 1901); Lynd, *Anti-Federalism in Dutchess County*; idem, "The Tenant Rising at Livingstone Manor, May, 1777" in *Class Conflict, Slavery and the Constitution*, 63–71.

Figure 1   Forms of Upheaval in New York by Counties, 1775–1781

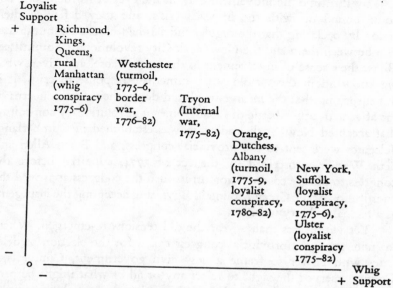

Based on the categories developed in Ted Robert Gurr, *Why Men Rebel*, Ch. 8.

the early 1770s.[23] So serious was the situation that in 1774 the New York Assembly passed a draconian riot act for the region, attainting eight of the movement's leaders by name and providing the death penalty for a host of their activities.[24] Adherents of New York sought the use of Royal troops to suppress the movement in 1774 and 1775, but General Thomas Gage, who had other problems on his mind, refused. The situation reached a crisis in March, 1775, when some ninety insurgents occupied the Cumberland County courthouse and came to blows with a party led by the county sheriff. Their numbers swelled to an estimated 500 and they took prisoner the judges, justices of the peace, sheriff, and county clerk. One of the justices suffered two hundred lashes for exercising New York authority, for the insurgents "would not, under the present circumstances, suffer any Magistrate at all."[25]

23   See Irving Mark, *Agrarian Conflicts in Colonial New York, 1711–1775* (New York, 1940), Ch. 6.
24   *New York Session Laws*, Provincial Government, microfilm ed., *RSUS*, N.Y. B 2, Reel 6, Unit 1 (Washington, D.C., 1949), 29th Assembly (1774), Ch. 22.
25   I. N. Phelps Stokes, *The Iconography of Manhattan Island, 1619–1909* (New York, 1967, reprint ed.), IV, 867; Lord Dartmouth to Cadwallader Colden, December 10, 1774, Force, *American Archives*, 4th Ser., I, 1035; Deposition of Benjamin Hough before Daniel Horsmanden, March 7, 1775, *ibid.*, II, 215–218.

By this time the movement had, in the eyes of its members, become bound up with the imperial crisis, and they defended their action by declaring that the regular officials had blocked communication between them and the New York City revolutionary committee. Given their sense of involvement in the larger cause, and given what we know about the sociology of immediate response to crisis, it is not surprising that the insurgents played down their own concerns in the aftermath of the battle of Lexington.[26] A revolutionary committee that accepted New York leadership was established in Cumberland, delegates were sent to the provincial congress, and Ethan Allen and Seth Warner, proscribed by the act of 1774, appeared before the congress to pledge co-operation. In its turn the congress approved the constitution of the Green Mountain Boys, thus accepting the insurgents as a formal military unit.[27]

Yet within less than a year the old tensions re-emerged. When, in June, 1776, the provincial congress called for the election of delegates with power to frame a new civil government, Cumberland County reserved the right to reject any or all of what might be produced. At the same time local committees there were seeking military supplies from Massachusetts and Connecticut. In July a convention of delegates from towns in Charlotte, Cumberland, and Gloucester counties met and declared that the long conflict with New York made continued association with it impossible; in September another convention, representing thirty-three towns, declared the region's independence from New York.[28] Eventually the insurgents adopted a state constitution and in the early 1790s finally gained admission to the union. The important point is that by the end of 1776 they had broken their ties with New York.

---

26 "A Relation of the Proceedings of the People of the County of Cumberland and Province of New York," Force, *American Archives*, 4th Ser., II, 218–222. For the sociology of crisis see Ralph H. Turner, "Integrative Beliefs in Group Crisis," *Journal of Conflict Resolution*, XVI (1972), 25–40.
27 Report of Cumberland County Committee, June 23, 1775, Force, *American Archives*, 4th Ser., II, 1064–1066; minutes of New York Provincial Congress, June 21, 1775, July 4, 1775, *ibid.*, 1309, 1338–1339.
28 Cumberland County Committee to New York Provincial Congress, June 21, 1776, *ibid.*, VI, 1014; Committees of Newbury, Haverhold, Bath, and Mooretown to Massachusetts Assembly and Council, June 25, 1776 *ibid.*, 1076; David Galusha, Chairman of Bennington, New Hampshire Grants, to Governor Trumbull, June 30, 1776, *ibid.*, 1151–1152; Votes and Proceedings of convention of 59 delegates, Dorset, July 24, 1776, *ibid.*, 5th Ser., I, 564–566; Minutes of convention of towns on the New Hampshire Grants, Sept. 25–27, 1776, *ibid.*, II, 526–530.

When the new state constitution was proclaimed in the spring of 1777, New York was a very different place from what it had been in 1774. Suffolk, Kings, Queens, Richmond, New York, and half of Westchester were under British control, a situation fully acceptable to most of their inhabitants. Cumberland, Gloucester, and much of Charlotte were in the process of becoming Vermont. Westchester, Dutchess, Albany, and Tryon were wracked by loyalism and only Orange and Ulster could be counted as thoroughly whig. Table 1 shows how the population, as of 1771, was affected by these different forms of disturbance.

Coping with these problems was often beyond the capability of the state government. The southern district remained in British hands until the end of 1783 and although the new government did what it could to restore the Vermonters to New York allegiance they failed.[29] But even with New York redefined as seven counties instead of fourteen, consolidating the power of the new government was no easy matter. The loyalist presence was one problem, and it was met by as much repression as the government could muster, using both continental troops and local militia. Loyalists were occasionally hanged and more often forced into exile. Boards of Commissioners for Detecting and Defeating Conspiracies were established; these political police imprisoned many suspects and, for lack of jail space, put far more under bond for good behavior, all without a hint of common-law due process. The Albany County board made a regular practice of imposing a bond on practically everyone who came before it, even if the person were proven innocent on the particular charge that had brought him there.[30]

[29] The legislature passed three laws between 1777 and 1783 that were intended to deal with the Vermont situation. The first, in the third session, referred the matter to the Continental Congress. The other two, in the fifth session, pardoned "crimes" committed under Vermont authority and attempted to "quiet the minds" of the region's residents by confirming their land titles. *New York Session Laws*, State Government, microfilm ed., *RSUS*, N.Y. B.2, Reel 6, Unit 2 (Washington D.C., 1949), 3rd Sess., Ch. 24, 5th Sess., Chs. 43, 44. For a full discussion of these laws and of other actions taken by the New York government see Countryman, "Legislative Government in Revolutionary New York," 187–196.

[30] The hanging of seven loyalists is reported in Smith, *Historical Memoirs*, June 8, 1778, II, 397; for other repressive efforts see *Conspiracies Commissioners Minutes, Albany County Sessions* and *Minutes of the Committee and of the First Commission for Detecting and Defeating Conspiracies in the State of New York, Dec. 11, 1776–Sept. 23, 1778*, Dorothy C. Barck (ed.) [*Collections* of the New-York Historical Society, LVII] (New York, 1924), both *passim*.

Table 1 New York Population, 1771, Arranged by Forms of Upheaval During the Revolution

I	Nearly Wholly Loyalist	
	Kings	3,623
	Queens	10,980
	Richmond	2,847
		17,450
II	Vermont Secession[a]	
	Cumberland	3,947
	Gloucester	722
		4,669
III	Turmoil	
	Dutchess	22,404
	Albany[b]	42,706
	Westchester	21,745
		86,855
IV	Predominantly Whig, Seized by Britain in 1776	
	New York	21,863
	Suffolk	13,128
		34,991
V	Predominantly Whig	
	Orange	10,092
	Ulster	13,950
		24,042

SOURCE: E. B. O'Callaghan, M.D., *The Documentary History of the State of New York* (Albany, 1849), I, 697.

a To this should be added the population of the eastern two-thirds of Charlotte County, but no figures are available for either the county as a whole or for its secessionist portion.

b The Albany figure includes the totals for Tryon and Charlotte, which were set off from Albany County after 1771.

Another difficulty that could not be handled by simple repression was the continued exercise of direct popular power that had destroyed royal government in 1775 and made the situation revolutionary in the first place. In no little part this meant the persistence of the extra-legal revolutionary committees after the new regular institutions were supposed to have taken power. Hints of the possibility of tension between the local committees and the central revolutionary leadership had been present from the start. After Tryon County whigs had run their loyalist sheriff out in 1775, they elected a replacement and then referred the question to the provincial congress. The congress, which was trying to maintain relations with the royal governor, passed the matter on to him and he ordered the reinstatement of his appointee. The Tryon committee, however, simply refused to have him back.[31] A year later the congress ordered the county committees to begin sending it two nominations for each vacant post. This practice, an old New York custom, served to make appointment by higher authority something more than a mere ratification of a decision actually taken at a lower level, but when two county committees cited practical objections and refused to comply, the congress dropped the idea.[32]

More striking and self-conscious was a declaration by the New York City Committee of Mechanics in the spring of 1776. This informal body had become a powerful factor in the city's politics and when the idea of a new constitution was first bruited it sent a message to the provincial congress demanding popular ratification of whatever constitution was produced. The mechanics, however, went beyond the idea of a plebiscite. They wanted the people at large to retain "an uncontrolled power to alter the constitution in the same manner that it shall have been received" and thus they proposed that localities should retain the right "occasionally to renew their Deputies to Committees and Congresses, when the majority of such district shall think fit," without interference by any "power foreign to the body of the respective electors." Only through this eighteenth-century version of permanent revolution, thought the mechanics, could the people be

31 *Tryon Minute Book*, Sept. 9, 1775, 66–68; Tryon Committee to Provincial Congress, Sept. 7, 1775, *Journals of the Provincial Congress, Provincial Convention, Committee of Safety and Council of Safety of the State of New-York, 1775–1776–1777*, II (Albany, 1842), 81–82; Tryon Committee to Provincial Congress, Oct. 28, 1775, *ibid.*, 96–97.
32 Stokes, *Iconography*, IV, 311; Egbert Benson to Provincial Congress, Feb. 8, 1776, *Journals of the Provincial Congress*, 136; Tryon Committee to Provincial Congress, Feb. 17, 1776, *ibid.*, 191.

sure that the government would always stem from their own "voluntary choice."[33]

The constitution of 1777 contained no provision for anything of the sort, but circumstances kept the committee system alive until the middle of 1778, and a fresh crisis brought its resurgence in 1779. As one of its first acts the new state legislature moved to provide for the continuation of the committees; meanwhile local committees were declaring on their own authority that they would not immediately disband. The new government began operations in September, 1777; a month later, during the Saratoga crisis, an invasion of the Hudson Valley by British troops sent its legislators running to their homes and militia posts. Until early 1778 what central power existed was in the hands of an utterly irregular "Convention of the Members of the Senate and Assembly" and a council of safety appointed by it. Although the legislature reassembled in January, 1778, the committees, given a new popular mandate by an election at the end of 1777, continued to operate at least until June.[34]

When it was founded in 1774 and 1775 the committee system served primarily to co-ordinate resistance to Britain, but it increasingly came to exercise purely internal functions, both legislative and executive. The Albany Committee tried offenders, established jails for loyalists, assumed police functions, printed paper money, conducted Indian negotiations, and forbade smallpox inoculations. The New York City Committee tried to found a manufactory for the employment of the poor. In Schenectady the committee interfered in domestic disputes and in 1777 it ordered the arrest of the town constable when he refused to obey it despite his election in an apparent effort to restore regular authority. But most important was the work of the committees in regard to the marketing of food and supplies. As early as 1776 the

---

33 Lynd, "The Mechanics in New York Politics, 1774–1785," in Lynd, *Class Conflict, Slavery, and the Constitution*, 79–108. "The Respectful Address of the Mechanicks in Union, for the City and County of New York, represented by their General Committee," Force, *American Archives*, 4th Ser., VI, 895–896.

34 *Journal of the Senate of the State of New York*, microfilm ed., *RSUS*, N.Y. A.1a, Reel 2, Unit 1 (Washington D.C., 1949), Sept. 30, 1777; *Assembly Journal*, Sept. 29–Oct. 10, 1777; *Albany Committee Minutes*, Sept. 30, 1777, I, 849. *Assembly Journal*, Jan. 5, 1778; resolutions of the convention, October 7, 1777, and Pierre Van Cortlandt, president of the convention, to George Clinton, Oct. 7, 1777, Hugh Hastings (ed.), *Public Papers of George Clinton, First Governor of New York*, (Albany, 1911), II, 376–380. The last mention of committees in the records of the legislature was on Mar. 12, 1778, and the last recorded meeting of the Albany committee was on June 10, 1778.

Albany Committee was fixing prices and jailing merchants for profiteering. When wartime damage and the British blockade brought a grain and salt crisis in 1777, the committee played an active role in combatting it, putting embargoes on needed supplies, setting prices, punishing hoarders, and regulating distribution.[35]

The movement to revive the committees in the summer of 1779 sprang purely from such internal considerations, its root cause being the crisis of subsistence that accompanied the collapse of the continental dollar. The crisis, striking hardest at people who bought their food instead of growing it, was an "urban" phenomenon, afflicting town dwellers, tradesmen, and refugees from New York City rather than farmers. The movement to cope with it through popular committees began in Philadelphia, which issued a call in May for the establishment of committees "in every State and County," and in Boston, and it swept through the northern states. In New York its focal points were the City of Albany and the Dutchess County town of Fishkill. From these centers it spread out to most of the towns of Albany and Dutchess Counties and to some in Ulster and Orange. The new committees operated until mid-August, once again setting prices, distributing produce, forbidding distilling in order to conserve grain, interfering with interstate trade, exercising police functions, and even calling out the militia. The movement culminated with a state convention that met at Claverack, Albany County, in August.[36]

35 *Albany Committee Minutes*, May 3-4, 1775, I, 24-25, May 22, 1775, I, 33-34, June 10, 1775, I, 71-74, Sept. 13, 1775, I, 240-241; *ibid.*, Schenectady Committee Minutes, June 17, 1777, II, 1103, June 23, 1777, II, 1104, Feb. 1, 1778, II, 1140, Nov. 22, 1777, II, 1128; Philip Schuyler to Albany Committee, July 11, 1775, Schuyler Letter Book, Philip Schuyler Papers, Manuscript Division, The New York Public Library, The Astor, Lenox, and Tilden Foundations; New York City Committee Minutes, Nov. 10. 1775, Force, *American Archives*, 4th Ser., III, 1423-1424. *Albany Committee Minutes*, Mar. 6-8, 1776, I, 351-353, Apr. 18-Apr. 24, 1776, I, 384-387, May 2-8, 1776, I, 395-400; Albany Committee to Council of Safety, Dec. 29, 1777, *Journals of the Provincial Congress*, 351; Henry Luddington *et al.* to Council of Safety, Dec. 3, 1776[7], *ibid.*, 355; Abram P. Lott to Council of Safety, Dec. 9, 1777, *ibid.*, 355-356; *Albany Committee Minutes*, Nov. 18, 1777, I, 869; *ibid.*, Schenectady Committee Minutes, Jan. 17, 1778, II, 1137.

36 *New York Packet*, July 15, 1779, quoted in Lynd, *Class Conflict, Slavery and the Constitution*, 45. For the movement in Philadelphia see Sam Bass Warner, *The Private City: Philadelphia in Three Periods of Its Growth* (Philadelphia, 1968), 34-45; and esp. John K. Alexander, "The Fort Wilson Incident of 1779: A Case Study of the Revolutionary Crowd," *William and Mary Quarterly*, XXXI (1974), 589-612. For its spread from Philadelphia see Richard B. Morris, *Government and Labor in Early America* (New York, 1965), 110-114. *New York Packet*, July 29, 1779; *New York Journal*, Aug. 16, 1779, quoted in Morris, *Government and Labor*, 111; "Instructions Agreed to & Approved by the Inhabitants of Poughkeepsie Precinct . . . to their Committee," Broadside, New-York

Parallel with these committees were less formal, less structured outbursts of popular energy. Initially popular outbursts had been directed against important loyalists, such as the sheriff of Tryon County and the Dutchess County judge who was tarred and feathered in September, 1775, for undertaking a lawsuit to recover arms seized by the local committee. Action of this sort continued after independence. In the middle of 1778 residents of part of Albany County formed "a Combination to lessen the number of the disaffected by sending them orders to move off and threatening them to abide by the Consequence in Case of Neglect." In Tryon there were seizures in 1778 of the goods of loyalists who had not left. In western Albany County crowds were pulling down the houses and destroying the property of the wives of "disaffected" men. In the northern part of the same county, where many loyalists were free on bail in early 1779, a crowd gathered to make them run the gauntlet, and when the local committee intervened its members were forced to do the same, though without being beaten.[37]

But, like committee action, such informal popular energy was increasingly directed at targets other than overt political enemies of the movement. As early as late 1775, a public meeting in Albany complained that the city's merchants "in a great measure imposed upon" the people, and in the autumn of 1776 there were outbursts of direct action against the growing scarcity of tea and salt. By 1777, when engrossers in Albany were buying grain at 23/6 in order to sell it at 40 shillings, and when farmers were refusing to sell grain in small lots or at low prices, refugees from New York City were stopping loaded wagons and searching them. In several places there were instances of popular price-setting, the people involved behaving precisely as Thompson, Rudé, and Soboul suggest their counterparts

---

Historical Society; Minutes and Papers of the Albany Committee, Albany Institute of History and Art, Albany; *Albany Committee Minutes*, Schenectady Committee Minutes, June 16–Aug. 18, 1779, II, 1145–1159. I wish to thank Edna L. Jacobsen for bringing the manuscript Albany Committee minutes for 1779 to my attention. Records of the Claverack Convention, Albany Committee Papers, Albany Institute.

37 Report from Dutchess County, Sept. 27, 1775, Force, *American Archives*, 4th Ser., III, 823. *Conspiracies Commissioners Minutes, Albany County Sessions*, July 30, 1778, 185, Sept. 28, 1778, 244, July 19, 1779, 388; John Younglove to Albany County Committee, Feb. 26, 1778, and accompanying documents, *Clinton Papers*, II, 854–858. The experience of the committeemen who were made to run the gauntlet comes close to being an occupational hazard of men in their position. See James V. Downton, *Rebel Leadership* (New York, 1973), 98–99.

did during time of shortage in England and France. Plainly the resurgent committees of 1779 were built on real popular feeling, especially among the "urban" parts of the state's population. ("Urban" means either the people of towns like Kingston, Fishkill, Newburgh, and Albany, or refugees from occupied New York City; it is necessary to stress that these people were the source of this particular discontent.) Rural Americans had, by the time of the Revolution, a long tradition of direct action, but in New York, at any rate, their concern was much more likely to be over the ownership of land than the supply of bread or salt. It was people who did not produce their own food, who depended—literally—on merchants and farmers for their survival, who were behind the committee resurgence.[38]

Unlike loyalism and the Vermont insurgency the continuation of the committees and popular direct action did not challenge New York's basic integrity. It did, however, militate against the stabilization of the new government. It has been argued that in eighteenth-century America such activity was extra-governmental rather than anti-government, supplementing institutions rather than opposing them.[39] In the revolutionary context, however, it took on special meaning because of the way in which it blended unstructured, transient outbursts of social energy with overtly political and relatively sophisticated organizational forms, the committees and conventions. As Wood has shown, in the eighteenth-century Anglo-American world the term convention carried strong overtones of ultimate constituent power, and that its use to describe the 1779 gathering at

---

38 *Albany Committee Minutes*, Oct. 31, 1775, I, 282–283; Ulster County Committee to New York Convention, Nov. 18, 1776, *Journals of the Provincial Congress*, 229–230; Memorial of John Hathorn, Dec. 2, 1776, *ibid.*, 335. Albany Committee to Council of Safety, Dec. 29, 1777, *ibid.*, 351; Andrew Billings and Peter Tappen to Council of Safety, Dec. 9, 1777, *ibid.*, 354–355. James H. Kip to James Caldwell and John Maley, July 14, 1777, *ibid.*, 506; deposition of Peter Messier, Storekeeper, May 23, 1777, *Minutes of the Committee and First Commission For Conspiracies*, 301–303. For parallel behavior in eighteenth-century England and France see E. P. Thompson, "The Moral Economy of the English Crowd in the Eighteenth Century," *Past & Present*, 50 (1971), 76–136; George Rudé, *The Crowd in History, 1730–1848* (New York, 1964), 19–46; Albert Soboul, *Les Sans-Culottes Parisiens en L'An II: Mouvement Populaire et Gouvernement Révolutionnaire, 2 Juin, 1793–9 Thermidor, An II* (Paris, 1962), 482–491. Edward Countryman, "Out of the Bounds of the Law: Northern Land Rioters in the Eighteenth Century," in Alfred F. Young (ed.), *The American Revolution: Explorations in the History of American Radicalism*, forthcoming.

39 See Maier, *From Resistance to Revolution*, esp. Ch. 1.

Claverack was not entirely happenstance is borne out by several comments made at the time.[40]

The appearance and persistence of popular committees that came close to exercising all governmental functions takes on greater interest when considered in the comparative dimension. In political terms these committees were "revolutionary manifestations of the most fundamental sort"[41] and the emergence of something like them seems characteristic of what Huntington calls the "western" model of Revolution.[42] Their formation is both a means of dissolving the authority of an old order and a bulwark against revolution becoming chaos. One might say that to form them is the sensible thing to do in a revolutionary situation.[43] Such scholars as Soboul, Anweiler, and Carsten have considered their roles in the revolutions of eighteenth-century France and twentieth-century Russia, Germany and, most

40 Wood, *Creation of the American Republic*, Ch. 8. The comments referred to were made about the committee movement in general and reflect a strong sense that the failure of institutions to cope with the crisis would lead quickly to a resumption of active popular sovereignty, an event which would have drastically weakened whatever moral authority the institutions had. Thus "W.D. in Orange County" advised the people that "as soon as the authority of your committees ended, knavery showed its head, villains of every class came forth and practiced with impunity," *New York Packet*, Aug. 12, 1779. Associators in Ulster County, although stating their intention of supporting "our Young Government to the Utmost of our Power," prefaced that statement with a declaration that "the Origin of all Power is in the free Choice of the People," Association of Hanover, Wallkill, New Windsor, and Shawangunk, Albany Committee Papers, Albany Institute. The chairman of the committee there stated that "if the Legislature does not take decisive measures this session the Virtue and Patriotism of the People at Large must once more be roused . . ." James Hunter to Albany Committee, Sept. 7, 1779, Albany Committee Papers, Albany Institute. The suggestion is not that people were anxious to overturn the government; rather it is that people in several parts of the state thought that a real possiblity, if the government took no action. Analysts of both right and left agree that people do not abandon existing institutions and channels for as long as institutions can operate and channels remain open. See Johnson, *Revolutionary Change*, 53–58 and Trotsky, *History of the Russian Revolution*, 1017.

41 This point was made emphatically by Gurr at the J. I. H. conference on the American Revolution, May, 1975.

42 "Two general patterns [of revolution] can be identified. In the 'Western' pattern, the political institutions of the old régime collapse; this is followed by the mobilization of new groups into politics and then by the creation of new political institutions. The 'Eastern' revolution, in contrast, begins with the mobilization of new groups into politics and the creation of new political institutions and ends with the violent overthrow of the political institutions of the old order." *Political Order in Changing Societies*, 266. One does not find popular committees coexisting with the highly organized guerilla organizations that are a key element in the 'Eastern' model. Since there is in it no power vacuum comparable to 1917, or 1793, or 1775–1776, there is neither occasion nor need for them.

43 I wish to thank William Harper, for phrasing the generalization this way.

recently, Eastern Europe.[44] Radical thinkers have looked to them for the structural basis of an alternative to parliamentary democracy, or capitalism, or both.[45] Anweiler, although doubtful that popular committees can become the basis of a lasting order, stresses both the tension between them and more orthodox political institutions, and their articulation of social protest under "ever-different concrete historical circumstances." To use his categories, there existed in revolutionary New York both a well-developed and persistent committee system and elements of "council thought."[46] It would be overstating the case to suggest that the New York movement compares directly with the *soviet* movement in Russia; the latter was far more powerful and far more aware of itself. Yet the question of how informal tendencies were eliminated and regular institutions bolstered in the state is worth discussion; it represents a case of a much larger problem.

There were men among New York's revolutionary leaders who recognized that establishing general acceptance of the new state government would require more than the proclamation of a constitution. Their names—John Jay, Robert R. Livingston, Egbert Benson—are familiar even to the non-specialist and they held strategic positions during the early years of the new order. Jay was the first chief justice

44 Albert Soboul, *Les Sans-Culottes Parisiens*, 21–175, 582–585; Oskar Anweiler, *Die Rätebewegung in Russland, 1905–1921* (Leiden, 1958), *passim* (now translated as *The Soviets* [New York, 1975]), "Die Arbeiterselbstverwaltung in Polen," *Osteuropa*, VII (1958), 224–232, and "Die Räte in der ungarnischen Revolution 1956," *ibid.*, VIII (1958), 393–400; F. L. Carsten, *Revolution in Central Europe, 1918–1919* (London, 1972).
45 Marx and Lenin both saw popular councils—proletarian, in their view—as the basis of the new order that was to succeed the socialist revolution. See Karl Marx, *The Civil War in France* (Moscow, 1948); Lenin, *The State and Revolution* in *Collected Works* (London, 1964), esp. Ch. 3. There is a full discussion of their position in Anweiler, *Die Rätebewegung in Russland*, Erstes Kapitel, 3–4, Viertes Kapitel, 1. For similar ideas expressed by a non-Marxist see Hannah Arendt, "Thoughts on Politics and Revolution," *The New York Review of Books* (22 Apr., 1971), 8–20, esp. 19. A major aspect of the thought of the continental European New Left has been a resurgence of interest in the idea of popular councils. For a discussion and a critique see Anweiler, "Der Revolutionsgeschichtliche Zusammenhang Des Räteproblems," *Politische Vierteljahresschrift*, XI (1970), 56–69. See also Anweiler's article "Rätebewegung" in *Sowjetsystem und Demokratische Gesellschaft, Eine Vergleichende Enzyklopadie* (Freiburg, 1972), V, 429–444.
46 Anweiler, "Der Revolutionsgeschichtliche Zusammenhang Des Räteproblems," 67. Anweiler distinguishes *council movements* ("The concrete political social appearance of councils, their beginnings, their reality and their conclusions"), *council thought* ("the articulated theoretical ideas which stand in relationship with council movements"), and *council system* ("either the political or legal form of a victorious and stabilized council movement [in Soviet Russia after 1918] or a structure traced out in theory for a social order based on councils"), *ibid.*, 57.

of the state supreme court, Livingston the chancellor, and Benson a powerful figure in the state assembly. The first two were, in addition, members of the council of revision, a peculiar body with a qualified veto on legislation. These "constitutionalist patriots," as they may be called, bent every effort in 1777, 1778, and 1779 to restore the boundary between system and environment. Their old friend William Smith summed up their attitude when he commented in 1776 that, "the essential Properties of Civil Government are Power in the Magistracy ... and the Establishment of that Power free from the arbitrary Exertion of a Few or the Capricious Wantoness [sic] of the Multitude."[47]

Of particular concern, in the view of men like Jay and Benson, was a series of bills that went through the first session of the legislature, bills that recognized the existence and authority of the committees and conventions. Jay and his colleagues on the supreme court, who were named to the bench by the convention that had written the constitution, refused even to exercise their functions until they were reappointed under constitutional procedure. Jay and Livingston used their positions on the council of revision to force the rejection of such bills as the one continuing the embargo that had been imposed by the convention that took power in October, 1777. Jay, who wrote the veto message, objected to the bill because it "recognizes the late supposed Council of Safety as a Legislative Body" and because the bill recognized the committee system, which was unknown to the constitution. Benson worked in the assembly to expunge mention of extra-legal authority from legislation and even brought in a bill to indemnify the legislators who had taken part in the emergency convention. Similar attitudes greeted the resurgent committees of 1779. Benson was convinced that they threatened the "Subversion of the Constitution," and one official tried to get an indictment against the Albany Committee in order to force it to disband. Yet the efforts of such men met with little success. Only on the most minor points would the assembly accept Benson's position in 1778, and the legislature overrode most of the vetoes handed down by the council of revision.[48]

47 William Smith, *Historical Memoirs*, Oct. 14, 1776, II, 18.
48 *Assembly Journal*, Oct. 2, 1777. *Minutes of the Council of Revision of the State of New York*, microfilm ed., *RSUS*, N.Y. E.1x, A. X., Reel 8, Unit 1 (Washington D.C., 1949), Feb. 20, 1778. See also *ibid.*, Mar. 25, 1778 and Mar. 30, 1778. *Assembly Journal*, Feb. 4–5, 1778. John Lansing to Philip Schuyler, Aug. 4, 1779, Schuyler Papers, NYPL. In March, 1778, the senate sent to the assembly a bill bearing the title, "An Act to authorize the several County Committees within this State, to procure a Supply of Shoes and Stock-

The end of popular direct action came not from principled argument but rather from several dramatic demonstrations by the new government that it could and would respond to popular pressure. During its first two sessions, in 1777, 1778, and early 1779, the legislature confined itself almost exclusively to war measures; it had, needless to say, good reason for doing so. But in the third session, which followed hard on the resurgence of the popular committees, it made sweeping policy changes in several areas of intense popular concern. One was the loyalist problem, and particularly the question of loyalist property. A confiscation bill was passed by the legislature in 1778, but its opponents were strong enough to delay it by using parliamentary tactics and, when the council of revision rejected it, its supporters lacked the strength to override the veto. In the third session, however, a new bill was approved by the legislature and the council, meeting virtually no opposition on its way to becoming law. In a similar vein, a law was passed to provide recompense for robbery victims from a special tax to be imposed on loyalists. The highly political nature of the robberies in question has been shown; the response was appropriate. Up to this point New York's tory laws had been concerned solely with guaranteeing military security, but henceforth they would aim at punishment and at victimizing tories in favor of whigs.[49]

The concerns of the town dwellers and non-producers of food who were directly responsible for the committee resurgence were met by a fresh effort at the imposition of state-wide price controls. These had been tried before and found inadequate to the task of taming the wild continental dollar; they were no more successful this time.[50] The point, however, was not so much the material achievement as the demonstration of responsiveness. As Huntington suggests, revolutionary governments can lead their populations through the most dire economic straits if they are able to create a popular sense of

---

ings for the Troops . . ." When it left the assembly it had become "An Act to procure a Supply of Shoes and Stockings for the Troops . . ." and all mention of committees had been eliminated from it. *Assembly Journal*, Mar. 5–10, 1778.

49 See *Laws of the State of New York*, 1st Sess., Chs. 3, 27, 31, 43, 2nd Sess., Chs. 3, 10, 28. *Senate Journal*, Mar. 9–15, 1779; *Assembly Journal*, Nov. 2, 1778–Mar. 15, 1779, Sept. 14–16, 1779; *Laws*, 3rd Sess., Ch. 25. *Assembly Journal*, Sept. 28–29, 1779; *Laws*, 3rd Sess., Ch. 19.

50 *Laws*, 3rd Sess., Ch. 43; Thomas C. Cochran, *New York in the Confederation; An Economic Study* (Port Washington, L.I., 1970, reprint ed.), 31–32.

identification with the government—of possession and control of the institutions of power.[51]

Price controls, however, were anathema to the farmers who grew the grain, and it was the rural population's support that was most vital if the new institutions were to stand. Few farmers had become involved in the committee resurgence—a fact that distinguishes it from the popular conventions of Massachusetts in the 1780s—but rural discontent was nonetheless real. The legislature coped with it and, in a sense, brought consumers and small producers under one umbrella by means of a drastic change in the taxation system. Collecting taxes at all was no easy matter, given the fact that none had been directly imposed for years, and the initial tax laws of 1778 and early 1779 imposed different rates on personal and real property. In the third session, however, the legislature began imposing taxes on the basis of county quotas and, at the local level, ". . . according to the Estate and other Circumstances and Abilities to pay Taxes, of each respective Person, collectively considered." This, needless to say, amounted to an invitation to assessors to soak the local rich, which they proceeded to do. This system of taxation was far from elegant; observers in succeeding years regularly noted the logrolling that took place when county quotas were being decided and bemoaned its class content.[52] Yet there can be no doubt of its popularity with the vast bulk of the population, both rural and urban.[53] The Confiscation Act, too, was important in winning rural support. Whether its passage was rooted in class antagonism or, as seems at least equally likely, in the desire to punish prominent tories for their political attitude, it destroyed the economic, social, and political power that men with names like Frederick Philipse, James DeLancey, Sir John Johnson, and Philip Skene had wielded before the Revolution. In doing so it endeared the state government to many small farmers and tenants who had hated the great holders. Men of this sort had lent willing ears to the overtures of British agents when the war first broke out and they had formed the

---

51 Huntington, *Political Order in Changing Societies*, 308–311.

52 *Assembly Journal*, Feb. 25–Mar. 27, 1778, Oct. 20, 1778–Feb. 6, 1779, Sept. 7–20, 1779, Jan. 31, 1780; *Laws*, 1st Sess., Ch. 17, 2nd Sess., Ch. 16, 3rd Sess., Ch. 47. Lynd, "Who Should Rule at Home?" in *Class Conflict, Slavery, and the Constitution*, 49. Alexander Hamilton to Robert Morris, Aug. 13, 1782, *The Papers of Hamilton*, III, 135–137; *Minutes of the Council of Revision*, Unit 2, Apr. 20, 1784.

53 The issue was regularly debated in subsequent years and was the cause of numerous divisions in both senate and the assembly. See Countryman, "Legislative Government," Chs. 6–9 for a full discussion and analysis of legislative divisions.

backbone of popular loyalism. Now, at the same time that forcible repression of loyalism was a real necessity, the state government was demonstrating that it could take an anti-landlord stance, both through radical taxation of whig landlords and through the destruction of tory ones. Lynd, indeed, sees confiscation as a potent factor in turning many tenants from reluctant rebels into enthusiastic ones.[54]

In retrospect it seems that the twelve months following May, 1779 were crucial; it was during this period that the institutions created by the state constitution "took hold" among the whig population. The problems faced by the government certainly were great; the simultaneous upsurge of militant loyalism in Dutchess and Albany Counties, the deterioration of the paper money with its concomitant soaring of prices, the outbursts of popular energy, and the rebirth of the revolutionary committees were the elements of a general social and political crisis. The strength that the system gained in coping or publicly attempting to cope with these problems can be seen in the events of subsequent years. Loyalism remained a problem, but from 1780 onwards it was a matter of plots to escape to Canada and to kidnap prominent whigs; tories were no longer capable of attempting quasi-insurrection and the conspiracies commissioners could begin to devote their energies to such relatively minor problems as sectarian pacifists who opposed the war on religious grounds.[55] Similarly, the economy remained in such frightful condition that in 1781 there was another brief flurry of committee activity. This time, however, it was confined to southern Albany County, and although it certainly frightened Robert R. Livingston, it was subtly different from the more widespread movement of two years before.[56] The people involved declared that their many grievances "unless soon remedied will tend to alienate the minds of the people from the Legislature" but they were working on the assumption that the legislature would act. There is no evidence that they attempted or thought of direct action on the model of 1779. Elements of pressure-group politics as well as of revolutionary action had been there in 1779, but this time they were clearly predominant. And, what is more, there was little response elsewhere in the state.[57]

54 Lynd, "Who Should Rule at Home?" 33–34.
55 This generalization is based on *Conspiracies Commissioners Minutes, Albany County Sessions*, minutes for 1780 and 1781.
56 Robert R. Livingston to Gouverneur Morris, Jan. 19, 1781, and to George Washington, Jan. 8, 1781, Robert R. Livingston Papers, New-York Historical Society, quoted in Lynd, *Class Conflict*, 55.
57 *New York Packet*, Jan. 18, 1781.

Consolidating the power of the new institutions that were set up to govern revolutionary New York was thus a process of considerable complexity. The state in which the process took place was very different from the pre-revolutionary province, for New York had, in effect, been redefined through the secession of Vermont, the temporary loss of the heavily loyalist southern district, the migrations, forced or voluntary, of many loyalists to Canada, New England, or New York City, and the civil war on the western frontier. The populace that was politically relevant for the new institutions during the war years consisted, then, of those loyalists who remained in the whig zone, of upstate whigs, and of refugees from the southern district. In a way this fragmentation of what had been New York made the task of the new institutions easier, for it saved them from having to deal with several large concentrations of people who denied the legitimacy of either the revolution or the community. The Vermonters were gone for good, and when the southern district was restored to the state at the end of 1783, large scale emigration and the unquestionability of the Revolution's triumph made its reintegration into a political community relatively easy. And ultimately, repression proved able to cope with the serious problems of loyalists who remained within the whig zone.

The immediate problem thus lay within the whig population that neither denied the propriety of the revolutionary movement nor threatened the state's basic integrity, and with loyalists and neutrals whom the new system could "reach," one way or another. That a problem existed, that legitimizing the regime was a different matter from legitimizing the state, was recognized by the men identified in this article as "constitutionalist patriots," but it was the actions of the legislature rather than the arguments that John Jay wrote into the council of revision's veto messages that moved toward solving the problem. And perhaps most significant for making the new stability permanent, it was those actions that led to the development of a modern party system in the state.

It is customary among students of New York history to think in terms of well-formed "Clintonian" and "anti-Clintonian" groups existing from independence onwards, the touchstone being approval or disapproval of the populist policies of Governor George Clinton.[58]

58 See Jackson Turner Main, *The Upper House in Revolutionary America* (Madison, 1967), Ch. 5; Main, *Political Parties Before the Constitution* (Chapel Hill, 1973), Ch. 5; Alfred F. Young, *The Democratic Republican in New York: The Origins, 1763–1797*

234

That such parties came to be is undeniable, but during the war years the situation was by no means that simple. The governor himself worked hard during his first years in office for policies that were anything but populist, and his actions had the full approval of figures like Jay and Livingston. He pressed the legislature for heavy taxation, despite the resistance of his Ulster County neighbors; he quietly opposed the 1778 confiscation bill; he worked against wage and price controls.[59] Similarly, within the legislature there was no such thing during the first years after independence as a stable partisan alignment.[60] But social and economic discontent are the very stuff of party organization just as they were of popular committees and crowd action, and the legislative actions that began as a result of popular pressure in 1779 served to build a party system in two ways. On the one hand they ran against both the social philosophy and the personal interests of men such as Jay and Livingston. It was men of this sort who formed the core of the movement that by the mid-1780s was working to oust Clinton and his supporters and to strengthen federal institutions at the expense of the states. Whether one looks, with Wood, at their ideological concerns or focuses, with Young, Lynd, and Main, on their material circumstances, it is undeniable that they sought to counter the power of the state government to do things like harass loyalists and tax according to "circumstances and abilities."[61]

(Chapel Hill, 1967); E. Wilder Spaulding, *His Excellency George Clinton, Critic of the Constitution* (Port Washington, L.I., 1964, 2nd ed.); Spaulding, *New York in the Critical Period, 1783–1789* (Port Washingson, L.I., 1963, 2nd ed.). I wish to thank Main for making a pre-publication copy of the relevant parts of *Political Parties Before the Constitution* available to me. It should be noted that Young sees politics during the Confederation Period in terms of coalitions that shifted, divided, and gradually hardened, not in terms of steady polarity.

59 Gouverneur Morris to Clinton, Feb. 20, 1779, *Clinton Papers,* IV, 584–585; James Duane to Clinton, June 2, 1779, *ibid.,* V, 10–11. For Clinton's attitude on taxation see Charles Z. Lincoln (ed.), New York State Governors, *Messages From the Governors,* II, 1777–1822 (Albany, 1909), 9, 46–47, 52; Clinton to John Jay, Feb. 9, 1779 and Clinton to Gouverneur Morris, Feb. 9, 1779, *Clinton Papers,* IV, 554–557; Clinton to Robert R. Livingston, Feb. 22, 1780, Mar. 9, 1780, Robert R. Livingston Papers, NYHS. For his attitude on confiscation of loyalist property see Clinton to John Jay, Mar. 17, 1779, *Clinton Papers,* IV, 641–642. For his attitude on price controls see *Messages From the Governors,* II, 52.

60 This point is established by means of scale analysis of all roll-call votes taken in both houses, 1777–1783, in Countryman, "Legislative Government," Chs. 7, 8.

61 Wood, *The Creation of the American Republic;* Young, *The Democratic Republicans in New York;* Lynd, *Anti-Federalism in Dutchess County;* Main, *The Upper House* and *Political Parties Before the Constitution,* all *passim.*

Governor Clinton, on the other hand, came to realize that the continuation of his power at the state level turned on his ability to create and control a political majority within the state and that that meant being responsive to popular demands. He began moving in this direction in 1779 when he advised the third session of the legislature to pay attention to its constituents. He completed his political divorce from the group that was moving towards Federalism when he publicly endorsed taxation by circumstances and abilities in 1783.[62] As a result organizations were formed dedicated to the task of capturing and controlling the state government, organizations that played on popular discontents and at the same time directed them toward solutions within the system. With people concentrating on who the governor and legislators were to be and on what policies these officials should follow, there was no room for debate on whether they should exist until Hamilton, Robert Livingston and the rest of the opposition decided that their chances of success were so small that their only hope was to create a new national system that would render the state either impotent or unimportant.

This emergence of a party system completed the revolutionary transformation of New York's public life and finally achieved stability of the state government. At the same time, that emergence demonstrated some inadequacies of the analytical model of "political system" and "environment." That model in its stark simplicity came close to describing the structure, if not the operations, of the New York government in 1777 and 1778. There were contests for office, and there was jockeying for position, but, with the possible exception of the election of Clinton to the governorship, there was little meaning to elections. Local notables were chosen and in the legislature they voted without pattern or program.[63] The system existed virtually in name only.

The party system that was germinated in 1779 and 1780 and that reached maturity by 1786 and 1787 was a basic and necessary prop for the republican political system that had been created in 1777. It gave structure and direction to the operations of the legislature and it helped give to the act of voting for one's representatives a larger

62 *Messages From the Governors*, II, 77. In urging the legislature to review the state's tax laws at the end of the war Clinton commented that the existing laws, inefficient as they might be were just and proper. ". . . as far as they are calculated to compel the members of the community to contribute towards the public burthens, according to their respective abilities." *Messages From the Governors*, II, 183.
63 See Countryman, "Legislative Government, Chs. 4–9.

meaning than the mere choice of a local chieftain on the basis of his prominence. Because it "aggregated interests" with a view to getting action out of the political system, it helped render unnecessary the direct action of the committees and crowds that competed with the system in its early years and made those years a time of instability and doubtful legitimacy.

The comparative point is worth noting: Bolshevik party domination of the Soviets of post-revolutionary Russia would eventually make impossible direct action by them in the manner of 1917, and the competition of Clintonians and Nationalists for control of the New York government would make unnecessary direct action by committees in the manner of 1779. Hence that is one reason for suggesting that a party system, Western or Leninist, is the "best friend of modern political institutions." In each case stability was the result of the practical and creative responsiveness of political leaders who looked downward for the source of their authority and were genuine products of the preceding revolutionary ferment.[64]

But the revolutionary populace that was mobilized in the 1760s and 1770s and whose mobilization received institutional form through the development of a party system was not thinking in terms of the abstractions suggested by the systemic model of "political system" and "environment." Rather, people took to the streets, fields, and committee chambers because they had real interests at stake, interests that in New York turned on the imperial question, on ethnicity, on sectionalism and, not least, on class. Benson and Robert R. Livingston used the language of neutral political science in the late 1770s to describe their hostility to committees and crowds, and there is no reason to doubt their sincerity. Yet Benson was worried about interference in the rights of private property and commerce, as well as about constitutional irregularity, and the Livingstons were plagued with radical taxation as the price for no longer being plagued with rebellious tenants. What member of the elite could not have been worried when in 1779 a Poughkeepsie newspaper essayist called for a state monopoly of foreign trade and for special favoritism for the yeomanry? "A more equal distribution of property" was his goal.[65]

64 The comments on Russia are drawn from Anweiler, *Die Rätebewegung in Russland*. Anweiler is particularly concerned about the relationship between popular councils and party systems.
65 *The New York Journal, and the General Advertiser* (Poughkeepsie), Jan. 18, 25, Feb. 1, 8, 15, 1779, quoted in Main, *Political Parties*, 127.

Internal tensions of the sort that Benson feared had played a major role in both the creation and the continuation of the committee system. In Tryon County the very act of founding the committee was a gesture of defiance to the family of Sir William Johnson. Christopher P. Yates, Isaac Paris, John Frey, and Andrew Finck, Jr., the members of the first tiny committee of correspondence, functioned as a more or less underground body from August, 1774 to the arrival of the news of Lexington and Concord.[66] None of these four were among the Grand Jurors and other county leaders and officials who ostentatiously declared their loyalty to the King in March, 1775; all of them were to be local officials, militia officers, and state legislators after independence; all four were probably middling farmers. Later the committee would operate on the principle that old friendship for the Johnsons was tantamount to loyalism.[67] In New York City the successive Committees of Fifty-One, Sixty, and One-Hundred drew the newly politicized mechanic class into public life and the militant Committee of Mechanics drove the point home.[68] Of the forty-eight people who formed the first committee of Ulster County nearly half bore neither the title of Esquire nor a rank in the old militia, and of the nineteen men on the committee that succeeded it there were only five with honorifics. None of the fourteen members of the first committee in Charlotte County had titles, and one can say with surety that, for most of the roughly 435 people who served at one time or another on the Albany Committee, their service was their pinnacle of political involvement.[69] Detailed collective biography, though necessary in a full-length study, has not been the goal here but it seems safe to say that in New York, as in Ryerson's Philadelphia and Maier's Charleston, the committee system was the means of the mobilization of people for whom politics had previously been closed territory.[70] Obviously this point applies in a different way in Livingston Manor,

66 *Tryon Committee Minute Book*, Aug. 27, 1774–May, 1775, 4–6.

67 Tryon Committee to George Clinton, Sept. 7, 1777, *Clinton Papers*, II, 283–286; "Loyal Persons in Tryon County Fitted for Civil Office Under the New State Government", *Ibid.*, 621–622.

68 See Lynd, "The Mechanics in New York Politics"; Becker, *The History of Political Parties*, both *passim*.

69 Ulster County Committee, May, 1775, Force, *American Archives*, 4th Ser., II, 833; Charlotte County Committee, May 12, 1775, *ibid.*; *Albany Committee Minutes*, I, 19, 287–288, 420ff., 618ff., 777ff., 894ff.

70 Richard A. Ryerson, "Political Mobilization and the American Revolution: The Resistance Movement in Philadelphia, 1765 to 1776," *William and Mary Quarterly*, XXI, (1974), 565–588; Maier, "The Charleston Mob and Popular Politics."

where the committee worked actively to suppress the loyalist tenantry, and in Tryon, where the committee led the sundering of the "World Sir William Made," but the point holds.[71]

Committees, even the huge body in Albany County, were not of course the whole revolutionary populace, but the relationship between men in committee chambers and people in streets and fields might best be noted by pointing to the congruent complexities of committee behavior and crowd behavior, and by reinforcing the point that the existence of a committee system gave new meaning to crowds themselves. It was, after all, while watching a committee election that Gouverneur Morris made his oft-quoted remark about the mob beginning to "think and reason."[72] It was not the mob's existence that bothered him; it was the thinking and reasoning, the independent political action. Like the revolutionary committees, New Yorkers in the 1770s could be militant against the British enemy, tories, landlords, hoarders, and aggrandizing merchants. The colonial predecessors of these crowds, particularly the urban ones, had so long a tradition and so accepted a social role that they can properly be termed an institution,[73] but at least part of their colonial social legitimacy had rested on a relationship of mutuality with their social and economic betters.[74] Though they work from different perspectives, it would seem that Maier's legitimate popular uprisings and Thompson's moral economy of the English poor had much in common.[75] But by the time of the Revolutionary War many elitists, like Benson, who once would have responded to crowd action over shortage or high prices with efforts to increase distribution and control costs, were becoming free traders. They were now convinced of the folly of relying on anything but the market mechanism and some of them, at least, were looking forward toward the jostling, fluid world of James Madison, and Adam Smith. Hence one reason for Benson's concern at both crowds and committees. A food riot in Poughkeepsie or popular price controls in

71 On Sir William's world see James T. Flexner, *Mohawk Baronet, Sir William Johnson of New York* (New York, 1959), Ch. 22.

72 Morris to Mr. Penn, May 20, 1774, Force, *American Archives*, 4th Ser., I, 258.

73 This point is developed by Dirk Hoerder in *People and Mobs: Crowd Action in Massachusetts During the American Revolution, 1765–1780* (Berlin, 1971) and in his essay in Alfred Young's forthcoming anthology, *The American Revolution.*

74 In Countryman, "Out of the Bounds of the Law," a different attitude towards rural crowds is suggested. See also Elizabeth Fox Genovese's criticism of Thompson's "Moral Economy of the Crowd," *Past & Present*, 58, 161–168.

75 See Maier, *Resistance to Revolution*, Ch. 1; Thompson, "The Moral Economy of the Crowd."

Albany would not necessarily mean internal revolution, but they did indicate profound disagreement with the economic ideas and posed a significant threat to the social and political dominance of men who fancied themselves fit to lead.[76]

Many of the legislators who became Clintonians were involved directly in this upsurge. From the four original Tryon County committeemen, laying the groundwork in 1774 for the armed assault on Sir John's mansion, to Gilbert Livingston, Jacobus Swartwout, and Melancton Smith of Dutchess, James Hunter of Ulster, and Matthew Adgate and John Lansing of Albany playing their roles on the committees of 1779, one finds men who would be the governor's supporters in the 1780s involved in the internal aspects of the political mobilization of New York. Some of these were already legislators in 1779, elected, one suspects, on the basis of militia rank or modestly superior property. Most of them would never go so far as that Poughkeepsie call for socialized foreign trade and a redistribution of property, but they were in sympathy with the movement from which it sprung and it was in response to that movement that they began to come together. As a result the "governing class on the defensive" that opposed popular action in 1777, 1778, and 1779 found itself confronted in the years that followed by a legislative and popular party that rested on the sources of that action and that provided effective linkage between popular feeling and the formal institutions of government. It created stability both because it regularized the popular upsurge that had been the revolutionary movement and because it reflected the social aspects of that movement even as it tamed them. The irony is that it was the way in which this stability was achieved that drove the Federalists-to-be away from state political life and into the movement for a larger republic.

Social tensions and class conflict were part, though only part, of the American Revolution in New York. It can nonetheless be seen how Huntington's model of the revolutionary process aids in understanding events as they unfolded.[77] Scholars from Becker to Bonomi

---

76 Eric Foner will develop the problem of changing elite attitudes toward traditional crowd concerns in his forthcoming study of Thomas Paine and the American Revolution. I wish to thank him for permission to cite a draft essay containing many of his ideas.

77 Huntington, *Political Order in Changing Societies*, esp. Chs. 5, 7. For other comments on popular mobilization see Kenneth Lockridge, "Social Change and the Meaning of the American Revolution," *Journal of Social History*, VI (1973), 403–439; Ryerson, "Political Mobilization and the American Revolution."

have shown how the political life of the late colonial period was marked by the mobilization of new groups, a mobilization with which the existing political system could not cope. The final upheaval completed the process in terms of bringing out rural populations that had hitherto been quiescent, and led to a redefinition of the political community through the elimination from it of loyalists and Vermonters. The structure of government, in turn, adjusted to the new realities, both through enlarged and rationalized formal institutions and through the generation of a party system.[78] The system, in turn, which may better be described as one-party (the Clintonians) dominant than as two-party, contributed to the internal political stability which New York enjoyed while neighboring Massachusetts was undergoing the upheavals that culminated in Shays Rebellion.[79] The whole process was violent and rapid, and by the time it finished it had created a New York that was new in leadership, institutions, population, consciousness, and even geographical boundaries. Little more than the name, and the continuing fact of private property, remained the same.

[78] The state assembly created by the constitution was more than double the size of the pre-revolutionary provincial assembly, and the state senate was more than twice as big as the old provincial council. In addition representation was rationalized through the elimination of the corporate representation which had been allowed to three Hudson Valley Manors and one town and one borough under the old order, through the allotment of seats in the assembly to counties on the basis of population rather than of county equality and through provision for regular reapportionment and enlargement of both assembly and senate.

[79] That Clinton's party achieved a decided majority in the 1780s is shown by the reluctance of New York to accept the Federal Constitution, to which the governor was opposed, in 1788. The decidedly minority status of his opponents was certainly one reason for their decision to circumvent the state system by driving for a stronger federal government. As Huntington suggests, a dominant party system is less effective as a guarantor of political stability than a two-party system in which either party has a good chance of achieving power. *Political Order in Changing Societies*, 432.

"Parade of the Stamp Act in New York." *From Lossing,* Seventeen Hundred and Seventy-Six.

Hugh Hughes, A Study in Revolutionary Idealism

By BERNARD FRIEDMAN

A fresh examination of one of New York's Liberty Boys further explains the social and economic views of the province's radicals in the era of the American Revolution. Bernard Friedman is in the Department of History, Indiana University-Purdue University at Indianapolis.

HUGH HUGHES IS AMONG the less conspicuous of New York's cadre of Revolutionary radicals. In that respect he is rather more characteristic of the group than otherwise. Excepting that doughty pair, Isaac Sears and John Lamb, both of whom better fitted the conventional image of the radical agitator, there is really very little known about those other individuals whom the evidence places among the Liberty Boys.[1] It was the fate of these men to be subordinated in the final resolution of the crisis to a higher level of leadership, and then later to be further diminished in stature by nationalist historians intent upon legitimizing the American Revolution as an exercise in restraint and moderation.[2] The more prominent radicals, as

The author thanks the Center for American Studies, Indiana University-Purdue University at Indianapolis, for a grant-in-aid of research which contributed substantially to making this paper possible.

1. Pauline Maier, *From Resistance to Revolution: Colonial Radicals and the Development of American Opposition to Britain, 1765–1776* (New York, 1972), p. 303, lists ten men for whom there is documentary evidence as having been actively involved with the Sons of Liberty at the time of the Stamp Act dispute. Her list, with one exception, is taken from Isaac Q. Leake, *Memoir of the Life and Times of General John Lamb* (Albany, 1850), p.4, who gathered his names from the correspondence now available in the Lamb Papers, New-York Historical Society. Lamb, of course, is one of the gentlemen listed, as is Isaac Sears, the subject of a substantial monograph: Robert Christen, "King Sears: Politician and Patriot in a Decade of Revolution" (Ph.d. diss., Columbia University, 1968). But otherwise there are only some biographical sketches in John Austin Stevens, Jr., *Colonial New York: Sketches Biographical and Historical 1768–1784* (New York, 1867) which are drawn from the colonial records of the New York Chamber of Commerce, and which leave four of the ten men on the Maier-Leake list totally unaccounted for biographically. In truth, apart from Lamb and Sears, historians know very little that is useful about the other eight alleged radicals.

2. David D. Van Tassel, *Recording America's Past: An Interpretation of the Develop-*

Pauline Maier has aptly observed, were "mythologized over time into symbols of all that had to be rejected in the revolutionary heritage." The rest were left to the antiquarians.[3]

We have had some restitution recently for at least a few of those lost heroes, but there still remains the principal task of reclaiming that shared sense of purpose and conviction that allowed the radicals to perform their role as a revolutionary vanguard and then sustained them through the long years of revolutionary struggle.[4] It is in this last connection that the inconspicuous Hugh Hughes can make a contribution—in part because his obscurity, as it happens, is not nearly as impenetrable as seems the case with most of his associates, but more relevantly because his personal history incorporates a good deal of the common experience of that middling stratum of urban tradesmen and entrepreneurs from whose ranks came the radical leadership in New York.

The references to Hugh Hughes in the secondary literature are few and meager, and understandably so. He is hardly visible in the stream of events leading to the outbreak of armed rebellion in New York. His name appears early in the crisis years as an emissary to the Connecticut Liberty Boys in negotiations leading to an understanding regarding mutual military assistance in the event that Britain sought to impose the Stamp Act on the colonists by force of arms. But even this piece of vital information is available only through the chance presence of a crown informant.[5] Hughes simply does not appear in any

ment of Historical Studies in America, 1607–1884 (Chicago, 1960), pp. 37–40, 44–46, 78–86, 91, and passim; Michael Kammen, A Season of Youth: The American Revolution and the Historical Imagination (New York, 1978), pp. 35–75.

3. Pauline Maier, The Old Revolutionaries: Political Lives in the Age of Samuel Adams (New York, 1980), p.14.

4. The essays dealing with Isaac Sears and Thomas Young in Pauline Maier, Old Revolutionaries, represent such an effort, but her emphasis on the uniqueness of each of her characters, apparently designed to demonstrate the lack of a coherent Revolutionary radicalism, seems to me to finally trivialize her subjects by making their relationship to the larger revolutionary movement seem almost incidental.

5. Francis Bernard to Henry Conway, Jan. 19, 1766, "The Fitch Papers," Connecticut Historical Society Collections (1920), pp. 384–385; see also, Francis Bernard to Sir Henry Moore, Feb. 23, 1766, "Papers Relating to New York, 1764–1768," British Museum. Add. Mss. 22679. The episode is related in detail in Roger Champagne, "The Military Association of the Sons of Liberty," New-York Historical Society Quarterly XLI (1957), 338–350. There is one other direct reference to Hughes as a Liberty Boy in this opening phase of the crisis. Hughes is mentioned as one to whom a confidential letter should first be shown. Joseph Allicocke to John Lamb (?), Nov. 21, 1765, Lamb Papers, New-York Historical Society.

public capacity as a figure of consequence among the Sons of Liberty until the summer of 1776 when he received his appointment as deputy quartermaster general for the New York district with the rank of colonel in the Continental army. Obviously, Hughes must have stood fairly high in the esteem of his revolutionary brethren to have been entrusted with a position of such responsibility, but there is little in the recorded transactions of the preceding years to suggest as much.

It is rather likely that we would not know anything more about him than the bare facts recited above were it not for a brief sketch of Hughes appended to Isaac Q. Leake's *Memoir of the Life and Times of General John Lamb* (Albany, 1850). As might be expected from a work of this vintage, the author was mostly concerned with magnifying Hughes' military contributions and exemplary patriotism. But Leake did have access to manuscript materials and was personally acquainted with family descendants from whom he evidently derived the crucial information he passes along concerning Hughes' antecedents and concluding years.

Hugh Hughes was born on April 20, 1727, the youngest of the three male offspring of Hugh and Martha (Jones) Hughes. According to family tradition, the elder Hugh Hughes had run away to America at the tender age of nine, and had then been followed by his Welsh parents to Pennsylvania where they had taken up a sizeable tract of land in the heavily Welsh district of Upper Merion in what was then Philadelphia (and later Montgomery) County. An only child, the elder Hugh Hughes eventually inherited the family farm (which would be later called "Walnut Grove"), but not before he had pursued the trade of a tanner in Philadelphia in his earlier years.[6] The younger Hugh Hughes—our principal—was to follow this same craft so that it is reasonable to conjecture that he had served his apprenticeship with his father.

The family condition was seemingly one of modest well-being. The Hugheses were not so affluent as to exempt their sons from the necessity of taking up a trade, but they were sufficiently well-off to encourage a distinguishing measure of cultivation in

---

6. Leake, *John Lamb*, p. 360, identifies Hughes as of Welsh extraction and establishes the fact that John Hughes was his brother. With that information it was possible to locate a family history in Ellwood Roberts, ed., *Biographical Annals of Montgomery County, Pennsylvania* (2 vols.; New York, 1904), 1:282–286, from which the biographical information above is taken.

their children and an accompanying expectation of upward mobility. Hugh's older brother, John Hughes, offers a case in point. His political opponents in later years derisively referred to him as "the baker" and the "Welsh Squire," which suggest both his origins and his aspirations. John rose rapidly in station after his marriage in 1738, becoming a successful businessman and then a leading politico. He was first elected to the Pennsylvania Assembly in 1755, where he served for the next ten years as one of Benjamin Franklin's closest political associates. It was that latter relationship, ironically, which finally led to John Hughes' downfall, Franklin having recommended his good friend to the Grenville ministry for the ill-fated post of stamp master for Pennsylvania. Thus it was that John would be withstanding the pressures of the Philadelphia mob at the same time that his brother Hugh was travelling the opposite road to Connecticut in the service of the Sons of Liberty.[7]

The records with respect to Hugh Hughes' earlier years have much less to offer than they do for John, presumably because there was much less to report. He married a Charity Smith of New York City in 1748, though the date of his arrival in that city is not anywhere noted, nor the occasion for his departure from home.[8] Since he was only twenty-one when he married, we may assume that he was not too long gone from "Walnut Grove." The earliest evidence of Hughes' presence in New York is an entry of May 5, 1752, in the rolls of the freemen of the city in which it is noted that a "Hugh Hughes, Currier," had paid the necessary fee entitling him to ply his trade in that community. The purchase of the freedom of the town, it should be remarked, had become by that date little more than a formality with respect to the enforcement of economic sanctions, so that it is more than probable that Hughes' motive for registering was related to his appointment a month later as "one of the Corn Measurers of this City" by the Common Council.[9] There is a hint in this last event

7. Ibid. See also Theodore Thayer, *Pennsylvania Politics and the Growth of Democracy, 1740–1776* (Harrisburg, 1953), pp. 96, 106, for references to John Hughes as "the baker" and "the Welsh Squire." Edmund S. and Helen Morgan, *The Stamp Act Crisis: Prologue to Revolution* (New York: Collier Books, 1963), pp. 301–324, devote a chapter to John Hughes' embroilment in the Stamp Act controversy. Surprisingly, John Hughes' career has not yet been examined in its entirety.

8. Roberts, *Montgomery County*, 1:283.

9. *The Burghers of New Amsterdam and the Freemen of New York*, New-York Historical Society *Collections* (New York, 1885), and Appendix, No. 79. See also Beverly McAnear, "The Place of the Freeman in Old New York," *New York History* XXI (October 1940), 423–424.

of a somewhat superior standing in the community than that of the ordinary journeyman-artisan. But there is nothing more to go on until the latter months of 1762, when advertisements began appearing in the local press informing the public that "Hugh Hughes . . . has a Tan-Yard, and Currying Shop, in Ferry Street, near Peck's Slip, where the Business is carryd on as usual."[10]

Hughes can now be placed with some measure of assurance among that smaller body of artisan-proprietors whom contemporaries frequently referred to as the "middling sort," or whom General Thomas Gage rather more condescendingly described as "inferior Burghers" in his reports on the Stamp Act disorders in New York in 1765. These "inferior Burghers," in Gage's opinion, had been very much implicated in the public demonstrations against the Act, but he held in the usual fashion of his class that the "inferior sort" had been stirred up by their betters among the provincial gentry without whose "Influence and Instigation" the ordinary folk "would have been quiet."[11] A closer look at the condition of one such "inferior Burgher," Hugh Hughes, suggests a less devious scenario.

The economic recession which struck the colonies at the close of the French and Indian War was initially felt as a decline in the price of domestic goods, which is to say that tradesmen such as Hugh Hughes, whose market was almost entirely internal, were most vulnerable.[12] Hughes was unmistakably in serious financial trouble by the spring of 1765, but there is an intimation of difficulties as much as a year earlier when his name appears with those of a local distiller, Benjamin Blagge, and James Parker, the printer, in a letter to John Hughes indicating a willingness "with many of our friends, Relations, and Neighbors to Remove to Nova Scotia and Settle there."[13] John Hughes

10. *New York Gazette; or The Weekly Post Boy,* Oct. 7, Dec. 30, 1762.

11. Clarence E. Carter, ed., *The Correspondence of General Thomas Gage* (2 vols.; New Haven, Conn., 1931–1933), I:67–68, 72, 78–79. I have chosen to call Hughes an artisan-entrepreneur to distinguish him from the more numerous body of artisan-mechanics. For a fuller discussion of what is implied by that distinction, see pp. 237–238 below.

12. Herman M. Stoker, "Wholesale Prices at New York City, 1720–1800," *Cornell University Agricultural Experimental Station Memoirs,* no. 142 (November 1932), p. 203; Arthur H. Cole, *Wholesale Commodity Prices in the United States, 1700–1861* (Cambridge, 1938), pp. 12–14.

13. Hughes, Blagge, Parker, to John Hughes, May 20, 1764, John Hughes Papers, microfilm, Historical Society of Pennsylvania.

Benjamin Franklin. From Appleton's Cyclopaedia
of American Biography.

was involved at this time with a group of Philadelphians, including Franklin, in a grandiose land speculation in Nova Scotia, from which ultimately little would issue. One can sense the eagerness with which Hugh Hughes and his fellow Yorkers approached this proposition. They assured John Hughes "that at least Thirty families will follow our Example ... it is therefore our Earnest Request that you will use your Endeavors ... to have one Township Reserved for us ... and whenever that is Done, and we have Notice of it, shall use all our Influence to have it settled Immediately. ... " [14]

By April of the following year, 1765, Hugh Hughes was advertising the sale, or rental, of his business property, but as it turned out not in preparation for a removal to Nova Scotia. James

14. Ibid. The Nova Scotia venture is described in some detail in an informative headnote in Leonard Labaree, *et al.*, eds. *The Papers of Benjamin Franklin* (23 vols. to date; New Haven, Conn.: 1959–1983), 12:345–350.

Parker was the bearer of the sad news in a letter to Franklin that their "Old Friend" was "in a State of Ruin occasioned by his Security for one Mr. Blagge in New York for upwards $500, Blagge having been his some Time before for about $200, and Blagge being ruined, Mr. Hughes is fell upon, he keeps close this Instant: but is trying to get all delivered up and become entirely Insolvent, rather than go and lye in Jail, which will be his Fortune, if he is catch'd."[15] Hughes was never caught, but he was obliged in the years following to stay "close," confining himself to his home, and thus his role as an ardent Liberty Boy was necessarily played out in the shadows. We catch only occasional glimpses of him on secret missions or in private correspondence in which he is very much the confidential informant. But he is never to be seen in the public places where the committeemen served and where the plaudits of the crowd were to be had.

Franklin's interest in his "Old Friend," it should be noted, was more than sentimental. Hughes had ordered an "Electrical Machine" and other scientific apparatus from the London-based Franklin and could not now accept the consignment. He was soon complaining, Parker wrote, that "he had not requested a 10th part of them and the Electrical Machine; he understood was not to exceed two Guineas."[16] The "Old Friend" was obviously not in a friendly mood. But the incident does afford us another opportunity to gauge the breadth of Hughes' intellectual interests, as was soon manifested in a more practical context.

Hughes' creditors, according to Parker, were not prepared to accept a settlement based upon the liquidation of his assets "in Hopes if he is sent to Goal, that his Brother would relieve him: This he says he will by no Means allow of."[17] It cannot be said whether Hughes' reluctance was more a matter of pride or politics, but he was certainly much offended "being one of the Sons of Liberty, at the general Odium cast upon his Brother in Philadelphia," and extended his opprobrium even to Franklin, who was at the time under a cloud for having too easily capitulated to the Stamp Act. Months after the repeal of the Stamp Act Parker found Hughes still "keeping close" and "very much

---

15. Parker to Franklin, Aug. 8, 1765, *Franklin Papers*, 12:232. See also *New York Gazette*, April 18, 1765.

16. Parker to Franklin, Jan. 9, 1766, *Franklin Papers*, 13:13–14.

17. Ibid.

displeased both with his Brother and You. . . . Maugre all I can say to the contrary: But I observe, those who have little or nothing to lose, are the greatest Sons of Liberty."[18] Which last impertinence raises a crucial issue.

It would be the worst sort of reductionism to hold that Hughes' radicalism was nothing more than a response to financial adversity. What does bear consideration are the larger circumstances mirrored in Hughes' personal affairs which may be said to have contributed to that community of interest and outlook from which issued the radical politics of the Sons of Liberty. The leading radicals at the time seem to have been men cut from the same middle-class cloth. There were tradesmen like Hughes or Marinus Willett, or former tradesmen such as John Lamb, aspiring to greater place in the ranks of the local burghers; privateers like Isaac Sears turned merchant in the aftermath of the French war; drygoods merchants like Edward Laight seeking to expand their sphere of operations into the manufacture of ironware; failed merchants like Joseph Allicocke desperately clinging to illusions of gentility.[19] "Business is here very languid," reported a leading New York merchant in August, 1765, "the weak must go to the Wall, frequent Bankruptcies and growing more frequent."[20] More to the point, the weak were all too frequently just such enterprising individu-

18. Parker to Franklin, Nov. 11, 1766, *Franklin Papers*, 13:494.

19. Lamb had been an instrument maker before turning to the wine trade in the halcyon years of the French and Indian War. Isaac Sears was similarly in the wine trade in the post-war years,* as well as in ironware, according to Robert Christen, "King Sears." Sears' maritime background is treated extensively by Christen, but see also "Isaac Sears and the Business of Revolution," in Maier, *Old Revolutionaries*, pp. 51–100, in which Sears' revolutionary radicalism is, in fact, reduced to a matter of vulgar self-interest. It should be noted that the trade in Madeira wines slumped badly after the conclusion of the French war and that this condition was attributed at least in part by New York merchants to the impending Parliamentary duty on wines. (*Letter Book of John Watts of New York, 1762–1765*, New-York Historical Society *Collections* [1928], pp. 286, 381). Marinus Willett is listed as a cabinetmaker in 1765 (*Burghers of New Amsterdam*, p. 207), but within a few years was calling himself a merchant. See *Dictionary of American Biography* sketch on Willett. Edward Laight is an interesting case of a merchant who was earlier associated with the Liberty Boys but ultimately chose loyalism. For his business interests see the *Archives of the State of New Jersey*, First Series (Newspaper Extracts, 11 vols., 1884–1928), XXVI:553; *The Arts and Crafts in New York, 1726–1776*, New-York Historical Society *Collections* (1938), pp. 219, 220; Virginia D. Harrington, *The New York Merchant on the Eve of the Revolution* (New York, 1935), p. 151. Joseph Allicocke's fallen state is described in the *Watts Letter Book*, p. 372. Allicocke's social pretentions are indicated by the fact that he registered as a "Gentleman" in the roster of freemen, *Burghers of New Amsterdam*, p. 217.

20. *Watts Letter Book*, p. 368.

als who had overextended themselves in the flush of wartime prosperity only now to be brought back to the reality of their limited resources in capital and credit. But these men were not simply the victims of their own poor judgment. They were, after all, the casualties of an economic order that demanded risk-taking as the price of success. It is not surprising that some of them would begin to reason that success was not necessarily a measure of worth and that government should withdraw from the marketplace as it should also withdraw in matters of conscience.[21] These were the related concerns of a generation of hard-pressed colonials who had been reared to middle-class expectations of worldly success but also to a Protestant suspicion of worldly values, from which contradiction emerged the tenets of an American liberalism.[22]

There was still another dimension to Hughes' circumstances. He was not just suffering the consequences of an ill-fated economy, he was also an artisan-entrepreneur caught up in the stresses of an evolving system of production that would in time outmode such craft proprietorship. But even in this earlier period of small-scale shop production, the process of functional differentiation was sufficiently underway to foster divisions within the ranks of the artisan class, some few beginning to see themselves in a more exclusively entrepreneurial role while the greater number struggled to preserve their traditional status as

21. A piece in the *New-York Journal*, October 23, 1766, on "The ill Policy and Inhumanity of imprisoning insolvent Debtors," clearly delineates the developing middle class ethic of a morally neutral market place. After remarking that "a man without money, is next to nothing," the writer notes that "the arbitrary value which the tyranny of custom has unjustly fixed upon money, is the reason that mankind run such risques, and embrace such danger to obtain it; and men are so united and dependent upon one another in society, and especially in trade, that one individual cannot suffer, but some other must suffer with him. This is the case more especially with regard to merchants and traders who are every moment liable to misfortunes. ... Hope of gain induces traders in general, to hazard much and to enterprise too deeply ... if they succeed, they are ... outwardly applauded and caressed." Others are induced "to attempt and venture upon such like enterprises, but alas! they are dashed to pieces in a moment! And the unfortunate persons immediately deemed and called rogues and villains and treated as such. ... Therefore to judge a man's principles, or Conduct, to be good or bad merely from his success and prosperity or his misfortunes and adversity is a very weak (if not wicked) conclusion and judgement."

22. Joyce Appleby, "The Social Origins of American Revolutionary Ideology," *Journal of American History* LXIV (March, 1978), 935–958, offers a cogent analysis of the relationship of marketplace concerns to an emergent American liberalism. See also her "Modernization Theory and the Formation of Modern Social Theories in England and America," *Comparative Studies in Society and History* 20 (April, 1978), 259–285.

craftsmen against a rising tide of wage labor. These were not imagined issues but played themselves out in a variety of disputes over public policy, ranging from the regulation of prices and wages to the exclusion of unlicensed or non-resident laborers.[23] We cannot know in detail where Hughes stood with respect to these specific issues, but we can surmise from both his political associations and his later statements on related matters that he perceived the contest with the Mother Country within an anti-mercantilist framework. At the same time, Hughes' attachment to the mechanic class occasionally outweighed the imperatives of an emergent free enterprise ideology, as he was to demonstrate during the war years by his advocacy of some system of price controls.[24] James Parker's acerbic retort that those who had the least to lose were "the greatest Sons of Liberty" therefore has some merit but only when amended to read the least to lose and the most to gain.

In the same letter of January 9, 1766, in which Parker referred to Hugh Hughes' refusal of possible assistance from his brother, John, there is an intimation of a new livelihood: Hugh was keeping school.[25] The tradesman had assumed the role of pedagogue, more evidence of an expansiveness of mind which seems to have been characteristic of many such upward bound "middling" men in the fluid environment of Revolutionary America. Another correspondent summed up Hughes' status towards the close of 1771, presumably the situation in which he was to remain until the outbreak of rebellion: " . . . to avoid an

23. Charles S. Olton, *Artisans for Independence: Philadelphia Mechanics and the American Revolution* (Syracuse, 1975), pp. 7–18, believes that "the mechanic class was preponderantly composed of independent entrepreneurs, not employees, and that in any event the behavior of the class was almost wholly determined by the entrepreneurial element." Eric Foner, *Tom Paine and Revolutionary America* (New York, 1976), pp. 29–32, concludes differently that "at any one time, the majority of the men engaged in these trades were probably wage-earning journeymen" even if they could reasonably look forward to independent status at some future time. Richard B. Morris, "Labor and Mercantilism in the Revolutionary Era," in Morris, ed., *The Era of the American Revolution* (New York, 1939), p. 78, notes "that by the eve of the Revolution the conflict between *laissez faire* and mercantilism was becoming sharper," and in his succeeding pages offers evidence of that contest.

24. See pp. 252–253 below.

25. *Franklin Papers,* 13:14, is the first reference to Hughes keeping a school. Thereafter the reports are regular. Parker to Franklin, Sept. 11, Oct. 25, 1766, ibid., pp. 413, 475. Hughes advertised in the *New York Journal or General Advertiser,* March 12, 1767, that he was offering "Morning and Evening School, for the Instruction of Youth in Writing and Arithmatic," commencing April 1, which would seem to indicate an expanded enterprise.

Arrest, [Hughes] has, for many years past, made himself a voluntary Prisoner in his own House, where he has supported a numerous Family of Children, by teaching School, given his Children a very good Education, and greatly improved his own Knowledge; his being the best, as well as the most considerable English School in Town." Not surprisingly, Hughes was barely getting by, and, according to this informant, had "greatly impaired his Health and Constitituion" for reason of leading "a life so sedentary for so long a Time."[26] (This is the first in a series of reports of ill health which continued through the war and post-war years, nothwithstanding which Hughes lived to the fairly ripe old age of seventy-five.)

John Holt, the writer of the above letter, and another of Franklin's printer associates, gives us the closest account of the rift in the relations of the Hughes brothers, blaming himself in part for the outcome. Hugh Hughes, Holt informed Franklin, had from the first strongly opposed the Stamp Act. "There had till then subsisted the greatest Cordiality between the two Brothers," but that harmony was abruptly sundered by their differing responses to the measure. An exchange of letters precipitated the break, according to Holt, with Hugh showing "an affectionate Concern for the Rectitude of his Brothers Conduct," while on the other side John adopted "the dictatorial Stile, destitute of Argument, mixt with reproach, and tinctured with that overbearing Haughtiness, assumed by fancied Superiority, not only of Fortune, but Intellects"; so the break occurred, claimed Holt, with the fault clearly lying with the imperious John. Holt recounts his attempt to mediate the quarrel by writing John Hughes a letter, which by his own description would appear to have been half political cajoling and half personal appeal. But "unluckily" the letter was delivered to John Hughes by the hand of a political foe, which led John to believe that his brother and Holt had lent themselves to "a concerted Plan of the Party who opposed him."[27]

All this sorry history was clearly designed by the writer to enlist Franklin's assistance in behalf of the unfortunate Hugh Hughes. Holt closes on that note by referring to John Hughes' offer of help to his brother as such that "no Man of Spirit or Sense could accept ... and so humiliating ... that any As-

26. John Holt to Franklin, Oct. 2, 1771. *Franklin Papers,* 18:227.
27. Ibid., 225–227.

sistance he should receive, would have been at the Price of his Freedom and Independency." Nonetheless, there is evidence that Hugh did in fact borrow a sum of money from his brother some months before friend Holt sent off his appeal to Franklin. In any case, the fraternal conflict was shortly terminated with the death of John Hughes in February, 1772.[28] Thus was the elder brother spared the final humiliation of the War for Independence, an event that would briefly elevate the younger Hughes into a position of some dignity and consequence before an unkind fate once again discarded him.

On July 12, 1775, the die having been cast a few months earlier at Lexington and Concord, Samuel Adams was writing from Philadelphia to James Warren at Watertown in behalf of "Mr. Hugh Hughes of New York, a worthy sensible Man, whose Virtue has rendered him obnoxious to all Tories of that City. . . . He is perhaps as poor as I am but 'he goes about doing good.'" Warren replied shortly thereafter indicating that he had seen Hughes and would indeed "Introduce him to our friends . . . ."[29] In a series of letters from Hughes to Samuel and John Adams written in the closing months of that year and into the next we are afforded some better explanation of Hughes "going about doing good." Writing under the *nom de plume*, "The Intelligencer," Hughes passed along to the Adamses a medley of facts and impressions concerning the political climate in New York and environs. The information delivered is interesting in itself, but also revealing as an insight into Hughes' own perspective on events. In a letter of October 17, 1775, for example, he comments on the local resistance to the authority of the Continental Congress, remarking that "this is not a little owing to the Timidity of a Set of Creatures call'd Whigs, but who are neither Whigs nor Tories, in reality, — a Sort of political 'Maphrodite'," and then concluding, "I much question if any Thing will save us, but immediate and open Force, and that under the Direction of a discerning and vigilant Commandant. Nay, I some Times think, it is such an important Post, it might be

28. Ibid., 227. John Hughes Papers contain a document, dated Dec. 8, 1770, listing obligations owed to John Hughes, one of which includes the notation, "Hugh Hughes is to pay his brother John ... 250:0:0." Morgan, *Stamp Act Crisis*, pp. 371–373, recounts John Hughes' last years. His end came in Charleston, South Carolina, where he had been serving as a collector of customs, no doubt as a reward for his resistance to popular pressures in 1765–1766.

29. "Warren-Adams Letters," *Massachusetts Historical Society Collections*, 72 (1917), 82; Warren to Adams, July 27, 1775, ibid., 73 (1925), 416.

John Lamb asking a New York gathering if East India Company tea should be landed. From Lamb and Harrison, History of the City of New York.

safer for the Continental Congress to take it under their sole Authority, especially when I consider the Conduct of the Provincial Congress."[30]

Two months later "The Intelligencer" sounds again the authentic voice of the revolutionary radical on a rather different issue—slavery.

Would it answer a good Purpose, if the Congress should spare a few Moments to reply to that Scoundrel Dunmore's infamous Proclamation, by showing that the former Congress, as well as the several Assemblies, especially Virginia, Pennsylvania Etc., Etc., have endeavour'd to put a total stop to the disgraceful and inhuman Practice of enslaving our Fellowmen, and that it was defeated by his Master and his Creatures?

It would, at least, I think, have a salutary Effect in all the Colonies, by affording the poor desponding Sufferers a gleam of Hope that whenever we have it in our Power, we shall give them all the Relief their and our Circumstances will permit. This I hope we shall never lose Sight of till it is happily completed.

I don't like those half pac'd Sons of Liberty that only want Freedom for themselves; if we contend for Liberty, let us show that we are worthy of it,

30. Samuel Adams Papers, New York Public Library.

by diffusing the Blessings of it to the whole human Race, within our Influence. . . . [31]

Hughes appealed again to Samuel Adams in a subsequent letter to use his influence with the Congress in behalf of these "unhappy Sufferers," the black slaves, and would continue to lament the incongruity of slavery with American pretentions to freedom in the post-war period.[32]

In the same letter of January 8, 1776, Hughes was again critical of the timidity of his fellow provincials, remarking upon "the absolute Necessity . . . for adopting some national System of Government." It was shortly thereafter that Tom Paine's *Common Sense* brought such latent sentiments to the surface, and Hughes predictably was among the first to step forward in defense of that clarion call to independence. He rebuked Alexander McDougall, one of those "half-pac'd Sons of Liberty," for trying to stop the local publication of *Common Sense,* remarking that the people "are constantly treading on their leaders heels" and asserting "that there never was anything published here within these thirty years . . . that has been more universally approved and admired."[33]

Whatever Hughes' impatience with Alexander McDougall, the latter appears to have played a role in the sequence of events that led to Hughes' appointment as a deputy quartermaster general. Hughes had himself broached the possibility to Sam Adams in an earlier letter, the contents of which are revealing with respect to the inner workings of the revolutionary movement.

Since I wrote to you last, I have considered your kind offer of using your Influence in my favour. . . . As I told one of you then, my Circumstances are such, that I cannot accept of any thing that will not afford a small Surplusage for my Family. If anything offer that will do that, I am most heartily dispos'd to serve my suffering Country, and shall gratefully acknowledge your Favour in my Behalf. I just mention'd a Secretaryship to you, when present, but, as that may be somewhat precarious, every General having his Favourite, I think

31. Hughes to Samuel Adams, Dec. 22, 1775, ibid. Most of Hughes' letters to the Adamses were dated Fairfield, Connecticut, but he seems to have been moving around at intervals. Hughes to Alexander McDougall, Philadelphia, Nov. 2, 1775, McDougall Papers, New-York Historical Society, has him meeting with Charles Thompson, delivering a letter to John Jay and going over "the State of Affairs in our Province" with him, and visiting with other members of Congress.

32. Hughes to Samuel Adams, Jan. 8, 1776, Samuel Adams Papers.

33. Hughes to Samuel Adams, Feb. 4 (?), 1776, ibid.

a Deputy Quartermastership General preferable to it. However, if you know of any thing better, and think I can discharge the Trust, to the Satisfaction of the Publick, I submit to your Decision.[34]

The stage was obviously well set for Hughes' recruitment by the Quartermaster Department when the New York Provincial Congress acted favorably on a report brought out by a committee headed by Colonel McDougall recommending Hughes for the new post of commissary of military stores in New York. It was shortly thereafter that Hughes received his commission as a colonel in the Continental army and appointment as deputy quartermaster general for the New York district.[35] The system of republican patronage, it would appear, was well underway.

It proved to be a grinding duty for Hughes, with little of the glamour of military service attached to it, and certainly little in the way of acknowledgement or reward from his fellow countrymen in the aftermath. Hughes' finest moment as a soldier probably came with the American defeat on Long Island on August 27–28, 1776, when Washington's shattered forces had somehow to be ferried across the East River to Manhattan Island. "I recollect very well," the general recalled for Hughes' benefit years later, "that it was a day which required the greatest exertion, particularly in the quartermaster's department, to accomplish the retreat which was intended under cover of the succeeding night."[36] But such heroics were for the most part exceptional for Hughes. A reading of his wartime letterbooks discloses a tedious round of assignments, endlessly plagued by the frustrations of poor organization, meager resources and insatiable demands. Hughes seems to have borne it all with a combination of tact and fortitude, occasional flashes of exasperation but also good humor. He wrote to an associate at Albany, "If you can procure but half a Dozen Barrels of Tar, pawn your old Cap and send them here," and to that same gentleman who had been remonstrating about the urgent need for "Money, Money, Money," "Yours of the 6th Current overtook me here last Evening, and . . . it is full of an Article that I

34. Hughes to Samuel Adams, Dec. 22, 1775, ibid.

35. *Journal of the Provincial Congress . . . of the State of New-York* (2 vols.; Albany, 1842), I:302. See also *The Memorial and Documents in the Case of Colonel Hugh Hughes . . . Respectfully Submitted to Congress, by the Memorialist* (Washington city, January, 1802), p. 3.

36. Washington to Hughes, Aug. 22, 1784, *Hughes Memorial,* p. 10.

have had Nothing to do with for some time past, I mean *Money,*" but he offered as consolation "that the whole York Line embark'd at West Point the Day before yesterday for your Quarter, which will find you employment enough *without Money.*" In a similar vein of irony he informed Colonel Henry Dearborn, "Let me know all your Wants at once, as it is just as easy to disappoint you of the whole . . . as one or two." With another subordinate, Hughes' wit cut more sharply. "Don't fill your letters with such c———d longtail'd Words, Similes, Tropes and Figures. Write to the Purpose in good plain Style, and you'll be much more regarded. You only raise laughter by your Flights and c. which are out of character for a Man of Business." The canon of an emergent republican culture is thus delineated.[37]

Hughes' correspondence deals with boards and planks, horses and hay for the horses, tar, paper, and sealing wax, and canteens, of "which there is not any thing of greater Importance to an Army . . . at this Drouthy Season."[38] And in season and out there was always the maddening shortage of funds. Hughes was continually under pressure from his assistants for cash with which to satisfy the demands of suppliers, and he was continually obliged to caution his harried agents "against making Promises of payment." Deferred payment was the rule. "The office here don't pay more than 4th or 8th and give specie Certificates for the Residue. We shall not keep the *Great Wheel* in Motion, if we don't observe the greatest Frugality in our Expenditures." But frugality was hardly the issue where "Every Door is shut up at paper money, and nothing but Solid will enable us to carry on Business," which was the leit motif in almost every communication from his subordinates in the field.[39]

The Man of Business was sustained in the final analysis by the revolutionary idealist. "Never were Exertions more requisite

37. Hugh Hughes Letter Books in the New-York Historical Society consist of 19 manuscript volumes of varying length organized more or less by correspondents, and are a mine of information about the operations of the Quartermaster Department. For the references above see Hughes to Major Nicholas Quackenbush, Oct. 17, Nov. 11, 1780 (Letter Book 8); Hughes to Colonel Henry Dearborn, July 28, 1781 (Letter Book 14); Hughes to Major Daniel Carthy, Feb. 27, 1781 (Letter Book 3).

38. Hughes to Peter De Haven, July 18, 1776 (Letter Book 2). Hughes was here seeking to purchase 5,000 wooden canteens and 3,000 pails.

39. Hughes to Major Nicholas Quackenbush, Feb. 1, 25, 1781, Quackenbush to Hughes, Feb. 24, 1781 (Letter Book 8); Major John Keese to Hughes, Aug. 27, 1781 (Letter Book 15).

than at this time," Hughes informed Major Nicholas Quackenbush, his assistant at Albany, "immense Quantities of every
species of Stores to procure, both for the Main Army and the
Department in the State, when the Season is greatly advanced
and our Finances totally deranged. But this must not discourage
us, the greater the Difficulty the more Credit in surmounting
them. We must succeed or Perish and if we die, let it be
gloriously, not in a Ditch." To the long-winded Major Carthy he
mused on the "mysterious" manner in which "we get along
from year to year without money Stores or Credit at Times," and
then provides the ultimate explanation. "But the Country is to
be free and it's not essential whether we have them or not, use
them frugally or profusely, we are to prepare an Asylum for the
small Remains of expiring Liberty in the old World, where
Anarchy and aristocracy, those implacable Enemies to the
Rights of Men have long stalked Truth and Justice out of
countenance." And then Hughes catches himself up— "so
much by way of Rhapsody," and he is back to being the Man of
Business.[40]

Hughes' dedication to the American cause was severely tested
when General Nathanael Greene was placed in command of a
reorganized quartermaster department, involving alterations in
the chain of command which the sensitive Hughes construed as
a downgrading of his post, and which it may very well have
been.[41] In any case he resigned his position, whereupon followed a round of correspondence with Greene which reveals the
curious mixture of high-minded idealism and rather petty ego-
ism that so often turns up in the revolutionary character.

Greene responded to Hughes' letter of resignation by strongly
urging him "to reconsider the matter — I am induced to request
this, from your general Character and the Satisfaction you have
given in transacting the business of the Department." Having
flattered his man, Greene then baited the hook with expectations
of material advantage. Hughes' "situation," the General
pointed out, would be "both honorable and profitable," and "if
you are not wounded on the one hand, and not too wealthy to

40. Hughes to Quackenbush, Feb. 1, 1781 (Letter Book 8) and to Major Daniel
Carthy, Nov. 28, 1781 (Letter Book 3).

41. See Richard Showman, ed., *The Papers of General Nathanael Greene* (2 vols. to
date; Chapel Hill, 1976–   ), II:307–313. For an account of the operations of the
Quartermaster Department that is somewhat more comprehensive, see Louis Clinton
Hatch, *The Administration of the American Revolutionary Army* (New York, 1904), pp.
86–123.

Nathanael Greene. From Appleton's Cyclopaedia.

regard profit on the other, I should think you an Enemy to your own Interest to reject so considerable an appointment."[42] Hughes' reply was all wounded vanity and noble sentiments. In the first instance he had been "deprived of rank and left at the will and pleasure of those just over me"; and then drawing himself up to his full patriotic height, Hughes expostulated,

42. Greene to Hughes, April 16, 1778, *Papers of General Nathanael Greene*, II: 342–343.

You speak of Profits & Emoluments—that I am an entire stranger to, I assure you Sir.—I never derived any benefit from the Office but my Wages & Rations.—I have heard that the Gentlemen of the new Arrangement are so happy as to have it in their power to enjoy very great Profits & Emoluments, which, if so, may perhaps give Rise to the Idea of others having had the same, or similar advantages—and as to the Honorary Part, whatever was, is now done away, as far as concerned me.[43]

Hughes came down to earth somewhat in a subsequent letter to General Greene in which he gave a frank appraisal of the problems of the department, the principal one of course being the lack of cash, a commodity that could only be "procured by negotiating Loan Office Certificates, where a Friend could be found that has a little to Spare, and that is call'd for much faster than collected, by public Creditors of long standing." Rather apologetically, Hughes remarked that he offered his comments out of a sense of "The Duty I owe my Country," and that "tho' I quit the Department, it does not follow I shall the Country, or cause."[44] And indeed he did not.

Hughes' resignation from the Quartermaster Department in the spring of 1778 did not by any means terminate his business with that department. He was obliged to go on settling up accounts, almost, it would appear, indefinitely. In this, he was at least in part the victim of the indiscretions of his former superior, General Thomas Mifflin, which had precipitated the appointment of General Greene as the new quartermaster general. A circular, dated March 5, 1779, addressed to Hughes from Mifflin's adjutant, alerted him to "the Necessity of having Accounts and Vouchers perfectly arranged against the time they may be Called upon for a Settlement, which must be shortly." Mifflin thought it "just" to inform his late deputies "that as his Department has had its Enemies, and in some cases been very maliciously traduced, the Strictest Scrutiny will be observed with the Accounts."[45] Hughes was soon writing to complain that his constituents in New York were either being misled or unfairly treated by Mifflin's plan of settlement. It would appear that the latter was offering to settle accounts with certificates rather than hard money and calling that "immediate payment." Creditors were refusing "to bring in their Accots on those

---

43. Hughes to Greene, April 23, 1778, ibid., 352–353.

44. Hughes to Greene, May 3, 1778, ibid, 373–375.

45. Circular, Philadelphia, March 5, 1779, Anthony Butler to Hughes (Hughes Letter Book 1).

terms," Hughes noted, all of which could have been avoided, he lamented, "If the money I drew for, had been sent me" in the first place. With or without the slippery Mifflin, the affairs of the Quartermaster Department were bound to remain a tangled mess from which Hugh Hughes would never entirely extricate himself.[46]

In the following summer of 1780, Hughes was again called upon to assume the duties of deputy quartermaster general for the New York district, an assignment he accepted when still another quartermaster general, Colonel Timothy Pickering, put it to him as a matter of "absolute necessity" rather than pecuniary opportunity. In his later memorial to Congress seeking reimbursement for wartime incurred expenditures, Hughes noted that his acceptance of the post "prevented a delivery of accounts as intended."[47] But whatever the circumstances, Hughes renewed involvement was to push him even more deeply into a financial quagmire.

Hughes' second tour of duty in the Quartermaster Department was to prove even more demanding than his first. His letterbooks indicate a marked improvement in the organization of the department, and Hughes seems much more in control of his staff, but the problems of supply and morale had considerably deepened with the passage of time. The *rage militaire* which had characterized the opening phase of the rebellion had long since faded to be replaced by a spirit of cynicism and narrow self-interest.[48] Hughes responded by insisting even more firmly that the men serving under him perform their tasks conscientiously. "Where are you and what are you about?" he queried Major Quackenbush in mid-October, 1780. "I am in great Anxiety to know the State of the Department. . . . I hear you have met with some Difficulties . . . but Time, Industry and Perseverance will carry us through triumphantly, there is no doubt. We have seen darker Days than these." And again to Quackenbush the follow-

46. Hughes to Anthony Butler, June 13, 1779, ibia. Hughes did comply with Colonel Butler's request for a full accounting of transactions undertaken under Mifflin's command. Butler to Hughes, June 14, 1779, Hughes to Butler, June 23, 1779, ibid.

47. Pickering to Hughes, Aug. 31, 1780, and "To the Honorable the Senate and House of Representatives of the United States," Feb. 18, 1793, in *Hughes Memorial*, pp. 4, 14–15.

48. Charles Royster, *A Revolutionary People at War: The Continental Army and American Character, 1775–1783* (Chapel Hill, 1979), pp. 25–53, employs the term *rage militaire* to describe the enthusiasm for military service and ritual that swept through the colonies with the outbreak of fighting in 1775. The trauma of the later years of the war is described in the chapter entitled "Division," pp. 295–330.

ing month on a matter of disposing of some unfit horses, "Let the Person that sells them have no Connection with the Department. ... It is not enough to avoid evil, but we must avoid every appearance of it." To another of his field assistants who had allowed one of his men compassionate leave, Hughes remarked sarcastically "Perhaps you have more Humanity than I" as it is said "that we lose much of our sympathetic Tenderness by Age .... Yet, you will readily allow, I am persuaded, that it is my duty to endeavour to prevent even your most laudable Virtues from prejudicing the Public Service under my direction, and I really esteem it a cardinal virtue to [be] compassionate [to] the Sufferings of our Fellow Creatures ... and not by a partial present Sympathy for one, lose Sight of thousands."[49]

Hughes was in fact a sensitive man, obviously torn by the conflicting claims of his office and his strong human sympathies. "Let me give you one friendly caution more," he remarked to another of his assistants. "If you cannot refrain from Liquor and give greater attention, you will not answer your Appointment." Then emboldened by having broken the ice, he launched into a diatribe. "There must be an *Attention* and a Desire to promote Service allotted you, by endeavouring to enter into the very Spirit of it, with Mind as well as Body. This I have not seen you attempt. Nay, the whole seems an irksome affair to you, especially if any body will trifle away time with you. Another practice you are in ... is quitting Business the Moment I step out," and then back to the "inordinate Lust for Spiritous Liquors." But then Hughes rather lamely concludes, "Yet I don't mean to infringe on the Rights of Nature."[50]

It was this strong sense of duty that made Hughes particularly sensitive to the criticisms that were continually directed at the Quartermaster Department, criticisms he felt were unjust in the light of the department's inadequate support. "It is most unreasonable conduct of the publick to suffer the service to be retarded for what there is plenty of in the Country," he charged more than once. "Nay, even of cash there is no real scarcity, whatever they pretended may be." But most of all Hughes reacted to complaints from his comrades-in-arms. "The Gentlemen of the Line, or State," he observed bitterly in a letter to General William Heath in which he tendered his resignation as

49. Hughes to Quackenbush, Oct. 17, Nov. 7, 1780 (Letter Book 8) and to Major Keese, Nov. 9, 1781 (Letter Book 15).

50. Hughes to John Tyson, Nov. 9, 1781 (Letter Book 15).

Quartermaster for the Main Army, failed to "make sufficient allowances for the want of Cash or Stores in the Quartermaster Generals' Department." They behaved as if "the Department was crowded with Stores and drew cash by Millions." Hughes refused to "be answerable for the deficiencies of Supplies of any kind whatever where they are occasioned by a want of Cash. Neither is it practicable to organize either Department, Army or State in such a manner as if expenses or wages were paid in reasonable time." The people he employed as day laborers all too frequently left their jobs "when push'd too hard," and it was difficult to find adequate replacements under the circumstances. Hughes summed it all up in a subsequent letter to Heath: "It is not possible to give satisfaction to all in the present situation of publick affairs. . . . No allowance is made, nay the most trivial circumstance is exaggerated, and painted in the most odious Colours."[51]

General Heath sought to sooth Hughes' injured feelings by insisting that he could not be spared and by complimenting him on his "abilities . . . zeal and attention," but the obviously weary Hughes did step down in December, 1781, as deputy quartermaster general for the Continental army.[52] He remained, however, as deputy for the district, which at this stage of the war took in Massachusetts and part of Connecticut as well as New York. Indeed, Hughes remained in communication with Heath well into 1782 in what seems to be almost the same relationship as before, but that simply illustrates how peculiarly the Quartermaster Department was organized at this time, a state of affairs which Hughes accepted as inevitable under the circumstances.[53]

Hughes' later account to Congress states that he remained with the Quartermaster Department "till sometime in 1783"

51. Hughes to General William Heath, Nov. 26, 28, Dec. 6, 1781 (Letter Book 17).

52. General Heath to Hughes, Nov. 27, Dec. 5, 1781; Hughes to General Heath, Dec. 3, 1781 (Letter Book 17).

53. The letter books clearly indicate that Hughes continued to serve as the deputy quartermaster general for the New York district. He had been doubling before as quartermaster for the Continental army quartered on the Hudson River. See note 54 below, for his further correspondence with General Heath. Hughes' resignation as quartermaster for the army may have been speeded up by a procurement crisis in forage which placed him in the middle of a tug-of-war involving Robert Morris, the superintendent of finance. For the latter see his letter to William Denning, Nov. 30, 1781, and Denning's letter to Robert Morris, Nov. 23, 1781 (Letter Book 18). The Denning letter, with appropriate notes, appears in E. James Ferguson, ed., *The Papers of Robert Morris* (5 vols. to date; Pittsburgh, Pa., 1973–   ), III:241–243.

when his branch of the department was disbanded. In this last period of service he managed one last notable contribution to his country by taking the initiative in rescuing a considerable store of arms and powder that had somehow been left on the wrong side of the Hudson River and was thus vulnerable to seizure by Tory sympathizers. For this action he was warmly commended by General Heath who also informed General Washington.[54] But disaster again struck Hughes, setting the stage for his leaving the Quartermaster Department as he had entered it— in financial difficulty. Having received from the department a sum of money with which to purchase boards, the indefatigable deputy was returning to Albany one cold November evening, and, as he tells the story, went off in search of some means of transport across the Hudson, having "fastened his horse near the landing, leaving the saddle bags in which were 1001 dollars," only to discover on arriving at his destination that his bags had been pilfered. Efforts to recover the stolen funds were unavailing.[55] Thus was poor Hughes literally left holding the bag.

Hughes' memorial to Congress in 1793 recounts his continuing efforts after the war for reimbursement of debts "incurred in his private capacity, when supplies could not be procured, by any means on public credit," all to no avail. Not only was he rebuffed by an unsympathetic superintendent of finances, Robert Morris, who found Hughes' affairs much too "deranged" to give satisfaction, but later suffered further misfortune when a fire destroyed almost all of the documentation that he had painfully assembled in anticipation of that final day of reckoning. He was thereupon advised by a federal auditor to solicit statements from wartime associates who might confirm his claims. But as Hughes plaintively pointed out in his 1793 memorial to Congress, a good many of those men were dead and gone and that "the gentlemen at the head of the treasury department" had therefore suggested that a settlement of his claims required an act of Congress.[56] As might have been expected, his appeal went for naught.

54. Hughes to General Heath, Feb. 15, 20, 1782; General Heath to Hughes, Feb. 18, 22, 1782; General Heath to Washington, Feb. 23, 1782 (Letter Book 17).

55. *Hughes Memorial*, pp. 4–6.

56. Hughes to Colonel Tomothy Pickering, July 19, 1784, ibid., pp. 20–24; in his 1793 memorial to Congress Hughes reported the "disastrous accident by fire" which occurred in January, 1789, destroying his home and along with it all the papers he had been gathering to support his case, ibid., pp. 6–7.

Hughes' lack of success with Congress was a manifestation of more than his own ill luck and messy bookkeeping. He was in a very real sense the victim, as were thousands of other war veterans, of an ongoing struggle for the control of fiscal and economic policy. He may also have been particularly singled out because of his continued affiliation with the old Liberty Boys, most of whom had aligned themselves with the dominant Clinton faction in New York during the war years and who seem to have retained some degree of cohesiveness as a group even in the midst of hostilities.[57] The revolutionary coalition was clearly most fragile on issues of economic policy, and it was on just such an issue that Hughes made his presence felt for the brief period during which he was relieved of his military duties.

The Revolutionary was very much the social radical when he renewed his correspondence with Sam Adams in the summer of 1779. As chairman of the "Committee of Refugees" from the lower counties of New York, which were at the time still occupied by British forces, Hughes suggested a plan for "breaking up an infamous Gang of Monopolisers and Extortioners, who have too long preyed upon their distressed Country." It was the intention of Hughes' committee to undercut the profiteers by purchasing and distributing such goods as were in short supply at a fixed rate of 8 percent profit. To that end they had gathered a sum of money with which they hoped to make their purchases in Boston, but as Hughes cautioned Adams, the profiteers "it is imagined are now flocking to your Metropolis with a Design of Forestalling all the most necessary articles of Trade, thereby defeating the salutary Intentions of the Inhabitants of these Parts, as well as others." As a countermeasure, Hughes suggested to Adams that such outsiders coming to trade in the Boston mart be required to show vouchers that would be issued by such committees as his own. "Most certainly Something ought to be adopted immediately or all our Endeavors will be in vain to save the Currency."[58]

The currency, of course, was not saved by such voluntary measures, but the groundwork was laid for the political partisanship of the post-war years, a partisanship to which Hughes, as it happened, lent himself only briefly as an active participant.[59]

57. Alfred F. Young, *The Democratic Republicans of New York: The Origins, 1763–1797* (Chapel Hill, 1967), pp. 10–32.

58. Hughes to Samuel Adams, Aug. 23, 29, 1779, Samuel Adams Papers.

59. Young, *Democratic Republicans*, pp. 28–29; Morris, "Labor and Mercantilism."

He was to be once again much too concerned with financial survival to play a leading part, and perhaps at this time of his life he preferred the more anonymous role of "The Intelligencer." In any event, Hugh serves as a concerned witness to those highly charged times, both by virtue of his personal connections with some of the men who did play a more direct part and perhaps even more importantly because he brings to bear a singularly consistent point of view, relatively undisturbed by considerations of private advantage or party expediency.

Before he stepped aside, Hughes did have one last encounter with public office. With the British evacuation of New York City in November, 1783, the stage was set for the return of revolutionary refugees and the subsequent election at year's end of a slate of "warm and hot headed whigs," as an alarmed Robert R. Livingston described them, to represent metropolitan New York in the State Assembly.[60] Hughes was among that group, which numbered such old associates as Isaac Sears and John Lamb. This was to be perhaps the last such occasion of unity among the men who had taken the lead in the forging of the revolutionary coalition in the port city. A remnant of the old radical leadership, led by a rather more complacent John Lamb and certainly supported by Hugh Hughes, would persevere in an awkward alliance with the upstate landed interests gathered around George Clinton, but within a few years these former Liberty Boys would lose their natural constituency among the mechanics and shopkeepers of the city. It has been suggested that patronage was the cement that bound Lamb and his friends to an alliance that was increasingly viewed as detrimental to the commercial interests of the City of New York.[61] That may have been the case with Lamb, who owed his appointment as Collector of the Port of New York to Governor Clinton, but it can hardly be said of Hughes, who had settled into the life of a

---

pp. 115–139. Foner, *Tom Paine*, pp. 145–182, shows Paine caught up in much the same predicament as Hughes in holding to a generally laissez faire attitude toward government involvement in the economy but still supporting price controls as a matter of equity.

60. Roger Champagne, *Alexander McDougall and the American Revolution in New York* (Schenectady, 1975), pp. 200–204.

61. Young, *Democratic Republicans*, pp. 47–48. Young has by far the best analysis of the Clintonians, adjudging them to be mostly "new men" of the "middling classes," mostly from the counties north of New York City and accordingly more small town and rural than urban. See also Jackson Turner Main, *Political Parties before the Constitution* (Chapel Hill, 1973), pp. 126–154, for an assessment of the issues and voting patterns in post-Revolutionary New York.

country schoolmaster after his single session in the state legislature in 1784. With Hughes it was much more clearly a matter of a
sustained revolutionary idealism which left him abidingly suspicious of the elitist pretentions and privileges of the old ruling
families.

Hughes' brief career as a legislator yields little in the way of a
personal political testament. As might be expected, he took the
hard line on the treatment of Tories, an issue that was very much
tied into the larger question of elitist politics in New York. He
appears also to have voted rather consistently in support of the
commercial interests of his constituents, which at the moment
seems not to have constituted any serious breach of faith with his
loftier principles.[62] But that was not long to be. The mercantile
interests of New York City increasingly lent themselves to the
movement for a stronger national government, a movement
viewed by Hughes and a few radical colleagues of old as designed to restore the primacy of the old ruling families. By
March, 1785, Hughes was vigorously contending "how *absolutely requisite* it is, to continually guard against power, for
when once Bodies of Men, in Authority, get Possession, or
become invested with, Property or Prerogative, whether it be by
Intrigue, Mistake, or Chance, they rarely ever relinquish their
claim, even if found in Iniquity itself."[63]

If Hughes adhered to the conventional wisdom that men were
too easily corrupted by power, he was nonetheless sanguine
about the good sense and civic rectitude of ordinary folk (at least
on these shores) when left to their own devices. Complaining
about the "administration of the General Government" during
Washington's second term in office, Hughes found it ironic that
if the people are the basis of government, the administration did
"not consult their Genius and Conciliate their affections."

I am Confident that a very great Majority of the Inhabitants of the U. States are
as easily governed, if I may use a Phrase that I don't approve, as any People in
the World of equal Knowledge and sense of what is just and right. What
support can administration expect from the people, when they treat them with
Contempt in not thinking them worthy of Notice?

62. Main, *Political Parties*, p. 42, Table 2.5, shows that Hughes voted rather consistently as a "cosmopolitan," a category devised by Main to describe a legislator of a
broad world outlook. But it should be noted that in this first session following the close
of hostilities the issues that would shortly form the basis for political coalitions had not
yet fully crystalized.

63. Hughes to Charles Tillinghast, March 7, 1785, Lamb Papers.

But then, what more could be expected of a government grounded in "biennial Representatives and sextennial Senators, and the Executive being chosen by Proxy &c."[64]

It goes without saying that Hughes opposed the ratification of the Constitution when that issue was debated in New York. His opposition was grounded in a radical perception of government as an instrument of privilege.[65] It was from that perspective that he was "not greatly in Favour of corporate Bodies," even if he was prepared to make an exception of the Society of Mechanics when that body sought a charter from the legislature in 1785. With respect to these same mechanics, it should be noted that though he saw them as the salt of the earth, he was nonetheless somewhat condescending in recommending that they "attend properly to the education of their Children" if they wished to make themselves less susceptible to the wiles of political demagogues "as well as render them more truly respectable."[66] Hughes' virtuous mechanics had more than a little in common with Jefferson's virtuous yeomanry in that both groups required some intellectual reinforcement in the enduring contest with wealth and privilege.

Hughes was clearly Jeffersonian in his creed, then, even before that notable arrived on the scene as the recognized leader of the anti-federalist opposition, and without benefit of an agrarian mystique to justify the self-governing capacities of the people. Nor was his republican faith simply an endorsement of state's rights (as Isaac Q. Leake makes it out), but was much more fundamentally attached to a conception of the state itself as inherently threatening to the rights of the individual. In the midst of the War for Independence, sharing in the problems of administering the war effort, he had been quite prepared to embrace a larger vision of national development. "We must extend our Views beyond the Verge of little separate paltry Provinces," he exhorted in a letter concerning ironware, "to that of a Free and United States, calling for every thing necessary for its extended Defenses, and internal Support."[67] But the free and United States he envisioned did not take in any Hamiltonian

64. Hughes to Tillinghast. Aug. 19, 1794, ibid.

65. Hughes to Tillinghast. Nov. 22, 1787, ibid.

66. Hughes to Tillinghast, March 7, 1785, ibid. The political ramifications of the dispute about the Society of Mechanics charter are dealt with in Sidney I. Pomerantz. *New York: An American City, 1783–1803* (New York, 1938), pp. 95–97.

67. Hughes to John Jacob, July 23, 1777 (Hughes Letter Book 2).

John Lamb. From Leake. Memoir of the Life and Times of General John Lamb.

system of economic regulation that wedded the powers of the national government to the interests of a few privileged speculators. Hamilton in this fashion sought to develop an enlightened ruling class; Hughes sought an enlightened people who could be left mostly to their own devices.

Hughes' opposition to slavery was, of course, entirely consistent with his emphasis on the rights of the individual. In this respect it was the states who deserved "the *severest Reproach*" for not yet acting to free the "poor Negroes" from their condition of "perpetual Bondage," a condition that was "Cruelty in the Extreme." Hughes did not hedge his distaste for slavery with the racist qualifications offered by Jefferson. But it is interesting to note that he does attach a condition to his call for the freeing of the slaves "as early as possible it can be done, *with safety*" (my italics). It may be suggested that it was easy enough for Hughes, not having anything to lose by it, to assume so noble a stance in defense of the "poor Negroes," but he was the owner of several slaves in 1790, according to the census of that year.[68]

These slaves more probably belonged to, or were the gift of, John Lamb, on whose farm in the same town of Yonkers, in Westchester County, as reported in the 1790 census, Hughes had settled down to school teaching at least half a decade earlier. He had come out of the Revolution insolvent, so that he was obliged to support himself by teaching the children of a few old friends and political allies. Chief among his patrons were General John Lamb, who had been a leading figure among the Liberty Boys from the outset, and Lamb's son-in-law, Charles Tillinghast, who had served as Hughes' secretary during the war years. Both of these men were Clintonians and anti-federalists, and were themselves still in active communication with other partisans of old, so that we may surmise in these relationships some degree of continuity in the revolutionary radicalism that had once bound them.[69]

It is sometimes asserted that the old radicals were by this time out of step with their former constituency among the mechanics and shopkeepers of New York, but that is to assume a close-knit body of followers of the sort that describes a party more than a revolutionary vanguard whose role it was to cement an alliance of forces considerably larger than itself. Inevitably, with the successful termination of the War for Independence, that coalition dissolved into its constituent elements leaving the radicals of old as no more than a splinter element, particularly because these men were more inclined than most to persist in the principles which had sustained them in the course of the long struggle with England. In any event, time was running out on the generation of Liberty Boys in matters of the flesh as well as of the spirit.

Hughes was among the pallbearers who laid to rest the worthy printer, John Holt, coincidentally with the opening of the polls for the first post-war election in New York City, the election which brought Hughes and his radical colleagues briefly into the ascent in the state legislature. Shortly thereafter, Isaac Sears, the

---

68. Hughes to Tillinghast, March 7, 1785, Lamb Papers.

69. See the letters from Hughes to Tillinghast cited above for personal references to John Lamb and others. Lamb served as chairman of the Federal Republican Committee in opposition to the ratification of the new Constitution in New York. Tillinghast was secretary for that body, and among other adherents were James Miles Hughes, Hugh's younger son, Marinus Willett, one of the original Liberty Boys, and a Major John Wiley who had served under General Lamb in the war and was one of those to whom Hughes sent greetings in his letters to Tillinghast. (A William Wiley had been a member of the radical committee of correspondence in 1766, but the family connection remains to be established.)

notorious "Captain of the Mob," sailed off to the Orient in search of elusive fortune, never to return. General John Lamb passed away in 1800, but not before he too suffered the ignominy of a bankruptcy brought on by too much faith in his fellow man, or at least one of the species. The younger Tillinghast, with whom Hughes had carried on a warm correspondence, had succumbed to yellow fever in the preceding year. It must have been with some considerable fortitude that Hughes, in his seventy-fifth year, mounted one last campaign—for a "settlement of his claims, and a full payment of the balance justly due him."[70]

Reasoning, perhaps, that with the Jeffersonians now in power his chances of success were considerably better than they were in 1793 when he had been turned away by an inhospitable secretary of the treasury who declared himself "so much occupied by other concerns," Hughes journeyed to the new national capital at the close of 1801 to personally attend to his latest appeal to Congress. In his last surviving letter—dated the District of Columbia, January 27, 1802—he refers to a delay in the printing of a small volume of testimonials and documents he had privately undertaken in hopes of expediting his case. It must have been within a few days of his writing that the book appeared in print, but as it turned out it hardly mattered. Hughes died on the fifteenth of March, three days after returning to his residence at Orange-Town, Rockland County, New York.[71] He had finally settled his accounts.

Set against the background of his time and place, Hugh Hughes allows us a better understanding of the cause for which he fought. His was the perspective of a "middling" element of advancing tradesmen and merchants whose earnest espousal of liberty was a harbinger of a new republican order predicated upon the emancipation of class interests from the ancient restraints of rank, estate and privilege. If that project sounds to our modern ears both contradictory and vulgar we would be advised to heed the example of Hughes for whom the American cause was manifestly much more than the narrow pursuit of personal gain. As Joyce Appleby remarks perceptively, the liberalism incorporated in the radicalism of the American Revo-

---

70. Champagne, *Alexander McDougall*, p. 204; *Hughes Memorial*, p. 2.

71. *Hughes Memorial*, p. 2; Hughes to Anthony Lamb, Jan. 27, 1802, Lamb Papers. The *New York Evening Post*, March 20, 1802, carried the report of Hughes' death. Leake, *John Lamb*, p. 370, places his death three days after his return from the District of Columbia, and indicates that his mission had failed.

lution was "more than an ideological gloss on market economics; it was a description of a modern utopia which could garner
the loyalties of a broad range of Americans."[72] Liberty may
have been "good business," as Pauline Maier puts it in her
assessment of Isaac Sears and his radical associates in New
York, but it was also an expression of faith in the self-governing
capacities of ordinary human beings.[73] In this last respect,
Hugh Hughes' sense of the American Revolution as a "super-
natural conflict" may still serve us as we continue to strive, as he
did, "for a part of the miraculous."[74]

72. Appleby, "Social Origins of American Revolutionary Ideology," p. 958.

73. Maier, *Old Revolutionaries,* pp. 97–100.

74. Hughes to Major Keese, Sept. 1, 1781 (Letter Book 15).

Impact of Class Relations and Warfare in the American Revolution: The New York Experience

Sung Bok Kim

Class conflict between landlords and tenants on the great Hudson River estates has been the central theme in the historiography of the American Revolution in New York since the publication in 1909 of Carl Becker's classic study of the province. It has been argued that the lease system as practiced by landlords like the Livingstons, Beekmans, Van Rensselaers, Philipses, and Van Cortlandts in the mid-eighteenth century was onerous, oppressive, and exploitative, with the result that the tenants became impoverished, resentful, and radicalized socially and economically, and that their radicalism, first manifested in the widespread antirent agitation in the 1750s and 1766, was carried on into the revolutionary period, affecting both the course and outcome of the Revolution. The stubborn pursuit of socioeconomic justice by the tenants not only made their Whig landlords reluctant revolutionaries but also accounted for several democratic achievements, such as the confiscation and distribution of the huge Loyalist estates and the establishment of the secret ballot as a mode of voting in elections. In the evolution of the historical drama, the tenants were never passive agents. Although they were not the precipitants of the Revolution at its beginning as the urban radicals in New York City were—so the argument goes—they nevertheless consciously used the Revolution as a vehicle for obtaining socioeconomic justice, a freehold estate, at the expense of their landlord's land title. In sum, because of the radical behavior of the tenant class, historians have maintained that the Revolution in New York was a struggle for "who should rule at home" as well as for home rule.[1]

Sung Bok Kim is associate professor of history at the State University of New York at Albany.

[1] Staughton Lynd more than anyone else has expanded and elaborated on Carl Becker's dual revolution thesis in the New York context. Staughton Lynd, "Tenant Rising at Livingston Manor, May 1777," *New-York Historical Society Quarterly*, 48 (April 1964), 163-77; Staughton Lynd, "Who Should Rule at Home? Dutchess County, New York, in the American Revolution," *William and Mary Quarterly*, 18 (July 1961), 330-59. The following works subscribe in part or in whole to what has become the social-conflict view of life in revolutionary New York: Irving Mark, *Agrarian Conflicts in Colonial New York, 1711-1775* (New York, 1940); Irving Mark, "Agrarian Conflicts in New York and the American Revolution," *Rural Sociology*, 7 (Sept. 1942), 275-93; George

The range and complexity of the subject prohibit a full discussion of all the points raised here. This essay will limit itself to two important questions. First, did the tenants' class relations with their landlords on the Hudson and Mohawk rivers affect their choice of loyalism or whiggism in the revolutionary war? Did they ever take the opposite side of their landlords in the contest because of their alleged traditional class hatred and commitment to a radical socioeconomic plan? Second, in what way did the war influence their attitude toward the Revolution?

Before turning to these questions, it is necessary to outline the general conditions of New York tenantry in the decade preceding the Revolution. By 1775 there were at least six or seven thousand tenant families on about thirty large estates. A considerable number of them were situated on seven large patents, Rensselaerswyck Manor (750,000 acres with about 1,000 tenants), Livingston Manor (160,000 acres with about 500 tenants), Philipse's Highland Patent (200,000 acres with about 500 tenants), Henry Beekman's two patents (100,000 acres with 359 tenants), Philipsburgh Manor (92,000 acres with 272 tenants), Cortlandt Manor (45,000 acres with about 100 tenants), and the Johnson family land (200,000 acres with about 450 tenants).

As I have discussed elsewhere, these tenants, generally unencumbered by feudal obligations and exactions, enjoyed a secure lease tenure. Since they were entitled to an equity in whatever they improved on their leaseholds, they became enviable property owners. Indeed, by 1775 the value of such improvements as house, barn, orchard, nursery, fences, pasture, and cultivated land had generally grown to the point where it rivaled their landlord's soil rights. This equity provided the tenantry with a shield against the landlord's possible tyrannical inclination, for the latter could not threaten eviction to tenants for their delinquent behavior unless he was prepared to pay for the equity. The leaseholds were coveted objects of transactions, like any other commodity, in the real estate market. Newspaper advertisements for leaseholds on sale clearly show that their owners exhibited the usual pride characteristic of property holders. Contemporary observers too perceived the mid-eighteenth-century tenancy to be "profitable," "rich," "thriving," "prosperous," "easy," and, above all, "independent."

The prosperity of the tenantry was related as much to the booming economy of New York during the 1760s and early 1770s as to their liberal leases. Its main staple, food products, commanded high prices both at home and abroad, especially in New England, the West Indies, Ireland, and southern Europe. While the New Englanders were bemoaning land shortage and depression in

Dangerfield, *Chancellor Robert R. Livingston of New York, 1746-1813* (New York, 1960), 20, 57, 81–82; Alice P. Kenney, "The Albany Dutch: Loyalists and Patriots," *New York History*, 42 (Oct. 1961), 339–41; Beatrice G. Reubens, "Pre-Emptive Rights in the Disposition of a Confiscated Estate: Philipsburgh Manor, New York," *William and Mary Quarterly*, 22 (July 1965), 436; Merrill Jensen, *The American Revolution within America* (New York, 1974), 15–16; Edward Countryman, "'Out of the Bounds of the Law': Northern Land Rioters in the Eighteenth Century," in *The American Revolution: Explorations in the History of American Radicalism*, ed. Alfred F. Young (DeKalb, Ill., 1976), 56–57; Richard B. Morris, *The American Revolution Reconsidered* (New York, 1967), 60–61.

their region's economy, New Yorkers were singing a rhapsody of good times. These circumstances explain why so many Yankees and foreigners sought land and settlement in New York, which resulted in the doubling of the province's population from 100,000 to 200,000 in the prerevolutionary decade. It is worth noting that the great Hudson and Mohawk river estates, which had remained sparsely settled in the first half of the century, took a lion's share in this rapid demographic expansion.

To be sure, the record of New York landed society was not all rosy. Several of the estates had been the scene of riots—notably John Van Rensselaer's Claverack (80,000 acres), Livingston Manor, and Philipse's Highland patent in the 1750s and, in 1766, Cortlandt Manor as well. But, with the exception of the last, the conflict revolved around rival land claims and titles between manorial proprietors and squatters. The bone of contention was land itself, not the prevailing lease conditions. Besides, the disturbances were extremely localized events in the areas adjoining the New England colonies of Massachusetts and Connecticut. The outbreaks in Albany County (at Claverack and Livingston Manor) essentially involved aggression by the people from Massachusetts against New York's territory. In the case of the Highland estate, it was simply an insurgency inspired and led by squatters. Only in Cortlandt Manor was there an antilandlord struggle waged by aggrieved tenants, but the conflict was very limited in scale, involving a dozen or so tenant families and one of ten Van Cortlandt proprietary families. Besides, the riot was never directed against the lease system itself but against what the rioters perceived to be an unfair abuse of it by a landlord.

During the first half of the eighteenth century manorial society remained tranquil and orderly. An unusual fact about New York agrarian society is, not that the disturbances occurred in mid-century, but that when violence did occur it failed to spread and spawn a general uprising involving a larger number of tenants. Why was this? The tenantry seems to have had too much at stake in the lease system to rebel. Moreover, the tenant society, composed of individuals holding varying degrees of equity in improvements and subject to frequent turnover of its membership, was not conducive to the growth of class consciousness. Spurred on by the higher expectations of the New World, some tenants, like indentured servants, refused to accept their present lot as their permanent station. Tenancy naturally failed to engender a sense of enduring connection and cohesion among the tenants or to cause them to initiate a collective action on their own. The mentality of the farmers was typically that of petit landed bourgeois; it was conservative, traditional, and apolitical.[2]

After the so-called Great Rebellion of 1766, New York manorial society was politically in the doldrums for nearly a decade. The acute constitutional controversy about Anglo-American relations between Whigs and Loyalists was too academic and too complex to interest ordinary farmers. J. Hector St. John de Crèvecoeur, a farmer-intellectual with 370 acres of well-improved land in

---

[2] For a more detailed account, see Sung Bok Kim, *Landlord and Tenant in Colonial New York: Manorial Society, 1664–1775* (Chapel Hill, 1978).

Orange County who was married to a daughter of a Philipsburgh manor tenant, gave us an insight into the attitude of the country farmers in general when he wrote of his own plight and confusion in the controversy: "As to the argument on which the dispute is founded, I know little about it. Much has been said and written on both sides, but who has a judgment capacious and clear enough to decide? The great moving principles which actuate both parties are much hid from vulgar eyes, like mine."[3] The farmers' intellectual indifference was also matched by their apathy toward any of the political issues that generated so much heat and emotion in New York City. Accustomed to the deferential way of politics in which their social and economic betters thought and acted for them in imperial and provincial affairs, the farmers were not disposed to step forward and try to affect the course of events involving the fate of America in the British Empire.

This apathy and inaction were exemplified by the Cortlandt Manor inhabitants. Both the Whig and Loyalist leaders were equally exasperated with the tenants' "inattention to political matters" and "lethargy." In the early months of 1775, partisan newspaper articles warned the residents of the danger of such indifference and asked them to express their political "sentiments" publicly by action. It is doubtful that these appeals made any lasting impression upon the farmers. The persistence of this apathy was evidenced in another "Address" by a partisan to the same constituents in midsummer in which he denounced them as "very indolent inhabitants."[4]

The farmers' attitude was partly a conditioned reflex of their traditional conservative frame of mind. But it also appears to have been a defensive posture at a time of gathering political storm, consciously adopted against anything that might interfere with their ordinary life. To these farmers, politics without immediate local implications and material benefits was at best a burden and nuisance. This was especially true of the poorest farmers. They always exhibited an extreme aversion to any distraction from farm business, like militia muster, for the loss of time on such occasions could mean the difference between famine and survival for their families.

The Cortlandt Manor farmers were fortunate in that they could continue to enjoy inaction with only a mild rebuke from a chagrined Whig. This was due to the absence of an aggressive leader on either side of the contest. Pierre Van

[3] J. Hector St. John de Crèvecoeur, *Letters from an American Farmer* (New York, 1963), 198. For an excellent discussion of J. Hector St. John de Crèvecoeur's perception of the war and farmers' attitude in general, see R. H. Gabriel, "Crèvecoeur, an Orange County Paradox," *Quarterly Journal of the New York State Historical Association*, 12 (Jan. 1931), 49. For farmers' poor knowledge of the constitutional issues, see also Richbill Williams to Legislature of New York State, June 23, 1781, *Public Papers of George Clinton, First Governor of New York*, ed. Hugh Hastings and J. A. Holden (10 vols., New York, 1899-1914), VII, 39-40; John Grant et al. to George Clinton, May 12, 1781, *ibid.*, VI, 857; and *Calendar of Historical Manuscripts Relating to the War of the Revolution* (2 vols., Albany, 1868), I, 349.

[4] Robert R. Livingston to Margaret Beekman Livingston, May 3, 1775, Livingston Family Papers (New York Public Library, New York, N.Y.); Crèvecoeur, *Letters*, 200-02; *Rivington's New York Gazetteer*, Feb. 16, March 9, 1775; "Address," May 19, 1775, in *American Archives: Consisting of a Collection of Authentick Records, State Papers, Debates, and Letters and Other Notices of Publick Affairs*, 4th series, ed. Peter Force (6 vols., Washington, 1837-1846), II, 644.

Cortlandt, by virtue of his being one of the two resident landlords and the manor representative in the General Assembly since 1768, was the person most likely to have assumed a leadership role. But his influence was checked not only by his lack of vigor but also by the efforts of several Loyalist absentee landlords, including the powerful Delanceys. He was certainly known as a warm advocate of American liberties. But his attitude at this time was ambivalent. While New York City was seething with revolutionary ferment after the Lexington-Concord incidents, Van Cortlandt, the only Whig member of the assembly, joined his Loyalist colleagues in petitioning Gen. Thomas Gage, the commander-in-chief of the British forces in North America, not to take a step that he feared would inevitably lead to the breakup of the empire.[5] His moderation, one might add, mirrored as well as reinforced the complacency of the manor inhabitants.

The tenant farmers in other areas could not remain as inert as those at Cortlandt Manor, because their landlords did not permit it. In marked contrast with Van Cortlandt, other proprietors were activists of one persuasion or the other. Frederick Philipse III, the owner of Philipsburgh Manor in Westchester County, was an aggressive Loyalist. So were Beverly Robinson and Roger Morris of Philipse's Highland Patent in Dutchess County and Sir John Johnson and Guy Johnson in Tryon County. Aligned against them were such Whig leaders as Robert Livingston, Jr. of Livingston Manor ("upper manor"), Robert R. Livingston of Clermont, John Van Rensselaer of Claverack, and Abraham Ten Broeck, manager of Rensselaerswyck. While Van Cortlandt was cautious and his whiggism barely noticeable, these partisans were vocal and vigorous in pushing their tenants to action.

When landlords took a firm course, their tenants generally followed them. In April 1775, Philipse "used all his Influence" to mobilize 300 farmers—at least 68 of whom were his tenants—at White Plains in order to reaffirm their loyalty to George III and to reject the "authority of the congress." In the opinion of the New York Committee of Safety, Philipse's "great estate" in Westchester County inevitably "created a vast number of dependents on his pleasure," and "the shameful Defection" of his tenants and the county inhabitants was "in great measure owing to his influence."[6] Following the order of the Provincial Congress, dated May 27, 1775, Robert Livingston, Jr., a staunch Whig, ordered all of his tenants to assemble with arms at the manor seat on June 16, and he

---

[5] Members of the General Assembly of New York to Thomas Gage, May 5, 1775, *The Letters and Papers of Cadwallader Colden* (9 vols., New York, 1917–1937), VII, 291–93.

[6] Frederick Philipse's testimony, Oct. 25, 1784, class 12, vol. XIX, pp. 385–86, Audit Office Series (Public Record Office, London, Eng.); *New York Gazette and the Weekly Mercury*, April 17, May 15, 1775. Frederick Philipse contended that the "friends to order and government" consisted of two-thirds of Westchester County's inhabitants. See also *Calendar of Historical Manuscripts*, I, 555; *American Archives: Consisting of a Collection of Authentick Records, State Papers, Debates, and Letters and Other Notices of Publick Affairs*, 5th series, ed. Peter Force (3 vols., Washington, 1848–1853), III, 1205–07. Echoing the view that the wealthy exerted strong influence on other men, Abraham Yates, Jr., a fervent Whig in Albany, stated that "we know by experience that there would not have been a Tory in fifty in our late struggles if they had not been disaffected by the rich." Speech to Delegates in Congress, 1786, box 4, Abraham Yates Papers (New York Public Library).

persuaded "about two thirds" of them to sign the "Association," a manifesto adopted by the Congress, which vindicated the American right to resist the parliamentary "tyranny" with force, if necessary. The meeting was adjourned with "the rest" promising to "consider of it" in two weeks. Available evidence indicates that "many" of those uncommitted opposed it "warmly."[7] Nevertheless, it is significant that a great majority of the Livingston tenants took their landlord's side and that the landlord at this time was confident enough about his tenants' sympathy with his whiggism to leave them under arms.

Tenants elsewhere displayed a similar pattern of behavior. In the spring of 1775, the farmers on Philipse's Highland Patent—comprising three southern precincts (Fredericksburg, Charlotte, and South-East) in Dutchess County— followed the lead of their Tory landlord and "almost unanimously" opposed what they called "all nonconstitutional representation" to a provincial congress, while northern precincts under the whiggish influence of Judge Robert R. Livingston of Clermont supported it. One unhappy Whig leader, reporting on the situation in southern Dutchess County, stated that the "British agents" in the county "have corrupted the minds of many of the ignorant and baser sort of men among us, maliciously telling them the whigs are in rebellion: the King would conquer them, and their estates be forfeited; and if they take up arms against them, the King for service will give them the whig's possessions." By "British agents," they undoubtedly meant Robinson and Roger Morris, two principal Loyalist landlords.[8] No dissension on the part of tenants from their Whig landlords' position was evidenced in either Claverack or Rensselaerswyck throughout 1775. Although lists of the associators from these districts are not available, the reports that they were returned promptly, while those from other Albany Court districts were not, suggest that a Whig solidarity there was firm.[9] Furthermore, a fairly complete record on the two districts' revolutionary committee's activities turns up not a single instance of Loyalist opposition. Jarring disputes occasionally developed between Robert Van Rensselaer and George Smith of Claverack, but they concerned the issue of a militia organization, not political ideology. In every instance, Smith was badly outvoted by the tenants in favor of the landlord.[10] In Tryon County, the home of the huge estate of the Johnson family, the Loyalist landlords were once again supported by their tenants and pro-British Indians. No evidence is available to show that this pattern of tenant behavior differed elsewhere. J. Franklin Jameson was correct, as far as the pre-1776 conditions were con-

---

[7] Robert R. Livingston to Robert R. Livingston, Jr., June 17, 1775, roll 31, Historical Collections (Morristown Historical Park, Morristown, N.J.).

[8] Robert R. Livingston to William Gordon, Nov. 27, 1778, box 4, Robert R. Livingston Collection (New-York Historical Society, New York, N.Y.); New York Gazette and the Weekly Mercury, April 24, May 1, 1775; Samuel Dodge to President of the New York Provincial Congress, Dec. 5, 1775, Journal of the Provincial Congress of the State of New York, 1775–1777 (2 vols., Albany, 1842), II, 106.

[9] Minutes of the Albany Committee of Correspondence, 1775–1778 (2 vols., Albany, 1923–1925), I, 124, 211, 231.

[10] Ibid., 232–33, 250–51, 254–55, 380.

cerned, when he observed in a seminal study that "on the large manorial estates the tenant farmers sided with their landlords if they took sides at all."[11]

It would be a mistake, however, to assume that the tenants quickly became vigorous Loyalists or Whigs with strong intellectual convictions. Their action was passive at best. It largely reflected the wishes of their landlords who were then the most powerful force in their midst and with whom they had maintained good relations in the past. It did not necessarily indicate willing engagement in the emerging revolutionary situation, the full range and implications of which they did not always understand. The view of Conrad Van Dusen, a Rensselaerswyck tenant, was probably typical of the majority of the tenant farmers when, after the war, he said that he "took the oath" of allegiance to America, "but he does not know what was the substance of it."[12] He did what he did because he was told to do it. Indicative of the character of tenants' behavior was the conspicuous absence of anything remotely resembling a collective deed under their initiative; they took steps neither to enlist in military service nor to articulate their views.

During the subsequent war years, however, tenants did at times reject their landlords' leadership. Even in these instances, their attitude did not systematically exhibit the hallmarks of class conflict. Instead, their behavior can best be understood as a reaction to shifts in the local military balance of power or to threats (such as the military draft) to their preferred condition of noninvolvement. Nothing animated them more than fear for their estates and families.

The Whig landlords' hold on their tenants' support underwent its most severe test in 1776 and 1777. The occasion was the British army's massive three-pronged invasion of New York following the disastrous American campaign in Canada. In the spring and summer of 1776, the pro-British Indians and Loyalists under the command of Sir John Johnson and Joseph Brant became more ominous on the western frontier as the British army under Sir Guy Carleton pushed southward along the Lake Champlain–Lake George corridor. These movements were soon followed by the Howe brothers' successful occupation of New York City, Long Island, and the neighboring areas. When the British resumed their march southward from Canada in the summer of 1777 under Gen. John Burgoyne, New York's Whig leadership found itself controlling "little more than 4 Counties . . . out of 14" that it has once possessed.[13] The state was literally under siege. The Continental army, shattered by the defeat in Canada and on Long Island, was reeling back in the face of the advancing enemy forces. Until the battle of Saratoga, the American army was very weak in every military sense, suffering from poor supplies of men and

[11] J. Franklin Jameson, *The American Revolution Considered as a Social Movement* (Princeton, 1926), 16.

[12] Conrad Van Dusen's testimony, Nov. 9, 1787, class 12, vol. XXXI, pp. 1-3, Audit Office Series.

[13] Robert R. Livingston to Alexander Hamilton, Aug. 10, 1777, *The Papers of Alexander Hamilton*, ed. Harold C. Syrett and Jacob E. Cooke (26 vols., New York, 1961-1979), I, 311.

material, poor morale and discipline, a high desertion rate, and contagious diseases like smallpox and "putrid fever." In short, they appeared to be a broken reed incapable of protecting good Whig inhabitants and overawing Loyalists.[14]

The effect of the British military presence and might was felt everywhere in New York. It emboldened the Loyalists, who had long been in disarray and timid, and increased their number, and it threw the Whigs deeper into what Lewis Morris called the "Sin of Fear." A consequence of this situation was that the British army threatened to displace the Whig landlord as a primary influence in his tenants' lives, while the Tory landlord's solidarity with his tenants was strengthened.[15] Indeed, as the war intensified in New York in 1776 and 1777, some of the tenants in Whig-landlord-controlled Livingston and Renasselaerswyck manors became increasingly "disaffected" from the American cause and their landlords' views. Significantly, few, if any, of the tenants on the Johnson estates, Philipse's Highland Patent, and Philipsburgh defected from their landlords' loyalism in the course of these changing circumstances.

The first sign of an open breach in tenant-landlord unity appeared in Livingston Manor in mid-February 1776 when an unknown number of tenants in the Taconic area were reported to have voiced Tory sentiments. The situation was grave enough for the Albany County Committee of Safety to dispatch three militia companies from neighboring districts (including Claverack) in order to arrest and disarm "all such suspected persons" there.[16] A month later the committee was also alarmed by a rumor that four or five tenants in Stephentown in the easternmost section of Rensselaerswyck had disrupted the local committee of safety. Then, in May, it came to the committee's attention that a tenant named Daniel Litts had "Cursed" the Albany committee and spoken "disrespectful" of the Whigs in general. These were, however, all sporadic and isolated incidents which the committee felt the Rensselaerswyck committee could handle administratively by itself. As it turned out, the

[14] Samuel Blachley Webb to Joseph Trumbull, Dec. 16, 1776, Correspondence and Journals of Samuel Blachley Webb, ed. Worthington Chauncey Ford (3 vols., New York, 1893–1894), I, 174–75; John Trumbull to Jonathon Trumbull, July 12, 1776, Letter Book "B," William Livingston Papers (Massachusetts Historical Society, Boston, Mass.); Harry B. Livingston to William Livingston, July 17, July 24, Aug. 6, 1777, ibid.

[15] Regarding the change in the Whigs' attitude, see John Jay to Alexander McDougall, Dec. 22, 1775, Alexander McDougall Papers (New-York Historical Society); William Duer and Jonathan G. Tompkins to Lt. Col. Van Rensselaer, Feb. 24, 1777, ibid. For the Loyalists' attitude, see William Smith, Jr., to Gen. Frederick Haldimand, Oct. 6, 1775 , box 4, William Smith Papers (New York Public Library); Nathaniel Merrit to William Tryon, Oct. 18, 1775, vol. 55, pp. 1106, 708, Colonial Office Series (Public Record Office); Minutes of the Committee and of the First Commission for Detecting and Defeating Conspiracies in the State of New York, December 11, 1776–September 23, 1778, with Collateral Documents (2 vols., New York, 1924–1925), I, 12–13; Johannes J. Blauveldt to George Clinton, April 26, 1777, Public Papers of George Clinton, ed. Hastings and Holden, I, 734–35.

[16] The only person specifically named to be apprehended was Christopher Cooper, who had been on a small lease farm since 1771. Minutes of the Albany Committee of Correspondence, I, 336. His lease indenture is in roll 8, Livingston-Redmond Papers (Franklin Delano Roosevelt Library, Hyde Park, N.Y.).

Rensselaerswyck Whig leadership, composed largely of tenants, was effective in policing internal affairs. By June 1776, the Whig leadership there had achieved such a reputation for its vigor that the Albany committee even asked its manor tenant militia under Kiliaen Van Rensselaer to discipline the manor's freehold neighbor, Loyalist-infested Kinderhook Township.[17]

The disaffection in Livingston manor had spread farther than in Rensselaerswyck; so its committee found it necessary in late May to invite in 400 Dutchess County militiamen and 6 Albany County committeemen to "assist in the management" of the growing evil. In September, the committee was informed that Jury Wheeler, a tenant, had boasted that if he were forced into military services the "first" person he would "shoot" would be his captain. Many other tenants, like any ordinary country farmers, would rather have been fined than drafted.[18] The reason for their antidraft sentiment is hard to determine. It was perhaps too early for overt toryism to be a factor. Probably, the general political apathy and concerns for their farms and families were the overriding considerations.

By October, Tory activities among the Livingston Manor tenants completely overshadowed their antidraft sentiment as a critical issue for the committee to handle. It was reported that "a number of Disaffected persons" were hiding in the woods in the "South East Corner" of the manor where some of them had signed "a Kings Book," pledging allegiance to the king. It was also reported that these secretive Loyalists believed that the American army was "Defeated at Port Washington," that the "Kings Troops" were "Expected at Poughkeepsie," and that "if the Regulars should come up in the Country they would be rejoiced" and reimbursed for all the fines they had paid for their delinquencies in militia service. The Tory actions soon became more menacing: shots were fired at two "Young men" walking home and into the "very beds" of some active manor committeemen like Dirck Jansen at night.[19] Even one Tory relative of Robert R. Livingston, the Clermont proprietor, hatched a "regular plan" to kidnap his kinsman, but it was aborted by "a discovery that very night" when it was supposed to have been executed.[20]

[17] Minutes of the Albany Committee of Correspondence, I, 353, 403, 450.

[18] Dirck Jansen to Abraham Yates, Jr., May 19, 1776, Yates Papers; "The Minutes of the Committee of Safety of the Manor of Livingston, Columbia County, New York, in 1776," New York Genealogical and Biographical Record, 60 (1929), 325-28; Documents Relating to the Colonial History of the State of New York, ed. E. B. O'Callaghan and Berthold Fernow (15 vols., Albany, 1856-1887), XV, 131, 136, 142-43; Philip Schuyler to McDougall, Feb. 15, 1776, roll 1, McDougall Papers; Minutes of the Albany Committee of Correspondence, I, 681.

[19] "Minutes of the Committee of Safety of the Manor of Livingston," 328-31. The northern-frontier Tories at this time believed that two of the "king's Armies" were coming down, John Burgoyne by way of the "Lake" and John Johnson by the Mohawk River with another British army, and that some of their "Kinderhook Friends" had already marched north to join them. Calendar of Historical Manuscripts, I, 528-29.

[20] Robert R. Livingston to Edward Rutledge, Oct. 10, 1776, vol. I, Robert R. Livingston Papers (New York Public Library). I have searched in vain for the identity of this "relative." Several of the Livingston relatives were suspected Tories: John Patterson, married to a daughter of Robert Livingston, Jr.; William Smith, Jr., married to Janet Livingston, a cousin of Robert R. Livingston; and Samuel Hake, married to a daughter of Robert Gilbert Livingston of Rhinebeck. See class 12, vol. XIX, pp. 237-39, 245-46, 253-66, 274-75, Audit Office Series; Minutes of the Committee and of the First Commission for Detecting and Defeating Conspiracies, I, 89.

Fearful of an impending Tory "Rising" against "Members of the Committee," the manor committee on October 10 sent an urgent appeal to Peter R. Livingston, the eldest son of the manor proprietor and president of the state convention, which stated that unless a militia company composed of at least "Sixty Men" was raised "very soon" in the district, they would be "a ruined people." They also noted that the Tories "Increase daily." If the disaffected ranks swelled, the new recruits seem to have come largely from those passive Whigs like Henning N. Loester, a tenant, who soon regretted that "he had signed the Association, as he Expected that the Kings Troops would Conquer America" shortly. The political vacillation of the manor tenants according to changing military dynamics was and would be duplicated by many other Whigs elsewhere.[21] In any event, the convention quickly authorized the committee to raise a ranger company of forty-nine. The company proved to be fairly adequate to the tasks for which it was raised, arresting several Tories, protecting committeemen, and preventing any further overt actions by the disaffected.[22]

In mid-October, Rensselaerswyck also suffered a moment of alarm because of some unrest among its farmers. As it turned out, there was an insurgency of about ninety people concentrated at the rough Hellebergh escarpment and at Beaver Dam, locations on the westernmost part of the manor which only recently had come under settlement. It was no more than an expression of resistance to an order for the militia to march toward Fort Edward. According to a Whig spy at their meetings, a majority (about twenty) of those at Hellebergh were "friends to the Country," but they "won't fight if they [could] help it," nor would they be "against the King." This neutral sentiment had been cultivated aggressively by John Read of Hellebergh and John Cummins, a Scottish merchant who in 1774 had settled in the Catskills just south of the manor with "above 200" countrymen of his. It was Cummins who persuaded some of his tenants in the Catskills to "join the Kings army" under General Carleton and Sir John Johnson, on the condition that he, remaining at home, would support and protect their wives and children. On October 21 Cummins also invited to his Catskill house some of the Rensselaerswyck militia men and warned them not to march by threatening them with ruin when the British army conquered "this Country in a months time." Apparently, the manor draft dodgers were persuaded, for by October 25 three companies of thirty men were organized in the manor settlements of Hellebergh,

[21] "Minutes of the Committee of Safety of the Manor of Livingston," 332, 334; *Journal of the Provincial Congress*, II, 319–20. Reporting on the situation in the Schohary area, John Barclay, chairman of the Albany County committee, stated that "nearly" one-half of the Whigs there "have laid down their arms, and purpose to side with the Enemy all which change has taken its origin from the desertion of Tyconderoga, the unprecedented loss of which we are afraid will be followed by a Revolt of more than the one half of the Northern part of this [Albany] county." John Barclay to Schuyler, July 22, 1777, box 2, Schuyler Family Papers (New-York Historical Society); *Journal of the Provincial Congress*, I, 1010, 1006, 1019, II, 507, 518; Duer to Abraham Ten Broeck, Feb. 25, 1777, roll 2, McDougall Papers.
[22] Peter R. Livingston to Petrus Van Goosebeck, Oct. 12, 1776, roll 31, Historical Collections; "Muster Roll of a Company Raised in the Manor of Livingston . . . Oct. 19, 1776," Livingston Manor Papers (New-York Historical Society).

Niscuthay, and Normans Kill to resist the draft and other Whig directives that threatened local neutrality. The groups also agreed to keep up "a correspondence" with those Scottish Tory tenants in the Catskills.[23]

Informed fully of almost every detail of this ominous development, the Albany County Committee of Safety promptly dispatched several militia companies, including a manor company, to the different places where insurgents were reported to have assembled. Contrary to the committee's expectations, these Whig forces numbering about 185 did not encounter resistance from the insurgents and were able to capture suspected persons. Upon the information that there were about 300 Loyalists at "a Certain Place," a militia detachment set off "in high spirits" only to find not a single person there. As its commander ruefully confessed, the information was entirely faulty. Robert Yates, the county committee chairman, also concluded several days later that the "Defection in that Quarter has as usual been much exaggerated" and that even those who were apprehended "as Tories" were not "Dangerous." The Rensselaerswyck committee, to which the cases of those arrested were referred, discharged all of them because it had "proof" that they were "ignorant," "deluded," and willing to "return to their Duty" once their "past misconduct" was forgiven. It attributed the entire episode to "some designing men" trying to "sow the seeds of a Revolt."[24]

There had been a real possibility the Loyalists might exploit the increasing antidraft sentiment and convert it into explicit toryism. The timely countermeasures by the county revolutionary leadership, however, prevented this from happening. The disturbances were in no way connected with an antilandlord struggle. Cummins, the principal leader in the conspiracy, was a landlord himself and would not have instigated and directed the insurgency if he had perceived it to be directed against the very lease system upon which his fledgling economic enterprise was built. Besides, the Slingerlandts and others of Normans Kill, the arrested insurgents who contributed a dozen or so men to the attempted revolt, were not even tenants. They were freeholders of the ancient Baals Patent, one pocket of freehold landholding containing about 700 acres within the manor jurisdiction, and therefore had no socioeconomic reason to rise against the landlord Van Rensselaers.[25]

[23] Deposition of John Vanderburg, Oct. 25, 1776, *Calendar of Historical Manuscripts*, I, 515–16, 523; John Cummins's testimony, Nov. 12, 1783, class 12, vol. XX, pp. 37–39, Audit Office Series. On July 10, 1776, John Read leased, for two years, a farm of 100 acres in Rensselaerswyck for the annual rent of 3 schepels and one day's work. Rensselaerswyck Rent Ledger, 1768–1789, pp. 75, 256, Rensselaerswyck Manuscripts (New York State Library, Albany, N.Y.).

[24] Lynd and Alice P. Kenney both give the impression that 400 disaffected men were in arms and that toryism in the manor was widespread. Yet, as Robert Yates, the county committee chairman, testified repeatedly, this was simply untrue. Lynd, "Tenant Rising," 169–70; Kenney, "Albany Dutch," 340; *Calendar of Historical Manuscripts*, I, 505–13, 521–25.

[25] On August 21, 1671, the Normans Kill land was granted to Jan Hendrick Van Baal. Sometime in the 1710s his heirs sold it to the Slingerlandts and others. A protracted dispute regarding the exact bounds of the patent developed between the Normans Kill people and the Van Rensselaers in subsequent years. See Land Papers, 1642–1803, vol. VI, p. 180, vol. VII, pp. 44, 64, vol. VIII, pp. 30, 32–34, New York Colonial Manuscripts (New York State Library); James Duane to Abraham Yates, Jr., May 26, 1767, Letters, 1767–1794, Rensselaerswyck Manuscripts; Ten Broeck to

The backwardness of the militiamen in responding to calls for action continued to perplex the Albany County Whig leaders. It was especially serious in Livingston Manor, where that committee's main business reverted to coping with the enlistment problem. Peter R. Livingston, commander of the manor regiment, was ordered on December 21 to march three manor companies to North Castle, Westchester County. He sadly reported that only "45 men could possibly have been sent at this Season" because he had to excuse 105 men from the draft for one reason or another. In January 1777, a recruiting officer for the manor was threatened with physical violence by several draft resisters. One corporal named John Concklin bitterly complained that the drafting was "unfair." The most common excuse that the potential draft dodgers gave was illness, but the skeptical committee tried in March to eliminate this loophole by having a physician examine every draft-age person who feigned illness. Because of this action and its exercise of revolutionary authority, the committee inevitably became a source of resentment to the manor inhabitants, whose principal desire was to remain uninvolved in public affairs.[26]

In the first three months of 1777, Livingston Manor appeared to be calm despite or perhaps because of the disbanding of the ranger company in mid-January. A militia call in February to march northward stirred not a single person. The manor remained calm largely because the Albany County Tory leadership—Cummins of Catskill, John Hueston of Lunnenbergh (a retired British half-pay officer), Capt. Andrew Palmetier of Kings District, and Alexander Crookshank of Albany City—believed that it was best for them to wait until the expected arrival of the British army, both by land and water, sometime in the spring or, at the latest, by the middle of June.[27] In the meantime, however, the manor Tories kept up their underground activities. They combed the manor and neighboring districts for new converts and proved to be very good at recruiting. Aernout Viel, a twenty-year-old Tory who had never been

Teunis Slingerlandt, March 8, 1769, June 30, 1770, Letters to Abraham Ten Broeck, 1753–1783, *ibid.* The history of the Baals Patent is in "James Jackson ex dem Barnardus La Grange vs Robt. Freeman and Catherine Van Rensselaer, 1774," Sorted Legal Manuscripts, John Tabor Kempe Papers (New-York Historical Society).

[26] "Minutes of the Committee of Safety of the Manor of Livingston," 335, 338–40; Peter R. Livingston to Provincial Congress, Jan. 2, 1777, *Documents Relating to the Colonial History of the State of New York,* ed. O'Callaghan and Fernow, XV, 144. According to Smith, who was then staying at Peter R. Livingston's house in the manor, the manor militia regiment had about 500 men. William Smith, *Historical Memoirs of William Smith: Historian of New York, Member of the Governor's Council and Last Chief Justice of that Province under the Crown, Chief Justice of Quebec,* ed. William H. W. Sabine (2 vols., New York, 1956–1958), II, 83.

[27] John Cummins and Alexander Crookshank, who had returned from their trips to New York City in early February, spread the word about the coming of the British army among the Tories on both sides of the Hudson River. While in the city, they met Gen. James Robertson and Col. Allen McLean of the British army and Abraham C. Cuyler, former Tory mayor of Albany, and were instructed to prepare the upstate Tories for the British invasion. Although they were imprisoned soon after their return home, it is reasonable to assume that Livingston Manor and Rensselaerswyck Tory elements heard of the story. Deposition of John Cummins, Alexander Crookshank, and Hugh Denniston of Catskill, March 1777, *Calendar of Historical Manuscripts,* I, 672–75, 677–78. Regarding John Hueston and Andrew Palmetier, see *ibid.,* I, 527, 530, II, 225–28. On the tenant-Tory activities, see *ibid.,* II, 83, 199–200, 229; Smith, *Historical Memoirs,* II, 83.

"backward in turning out with the militia," alone converted sixty to seventy men in the manor, at Claverack, and in Kings District. Each of these new converts was promised standard compensations for military service—a bounty of five dollars, British regulars' pay from the time of their joining the king's army, and 200 acres of land. They were also given to understand that Hueston had orders from Gen. Sir William Howe, Gov. William Tryon, and Sir John Johnson to grant such promises and to organize them into "a Battalion of Loyal Volunteers" in Albany County.[28]

By the middle of April, it appears that "Almost every body" in the manor, especially in the Taconic area, including "one third" of the manor militia officers, had pledged either the oath of secrecy or allegiance to the crown. Encouraged by their success in recruitment and by the gloomier turn of military events for Americans, the manor Tories became more audacious than ever. They "publickly" plundered and disarmed Whig tenants like "Mr. Van Veghten" and his sons and "many of his neighbours." Robert R. Livingston, the Clermont proprietor, was "more and more convinced that something [was] in agitation among the Tories." Late in the month, while the inhabitants were busy with their farm work and were complaining about the recent orders to impress twenty-four wagons and to draft fifty-two militiamen for the northern frontier defense, the Tories fired "several" shots into the house of a committeeman at night obviously to "terrify" the "whole" committee. About the same time, Nine Partners's Tories stole 900 pounds of powder from Robert R. Livingston's powder mill, and they took lead from the nets strung across the Hudson to obstruct the British ships.[29] No Whig with any sense at all could miss the grave implications of this last deed coupled with the intelligence provided by the arrested Tories on the expected arrival of the British: a Tory uprising against the committee and Whigs was imminent.

The state convention's reaction was swift. On May 2, it ordered the militia units of Claverack, Dutchess, and Ulster counties and of Egremont, Massachusetts, into the Taconic section of Livingston Manor to crush the Tory conspiracy. A series of skirmishes ensued there lasting three days, and the armed Tories, constituting no more than 150 men, were outnumbered, outgunned, and outsmarted by the Whig forces. Three Tories were killed and several were wounded, but the Whigs suffered no casualties. In the course of the mopping-up operation afterward, about 300 "sworn" and "not sworn" Tories in the manor, Nine Partners, and Kinderhook were arrested and sent away for interrogation. A majority of them were "upper" manor tenants, but their exact number cannot be verified.[30]

The spread of toryism at Livingston Manor has convinced some historians of

---

[28] Class 12, vol. XXXI, pp. 1-3, Audit Office Series; *Calendar of Historical Manuscripts,* I, 190-94, 198-99, 334-35, 361; Smith, *Historical Memoirs,* II, 131; *Minutes of the Committee and of the First Commission for Detecting and Defeating Conspiracies,* I, 136-37.

[29] Robert R. Livingston to Clinton, April 11, 1777, *Public Papers of George Clinton,* ed. Hastings and Holden, I, 709-10; Smith, *Historical Memoirs,* II, 126; Robert R. Livingston, Zephaniah Platt, and Matthew Cantine to Provincial Congress, May 8, 1777, *Journal of the Provincial Congress,* I, 918-19; *Calendar of Historical Manuscripts,* II, 193.

[30] Smith, *Historical Memoirs,* II, 129-30; Deposition of Richard Esselstyn, [May 1777], *Calendar of Historical Manuscripts,* I, 581.

the existence of class conflict between the tenants and their Whig landlord. Close examination of the Tory insurgency and its aftermath does not bear this out. Ironically, the most effective Whig troops in combating and apprehending the Livingston tenants were about "100 and odd" tenant militiamen under Robert Van Rensselaer of Claverack and John R. Livingston of Clermont and the Yankees from Massachusetts who, in partnership with the Taconic tenants, had fought the Livingstons over the Taconic land in the 1750s and 1766. Moreover, it was their Whig landlord, especially his sons Peter R., Walter, and Henry Livingston, to whom the suspected, hiding, or arrested tenants did "fly" for "favors" and protection from the revengeful committee shortly after they were routed. On May 5, even before the gunsmoke dissipated, the hiding tenants contacted the proprietary family with an overture that they would surrender their arms to the landlord and submit themselves to a "Trial by the Manor Committee," provided they were guaranteed against eviction from their leases. These farmers were willing to exchange toryism for their tenant farms, which they apparently valued more. The committee's instant response was to reject the proposal, but such a recourse "greatly" upset the proprietary family, who thought the tenants were "sincere" and dreaded the consequences of a punitive measure. By the end of June, the landlord's conciliatory policy prevailed, and all but three of the manor Tories were discharged of their disloyalty by taking an oath of allegiance to America.[31]

The tenants seemed very appreciative of the Livingston family's good offices as was demonstrated by the fact that in early July when Burgoyne's army was pushing toward Albany, an unprecedented number of manor militiamen, "above 200," were willing to march north despite the pressing demand of labor at their farms. The landlord was probably unsure in this plowing season whether he should rejoice in the militia turnout for the cause of liberty or fear a "Famine" from it.[32] The militia zeal proved to be ephemeral, however. A month later, following the loss of Fort Ticonderoga, an event that "dejected" the people "in general," the militia was called up again to march for Stillwater, but the manor committee found it "impossible to get any of them to go." Their old habit of apathy—not necessarily their "disaffection" as Jansen, a manor committeeman, suspected—seized them again, this time for good. The manor militia-farmers' behavior was nothing peculiar because farmers in Schenectady, Schohary, Dutchess County, and Orange County, were also very backward in militia service at this time.[33]

[31] Smith, *Historical Memoirs*, II, 131–32, 136–37, 139, 143, 145, 147; *Calendar of Historical Manuscripts*, II, 194.

[32] Smith, *Historical Memoirs*, II, 168–69, 172; Robert R. Livingston to Hamilton, June 7, 1777, *Papers of Alexander Hamilton*, ed. Syrett and Cooke, I, 268.

[33] Jansen to Council of Safety, Aug. 7, 1777, *Public Papers of George Clinton*, ed. Hastings and Holden, II, 193–94; John R. Livingston to "Dear Robert," Aug. 12, 1777, *ibid.*, 219; Schuyler to Clinton, Aug. 6, 1777, *ibid.*, 199–200; Reynes Mynderse to Schuyler, Aug. 5, 1777, *ibid.*, 187; Clinton to George Washington, Aug. 9, 1777, *ibid.*, 195–96; William Humfrey to Clinton, Aug. 28, 1777, *ibid.*, 262; Pierre Van Cortlandt to Clinton, Aug. 12, 1777, *ibid.*, 215–18; John McKesson to Washington, July 29, 1777, *ibid.*, 144; Clinton to [Gen. Israel Putnam], July 9, 1777, *ibid.*, 92; Smith, *Historical Memoirs*, II, 293.

Rensselaerswyck too was not entirely free of Loyalist activity during the spring and summer of 1777. Its committee, which had been more concerned about the Tory strength in Kinderhook than about its own situation since the last disturbances in Hellebergh, was freshly alarmed by a report on April 19 that a "Party of 46" suspected persons "lay concealed in the Woods about three Miles" from Albany.[34] A Loyalist party of twenty-four under Captain Palmetier from Kings District, which adjoined Rensselaerswyck on the southeast, was indeed meeting at the house of John Ebes, a manor tenant. The objective of the outsiders moving into the manor was to proselytize the manor tenants and form a Tory company to prepare for the junction with the British army. Palmetier and his men fed some manor residents with a scary tale that the reason for "raising the Company" and for administering the loyalty oath was to "prevent our being destroyed by the Indians, who . . . were coming down in Great Numbers" and "would destroy all that had not a certificate of their being true to the King." The Kings District men, as the Catskill Tories had done earlier, also tried to get across the idea that Americans would never be able to win their "Cause." In the evening of April 20, the manor militia under one Capt. James Dennison encountered the Tory contingent at the house of Thomas Blewer, another manor tenant, and routed the Tories, but not without suffering the humiliation of seeing two of their men taken away by their enemy.[35]

A month later, the manor and Albany County committees were disturbed again by a report that "a number of disaffected Persons [who] skulk in and about the Hellebergh . . . [have] induce[d] many of the wellmeaning tho' misguided Inhabitants to enter into Combinations against . . . the United States."[36] In August, when Burgoyne's army was near Saratoga, the manor suffered another intrusion into its "East part" by the Palmetier men from Kings District who robbed the manor inhabitants of clothes and furniture. In both instances the manor revolutionary authority, which was praised earlier by the Albany County committee for its vigor and commitment to whiggism in "detecting and defeating . . . our internal Enemies," brought the situation under control.[37]

The British army and Loyalist elements in New York, however, persisted in their campaign to stir up the Hudson River tenantry against their Whig landlords. John Watts, a Cortlandt Manor Tory proprietor related to the Delanceys, recommended to the British ministry through a Philadelphia newspaper and Samuel Loudon's *New-York Packet* that the Whig estates be vacated by a parliamentary action. He urged the crown "by proclamation" to declare that the tenants presently in "an absolute state of vassalage, being all tenants at will to Rensalear, Livingston, Beckman, and Philipse," be given freehold

---

[34] *Minutes of the Albany Committee of Correspondence*, I, 727.

[35] *Ibid.*, 593–94; *Calendar of Historical Manuscripts*, I, 527, 530, II, 204–05, 229–31.

[36] Harry B. Livingston to William Livingston, June 10, 1777, box 13, William Livingston Papers; *Minutes of the Albany Committee of Correspondence*, I, 740–42.

[37] Gershom French was captured soon. *Minutes of the Albany Committee of Correspondence*, I, 740, 821, 823, 839.

farms "for ever" on condition that "they in person take up arms" in the British service. Watts was confident that these measures would "instantly" bring out "at least" 6,000 tenant Loyalist soldiers.[38] Obviously written shortly after he heard of Burgoyne's surrender at Saratoga, Watts's recommendation reflected his desperation, wishful thinking, and vindictiveness toward New York's landed Whig leadership rather than a correct reading of the prevailing tenant-landlord relationship and the mood of tenantry. He was disappointed in his scheme, for neither did the British government adopt it nor did the tenants, whom he wrongly characterized as holding leases at the will of their landlords, respond enthusiastically to his idea.

Nevertheless, as British strategy shifted in 1778 toward heavier dependence on loyal Americans for their manpower needs, Sir Henry Clinton and Tryon kept sending agents to the upstate area in order to recruit soldiers and agitate, especially among the Livingston tenants. But they were not very successful in disturbing the tenants out of their entrenched apathy.[39] Despite the widely publicized disaffection among them and the promised bounty of freehold land, the Livingston tenant families sent only five sons to the British army during the 1779–1780 period. The number is dismally few compared with the contributions from much smaller precincts in Dutchess County—twenty-one from Rumbout, nineteen from Beekmans, twenty-one from Poughkeepsie, sixteen from Fredericksburg, and fifty-five from Charlotte (the last two were under the influence of Robinson and Roger Morris). The "spirit" of disaffection in the manor was virtually dead, and it would never raise its head again even though the manor landlords became tougher in enforcing the rent collection and the committee continued its vigorous war efforts.[40]

Elsewhere, the pronounced solidarity between landlords and tenants continued. Robinson, a notable Tory landlord with 166 "thriving tenants" on his estate in Dutchess County, could boast that he had raised a Loyalist regiment of 250 men during the war, "many" of whom were "his own Tenants and most of them from his own County." James Fallon, a senior physician of the General Hospitals at Quaker Hill, the heartland of the Robinson estate, reported in 1779 that there were "only 4 whigs" there and that the rest were the "very essence and quintessence of Tories." A militia regiment of Philipse's Highland Patent, like its counterpart in other Whig-controlled areas, was largely nonfunctional since the "greater part of them by farr Refuse to

[38] *Pennsylvania Ledger: Or the Weekly Advertiser*, Oct. 29, 1777; Smith, *Historical Memoirs*, II, 274–75.

[39] For full discussion of the shift in British strategy, see John Shy, *A People Numerous and Armed: Reflections on the Military Struggle for American Independence* (New York, 1976), 185; John M. Beeckman to Clinton, April 1, 1778, *Public Papers of George Clinton*, ed. Hastings and Holden, III, 109–10. In April 1778, the Livingston Manor proprietors were alarmed by a Tory rising in Nine Partners, but it ended short of affecting the manor. Margaret Livingston to Susan F. Livingston, April 11, 1778, box II, William Livingston Papers; Robert R. Livingston to John Livingston, April 11, 1778, box J-M, Livingston Miscellaneous Manuscripts (New-York Historical Society)

[40] *Public Papers of George Clinton*, ed. Hastings and Holden, VI, 593–94, 567, 516, 585–86, 286, 576; Margaret Livingston to Robert R. Livingston, Feb. 4, 1780, box 5, Livingston Collection.

March" when ordered to do so, either because its men disliked service or because they were loyal to their Tory landlords.[41]

Similarly, the behavior of the Philipsburgh tenants indicates that the war was an occasion for them to demonstrate their deference to their landlord. Although their landlord, Philipse, had been exiled from the manor since August 1776 and the area was contested and thus subjected to extreme devastation by the contending armies and bandits like "Skinners" and "Cowboys," many of those tenants remaining at their farms faithfully paid their annual rents to their landlord. Extant rent rolls show that 80 of them paid their 1777 rents and 173 their 1778 rents to the landlord in New York City. The tenants' conduct, risking their lives and the wrath of the American army by going across the American lines, is a remarkable testimony to their unwavering commitment to their landlord even at the height of war.[42] It is indeed remarkable because they could have easily gotten away with nonpayment on one pretext or another, by arguing that they were impoverished by war or that they lacked means to reach the landlord behind the British lines. This does not mean, however, that every one of the Philipsburgh tenants was a Loyalist or antiwhiggish in sentiment. There were several active Whigs like Peter Van Tassell, Jonathan G. Graham, John Relyea, and James Hammond among them, but it is fair to say that the overwhelming majority of the tenants were either active or indifferent adherents to their landlord.[43]

The story of the tenants on Sir John Johnson's estate on the Mohawk River was much the same. They continued to fight together with their landlord and their Indian allies, terrorizing and devastating the scattered Whig settlements in the western frontier throughout the war. One concerned militia officer stationed at "Caughnawaga" reported in 1779 that "we have upwards of 300 Disafected familys back of us, mostly tenants" of the landlord.[44] Even in Cort-

[41] Beverly Robinson's testimony, Dec. 16, 1785, class 12, vol. XXI, pp. 147, 149–163, Audit Office Series; James Fallon to Clinton, Jan. 3, 1779, *Public Papers of George Clinton*, ed. Hastings and Holden, IV, 460–72; John Field to George Clinton, Nov. 19, 1777, *ibid.*, II, 529–30. The phrase "thriving tenants" was voiced by one of Beverly Robinson's tenants. See class 12, vol. XXI, p. 180, Audit Office Series.

[42] The ratio between those remaining and those absent is unknown. Many of the tenants, however, took refuge in Dutchess County in order to avoid the ravages of war. See the "petition" of thirty tenants to New York State Legislature, March 12, 1782, in *Tarrytown Argus*, April 28, 1894. In August 1776, Philipse was imprisoned by the order of George Washington and taken to New Rochelle, to New Haven, and then to Norwich, Connecticut. In 1777 he was banished to New York City. See Frederick Philipse to Elizabeth Philipse, Aug. 14, Aug. 20, Aug. 22, 1776, PA 824, 825, 826, Philipse Papers (Sleepy Hollow Restorations Library, Tarrytown, N.Y.). For tenants' rent payment records, see files PA 817, PA 822, PA 823, *ibid.* For additional information about Philipsburgh and its tenants, see class 12, vol. XIX, pp. 370–83, Audit Office Series.

[43] Regarding Peter Van Tassell's active role in the American cause, see *New York Gazette and Weekly Mercury*, Nov. 24, 1777. There was a Philipsburgh militia regiment during the war, but it was not operational, as suggested by the fact that its fourteen officers had neglected to swear the oath of allegiance to the United States until July 8, 1778. *New York Genealogical and Biographical Record*, 28 (1897), 2; *Journal of the Provincial Congress*, I, 159, 304, 331; Gilbert Van Cortlandt et al. to Philip Van Cortlandt, Nov. 13, 1775, Mss. no. 11326 (New York State Library); Cornelia Beekman to Philip Van Cortlandt, Nov. 12, 1775, Van Cortlandt-Van Wyck Papers (New York Public Library).

[44] Jelles Fonda to Clinton, March 26, 1779, *Public Papers of George Clinton*, ed. Hastings and Holden, IV, 669; "Extracts from Capt. Bloomfield's Journal," *Proceedings of the New Jersey Historical Society*, 2 (no. 3, 1847) 115, 119.

landt Manor, where apathy and lethargy were most conspicuous in 1775, tenants by and large tended to side with their landlord in subsequent years. As the war escalated and the militancy of the partisans from within and without mounted, some of them probably found overt neutrality to be a luxury in which they could no longer indulge, unless they were prepared to antagonize both Tories and Whigs. Of the manor's one hundred or so tenants, twenty-seven were active and the rest managed somehow to stay outside the vortex of conflict. Of those active partisans, it appears that twenty-one (78 percent) were on their landlord's side, while only six (22 percent) rejected the cause of their landlord.[45]

In Claverack, the overwhelming number of the approximately 150 tenants stayed with their Whig landlord, if they took sides at all. Throughout the revolutionary period, not once was Claverack under John Van Rensselaer and his son Robert Van Rensselaer threatened by an organized Tory conspiracy. Its tenant militia was regarded by the county revolutionary authorities as most dependable not only for policing Tories in the surrounding areas like Livingston Manor, Kings District, Kinderhook, and even the western part of Rensselaerswyck across the Hudson River but also for defending the northern frontier. Their reputed readiness to serve the Whig cause, however, led to their frequent mobilization, which in turn "Harrassed" and exhausted them "exceedingly" by the middle of 1778. To be sure, they were reluctant to march at the time of pressing labor demands at home, but every farmer displayed this understandable characteristic.[46] Claverack lost about fifteen of its inhabitants to the Tories in the spring of 1777 when Tory activity in southern Albany County was at its peak. Most of them, however, appear to have come from the western part of Claverack where the Van Rensselaers' land claim clashed with that of other settlers.[47] Much of the Whig cohesion and control in Claverack was due to the zeal and leadership of Robert Van Rensselaer, which Gen. Philip Schuyler contrasted with the "inactivity" of Peter R. Livingston at Livingston Manor.[48]

Although there were sporadic disturbances in Rensselaerswyck in 1776 and 1777, a great degree of amiability existed between Stephen Van Rensselaer and his 1,000 tenants. The major pockets of defection were in Hellebergh, Stephentown, and Normans Kill. Almost all of the settlers in the first two settlements

[45] Sung Bok Kim, "The Manor of Cortlandt and Its Tenants, 1697–1783" (Ph.D. diss., Michigan State University, 1966), 246–61. For additional information on the situation in Cortlandt Manor, see class 12, vol. XXVI, pp. 1, 13–15, 17, 394, vol. CX, p. 32, Audit Office Series.

[46] *Calendar of Historical Manuscripts*, I, 530–31, 581; *Minutes of the Albany Committee of Correspondence*, I, 725, 795–96; Smith, *Historical Memoirs*, II, 127, 293, 422; Robert Van Rensselaer to Clinton, May 2, 1778, *Public Papers of George Clinton*, ed. Hastings and Holden, III, 255–56.

[47] A case in point is Christian Wehr, a Tory from Claverack. He had two pieces of land, one of 30 acres and another of 100 acres, in western Claverack for which he had no legitimate deed. The first tract in his possession was, however, claimed by the Van Rensselaers. See his testimony [1784], class 12, vol. XXVI, p. 326, Audit Office Series. For the other Loyalists, see class 12, vol. XXVIII, p. 274, ibid.; *Calendar of Historical Manuscripts*, I, 187, 222–23, II, 199; *Minutes of the Committee and of the First Commission for Detecting and Defeating Conspiracies*, I, 48, 95, 156–57, 203, 219.

[48] Smith, *Historical Memoirs*, II, 293.

were recent arrivals. Twenty-four tenants actually joined the British army and John Johnson's Loyalist troops, mostly in 1777 during Burgoyne's southward march; and forty-one residents, nine from East District and thirty-two from West District of the manor, were "indicted for adherence to the Enemies of the United States" throughout the war.[49] That the disproportionately large number of Tories came from the western part of the manor, which was exposed to the ever-present menace of John Johnson's strong Tory arms and pro-British Indians, shows the extent to which the military situation affected the attitude of the manor inhabitants. In any event, these statistics and other circumstantial evidence suggest that a maximum of only about 100 tenants were Tories or Tory sympathizers. This manor's Tory strength, however, pales into insignificance when one considers the situation in Albany County as a whole, where "almost half" of the inhabitants were known to be "disaffected."[50] Without the willing majority (90 percent) of the manor tenantry, its revolutionary leadership could not have silenced its internal and external foes as effectively as it did. Behind the Whig predominance were the powerful stature and influence of the landlord and especially his uncle, manager of the estate, Brigadier General Ten Broeck, commander of the Albany County militia which the British army threatened but failed to break.

The years 1776 and 1777 were the crucial period of the Revolution in New York. With the recession of a serious British threat thereafter, landlord-tenant relations were largely harmonious. In general, tenants in New York adopted the political position of their landlords. The only conspicuous exception was the widespread defection by the Livingston Manor tenants. Where the tenants on the Whig-owned estate became Tories, was this due to their socioeconomic antagonism toward their landlord? The Livingstons indeed suspected and feared at the outset of the war that "Some" of the tenants would "take advantage of the times and make their Landlords give them Leases forever" on the kind of terms that the Rensselaerswyck and Claverack tenants were enjoying.[51] Their fear at the time was natural, a reaction that we could expect of the family who had repeatedly been harassed by the persistent attempt of western Massachusetts men to challenge their manor titles in the 1750s and 1760s. They knew that the disaffection was centered in the Taconic area where the Yankees' tenant collaborators (about twenty) resided. As subsequent events demonstrated, such suspicions and fears were totally groundless. The Taconic Tories received no help from the whiggish Yankees across the border, and they never targeted for attack their landlords' persons or houses or Robert Livingston, Jr.'s four nearby iron works, which produced cannon balls for the

[49] Seventeen of the Tories joined the British or Loyalist army in 1777, two in 1778 and 1781 respectively, and on the rest no information exists. See class 12, vol. XXIII, p. 153, vol. XXVI, pp. 147, 304–05, vol. XXVII, pp. 9, 340–41, 417–18, vol. XXVIII, pp. 1, 25–26, 38, 42, 94–95, 198, 245, 298, vol. XXIX, pp. 165, 298, vol. XXXI, pp. 1–3, 143, 341, vol. XXXII, pp. 95–98, 213, vol. CXLIII, pp. 17, 21, Audit Office Series; class 13, vol. XVI, p. 206, *ibid.*

[50] Walter Steward to Ebenezer Hancock, April 26, 1777, roll 53, Historical Collections.

[51] Lynd, "Tenant Rising," 168.

American army. Unlike William Predergast's 1766 rebels, they did not issue a manifesto against their landlords and the land system they represented, not even for the purpose of garnering support from fellow tenants elsewhere. To judge from the vengeance with which the Yankees (the people from Egremont) attacked and plundered the Taconic Tories—their former allies—in May 1777, the Yankees apparently did not believe that the manor tenants were continuing the socioeconomic struggle they had started and directed before the Revolution. However, there was definitely no love lost between the Livingstons and the Yankees who still coveted the manor's Taconic land.

Nowhere in the voluminous testimonies, depositions, and confessions by the manor Tories, Tory soldiers, and witnesses for or against them was a single reference to a lease system or tenant-landlord relations in Livingston Manor and Rensselaerswyck made in explaining the origin of tenant toryism.[52] If hatred of their landlords and the lease system had been the main cause of their pro-British conversion, it would have been a travesty of their alleged "socioeconomic radicalism" to fly, soon after their cause was aborted, to their landlord family for favors and protection fom the fury of committeemen and to ask for an assurance against eviction from their leases.[53]

The political choices the New York tenants made during the Revolution were at once more simple, more mundane, and more subtle than many scholars have suggested. The least important was the role of republican or Tory ideas and radical class interest. The tenants' leanings in 1775 were determined by their traditional apathy, by their preference for noninvolvement in public affairs, and, above all, by their respect for their landlord. When their landlord was firm and forcible, and remained as a primary influence in their lives, they generally followed his direction as they had done in the prerevolutionary period. In the war years, when the British threatened to invade New York, many tenants, especially those on the Whig-owned estates, defected from the Whig cause. At first, their disaffection took the form of draft resistance, and it gave way to toryism as the British and Indian conquest of the state seemed to be imminent. To these tenants, conversion to toryism appeared to be the best means of survival.

In January 1778, the Albany County Committee of Safety observed that "many Persons" under its jurisdiction "went over to the Enemy and took an Active part in their favour some thro' Fear, some thro' the persuasions of artful and designing Persons, others thro' the Allurements of Gain and the prospect of seeing their oppressed Country in the Hands of its base Invaders." This official version seems well supported by available evidence. The reason that tenant Tories most frequently gave was, not their love of the British, but their concern for self-preservation. They sought protection of their families and estates from the possible violence of the British army and their Indian allies,

[52] Smith, *Historical Memoirs*, II, 129, 131. Many testimonies given very freely by the former Tory soldiers before the Parliamentary Commission on the Loyalist claims were similar to those given before the American courts.
[53] Lynd, "Tenant Rising," 177.

who they believed would easily conquer New York if not America.[54] The paramount importance of the British-Indian factor is clearly underscored by the fact that the ebb and flow of Tory strength and activities in the manors, as well as in other areas, between the fall of 1776 and the spring and summer of 1777 exactly coincided with the ebb of the British-Indian invasion threat and the flow of the perceived American military strength. Apart from the cause of self-preservation, the wish to be on the winning side and to be compensated generously in money and land for their service was probably an attraction that some tenants could not resist.

All in all, too much has been read into the toryism of the Livingston Manor tenantry in efforts to generalize about the nature of the Revolution in New York. There was no internal socioeconomic conflict going on there or in Rensselaerswyck, although toryism as a political issue affected both places. On the estates of the Tory landlords, none of the aspects of conflict was ever present throughout the war, although the lease system there was almost the same as on the Whig-owned estates. Therefore, from the broad perspective of both Tory and Whig landed estates, one can argue that the *political* dissension on the northern manors was an aberration rather than a norm in the overall experience of New York agrarian society during the American Revolution and that the New York lease system under Whigs' control was still strong and mutually beneficial for landlord and tenant. Consequently, the system was capable of withstanding the convulsions of the revolutionary era. The Tory estates were confiscated not because they represented a socioeconomic injustice but because their owners were on the losing side. As for the tenantry, they generally proved to be neither Emelyan Ivanovich Pugachevs nor Mariano Azuelas, but petit bourgeois conservatives.

[54] *Minutes of the Albany Committee of Correspondence*, I, 901–02; *Journal of the Provincial Congress*, I, 1010, 1006, 1019, II, 507, 518; *Calendar of Historical Manuscripts*, II, 190–91, 204–06, 229–31.

Patriots by Default:
Queens County, New York, and the
British Army, 1776-1783

Joseph S. Tiedemann

TWENTIETH-CENTURY insurgency warfare and the involvement of the United States in Vietnam have made historians more aware of the political dimension of the War for American Independence.[1] The mother country had not only to defeat rebellious armies but to pursue a policy of reconciliation and to cultivate support in areas that her forces occupied. Success in this noncombative phase of the conflict could not substitute for military victory, but the British war effort stood to benefit greatly from the manpower and matériel civilians could provide. It was advisable, therefore, that strict discipline be maintained over the army. British soldiers could not be permitted to treat American civilians as harshly or recklessly as most eighteenth-century European armies dealt with enemy noncombatants.[2] Such misconduct would only create enmity

Mr. Tiedemann is a member of the Department of History at Loyola Marymount University. A version of this article was presented at the annual meeting of the Pacific Coast Branch of the American Historical Association, August 1981. Acknowledgments: I wish to thank Thomas E. Buckley, S.J., Robert M. Calhoon, Angus B. Hawkins, Lawrence J. Jelinek, Milton M. Klein, John N. Shaeffer, and David Syrett for their comments and suggestions. I am also grateful to the late Harold C. Syrett for his support.

[1] See John Shy, "The American Revolution: The Military Conflict Considered as a Revolutionary War," in Stephen G. Kurtz and James H. Hutson, eds., *Essays on the American Revolution* (Chapel Hill, N.C., 1973), 121-156; "The American Revolution Today," in his *A People Numerous and Armed: Reflections on the Military Struggle for American Independence* (New York, 1976), 1-19; and "British Strategy for Pacifying the Southern Colonies, 1778-1781," in Jeffrey J. Crow and Larry E. Tise, eds., *The Southern Experience in the American Revolution* (Chapel Hill, N.C., 1978), 155-173. Also important are Piers Mackesy, *Could the British Have Won the War of Independence?* (Worcester, Mass., 1976), and Ira D. Gruber, "Britain's Southern Strategy," in W. Robert Higgins, ed., *The Revolutionary War in the South: Power, Conflict, and Leadership* (Durham, N.C., 1979), 205-238. For criticisms of this approach see Don Higginbotham, "Reflections on the War of Independence, Modern Guerrilla Warfare, and the War in Vietnam," in Ronald Hoffman and Peter J. Albert, eds., *Arms and Independence: The Military Character of the American Revolution* (Charlottesville, Va., 1984), 1-24.

[2] For armies as a scourge to society see Tony Hayter, *The Army and the Crowd in Mid-Georgian England* (London, 1978), 21; André Corvisier, *Armies and Societies in*

and hinder the effective prosecution of the war. Given the significance of the political dimension of the conflict and Britain's inept handling of it, the topic merits further examination.

Queens County, Long Island, New York, provides an appropriate locale. As one of the first areas recaptured by the British, it was a logical place to initiate the work of reconstruction and signal the government's good intentions for the future.[3] Revolutionary Queens County constituted what is today the Borough of Queens in New York City and the adjacent County of Nassau. It was bounded on the north by the Long Island Sound, on the south by the Atlantic Ocean, on the east by Suffolk County, and on the west by Brooklyn and the East River. In 1776 it consisted of five towns—Newtown, Flushing, Jamaica, Hempstead, and Oyster Bay—and had a population of approximately 11,000, most of whom were farmers.[4]

If the people of Queens County had had their way, there would not have been a Revolution in 1776. A decisive majority of the adult male residents, 60 percent, were neutral in the period immediately before the war. Furthermore, most neutrals were also probably apolitical in outlook.[5]

Europe, 1494-1789, trans. Abigail T. Siddall (Bloomington, Ind., 1979), 77-79; and Geoffrey Best, *War and Society in Revolutionary Europe, 1770-1870* (New York, 1982). These sources also provide a good starting point for comparing the conduct of the British army in New York with that of European armies elsewhere than America. See also John Phillip Reid, *In a Defiant Stance: The Conditions of Law in Massachusetts Bay, the Irish Comparison, and the Coming of the American Revolution* (University Park, Pa., 1977), and Correlli Barnett, *Britain and Her Army, 1509-1970: A Military, Political and Social Survey* (London, 1970). For comparison with the Continental army see Charles Royster, *A Revolutionary People at War: The Continental Army and American Character, 1775-1783* (Chapel Hill, N.C., 1979).

[3] Recent studies that consider this issue in New York include Milton M. Klein, "An Experiment That Failed: General James Robertson and Civil Government in British New York, 1779-1783," *New York History,* LXI (1980), 229-254, and "Why Did the British Fail to Win the Hearts and Minds of New Yorkers?" *ibid.,* LXIV (1983), 357-375. Of great value are Milton M. Klein and Ronald W. Howard, eds., *The Twilight of British Rule in Revolutionary America: The New York Letter Book of General James Robertson, 1780-1783* (Cooperstown, N.Y., 1983), and K. G. Davies, "The Restoration of Civil Government by the British in the War of Independence," in Esmond Wright, ed., *Red, White and True Blue: The Loyalists in the Revolution* (New York, 1976), 111-133. See also George Smith McCowen, Jr., *The British Occupation of Charleston, 1780-82* (Columbia, S.C., 1972), and John W. Jackson, *With the British Army in Philadelphia, 1777-1778* (San Rafael, Calif., 1979).

[4] The northern half of the county, where the soil was very fertile, was then a thriving commercial agricultural region that supplied the growing New York City market. Inhabitants of the island's south shore engaged in subsistence agriculture and did not enjoy the same degree of prosperity. Nonetheless, the county did not divide by class over the issues of the Revolution.

[5] Evidence concerning the statistical data and my arguments about the political situation in Revolutionary Queens County can be found in my "Communities in

Popular participation in town government had declined during the eighteenth century, and town meetings no longer acted with the vigor of a century earlier.[6] It is not surprising, therefore, that by 1776 only 12 percent of adult males had publicly renounced their allegiance to the crown. Since there was so little evident support for the American cause, contemporaries believed Queens to be a pro-British stronghold, though by 1776 only 27 percent of the adult males had declared themselves to be royalists.[7]

After the British victory at the Battle of Long Island in August 1776, the county remained under military rule until the end of 1783. Royal officials consequently had ample time to devise an effective program of reconciliation.[8] By war's end, however, the people of Queens had become, not loyal subjects, but patriots—as much by British default as by personal choice. To explain why, this article will explore the relationship that developed between the British army and Queens County civilians. It will examine the aftermath of the Battle of Long Island; the army's abuse of private property and its demands on residents for supplies; the insolent and abusive behavior of British officers; the imposition of martial law and the governance of Queens between 1776 and 1780; the debate among British officials after 1777 about martial law; the arbitrary rule by the

---

the Midst of the American Revolution: Queens County, New York, 1774-1775," *Journal of Social History*, XVIII (1984), 57-78.

[6] For the evolution of town government in one of these communities see Jean B. Peyer, "Jamaica, Long Island, 1656-1776: A Study of the Roots of American Urbanism" (Ph.D. diss., City University of New York, 1974), chap. 3. Also important is Jessica Kross, *The Evolution of an American Town: Newtown, New York, 1642-1775* (Philadelphia, 1983), 68-70, 140-141, 198.

[7] Even the British recognized that many New Yorkers were not royalists but inclined toward neutrality. Gen. William Howe, for example, argued that "many wish for peace, but are indifferent which side prevails"; he believed that many people's "submission" to the crown after the Battle of Long Island sprang "from no other motive, than that of [the army's] success" (*The Narrative of Lieut. Gen. Sir William Howe, in a Committee of the House of Commons, on the 29th of April, 1779, Relative to His Conduct, during His Late Command of the King's Troops in North America: To Which Are Added, Some Observations upon a Pamphlet, Entitled, Letters to a Nobleman* [London, 1780], 39, 44). Ambrose Serle was worried about the "many pretended Friends in N. York, who are ready enough to do any Mischief" (Edward H. Tatum, Jr., ed., *The American Journal of Ambrose Serle, Secretary to Lord Howe, 1776-1778* [San Marino, Calif., 1940], 134, hereafter cited as *Serle Journal*).

[8] Concerning the initial efforts made to secure public support, Gov. William Tryon reported that he "took much pains in explaining to the people (having formed them into circles) the iniquitous arts ettc [*sic*] that had been practiced on their credulity to seduce and mislead them, and I had the satisfaction to observe among them a general return of confidence in govern[men]t" (Tryon to Lord George Germain, Dec. 24, 1776, in E. B. O'Callaghan *et al.*, eds., *Documents Relative to the Colonial History of the State of New-York . . .* [Albany, N.Y., 1856-1887], VIII, 693).

Court of Police on Long Island commencing in 1780; and, finally, the consequences of Britain's occupation of Queens County.

A considerable cast of characters participated in these developments. The most important were Lord George Germain, secretary of state for the American Department; Generals William Howe, Henry Clinton, and Guy Carleton, who served in turn as commander in chief of the British army in America; William Tryon, governor of New York from 1771 to 1780, and his replacement Gen. James Robertson; Col. Archibald Hamilton, aide-de-camp to Tryon and commander of the county militia; and George Duncan Ludlow, superintendent of the Court of Police on Long Island.

These officials had the power to institute an effective program of reconciliation. They failed dismally. As a British officer observed, "We planted an irrecoverable hatred wherever we went, which neither time nor measures will be able to eradicate. What, then, are we to expect from it, conciliation or submission?"[9] By ordering troops into Queens County, the British government set in motion a chain of events that could not be controlled and that in the end defeated the very purpose for which military forces had originally been sent. Instead of destroying the Revolution, the British army became one of its agents.

I: AFTER THE BATTLE

Great Britain's problems began immediately after the Battle of Long Island. County folk had expected British victory and presumed that it presaged a quick end to the war and the expeditious reestablishment of civilian rule. But the military abruptly disabused them of their hopes.[10] One British officer, for example, argued that "we should (whenever we get further into the country) give free liberty to the soldiers to ravage it at will, that these infatuated wretches may feel what a calamity war is."[11] Another

[9] Charles Stuart to Lord Bute, Sept. 16, 1778, in E. Stuart-Wortley, ed., *A Prime Minister and His Son . . .* (London, 1925), 132.

[10] For an account of sentiment within Queens at this time see Rev. Joshua Bloomer to the Secretary, Apr. 9, 1777, American Material from the Records of the Society for the Propagation of the Gospel in Foreign Parts, Letter Ser. B, III, 236, Library of Congress (microfilm), hereafter cited as S.P.G., Letter Ser. B. Also valuable are the "Declaration of the Inhabitants of Queens County," *New York Journal; or, the General Advertiser,* Dec. 14, 1775, and the "Petition and Representation of Queens County, in New-York," to the commissioners for restoring peace, Oct. 21, 1776, in Peter Force [ed.], *American Archives: Consisting of a Collection of Authentick Records, State Papers, Debates, and Letters and Other Notices of Publick Affairs, . . . ,* 5th Ser. (Washington, D.C., 1848-1853), II, 1159-1164. See also Benjamin F. Thompson, *History of Long Island from Its Discovery and Settlement to the Present Time,* 3d ed. rev. (New York, 1918), I, 193, and *History of Queens County, New York, with Illustrations, Portraits and Sketches of Prominent Families and Individuals* (New York, 1882), 32, 198-199.

[11] Lord Rawdon to [the earl of Huntington], Sept. 23, 1776, in Francis Bickley, ed., *Report on the Manuscripts of the Late Reginald Rawdon Hastings, Esq.. of the Manor House, Ashby de la Zouch,* III (Historical Manuscripts Commission, *Twentieth Report* [London, 1934]), 185, hereafter cited as *Hastings MSS.*

believed that "the old Hatred for Kings and the seeds of sedition are so thickly sown against them, that it must be thrash'd out of them[.] New England has poyson'd the Whole."[12] A third hoped the army would "cut them up a little" before peace was declared.[13]

Obviously, not every officer shared these sentiments, but enough did, and the consequences were inevitable. During the battle, crews from the ships transporting the army to Brooklyn interrupted their mission to plunder inhabitants.[14] Officers of lower rank and enlisted men, who did not understand how they could wage war when they could not tell patriot from loyalist, began abusing all as rebels. The army's "want of discipline" led one officer to remark that "those poor unhappy wretches who had remained in their habitation through necessity or loyalty were immediately judged . . . to be Rebels, neither their cloathing or property spared, but in the most inhuman and barbarous manner torn from them."[15] Maj. Gen. James Robertson, commandant of New York City from 1776 to 1778, later commented, "When I first landed I found in all the farms poultry and cows, and the farms stocked; when I passed sometime afterwards I found nothing alive."[16]

Debate began almost at once over who was responsible for the breakdown in military discipline. A Hessian commander wrote in September 1776 that all the British regiments already had their full quota of horses and that his own units were not far behind, for "an officer can acquire them for little money and often for nothing."[17] The British, however, charged that German soldiers had come to America with the expectation of making a fortune and were responsible for the abuses. Ambrose Serle, Adm. Richard Lord Howe's secretary, noted on August 25 that Hessians "had committed already several Depredations, and even upon the Friends of Government"; he would "have rejoiced if the Rebellion could have been reduced without Foreign Troops at all."[18]

[12] William Bamford, "Bamford's Diary: The Revolutionary Diary of a British Officer," *Maryland Historical Magazine,* XXVIII (1933), 13.

[13] Letter from Capt. John Bowater, July 23, 1777, in Marion Balderston and David Syrett, eds., *The Lost War: Letters from British Officers during the American Revolution* (New York, 1975), 138-139.

[14] *Serle Journal,* 74.

[15] Stuart to Bute, Feb. 4, 1777, in Stuart-Wortley, ed., *Prime Minister and Son,* 96-99.

[16] *The Detail and Conduct of the American War under Generals Gage, Howe, Burgoyne, and Vice Admiral Lord Howe: With a Very Full and Correct State of the Whole of the Evidence as Given before a Committee of the House of Commons . . . ,* 3d ed. (London, 1780), 119. Robertson not only understood the need for conciliation but apparently sought to let this principle guide his conduct while military commandant of New York City during the first year and a half of British occupation; see Klein and Howard, eds., *Twilight of British Rule,* 32, 35-38.

[17] Bernhard A. Uhlendorf, ed., *Revolution in America: Confidential Letters and Journals, 1776-1784, of Adjutant General Major Baurmeister of the Hessian Forces* (New Brunswick, N.J., 1957), 45.

[18] *Serle Journal,* 77. See also Serle to Lord Dartmouth, Sept. 5, 1776, in Benjamin F. Stevens, comp., *Facsimiles of Manuscripts in European Archives*

Another writer commented more forthrightly that "the Hessians bore the blame at first, but the British were equally alert."[19]

Responsibility for the behavior of both British and German soldiers rested with Gen. Sir William Howe, the army commander in chief. Eighteenth-century army officers took their cue from their commanding general when determining how strictly to enforce discipline.[20] Howe certainly understood the need to control plundering, and he later defended himself by arguing before Parliament that he had issued a series of proclamations against such misbehavior.[21] But orderly books from the period tell a different story: he often pardoned or commuted the sentences of soldiers found guilty by court-martial of crimes against civilians.[22] Perhaps he was reluctant to punish his troops for conduct that was generally tolerated in European warfare.[23] Nonetheless, some observers believed that his leniency by itself explained the army's lawlessness. Once discipline was lost, it was never satisfactorily reestablished, although Howe issued orders threatening summary execution of soldiers caught looting.[24]

The military's approach to reconciliation was troubling in yet another way. County residents had expected the British to punish whigs and reward tories. But when royalists pressed their grievances against rebels who had injured them, it was often the complainants who were maltreated

---

Relating to America, 1773-1783 (London, 1889-1895), No. 2042, and Maj. Francis Hutcheson to Sir Frederick Haldimand, Sept. 1, 1776, Feb. 16, 1777, Haldimand Papers, Additional Manuscripts, 21680, IV, 148, 175, British Library (Library of Congress photostats).

[19] Thomas Jones, *History of New York during the Revolutionary War, and of the Leading Events in Other Colonies at That Period,* ed. Edward Floyd De Lancey (New York, 1879), I, 114.

[20] Best, *War and Society,* 104.

[21] Ira D. Gruber, *The Howe Brothers and the American Revolution* (Chapel Hill, N.C., 1972), 113, 145; *Howe Narrative,* 58-60.

[22] For information about courts-martial see "Three Orderly Books Written by Captain Henry Knight, Aide-de-Camp to Lord Howe from September 26, 1776 to June 2, 1777," New-York Historical Society, New York City; British Orderly Book, Headquarters Orders, New York City, Aug. 1781 to Feb. 1782, *ibid.;* and *General Sir William Howe's Orderly Book at Charlestown, Boston and Halifax, June 17, 1775 to 1776, 26 May* . . . , ed. Benjamin Franklin Stevens (London, 1890).

[23] Best, *War and Society,* 102-105; Corvisier, *Armies and Societies.* trans. Siddall, 77-79, 179-180; Hayter, *Army and Crowd.* 21, 52.

[24] Stuart to Bute, Feb. 4, 1777, in Stuart-Wortley, ed., *Prime Minister and Son.* 99; [Allen French, ed.], *Diary of Frederick Mackenzie: Giving A Daily Narrative of His Military Service as an Officer of the Regiment of Royal Welch Fusiliers during the Years 1775-1781, in Massachusetts, Rhode Island, and New York* (Cambridge, Mass., 1930), I, 40. Sylvia R. Frey believes that discipline soon began to take hold among British but not German soldiers; as a result the number of complaints against the former declined (*The British Soldier in America: A Social History of Military Life in the Revolutionary Period* [Austin, Tex., 1981], 75).

by the British.[25] Thomas Jones, a county loyalist, justice of New York's Supreme Court before the Revolution, and author of the partisan *History of New York during the Revolutionary War and of the Leading Events in the Other Colonies at That Period*, argued that rebels should have been promptly prosecuted in the courts for treason.[26] Instead, on November 30, 1776, William Howe and his brother, Adm. Richard Lord Howe, the naval commander, issued a proclamation pardoning all who would submit within sixty days to royal authority. Even whig leaders could receive free and full pardon, provoking Lord George Germain to grumble that it would alienate royalists to find that rebels who had caused so much suffering were now on an equal footing with those who had persevered in their loyalty.[27]

II: ARMY ABUSES

Affairs had gotten off to an inauspicious start, but the situation was not irreversible. If the military had quickly restored order, local cooperation would still have been possible. Instead, the abuses the army committed against private property and the demands it made for supplies over the next several years exacerbated the discord. In planning the New York campaign the ministry had expected that the city and its environs would

[25] Henry Onderdonk, Jr. [comp.], *Documents and Letters Intended to Illustrate the Revolutionary Incidents of Queens County* . . . (New York, 1846), 100, 114.

[26] Jones, *History*, ed. De Lancey, I, 127, II, 116, 145. An ardent loyalist, Jones was convinced that the blunders and corruption of the army caused its defeat. It has been pointed out that he was not unbiased and that his work contains factual errors (Henry P. Johnston, *Observations on Judge Jones' Loyalist History of the American Revolution, How Far It Is an Authority* [New York, 1880]). The present article disagrees with some of his conclusions. For example, his belief that one-third of the county's residents became refugees is without doubt an overestimation (Jones, *History*, ed. De Lancey, I, 108n); but for the period before 1781, when he became a refugee, he is usually a reliable chronicler of events in Queens. Obviously, some of his facts are incorrect, for he was writing in England after the Revolution and cannot be expected to have had total recall. However, other commentators, both English and American, have made the same general observations that he did concerning British misconduct; what Jones added to such accounts is local color. Many of the incidents he recounted can be documented or at least partially verified in other contemporary sources. It is fair to assume that his anger against the British resulted at times in exaggerations, but his opinions are still worth considering, for they were manifestly widely shared.

[27] Proclamation by the Peace Commissioners, Nov. 30, 1776, C.O. 5/177, Public Record Office (Library of Congress microfilm); for an example of a pardon granted a Long Islander see Henry A. Stoutenburgh, *A Documentary History of the Dutch Congregation of Oyster Bay, Queens County* . . . . IX (New York, 1906), 778-779. Germain to William Knox, Dec. 31, 1776, *The Manuscripts of Miss M. Eyre Matcham; Captain H. V. Knox; Cornwallis Wykeham-Martin, Esq.; etc.* (Historical Manuscripts Commission, *Report on Manuscripts in Various Collections*, VI [Dublin, 1909]), 128.

feed the forces being sent to America. But the British defeats at Trenton and Princeton forced the army to evacuate New Jersey, and for the remainder of the war the government provisioned the army from Europe. Still, the military relied on America for fresh food, animal fodder, fuel, horses, and other resources the occupied areas could yield.[28] Queens County not only supplied its own residents, the expanding refugee population within its borders, and the soldiers quartered there; it also helped to feed the civil and military population of New York City and to outfit the army for each campaign. Establishing efficient and equitable arrangements for procuring war matériel would have been a good first step toward winning the allegiance of county residents.[29] Yet the collection of supplies was never efficiently organized, and the methods employed often exhibited a cavalier disregard for citizens' rights and feelings.

When the American forces retreated from Queens, they left behind cattle they had collected there. General Howe instructed owners to present a claim and affirm their loyalty in order to recover their animals. From the standpoint of civil-military relations this was a positive step. However, when a claimant did as instructed, the military did not always return his cattle but kept some for the army's use. The owners were promised compensation, yet when they requested it, they were not paid. Military officials damned a few for being rebels, threatened some with jail, and told others that redress must come from the patriots. The commissary department then billed the government for the cattle, and royal officials pocketed the money.[30]

Similar abuses continued throughout the war. Commissary officials sometimes used intimidation to seize cattle without paying or at prices below those set by the commander in chief; yet the crown still paid full price.[31] Little ingenuity was needed to falsify financial records in order to defraud the government. Ambrose Serle reported that commissary employees often forced inhabitants to sign blank receipts to secure payment for supplies taken by the army; if a farmer refused, he was not paid.[32] Officials could then make a profit by writing in inflated sums of money.

[28] R. Arthur Bowler, *Logistics and the Failure of the British Army in America. 1775-1783* (Princeton, N.J., 1975), 41-91.

[29] For the consequences Great Britain faced when the army failed to maintain discipline and as a result neglected the political dimension of the war, see Shy, "American Revolution," in Kurtz and Hutson, eds., *Essays on the Revolution.* 134, 141, 142, 145, n. 36.

[30] Jones, *History,* ed. De Lancey, I. 115-118; Bowler, *Logistics.* 80-81; Oscar Theodore Barck, Jr., *New York City during the War for Independence. with Special Reference to the Period of British Occupation* (New York, 1931), 100-101.

[31] Bowler, *Logistics.* 80-81.

[32] *Serle Journal,* 293. Until 1780 army regiments were permitted during military operations to confiscate the cattle of rebels and turn these animals over to the commissary department for a dollar-a-head bounty, but soldiers rarely cared whose property they took, and the commissaries not infrequently sold these cattle to the government at the full price and kept the profit (Bowler, *Logistics.* 180-181).

Such practices not only cost the government but encouraged residents to view the British and not the American army as the enemy. The guilty officials do not even appear to have been very discreet in conducting their business. Sir George Rodney, a British naval officer, was so disgusted by the corruption at New York that he wrote Germain in 1780 complaining "of a long train of leeches, who suck the blood of the State, and whose interest prompts them to promote the continuance of the war."[33]

The army also needed horses, wagons, and drivers. Troops blanketed the county in 1776 impressing what was wanted. The drivers and wagons remained with Howe for the duration of that year's campaign, and much equipment was lost. When the army returned, the quartermaster refused to pay owners whose property was missing unless a driver swore to its loss and the exact period of time it was used in government service. Since a large number of drivers had died or deserted, many owners were not compensated. Instead, the quartermaster billed the government and kept the proceeds.[34] The army again needed baggage trains for the campaign of 1777, and justices of the peace in each town summoned inhabitants to determine how the burden was to be distributed. At these meetings, residents complained bitterly about the treatment they had received the previous year. A compromise was finally reached: the horses and wagons were to be appraised by an impartial judge, and the owners' names and the value of the seized property recorded in a special book.[35] A clerk employed by the quartermaster was to keep an account so that compensation could be made for the period from the date of entry to the time of loss or return. If the property was lost, the owner was entitled to its assessed value. When the campaign was ended, the quartermaster notified owners that the date of entry was a date of sale by the owner and that he was prepared to pay the original valuation. Many inhabitants rejected the offer, expecting eventually to go to court, but the opportunity never arose, for Queens County remained under martial law until 1783. British officials next had the drivers, many of whom were illiterate runaway slaves, sign reimbursement receipts for the wagons. The ruse was simple. The quartermaster, Gen. Sir William Erskine, and his two senior deputies,

---

[33] George Rodney to Germain, Dec. 22, 1780, in *Report on the Manuscripts of Mrs. Stopford-Sackville, of Drayton House, Northamptonshire,* II (Historical Manuscripts Commission, *Fifteenth Report* [London, 1910]), 191, hereafter cited as *Stopford-Sackville MSS.*

[34] Jones, *History,* ed. De Lancey, I, 330-332; Onderdonk [comp.], *Documents,* 108-109, 203-204; *New-York Gazette: and the Weekly Mercury,* Dec. 2, 1776; for examples of claims by residents for unpaid bills see Testimony of Daniel Whitehead, June 3, Oath of Henry Wiggins and Simon Voris, June 3, Oath of Israel Powell, July 9, 1783, A.O. 13/92, 153, 154, 175, P.R.O. (Library of Congress microfilm).

[35] Jones, *History,* ed. De Lancey, I, 332-336; William Shirreff, "Manuscript List of Wagons and Horses, and Owners' Names, All Living on Long Island," n.d., Long Island Historical Society, Brooklyn, N.Y. Shirreff's manuscript is most likely the book to which Jones was referring, and it substantiates his major points.

Col. William Shirreff and Maj. Henry Bruen, rented the baggage trains to the government and used the proceeds to buy the teams from county residents. When Erskine and Shirreff returned to England in 1779, after collecting twelve shillings per day for each animal and feeding them at government expense, they sold their wagons and horses to the new quartermaster, Maj. Lord William Cathcart, and his assistant, Capt. Archibald Robertson, who also became wealthy by following the established practice.[36]

The military's need for fuel also provoked discontent.[37] At first, wood cut from the estates of absentee rebels, supplemented with coal from mines on Cape Breton Island, largely satisfied British requirements. However, contractors licensed by the army laid bare entire farms without regard for future needs. Little supervision was exercised over licensees, who sometimes cut their quotas from the most accessible woodlands without authority to do so. Farmers protested, but the lumbermen were gone. Officials were callously indifferent, for the barrackmaster department, which was responsible for fuel, was sharing in the spoils. Wood taken from rebel land was free except for cutting and transportation costs. Unprincipled officials, however, sold these supplies to the government at the market price. Furthermore, even though wood was purchased in four-foot nine-inch "country cords," the department distributed it in four-foot cords. The barrackmaster general defended this practice, but once it was stopped, the government saved £55,000 annually or one-sixth of the

[36] Erskine and his two deputies together owned three-quarters of the baggage train. Whenever a participant left office, he sold his interest to his successor. The profits were large: the total cost of wagon hire to the government from Jan. 1777 until May 1782 was £642,192 sterling. This episode can also be traced in Bowler, *Logistics*, 24-25, 183-185, 190-199, and *Proceedings of a Board of General Officers of the British Army at New York*, 1781 (New-York Historical Society, *Collections*. XLIX [New York, 1916]), 70-79, hereafter cited as *Proceedings of a Board*. The military's demands on county residents for wagons and teams did not cease at this time but continued until the war's end; see "The Examination of Colonel Archibald Hamilton Taken on Oath, April 20, 1789," Misc. MSS. N.-Y. Hist. Soc., and Onderdonk [comp.], *Documents*. 209. Information about this aspect of civil-military relations can be found in A.O. 13/92, 176, 187-189, A.O. 13/97, 525-526, and A.O. 13/99, 208, 209, 211, 229, 261, 265, 277, 312, 318-320, 324, 325, 334-335. James Thomas Flexner describes the operations of the quartermaster department in New York during the Revolution (*States Dyckman: American Loyalist* [Boston, 1980], 25-38).

[37] For the methods used to collect firewood see Jones, *History*. ed. De Lancey, I, 337-338; *Proceedings of a Board*, 97-103; Rivington's *Royal Gazette* (New York), Nov. 14, 1776, Nov. 11, 1778, Feb. 6, Mar. 13, Dec. 9, 1779; *New-York Gaz.*, Jan. 5, 1778; "Original Order Book of Colonel [Archibald] Hamilton, Commandant of the Queens County Militia," Feb. 1780, L.I. Hist. Soc.; Henry Onderdonk, Jr., ed., "Correspondence of Major John Kissam Illustrating the Revolutionary History of Queens County on Long Island," 31, 33, 36, 37, 39, 43, L.I. Hist. Soc.; "Captain [Daniel] Youngs's Forage Book," Apr. 15, July 17, July 19, 1780, Nassau County Historical Museum, East Meadow, N.Y.; and Bowler, *Logistics*. 60-63.

cost.[38] A crisis developed in the unusually cold winter of 1779/80, when coal shipments ceased, the supply of wood cut from the property of whig refugees had been depleted, and the contracting arrangement was unable to satisfy the army's needs. The price of wood then soared 250 percent; during the most critical period soldiers were reduced to half-rations of fuel.[39] In 1780 efforts were made at last to reform the system. From this time onward, captains from the local militia units determined the amount of wood to be cut in each district of the county. Inhabitants then cut their quotas and carted the logs to selected landing places.[40] Although an improvement, the method was never entirely satisfactory, and after the war the county of necessity became an importer of wood.[41]

The British saw little injustice in their demands on civilians who had benefited for years from the crown's protection and who must now make the effort the crisis required. But the army intruded upon almost every aspect of life.[42] Farmers were told when to thresh grain and cut hay. Things not needed for a family's personal use were often taken at prices set by the commander in chief. One year, residents did not have sufficient seed remaining to plant their next crop and had to purchase it at exorbitant rates. In winter, soldiers were often billeted in private residences, and farmers sometimes had to lock up their animals to prevent thievery by troops who were ever on the prowl for food. During the winter of 1778/

[38] Bowler, *Logistics*, 167-168, 173.

[39] Proclamation by Sir Henry Clinton, Nov. 24, 1779, British Headquarters Papers, No. 2446, P.R.O. (New York Public Library, photostats); Frey, *British Soldier*, 40.

[40] In the winter of 1780/81 Queens supplied 4,500 cords. In February the military demanded another 6,000 cords from residents of the north shore; additional demands were also made on other parts of Queens where soldiers quartered. In July 1781 the British again requisitioned 4,500 cords. This pattern continued until the evacuation. Developments in 1780 and after can be traced in *New-York Gaz.*, July 24, Sept. 18, Dec. 3, 1780; *Royal Gaz.*, Dec. 9, 1779, June 17, 1780, July 15, Nov. 28, Dec. 5, 1781; Onderdonk, ed., "Correspondence of Kissam," 44, 55-58, 60, 73, 75, 77, 79; "Youngs's Forage Book," June 28, 1780, Mar. 8, 1781; Copy of a Wood Contract, Feb. 14, 1781, Queens County, New York Box, N.-Y. Hist. Soc.; "Return of the Inhabitants of Jericho Who Have Furnished Fire Wood from 30 December to 8 January, 1783, Being 10 Days," N.-Y. Hist. Soc.; "List of Inhabitants of Oyster Bay on Long Island Who Have Furnished Hessians with Firewood, Jan. 7 to Feb. 2, 1783," Documents Book, I, 37, East Hampton Free Library, East Hampton, L.I.; and William Crosbie to Kissam, Mar. 29, 1781, Documents Relating to the Revolutionary War and Civil War, L.I. Hist. Soc.

[41] Bernice Schultz Marshall, *Colonial Hempstead: Long Island Life under the Dutch and English*, 2d ed. (Port Washington, N.Y., 1962), 116.

[42] The military's interference with daily life can be traced in *Royal Gaz.*, Nov. 21, Dec. 27, 1777, Sept. 23, 1778, Jan. 27, Oct. 2, 1779, Nov. 18, 1780, July 14, 1781; *New-York Gaz.*, June 23, 1777, Sept. 14, 1778, Jan. 25, 1779, Oct. 30, 1780; Onderdonk, ed., "Kissam Correspondence," 15, 21; and Jones, *History*, ed. De Lancey, II, 27-29. Also see Barck, *New York*, 102-104.

79 the army faced a provisioning crisis; hunger consequently aggravated the tensions between civilians and their uninvited guests. Since officers sometimes sold the firewood residents had provided, soldiers tore down fences to keep warm, and herds of animals strayed through unfenced fields destroying the crops.[43] Officers then disclaimed responsibility, arguing that the farmers had not provided sufficient firewood.[44]

The county was also plagued by raids of privateers engaged in whaleboat warfare on the Sound. These attacks began with American attempts to interdict the Royal Army's exposed supply lines on the north shore but soon degenerated into brigandage.[45] Legitimate whaleboaters pillaged private property and were quickly joined by lawless freebooters—"skinners" who claimed to be whigs and "cowboys" who were pro-British. The situation became especially perilous after 1778. At the beginning of the war General Howe made Oliver De Lancey a brigadier general with authority to raise three battalions "for the defense of Long Island" and "other exigencies";[46] the third was to consist of officers and enlistees from

[43] "Order Book of [Archibald] Hamilton," Nov. 12, 17, 1779, Jan. 7, May 15, 1780; Onderdonk, ed., "Kissam Correspondence," 50; "Youngs's Forage Book," Aug. 1, 1781; Hamilton to John Suydam, n.d., Misc. MSS, N.-Y. Hist. Soc.; John Leland to Hamilton, Jan. 24, William Loewenstein to Hamilton, Nov. 23, Hamilton to Loewenstein, Nov. 24, 1780, A.O. 13/99. For the provisioning crisis see David Syrett, *Shipping and the American War. 1775-83: A Study of British Transport Organization* (London, 1970), 31. Inhabitants also periodically had to leave their property and families unprotected against the soldiers when called upon to stand guard or do fatigue duty. Hamilton, for example, complained that on one of his absences "the Stone Walls were pulled down, the Rail Fences destroyed, and Burned, all of which occassioned the Loss of his Cattle or his farm being otherwise damaged to the Amount of at least £400 Currency" (Memorial of Archibald Hamilton to Sir Guy Carleton [1783], Transcript of Various Papers Relating to the . . . American Loyalists . . . in the Royal Institute of Great Britain, 1777-1783, VI, 513-514, N.Y. Pub. Lib.).

[44] Eighteenth-century officers paid scant attention to the physical needs of their soldiers; see Eric Robson, "The Armed Forces and the Art of War," in J. O. Lindsay, ed., *The New Cambridge Modern History*. Vol. VII: *The Old Regime. 1713-63* (Cambridge, 1957), 176. This neglect was an underlying cause of the soldiers' maltreatment of civilians. Bowler shows that the army's logistics problems were exacerbated by "the inability of the British administration to respond adequately to the war" (*Logistics*, 243-260, quotation on p. 243). See also Hew Strachan, *European Armies and the Conduct of War* (London, 1983), 10-12, and Piers Mackesy, "What the British Army Learned," in Hoffman and Albert, eds., *Arms and Independence*, 199-200.

[45] Wallace Evan Davies, "Privateering around Long Island during the Revolution," *New York Hist.*, XX (1939), 283-294; James F. Collins, "Whaleboat Warfare on Long Island Sound," *ibid.*, XXV (1944), 195-201. See also Catherine S. Crary, "Guerrilla Activities of James DeLancey's Cowboys in Westchester County: Conventional Warfare or Self-Interested Freebooting," in Robert A. East and Jacob Judd, eds., *The Loyalist Americans: A Focus on Greater New York* (Tarrytown, N.Y., 1973), 14-21, and Jones, *History*, ed. De Lancey, I, 301-302, 314-315.

[46] William Kelby, comp., *Orderly Book of the Three Battalions of Loyalists. Commanded by Brigadier-General Oliver De Lancey. 1776-1778; to Which Is Appended*

Queens County. But in the fall of 1778 the British ordered the first two battalions to Georgia, only the third remained on Long Island. Inhabitants' anger at this alleged breach of trust was heightened by the increased number of whaleboat raids that followed.[47] British officials argued that protection against privateering was a militia responsibility, while residents protested that warships should patrol the coast.[48] The navy did in fact attempt to protect the supply routes but assigned too few ships. In 1780 and again in 1781 Clinton himself complained that the navy was not providing any ships at all for this important service.[49] The government's response to the raids—the launching of its own attacks—only increased their scope and intensity.[50]

III: MISCONDUCT OF OFFICERS

The behavior of British officers bore out Benjamin Franklin's description of British colonial officials before the Revolution: "Their office makes them proud and insolent, their insolence and rapacity makes them odious, and, being conscious that they are hated, they become malicious."[51] Some of the misconduct, although degrading, was trivial: men of the county had to dismount and remove their hats when passing the residence of an army commander. Other actions were more serious. An officer on a foraging party led fifty horses into an orchard where apples were piled for making cider. The farmer pleaded with the officer to use another field where the pasture was better, but the request was denied and the farmer called a "damned old rebel." The loss amounted to £200.[52] Paul Amberman, a miller, sold flour to Maj. Richard Stockton, but when he applied for payment, Stockton took personal offense. The next day, after watching a fellow officer horsewhip Amberman, Stockton killed the miller with a

---

a List of New York Loyalists in the City of New York during the War of the Revolution (New York, 1917), x; Barck, New York, 192. For muster rolls of De Lancey's Brigade see the photostatic copies in the Library of Congress of the Public Archives of Canada, Ser. C, vols. 1878, 1879, 1882. These records indicate that few prewar county residents joined the brigade.

[47] Kelby, comp., Orderly Book, x-xi. It apparently did not dawn on the British that to win the minds and hearts of county residents they needed to defend the local population from such attacks. Failure to do so underscored Britain's military weakness and undermined the legitimacy of her continued rule over New York.

[48] Jones, History, ed. De Lancey, I, 270-271; Marshall, Hempstead, 331.

[49] Clinton to Arbuthnot, Dec. 9, 1780, Mar. 8, May 1, 1781, Arbuthnot to Clinton, Apr. 12, 1780, May 1, 1781, Clinton Papers, William L. Clements Library, Ann Arbor, Mich.

[50] Tryon, however, believed that these raids would result in the collapse of the rebellion; Tryon to Germain, July 28, 1779, C.O. 5/1109.

[51] Franklin to the Massachusetts House of Representatives Committee of Correspondence, May 15, 1771, in William B. Willcox et al., eds., The Papers of Benjamin Franklin, XVIII (New Haven, Conn., 1974), 102.

[52] Jones, History, ed. De Lancey, II, 87-88; Onderdonk, ed., "Kissam Correspondence," 13.

sword. Court-martialed for murder, Stockton was found guilty. Gen. Henry Clinton, who was then commander in chief of the army, asked the miller's widow to sign a petition to pardon the convicted officer. Despite her refusal, he released the murderer.[53]

The outrages committed by Col. Samuel Birch of the Seventeenth Dragoons, stationed in Hempstead, led the Reverend Leonard Cutting, an S.P.G. missionary and pastor of the local Anglican church, to complain to his religious superiors in London of Birch's "various Acts of Violence and Oppression." His "worse than useless Regiment," which had been "scarce out of the Smoke of Hempstead," seized whatever it wanted including the society's school and land in the town. "This is," Cutting declared, "perhaps the most trifling Instance of a thousand that might be produced of the Tyranny we are under; Where the Army is, Oppression, such as in England you can have no Conception of Universally prevails. We have nothing, We can call our own; and the Door to Redress is inaccessible. What a state must that people be in, who can find Relief from neither Law, Justice, or Humanity Where the Military is concerned."[54]

The behavior of one officer, in particular, explains much about the failure of reconciliation. Archibald Hamilton, colonel of the county militia and aide-de-camp to General Tryon, held immense authority in Queens until 1780. He was a retired British officer who had served in America before the Revolution and married a daughter of Lt. Gov. Cadwallader Colden. As militia commander he made and enforced regulations for the conduct of the war and supervised the activities of town officials, justices of the peace, and militia officers. While his chief task was overseeing supply arrangements, he made it his "Duty to See Justice Done" and acted as judge in disputes between inhabitants that in the past had been settled in the courts.[55]

In 1779 twelve residents made sworn complaints to Tryon concerning his aide-de-camp, whom they accused of conducting himself with "all the fury of a mad man" and attempting to kill one of the complainants who was a noted tory and judge. When the attempt failed, the colonel is reported to have "got down on one knee in the dung in the Cow Yard" and prayed to his maker. The same day he attacked another man with a sword, gave a third thirty blows for no apparent reason, then horsewhipped yet another inhabitant. Tryon requested David Colden, son of Cadwallader, to

[53] Jones, *History*, ed. De Lancey, II, 92-93; Klein and Howard, eds., *Twilight of British Rule*, 103, n. 21.

[54] Cutting to the Secretary, Dec. 9, 1781, S.P.G., Letter Ser. B, II, 546-549. See also Jones, *History*, ed. De Lancey, I, 324-325, II, 70-75.

[55] Memorials of Archibald Hamilton, Feb. 20, 1784, n.d., A.O. 13/114, 280, 282-283; Benjamin Hewlett to Elijah Sprag, Feb. 20, 1780, Landon Papers, Documents Related to Long Island Persons, Estates, and Businesses, XXV, L.I. Hist. Soc.; Hamilton to Kissam, May 15, 1780, Documents Relating to the Revolutionary War and Civil War, XIII, 24, L.I. Hist. Soc.; "Youngs's Forage Book," Apr. 28, July 17, July 19, Sept. 10, 1780; Onderdonk, ed., "Kissam Correspondence," 7, 13, 33, 41, 47; "Order Book of Hamilton," Aug. 13, 1779.

investigate the charges against his brother-in-law, but Colden understandably declined, and no further action was taken.[56] In 1784 Tryon wrote that Hamilton "had served with great credit and reputation during the war."[57] In truth, Hamilton was an outsider, a man unfamiliar with local customs and unwilling to accept residents as compatriots in a war to save the empire. By relying on him rather than local leaders, the British squandered an opportunity to foster a spirit of cooperation between the army and civilians.

Army officers came from the English upper crust and viewed the colonists as social inferiors, greedy and ill-bred. They were "a Levelling, underbred, Artfull, Race of people that we Cannot Associate with them. Void of principal, their whole Conversation is turn'd on their Interest, and as to gratitude they have no such word in their dictionary and either cant or wont understand what it means."[58] This prejudice was aggravated by the officers' belief that many residents were crypto-patriots and by plain evidence of resentment against the army's presence. In addition, diaries, court-martial records, and the conduct of individual officers also suggest that many junior officers did not take army discipline seriously enough; but their mischief-making became malicious when the military's pride was stung by the humiliation of defeat. Cooped up in camp on Long Island, some officers sought to relieve boredom and prove their superiority by bullying defenseless civilians. It is impossible to state how many acted this way, but the number was sufficiently large to alienate inhabitants, and the entire officer corps shared responsibility by failing to punish offenders. Instead, officers too often overtly sanctioned misconduct by defending their fellows who broke military discipline.[59] On the whole, the deportment of these officers was not dissimilar to that of those who served in America between 1763 and 1776 and whose concern was also with "honor and affluence, not obedience or honesty."[60]

IV: Martial Law and the Governance of Queens

Day-to-day experiences with the military caused Queens County folk to echo Cutting's protest that they were living under a tyranny and not a government of laws. Patrick Ferguson, a loyalist officer, wrote in 1779 "that the People in general are become indifferent, if not averse, to a Government which in place of the Liberty Prosperity safety and Plenty,

[56] Statement of John Willett, Feb. 24, Statement of John Morrell, Feb. 25, Willett to Oliver De Lancey, Mar. 18, Hamilton to De Lancey, Mar. 29, 1779, Landon Papers.

[57] Testimonial by Tryon for Hamilton, May 25, 1784, A.O. 13/114, 284.

[58] Letter from Capt. John Bowater, Apr. 4, 1777, in Balderston and Syrett, eds., *Lost War*, 122.

[59] Such behavior was considered by European soldiers to be a part of an esprit de corps (Corvisier, *Armies and Societies*, trans. Siddall, 179).

[60] John Shy, *Toward Lexington: The Role of the British Army in the Coming of the American Revolution* (Princeton, N.J., 1965), 290.

under promise of which it involved them in this war has established a thorough Despotism."[61] Oppression was possible because martial law was in force, and civilians had no means of bringing suits against military personnel who abused them. As time passed, therefore, they channeled their indignation into demands for the abolition of martial law. But from the outset the military refused to reestablish civil institutions and persistently ignored evidence of public disaffection until it was too late to take remedial action.

General Howe and his brother, Admiral Lord Howe, who were appointed in May 1776 as king's commissioners for restoring peace, had power not only to negotiate an end to the war but to pardon rebels and restore civil government in areas retaken from the enemy.[62] The Howes understood that reconciliation was necessary, that undue bloodshed should be avoided, and that public support would help bring a happy ending to the conflict.[63] Yet General Howe had few concrete ideas about how to win the allegiance of inhabitants and did not see that the revival of civil government might pay dividends as a form of political warfare.[64] He wrote Germain on April 26, 1776, that it could not "be denied that there are many inhabitants in every province well affected to Government, from whom no doubt we shall have assistance, but not until his Majesty's arms have a clear superiority by a decisive victory."[65] The victory in New York was evidently not decisive enough, for the peace commissioners declined to reestablish civil authority but instead placed Long Island and New York City under martial law so that the military could act without civilian interference.[66]

In October 1776, Queens County petitioned Governor Tryon for the revival of civil institutions, yet his hands were tied. The Howes had reappointed him governor in September under orders to keep "the Executive Powers of Civil Government Dormant."[67] In hindsight, the

---

[61] Patrick Ferguson to Henry Clinton, Nov. 22, 1779, Clinton Papers. See also Robertson to Lord Amherst, July 1, 1780, in Klein and Howard, eds., *Twilight of British Rule*, 130-134.

[62] Instructions to the Commissioners for restoring peace in America, May 6, 1776, Additional Instructions to the Commissioners, May 6, 1776, C.O. 5/177. See also Lord Howe to Germain, Apr. 1, 1776, Germain to Lord Howe [Apr. 2, 1776], *Stopford-Sackville MSS*. II, 26-27, 28.

[63] Gruber, *Howe Brothers*, 52, 58, 59; W. Howe to Germain, Dec. 20, 1776, W. Howe to Guy Carleton, Apr. 5, 1777. *Stopford-Sackville MSS*. II, 52-53, 65-66.

[64] Davies, "Restoration of Civil Government," in Wright, ed., *Red. White and True Blue*, 114.

[65] Howe to Germain, Apr. 26, 1776, *Stopford-Sackville MSS*. II, 30.

[66] Commissioners to Germain, Sept. 20, Lord Howe to Germain, Sept. 20, 1776, C.O. 5/177; Davies, "Restoration of Civil Government," in Wright, ed., *Red. White and True Blue*, 113.

[67] Tryon to Germain, Sept. 24, Petition of Freeholders and Inhabitants of Queens County to Tryon, Oct. 21, David Colden to Tryon, Oct. 21, Tryon to Colden, Nov. 12, 1776, C.O. 5/1107.

determination seems inevitable. The power granted General Howe and his successors over civil affairs and the government's maintenance of martial law were in part outgrowths of a tendency that had developed in America after 1763 for British military authority to expand at the expense of the civilian establishment. What had emerged after the Seven Years' War as "military centralization" evolved by early 1775 into a decision to crush the rebellion with force and then ripened in 1776 under wartime circumstances into martial law.[68]

At first, the Howes based their refusal to restore civil authority on the premise that the occupation of New York City would precipitate the rapid collapse of resistance throughout the province and that they should wait for that moment to act.[69] General Howe was so confident of victory in 1776 that he likewise neglected to make an earnest effort to win the assistance of New York loyalists.[70] When it became evident that the war would continue for at least another year, the Howes found other reasons to keep civil government dormant. If they declared a district at peace, the Prohibitory Act of 1775, which forbade rebellious colonies to engage in trade, could no longer be enforced, and the enemy would benefit by the resumption of trade.[71] They also argued that civil government would be advantageous only if restored at a stroke to the entire province, for the General Assembly could then be called into session. Germain approved their decision, for he had reservations about the strength of loyalism in the region. Only a minority of the inhabitants in Queens and other counties of British-occupied New York had signed declarations renewing their allegiance to the crown.[72]

The Howes were responsible both for waging war and for securing peace, and the former took precedence in their minds. Reviving civil government would hinder their prosecution of the war, jeopardize a quick triumph, and as a result possibly tarnish General Howe's reputation. They did not sufficiently understand that reconciliation was as essential an objective as military victory.[73] They consequently failed in the campaign

[68] Shy, *Toward Lexington*, 422; Paul H. Smith, *Loyalists and Redcoats: A Study in British Revolutionary Policy* (Chapel Hill, N.C., 1964), 8.

[69] Commissioners to Germain, Sept. 20, 1776, and Lord Howe to Germain, Sept. 20, 1776, C.O. 5/177.

[70] Memo of Henry Clinton's Interview with General Howe, [Nov. 1776], Clinton Papers. See also Howe to Germain, Aug. 10, 1776, *Stopford-Sackville MSS.* II, 37-38, and Smith, *Loyalists*, 168-169.

[71] The Prohibitory Act did not in fact prohibit the restoration of civil authority. See Barck, *New York*, 50, and Thomas Jefferson Wertenbaker, *Father Knickerbocker Rebels: New York City during the Revolution* (New York, 1948), 152. In 1780, Parliament exempted New York from the Prohibitory Act (*Royal Gaz.*, Nov. 1, 1780), but martial law continued in force.

[72] Commissioners to Germain, Nov. 30, 1776, Germain to Commissioners, Jan. 14, 1777, C.O. 5/177. About 40% of the county's adult male residents signed the declaration, for which see Force [ed.], *American Archives*, 5th Ser., II, 1159-1164.

[73] The Howes were evidently sincere in seeking to fulfill their mission as peace commissioners and recognized that the use of military force had its limitations; see

of 1776 not only because Washington's army survived to fight again at Trenton and Princeton, but because civil-military relations were not established on a firm foundation at the outset. The belief that the patriots were a small minority and that military defeat would force colonists to their senses blinded the Howes to the need for political action. Military reverses only complicated matters. Defeat in New Jersey, for example, necessitated a greater dependence on Long Island for supplies and thus made military officials even less tolerant of civilians, and civilians, accordingly, less cooperative.

The military's myopia might possibly have been overcome had the commission worked closely with civil officials. Governor Tryon, for example, was popular with the people and conscious of the dignity of civil institutions.[74] In 1775 he had asked the ministry to clarify the proper relationship between civil and military officials, because he feared that the power of the latter was being strengthened unnecessarily at the expense of the former.[75] In early 1776, confessing the inability of civil magistrates to manage the crisis, he recommended appointment of a viceroy with authority over the civil and military departments in each province. In calling for a "great and distinguished person" to fill the post, he apparently hoped to avoid the perils of military misrule by bringing in a powerful personage to mediate between the two departments.[76] The nomination of the Howes as commissioners seemingly followed Tryon's suggestion but in reality placed power squarely in military hands. The Howes, moreover, were disinclined to heed civilian advice. In fact, General Howe recommended to Germain in early 1777 that the remaining civil governors be recalled and a military officer put in charge in each province.[77]

Tryon's own views were ambivalent. Several times during the fall of 1776 he wrote the ministry acquiescing in the decision not to restore civil government as long as the enemy threatened southern New York; nonetheless, he was preparing a new civil list and had the strongest expectations that martial law would end as quickly as possible.[78] His primary concern as time passed, however, was with his own power and interest. Chafing at his imposed inactivity and the meaningless tasks he was given to perform, he sent a private letter to Germain in April 1777, expressing a desire to retire if the government would make adequate provision for him. The secretary denied this request. That same month Tryon secured appointment as major general of provincial forces. He then

---

Troyer Steele Anderson, *The Command of the Howe Brothers during the American Revolution* (New York, 1936), 92-95, and Gruber, *Howe Brothers*. 52. See also Klein and Howard, eds., *Twilight of British Rule*. 6.

[74] Bernard Mason, *The Road to Independence: The Revolutionary Movement in New York, 1773-1777* (Lexington, Ky., 1966), 77-78.

[75] Tryon to Dartmouth, Mar. 29, 1775, C.O. 5/1106.

[76] Tryon to Dartmouth, Jan. 3, 1776, C.O. 5/1107.

[77] Howe to Germain, Jan. 17, 1777, C.O. 5/94.

[78] Tryon to Germain, Sept. 24, Nov. 26, 28, Dec. 24, 1776, C.O. 5/1107.

spent the next year protesting his place in the chain of command. In December he again asked permission to resign, this time in exchange for command of a regular army regiment.[79] He finally retired from the governorship in 1780. Unfortunately, his constant preoccupation with his own career had denied local residents the support he might otherwise have given them and forced inhabitants to fall back on their own meager resources in combating the rigors of martial law.

While insisting on martial law, the Howes failed to establish a uniform policy of implementation; it varied by time and place within British-occupied New York.[80] In matters relating to the conduct of the war, Archibald Hamilton had overall responsibility. Under him were not only the officers of the county militia but the local justices of the peace. The latter could likewise be directed by the commissary, quartermaster, and barrackmaster departments to assist in their operations.[81] At the beginning of the war justices at times called residents together to determine how the army's demands were to be met, but by 1779 decisions were also being made at meetings of the justices and the county militia officers, who then enforced what they had agreed upon.[82]

Inhabitants did what they could under these circumstances to preserve as many of their former liberties as possible. Most of the prewar governmental institutions, such as the town meeting, were allowed to continue functioning so long as they did not hinder military operations. Towns held annual meetings and elected local officials. However, it was impossible for the prewar leadership to maintain control over local affairs. A large percentage of the men who held important town offices before August 1776 were whigs, and they lost their positions in the elections of 1777.[83] Very few patriots held public office during the British occupation.[84] Seventy-six percent of those holding significant town offices in 1777 and 1778 were tories; thereafter the proportion of loyalist office-

---

[79] Tryon to Germain, Apr. 9, Dec. 1, Germain to Tryon, May 19, Tryon to William Knox, Apr. 21, 1777, C.O. 5/1108.

[80] See Jones, *History*, ed. De Lancey, II, 128-133.

[81] *Ibid.*, 130.

[82] See Resolutions for the Captains of Militia and Justices of the Peace in Queens County, Nov. 27, 1779, Documents Collection, Nassau County Historical Museum, and Onderdonk, ed., "Kissam Correspondence," 25, 47, 48.

[83] Although only 12% of the adult male county residents became whigs, 45% of important town officeholders in 1774, 32% of these same officeholders in 1775, and 37% of those in 1776 did so. All officeholders were studied for this period, but consideration here is restricted to persons holding important positions such as supervisor, constable, collector, assessor, clerk, and overseer of the poor, as well as persons assigned a special office or duty by a town meeting. The data on officeholding do not include Flushing, for its records were destroyed by fire in the 1790s. There are also no records for Jamaica in 1780 and 1783 or for Oyster Bay in 1774 and 1783.

[84] In no single year during the occupation did whigs constitute more than 5% of the important town officeholders.

holders declined in each succeeding year except 1781, when residents wrongly surmised that civil government would soon be restored. The yearly April town elections serve as a barometer of public opinion, registering growing alienation, for people expressed their distaste for martial law by electing men who had been neutral before 1776. In 1777 these neutrals constituted only 20 percent of the major officeholders; by 1783 their proportion had increased to 50 percent.[85] These neutral officeholders could not compel the military to change, but their election demonstrated that Great Britain was losing the political contest.

The county's other governing institutions likewise attempted to function as before. The Board of Supervisors held meetings, the mortgage office remained open, and land conveyances were recorded.[86] Although a civilian could not sue a soldier, the Queens County Court of Common Pleas continued to hear cases until 1779, and justices of the peace performed at least some of their customary responsibilities.[87] Still, local officials were not permitted to interfere with military operations or to challenge Britain's control. They had to accept that they had in effect become collaborators who could be ignored or overruled.

V: MARTIAL LAW DEBATED

Defeat at Saratoga in October 1777 and the worrisome prospect of a Franco-American alliance convinced Whitehall that the time had come to review its American strategy and pay greater heed to the war's political dimension.[88] In February 1778 the government established a new peace

[85] Loyalists constituted 77% of important town officeholders in 1777 and 1778, 71% in 1779, 64% in 1780, 75% in 1781, 56% in 1782, and 50% in 1783; for the same years in the same order, neutrals constituted 20%, 19%, 29%, 32%, 25%, 44%, and 50%.

[86] "Queens County Supervisors' Book [1709-1787]," Museum of the City of New York; Jones, History, ed. De Lancey, II, 129; Queens County Mortgages, 1754-1797, microfilm, Reel QMG2, and Queens County Conveyances, Liber E, 1764-1788, microfilm, Reel QCV3, Queens College Historical Documents Collection, Flushing, N.Y. There are no entries in Liber E from June 1776 until May 2, 1778, six days before Clinton relieved Howe as commander in chief. Perhaps there was a connection between Howe's departure and the resumption in the recording of deeds, but that leaves unexplained why mortgages were recorded during his period of command.

[87] Jones, History, ed. De Lancey, II, 119. For information about justices of the peace see Proclamation by Andrew Elliot, Nov. 19, 1783, A.O. 13/47, 314, and Petition of Benjamin Eldert, n.d., Documents Collection, III, 45, L.I. Hist. Soc. Justices also continued to try petty larcenies, "but in civil causes, of which they had cognizance by their commissions, and the laws of the province, they were forbid acting" (Jones, History, ed. De Lancey, II, 130).

[88] Disaffection was not solely a consequence of events occurring within Queens. Residents were also reacting to military developments, and their alienation grew as the crown's inability to win the war became more and more apparent. See, for example, Cutting to the Secretary, Dec. 9, 1781, S.P.G., Letter Ser. B, II, 546-549; Jones, History, ed. De Lancey, I, 365; and Onderdonk [comp.], Documents, 142.

commission.[89] Three of the five members were civilians: Frederick Howard, 5th earl of Carlisle, who headed the commission; William Eden, an undersecretary of state who had championed a change in policy; and George Johnston, a former governor of West Florida. The Howes were also appointed, but the admiral declined to serve, and the general was soon supplanted by Sir Henry Clinton, who became army commander in chief in March 1778. The Carlisle Commission had power to revive civil institutions, yet it declined to do so in New York.[90] Even though the commissioners recognized the harm already done the British cause in the province, the army insisted on maintaining martial law.[91] However, on returning to England, two of the civilian commissioners argued before a cabinet council that civil government should be restored to New York.[92] Germain agreed and began to make his military plans accordingly. On January 23, 1779, he instructed Clinton to engage Washington in battle. If the American forces refused combat, Clinton was to drive them into the highlands of New York, so that residents of the province would be "at liberty to follow, what the Commissioners represent to be their Inclinations, and renounce the Authority of the Congress, and return to their Allegiance to His Majesty."[93] A majority of counties could then elect deputies to a revived general assembly.

In July 1779 the ministry appointed Clinton sole peace commissioner and instructed him to restore civil government in New York.[94] To meet criticisms of military misconduct, a civilian-military council was established "to assist" the commissioner though without authority to act

[89] For the activities of the commission in America see *The Manuscripts of the Earl of Carlisle, Preserved at Castle Howard* (Historical Manuscripts Commission, Fifteenth Report, Appendix, VI [London, 1897]), 322-429, hereafter cited as *Carlisle MSS.* and Weldon A. Brown, *Empire or Independence: A Study in the Failure of Reconciliation, 1774-1783* (Baton Rouge, La., 1941), 244-292.

[90] Instructions to Commissioners, Apr. 12, 1778, C.O. 5/180. See also Germain to Clinton, Mar. 11, 1778, Clinton Papers. Civil government was restored in Georgia in 1779, and an assembly was elected in 1780 (Davies, "Restoration of Civil Government," in Wright, ed., *Red, White and True Blue,* 117, 119-120).

[91] Sentiment against martial law was building in New York, and in August 1778 New York merchants petitioned unsuccessfully for a restoration of civil authority and an end to the commercial restrictions imposed by the Prohibitory Act. See Address of New York Merchants, Traders, and Others to the Commissioners [Aug. 1778], Commissioners to Merchants, Aug. 29, 1778, Commissioners to Germain, Sept. 21, 1778, C.O. 5/180; Andrew Elliot to Lord Commissioners of the Treasury, Sept. 12, 1778, C.O. 5/175; Notes upon Elliot's Paper by Lord Carlisle, Sept. 20 [1778], *Carlisle MSS,* 367; and Address of the Inhabitants of the City of New York and Its Dependencies to Commissioners, Nov. 25, 1778, Commissioners to Germain, Nov. 16, 27, 1778, C.O. 5/181.

[92] Smith, *Loyalists,* 114.

[93] Germain to Clinton, Jan. 23, 1779, Clinton Papers. See also Klein and Howard, eds., *Twilight of British Rule,* 40-43.

[94] In 1780 the naval commander, Vice Adm. Marriot Arbuthnot, was also appointed peace commissioner, but Clinton made certain that Arbuthnot could not independently restore civil government; see Clinton to Germain, June 3, 1780, C.O. 5/99, and Germain to Clinton, Aug. 3, 1780, C.O. 5/178.

independently.[95] In effect, affairs reverted to the status quo under the Howes with the military in complete control, for nothing significant could be done without Clinton's approval. The ministry thus granted wide latitude in civil and military affairs to a commander three thousand miles away who could then evade orders, claiming that the exigencies of the situation required him to do so. The government, in fact, had no realistic alternative: dispatches were slow in crossing the Atlantic, knowledge of the American situation was limited, and an unexpected event could upset the best-laid plans.

Clinton thus took charge of implementing and overseeing the government's new civil policy, yet he opposed it. Germain wrote in February 1780 expressing the hope that New York had already been restored to civilian rule. Clinton's reply, in May, was evasive. He had not received his commission until after he had departed the province for South Carolina; he consequently could not have acted, even if he thought the measure proper. He would certainly "prevent as far as possible, any inconvenience to the loyal Inhabitants, in the places Possess'd By the King's Troops," but he made no more specific commitment.[96] In a letter of May 30, Clinton confided to William Eden that civil government was "too great a blessing to bestow upon them at once; it will intoxicate, as it has done in Georgia. At New York it will ruin us." He was so adamant about New York that he threatened to resign if overruled.[97] In June he asked the ministry whether he could "partially" restore civil authority in a province but drew a narrow line, for "to open the Courts of Civil Law would increase the Confusion, and be productive of many other bad Consequences."[98] Although he did not explicitly say so, he feared that New York residents would begin bringing civil suits for redress of grievances against military officers.

Clinton had the backing of Andrew Elliot, a well-connected New York politician who had won the confidence of the successive army commanders and peace commissioners.[99] Elliot acknowledged that abuses did exist; at the same time, as a placeman whose influence depended on the continuance of martial law, he balanced his criticisms with support for the

[95] Instructions to Clinton as Peace Commissioner, July 22, 1779, C.O. 5/178. A special act of Parliament had granted the Carlisle Commission its authority; the Howes and Clinton received theirs from the king under power granted him by the Prohibitory Act. See Germain to Commissioners, Aug. 3, 1780, C.O. 5/178. Concerning the origins of the advisory council see Advices from Mr. Elliot, Dec. 12 [William Smith to Carlisle], Dec. 19, 1778, *Carlisle MSS.* 390-394, 395-397, and Commissioners to Germain, Mar. 8, William Eden to Knox, Apr. 30, 1779, C.O. 5/181.

[96] Germain to Clinton, Feb. 15, Clinton to Germain, May 15, 1780, Clinton Papers.

[97] [Clinton to Eden], May 30, 1780, *ibid.*

[98] Clinton to Germain, June 2, 1780, *ibid.*

[99] For Elliot's career see Robert Ernst, "Andrew Elliot, Forgotten Loyalist of Occupied New York," *New York Hist.*, LVII (1976), 285-320. Born in Scotland, Elliot sailed for America in 1746 and was appointed Receiver General of His Majesty's Revenue and Collector of Customs for the Port of New York in 1764.

military. In seeking a solution to what had become an intractable problem, he explained the failure of martial law and clarified why British commanders were so averse to change. He believed that civil government could not be revived while military operations were in progress (or might be resumed at any moment, as in New York) or before the army had recaptured all or the greater part of a province. In the meantime, when the army entered a new province, the commander should institute a comprehensive plan governing the treatment of inhabitants and their property. The commander in chief should then appoint a commandant and a three-member civilian council to resolve civil-military disputes and establish regulations governing the army's impressment of supplies. Such regulations should be issued as regimental orders and advertised in the newspapers.[100] With order thus maintained, civil institutions could be reconstituted as soon as military operations were concluded.

Elliot's proposals were a verdict on what had gone wrong in New York. He believed that the damage done there was so extensive and irremediable that the province must remain under martial law until war's end. Restoring civil government would cause "discontents and riots amongst the civil, confusion and disorders in the Army, and the hands of the Commander-in-Chief [would] be entirely tied up from doing legally what the situation of the Army might make absolutely necessary," for "property" was in "confusion."[101] This comment hit the essence of the matter, for by 1780 there were a large number of civilian-military property disputes that could be brought to trial if civil government were reestablished.

Clinton's policy, rationalized by Elliot, brought him into conflict with Maj. Gen. James Robertson, whom the ministry appointed to replace Tryon as governor.[102] Sworn into office on March 23, 1780, Robertson issued a proclamation on April 15 declaring that it was the king's "wish" that civil government be restored in New York "to prove" that it was "not his Design to govern America by Military Law." Robertson promised to end martial law and call an assembly once Clinton approved and circumstances allowed.[103] The proclamation infuriated Clinton, who had already made his position clear to the governor.[104] Ignoring the fact that Robert-

---

[100] "Heads of Civil Regulations by Andrew Elliot and His Reasons for Proposing Such Regulations, Dec. 22, 1779," in [Lord Cornwallis] to Capt. Russel, Cornwallis Papers 30/11, P.R.O. (Library of Congress microfilm); Elliot to Robertson, Jan. 19, 1781, C.O. 5/175.

[101] Newsletter from Elliot, No. 4, May 4, 1779, *Carlisle MSS.* 425-427.

[102] Robertson had served in America since 1756 and had been military commandant of New York City from 1776 to 1778.

[103] *Royal Gaz.*, Apr. 19, 1780. For the drafting of this proclamation see Klein and Howard, eds., *Twilight of British Rule.* 94, n. 1. See also Klein, "An Experiment That Failed," *New York Hist..* LXI (1980), 236.

[104] Minutes of a Council held on March 23, 1780, C.O. 5/1109; William H. W. Sabine, ed., *Historical Memoirs from 26 August 1778 to 12 November 1783 of William Smith . . .* (New York, 1971), 245; Robertson to Clinton, Mar. 29, 1780, Clinton Papers. For Clinton's reaction to the proclamation see [Clinton to Eden and Carpenter], Aug. 14 [1780], Clinton Papers.

son had a vested interest in reviving civil institutions, Clinton believed him to be engaged in a ruse aimed at embarrassing the commander in chief.[105] Then, on May 3, Robertson privately conceded to Clinton that the decision not to end martial law had been correct.[106] In the months that followed, Robertson won permission to perform his civil duties in a military capacity under orders issued by Clinton.[107] Still, the commander persisted in his mistrust of the governor, for he suspected that Robertson's continued public protestations of support for civil government would last only as long as his own opposition continued.[108] Clinton was so certain of this point that he offered in 1782, after the defeat at Yorktown, to terminate martial law in order to expose the governor's supposed duplicity.[109] As matters eventually turned out, the commander believed himself vindicated.[110] On March 21 Robertson's council recommended that martial law be continued: reviving civil government would mean calling an assembly; such a step would embarrass the government if the ministry decided as a result of Yorktown to evacuate New York.[111]

In the end, Cornwallis's defeat caused the fall of North's ministry in London, Clinton's recall, and Robertson's temporary appointment as commander in chief. The governor never did, in fact, serve in this capacity, for Clinton broke his orders and remained in America long enough to turn over command to his permanent successor, Sir Guy Carleton. Clinton also got his revenge in another way, for Germain's successor, Welbore Ellis, was "surprised" that Robertson had not acted

[105] For Clinton's complaints about Robertson see [Clinton to Eden], May 30, Aug. 26, 1780, Clinton Papers, and Clinton to [Eden], Oct. 15 [1780], in Stevens, comp., *Facsimiles*, no. 741.

[106] Robertson to Clinton, May 3, 1780, Clinton Papers. For the governor's possible motives in making this statement see Klein and Howard, eds., *Twilight of British Rule*, 101, n. 1.

[107] Robertson to Clinton, May 3, June 25, 27, 1780, Clinton Papers.

[108] See, for example, Robertson to Germain, Jan. 28, 1781, in Klein and Howard, eds., *Twilight of British Rule*. 175-176. Clinton was not the only person suspicious of Robertson. William Smith had also come by 1782 to believe that the governor had been opposed to civil government from the outset (Sabine, ed., *Historical Memoirs*. 477-478).

[109] Clinton to [the duke of Newcastle], Mar. 18, 1782, Clinton Papers. Clinton also sought to make Lord Cornwallis share responsibility for not ending martial law; see Clinton to [?], Jan. 24, 1782, Clinton Papers.

[110] For the highlights of this dispute see Substance of a Conversation between Clinton and Robertson before a Board of General Officers, Jan. 20, 1782, C.O. 5/175; Clinton to Germain, Jan. 24, 1782, C.O. 5/104; Commissioners to Germain, Jan. 25, 1782, C.O. 5/178; Clinton to Robertson, Mar. 14, 1782, Clinton Papers; and Board of General Officers, Jan. 20, 1782, in Historical Manuscripts Commission, *Report on American Manuscripts in the Royal Institution of Great Britain* (London, 1904-1909), II, 385.

[111] Robertson to Clinton, Mar. 21, 1782, C.O. 5/105; Minutes of a Council Meeting, Mar. 21, 1782, Council's Observations on the Question of Civil Government [Mar. 21, 1782], C.O. 5/175.

favorably on Clinton's offer after Yorktown to revive civil government. He called on the governor for a full explanation and directed him to end martial law as soon as possible.[112] But on May 4, 1782, Robertson's council advised that martial law be continued.[113]

The preference of Generals Howe and Clinton for martial law is understandable, for both were afraid that civil government would impede military operations. Nonetheless, their inability to win the war by conventional means should have caused them to explore different alternatives. In fact, Germain's willingness to support the revival of civil government demonstrates that a change in outlook was possible. At the same time, his refusal to order the termination of martial law at New York only made the situation worse. The arguments among British officials in America over this question and the raising of false hopes served no purpose except to further alienate public opinion.

VI: Court of Police

While the British debated, Queens County suffered. At the beginning of Robertson's tenure as governor, residents honestly, if perhaps naively, believed that he would fulfill his initial pledge and restore civil authority.[114] Instead, in July 1780 Robertson, with Clinton's approbation, appointed George Duncan Ludlow, a county resident, superintendent of the newly created Court of Police on Long Island. The superintendent had power "to hear and determine peace and good order"; all officials on Long Island were to assist and obey him.[115] Ludlow's power even exceeded that of Colonel Hamilton, the county militia commander. He forwarded orders from General Tryon to militia officers and issued decrees on such varied matters as road and fence repairs, the weight and quality of bread, and the time for harvesting. In its judicial capacity his office combined the functions of police, judge, and jury.[116]

Robertson extolled the Court of Police as a partial restoration of civil government and a benefit in that Long Islanders no longer had to go to New York City to settle legal disputes.[117] But the situation was not so

[112] Welbore Ellis to Robertson, Mar. 6, 1782, C.O. 5/175.
[113] Minutes of a Council, May 4, Robertson to Shelburne and Smith to Robertson, May 9, 1782, *ibid.*
[114] *Royal Gaz.*, Aug. 12, 1780.
[115] *Ibid.*, July 15, 1780.
[116] *Ibid.*, Aug. 15, Sept. 19, 1780; Onderdonk, ed., "Kissam Correspondence," 7; "Youngs's Forage Book," Jan. 31, Apr. 7, 1781; Order for Aaron Van Nostrand, Aug. 14, 1781, Appointment of Aaron Van Nostrand, Marshall of the Police Office at Jamaica, as Inspector of Weights and the Quality of Bread, Oct. 16, 1782, Collection of Miscellaneous Documents Removed from the Henry Onderdonk, Jr., Papers and from the Pierrepont Family Papers, CXXIII, L.I. Hist. Soc.
[117] Robertson to Germain, Sept. 1, 1780, C.O. 5/1110; Robertson to Carleton, Apr. 11, 1783, British Headquarters Papers, No. 4686. After May 4, 1778, Long

advantageous for inhabitants as he pretended. Although Ludlow had been a justice of New York's Supreme Court before the war, the Court of Police represented nothing more than martial law under a different guise. Trial by jury was not restored, local justices of the peace lost their power to try petty larcenies, and the superintendent remained directly responsible to military authorities. The county Board of Supervisors also ceased meeting.[118] Ludlow became known as "the little tyrant of the island." To the protests of Daniel Kissam, the county's representative in the General Assembly from 1764 to 1776, and Thomas Jones that the civil courts should be opened, Ludlow replied that doing so "would be inconvenient, prejudicial, and injurious to the king's service." Jones believed that the courts were not opened because "barrack-masters, quarter-masters, and commissaries would have been prosecuted, and punished for the plunder, robberies, and other illegal acts, daily committed by them, and their dependents, upon his majesty's loyal subjects."[119]

Since the Court of Police was responsible for order on Long Island, Robertson and Ludlow were free to exploit the situation, and they began to do so at once, if Jones can be believed, by participating in the lucrative smuggling trade between Long Island and New England.[120] A proclamation by General Howe, published in November 1776 and continued in force by Clinton, prohibited the shipment of goods from British-occupied New York without a permit from the Superintendent of Imports and Exports.[121] The number of requests for permits soon became so great that each applicant was required to submit a "recommendation" verifying his loyalty to the government. Although permits could not be issued for trade with areas still in rebellion, an illicit trade with New England did exist, and Robertson apparently wanted to profit from it. He consequently had the power of issuing recommendations vested in Ludlow, who began charging an unauthorized fee for these recommendations that now also served as unofficial permits for the illegal commerce with New England.[122]

In July 1780 Robertson, with General Clinton's approval, ordered the

Islanders could try minor civil and criminal cases in a city court presided over by Superintendent of Police Andrew Elliot, David Mathews, and Peter Dubois.

[118] Barck, *New York*. 68-70; Jones, *History*. ed. De Lancey, II, 1-2, 30-32, 118-119, 128-132; "Queens County Supervisors' Book [1709-1787]." The Oyster Bay highway commissioners noted in 1780 that their authority came not from the town meeting but "By Virtue of an Order of Police" appointed by the military (John Cox, Jr., ed., *Oyster Bay Town Records* [New York, 1916-1940], VI, 640).

[119] Jones, *History*. ed. De Lancey, II, 12, 24, 23.

[120] *Ibid.*, 12-15.

[121] Concerning permits for importing and exporting and the extent of smuggling around New York City see Barck, *New York*. 123-124, 134-136; Wertenbaker, *Father Knickerbocker*. 206-207, 211-212; and Klein and Howard, eds., *Twilight of British Rule*, 162, n. 9, 190, n. 5.

[122] Although Jones could be very biased, he was not alone in challenging the governor's honesty. See Clinton to [Newcastle], Mar. 18, 1782, Clinton Papers, and Bowler, *Logistics*. 173-175. For a judicious treatment of the matter see Klein and Howard, eds., *Twilight of British Rule*. 48-52.

confiscation of the lands of absentee rebels, which were to be assigned, when possible, to refugee families on application to Philip Livingston, the newly appointed Superintendent of Derelict Properties on Long Island.[123] Such land could also be rented out, with the proceeds to go into a fund for refugee loyalists.[124] The procedure was simple. Livingston would appear as plaintiff before the Court of Police and claim a parcel of rebel property. Since the owner was not called to testify, judgment was by default.[125] Altogether, Livingston and the Court of Police assigned 2,807 acres, belonging to more than forty residents, to 468 refugees. Ten other estates were rented to raise relief funds. The fact that the rents amounted to only £291 per annum, however, suggests that the chief concern was not, as it was supposed to be, the raising of funds for refugees. Governor Tryon had previously given a friend, Joseph French, use of an estate valued at £2,000. The Court of Police now rented it to French for only £10. Yet another renter paid £50 for property valued at £1,000. A British officer rented land worth £3,000 for only £20. Officials concealed such discrepancies in the rents by neglecting to note the assessed valuations of these lands in the rent rolls, a procedure that was followed when land was assigned to refugees.[126]

Ludlow and Livingston, according to Jones, did everything possible to increase the amount of land confiscated.[127] John Rodman, a farmer who died before the war, had willed his farm to his wife with the proviso that it go, at her death, to his eldest son in fee or, if he died under age, to the legator's second son. By the end of 1776, the first son, who had become a whig committeeman and fled Long Island, had died under age. Although the mother and second son were still living on the farm, the Court of Police seized the estate, ejected the widow, cut down the woods, and gave the farm to refugees.[128] Another farmer who had moved to Dutchess

[123] *New-York Gaz.*, July 17, 1780; *Royal Gaz.*, July 19, Nov. 29, 1780; Robertson to Carleton, Apr. 11, 1783, Memorial of Philip Livingston to Carleton, May 10, 1783, British Headquarters Papers, Nos. 4686, 7655.

[124] Germain to Robertson, Sept. 3, 1779, C.O. 5/1109. Confiscation was not a new policy, for the army had previously taken the woodlands and movable estates of rebels. By 1778 the British had also confiscated nine Queens County farms valued at £15,600. Though some provision was made for refugees, most of this land was assigned to royal officials and their favorites. See "Estimate of the Value of Real Estate on Staten Island and in the Counties of Kings and Queens on Long Island" [1778], Stevens, comp., *Facsimiles*, No. 1234.

[125] Jones, *History*, ed. De Lancey, II, 35-37, 144-149; Barck, *New York*, 87.

[126] Testimony of William Tryon for Joseph French, Mar. 10, 1777, A.O. 13/114; "Return of Derelict Property within British Lines, 1783," "Derelict Property on Long Island Leased for the Relief of His Majesty's Loyal Subjects, 1782," and "Property on Long Island Assigned to His Majesty's Local Subjects Not Being Refugees, 1782," British Headquarters Papers, No. 9733.

[127] Jones, *History*, ed. De Lancey, II, 35-47.

[128] The records indicate that the property of a Thomas Rodman was seized and assigned to a refugee. The only Rodman on the list, he was perhaps the son of John Rodman to whom Jones referred; see Return of Derelict Property within British Lines, 1783, 1782, British Headquarters Papers, No. 9733.

County fifteen years before the war still owned woodland in Queens. The Court of Police declared him a rebel and had the wood cut down. A third farmer, Daniel Pine, willed his land to two infant nephews living in Dutchess County. This land, too, was confiscated.[129] Jones's allegations most likely were correct; in 1778 only nine farms were listed as having been confiscated, but under Livingston the total climbed to more than fifty.

Although eighteenth-century officeholders often employed public office for personal advantage, the officials at the Court of Police were perhaps too greedy. In the two years and eleven months of its existence, the court collected about £7,660 but used most of the money not to support loyalist refugees but to pay salaries. Ludlow received more than £1,825 for working one day a week for thirty-five months. His assistant, David Colden, and the treasurer, Charles M'Evers, were each paid £1,000. Ludlow's secretary was given £500. Livingston's share was £1,000 plus another £250 for travel expenses. Four other men were paid a total of about £445. After all expenses were paid, the refugees received only £300.[130]

VII: INDEPENDENCE

When the Court of Police was created, the people of Queens seem generally to have viewed it as a step toward the reinstitution of civil government. But Ludlow's tactics and the American victory at Yorktown fired disaffection afresh, and this time the estrangement between crown and county was complete and irreversible. After 1781 Queens County elected fewer royalists each year to public office. Even more telling was the way inhabitants adjusted to the war's outcome. If there had been continued resistance to Independence or if the mother country had won their allegiance, many might have become loyalist refugees. But probably only 5 to 6 percent of the prewar county population left New York with the British and became émigrés.[131] The vast majority remained to make

---

[129] *Abstract of Wills on File in the Surrogate's Office, City of New York* (New-York Historical Society, *Collections,* XXV-XXXIX [New York, 1892-1906]), X, 90-91, 108-109. British records indicate that the Pine land was assigned to four refugee families; see Return of Derelict Property within British Lines, 1783, 1782, British Headquarters Papers, No. 9733.

[130] Refugee Fund on Long Island, Philip Livingston, July 16, 1780, to May 20, 1783; Contingency Expenses on Long Island [1780-1783]; and A General Account of the Receipt and Disbursement of the Funds on Long Island from July 16, 1780, to June 16, 1783, British Headquarters Papers, Nos. 6261, 13065, 10366.

[131] This estimate is based upon findings from a collective biography of the 3,074 adult male inhabitants residing in the county at the outset of the war. In 1784, 56% were still living in Queens; another 3% are known to have become tory refugees; and 41% cannot be accounted for. The vast majority of this 41% are probably unlocatable, not because they became tory refugees (there is simply no evidence to indicate so massive an exodus), but because they were landless folk

their peace with the new government. It was, in fact, a group of county whigs who most accurately expressed public sentiment when they sent a petition in April 1783 to Gov. George Clinton arguing that residents were "entitled to a voice with our fellow citizens of the State in the approaching election."[132] Nor were these whigs disappointed: civil government was quickly restored in the county. Elections held in December 1783 to fill local and state offices marked the divide within Queens between war and peace. By voting, residents not only accepted the new order; they became part of it.[133]

Queens County is a test case. From the outset the top British officials in America recognized the need for reconciliation by cultivating public support. But they were never able in Queens County, although the odds were favorable, to devise an effective strategy for waging political warfare. Such efforts as they made were compromised by avarice, ambition, and prejudice. More energy was devoted to defending their mistakes than to seeking a solution. As a result, Great Britain lost the war not only on the battlefield but in the minds and hearts of the people of Queens. In the end, most residents of the county, especially those who had been neutral before the war, became patriots, less by choice or conviction than by British default. Seven hard years of military misrule had readied them for Independence.

---

who cannot easily be traced in the records. These unlocated people had little reason to become émigrés: 66% had been neutral in 1776, 11% had been patriots, and only 22% had been loyalists. Since county residents did not divide by economic class over the issues of the Revolution, it can be assumed that they acted at the end of the war in roughly the same manner as those for whom there is information. If this assumption is correct, then approximately 5% to 6% of the prewar population became émigrés.

[132] Henry Onderdonk, Jr., comp., *Documents and Letters Intended to Illustrate the Revolutionary Incidents in Queens County*, 2d Ser. (Hempstead, N.Y., 1884), 68.

[133] *Independent Journal* (New York), Dec. 15, 1783; *Independent Gazette* (New York), Dec. 13, 1783. Postwar voting and officeholding are interesting. First, neutrals continued the pattern developed during the British occupation; they constituted 44% of significant officeholders in Nov. 1783, 46% in 1784, and 47% in 1785. Second, loyalists also continued to hold office and vote. They constituted 5% of the significant officeholders in Nov. 1783, 12% in 1784, and 13% in 1785. For evidence that loyalists also voted see *New-York Packet*, Feb. 20, 1786.

Engraving showing the uniforms of an American general (*left*) and an American rifleman (*right*), from Edward Barnard's *The New Comprehensive and Complete History of England* (London, 1782). [*NJHS*]

The Conscripted Line: The Draft in Revolutionary New Jersey

MARK EDWARD LENDER

TROOP SHORTAGES were a particular bane of the Continental Army throughout the War for Independence. As early as 1776, Gen. George Washington became convinced that voluntary enlistments could not keep the Continental Line at operational strength; in a thinly veiled suggestion that the individual states resort to conscription, he questioned "whether it may not be prudent, to devise some other way" to raise men.[1] At least two states, Massachusetts and New Hampshire, had come to the same conclusion and started drafting men early in the war. Most, however, showed little enthusiasm for conscription, even as recruiting problems deepened. In April 1777, after the Continental Congress and the states failed to provide what he considered a satisfactory answer to his call for reinforcements, Washington again addressed the issue; this time he bluntly called for compulsory military service. "The government must have recourse to coersive measures," the commander-in-chief insisted, "for if the [manpower] quotas required of each State cannot be had by voluntary inlistment, *in time*, and if the Powers of Government are not adequate to *drafting*, there is an end of the Contest, and opposition becomes vain."[2]

Congress received this message with considerable ambivalence. They readily conceded the severity of troop shortages and called on the states to consider a draft if all other recruiting measures failed; but, reflecting the delegates' fear of the potential uproar inherent in the measure, this was hardly a ringing endorsement.[3] Finally, however, with the army crumbling at Valley Forge, congressmen could no longer skirt the issue. On February 26, 1778, they gave Washington what he wanted: a resolution calling on the states to draft men, or enlist them in any way they could, for service in the Continental Army.[4]

The conscription drive that followed was one of the most interesting attempts to reinforce the Patriot military and marked the nation's first effort to institute compulsory service in its regular forces. The broad outlines of what happened are familiar. Over the spring of 1778, eleven states framed recruiting laws with draft provisions and, with varying degrees of success, put them in motion. Thousands of men, either draftees or substitutes, subsequently reported for duty and enabled the Continental Army to take the field with credible strength. Beyond these observations, however, a range of interesting questions remain on the Revolutionary draft.[5] How effectively, for example, did the states organize and implement their conscription efforts, and, as they did so, what meaning—if any—did they attach to compulsory service in the ideological debates of the era?[6] This essay is concerned with how the state of New Jersey faced these issues, and thus sheds additional light on how the revolutionary generation grappled with an issue that continues to provoke pointed national debate.

Recruiting until 1778

By late 1776 Continental recruiting efforts were in serious trouble across the thirteen states, and New Jersey was no exception. In the early months of the war, the state easily raised three regiments of volunteers. Enthusiasm for the contest was at fever pitch, and the one-year enlistments imposed only a limited tour of duty.[7] The disastrous fortunes of Patriot arms in late 1776, however, all but destroyed rebel morale; and with ranks thinned by combat, disease and desertion, all of the original New Jersey Continentals mustered out by February 1777.[8] The impact of this loss was profound. Bitter memories lingered; most of the New Jersey veterans of 1776 never returned to Continental ranks in any numbers. Worse, the tales of their defeat and privation clearly discouraged new volunteers from coming forward.

Yet as recruits became less plentiful, demands on state manpower increased. In an effort to repair the damage of the previous year, Congress called on the states to provide Washington with a larger and a more stable regular army for 1777. The new military arrangement required an additional New Jersey regiment, hardly welcome news. Still reeling from the fighting of 1776, the state faced having to raise not three, but four Continental regiments (or just over 2,900 men). Moreover, Congress now wanted men for at least three years of service, and preferably for the duration of the war.[9] Under the best of circumstances, the new troop quota was a tall order. But as local Patriots gloomily pointed out, circumstances were hardly the best.

In the legislature, Patriots protested that Congress had asked too much. The disruption wrought in the 1776 campaign, they noted, and the fact that New Jersey was still an active theater of war, had stretched state human and financial resources to the limit.[10] The British invasion had killed relatively few people, but the enemy had captured many Whigs and driven others into exile, thus reducing the rebel manpower pool. And while it is impossible to assign a precise figure, it is entirely likely that upwards of 30 percent of the state's men of military age were Quaker pacifists or Loyalists, a high proportion of whom actually bore arms against their Patriot brethren.[11] Local defense needs also discouraged Continental enlistments. In the face of continuing enemy activity, many citizens, if they still cared to serve at all, chose duty in local militia outfits where they could keep an anxious eye on homes and families.[12] There was a basis in fact, then, to protests that congressional manpower demands were simply beyond the state's ability to provide.

Other wounds to the New Jersey recruiting service, however, were self-inflicted. The most serious was a section in the state militia law that exempted militiamen from duty if they hired substitutes to take their places.[13] The practical result of this provision was to drain potential recruits from the regular army. Men had little motive to enlist for long-term duty as Continentals, for a single bounty and notoriously irregular pay, when they could serve short militia tours for men who were willing—even anxious—to pay them well. Indeed, the business in substitutes was brisk and lucrative. Washington found the entire situation exasperating, and argued that eliminating the substitute laws would prove a splendid reform. "A number of idle, mercenary fellows would be thrown out of employment," he wrote, "precluded from their excessive wages, as substitutes for a few weeks or months; and constrained to enlist in the Continental army."[14] From a strictly military point of view, the commander-in-chief's argument made sense, and Gov. William Livingston was sympathetic. On a practical level, however, the governor could never convince the legislature to compel the personal service of militiamen. Such a step would have been highly unpopular; New Jersey lawmakers, who clearly understood the grave state of Continental manpower, simply were not willing to change the substitute laws at the cost of provoking the wrath of their constituents.[15]

Yet dissatisfaction with congressional manpower requests did not prevent an intensive recruiting effort. The New Jersey Brigade frequently detached officers for recruiting duty, and they were a familiar sight as they traveled the state offering potential troops free drinks, Continental bounties, and promises of martial glory.[16] Civil authorities were just as active. Frequently prodded by Governor Livingston, the legislature framed enlistment laws annually until 1783 and maintained a permanent recruiting service. By 1777, legislation had assigned full-time enlistment personnel to fixed recruiting districts.[17] All of this was expensive, and the state went deeply into debt to fund the search for its Continentals. It even borrowed funds to offer bounties substantially above those allowed by Congress to men willing to enlist for the duration of the conflict. Thus if New Jersey officials complained to Congress about troop quotas—as they did virtually throughout the war—they at least did not shirk the duty of trying to enroll volunteers.[18]

The best efforts of military and civilian recruiters, however, could not overcome the fact that there were simply not enough volunteers. Throughout 1777, the New Jersey battalions were never at full strength, and their numbers dwindled as the campaign (in which New Jersey casualties were quite heavy) took its toll.[19] By late 1777, when plans for the following year should have been well in hand, the New Jersey Brigade was barely at operational strength. Muster rolls for the four regiments in December showed 1,378 New Jersey infantry, over 700 men short of the state quota.[20] Of these, however, only 872 were listed as actually present and fit for duty at Valley Forge; the rest were sick, without equipment, away on detached duty, furloughed, or lost to desertion. All of this meant that none of the regiments had even half their complements, which was bad enough, but things quickly got worse. Not a single recruit joined the New Jersey Brigade in December, and the first three months of 1778 brought so few volunteers that the strength of the Jersey Line fell to some 550 effective men by March.[21] The recruiting situation, always a problem, had become a genuine crisis.

The Call for the Draft

It was in this atmosphere that Patriots finally confronted the conscription issue. As before, Washington took the lead. In January 1778, the general raised the question in a lengthy communication on the state of the army to a special investigating committee of Congress.[22] He suggested that the states draft men annually from their militia for a year of service in the Continental

Line. Near the end of each year, the army would try to reenlist these men for another annual tour, and would reduce the new draft quota of a state in proportion to such reenlistments. First-time draftees should not, Washington argued, receive either Continental or state bounties (and he wanted "solemn" promises of agreement from the states on this point), although troops signing on for the additional year would get twenty dollars. Thus Washington saw conscription not only as a means of short-term reinforcement, but as a step toward building a veteran corps as well. "This method," he noted, "though not so good as that of obtaining Men for [the duration of] the war, is perhaps the best our circumstances will allow."[23]

The commander-in-chief's proposals won immediate and articulate support in New Jersey. Writing under the pseudonym "Adolphus," Governor Livingston was probably Washington's staunchest partisan as he took up the fight for an effective draft in the January 21st issue of the *New-Jersey Gazette*.[24] Offering the public what he titled "Thoughts on the Situation of Affairs," Livingston dealt not with the mechanics of conscription, but with the need to reinforce the American regulars and, significantly, the ideological basis for compulsory service. A successful recruiting drive, he predicted, could lead only to victory, and if drafting men to achieve that goal gave "umbrage to some who never look beyond themselves," Adolphus had a ready answer. "It is a maxim in government which I never heard a man of sense deny," he wrote, "that every state hath a right to demand the personal service of its members or an equivalent, whenever the public weal demands it." Compulsory service in the militia was already a tradition "conformable to the genius of a free people," and now the times demanded that patriots accept the same obligations for service in the Continental army. Let "the yeomanry of a country" be conscripted into the regulars, the governor insisted, or serve as substitutes for other draftees, and they would quickly be the equals of veterans.[25]

Livingston's tract was a minor republican masterpiece. Even while conceding that draftees might hire substitutes to escape personal duty, he nevertheless couched support for the draft in terms of patriotic obligation and drew on the vocabulary of sacrifice, unity, and the "folly" of not rising to the public duty. "Peace, liberty and safety," he proclaimed, "lie before us as the reward of our exertions—Infamy, distress, and all that we have felt or feared from the tyranny of Britain, may be the consequence of supineness and inaction."[26] Conscription, as far as Livingston's Adolphus was concerned, was as much a matter of political principle, one more sign of patriotic virtue, as it was a military measure.

Throughout the war, Livingston generally favored stern military measures, and there seems little question that he wanted to help Washington in any way he could. There is also a strong likelihood, however, that he intended the Adolphus message for the particular attention of New Jersey. He was well aware that conscription would face strong opposition in some parts of the state, and that at least a measure of antidraft sentiment was already a part of New Jersey's heritage. The colonial militia laws, for example, had included provisions for short-term compulsory service, but not all residents had approved. In South Jersey, Quaker influence had slowed efforts to draft men for duty in the French and Indian War, and the provincial assembly went on record at one point as being "determined not to oblige or compel any of the Inhabitants by Force to serve as Soldiers."[27] Even the crisis of revolution found local Whigs unwilling to resort quickly to conscription. In 1775, Patriot authorities in Newark urged militia to volunteer for short tours of duty, lest "the disagreeable measure of draughting" prove necessary.[28] Thus if the draft was part of militia tradition, it was by no means a popular part; and Adolphus was virtually the only New Jersey voice to argue that militia precedent justified conscription for a regular army.

The draft faced other problems as well. Indeed, in February events threatened to put all Continental recruiting efforts at risk. On February 16, the governor urged the assembly to adopt "the most expeditious and vigorous Measures" to complete the four New Jersey Continental regiments.[29] Five days later, however, a joint committee of the assembly and council sent a disheartening reply. They did not see how the state could enlist enough men; furthermore, in what may have been an oblique reference to the Adolphus essay, they insisted that New Jersey attempt no recruiting by "other Means than those already adopted." That, plainly, precluded conscription. In fact, the Patriot lawmakers wanted to discuss fewer troops, not more. They concluded their response with a request that the state petition Congress for a reduction of Continental manpower obligations, once again pleading the exhaustion of local human and material resources.[30] Justified or not, the legislature's position left unaddressed the vulnerability of Washington's forces.

Indeed, the call for a petition to Congress dismayed a number of Patriots. In Philadelphia, the suggested memorial appalled Elisha Boudinot, the attorney brother of New Jersey Congressman Elias Boudinot: "Will it not disgrace us?" he wrote to state Chief Justice Robert Morris. "Is it not only protracting the War and consequently increasing our Grievances?"[31] Back in New Jersey, the governor was not pleased either. But with the legislature in such a frame of mind, he plainly needed to make a more convincing case if he wanted any kind of effective enlistment drive, much less legislative and popular support for a conscription law.

Trying to avoid an open clash with the assembly and council, Livingston—at least it was probably Livingston—again took up the pen. This time he wrote as "Persius," and on February 18, while the legislature was still framing its reply to his message on recruiting, he published another column in the *New-Jersey Gazette*.[32] The ostensible purpose was to applaud the arguments of Adolphus, which, Persius held (albeit lamely), "gave pleasure to thousands." The "thousands," however, as Livingston had become acutely aware, needed a bit more convincing. Putting ideological matters largely aside this time, he argued that the Continental Line needed men, and the draft was the only timely way to get enough of them. Stating that his remarks had "a particular application" to New Jersey, he also suggested the actual mechanics of conscription. Draft a tenth of the militia by lot for a nine-month tour of duty with the regulars, he said, and give the draftees a bounty and the same clothing allowances as Continentals. If drafted men did not want to serve, they could hire substitutes, many of whom had considerable military experience. It was a good plan, he concluded, for "the time of service will be short, the inducements great, and the cause is glorious."[33]

The Persius essay, however, was more than an effort to prod a reluctant legislature or to provide a blueprint for compulsory service; it was probably Livingston's attempt to prepare New Jersey for impending congressional action. In Philadelphia, Congress had reacted to Washington's January message by establishing a committee to frame a conscription resolution. One of the committee members was Nathaniel Scudder, delegate from New Jersey, who may have kept Livingston informed on committee deliberations.[34] If the governor's source was not Scudder, then in all likelihood someone else was passing him information, for the committee's final resolution bore a remarkable resemblance to the plan that Persius had put forward. One suspects that Livingston knew full well what would happen.

On February 26, the full Congress approved the resolution in substantially the form in which Scudder and his colleagues had presented it.[35] The measure conceded that volunteering had failed, and stipulated that the states "be required forthwith to fill up" their Continental battalions "by drafts from their militia, or in any other way that shall be effectual." The draft, however, as in the Persius essay, was to be a one-time affair, not an annual event, and conscripted militiamen were to serve for only nine months. In a provision that Persius had suggested—and one that Washington had specifically warned against in January—Congress allowed the states to offer bounties to draftees. On the other hand, as the general had hoped, there were inducements for the states to recruit long-term soldiers: the army was to send drafted troops home early in numbers equal to the enlistments of men willing to serve for three years or for the duration of the war. Draftees from New Jersey and the other Middle Atlantic states were to report directly to Valley Forge, while the resolution directed men from more distant areas to muster at regional military centers.[36]

The congressional resolution did not give the commander-in-chief all he had asked for, but he got a good deal of it. If Washington was disappointed, he never revealed this publicly; from the army's point of view, the resolution, however imperfect, was at least a step in the right direction.

The New Jersey Debate

On March 16, Governor Livingston put the congressional resolution before the New Jersey Assembly. "I conceive," he noted in what was an implicit endorsement, that the measure "requires your speedy Consideration."[37] Speedy the debate generally was, but amicable it apparently was not. Faced with the wishes of Congress and the governor, the legislature promptly took up the conscription question, although it did not drop the idea of asking Congress to reduce the New Jersey regiments. The bickering drove Livingston to the point of distraction, and on the 20th he complained privately to Scudder that the conduct of "that august assembly . . . would have chagrined me to death." The "fatal clause in the constitution respecting a majority of voices," he asserted, "will yet prove our ruin."[38] Later, he wrote Washington that "Our Legislature has been so dilatory in framing the law for raising our Quota of Troops destined to reinforce the grand army, that it puts me out of all Patience."[39]

The debate ended in early April. Large majorities in both the assembly and the council approved a recruiting law with conscription provisions; the former voted twenty-two to five on March 27, and the latter concurred, six to two, on April 3. Most of the seven "no" votes came from South Jersey, where traditional Quaker influence may have told. But two negatives also came from Somerset and Sussex counties, and support for the draft law was strong among legislators from all sections of the state.[40] It is difficult, then, to determine precisely why the vote went as it did. But in light of prior legislative reluctance to embrace any strong recruiting measure, it is somewhat surprising that the measure passed so easily. In fact, proponents of conscription may have carried the day only after striking a political deal.

The recruiting bill was not the only measure to win legislative approval on April 3. The other was the much-discussed petition to Congress, which argued strenuously for a reduction of the state troop quota. The document was a familiar litany, pleading that the British invasion of 1776 had seriously impeded New Jersey recruiting abilities. It reiterated that many Patriots had been captured and large numbers of the disloyal had fled to the British or enlisted in Tory battalions. Other Jerseymen willing to fight, it said, had joined regiments from other states. Besides, if militia drafts were to reinforce the Continental Line, who would be left back home for local defense? Finally, the petition asked that the army send Continental regiments to protect the area, and suggested that a reduction in the additional New Jersey regiments would better allow any new recruits to fill up the old units.[41] The legislature duly sent the memorial to Congress, which in turn referred it to a special committee on April 8.[42]

Approval of the petition and the draft on the same day was probably no coincidence. Indeed, one can easily surmise a "package deal": conscription to satisfy Congress and Washington (not to mention Livingston); a plea for relief for those who thought the war-ravaged state could do no more. The legislative record is not clear enough to state with certainty that things actually happened this way; and it is probably true that some lawmakers, otherwise opposed to compulsory service, supported the draft solely in the belief that it was the only practical way to reinforce the Continental Army. The likelihood of a compromise, however, is entirely plausible given the legislature's demonstrated reluctance to undertake stern recruiting measures and the state's previous aversion to conscription.

Nevertheless, conscription was finally on the books, and while Congress dealt with the legislature's petition, the state prepared to set its new draft law in motion. Entitled "An Act for the speedy and effectual recruiting of the four New-Jersey Regiments in the Service of the United States," the statute named militia field officers and local justices of the peace as commissioners to supervise conscription procedures.[43] It then ordered the militia to prepare full returns of all enlisted personnel, and upon the certification of the returns, to conduct full regimental musters. Officers and commissioners would then divide each regiment into eighteen classes. Each class was allowed ten days to present a volunteer or a substitute to serve nine months in the New Jersey Brigade. To encourage volunteers, the law promised a $40.00 bounty, a blanket, and an allotment of clothing.[44] If, after ten days, a class did not present a recruit, one man would be drafted by lot; and he then had five days to either report for duty, hire a substitute, or pay a fine of three hundred pounds (or face jail upon refusal or inability to pay). The commissioners were to muster the recruits locally and send them on to Jacob Dunn, of Middlesex County, who was named agent to receive the draftees at army headquarters. The state was to finance the entire effort by borrowing, with the loans to be apportioned by county.[45]

To the extent that the legislature reflected popular opinion, support for the new measure was apparently grudging. Yet Congress and the state had bent over backwards to make the situation palatable. While compulsory service theoretically lay behind the congressional resolution and the New Jersey recruiting law, few Patriot leaders wanted to push the theory too hard. Indeed, it is worth recalling that the original resolution offered a ready alternative to conscription: it allowed the states to procure men by drafting "or in any other way that shall be effectual."[46] This clause, as everyone knew, was an invitation to include provisions for substitutes in state draft acts, thus allowing a way out for draftees who did not want to serve (provided, of course, that they could afford the price of a substitute). All of the states had such provisions and, like New Jersey, also levied fines on those who refused either to serve or to hire another in their place.[47] But even the fines provided a way out of the ranks. As inflation ravaged the currencies of the states, depreciation took much of the sting out of the penalties. The three-hundred-pound New Jersey fine, for example, was within the reach of many men of moderate means by 1778.[48] These built-in "escape" mechanisms probably made the draft law at least tolerable to the public; they also signaled that Whig legislators would actually compel service only as a last resort.

Nevertheless, the law had important implications. Previous military legislation, notably the colonial militia laws, had defined military obligations based on local duty and authority. The 1778 act was still based on militia participation. But this was simply a matter of convenience—it offered the quickest way to raise men— as the intention now was to use the draft in the service of a national army. Conscription had come at the request of Congress, and the law specified that men raised under the act were to serve under Continental and not state authority, "amenable to the [Continental] Rules and Discipline of War."[49] Moreover, unlike a number of the other states, which insisted that draftees serve in special units, New Jersey placed no restrictions on their duty.[50] For nine months, they belonged to General Washington, to do with as he would. For the first time in New Jersey, and in most of the other states, the draft was no longer a strictly local affair.

The British Response

As the rebels struggled to produce an effective recruiting law, the British watched with mixed emotions. The first enemy response was undisguised contempt. The day after Livingston first took the congressional draft resolution to the assembly in March, "A British Captain" launched a counterattack in the Tory *New-York Gazette*, taking the governor to task for his Adolphus essay. (It is worth noting that this was the only public response to Adolphus.) The writer had no trouble identifying the New Jersey leader as the true author of the draft proposal, and he responded with a mocking blast at the entire rebel war effort. For good measure, he dismissed Livingston himself as an "Ass which has put on a Lion's skin" and a "miserable pettifogging scribbler."[51] The man had a genuine flair for invective, and obviously enjoyed the spectacle of the New Jersey Whigs grappling with their manpower problems.

With the enactment of the New Jersey and other state draft laws, however, the British tone changed. There is little evidence that they feared the American effort might succeed, but they did see an opportunity to sow discord among the rebels. Thus while Patriots were still compiling militia returns in preparation for drafting, the British moved to disrupt their plans. On April 3, the Loyalist *Pennsylvania Evening Post* published a copy of what it claimed was the congressional draft resolution of February 26 (the *Post* had the date wrong, reporting it as February 20). It was a patent forgery, holding that Congress would compel all current Continental troops and all future draftees to serve for the duration of the war. In addition, the *Post* version maintained, Washington would try for desertion those soldiers leaving ranks after their legal enlistments had expired.[52] After this initial publication, the British did their best to circulate copies of the spurious resolution; in a cool display of arrogance, William Tryon, the deposed royal governor of New York, even sent a copy to Washington.[53]

Livingston was evidently the first Patriot to call the forgery to Washington's attention. Writing the commander-in-chief on April 17, he enclosed a copy of the *Post* and warned that it was "calculated to do the most extensive Mischief." The entire matter, he urged, "ought to be exposed & the public disabused as soon as possible."[54] The general, furious, agreed. The *Post* column, he replied to the governor, was an "arrant forgery," calculated to forestall a successful draft. He quickly informed Congress of Livingston's message and denounced the enemy ruse before the army in general orders. Privately, however, he conceded that the British had "industriously circulated" the forgery, and that it had indeed hurt the army by "alarming the fears of the Soldiery and Country."[55] Other Whigs were just as alarmed, with Charles Thomson, secretary of the Continental Congress, concisely summarizing most feelings: "If it was possible to be surprised by any chicanery of the enemy, this might perhaps have that effect."[56] Intended to spread consternation in Patriot ranks, then, the British ploy worked admirably.

The Draft in Practice, 1778–80

In late April and early May, militia commanders compiled the required returns of their men, and the draft commissioners initiated the processes of classification and conscription. Remarkably, despite enemy meddling and the resulting growth of public distrust, civil and military authorities had little difficulty enforcing the law. Most of the militia classes sent men, many of whom were substitutes. Indeed the substitute provisions of the law worked quite well, and perhaps as many as 40 percent of the men raised under the 1778 act were hired stand-ins for militiamen unwilling to serve themselves.[57] Some areas sent only substitutes. The draft classes of a Middlesex County militia regiment, for instance, submitted a roster of twenty-eight recruits—all hirelings. Some of these men, as the army hoped, later enlisted for three years or for the duration of the war.[58] In a few cases, draftees paid fines in order simply to buy off their obligations. This was not the norm, however, and over May and June, army rosters reflected a steady strengthening of the New Jersey regiments. All of this was a pleasant surprise to Washington. In April, the general had expected the worst from British propaganda. But by June he was convinced that New Jersey was one of the few states "likely to get their Regiments nearly compleated."[59]

Drafting days brought some interesting negotiations among the militia classes as they decided who would volunteer or how they would procure a substitute. In one case, a Somerset County class repeatedly refused to send a recruit. The militia company commander drew the lot twelve times, and each time the draftee paid the fine instead of agreeing to serve. Finally, the class settled on one Peter Post, who previously also had paid a fine when the lot fell to him. His ultimate selection, however, is suspicious: he was apparently in debt to his company commander, a situation which perhaps gave the officer a persuasive lever in Post's decision.[60] Private Joseph Plumb Martin, who enlisted as a substitute in Connecticut's draft, described a scene probably similar to those in other states. Once a class knew he was for hire, they wasted no time in buying his services. "I forget the sum," he recalled after the war. "They were now freed from any further trouble, at least for the present, and I had become the scapegoat for them. . . . I thought, as I must go, I might as well endeavor to get as much for my skin as I could."[61]

Happily or not, however, men came forward. In mid-June, Congress exhorted the state to keep the recruiting drive moving, proclaiming that "the public safety demands strong and united efforts."[62] And if the raising of men was the criterion for success, then New Jersey clearly gave Congress what it wanted. The state recruited more Continentals in 1778 than in any other year (see table 1); while the draft did not completely fill the four regiments of the New Jersey Brigade, it helped get them to three-quarters of their allotted strength, enough to let them operate effectively during the 1778 campaign.[63]

The draft also demonstrated how effectively the revolutionary government had consolidated its control of the machinery of state. Few New Jersey leaders were forthright in their endorsements of conscription, and certainly public opinion never clamored for it; but once enacted, the state enforced the law, perhaps more successfully than even the staunchest of Whigs had hoped. In fact, there is no record of even a single instance of public protest, let alone disruption, taking place as commissioners and militia officers went about their business. This is significant considering the many predictions—and complaints—to the effect that New Jersey was too exhausted and war-ravaged to levy a sizable body of soldiery. At least for 1778, then, the draft succeeded admirably.

If conscription raised men, however, it also may have raised a constituent backlash. Indeed, despite the evident success of 1778, New Jersey did not draft again in 1779. In fact, the legislature considered no recruiting measure at all until June of 1779, by which time some Patriots again had become gravely concerned. "The Publick is astonished," wrote Elisha Boudinot, "that we are so far advanced in the Spring and nothing done in our State toward filling up the Regiments or preparing for the next campaign. . . .

This is like men sleeping on the Point of a Precipice."[64] Finally, ignoring a congressional request that conscription continue, the legislature passed a recruiting act that reverted to the old reliance on volunteering.[65]

The roots of this seemingly perverse action are not hard to find. The lessons of 1778 aside, many New Jersey Patriots were still convinced that the state had to cut its manpower contributions to the regular army. Thus as the draft machinery went into motion in April and May, legislative leaders continued to press for congressional action on the troop reduction petition of April. Late in the month, they won their point: The congressional committee investigating their complaints recommended the elimination of one of New Jersey's regiments for the 1779 campaign.[66] Final action came in May when Congress, realizing it had too many thin battalions, voted to consolidate weaker units into stronger formations; under the new arrangement, the New Jersey Brigade would consist of only three regiments. Also in May, New Jersey delegates helped defeat a congressional attempt to increase regimental size to over 1,200 men, a change that would have effectively negated the reduction in state troop strength.[67]

The legislature had won its battle, and evidently saw no grounds to continue a draft that had evoked little popular enthusiasm anyway. Indeed, state leaders then chose to carry their manpower grievances beyond those addressed in the original petition. The new complaint involved quota credit for New Jersey regulars not serving with the New Jersey Brigade. These men saw duty in other state lines or detached units of horse or artillery; the legislature, however, wanted them to count toward completion of the New Jersey quota.[68] Congress reasoned that they already had credited the state with many men on whom it had only a dubious claim, and that if they counted detached units toward line quotas, the horse and artillery could only increase at the expense of the infantry battalions, which would remain seriously under strength.[69]

Having carried the argument in April, the legislature was not about to accept no for an answer. One assembly committee even suggested that the state adopt only a temporary recruiting law in 1779 unless Congress relented.[70] Finally, the delegates in Philadelphia did just that, leaving Washington to grumble that New Jersey Whigs would use the concession as an excuse not to complete the New Jersey Line. He was right, for in 1780 the legislature again delayed enacting a recruiting law until the commander-in-chief reported the total number of all New Jersey residents in the army.[71] Knowing what was coming, the general forwarded a troop return (which showed the state over five hundred men short),

Table I

NEW JERSEY CONTINENTAL REGIMENTAL QUOTAS

Year	Quota Regiments	Quota Men	Actual Men
1777	4	2,720	1,408
1778	4	2,088	1,586
1779	3	1,566	1,276
1780	3	1,566	1,105
1781	2	1,522	823
1782	2	1,522	660
1783	2	1,522	676

Source: Walter Lowrie and Matthew St. Clair Clarke, eds., *American State Papers: Military Affairs*, 7 vols. (Washington, D.C., 1832–61), 1:14–19. Each regiment (or battalion, the words were interchangeable) originally had an official strength of eight companies of 79 officers and men—728 men of all ranks including staff officers.

and promised to credit men in detached corps as he located them. He asked, though, that the absence of these men from the return not impede recruiting efforts, as the Jersey regiments were weaker than they looked on paper.[72]

Haggling over the quota ended only after 1780, when Congress became fully convinced that New Jersey simply would not complete its battalions. In fact, it may have believed that the state legislature was more interested in reducing the army rather than augmenting it. In February 1780, New Jersey was one of three states to support a Massachusetts bid to decrease her regiments; and Congress did not bother to ask for help from the Garden State when searching for men to make good the Patriot losses at Charlestown, South Carolina.[73] Finally, in October of the same year, Continental authorities reduced the New Jersey Brigade to two regiments, its strength for the rest of the war.[74]

As the state and Congress debated the quota issue, troop shortages unsurprisingly again became acute. With the reduction of a regiment in 1779, as well as the recruiting of some 150 volunteers (including reenlistments by a number of the nine-month draftees or their substitutes), the New Jersey Brigade maintained a functional strength for a year without conscription (see table 1). By 1780, however, military and civilian officials were issuing dire warnings over the loss of brigade manpower. In March of that year, the legislature ignored another congressional call for the draft; and shortly afterward it voted down a motion to force delinquent militiamen to serve three months of punitive duty in a Continental battalion.[75] Throughout the spring, the entire New Jersey Line (including Oliver Spencer's "Additional" regiment, brigaded with the other Jersey troops since the reduction of the Fourth New Jersey Regiment in 1779) numbered less than nine hundred men, just over half its authorized complement.[76] Finally, armed with a personal plea from Washington, Congress notified the legislature that the situation had become truly dangerous and asked that New Jersey reinstitute the draft.[77] Reluctantly, but conceding the necessity, the legislature complied in June.

The new conscription law was modeled on that of 1778, the major difference being that the 1780 term of service was only six months.[78] This effort, however, was less successful, apparently because of half-hearted attempts to enforce its provisions. Essex County, for example, drafted only half as many men as in 1778; and although men trickled into camp throughout the campaign season, the law produced fewer than two hundred recruits by August. Indeed, the 1780 draft brought derision from Loyalists. A Tóry editor remarked that the draft merely created refugees who fled rather than be conscripted or forced to hire a substitute.[79]

Conscripted militia and substitutes reported for duty in greater numbers later in the summer. But Congress, bewildered at the disappointing results of the recruiting effort, made no effort to hide its displeasure. In August, a special committee complained to Livingston of "the extraordinary backwardness of some states" in completing their battalions. Could it be, it asked, that "avarice, luxury and dissipation" had seduced "the boasted sons of American freedom" and persuaded them to forsake country and liberty? Were they ready for the slavery which "their generous nature but a few . . . years before would have revolted at the bare idea of?" The very thought, the message concluded, was contemplated only with "the extremest pain; nay, horror!"[80] Horror or not, though, this was New Jersey's last draft, and in 1781 the state reverted to seeking voluntary enlistments and tacitly accepting troop shortages.

The Draft in Perspective

There were no further calls to revive conscription in New Jersey, and even such proponents of the measure as Livingston must have known that fighting on was hopeless. Indeed, discussion of the issue ended so abruptly that state Patriots left a great deal

William Livingston (1723–90), a New Jersey delegate to the Continental Congress, assumed command of the state militia in 1776. In that year he began a fourteen-year term as governor of New Jersey. His many writings promoted the Patriot cause during the revolutionary war. [*NJHS*]

unsaid about the experience; there was no postmortem on the draft, no direct comment on whether New Jersey Whigs thought the entire effort worth the trouble or whether they had derived any particular lessons from it. Still, one can make a number of observations based on the record of 1778 and 1780.

On a strictly practical level, conscription proved an effective way to raise men for the New Jersey Brigade—despite protests from those Whigs who thought the state too war-weakened to maintain a sizable regular line. At the same time, however, one must take seriously many of those protests: the consequences of New Jersey's exposed strategic position and the battering its population and economy had absorbed were quite real. The state had suffered enormous damage.[81] This is not to say that Patriots would have been happier about the draft if the war had not hit them so hard, but the situation makes their feelings easier to understand. Besides, it is important to recall that many Patriots balked, not necessarily at the draft itself, but at all recruiting activity beyond what they considered the capabilities of the state.

There seems little question that the state would never have resorted to the measure by itself. The promptings of Congress and Washington, the undeniable seriousness of the manpower crisis facing the army, and the knowledge that most of the other states were also drafting all helped to bring reluctant legislators into agreement. The substitute provisions, and the fact that inflation made the fines affordable to all but the poorest residents, also acted to make the revolutionary drafts generally tolerable. Had the conscription statutes actually demanded personal service, unquestionably they would have provoked more political opposition, and may not have been so readily implemented in the field. Indeed, when Continental troop quotas fell, so did New Jersey's readiness to support any talk of compulsory military duty.

This is not to say, however, that New Jersey leaders necessarily were philosophically opposed to drafting men for national service—or even to enforcing their personal service. Indeed, some local Patriots accepted at least the principle of compulsory duty. Governor Livingston's views offer a particular case in point: He was one of the first Americans to characterize the draft in specifically ideological terms. When he argued, as Adolphus, that government could compel the military service of the citizenry, he presented the matter as an article of republican faith. The import of the tract was that submission to conscription was a civic obligation, and that the republic had every right to call its citizens to the colors.[82] This was a conception that, if carried to its logical conclusion, led eventually to the conscripted, popularly based armies of the Napoleonic and democratic futures—times when those who passed draft laws frequently did intend to compel actual service from individuals.[83]

The majority of New Jersey Patriots—or Patriots generally, for that matter—were probably not of the same mind on the subject as Livingston. But it is worth noting that, if many contemporaries opposed the governor's stand on the draft, they chose not to debate the issue on ideological grounds; rather, they stuck to such practical matters as the exhaustion of state resources or the need to preserve manpower for local militia outfits. This is hardly proof that Livingston's opponents conceded the argument of political principle, but the fact that no one publicly refuted the governor on his own terms is at least interesting. Thus if Patriots were reluctant to force their neighbors into ranks in 1778 or 1780, some also may have been hesitant to deny government's theoretical right to do so. The evidence is too thin for any firm conclusion on this, but it is too suggestive to ignore. Certainly, however, what happened in New Jersey does not support the contention, proffered by at least one other study, that the revolutionary generation was philosophically opposed to any but drafts for militia duty.[84]

It seems best to conclude that amid the turmoil of revolution and war, Patriots formed no real consensus on the ideological significance of conscription. In fact, when New Jersey Whigs took sides at all, their arguments usually were linked inextricably to others about the nature of citizenship and government, specific military necessities, the economic health of the state, local defense concerns, and the immediate demands of practical politics. The draft never stood alone as an issue. Even Livingston, who perhaps devoted more thought to the nature of conscription than anyone else in the state, looked at the matter from more than a single perspective. It is probably enough to note that the debate over the draft, at least in part, was yet another reflection of the broader ideological struggle that shaped revolutionary America—and that certain aspects of the controversy pointed toward a day when compulsory military service became a serious issue indeed.

Notes

[1] John C. Fitzpatrick, ed., *The Writings of George Washington from the Original Manuscript Sources, 1745–1799*, 39 vols. (Washington, D.C., 1931–44), 5:317.

[2] Don Higginbotham, *The War of American Independence: Military Attitudes, Policies, and Practice, 1763–1789* (New York, 1971), 392; Fitzpatrick, *Writings of Washington*, 7:355.

[3] Worthington Chauncey Ford, ed., *Journals of the Continental Congress*, 34 vols. (Washington, D.C., 1904–37), 7:262–63 (hereafter, *JCC*).

[4] Ibid., 10:199–203.

[5] Brief overviews of the draft in the revolutionary war are available in Higginbotham, *The War of Independence*, 392–93, and in Russell F. Weigley, *History of the United States Army* (New York, 1967), 41–42; more detail is in James Kirby Martin and Mark Edward Lender, *A Respectable Army: The Military Origins of the Republic, 1763–1789* (Arlington Heights, Ill., 1982), and in Jack F. Leach, *Conscription in the United States: Historical Background* (Rutland, Vt., 1952). Hugh F. Rankin, *The North Carolina Continentals* (Chapel Hill, N.C., 1971), has some material on conscription in that state. Although there are only a few state-level studies, the best are Arthur J. Alexander, "How Maryland Tried to Raise Her Continental Quotas," *Maryland Historical Magazine* 42 (1947):184–96; and Jonathan Smith, "How Massachusetts Raised Her Troops in the Revolution," Massachusetts Historical Society, *Proceedings*, 3d ser., 56 (1923):361–65.

[6] The studies dealing most directly with the ideological or policy issues inherent in the revolutionary war draft are Louis Morton, "The Origins of American Military Policy," *Military Affairs* 12 (1958):75–82; Leon Friedman, "Conscription and the Constitution: The Original Understanding," *Michigan Law Review* 67 (1969):1493–1552; Michael J. Malbin, "Conscription, the Constitution, and the Framers: An Historical Analysis," *Fordham Law Review* 40 (1972):805–26; and Charles A. Lofgren, "Compulsory Military Service under the Constitution: The Original Understanding," *William and Mary Quarterly*, 3d ser., 33 (1976):61–88.

[7] On early recruiting efforts in New Jersey, see Mark Edward Lender, "The Enlisted Line: The Continental Soldiers of New Jersey" (Ph.D. diss., Rutgers University, 1975), 67–69.

[8] Ibid., 69–70.

[9] New Jersey troop quotas during the revolutionary war are summarized in

Walter Lowrie and Matthew St. Clair Clarke, eds., *American State Papers: Military Affairs* (Washington, D.C., 1832–61), 1:14–19.

[10]See, for example, New Jersey Legislative Council, *Journal of the Proceedings of the Legislative Council* . . . [session of October 1777 to October 1778] (Trenton, N.J., 1778), 31 (hereafter, *NJLC*, with session dates).

[11]Lender, "Enlisted Line," 46–47. The number of men New Jersey lost to Loyalist regiments, while not precisely known, was considerable. Most of them served in the New Jersey Volunteers (Skinner's Greens) under the command of Brig. Gen. Cortland Skinner, New Jersey's last colonial attorney general. Skinner raised three battalions in 1776, and three more over the course of the war, with a combined strength approaching three thousand regular soldiers (and possibly more). They fought gallantly for the king, and were arguably among the best units either side fielded during the conflict. The West Jersey Volunteers, led by a Maj. John Van Dyke, were raised in 1778 around Philadelphia and numbered only some 200 men. See Philip R. N. Katcher, *Encyclopedia of British, Provincial, and German Army Units, 1775–1783* (Harrisburg, Pa., 1973), 93, 102.

[12]Lender, "Enlisted Line," 30–32.

[13]*Acts of the* . . . *General Assembly of the State of New Jersey* [session of May–June 1777] (Trenton, N.J., 1777), 52 (hereafter, *Acts*). New Jersey militia law is discussed in detail in John R. Anderson, "Militia Law in Revolutionary New Jersey," *New Jersey History* 76 (1958):280–96; ibid., 77 (1959):9–21.

[14]Fitzpatrick, *Writings of Washington*, 10:367.

[15]On the frustration of militia law reform, see Lender, "Enlisted Line," 32–42; on Livingston's sympathy with Washington's position, see Carl E. Prince and Dennis P. Ryan, eds., *The Papers of William Livingston, July 1777–December 1778* (Trenton, N.J., 1980), 2:189.

[16]The activities of local recruiters in New Jersey are traced in Lender, "Enlisted Line," 82–84.

[17]Permanent recruiting districts came at the request of Congress, and engendered considerable debate in the legislature, which thought the system administratively complex and expensive. The recruiting officer would also apprehend deserters. See *JCC*, 8:593–94; Minutes of the Governor's Privy Council of New Jersey, 1777–96, 1:7–8, bound manuscript, Division of Archives and Records Management, New Jersey Department of State, Trenton (hereafter, DARM); New Jersey General Assembly, *Votes and Proceedings of the General Assembly of the State of New Jersey* . . . [August–October 1777] (Trenton, N.J., 1778), 200–1 (hereafter, *Votes and Proceedings*, with session dates); *NJLC*, September–October 1777, 122–23; *Minutes of the Council of Safety of the State of New Jersey* (Jersey City, N.J., 1872), 149–50.

[18]The various financial arrangements to support recruiting operations can be traced in *Acts*, February–April 1778, 66; ibid., May–June 1779, 87; ibid., February–March 1780, 60; ibid., November 1780–January 1781, 20–21.

[19]New Jersey troop strength can be followed on a monthly basis for this period in Charles H. Lesser, ed., *The Sinews of Independence: Monthly Strength Reports of the Continental Army* (Chicago, 1976), 46–54.

[20]Ibid., 54.

[21]Ibid., 54, 58, 60.

[22]Fitzpatrick, *Writings of Washington*, 10:366–67.

[23]Ibid., 366.

[24]Adolphus, "Thoughts on the Situation of Affairs," *New-Jersey Gazette*, January 21, 1778.

[25]Ibid.

[26]Ibid.

[27]Quoted in Carl Raymond Woodward, *Ploughs and Politics: Charles Reed of New Jersey and His Notes on Agriculture, 1715–1774* (New Brunswick, N.J., 1941), 173.

[28]*Minutes of the Provincial Congress and the Council of Safety* (Trenton, N.J., 1879), 151–52.

[29]Prince and Ryan, *Livingston Papers*, 2:219.

[30]*NJLC*, October 28, 1777–October 8, 1778, 31.

[31]Elisha Boudinot to Robert Morris, February 26, 1778, Boudinot Papers, box 4, Rutgers University Library, New Brunswick, N.J.

[32]Persius [William Livingston?], "Thoughts on bringing to a speedy and happy end the present war," *New-Jersey Gazette*, February 18, 1778. Prince and Ryan, *Livingston Papers*, 2:529–30, tentatively have attributed the Persius essay to Livingston. They are almost certainly correct, and the information presented in this essay adds additional confirmation to the attribution.

[33]Persius, "Thoughts on the present war."

[34]*JCC*, 10:199–203. Livingston certainly discussed aspects of the draft situation with Scudder, although there is no direct evidence that they corresponded on the congressional resolution. See Prince and Ryan, *Livingston Papers*, 2:265–66.

[35]*JCC*, 10:199–203. Congress did delete, however, a committee recommendation that the states not offer bounties in addition to the existing Continental bounties. The committee had probably included this provision at the request of Washington. See Fitzpatrick, *Writings of Washington*, 10:366–67.

[36]*JCC*, 10:203.

[37]Prince and Ryan, *Livingston Papers*, 2:254.

[38]Ibid., 266.

[39]Ibid., 291.

[40]*NJLC*, October 28, 1777–October 8, 1778, 52; *Votes and Proceedings*, October 28, 1777–October 8, 1778, 92.

[41]For the text of the petition, and legislative action on it, see *NJLC*, October 28, 1777–October 8, 1778, 53–54; and *Votes and Proceedings*, October 28, 1777–October 8, 1778, 101.

[42]*JCC*, 10:322; "Representation of the Legislative Council and General Assembly of the State of New Jersey," Papers of the Continental Congress, item 68, 347, microfilm edition, Rutgers University Library (hereafter, PCC).

[43]*Acts*, October 28, 1777–October 8, 1778, 64–70.

[44]Ibid., 66.

[45]Ibid., 68–69.

[46]*JCC*, 10:200.

[47]The New Jersey fine provisions are in *Acts*, October 28, 1777–October 8, 1778, 67; for the situation elsewhere, see Higginbotham, *War of Independence*, 292–93.

[48]Inflation heated up in 1777, with Continental currencies depreciating to a three-to-one ratio with specie; the rate was one hundred-to-one by 1780, with one historian describing New Jersey's economy as in "total disarray" by 1779. See James H. Levitt, *New Jersey's Revolutionary Economy*. New Jersey's Revolutionary Experience, no. 9 (Trenton, N.J., 1975), 22–23. Greater detail on the state's wartime fiscal woes is in Richard P. McCormick, *Experiment in Independence: New Jersey in the Critical Period* (New Brunswick, N.J., 1950), Leonard Lundin, *The Cockpit of the Revolution: The War for Independence in New Jersey* (Princeton, N.J., 1940), and Edward A. Fuhlbruegge, "Abstract of New Jersey Finances during the Revolution," *Proceedings of the New Jersey Historical Society* 55 (1937):167–90. All testify to the dangerous state of inflation in the state by the late 1770s.

⁴⁹*Acts*, October 28, 1777–October 8, 1778, 66.

⁵⁰Lofgren, "Compulsory Military Service under the Constitution," 78.

⁵¹Prince and Ryan, *Livingston Papers*, 2:255–56.

⁵²*Pennsylvania Evening Post*, April 3, 1778.

⁵³Fitzpatrick, *Writings of Washington*, 11:296–97.

⁵⁴Prince and Ryan, *Livingston Papers*, 2:293. The British forgery was in fact a very good one; Livingston's letter to the commander-in-chief had a tone of doubt about what Congress had really done. He wrote that he "suspect[ed]" the resolution in the *Pennsylvania Evening Post* was a forgery, but then noted that, "Indeed if genuine," the public was going to be indignant.

⁵⁵Fitzpatrick, *Writings of Washington*, 11:296–97, 299, 301, 500.

⁵⁶Thomson's remarks are in the *Pennsylvania Packet*, May 6, 1778. Letters on the same subject by Congressional delegates are in Paul H. Smith, ed., *Letters of Delegates to Congress, 1774–1789*, 10 vols. (Washington, D.C., 1976–), 9:493, 508, 543, 568.

⁵⁷Mark Edward Lender, "The Social Structure of the New Jersey Brigade: The Continental Army as an American Standing Army," in Peter Karsten, ed., *The Military in America* (New York, 1980), 27–44.

⁵⁸"List of Substitutes . . . 1778 [from Middlesex County]," New Jersey Department of Defense MSS, no. 3620, DARM (hereafter, NJDOD).

⁵⁹See the various proceedings of the draft commissioners in May and June, and muster rolls of draftees or substitutes, for Morris, Essex, Cumberland, Cape May, Burlington, Gloucester, Hunterdon, Middlesex, and Salem counties in NJDOD MSS, nos. 1330, 3613, 3595, 3600, 3598, 3589, 3592, 3593, 3587, 3601, 3605, 3606, 3608, 3614, 3549, 3552, 3619–23. *JCC*, 11:853–54; Fitzpatrick, *Writings of Washington*, 12:42–43.

⁶⁰Militia Draft Class Rolls, [May–June] 1778, Ten Eyck Family Papers, box 1, Rutgers University Library; "A Bill of Sale of Peter Post for all his estate," November 24, 1783, ibid.

⁶¹George F. Scheer, ed., *Private Yankee Doodle: Being a Narrative of the Adventures, Dangers and Sufferings of a Revolutionary Soldier* (Boston, 1962), 61.

⁶²*Selections from the Correspondence of the Executive of New Jersey, from 1776 to 1786* (Newark, N.J., 1848), 116 (hereafter, *Correspondence of the Executive*).

⁶³Strength reports for 1778 are in Lesser, *Sinews of Independence*, 58–98. Yearly tabulations are in Lowrie and Clarke, *American State Papers: Military Affairs*, 1:14–19.

⁶⁴Elisha Boudinot to Robert Morris, March 6, 1779, Robert Morris Papers, Rutgers University Library.

⁶⁵*JCC*, 13:298; PCC, item 68, 451–52; *Votes and Proceedings*, April–June 1779, 125, 138, 141.

⁶⁶Gouverneur Morris to Robert Morris, April 16, 1778, Robert Morris Papers, box 4, Rutgers University Library; *Votes and Proceedings*, October 28, 1777–October 8, 1778, 118.

⁶⁷*JCC*, 11:514–15; 10:40–41, 67, 186.

⁶⁸*Votes and Proceedings*, April–June, 1779, n.p. [entry of May 19, 1779].

⁶⁹*Correspondence of the Executive*, 171–72.

⁷⁰*Votes and Proceedings*, April–June, 1779, 72.

⁷¹*JCC*, 14:157; PCC, item 147, 3:335; Fitzpatrick, *Writings of Washington*, 15:249–50; *NJLC*, October 1779–March 1780, 50.

⁷²*Correspondence of the Executive*, 207–9.

⁷³*JCC*, 16:123; 17:540; PCC, item 11, 65–66.

⁷⁴*JCC*, 21:1163–64; *Votes and Proceedings*, October–December 1782, 44.

[75] The trickle of 1779 recruits can be followed in Lesser, *Sinews of Independence*, 100, 104, 108, 112, 125, 140, 144. *Acts*, May–June, 1780, 105, 237–38; *JCC*, 16:150–51; *Correspondence of the Executive*, 242–43, 247.

[76] Lesser, *Sinews of Independence*, 156, 160, 164.

[77] *Acts*, May–June, 1780, 105–6; *Correspondence of the Executive*, 229–30.

[78] *Acts*, May–June, 1780, 105–6.

[79] The Essex County draft records for 1778 and 1780 are in NJDOD MSS, nos. 3595, 3596. New York *Royal Gazette*, August 26, 1780.

[80] *Correspondence of the Executive*, 251.

[81] For a convenient overview of war damage to the state, see Levitt, *New Jersey's Revolutionary Economy*.

[82] Adolphus, "Thoughts on the Situation of Affairs."

[83] On the relationship between democracy and conscription, see Richard A. Preston and Sydney F. Wise, *Men in Arms: A History of Warfare and Its Interrelationships with Western Society* (2d ed., rev.; New York, 1970), 181, 183–84, 192, 246, and Walter Millis, *Arms and Men: A Study of American Military History* (New York, 1956), chapter 1.

[84] Lofgren, "Compulsory Military Service under the Constitution," 79.

PROCEEDINGS OF THE
NEW JERSEY
HISTORICAL SOCIETY
VOLUME LXXIV, NUMBER 3, JULY 1956
WHOLE NUMBER 286

Suffrage Reform and the American Revolution in New Jersey

J. R. POLE

IN 1774 an elderly resident of New Jersey would have been able to recollect very little change in the laws that governed the suffrage of the Province. Yet the Revolutionary troubles were about to bring reforms that would place New Jersey well in advance of most of her sister states when the time came to draw up independent constitutions.

The foundations of manhood suffrage in New Jersey were laid in the political practices of the colonial era; and the reforms built upon these foundations were brought into being through the pressure of Revolutionary circumstances upon domestic politics. In New Jersey we thus have an opportunity to study the formulation of the earlier principles of American representative government without special reference to the ideals, or the instincts, of the frontier.

For nearly half a century the electoral process had been guided by an Act for the Better Regulation of Elections passed in 1725[1]; in this period the one constant factor governing property quali-

THE WRITER will be remembered for a 1953 PROCEEDINGS article on suffrage in New Jersey during the period 1790-1807. Having studied at the University of London, Oxford, and Princeton (where he was also an instructor), he has been in recent years lecturer in American History, University College London. At present he is in this country.

[1]Samuel Allinson, *Acts of New Jersey, 1702-1776* (Trenton, 1776), pp. 69-70.

fications for the suffrage was the requirement that voters be free-holders.[2] This restriction does not seem to have been very rigor-ously applied, for in the entire range of disputed elections, very few votes were challenged on grounds of inadequate property.[3] A movement away from democracy, dating from the settlements of 1644, has been noticed by one observer,[4] yet the franchise was liberal enough to permit non-freeholders to vote in the towns before the Revolution if they could fulfill the condition that they must be "inhabitants," a vague term which was declared in 1766 to mean "Freeholder, Tenant for years, or Householder and Res-ident in . . . Township or Precinct."[5] The right to vote at town meetings extended to householders throughout the Colony.[6] An early concession to Perth Amboy and Burlington, respectively the capitals of the Eastern and Western divisions of the Province, gave their householders the right to vote in provincial elections.[7] If high property qualifications maintained for admission to the Assembly were certainly a barrier against the populace,[8] the wide extent of this participation in local government exercised a pro-found influence on the course taken in framing the institutions of complete self-government when the time came.

A curious broadside, printed in March, 1772, in Salem County, tells us that candidates for office might have to take account of those who are frankly described as "lower class" people. The broadside is a spurious and satirical report of "the Weekly Meet-ing in G—N—H [Greenwich] to the Monthly Meeting in S—M [Salem]" of a political party; it purports to communicate "the wise schemes we have laid and the favourable reception they met with at the late election." These wise schemers relate that they

[2]R. P. McCormick, *The History of Voting in New Jersey, 1664-1911* (New Bruns-wick, 1953), pp. 60-61. Writs of summons to elections under George II and George III generally specified that electors were to be qualified by possession of a freehold and fifty pounds sterling in property. Misc. MSS. in Room 120, New Jersey State Library.

[3]B. H. Rich, "Election Machinery in New Jersey, 1702-1775," *Proceedings NJHS*, LXVII, 208.

[4]C. R. Erdman, *The New Jersey Constitution of 1776* (Princeton, 1929), p. 56, n. 81.

[5]Allinson, *Acts*, pp. 287-88; A. E. McKinley, *The Suffrage Franchise in the Thirteen American Colonies* (Phila., 1905), p. 257.

[6]Allinson *Acts*, pp. 287-88; McKinley, *Suffrage Franchise*, p. 257.

[7]*N.J. Archives*, 2nd Ser., II, 510. E. P. Tanner, *Province of New Jersey* (New York, 1907), p. 318.

[8]McCormick, *Voting in New Jersey*, p. 43; Allinson, *Acts*, pp. 306-07, for the same qualifications—a freehold and £500 personal estate, in 1768.

failed to get their friends into the Assembly on account of religious opposition, and so planned instead to divide their opponents by artifice.

The letter was in fact, of course, written by the enemies of the schemers, who are made to continue their report from the Greenwich meeting in the following terms:

We proposed our friend J—n S—d, who has been in trade for many years past, and has many of the people of the county in debt. He has made himself very popular here of late by joining a number of the lower class of people to oppose the Magistrates (which we call the court party) has likewise made a sham [?] purchase of some building lots at the bridge that the people would think he would be in their interest, in erecting the fairs there (which they have very much at heart) he being sensible an election would soon come on.[9]

The meaning of the broadside, from our point of view, can fortunately be discerned without the need to elucidate the obscurities of local politics. The lower class of people who had been joined by the prosperous trader-candidate were clearly voters, or he would not have taken the trouble to make himself popular with them; the fact that the report is really written by his opponents does not detract from the force of this argument.

Between the end of the French and Indian Wars and the outbreak of the Revolution, acute political and economic tension developed in East Jersey. In the period of currency restriction that followed the end of the wars, many mortgages were foreclosed; the struggle between landed proprietors and their tenants, between creditors with the law on their side and small holding, impoverished debtors, increasingly assumed the aspect of a class war, and in 1770 erupted into riots that caused Governor Franklin to call a special session of the Assembly.[10] The franchise may have been broader than it looked on paper, but it

[9]Broadside in Rutgers University Library, dated "The 25th of the 3d Month, 1772." Some of the references remain obscure. The greater part of the county residents are described as Presbyterians, the mortal enemies of those to whom the document is attributed; the writers, in all probability, therefore actually were Presbyterians. The paper claims that the artifice in the selection of candidates gained two Baptist congregations and the Dutch. There is a strong inference from this and from the fact that Salem County lies in the southwest, that the other major religious group, the Quakers, are those being attacked; that is, that the document was written by Presbyterians pretending to be Quakers. Non-religious factors might invalidate this suggestion.

[10]Leonard Lundin, *Cockpit of the Revolution: the War for Independence in New Jersey* (Princeton, 1940), pp. 64-65.

was still limited to freeholders except in the two capitals, and it was still nominally limited to freeholders with fifty pounds *sterling* in real and personal estate,[11] which (if strictly applied) would take no account of the proclamation money which had been current since the reign of Queen Anne.[12] It is not at all surprising that the Revolution should have brought early demands for suffrage extension.

Local government in New Jersey was run by local people. The freeholders, at their annual meetings, appointed from amongst themselves a cluster of officials responsible for such matters as care of the poor, the assessment and collection of taxes and the maintenance of the highways.[13] The system of local administration and the habit of local responsibility, were to be of profound importance when the time came to set up a new government; for it was the existence of this administrative system that made it possible for the Provincial Congress to take over the powers of government from the governor and General Assembly, with the co-operation and obedience of the local authorities and without any serious administrative dislocation.

The Continental Congress, by the eleventh article of its Association in September, 1774, recommended the establishment throughout the colonies of local committees of observation and correspondence.[14] The Congress itself was the product of a movement which had been in the making since early in the year; and in February, 1774, the General Assembly of the province of New Jersey had resolved to establish a standing committee to collect information about the measures of the British Parliament, and to maintain a permanent correspondence with the sister colonies.[15] In the summer of the same year, the freeholders and inhabitants

---

[11]An act of 1709 substituted "current money" for "sterling," and there was much subsequent variation (McCormick, *Voting in New Jersey*, p. 43 and pp. 60-61); but election writs seem to have followed the sterling formula. Misc. MSS., Room 120, New Jersey State Library.

[12]Curtis Nettels, *The Money Supply of the American Colonies before 1720* (Madison, 1934); W. M. Gouge, *Short History of Paper Money and Banking in the United States* (N.Y., 1835), p. 6.

[13]Votes of Elections, NJSL.

[14]*Minutes of the Provincial Congress and Council of Safety of the State of New Jersey, 1774-1776* (Trenton, 1879), p. 34 (to be cited as *Minutes P.C.C.S.*); *Journals of the American Congress, 1774 to 1788* (Washington, 1823), I, 25.

[15]*Minutes P.C.C.S.*, pp. 1-2.

of counties and townships began to place themselves in a position, not so much of defence, as of alertness and precaution. Meetings in both townships and counties expressed the determination of the freeholders to establish an association for the Province as a whole. Lower Freehold, in Monmouth County, held the first recorded township meeting, while Essex was the first county to declare itself.[16]

The representative character of this meeting and of the general movement was admitted by Governor Franklin in a letter to his home government. "Meetings of this nature," he wrote, "there are no means of preventing, when the chief parts of the inhabitants incline to attend them."[17] There seems to be no difficulty in accepting the view that the provincial gathering of July, 1774, to which this movement led, was at least as representative of the people of the Province as were the General Assemblies.[18] The article of the Congressional Association recommending the appointment of a committee "in every County, City and Town," said specifically that this should be done "by those qualified to vote for Representatives in the Legislature . . ."[19]

These township and county committees formed the basis of the government by Provincial Congress that developed in the next year. To understand the character of that government we must ask by whom the local committees were elected.

The Essex meeting of which Governor Franklin spoke "was occasioned by an advertisement, requesting the attendance of the inhabitants . . . and published in one of the New York papers, signed by two gentlemen of the law, who reside in that county." The call was not directed only to qualified electors, but to "All the inhabitants of the County of Essex, in New Jersey, friends to the Constitution, the liberties and properties of America." It was hoped, from the importance of the subject, that the

[16]*Minutes P.C.C.S.*, pp. 4-8. The Essex meeting, held on June 11th, declared its approval of a congress of deputies to form a general plan of union. It was ready to send a committee to meet committees of other counties to elect persons to represent the Province. William Livingston and Elias Boudinot, among others, were put on the committee.

[17]Franklin to Dartmouth, June 18th, 1774, *Minutes P.C.C.S.*, pp. 8-9.

[18]Erdman, *Constitution of 1776*, makes this point in answer to the statement of Charles and Mary Beard that the meetings were unrepresentative of the counties, p. 10, n. 50. He gives the date of the letter as June 28th.

[19]*Minutes P.C.C.S.*, pp. 34-35.

meeting would be general. The call was signed by order of a meeting of a number of the freeholders of the county of Essex.[20] Most of the reports refer to meetings of the freeholders and inhabitants. A call issued in Burlington County in January, 1775, was addressed "To the Freeholders, Electors for the County of Burlington," and those qualified to vote for members of the Assembly are mentioned in the text; the hope was again expressed that the importance of the cause would induce people in general to give their attendance.[21] Somerset County's freeholders chose a new committee of correspondence in July, 1775, on the expiration of the term of the old one.[22]

It is clear that these calls to action primarily concerned the freeholders and voters for the Assembly; but it should be remembered that inhabitants, meaning householders, tenants or merely "residents," were already voting on township matters in their own neighborhoods, and it seems highly probable that the local meetings, some of which from the beginning invited the attendance of inhabitants or people in general, came to admit of wider participation in the course of a year of increasing tension and need to rally the support of all patriotic Americans.

These committees formed the basis of both the authority and the membership of the Provincial Congress. Meeting in May, 1775, the New Jersey Congress soon made the first moves towards assuming the powers of government. To meet the military emergency a militia had to be raised, and money had to be procured from the counties for defence. Each township or corporation was recommended to form one or more companies; officers up to the rank of captain were to be elected by their companies, while company officers would appoint non-commissioned officers. Regimental officers would be appointed in meetings of company officers.[23]

[20]*Minutes P.C.C.S.*, p. 6. The call is printed in the *Minutes* without reference to its original mode of publication, but is presumably the same one as that mentioned by Franklin. The two gentlemen of the law, John De Hart and Isaac Ogden, were both subsequently elected to the county committee. It is notable that these preliminary steps did not imply revolutionary intentions: De Hart later resigned from the Continental Congress, to which he was a New Jersey delegate, apparently out of dislike for its radical course. D. L. Kemmerer, *Path to Freedom: the Struggle for Self-Government in Colonial New Jersey, 1703-1776* (Princeton, 1940), p. 336; *NJA*, 1st Ser., X, 680.

[21]*NJA*, 1st Ser., XXXI, 24-25.

[22]*Minutes P.C.C.S.*, pp. 162-63.

[23]*Minutes P.C.C.S.*, pp. 179-83.

Two points are notable in these proceedings. One is the indispensable co-operation of the township committees, whose task it was to acquaint themselves with the number of male inhabitants between the ages of sixteen and fifty and to form them into companies of eighty each. These committees were working for a government of their own, not for an alien authority, and as this government effectively superseded the royal authority it is important never to lose sight of its co-operative machinery and its representative, if limited, basis. The other characteristic of these events, a product of the same state of affairs, is the provision for the election of officers. This method was not adopted in European countries until after the French Revolution, when it is found, for example, in the Prussian Landwehr. It is characteristic of militia or citizen armies and is profoundly antipathetic to the professional soldier's cast of mind.

Governor Franklin failed in a series of skilful attempts to set the Assembly against the Congress, whose members included about two-fifths of the assemblymen. The Congress, adjourning on June 3rd, re-convened on August 5th, and from that time became the effective government of the province.[24]

The Assembly was losing control. Meanwhile the Provincial Congress developed its own administration, and in October it ordered the issue of bills of credit and the raising of ten thousand pounds for the year. The counties were to be taxed by quota.[25]

The Congress exercised the parliamentary function of determining the credentials of its members and enquiring into disputed elections. The *Minutes,* our only source for the proceedings of the Congress, unfortunately do not record the precise nature of the complaints in the batch of petitions challenging the results of elections held under the second Congress, between October, 1775, and June, 1776. These complaints challenged not

[24] Erdman, *Constitution of 1776,* gives a clear narrative of these events, pp. 1-24.
[25] *Minutes P.C.C.S.,* p. 252. The quotas of taxation indicate the relative wealth of the counties. Here is the table employed:

	£	s.	d.		£	s.	d.
Bergen	664	8	0	Hunterdon	1363	16	8
Essex	742	18	0	Cape May	166	18	0
Middlesex	872	6	8	Burlington	1071	13	4
Somerset	904	2	0	Gloucester	763	2	8
Monmouth	1069	2	8	Salem	679	12	0
Morris	723	8	0	Cumberland	385	6	8
Sussex	593	5	4				

only elections to the Congress but also to local committees—which reminds us of the very great importance of the committees in the life of the Province. In none of the four hearings conducted before the Congress rose in June, was the verdict overturned.[26]

The need for continuity in government was recognized. A Council of Safety had been appointed to be ready to handle urgent matters during recesses of the Congress,[27] and now the Congress determined that during the continuance of the unhappy disputes between Great Britain and America, there should be a new choice of deputies every year, in September. On the same day each year the inhabitants "qualified to vote" were to elect their committees of observation and correspondence, with full powers to direct the necessary business of the county, and to execute the resolutions and orders of the Continental and Provincial Congresses.[28]

The Congress which sat during the summer of 1775 terminated its proceedings with resolutions passed on August 12th, 1775, calling for elections to a new Congress. These resolutions dealt bluntly with the crisis. The horrors of civil war were likely and the tax burden would increase.

The inhabitants [of this Colony] should have frequent opportunities of renewing their choice and approbation of the Representatives in Provincial Congress—It is therefore resolved, that the inhabitants in each County qualified to vote for Representatives in General Assembly, do meet together at the places hereinafter mentioned, on Thursday the twenty-first day of September next, and then and there by plurality of voices, elect and appoint any number not exceeding five substantial freeholders as Deputies, with full power to represent such County in Provincial Congress to be held at Trenton . . . on . . . the third day of October next.

There followed a list of the places at which elections were to be held—in every case save that of Hunterdon, in the county courthouse. The house of John Ringo, presumably a tavern, would provide for the Hunterdon poll.

The inhabitants thus authorized to elect deputies to the Congress were identified with those qualified to elect county and township committees. Unfortunately we do not possess the poll

[26]*Minutes P.C.C.S.*, pp. 205-07, 211-14, 391, 452, 453, 463.
[27]On August 17th, 1775, with eleven members. *Minutes P.C.C.S.*, pp. 193-94.
[28]*Minutes P.C.C.S.*, pp. 186-87.

lists or other records that might tell us how many people availed themselves of the suffrage; but the local committees of the summer of 1774, like the provincial meeting of July, 1774,[29] had been elected in various ways—by regular procedure of the freeholders, or at town meetings. The resolutions of August 12th, for new elections, seem to have taken notice of the laxity of former methods; and it is distinctly stated that the electors of the local committees are to be those "qualified as aforesaid"—qualified, that is, to elect deputies to the Provincial Congress. Up till now, the "inhabitants," already entitled to vote in township elections, had helped to elect members of the local committees; but the voters for the Provincial Congress had been defined as those qualified to vote for the Assembly. This new provision, if it had any effect, would have tended to restrict the suffrage by excluding township voters from the franchise for township or county committees.

While it is doubtful whether the distinction was more than verbal tidiness, the possibility remains that it was enforced more literally, and produced more dismay, in some places than in others. An effective act of general suffrage restriction, however, would undoubtedly have produced floods of protest, and the petitions for suffrage reform reaching the Congress only two months later contained no reference to such a restriction, which would, indeed, have been most extraordinary tactics at this juncture of the crisis.

Six months later there is positive evidence, on the other hand, that one county, Middlesex, contained voters among the poor, who had exercised their suffrage in the elections for the Provincial Congress then sitting.

A letter from the constituents of the "Southward [i.e., South Ward] of New Brunswick" informed the Middlesex and other delegates that they had been chosen by the signers, and proferred advice in favor of taxation in the interests of the debtors. The writers requested that money at interest being clear estate be taxed, and proposed a scale that would

Prove a Great Easement to the Lower Class of men on whom the Burthen will fall the heaviest; many of whom to keep their familyes in Imploy has borrowed money to buy Lands and now pays tax for their Lands and In-

[29]And according to Erdman, *Constitution of 1776*, pp. 14-15, like the Provincial Congress of 1775 also, though he cites no *new* evidence for that Congress and merely refers back to the evidence on 1774.

terest for the Money while the man of Estate Goes free and whereas there is Large Sumes of money Due from the Inhabitants of this province to Gentlemen in New York Colony and pensylvania we think it within the Verge of your power to order the same Deduction as if the Credditor Lived in this province.[30]

The signers of the letter, having bought lands, were strictly landowners, but they were owners heavily encumbered by debt and would, in point of law, have failed to meet the provision of the constitution adopted later that year that voters must be worth fifty pounds clear estate, fifty pounds free of debt. They freely identified themselves with "the lower orders," and resented the privileges of the creditor class. By telling the delegates that they had chosen them, the signers identified themselves as voters to whom the delegates were responsible. The objection that they might have been non-voters posing as voters can be dismissed, for the fifty-nine signatures must have included a number that were known to the local delegates.

The mere failure of the Congress to take a more forthright stand in favor of suffrage extension in its election resolutions caused sharp disappointment and seems in one instance to have been regarded as a positive reactionary step. The Freemen of Salem County, in a remonstrance that seems to have been received on February 9th,[31] declared that they had taken up arms

at an early stage of the present glorious struggle, devoting both our time and our property to the Acquirement of Military Knowledge when called on to contribute both by pecuniary and personal service. Convinced of the Justice and importance of the Cause we cheerfully obeyed the summons— But how great the disappointment when we found that whilst we were spending our time and Money with a view to repelling the invaders of our Liberties we were deprived of the privileges we contended for by an Act of the late provincial Congress consisting of the very men we had intrusted as the Guardians of our Rights—Born to the same privileges with the rest of mankind we have a right to the free Exercise of them until divested thereof by some Act of our own . . . Was the sole design of Government either the security of Land, or Money, the possession of either or both these would be the only qualification for its members— but we apprehend the benign intentions of a well regulated Government extend to the security of much more valuable possessions—The Right and privileges of Freemen for the defence of which every kind of property and even Life itself have been Liberally expended.

[30]Provincial Congress papers, no. 78, February 9, 1776. NJHS.
[31]*Minutes P.C.C.S.*, p. 358.

The present measures were "an usurpation." The remonstrance closed with a bitter attack on the conduct of war without the moral sanction derived from defending the rights of the people.[32]

Unfortunately the remonstrants, in their indignation, omitted to give either the date of the petition or the precise cause of their grievance. Certain aspects of this document remain difficult to elucidate. Two petitions from Salem County are recorded in the *Minutes* as having been received by the Congress, in February and in August, 1776; the only date compatible with the reference to "the late Provincial Congress" would be February 9th. But what act of that Congress had deprived freemen of the rights they contended for? A possibility has been noticed that the election resolutions of August, 1775,[33] may have had a limiting effect on the suffrage, but the numerous petitions for suffrage reform that were soon to reach the Congress from East Jersey made no reference to such a restriction, as they would surely have done if it had been a matter of recent experience. The objection in these resolutions was, not so much that they denied existing privileges, but that in setting the same suffrage qualifications as had prevailed for Assembly elections, and in requiring that members elected must be "substantial freeholders," the Congress had failed to break decisively with the colonial past. In this latter point, however, the absence from the August resolutions of any definite designation of the *amount* of property to be possessed by freeholders standing for election, did represent a breach in traditional restrictions, and one that, significantly enough, the Provincial Congress repaired when a new constitution was framed in 1776.[34] The delay of six months between the action of the previous Provincial Congress and the receipt of this particularly vigorous protest is difficult to understand; the remonstrants presumably sent up their objections only when they heard that the

[32]Misc. MSS., Box 16, Room 120, NJSL.

[33]See pp. 180-81 below; *Minutes*, pp. 185-87.

[34]Below, p. 193. McCormick, *Voting in New Jersey*, pp. 43-45, 68.

[35]Dr. McCormick quotes from this document on p. 67 as evidence of the demand for suffrage reform. In note 12, p. 67, he gives the date in round brackets as Feb., 1776, but the MS. itself is undated. He cites the *Minutes*, p. 358 (Feb. 9th). He quotes the statement: "We cannot conceive the wise Author of our Existence ever designed that a certain quantity of Earth on which we tread shou'd be annexed to Man to compleat his dignity and fit him for society," a passage which strengthens the case for regarding the whole piece as primarily a protest against the land tenure qualification, but does not demonstrate that reform of the suffrage qualifications was its only purpose.

discussion of the subject was about to reach a critical stage. Though the full explanation may lie buried in the local politics of Salem County, some interferences can safely be drawn.[35] The remonstrants were voters—they had entrusted the members of the Congress as the guardians of their rights. They were freemen and had given money to the cause; they objected to being excluded from the government—meaning, in contemporary terms, the whole political system, not necessarily the administration alone—for want of the ownership of land or money, bearing in mind that the duties of government extended to the protection of the rights and privileges of freemen. The remonstrance, then, is an attack on property qualifications for participation in the government—for the suffrage franchise, but also, quite possibly, for membership of the Congress. The prime target of the attack was the requirement of land tenure as a qualification. The petitioners refrained from calling themselves "freeholders," as they would surely have done if they had been able to claim that title;[36] they were "Freemen" of their county. In the question of the landed property qualification, it was precisely the distinction between the freemen and the freeholders that was at issue.

The Congress that received these petitions had been elected, in September, 1775, under suffrage rules that gave dissatisfaction not only among the landless but among taxpayers. Six days before the opening date of the new Congress, a letter in the *New York Journal,* addressed to the people of New Jersey, stated the case for a reform that would bring American domestic practice into line with American propaganda. The letter bears so directly on the subject as to deserve full quotation.

To the Public. No. iii.

Dear Countrymen: In a day of public calamity like this, arising from oppression, every benevolent mind ought to be engaged for the defence of the rights of mankind, and in particular should endeavour to remove all cause of oppression, complaint and disunion among ourselves. And to stop, as much as possible, the mouths of our adversaries (who will omit the use of no plausible argument against the justice of our cause and the probability of its success,) such is the design of this letter. The Hon. Continental Congress, and the late Provincial Congress of the Province [i.e.,

36Many petitions came from "Freeholders" or "Freeholders and others"; the AM papers, NJSL, and the *Minutes,* are thick with examples.

the one that dissolved in August, 1775] have adopted the old mode of electing Representatives, who have power to tax those Colonies from whom they are chosen. By this mode, many true friends of their country, who are obliged to pay taxes, are excluded from the privilege of a vote in the choice of those by whom they are taxed, or even called out to sacrifice their lives. This is a real grievance; yet one that may easily be redressed, for many of the members of the Present Provincial Congress begin to give serious attention to the complaints of the people on this account, and all our Congresses know that one part of his Majesty's subjects have no right to tax another part of their fellow-subjects without their consent, given by themselves or their representatives. Nothing is therefore necessary in order to obtain a redress but a number of petitions from several towns and counties for that purpose. They will undoubtedly resolve that no-one shall be taxed, who is excluded from a vote in their elections, and will also resolve who shall for the future be esteemed proper electors. And by such resolve our enemies will be cut off from one of their most plausible arguments against us.

I am, My Countrymen,
Yours,

Essex

Morris County, New-Jersey, Sept. 26, 1775.[37]

This letter, it will be noticed, does nothing to suggest that the election resolutions of August, 1775, might have curtailed the suffrage, but it does express disappointment that the Congress should have adopted "the old mode of electing Representatives," the mode in use under the royal government. There is a clear call to make American practice conform with public American doctrine. Neither this letter nor the subsequent petitions throw direct light on the problems of the Salem remonstrance, though they perhaps add some weight to the suggestion that the bitter language of that protest, like the more persuasive tone of the "Essex" letter, is directed against the adoption of the "old mode" of representation, when such an opportunity existed for reform.

Nearly twenty petitions answered the call of "Essex," probably outnumbering petitions demanding any other one piece of legislation. Most of them demanded the vote for householders, or for taxpayers, while five mentioned either householding or tax-paying as alternative qualifications. Two requested the use of the ballot in elections; petitions from Essex County, and one from

[37]NJA, 1st Ser., XXXI, 200. From the *New York Journal*, Sept. 28, 1775.

Morris, linked a demand for the taxation of money put out at interest with the extension of the suffrage to taxpayers. There was conflict in Somerset, where the county committee, with John Witherspoon as its chairman, favored giving the vote to taxpayers and householders, while two counter-petitions opposed giving the vote to any others than freeholders; a petition from Monmouth objected to a decision at the present session. No county of West Jersey was represented in this movement; the great majority came from the wealthy county of Hunterdon, from populous Essex and from Sussex, all eastern.[38]

The pressure for suffrage reform that came from East Jersey, which had experienced so much serious social unrest in recent years, was supported in the Congress on October 25th by the delegates of Salem (West Jersey), who moved for a dissolution at the end of the current session and a new election upon more extensive principles. The question was postponed to the next sitting by a vote of seven to six, Essex for some reason voting for the delay.[39] When the motion came up for consideration again, on February 16th, 1776, it was given a wording that later produced unintended results. The question was put, "Whether every person of full age, who hath immediately preceding the elections, resided one whole year in any County of this Colony, and is worth at least fifty pounds in real and personal estate, shall be permitted to vote in the County wherein he resides, for Representatives in Provincial Congress, or not?"[40] This suffrage basis, when adopted in the new constitution, in July, provided a loophole which, from about 1790 until 1807, enabled women and Negroes to vote, and assumed an unexpected place in local political controversy.[41]

The new election ordinance, passed after four days of debate and amendment, extended the suffrage to all persons of full age, satisfying the year's residence requirement, and worth fifty pounds

[38]Minutes P.C.C.S., pp. 202, 207, 220-21, 228, 231, 340, 346, 355, 365, 372. V. Lansing Collins, President Witherspoon (Princeton, 1924), p. 182.

[39]Minutes P.C.C.S., p. 231.

[40]Minutes P.C.C.S., pp. 373-74.

[41]R. E. Turner, "Women's Suffrage in New Jersey, 1790-1807" (Smith College Studies in History, Vol. 1, No. 4, 1916), pp. 165-87; Marion J. Wright, "Negro Suffrage in New Jersey," Journal of Negro History, April, 1948, pp. 168-224; J. R. Pole, "Suffrage in New Jersey 1790-1807," Proc. NJHS, Jan., 1953, pp. 60-61.

proclamation money in personal estate, having signed the Association.[42]

This ordinance, which became in effect the first independent election law of New Jersey, was the most important act of the Provincial Congress preceding the new constitution. In dropping the freehold tenure clause, the Congress withdrew the lynch-pin from the structure of property qualifications. The delay from October to February, the four days of debate, and the opposition of four counties in the final vote,[43] all show that the delegates had a sense of the gravity of their action.

It is sad that we have no record of the debate on this intensely interesting problem.[44] Yet the political circumstances of the Congress show compelling reasons for its decision. These reasons will appear from a consideration of the nature of the Congress' authority in the uncertain state of the Province. Both the traditional social leadership, and the official colonial government, were deeply divided by the conflict with the Crown. Of the ten active members of the governor's Council, four pursued a doubtful neutrality while three supported the governor; the Assembly was no less conservative, perhaps more so. At the end of November, 1775, when it was proposed in the Assembly that the governor be asked for a dissolution, the vote was twelve—twelve, with the speaker, Cortland Skinner, a Tory, giving his casting vote in the negative because he knew that a new election would produce a more radical Assembly.[45] The Assembly, in the same month, resolved, in reply to a petition, "That reports of Independency, in the apprehension of this House, are groundless." The delegates to the Continental Congress were urged to use their utmost endeavors for a redress of American grievances, and for restoring the union between the colonies and Great Britain upon constitutional principles; but they were directed to reject utterly any propositions

[42]*Minutes P.C.C.S.*, pp. 407-10.

[43]The opposition consisted of Bergen, soon to reveal itself as infested with Toryism, Somerset, which has been seen to be divided, Monmouth, which sent up a petition for delay, and Cape May, traditionally conservative. See pp. 188 below, 186 above; McCormick, *Voting in New Jersey*, p. 68.

[44]Personal papers of the members seem too fragmentary to be of any help. The William Paterson papers in the Rutgers University Library and the AM papers in NJSL give no help. There is no official record.

[45]Kemmerer, *Path to Freedom*, p. 337, n. 39.

"that may separate this Colony from the Mother Country, or change the form of Government thereof."[46] Meanwhile the fears of some of the wealthier people about the consequences of social convulsion were openly expressed by the Council, in seeking to persuade Governor Franklin of the sincerity of its assurances to him. The members described themselves as "Persons who have too much at stake not to dread the consequences of a total subversion of government, order, and authority, who, while they lament the public disorders of the present times, are anxiously studious to lessen their effects on the inhabitants of this province . . ."[47] These Tory sympathies soon became still more explicit. The Province was beset with dissension, and numbers went over to the enemy early in the war.[48] Some of the members of the wealthy East Jersey Board of Proprietors went into retreat in New York, thus easing the immediate grievances of the debtors[49] and at the same time creating a breach in the political leadership of the community.

The principal Whigs in the meantime retained the leadership in their own communities by placing themselves at the head of the opposition to parliamentary measures.[50] Experience teaches us that even seemingly urgent reforms may be delayed rather than hastened in war-time until the emergency is over; but the members of the Provincial Congress, pressed for suffrage extension by the lower ranks, were in no position to bargain with the mass of their own supporters. The reasons for the reform of the suffrage, whose justice might not alone have been enough, were rendered more cogent by the pressure of events.

The Provincial Congress had come into existence through the action of the county and township freeholders, but not only of the freeholders but also resident householders and tenants for years, who, in the case of town-dwellers, were all enfranchised under the title of inhabitants. The Congress had no administra-

---

[46]*Minutes P.C.C.S.*, pp. 292-93, 300.

[47]*NJA*, 1st Ser., XXXI, 227.

[48]Minutes of the Governor's Privy Council (MSS), NJSL, Vol. I, p. 7, reports in Aug. 1777, that Bergen County is almost wholly disaffected and has refused to do any military duty for above a year. "Numbers have gone over to the enemy, and now serve in what they call the New Levies, or New Jersey Volunteers . . . "

[49]Lundin, *Cockpit of the Revolution*, p. 257.

[50]*Ibid.*, p. 92.

tive machinery of its own, no military force other than the militia raised by its own orders, and no funds other than its own assessments.

The coercive power of government may exact a temporary obedience, but no government can long survive, especially in times of divided loyalty, without the moral leadership which makes its agents willing to work for it and the community ready to accept its rule. Without a firm foundation of popular support in the counties and townships that elected the Congress, supplied the taxes and raised the militia, the government would have neither coercive power nor moral leadership. The extension of the suffrage to non-freeholders in New Jersey arose from the political logic of the revolutionary crisis.

The suffrage provisions of the Ordinance of February, 1776, were in force at the time of the election of the next Provincial Congress, and were substantially adopted by that Congress as part of the constitution of the independent state.[51]

There is no exact way of determining what proportion of the population was enfranchised by the new suffrage qualifications, but a good deal can be inferred.[52] Statistics of population are scanty, while polls, with rare exceptions, are not recorded. The vital step of removing the freehold tenure clause, however, makes the value of fifty pounds proclamation money the central problem.[53]

---

[51]*Minutes P.C.C.S.*, pp. 552-58.

[52]The effects of the removal of the qualification of freehold tenure are not a matter of agreement among scholars. Lundin, *Cockpit*, p. 258, considers that "The Constitution of 1776 made no drastic alteration in the franchise." Erdman (*Constitution of 1776*, p. 56), feeling that the undemocratic qualifications require a note of explanation, says: "It was a common requirement of the early State constitutions that the voter should show some evidence that he possessed a financial interest in the community . . . The new constitution was thus no more democratic than the government of the Royal Province." E. A. Fuhlbruegge, in a discussion of New Jersey finances, states that the agitation for the right to vote for all who paid taxes failed, though the constitution of 1776 popularized the suffrage slightly. ("New Jersey Finances during the American Revolution," *Proc. NJHS*, July, 1937, p. 175.) R. P. McCormick, in still more recent studies, puts the matter very differently: "The practical effect of the change was unquestionably a great increase in the number of eligible voters." (*Experiment in Independence: New Jersey in the Critical Period, 1781-1789* [New Brunswick, 1951], pp. 80-81; and similarly in *Voting in New Jersey*, pp. 70-71.)

[53]L. Q. C. Elmer, *The Constitution and Government of . . . New Jersey* (Newark, 1872), a reliable source, states (p. 25) in this connection that fifty pounds proclamation were worth $133 when the suffrage qualifications were changed. This is confirmed by

The greater part of New Jersey's approximately 150,000 inhabitants[54] made their living in connection with the land. There were iron foundries owned by wealthy masters in the northwest, merchants in towns in the eastern division, especially Perth Amboy, and the variety of occupations to be expected in any town or village community. But abstracts of wills show that the word "yeoman" was the most popular description of the occupation, and status, of those who died testate.

Yeomen differed widely in their possessions; of those claiming this title, a few evidently worked some diminutive allotment and were able to leave an estate which barely reached the voting qualification; and the slightly more prosperous-sounding name "farmer" does not always seem to stand for wealth. Inventories show a substantial proportion of estates reckoned between fifty pounds and two hundred pounds. The study of wills is limited to those who died testate. It was not common for an inventory of estate to register more than three or four hundred pounds. Though the number of those described as artisans is much smaller than of yeomen or farmers, a few of them ranked with the average yeoman in modest wealth. The village blacksmith, a carpenter, a weaver or a potter, of whom there would in any case be a smaller proportion in a community overwhelmingly devoted to agriculture, would have voted beside the farmers with a "stake in society" under the ordinance of February.[55]

The events of the war years and the early post-war period have great relevance to the question of the extent of the suffrage established in 1776. Currency depreciation was not an instrument advocated by promoters of democratic reform, yet it was startlingly

the fact that, in 1789, after the wartime inflation had subsided, one dollar was worth seven shillings and six pence in New Jersey, a value which corresponds precisely with that originally laid down for proclamation money in 1703. The steadiness of the currency outside periods of wartime inflation will be noticed. William M. Gouge, *Short History of Paper Money in the U.S.* (New York, 1835), gives the 1703 values, p. 6; Hamilton's *Report on the Public Credit*, appendix, gives those for 1789. Dr. Paul Trescott, of Princeton University Department of Economics, introduced me to this useful information.

54In 1784, the population was estimated, for purposes of taxation, at 138,934, plus 10,508 colored people. *New Jersey Guardian*, Dec. 6, 1784. See also, Greene and Harrington, *American Population Before the Federal Census of 1790* (N.Y., 1932), p. 113.

55*NJA*, 1st Ser., XXXIV (Abstracts of Wills), 339, 403, 431, 452, 589. It should be noted, in the interest of truth, that Thomas Pool, potter of New Brunswick, alluded to above, had died in 1775.

effective. It was well known and soon to be demonstrated again in the states that inflation could help debtors to pay their debts, but it is doubtful whether anyone realized that it might help citizens to cast their votes.

The history of the inflation during the Revolutionary War is familiar.[56] The effect was practically to annihilate the remaining property qualifications for the suffrage. This sweeping development should be carefully distinguished from the removal of the freehold tenure qualification in 1776. The inflation did not set in immediately, and in due course it subsided, so that it would be a mistake to lump the constitutional reform and the currency depreciation together; the one was the result of legislative debate, the other of economic forces far beyond legislative control. But it was precisely the removal of freehold tenure that made possible this political effect of the inflation.

Yet when the inflation had subsided to the point at which fifty pounds had regained its former value, the suffrage did not again become a political issue. There was no demand for the abolition of the remaining qualification. Neither in the legislative journals nor in the petitions preserved,[57] is there any indication of pressure on this subject. It is difficult to believe that any coherent political or economic group, left without the franchise in 1776, enfranchised by the inflation, and deprived again by the deflation, would have acquiesced in such a deprivation without a murmur of protest. Moreover, the legislature could have raised the property qualification had it so chosen; neither Provincial Congress nor state legislature felt itself restrained by the constitution in any matter not specifically excluded from future altera-

[56]See especially, A. Bezanson, *Prices and Inflation During the American Revolution* (Phila., 1951). The progress of inflation in New Jersey is well indicated in official records of salaries. Under the election law of June, 1777, the county clerk was ordered to be paid twelve shillings for his services at elections, and was liable to a fine of five pounds for neglect (*Laws*, 1 Sess., 2 Sit., pp. 54-61). By the law of December, 1779, under which these figures were brought up to date, a clerk was to receive six pounds—120 shillings—for election day duty, and could be fined thirty pounds for neglect (*Laws*, 4 sess., 1 Sit., pp. 34-40). Salary warrants tell the same story. In June, 1778, the governor's salary for half a year was £500; a year later it was £1,000 for half a year; by March, 1780, a salary warrant for four months authorized payment of £2,666. 13s. 4d. Justices and state officers received comparable increments. (Minutes Gov.P.C., Vol. 1, pp. 36, 59-60, 68-69, 74-75.) The point needs no laboring.
[57]AM files, NJSL.

tion.[58] Yet no such action was taken with regard to the property qualification. The legislature made no attempt to maintain a consistent exclusion of those without property. The fifty-pound qualification itself was an institution carried over from colonial days, merely a vestige of the traditional safeguard of propertied interests. The absence of agitation on the suffrage issue shows that the step taken in 1776 was decisive, and was never in practice reversed, leaving no pressure for reaction on the conservative side and no body of discontent among the reformers.

The records of elections from about the mid-1790's make it possible to assemble some statistics which go far to explain the decline of the suffrage question as a political issue. A very high proportion of the population of adult white men are found to be availing themselves of the suffrage just as soon as the polling places themselves became reasonably accessible.[59] In the interval since the war, not one measure had been enacted to reduce the property qualification, and it is only possible to infer that a nearly universal right of suffrage was no longer in dispute. The law of 1807 that formally established taxpayer suffrage merely confirmed existing practices.[60]

The constitution of 1776 was not intended to establish universal suffrage, and undoubtedly left a number of people outside the qualifications. The unemployed, the casual laborer, artistans' assistants, and the floating migratory population would still be excluded, and, in another category, younger sons living at home,[61] and younger men in general who, though making their way, might not yet have more than a daily subsistence. From the point of view of the structure of society, and of its reflection in political life, however, the most striking consequence of the constitution of 1776 is that it left no distinct social or economic group, and

[58]The Provincial Congress did in fact alter the qualifications after the constitution, with its suffrage clauses, had been adopted, when by an ordinance of July, 1776, the oath of allegiance was added for both voters and legislators. (*Minutes P.C.C.S.*, p. 560.) The legislature, in the election act of 1777, changed "Proclamation money" to lawful money," liberalizing the qualifications by including wealth in Continental money. (McCormick, *Voting in New Jersey*, p. 72, and n. 25.)

[59]McCormick, *Voting in New Jersey*, Ch. IV. Professor McCormick has found nearly seventy per cent adult white males voting in Essex in 1785 (p. 84). Pole, "Suffrage in New Jersey, 1790-1807," *loc. cit.*, pp. 60-61. Dr. McCormick demonstrates the importance of the township system in rendering the polls accessible, *Voting in New Jersey*, pp. 91-96.

[60]*Laws*, 32 Sess., 1 Sit., pp. 14-15; Pole, "Suffrage in New Jersey," *loc. cit.*, pp. 59-60.

[61]Pointed out to me by Professor R. P. McCormick.

no regional group, in a position of inferiority in the political system, in so far as power within the system was in the hands of the voters in local or state elections.

The same cannot be said of power exercised through membership of the state legislature. In this sphere a high scale of property qualifications was retained.[62]

John Rutherfurd, later United States Senator from New Jersey, observed in 1786 that most of the land in the state was divided into farms of from fifty to four hundred acres;[63] and Professor McCormick has estimated that in this period a farmer owning two hundred acres could qualify to sit in the Assembly.[64] But despite these restrictions, the question seldom arose, and never seems to have been the occasion of a political campaign or controversy. In September, 1777, one Edward Fleming, having been elected to represent Essex County in the Assembly, declared before taking his oath that he had not been a freeholder in the county for one whole year past. It was resolved that he could not be admitted to his seat.[65] An act of 1790 dropped the requirement that members of the Assembly must take an oath that they were freeholders, but it apparently continued to be administered until 1807.[66] In that year the two members elected from Sussex explained that, although of several years' residence, and now freeholders, they had not been freeholders for the whole year last past, "as seemed to be required by one of the oaths to be taken." A committee reported that the constitution did not require the oath, and that they have been able to discover no law enforcing it. It would be expedient to dispense with it, especially so far as it affected the gentlemen from Sussex. After a debate the clause referring specifically to the gentlemen from Sussex was dropped. The amended report was then carried by twenty-nine votes to six, Republicans and Federalists both voting in favor.[67]

[62]To be eligible for a seat on the Council under the new constitution, a candidate had to be an inhabitant and freeholder of his county of at least one year's standing, and to be worth one thousand pounds proclamation money, real and personal estate, within the county. For an assemblyman, a candidate must have been an inhabitant and a freeholder in the county for a year and be worth five hundred pounds real and personal. *Minutes P.C.C.S.*, pp. 552-58.

[63]John Rutherfurd, "Notes on the State of New Jersey" (1786), *Proceedings NJHS*, 2 Ser., I (1867-69), 79-89.

[64]McCormick, *Experiment in Independence*, p. 74.

[65]Assembly *Votes and Proceedings*, Sept. 15, 1777.

[66]McCormick, *Voting in New Jersey*, p. 96.

[67]*Votes and Proceedings*, 1807, pp. 6, 10-12.

The rule was thus relaxed; and the issue was finally disposed of by the constitutional convention of 1844, at which the Chief Justice asked when enquiry as to his qualifications had ever been made of a candidate.[68] The higher qualification for membership of the legislature was then abolished;[69] but the Chief Justice's rhetorical question does not mean that seats in Assembly and Council had been unrestricted as to personal property, for unqualified persons would probably not have sought election.[70]

The Republicans, who gained a majority in the legislature in 1801,[71] and ruled again from 1803 to 1812,[72] never moved to reduce the property qualifications for membership of the legislative bodies in the earlier period. It was not merely that their interest in retaining their privilege of membership as individuals was more than a match for their zeal for reform; they shared with their Federalist rivals the fundamental notion that government should remain primarily the concern of the gentry.[73]

Nevertheless, it is clear that the issue was never prominent; the campaigning of the Jeffersonian and Jacksonian periods alike fails to reveal any earnest demand for reform on this head. The absence of demand for suffrage reform, on the other hand, is explained when we realize that an almost universal white manhood suffrage had been exercised many years, perhaps fifty years, before the convention of 1844 gave it the stamp of constitutional authority. Neither Jacksonian democracy nor western pressure brought this suffrage into being. The Provincial Congress of 1775-76 was directly challenged to extend the legal right of suffrage; and the measure in which the constitution of 1776 answered the demand is reflected in the fact that this proved to be the only point throughout the period down to 1844 at which the extension of the suffrage was itself the object of an articulate and organized movement.

[68]*New Jersey Constitutional Convention of 1844* (N.J. Federal Writers' Project, Trenton, 1942), pp. 108-09.

[69]*New Jersey Constitutional Convention of 1844.* p. 435.

[70]The point could be finally settled only by extensive sampling of the financial histories of members, not at their deaths—through wills—but at the time of their membership, and material for this is decidedly scarce.

[71]*Trenton Federalist & New Jersey Gazette,* Jan. 6, 1801.

[72]Elmer, *Constitution and Government of New Jersey,* pp. 151-52.

[73]See L. D. White, *The Jeffersonians* (N.Y., 1951), especially pp. 548-50.

The Crux of Politics:
Religion and Party in
Pennsylvania, 1778-1789

O. S. Ireland

RECENT literature on politics in Pennsylvania during the Revolutionary era has emphasized the primacy of divisions based on class, sectional, and occupational differences. Ethnic and religious alignments, when present, are viewed as accidental or, at best, as secondary factors modifying or magnifying more fundamental social-economic divisions. Robert Brunhouse originally developed this interpretative framework in the 1940s, and Jackson Turner Main has refined, extended, and supported it with masses of quantitative documentation. Main finds that Pennsylvania's Constitutionalists tended to be rural, agrarian, localist, western, smaller property holders, Scotch-Irish, Presbyterian, and men "who were or posed as democrats." Their opponents, the Republicans, were apt to be urban, commercial, cosmopolitan, eastern, larger property holders, Quaker or Episcopalian, English, and less democratic in their political and social views. Main diminishes the salience of religious affiliations by suggesting that the political attachments of Episcopalians were "perhaps due as much to geographical location as to their peculiar history" and that the political preference of Presbyterians "seems to grow out of their location in the more western counties."[1]

Douglas Arnold's dissertation on the debates between the Republicans and the Constitutionalists in the 1770s and 1780s impressively elucidates the central ideological strains of this political argument without challenging Main's general description. Richard Alan Ryerson, building on Arnold

Mr. Ireland is a member of the Department of History, State University of New York at Brockport. Portions of this article were presented at the Social Science History Association annual meeting, Philadelphia, 1976; the Duquesne History Conference, Pittsburgh, 1981; and the Tricentennial Conference on Immigration and Its Impact on Pennsylvania, Pennsylvania State University, Delaware County Campus, Media, Pa., 1982. Acknowledgments: I wish to thank Randall Miller, William Shade, H. James Henderson, John E. Ferling, Michael Parella, and John F. Kutolowski for helpful comments and criticisms, and the State University of New York for a summer grant and a sabbatical leave to support my research.

[1] Brunhouse, *The Counter-Revolution in Pennsylvania, 1776-1790* (Harrisburg, Pa., 1942); Main, *Political Parties before the Constitution* (Chapel Hill, N.C., 1973), 174-211, quotations on pp. 207, 210.

and others, and drawing from his own monograph on the radical committees of Philadelphia (1765-1776), has published an essay on the confederation years that is sympathetic to this neo-Progressive perspective.[2]

There is abundant evidence that Revolutionary Pennsylvanians divided along regional, vocational, and economic lines over such questions as taxation, land prices, debtor relief, tariffs, and the location of the state capital. Disputes of this nature constituted distinct dimensions of political reality. They were not, however, the dominant ingredient in the acrimonious party competition between Republicans and Constitutionalists throughout the period.

The thesis of this article is that in Pennsylvania from 1778 through 1789 conflicts based in religious differences formed the most persistent and predictable component of political partisanship.[3] Major elected officials (the members of the General Assembly) and their constituencies divided primarily along religious lines over such issues as control of higher education, loyalty oaths, and the constitutional structure of the state government. The group identifications that these divisions reflected transcended sectional, occupational, and commercial/noncommercial differences and were the most fundamental and conspicuous element of partisan behavior.

In 1776 Pennsylvania underwent a tumultuous internal political revolution, and during the next two years overlapping conflicts produced political chaos.[4] While loyalists, neutrals, and Revolutionaries argued over the legitimacy of Independence, patriots fought patriots for control of the new government and the British invaded the state and occupied the

[2] Arnold, "Political Ideology and the Internal Revolution in Pennsylvania, 1776-1790" (Ph.D. diss., Princeton University, 1976); Ryerson, "Republican Theory and Partisan Reality in Revolutionary Pennsylvania: Toward a New View of the Constitutionalist Party," in Ronald Hoffman and Peter J. Albert, eds., *Sovereign States in an Age of Uncertainty* (Charlottesville, Va., 1981), 95-133, and *The Revolution Is Now Begun: The Radical Committees of Philadelphia, 1765-1776* (Philadelphia, 1978).

[3] As I will suggest below, this religion-based partisanship did not involve political disputes over such explicitly religious questions as dogma, liturgy, ritual, or church organization. Such differences did exist but were not the subject of legislation. Rather, religious groups reacted to each other and to specific political issues in terms of a nascent consciousness-of-kind rooted in their cultural backgrounds, religious heritage, and historical experience, especially in Pennsylvania. In turn, their reaction to particular political issues heightened and intensified their consciousness-of-kind. Over time, these religious groups approximated ethnic groups. For further elaboration of this view of religious groups as ethnic groups see Timothy L. Smith, "Religion and Ethnicity in America," *American Historical Review*, LXXXIII (1978), 1155-1185.

[4] This and the following paragraph summarize the principal conclusions of Wayne L. Bockelman and Owen S. Ireland, "The Internal Revolution in Pennsylvania: An Ethnic-Religious Interpretation," *Pennsylvania History*, XLI (1974), 125-159, and Owen S. Ireland, "The Ethnic-Religious Dimension of Pennsylvania Politics, 1778-1779," *William and Mary Quarterly*, 3d Ser., XXX (1973), 423-448.

capital. Not until the fall of 1778, with the election of the Third General Assembly, did a semblance of order return. As it did, a new political structure emerged.

By the end of the legislative year 1778-1779, Scotch-Irish Presbyterians and their Calvinist allies in the Constitutionalist party stood arm in arm against the Republican coalition dominated by Anglicans, Quakers, and their Lutheran and sectarian allies. Constitutionalists supported rigorous enforcement of the state loyalty oaths (the Test Acts) against the largely Quaker, Anglican, Lutheran, and sectarian neutrals. They also attacked the Anglican-dominated College of Philadelphia and championed the state constitution of 1776 under which they had come to power. Their opponents, the Republicans, urged moderation in the use of the Test Acts, defended the college, and challenged the constitution as an instrument of tyranny. Partisan alignments on these three issues divided the assembly into two cohesive and antagonistic voting blocs on a wide range of other disputes.

Once established, this pattern of religion-based partisanship persisted in each of six legislative bodies studied from 1778 to 1789.[5] Year after year,

[5] The Third (1778-1779), Fifth (1780-1781), Seventh (1782-1783), Ninth (1784-1785), Eleventh (1786-1787), and Thirteenth (1788-1789) General Assemblies. Guttman scale analysis was used to compare the entire body of roll-call votes for each year. All possible pairs of votes with a Yule's Q-Coefficient in excess of ±.80 were recorded in a matrix from which the largest single set of potentially scalable votes was extracted. A modified version of Alexander's computer program was used to construct actual scalable sets. No contrived items were created. Only those roll-call votes that fit into the scalable set with less than 10% error were retained. All legislators whose actual votes deviated from the expected vote on more than 10% of the roll calls in the scale were classified as idiosyncratic and were omitted. Each of the resultant empirically derived scales has a coefficient of reproducibility of .90 or greater.

Legislators were ranked by scale scores, and the array was divided into three equal parts such that each subset contained the legislators located at one-third of the scale score positions. The men in each third of the scale positions voted together at least 66⅔% of the time. These subsets thus constitute three distinct voting patterns with the bloc at the lower third of the scale opposing the bloc at the upper third of the scale, and the men in the middle taking a nonaligned or nonpartisan position.

Using Guttman scale analysis to identify voting blocs is more laborious than cluster bloc analysis, but it allows identification of scalable sets of roll calls regardless of the manifest content of any particular motion; it decisively identifies those issues that clearly do not belong in the scalable set, and it ranks the men and the motions according to the degree to which they approximate the polar cases of bloc identification. Including all roll-call votes, instead of preselecting those that seem important, allows the participants rather than the historian to determine which votes and thus which issues went together. I have cross-checked some years by running cluster bloc analysis. This produced roughly the same configuration but with less precision and refinement of internal ranking of both men and issues. For further discussion see Thomas B. Alexander, *Sectional Stress and Party Strength: A Study of Roll-Call Voting Patterns in the United States House of Representatives, 1836-*

the preponderance of assemblymen formed opposing blocs that squared off across a wide span of policy issues, including the majority of roll-call votes in four of the six years and no less than a third in the remaining two. In each of these six legislatures, no other voting patterns approached the magnitude of these alignments.[6] In four, all nonpartisan votes were idiosyncratic, and in the other two this was true of most nonpartisan divisions. The percentage of legislators voting consistently with one bloc or the other ranged from 73 to 94 and averaged 86. Maintaining a high degree of internal cohesion, 92.5 percent of each bloc voted together at least 80 percent of the time on partisan issues.

Description and analysis of the full range of issues producing partisan responses is beyond the scope of this essay, but the college, the Test Acts, and the constitution of 1776 remained central. Parallel divisions regularly occurred on such closely related matters as acts of attainder, the treatment of loyalists, and the distribution of power among the branches of government. Furthermore, each bloc achieved near unanimity on such questions as disputed elections, the qualifications for voting and office-

---

1860 (Nashville, Tenn., 1967); Lee F. Anderson, Meredith W. Watts, Jr., and Allen R. Wilcox, *Legislative Roll-Call Analysis* (Evanston, Ill., 1966); William O. Aydelotte, "The Disintegration of the Conservative Party in the 1840s: A Study of Political Attitudes," in Aydelotte, Allan G. Bogue, and Robert William Fogel, eds., *The Dimensions of Quantitative Research in History* (Princeton, N.J., 1972), 331-346; and Duncan MacRae, Jr., "A Method for Identifying Issues and Factions from Legislative Votes," *American Political Science Review*, LIX (1965), 909-926. For full details of this procedure see Ireland, "Political Development in Pennsylvania: Legislative Behavior and Political Parties in the Confederation Period, 1776-1789" (paper delivered at S.S.H.A. annual meeting, Philadelphia, Oct. 1976), available on request from the author. For a somewhat different approach see Main, *Political Parties*, chap. 2.

[6] These generalizations, as well as those that follow, are based on the scale analysis described above. Main's cluster bloc analysis produced a list of major partisan and nonpartisan issues similar to those described here. Both lists agree that the key partisan questions included the state constitution, the U.S. Constitution, loyalists and neutrals, the bank, the college, disputed elections, patronage, conflicts among branches of government, the creation of some new counties, and the state's assumption of that portion of the national debt owed to citizens of Pennsylvania. Major issues that did not consistently produce partisan divisions over time include moving the state capital west, stay laws, the civil list, arrearages on western lands, state subsidies for business, and the gradual abolition of slavery. The two approaches produced contrasting classifications on only a narrow range of topics, largely related to paper money and debtor-creditor legislation. Main defines these as partisan, but my analysis indicates a tendency toward party instability on such issues over time. The somewhat different time spans of the two studies may account for this, or we may be assigning different meanings to particular roll calls. More important, this probably reflects the ability of scale analysis to make finer distinctions and to define partisan votes with greater precision. However, only a full and detailed comparison of Main's data and mine can ultimately resolve these differences. See Main, *Political Parties*, 174-211.

holding, the subdivision of counties into election districts, and the annulment of the censure of the highly partisan secretary of the Supreme Executive Council for mishandling state funds. Disciplined party voting on issues with such manifest political salience suggests a high degree of political self-consciousness and a well-developed party spirit.

Among additional issues that produced partisan responses from time to time, some undoubtedly reflected substantive differences between the blocs. These include the regulation and maintenance of the state militia, relations with the king of France, state assumption of responsibility for that portion of the national debt owed to Pennsylvanians, and the incorporation of the Society for the Relief of Distressed Germans in Pennsylvania. Others appear to have had more symbolic significance—for example, the charter of the Bank of North America and the calling of a convention to act on the proposed United States Constitution.[7]

Some nonparty issues are also of particular interest. Many explicitly economic measures did not divide the legislators sharply along party lines. For example, in the Fifth General Assembly, approximately half of the votes on the question of legal tender for state and national paper money did not align with the thirteen party votes. Neither did the two blocs consistently oppose each other over time on paper money, stay laws, debtor relief, the size of the state civil list, economic relief for western areas, land policy, revenue measures, or the geographic distribution of tax quotas. While each of these issues divided the legislature at one time or another, no one of them alone, or any combination of them, produced cohesive and persistent partisan alignments.

Assemblymen did occasionally vote on issues that divided the state regionally, but neither party was able to maintain discipline on such issues over time. Bloc voting dissolved on such questions as moving the capital west to Harrisburg, adjusting county tax quotas, restricting the manufacture of whiskey, allowing late payments for western lands, meeting regional transportation needs, and holding the convention to ratify the proposed United States Constitution in Lancaster. On such obviously sectional issues Constitutionalists and Republicans broke ranks and voted their sectional interests, so that kaleidoscopic factionalism characterized voting on questions of this kind.

[7] Owen Ireland, "Partisanship and the Constitution: Pennsylvania, 1787," *Pa. Hist.*, XLV (1978), 315-332. The partisan nature of the division on the Bank of North America needs further study. George David Rappaport, "The Sources and Early Development of the Hostility to Banks in Early American Thought" (Ph.D. diss., New York University, 1970), and Arnold, "Political Ideology," contribute substantially to our understanding, but linkages between conflicting credit and currency needs, broad differences in political culture (court vs. country ideologies, for example), hostility between competing commercial banking groups in Philadelphia, and religion-based partisanship remain to be investigated. All that can be said with certainty at this point is that the bank became a partisan issue by the ninth assembly (1784-1785). I agree with Main that by 1786-1787 "the Bank . . . had come to prove, rather than cause, party divisions" (*Political Parties*, 188).

TABLE I
PARTISAN ASSEMBLYMEN,
1778-1789

Party	Calvinist		Non-Calvinist	
	N	%	N	%
Constitutionalist	55	71	11	18
Republican	23	29	50	82

C = .462, P = .0001, N = 139 of 239 or 58%. Contingency Coefficient (C) is a measure of the relationship between two nominal-level variables. It ranges from zero, when there is no relationship, to approximately .710 for a near-perfect relationship between dichotomized variables in a four-celled contingency table. Probability (P) is a measure of statistical significance. The lower the P, the greater the odds are that the observed relationship is not the result of a chance configuration. Here, for example, a P of .0001 indicates that this particular relationship could occur on a chance basis once in ten thousand times.

The religious basis of the partisan divisions remained strong and statistically significant throughout the period.[8] Two hundred eighty-seven men served in one or more of these six assemblies, and 239 voted regularly with one bloc or the other. Identifiably Calvinist legislators strongly supported the Constitutionalists (55 of 78: 71 percent), and non-Calvinist legislators strongly supported the Republicans (50 of 61: 82 percent). Thus Presbyterians and Reformed assemblymen voted better than two to one with the Constitutionalists; Anglicans and Quakers voted a little more than ten to one with the Republicans, and Lutherans followed suit less dramatically with slightly under two to one. (See Table I.)

This division transcended any and all regional configurations. Calvinists from Philadelphia voted Constitutionalist with Calvinists from nearby commercial-agricultural areas as well as from Lancaster on the east side of the Susquehanna River, from York on the west side, and from the western and northern frontiers. Non-Calvinists, whether urban or rural, east or west, north or south, commercial agriculturalists or frontier farmers, voted together in the Republican party.[9] The Calvinists and non-Calvinists who crossed party lines exhibited the same lack of geographic specificity.

Moreover, party voting displayed no persistent regional bias. York was the only county for which either bloc held a majority of the seats in all six legislatures. In all other counties, first one and then the other bloc dominated, and between 1778 and 1789 each faction completely reversed its geographic base. At the outset, in the third assembly (1778-1779), the

[8] For procedures and assumptions on which ethnic and religious identifications rest see Bockelman and Ireland, "Internal Revolution," *Pa. Hist.*, XLI (1974), 127n-128n. For full discussion of the details of this religion-based partisanship see O. S. Ireland, "The Ethnic-Religious Dimension of Pennsylvania Politics, 1776-1790" (paper presented at the Duquesne History Forum, Pittsburgh, Pa., Oct. 12, 1981), available on request from the author.

[9] Ireland, "Ethnic-Religious Dimension, 1776-1790."

Constitutionalists drew 78 percent of their members from the southeast: the city of Philadelphia, its three contiguous commercial farming counties (Bucks, Chester, and Philadelphia county), and the other three counties east of the Susquehanna (Lancaster, Berks, and Northampton). In the same year the Republicans drew only 33 percent of their supporters from this region. In the fifth, seventh, and ninth assemblies the relative geographic strength of each bloc fluctuated. In the eleventh a major shift began, and in the thirteenth (1788-1789) the Republicans doubled their eastern wing from 33 to 70 percent, while the proportion of Constitutionalists from the eastern commercial area was more than halved from 78 percent to 31 percent. The Constitutionalists thus lost control of their original heartland comprising Philadelphia and its three adjacent commercial-agricultural counties.[10]

Among the factors contributing to this radical realignment, the repeal of the wartime restrictions on the voting rights of neutrals and religious pacifists was probably of greatest importance. The reenfranchisement of substantial numbers of Quakers, Lutherans, Anglicans, and German sectarians in southeastern Pennsylvania dramatically changed the political orientation of a number of commercial counties. In addition, the subdivision of other counties may have provided new opportunities for previous minorities to gain political power.[11] Be that as it may, the central point remains: over this twelve-year period neither bloc maintained a stable geographic base. The religious base of partisanship persisted; the regional base did not. The first was independent of the second.

Were party alignments also independent of the wealth of legislators? Aside from the areas they represented, did the blocs differ collectively in relative wealth? Did one draw more heavily than the other from the economic elite? And was this the more fundamental or more plausible explanation of partisanship?

Sorting out and assigning relative weights to the factors that shaped political behavior is difficult for Pennsylvania, where a mosaic of regional, occupational, economic, and religious considerations must be taken into account. English Quakers arrived early, followed by Anglicans and Germans (both church people and sectarians), and then by Scotch-Irish Presbyterians. By the 1770s large numbers of Quaker families could trace back their American ancestry four or five generations, while many Scotch-Irish were first- or second-generation newcomers. Though few areas of homogeneous settlement existed in 1778, some broad tendencies are apparent. The English, both Quakers and Anglicans, dominated the eastern agricultural counties of Bucks and Chester, and the Germans held sway in the middle tier of counties on a crescent-shaped line from Easton on the Delaware River to York, west of the Susquehanna. The last to arrive, the Scotch-Irish, filled in the empty spaces. They also constituted a

[10] Ireland, "Political Development."
[11] Brunhouse, *Counter-Revolution*, 179-181. For further discussion of this point see the following analysis of voting in Chester and Lancaster.

sizable minority in the city and the adjacent counties, controlled the southeastern townships of Chester and the central portions of Bucks around Neshaminy, and probably composed a majority in northern Lancaster County (later Dauphin), Cumberland County, and western York (later Adams) County.[12]

Duration of residence and place of settlement affected occupation and social-economic standing. Not all Quakers and Anglicans were rich and not all Scotch-Irish and Germans were poor, but in general Quakers and Anglicans were probably better off than Scotch-Irish and Germans since they enjoyed the advantages of time and location. By the same token, not all Quakers and Anglicans were merchants, nor did Scotch-Irish or Germans shun commerce, but Anglicans and Quakers remained most conspicuous in the financial and mercantile sectors.

Given this historic relationship of religious groups, settlement patterns, and occupation, some differences in wealth between partisan groups might be expected. Surprisingly, however, no measurable and consistent inter-party wealth differences can be found. Within each political unit—that is, each county and the city of Philadelphia—both parties drew their leadership from essentially the same strata of society. This could be shown by comparing the wealth of all Republican and Constitutionalist assemblymen in the six legislatures, but the data are not easily susceptible to this kind of treatment. Variations in tax rates from year to year, and in assessment practices from place to place, create major difficulties, which are compounded by divergences in land values in widely separated areas and by the need for separate measures of urban and rural wealth. Thus no comparable data from all or even from most counties are available over time. The small numbers of assemblymen elected from each county usually preclude multivariate analysis within a single political district. However, studying several distinct, though sometimes overlapping, geographic subsets of assemblymen achieves much the same result. Such comparisons produce a similar pattern; each adds weight to the others; and their cumulative impact is persuasive.

The largest comparable collection of land data is for the representatives of 1778-1779 from the seven eastern and central counties—Bucks, Chester, Lancaster, York, Cumberland, Berks, and Northampton. Despite much local variation, these counties were basically involved in commercial agriculture. All produced staples for the market; all looked to Philadelphia as their commercial center; all were located primarily within the fertile heartland of Pennsylvania. Even though each county contained one or more villages of some 2,000 inhabitants, its people were overwhelmingly engaged in producing or processing foodstuffs for market. Bucks and Chester were part of the original seventeenth-century settlement. The rest were opened up during the first half of the eighteenth century. Despite a scattering of underdeveloped areas, none can be classified as frontier or subsistence agricultural counties.

[12] Joseph E. Illick, *Colonial Pennsylvania: A History* (New York, 1976), 22-43, 113-136, 164-195.

TABLE II
PARTISAN ASSEMBLYMEN, 1778-1779, IN
SEVEN COMMERCIAL-AGRICULTURAL COUNTIES

Party	Religion[a]		Wealth: Land[b]	
	Calvinist	Non-Calvinist	Top Half	Bottom Half
Constitutionalist	10	1	8	8
Republican	2	4	5	4

[a] C = .517, P = .025, N = 17 of 35 or 49%
[b] C = .053, P = .900, N = 25 of 35 or 71%

The religion of about half of the thirty-five partisan assemblymen from these seven commercial-agricultural counties in 1778-1779 is known. For them, as for the entire body of assemblymen, religious affiliation and party choice were strongly linked: Calvinists voted with the Constitutionalists, non-Calvinists with the Republicans. The strength of this relationship is suggested by the contingency coefficient (C) of .517. (See Table II.)

A second test produces similar results. Spearman rank-order correlation (Rho) measures the degree to which rank in one hierarchy corresponds with rank in a second hierarchy. Technically speaking, Rho is not an appropriate measure of the relationship between partisan scores (an ordinal-level variable) and religion (a nominal-level variable), since religion is not inherently hierarchical.[13] Still, a little contrivance allows us to approach legitimacy, if not respectability, in using it here. Ranking the legislators on a contrived religious scale of "most to least Calvinist" creates a hierarchy with just two ranks: all or none. Using this minor subterfuge to correlate voting scores with degree of Calvinism produces a Rho of .598. Since Rho may range from +1.000 (a perfect relationship) to −1.000 (a perfect inverse relationship), this is a strong association. By itself this technique would not command great confidence, but its results are consistent with those of the contingency coefficient, and it thus reinforces the conclusion that religion is a strong and reliable predictor of party.

Comparison of the available data on landholding for twenty-five of these thirty-five partisan legislators at first suggests some striking differences.[14] The largest individual landowners were Republicans; the smallest were Constitutionalists. Republicans averaged 935.5 acres; Constitution-

[13] Partisan scores are the scale scores used to assign legislators to one bloc or the other. See n. 5.
[14] Landholding by township within counties is listed in Samuel Hazard *et al.*, eds., *Pennsylvania Archives* (Philadelphia and Harrisburg, 1874-1935), 3d Ser., XII-XX, hereafter cited as *Pa. Archs.* This analysis is based on the total amount of land listed for each man in all townships in the county from which he was elected and in all counties adjacent to the county from which he was elected for the year 1779. If 1779 data were not available, 1778 or 1780 data were used. Some men with common names were excluded because indistinguishable from others with the same name living in the same county. Of the 41 representatives, 35 voted partisan patterns and 25 have been identified in the tax rolls. Religion is known for 17.

alists, 204.6. Comparing averages, however, is deceptive partly because the 6,920 acres held by Mark Bird of Berks distort the Republican figure. In addition, focusing on the extreme values diverts attention from the modest-to-substantial holdings of the bulk of the men in each bloc. In fact, landholding is a poor predictor of political choice. This is demonstrated by ranking assemblymen from the largest to the smallest landholders by quartiles. Each bloc proves to have had as many men in the top quartile as in the lowest. If the same array is divided in two, each bloc splits quite evenly between the top and lower halves. Putting these figures into a four-celled contingency table and calculating a contingency coefficient reemphasizes the lack of significant relationship between voting and landholding: $C = .05$, about as close to no relationship as it is possible to come. (See Table II.)

A more powerful test, Rho, produces similar results. In this case, Rho is a legitimate tool for measuring the relationship between rank in the landholding hierarchy and rank in the voting scale. Here it equals .073—again about as close to no relationship as it is possible to come.

Unfortunately, the data are too thin to establish statistically the predictive power of land ownership relative to religion. Nonetheless, what information we do have is suggestive. Two of the twelve Calvinists voted with the Republicans. One (with 40 acres) ranked in the bottom half of the landowners, the other (with 205) in the top half, and neither was at or near the extremes of the range. Although scarcely rigorous, this analysis is the best the data will allow. It is consistent with previous tests, all of which indicate that religion was the single most important independent variable associated with bloc voting by these assemblymen.

The investigation to this point has compared landholding patterns among Constitutionalists and Republicans from seven commercial-agricultural counties in the legislative year 1778-1779. Its tendencies are clear, but a number of considerations suggest caution. Most obviously, the analysis is limited to one year. Furthermore, although these counties participated in the commercial-agricultural economy of the state, they differed in age, in distance from the principal export markets, and probably in the market value of arable land. The small number in the subset also limits its usefulness. A detailed study of a second group of assemblymen, the legislators from Chester and Lancaster between 1778 and 1789, extends the analysis in time and space. Because both counties were located in the highly commercial southeastern corner of the state, the problems caused by variation in land prices and distances from market are also reduced. In addition, a dramatic shift in political control in each county in the mid-1780s provides insight into the electoral base of the legislative divisions.

On the eve of the Revolution, Chester and Lancaster counties constituted one of the most profitable grain growing and milling centers in British North America. Chester, stretching south from Philadelphia to the Maryland border, fronted the Delaware River and drew waterpower from Brandywine Creek. Its farmers and millers marketed their wheat and flour through Philadelphia and New Castle, Delaware, a small but vital port with special links to the Irish trade.[15] Lancaster, west of Chester and encompassing much of the remainder of the fertile coastal plain, extended to the Susquehanna River. Yeoman farmers in such townships as Conestoga and Paxton produced grain for the international market. The Philadelphia wagon road, the province's principal east-west artery, linked Lancaster to milling facilities in Chester and markets in Philadelphia. The Susquehanna provided direct access to the embryonic but expanding grain export market in Baltimore.[16]

Both Chester and Lancaster had highly mixed ethnic and religious populations. Quakers had originally dominated Chester County, especially in the area nearest Philadelphia, but immigration had reduced them to a minority by the mid-eighteenth century. An important Anglican community emerged in the region originally settled by Quakers, and large numbers of Germans moved into the northern and western townships. The southeast corner, within easy reach of the Irish-American trade center at New Castle, became a Scotch-Irish Presbyterian enclave. In Lancaster, Quakers had always been few. Germans of several religious persuasions constituted the bulk of the early settlers there, and by the mid-eighteenth century the Scotch-Irish made up the second largest identifiable group.[17]

The political affiliations of some of the most notable Revolutionaries of these two counties suggest a link between wealth, occupation, and party. Gen. Anthony Wayne owned large quantities of land in Chester and was one of its leading taxpayers in 1785. Wayne played a decisive role in organizing the Chester Republicans, as did Richard Willing, a brother of banker Thomas Willing, who himself was the partner of Philadelphia Republican leader Robert Morris. John Hannum, proprietor of one of the more noteworthy taverns in the county, owned over 400 acres and supported the Republican cause. Next door in Lancaster County, George Ross, a rich and prominent lawyer in the borough of Lancaster, helped organize the Republicans, and tavern keeper and mill owner Matthias Slough joined him in this enterprise.[18]

[15] J. Smith Futhey and Gilbert Cope, *History of Chester County, Pennsylvania* (Philadelphia, 1881); Charles William Heathcote, *History of Chester County, Pennsylvania* (West Chester, Pa., 1926); Henry Seidel Canby, *The Brandywine* (New York, 1941); "J. Smith Futhey Papers; Chester County, Pennsylvania," Historical Society of Pennsylvania, Philadelphia; *Chester County Collections* (West Chester, Pa., 1936-   ).

[16] Franklin Ellis and Samuel Evans, *History of Lancaster County . . .* (Philadelphia, 1883); Brooke Hindle, "The March of the Paxton Boys," *WMQ*, 3d Ser., III (1946), 461-486.

[17] For further details see works cited in notes 11, 15, and 16.

[18] *Pa. Archs.*, 3d Ser., XII, XVII. Landholding for assemblymen from Chester and Lancaster is based on all listings for the same name within the county the legislator represented. This may exaggerate the holdings for those cases in which another man with the same name lived in the county, and it may understate holdings of assemblymen with land in adjacent counties. See notes 14 and 24 for a somewhat different approach.

From this evidence it appears that the commercial, agricultural, and professional elite preferred the Republican party, but a view of some leading Constitutionalist assemblymen from these two counties suggests a different conclusion. John Flemming, the Chester legislator who ranked highest in land ownership in 1781 and highest in assessed taxes in 1785, was a Constitutionalist. For Lancaster, Constitutionalist David Jenkins ranked at the top of both indexes. John Culbertson of Chester lived in town, ran a store, owned a fulling mill and a sawmill, earned the title "Esquire" (at least from the tax recorder), and voted with the Constitutionalists. So, too, did Dr. Joseph Gardner, a graduate of the University of Pennsylvania, who practiced medicine in Chester. Constitutionalist tavern keeper Stephen Cochran held more land than Republican tavern keeper Hannum, and the tax paid by Constitutionalist paper-mill operator John Fulton in 1785 far exceeded that of Republican tanner David Thomas.

Large landholders, professional men, village merchants, manufacturers, and agricultural processors, as well as men with high tax assessments and large amounts of land, divided their support between the Republicans and the Constitutionalists. The most consistent difference lay not in the occupation of such men, in the acreage they possessed, or the amount of taxes they paid, but in their religion. National hero Wayne, businessman Willing, tavern keeper Hannum, lawyer Ross, miller Slough, and tanner Thomas were all Republicans and non-Calvinists. Wealthy John Flemming, businessman Culbertson, professional man Gardner, tavern keeper Cochran, and paper maker Fulton were all Constitutionalists and Calvinists.

The connections were not fortuitous. In both counties between 1778 and 1789, party identification and religion generally remained closely linked and independent of landholding and tax assessment. Chester legislators exhibited an almost perfect correspondence between party and religion. Among those for whom religious data are available (77 percent), every Constitutionalist was a Calvinist and all but one of the Republicans were non-Calvinists.[19] The data on wealth are less easy to interpret. Constitutionalists had a slight tendency to draw their legislators from the ranks of the larger landholders and from men toward the top of the tax hierarchy. (None of the Constitutionalists but a third of the Republicans were in the lowest quartile.) This is a bit surprising but probably meaningless since the tie to landholding is not consistently strong or statistically significant and since about equal portions of the men from each bloc appeared in the top and bottom halves of the tax assessment rankings of assemblymen.[20] (See Table III.)

The repeal of the Test Acts in 1785 further demonstrates the dominance of the religious factor in the partisan politics of Chester, where, as in

---

[19] C = .666 out of a possible .710; P = .0002.

[20] In Chester, (C) for party affiliation with landholding quartile in 1780 = .251 (P = .671); with landholding quartile in 1781 = .214 (P = .776); with tax assessment quartile in 1781 = .455 (P = .217).

TABLE III
CHESTER PARTISAN ASSEMBLYMEN, 1778-1789

Party	Religion[a]		Wealth: Tax 1785[b]	
	Calvinist	Non-Calvinist	Top Half	Bottom Half
Constitutionalist	6	0	4	4
Republican	1	13	7	7

[a] C = .666, P = .0002, N = 20 of 26 or 77%
[b] C = .000, N = 22 of 26 or 85%

a number of eastern counties, the reenfranchisement of Quaker, Anglican, Lutheran, and sectarian nonjurors produced a striking shift. To the third, fifth, seventh, and ninth assemblies (1778-1784) Chester sent nine Constitutionalists and ten Republicans, but beginning in 1786 this balance disappeared. All ten representatives in the eleventh and thirteenth assemblies were Republican, and six of the seven for whom data are available were non-Calvinists. Repeal of the tests reestablished the non-Calvinist majority in Chester and reduced the Scotch-Irish Presbyterian minority to political impotence.

The sectional distribution of the popular vote in Chester County suggests the degree to which the electorate divided along religious lines. Scotch-Irish Presbyterians in the second electoral district voted for Constitutionalist candidates; Quakers and Anglicans in the first district supported Republicans; and the more heterogeneous population in the third district split its vote.[21] These patterns, with the dramatic realignment and the weak tie between wealth and bloc choice, demonstrate the pervasive, independent, and powerful association between religion and partisanship in Chester.

A similar pattern appears in Lancaster. Calvinists overwhelmingly joined the Constitutionalists (nine of eleven); non-Calvinists were similarly Republican (seven of eight); and the link between wealth and partisanship was tenuous at best. Here, as in Chester, landholding and partisanship remained statistically unrelated, but the Constitutionalists tended to hold larger amounts of land. Although the top half of the tax assessment ranks of assemblymen contained a slightly higher proportion of Constitutionalists than Republicans, the difference is not marked or meaningful.[22] (See Table IV.)

In Lancaster, as in Chester, the political realignment of the mid-1780s further reflects the political importance of religion-based partisanship. From the third through the ninth assemblies Constitutionalists dominated

[21] For the close correspondence between religious settlement patterns and partisan voting in Chester and York see Ireland, "Ethnic-Religious Dimension, 1778-1779," WMQ, 3d Ser., XXX (1973), 442-447.

[22] In Lancaster, (C) for party affiliation with landholding quartile in 1779 = .263 (P = .617); with landholding quartile in 1782 = .239 (P = .596).

TABLE IV
LANCASTER PARTISAN ASSEMBLYMEN, 1778-1789

Party	Religion[a]		Wealth: Tax 1782[b]	
	Calvinist	Non-Calvinist	Top Half	Bottom Half
Constitutionalist	9	1	7	6
Republican	2	7	8	10

[a] C = .594, P = .005, N = 19 of 36 or 53%
[b] C = .093, P > .100, N = 31 of 36 or 86%

the Lancaster delegation by a three-to-two ratio, but this control disappeared after 1785. Repeal of the Test Acts and reenfranchisement of a number of nonjurors contributed to this major shift. Equally important, at about the same time the legislature subdivided Lancaster by combining its northern tier of townships with some in Berks to create the new county of Dauphin, thus removing from Lancaster a large Scotch-Irish enclave that had provided much of the support for the Paxton Boys in the 1760s.[23] These changes produced a non-Calvinist voting majority in Lancaster. Throughout the remainder of the period, while Dauphin elected a strong Constitutionalist delegation to the assembly, all eleven Lancaster assemblymen voted with the Republicans.[24]

[23] Brunhouse, Counter-Revolution, 115; Theodore Thayer, Pennsylvania Politics and the Growth of Democracy, 1740-1776 (Harrisburg, Pa., 1953), 85-88; Illick, Colonial Pennsylvania, 166-167, 172; James H. Hutson, Pennsylvania Politics, 1746-1760: The Movement for Royal Government and Its Consequences (Princeton, N.J., 1972), 25-26, 84.

[24] Repeal of the Test Acts produced an equally dramatic turnover in Bucks, another eastern commercial-agricultural county bordering Philadelphia on the north. Originally a Quaker stronghold, Bucks provided a "safe" legislative seat during the early 1770s for Joseph Galloway. From 1778 to 1784, the Scotch-Irish Presbyterian and German minority dominated its elections and turned Bucks into a Constitutionalist bastion with 13 of its 14 legislators voting with that bloc. After repeal of the tests, voter turnout in Bucks increased by approximately 90% and all Bucks representatives voted with the Republicans. No significant difference in relative wealth distinguished Constitutionalist from Republican legislators. All but one came from the affluent, solid, stable upper middle half of the landholding elite, but here, as in Chester and Lancaster, the largest landowner was a Constitutionalist. The small number of men involved and the lack of reliable religious identification for many make statistically significant generalizations difficult, but among those for whom data are available, predicting party on the basis of religious background would be successful at least two-thirds of the time. W. W. H. Davis, The History of Bucks County, Pennsylvania, from the Discovery of the Delaware to the Present Time (Doylestown, Pa., 1876); "Minutes of the Committee of Safety of Bucks County, Pennsylvania, 1774-1776," Pennsylvania Magazine, XV (1891), 257-290; Pa. Archs., 3d Ser., XIII. Landholding for assemblymen from Bucks County is based on listings in home township only. Listings for men with identical names in other townships are not counted. This differs somewhat from the criterion used to determine landholding of legislators from Chester and Lancaster,

TABLE V
PHILADELPHIA PARTISAN ASSEMBLYMEN, 1778-1789*

Party	Religion[a]		Quartile Rank Tax Assessment[b]			
	Calvinist	Non-Calvinist	Top	Second	Third	Bottom
Constitutionalist	8	4	4	1	5	4
Republican	3	19	6	9	5	6

* Includes Philadelphia city, Philadelphia County, and Montgomery County
[a] C = .480, P = .005, N = 34 of 46 or 74%
[b] C = .300, P = .266, N = 40 of 46 or 87%

To recapitulate, in these eastern commercial-agricultural counties Calvinists supported Constitutionalists and non-Calvinists voted Republican. The exceptions are few; the patterns are clear; the relationship is strong, and it is independent of wealth. These findings hold whether the focus is on a county or a region, whether the time span is a year or a decade, and whether the comparisons are with landholding or with tax assessments. Assemblymen of both parties came from the ranks of the well-to-do, and religion-based partisanship transcends two different measures of wealth and cuts across distinct political boundaries. It is an independent variable and the most important and reliable predictor of partisanship.

When we shift to the city and county of Philadelphia, the setting changes but the findings remain the same. The environmental contrast could not be more striking, since Philadelphia's assemblymen represented the largest and most economically developed urban center in the new nation. Yet here, too, religious affiliation proves, on examination, to be a reliable guide to party preference. Information on religious ties can be obtained for 74 percent of the metropolitan legislators who voted consistently with one party or the other. Of these, most Calvinists (73 percent) were Constitutionalists and most non-Calvinists (84 percent) were Republicans.[25] The link is strong and unequivocal, and it bears little relationship to differences in wealth. (See Table V.) The citizens of Philadelphia elected some very rich men such as constitutionalist William Coates and Republican Robert Morris but also chose representatives

which itself differs from the criterion used to determine landholding of the partisan legislators from seven commercial-agricultural counties in the Third General Assembly. Thus three different ways of counting landholding have been used: home township only, home county only, and home county and adjacent counties. All three produce similar conclusions. See notes 14 and 18.

[25] Between 1778 and 1789 in the six legislatures studied, Philadelphia city and county (and Montgomery County, separated from Philadelphia County in 1784) elected 55 different men to the assembly. Forty-six voted partisan patterns (16 Constitutionalists and 30 Republicans). Religious data are available for 74%, tax data for 87%, and both religious and tax data for 66%.

whose tax assessments were minuscule by comparison. Republicans Frederick M. Muhlenberg and William Hollingshead, for example, paid ten pounds or less in contrast to Constitutionalist Coates, who paid over five hundred pounds in 1785.[26]

Neither of these extremes, however, is typical. The bulk of the legislators came from the ranks of the well-to-do, and relative wealth is a poor predictor of political preference. When these forty assemblymen are arrayed from highest to lowest on the basis of tax assessments, 58 percent of the Republicans and 36 percent of the Constitutionalists are in the top half. This suggests a link between party and wealth, but its strength is low (C = .205) and the numbers are not such as to generate much confidence (P > .100). Breaking the array into quartiles strengthens the linkage (C = .300), but the peculiarity of the pattern clouds its political meaning. The differences in rank between the Republicans and the Constitutionalists occur in neither the top nor the bottom quartiles (the Republicans had 23 percent and the Constitutionalists 29 percent in each) but in the middle ranges where the Republicans are overrepresented in the second quartile and the Constitutionalists in the third. This configuration may well be random (P = .266) and thus meaningless. At best, it suggests a tendency for Republicans to draw more heavily from the upper half of the middle ranks of the array, a tendency in contrast with our findings for Chester and Lancaster legislators, and one whose political relevance remains obscure. In short, here as elsewhere the relationship between party choice and relative wealth is neither statistically nor substantively significant. (See Table V.)

The point can be further illustrated by comparing wealth and bloc choice while holding religion constant. Eighty-two percent of the non-Calvinist Philadelphia city and county assemblymen voted with the Republicans. If the tie between religion and party is independent of wealth, then we should find that approximately the same percentage holds for both wealthier and poorer non-Calvinists. This is in fact the case: ten of the twelve more well-to-do non-Calvinists voted Republican, and so did eight of the ten less well-to-do.[27]

This completes the comparisons of religion, wealth, and political partisanship among groups of legislators.[28] Further probes could modify

[26] Tax data from Pa. Archs., 3d Ser., XIV, XV.

[27] A similar pattern exists among the Calvinist legislators, but the total number is too small to justify systematic treatment. Overall, 73% of Calvinists voted with the Constitutionalists. Eighty-six percent of the poorer Calvinists voted this way, as did 50% of the richer Calvinists. Since only four men are involved in the latter and ten in the entire sample, a change of one individual could markedly alter this proportion. (Five of the six poorer voted with the Constitutionalists; two of the four richer voted with the Constitutionalists.)

[28] These conclusions about the relative wealth of Constitutionalist and Republican assemblymen differ from those of Main in Political Parties, possibly because his list of Constitutionalists and Republicans differs from mine. He concentrated his study on the 1780s whereas I have looked at the period from 1778 to 1789. Rapid

or refine but not alter fundamentally the conclusion that party preference based on religion permeated the politics of Pennsylvania between 1778 and 1789 and constituted its principal independent and autonomous dimension. Other factors could produce legislative divisions on particular issues and for short periods of time. Among these were sectional interest, clashes between merchants and manufacturers as well as between land-owners and land speculators, disputes about commercial and agricultural credit needs, and controversies over slavery.[29] Still, no one of these alone, and no combination of them, separated the legislators into two large, coherent, and cohesive voting blocs that carried over from one legislative year to the next. Religion-based partisanship alone exhibited this power.

The conclusion is clear. Explaining it is another matter. General models drawn from studies of religious influences on nineteenth-century American political behavior prove inapplicable. Anglicans, Quakers, Lutherans, Presbyterians, and German and Dutch Reformed cannot readily be arrayed in a politically meaningful way along the pietistic-ritualistic continuum Samuel P. Hays and Paul Kleppner developed to analyze late nineteenth-century politics, the puritan/non-puritan categories Lee Benson found in Jacksonian New York, or the evangelical/anti-evangelical distinction Ronald P. Formisano and William G. Shade used in their studies of early nineteenth-century Michigan and Northampton County, Pennsylvania. This is not altogether surprising. As Timothy Smith has reminded us, the development of group identities can be both complex and dynamic when heterogeneous populations meet and interact in new situations.[30] A new context may reshape or redirect old identities, or even

---

personnel changes in the legislature over time could produce substantially different compilations of partisans. More likely, we differ in how we made our comparisons. Main, apparently, compared the wealth of all known Republicans and Constitutionalists regardless of geographic base. I have made comparisons among Constitutionalists and Republicans within political or regional subdivisions. The difference in time span for our studies is the most probable cause of our differing interpretations of sectional considerations in partisanships. During the later years of the 1780s, after repeal of the Test Acts and the political reenfranchisement of Anglicans, Quakers, Lutherans, and German sectarians, Republicans dominated the eastern area. However, before repeal of the tests, the Scotch-Irish Presbyterian-based Constitutionalists had played a major role in this eastern commercial area.

[29] Owen S. Ireland, "Germans against Abolition: A Minority's View of Slavery in Revolutionary Pennsylvania," *Journal of Interdisciplinary History*, III (1973), 685-706.

[30] Hays, "History as Human Behavior," *Iowa Journal of History*, LVIII (1960), 193-206; Kleppner, *The Cross of Culture: A Social Analysis of Midwestern Politics, 1850-1900* (New York, 1970), *The Third Electoral System, 1853-1892: Parties, Voters, and Political Cultures* (Chapel Hill, N.C., 1979), and "Piety and Politics: The Structure of Religion and Politics" (paper delivered at the Brockport Conference on Social-Political History, fall 1969); Benson, *The Concept of Jacksonian Democracy: New York as a Test Case* (Princeton, N.J., 1961), 207, 293-

create a new sense of separate peoplehood among individuals with similar language, culture and religion, and thus produce a new basis for political response. To understand late eighteenth-century Pennsylvania we must look backward not forward, and consider not only the immediate context of political life but also the historical trends that created a very tangled bank of religion and ethnicity.

The roots of Pennsylvania's religion-based politics lay in the sixteenth- and seventeenth-century British Isles, where Anglicans, Quakers, Congregationalists, and Presbyterians emerged as antagonistic religious bodies. Their deep-seated hostilities were projected across the Atlantic. Quakers in Pennsylvania knew that Congregationalists in New England had killed Friends in the seventeenth century; the Anglican Society for the Propagation of the Gospel in Foreign Parts supported major missionary efforts to challenge not only the New England Puritans but also dissenting groups in the Middle Colonies; Calvinists, whether in Scotland, England, or Ireland, had not been noted for latitudinarianism and did not change their ways in America.

By the middle of the eighteenth century these groups, along with numbers of German church people and sectarians, had assembled in Pennsylvania, where the liberal franchise made them all potential participants in politics. The erosion of the initial Quaker hegemony, the Anglicanization of the Penn family and the proprietary interest, the precarious position and the missionary status of the Anglican church, the political awakening of the Germans, and the influx of Scotch-Irish Presbyterians, especially the virtual torrent of middle-class exiles from Ulster after mid-century, combined to create a volatile political mixture. Competition between the assembly and the proprietary governor in the 1760s, itself based partly on religious differences, contributed to widespread political mobilization, while vigorous, not to say brutal, electoral contests exacerbated ethnic and religious conflicts.[31]

317; Formisano, *The Birth of Mass Parties: Michigan, 1827-1861* (Princeton, N.J., 1971); Shade, "Pennsylvania Politics in the Jacksonian Period: A Case Study, Northampton County, 1824-1844," *Pa. Hist.*, XXXIX (1972), 313-333; Smith, "Religion and Ethnicity in America," *AHR*, LXXXIII (1978), 1155-1185.

[31] R. J. Dickson demonstrates that most Irish immigrants to Pennsylvania in the 1770s came not as poor indentured servants but as fee-paying passengers moving modest resources from a less promising to a more promising area (*Ulster Emigration to Colonial America, 1718-1775* [London, 1966], 97). He also shows that economic considerations, not religious conflicts, provided the primary motive for most of the 18th-century Ulster migration to America (pp. 11-13, 15-29, 33-34, 53-59, 65-80). Thayer, *Pennsylvania Politics;* Brunhouse, *Counter-Revolution.* 4; William S. Hanna, *Benjamin Franklin and Pennsylvania Politics* (Stanford, Calif., 1964); Hutson, *Pennsylvania Politics, 1746-1770;* Wayland F. Dunaway, *The Scotch-Irish of Colonial Pennsylvania* (Chapel Hill, N.C., 1944); David L. Jacobson, "John Dickinson's Fight against Royal Government, 1764," *WMQ,* 3d Ser., XIX (1962), 64-85; Benjamin H. Newcomb, "Effects of the Stamp Act on Colonial Pennsylvania Politics," *ibid.*, XXIII (1966), 257-272; Illick, *Colonial Pennsylvania.* esp. chaps. 9, 10.

The evolution of consciousness-of-kind among Pennsylvania's diverse peoples, and its translation into distinctive political perceptions and behavior in the crucial transition and realignment of 1776-1778, remain to be thoroughly researched, but broad outlines can be sketched and some probable causes examined. The imperial crises between 1765 and 1775, the outbreak of war, and the debate over Independence superimposed new configurations on old conflicts. Richard Alan Ryerson has argued persuasively that the patriot leadership consciously maintained a religious balance on the extralegal committees that served as the principal vehicle for bringing Pennsylvania into the Revolution (itself telling evidence of the political salience of these group identities at that time and place). However, by the winter of 1775-1776 Quakers in good standing with the Meeting no longer publicly supported the resistance movement. The moral agonies of both Anglicans and Lutherans increased as 1776 progressed, and when acceptance of Independence became a prerequisite for continued political participation in Pennsylvania, the earlier religious balance dissolved.

When a majority of Quakers opted for neutrality and a minority of Anglicans remained loyal to the crown, they left their coreligionists enfeebled vis-à-vis the Presbyterians, who sprang with near unanimity to the Revolutionary cause and, in a dramatic reversal, broke the long-established Quaker-Anglican political hegemony. Throughout the colonial period Quakers and Anglicans constituted about 80 percent of the legislature most of the time. In the first assembly elected after Independence, 58 percent of the representatives were Calvinists, and the next year, in the fall 1777 election, this proportion increased to 82 percent.[32]

The new state constitution deeply divided the patriot forces in the fall of 1776. Initially, the division represented an ideological cleavage. Some, like Thomas Paine, argued for direct, simple, and democratic government close to the people and immediately responsive to their demands. Others, like Benjamin Rush, believed that the preservation of liberty required balanced government and extensive constitutional checks on the power of officeholders. David Hawke, Eric Foner, and Douglas Arnold have done much to illuminate this debate, and Arnold, especially, has demonstrated its relatively narrow bounds.[33] Supporters and opponents of the constitution rested their public appeals on the same republican principles, and the

---

[32] Ryerson, *Revolution Now Begun*, 187-190, 192, 203; Illick, *Colonial Pennsylvania*, esp. chap. 11; Richard Bauman, *For the Reputation of Truth: Politics, Religion, and Conflict among the Pennsylvania Quakers, 1750-1800* (Baltimore, 1971), 134, 142-153, 160; Bockelman and Ireland, "Internal Revolution," *Pa. Hist.*, XLI (1974), 142-146, 154; David L. Holmes, "The Episcopal Church and the American Revolution," *Historical Magazine of the Protestant Episcopal Church*, XLVII (1978), 264, 265, 283.

[33] Hawke, *In the Midst of a Revolution* (Philadelphia, 1961); Foner, *Tom Paine and Revolutionary America* (New York, 1976); Arnold, "Political Ideology"; L. H. Butterfield, ed., *Letters of Benjamin Rush* (Princeton, N.J., 1951), I, 115, 137, 148.

decision of the anti-constitutionalists to call themselves "Republicans" in the spring of 1779 was of more than nominal significance.[34]

The social base of the original division on the constitution, however, remains unclear. No full analysis is possible here, but it is evident that substantial change took place over time. Although a number of prominent Presbyterians initially opposed the constitution, by 1778-1779 most had switched sides and become its champions. (Benjamin Rush was conspicuous among the few who remained Presbyterian and anti-constitutional.) Meanwhile, the Presbyterian majority in the legislature, and especially its Scotch-Irish core, increased its awareness of itself as a separate people while subtly redefining the criteria for group membership. Presbyterians became the staunch supporters of the form of government on which their ascendancy rested, then organized themselves as the Constitutionalists, and, under such leaders as Joseph Reed and George Bryan, lashed out at their opponents.[35] They first attacked their old enemies (Quakers and Germans) with the Test Acts and then turned on their former Anglican allies by assailing the charter of the College of Philadelphia.

This assault brought together an opposition coalition of new and strange political bedfellows. Anglican and Quaker supporters of the war and ultimately many of the Germans (especially those from non-Calvinist traditions) formed the core of this alliance. Fear of Scotch-Irish Presbyterians exercising unlimited power through the unchecked unicameral legislature held them together in an unusual political combination. Prominent non-Calvinists such as Robert Morris and James Wilson formed the Republican Society and gained the electoral support of other non-Calvinists, first those who were patriots and then, after 1785, those who had been neutrals.[36]

Political expediency and competition for power thus played major roles in the emergence of identifiable political alliances in the late 1770s, but religious factors were not irrelevant. Even though Pennsylvania Quakers, Lutherans, and Anglicans diverged on a range of theological issues, they shared a deep reservation about armed resistance to legitimate authority that led some to withdraw from the patriot cause as it moved from petition through protest to intimidation, war, and finally Independence. It also inhibited their compliance with the Test Acts, which demanded renunciation of allegiance to George III.

[34] Arnold, "Political Ideology," 7-8, 63.

[35] The process whereby this self-consciousness emerged and became politically salient needs detailed study. The Presbyterian majority in the First General Assembly chose as Speaker a Quaker with long pre-war political experience and strong patriot credentials, while at the same time future Constitutional leaders such as Presbyterians Joseph Reed and Thomas McKean railed against the evils of the constitution of 1776. Not until the Third General Assembly of 1778-1779 did the last vestiges of the pre-war coalition give way to the new alignments. See Bockelman and Ireland, "Internal Revolution," *Pa. Hist.*, XLI (1974), 148-151.

[36] The religious affiliation of James Wilson causes much confusion. He was born in Scotland and apparently raised as a Presbyterian. In Pennsylvania, however, he

Ecclesiastical polities also contributed. Although Quaker, Anglican, and Lutheran church organizations differed markedly, all three in Pennsylvania maintained close and vital links with their coreligionists in England. Pennsylvania's Quakers, for example, looked to their London counterparts for help against the Scotch-Irish and the Proprietary party in the 1760s; Lutherans in Pennsylvania enjoyed close, cordial, and supportive relations with the Anglican church in that province and with the Lutheran-oriented Hanoverian monarchy in England; and the Anglican church in Pennsylvania was largely a missionary endeavor dependent on English money and personnel. Extensive two-way communication maintained and nurtured a transatlantic identity that Independence could only threaten. These British ties also may have/dampened the enthusiasm of some Anglicans, Quakers, and Lutherans for continued resistance in 1776 and certainly heightened their unwillingness to renounce English citizenship and their English sovereign in 1778, thus contributing further to their internal divisions and political decline.[37]

In contrast, English-speaking Calvinists experienced no such inhibitions. They had never been noted for reluctance to take up arms in defense of truth, and respect for legitimate authority had not unduly limited their participation in just causes. Moreover, the Scotch-Irish Presbyterians in the 1760s and 1770s had no strong links to England. Ethnically distinct, speaking with a brogue, politically discriminated against in Ireland, abused (at least in their own eyes) by British mercantile legislation, and finally driven to America by the rack rents of absentee landlords (many of whom were English), these Ulster immigrants had few

---

associated himself with Anglicans and with the Anglican church. He arrived with letters to Anglican Richard Peters. Anglican minister (future bishop) William White was a close friend. Wilson married an Anglican woman in an Anglican church and is buried at Christ Church in Philadelphia. I have seen nothing to suggest that he maintained ties to the Presbyterian church in Pennsylvania.

[37] Illick, *Colonial Pennsylvania*, 190, 217-218; 236-244; Frederick B. Tolles, *Meeting House and Counting House: The Quaker Merchants of Colonial Philadelphia, 1682-1763* (Chapel Hill, N.C., 1948); Paul A. W. Wallace, *The Muhlenbergs of Pennsylvania* (Philadelphia, 1950). For a clear statement of the Quaker positions see the extracts from Philadelphia Yearly Meeting, Minutes of the Meeting for Sufferings, 1775-1785, printed in Richard K. MacMaster et al., *Conscience in Crisis: Mennonites and Other Peace Churches in America, 1739-1789* (Scottdale, Pa., 1979), 411-412, 434-435. For similarities and historic links between the Anglicans and the German Lutherans see Henry Eyster Jacobs, *A History of the Evangelical Lutheran Church in the United States* (New York, 1893), 278, 279, 280, 286, and Frederick Klees, *The Pennsylvania Dutch* (New York, 1950), 78, 81-82. For tensions and conflicting loyalties experienced by German Lutherans during the early days of Independence see Theodore G. Tappert and John W. Doberstein, trans., *The Journals of Henry Melchior Muhlenberg* (Philadelphia, 1942-1958), II, 735. For Quakers see J. William Frost, "The Trans-Atlantic Community Reconsidered" (paper delivered at the Philadelphia Center for Early American Studies Seminar, Feb. 17, 1984).

reasons to respect the English crown. In addition, they maintained few institutional connections with their coreligionists in the British Isles. Scotch-Irish Presbyterians in the Middle Colonies looked less to the old country and more to themselves for models, authority, and approval. In the same vein, the Dutch and German Reformed had few if any English attachments to lose and by the 1770s maintained no more than tenuous ties to Europe.[38]

Little in their theology, church organization, institutional linkage, or personal experience restrained the Scotch-Irish Presbyterians and their Calvinist allies from full participation in the resistance movement. They constituted a visible minority from the beginning but became a majority as others withdrew or were excluded. Once in power, their growing self-consciousness combined with wartime enthusiasms and emotions to provoke and justify a series of attacks on those who disagreed with them, whether old friends or old enemies.

This development suggests that theological orientation also may have contributed to the partisan behavior after Independence. Arnold's analysis of the political rhetoric of Republicans and Constitutionalists from 1776 to 1790 indicates that the factions differed markedly in willingness to tolerate dissent and to accept the diversity of a pluralistic society. The Constitutionalists "moved toward a politics of exclusiveness." They "embraced a narrow definition of the political community while their rivals . . . [became] committed to a far more inclusive definition of the political public." Arnold suggests a number of causes, including the heterogeneity of the Republican coalition, in contrast to "the greater social homogeneity of the Constitutionalists' support," and "the elitist perspectives of the Republican leaders, who saw governmental stability as the key to the maintenance of their own social and economic hegemony in the state." He does not explore the explanatory potential inherent in the theological differences between these partisan religious groups, but the Quakers' principled commitment to toleration, the historic latitudinarianism of Anglicans, and the Calvinists' reputation for exclusivity and conformity appear highly congruent with the political rhetoric of the party each supported. This congruity deserves further study.[39]

By the end of the Third General Assembly in September 1779 this nascent political polarization had come to term. Religion-based partisanship emerged full-fledged as the legislature struggled with the key issues of the revision of the constitution, the annulment of the charter of the College of Philadelphia, and the imposition of loyalty oaths. Once

[38] Illick, *Colonial Pennsylvania*, 120-122; Dunaway, *Scotch-Irish*, esp. 29-31, 58, 119, 140, 156-157, 181-183, 201; Maldwyn A. Jones, "Scotch-Irish," in Stephan Thernstrom, ed., *Harvard Encyclopedia of American Ethnic Groups* (Cambridge, Mass., 1980), 895-902. For insight into German and Dutch Reformed attitudes toward England, lack of links to Great Britain, and lack of attachment to the British crown see Klees, *Pennsylvania Dutch*, 79, 169-170.

[39] Arnold, "Political Ideology," 102-103, 145-146.

established and internalized, it persisted throughout the Confederation period. It was more visible and potent in some years than in others, but at all times it remained susceptible to rapid mobilization and reinforcement by the introduction of one or more of the three original issues or by legislation that assemblymen perceived as partisan.

This, in turn, raises a number of additional questions, including how politics and religious identity interacted in the minds of Pennsylvanians, what mechanisms organized and structured the expression of this religion-based political behavior, and how this behavior related to differences in world views, value systems, and group norms. All of these and more need to be explored if we are to move toward a fuller understanding of the role of religion in Pennsylvania politics in the 1770s and 1780s. What is clear at this point, however, is the degree to which these religious alignments lay at the root of a political partisanship as intense and long lasting as any in the new nation.

The Fort Wilson Incident of 1779:
A Case Study of the Revolutionary Crowd

John K. Alexander*

O
N the afternoon of Monday, October 4, 1779, a crowd—composed almost exclusively of militiamen who hated tories and supported price regulation—marched through the streets of Philadelphia. A number of men, believing that James Wilson and possibly they themselves were the targets of the crowd, armed themselves and gathered at Wilson's house. As the crowd passed the house, shots rang out. Six or seven people were killed; between seventeen and nineteen were "dangerously wounded."[1] This confrontation, which became known as the "Fort Wilson Riot," greatly alarmed many people, especially those who held positions of power. Major Samuel Shaw, a merchant in civilian life, wrote, "There has been hell to pay in Philadelphia. . . . It is hoped that a spirited interposition of the executive powers of the State will prevent a renewal of the tragedy."[2] Henry Laurens, merchant and past president of the Continental Congress, said, "We are at this moment on a precipice, and what I have long dreaded and often intimated to my friends, seems to be breaking forth—a convulsion among the people."[3] Samuel Patterson cried out, "God help us—Terrible times . . . The poor starving here and rise for redress. Many flying the city for fear of Vengeance."[4] The painful

---

* Mr. Alexander is a member of the Department of History, University of Cincinnati.

[1] The quotation is from *Pennsylvania Colonial Records*, XII: *Minutes of the Supreme Executive Council, 1779-1781* (Harrisburg, Pa., 1853), 122, hereafter cited as *Pa. Col. Recs.* The exact number of killed and wounded is in question, although it is clear that the great majority of casualties were members of the militia. See John K. Alexander, "Philadelphia's 'Other Half': Attitudes toward Poverty and the Meaning of Poverty in Philadelphia, 1760-1800" (Ph.D. diss., University of Chicago, 1973), 284-285, n. 2.

[2] Samuel Shaw to Winthrop Sargent, Oct. 10, 1779, in Nicholas B. Wainwright, ed., "Captain Samuel Shaw's Revolutionary War Letters to Captain Winthrop Sargent," *Pennsylvania Magazine of History and Biography*, LXX (1946), 300.

[3] Laurens to John Adams, Oct. 4, 1779, in Charles Francis Adams, ed., *The Works of John Adams*, IX (Boston, 1854), 499. Clearly this letter was written early on the morning of Oct. 5.

[4] Patterson to Caesar Rodney, Oct. 6, 1779, in George Herbert Ryden, ed., *Letters to and from Caesar Rodney, 1756-1784* (Philadelphia, 1933), 323. See also Benjamin Rush to John Adams, Oct. 12, 19, 1779, in L. H. Butterfield, ed., *Letters of Benjamin Rush*, I (Princeton, N. J., 1951), 240, 244.

memory of the Fort Wilson incident did not pass easily. "Valerius" of Philadelphia, writing in 1784 said, "The affair of Mr. Wilsons House, in 1779, . . . [was] the most alarming insurrection it [Philadelphia] had ever felt."[5]

The standard accounts of this traumatic experience in the life of Philadelphia explain it as a result of the political struggle between the Republican and Constitutional societies of Pennsylvania. The Republican Society was founded in March 1779 to oppose the constitution of 1776 because it was felt to lack the safeguards needed to check the potentially unreasonable will of the majority. Benjamin Rush, who was a Republican, described the Society's members as "in general the ancient inhabitants of the state and . . . distinguished for their wealth, virtue, learning, and liberality of manners." They were, as Robert Brunhouse called them, "the conservatives."[6] The Constitutional Society was formed in late March in response to the creation of the Republican Society. The leading Constitutionalists were, like the Republicans, typically men of wealth, but their wealth was usually "'new' money as opposed to 'old' money," and the Constitutionalists were often "persons marginal to the established merchant groups of Philadelphia." Thus Sam Bass Warner seems correct in noting that the difference between the members of the two societies "was political and social, not economic." The Constitutionalists, for example, did not fear giving the democratic majority the power to enact its will. Indeed, this was to them the essence of sound government, and they had formed to support the state constitution of 1776 which they believed embodied the principle of majority rule.[7] These two groups were "loose, nebulous affairs" rather than "highly organized political machines."[8] But they were political organizations and they were anathema to each other. The contest between the two societies supposedly led to the Fort Wilson incident because the deteriorating wartime economic situation allowed the Constitutionalists to heat the people's hostility toward wealthy Republicans. The Constitutionalists charged that the Republicans

[5] The Freeman's Journal: or, the North-American Intelligencer (Philadelphia), Apr. 7, 1784. See also the sources cited in n. 9.
[6] The quotations are from Benjamin Rush to Charles Nisbet, Aug. 27, 1784, in Butterfield, ed., Rush Letters, I, 337. See also Robert L. Brunhouse, The Counter-Revolution in Pennsylvania, 1776-1790 (Harrisburg, Pa., 1942), passim, and The Pennsylvania Gazette, and Weekly Advertiser (Philadelphia), Mar. 24, 1779.
[7] Sam Bass Warner, Jr., The Private City: Philadelphia in Three Periods of Its Growth (Philadelphia, 1968), 26-28, quotation on p. 28. For the view of the Constitutionalists see The Pennsylvania Packet or the General Advertiser (Philadelphia), Apr. 1, 1779, and Charles C. Sellers, Charles Willson Peale, I (Philadelphia, 1947), 193-194.
[8] Brunhouse, Counter-Revolution, 9-10.

and their merchant friends were gouging the people by artificially controlling the supply and price of goods. This "severe criticism" unleashed by the "radicals" "served as propaganda to inflame the emotions of the populace for an explosion." Fort Wilson was that explosion.[9]

In arriving at these conclusions historians have invariably called the crowd a "mob,"[10] thus adopting the terminology of contemporary accounts by persons who were neither members of the crowd nor supporters of its actions.[11] The historians, too, have not had much sympathy for the people they so easily dismiss as a "mob," nor have they tried diligently enough to understand and explain why the crowd marched on that October day.[12] Indeed, the standard explanation comes strikingly close to Peter Oliver's view that "the People in general . . . were like the Mobility of all Countries, perfect Machines, wound up by any Hand who might first take the Winch."[13]

The historians who offer this Oliverian analysis have not, as he would have, viewed the "mob" as mindless. Most carefully note that the leading "radicals" worked to stop violence. As Charles Sellers argued, the leaders of the Constitutional Society "without realizing it" had "raised" a "mob"

[9] The quotations are *ibid.*, 68. See also Sellers, *Peale*, I, 194, 195, 204-205; Warner, *Private City*, 25, 32-33, 38, 40, 42-43; Allan Nevins, *The American States during and after the Revolution, 1775-1789* (New York, 1924), 261; C. Page Smith, *James Wilson, Founding Father: 1742-1798* (Chapel Hill, N. C., 1956), 133.

[10] The important modern studies are listed in nn. 6-9. All of these sources use the word "mob" and none of them put the term in quotation marks when they speak of the incident. Although Warner, *Private City*, 43, in his description of the events of Oct. 4 does not use the term "mob," immediately after his account of the incident he writes that "the incident frightened both radical and moderate leaders. Both sides attempted to prevent further confrontation of mobs and merchants." See also n. 11.

[11] For the attitudes and actions of the eyewitnesses and of those who claim to be reporting eyewitness testimony see Shaw to Sargent, Oct. 10, 1779, in Wainwright, ed., "Shaw's Letters," *PMHB*, LXX (1946), 300; Patterson to Rodney, Oct. 6, 1779, in Ryden, ed., *Rodney Letters*, 322-324; Horace Edwin Hayden, ed., "The Reminiscences of David Hayfield Conyngham, 1750-1834," in Wyoming Historical and Geological Society, *Proceedings and Collections*, VIII (1904), 208-215; "The Attack on Fort Wilson, October 4, 1779," *PMHB*, V (1881), 475-476; Anna Wharton Morris, comp., "Journal of Samuel Rowland Fisher, of Philadelphia, 1779-1781," *ibid.*, XLI (1917), 169-171; and William B. Reed, ed., *Life and Correspondence of Joseph Reed . . .*, II (Philadelphia, 1847), for the following narratives: "Narrative of Allen M'Lane," 150-152; "Philip Hagner's Narrative," 426-428; "Statement of Charles Wilson [*sic*] Peale," 423-426.

[12] The lack of sympathy on the part of the historians is seen, I believe, in their uncritical acceptance of the term "mob." See n. 10. Smith, *Wilson*, who offered the most unsympathetic account, was not writing history, but historical fiction. See Alexander, "Philadelphia's 'Other Half,' " 337-338.

[13] Douglass Adair and John A. Schutz, eds., *Peter Oliver's Origin & Progress of the American Rebellion: A Tory View* (San Marino, Calif., 1961), 65.

that "not one of them *cared* or dared to use."[14] Thus, in the end, the "mob" marched on its own against the express wishes of those who had "raised it." The "Mobility" were not "perfect Machines." Once primed for violence, they could not be shut down.

Such an interpretation seems plausible and part of the scenario is above question. The leading Constitutional politicians did oppose the militia's actions. No less a person than Charles Willson Peale—president of the Constitutional Society—tried to dissuade the militia. But the standard argument about the militiamen—the people who marched on October 4—rests on two questionable Oliverian assumptions. It assumes first that the militiamen were indeed a mob moved by a base desire to destroy and possibly to commit mayhem. As we shall see, such does not appear to have been the case. More important, the standard historical analysis assumes that the militia had to be "propagandized" to act. But did the militia need to be inflamed? Or did they have their own, and as they saw it, logical reasons for action? These questions must be kept in mind as we examine the events that brought about that bloody Monday in Philadelphia.

The Fort Wilson incident calls for a detailed reexamination because our knowledge of the Revolutionary crowd is based almost exclusively on events in the years before 1776 when most "mobs" were aimed at a "foreign" enemy.[15] Obviously it is dangerous to generalize about the nature and significance of the Revolutionary crowd when we do not possess detailed case studies of crowd activity after 1776. We need as

[14] Sellers, *Peale*, I, 204-205 (emphasis added). See also Brunhouse, *Counter-Revolution*, 75, and Smith, *Wilson*, 133.

[15] The most important suggestive recent studies that give detailed accounts of "mob" action or actions are Pauline Maier, *From Resistance to Revolution: Colonial Radicals and the Development of American Opposition to Britain, 1765-1776* (New York, 1972), and her articles, "Popular Uprisings and Civil Authority in Eighteenth-Century America," *William and Mary Quarterly*, 3d Ser., XXVII (1970), 3-35, and "The Charleston Mob and the Evolution of Popular Politics in Revolutionary South Carolina, 1765-1784," *Perspectives in American History*, IV (1970), 173-196; L. Jesse Lemisch, "New York's Petitions and Resolves of December 1765: Liberals vs. Radicals," *New-York Historical Society Quarterly*, XLIX (1965), 313-326, and his "Jack Tar in the Streets: Merchant Seamen in the Politics of Revolutionary America," *WMQ*, 3d Ser., XXV (1968), 371-407; Hiller B. Zobel, *The Boston Massacre* (New York, 1970). Of these studies only Maier's essays purport to examine the "mob" during the Revolution. However, her "Popular Uprisings," *WMQ*, 3d Ser., XXVII (1970), 18n, does not discuss any "mob" action that occurred during the war, although she does refer the reader to an account of the Fort Wilson incident. In her "Charleston Mob," *Perspectives in Am. Hist.*, IV (1970), 186-187, Maier mentions disturbances that occurred in 1778, 1783, and 1784, but she does not examine these incidents in depth.

many such studies as we can possibly obtain if we are to substantiate or refine current views of the Revolutionary crowd.

For Philadelphia, 1779 was a very bad year.[16] The economy, racked by inflation even before the year began, grew worse as the value of continental currency dropped and prices rose.[17] In January the Supreme Executive Council of Pennsylvania renewed efforts to keep the price of "bread and other necessaries of life" at reasonable levels. Monopolizers and forestallers, whose "most heinously criminal" actions had become "ruinous to the industrious poor," were to be diligently searched out and prosecuted.[18] Orders, however, do not necessarily equal effective action. The "heinously criminal" manipulation of food prices, especially of bread, continued.[19] Early in April the General Assembly tried its hand at stopping "the forestalling and regrating of Provisions" in greater Philadelphia.[20] But the Assembly's legislation was as ineffective as the Council's order. Prices continued to rise; the continental currency continued to depreciate.

At least one important group, the militia, was angered by more than high prices. On May 12 the First Company of the Philadelphia Militia Artillery sent a long memorial to the Supreme Executive Council. Because the militia initiated the action that led to the Fort Wilson incident, this memorial deserves a close reading. The militia began by reminding the Council that they had once more been "call'd out in defence of . . . the Virtuous Cause of Freedom and Independency." While they "chearfully stepped forth . . . to act in a Military Capacity," they also felt compelled to point out certain "Circumstances and Grievances." Each time the militia had taken the field, they had had to leave their families "at the mercy of the disaffected, Inimical, or self Interested; and, we might presume to say, the most Obnoxious part of the Community." Each time the militia returned to the city from a campaign, they found that many had "taken Advantage of our Absence, and enormously advanced the prices on everything." The situation had deteriorated to the point

[16] The narrative presented here is based on a longer and more detailed version in Alexander, "Philadelphia's 'Other Half,'" 284-338.

[17] See Anne Bezanson, *Prices and Inflation during the American Revolution: Pennsylvania, 1770-1790* (Philadelphia, 1951), 12-25, 39-44, 83-88, and her "Inflation and Controls, Pennsylvania, 1774-1779," *Journal of Economic History*, supplement, VIII (1948), 14-19. There was some slight improvement in the price squeeze during the early summer when the committee was regulating prices. But the trend was almost steadily toward a worsening economic situation.

[18] *Pa. Packet*, Jan. 19, 1779.

[19] See *Pa. Gaz.*, Feb. 10, 1779.

[20] *Ibid.*, Apr. 7, 1779.

where "many of us are at a loss to this day what Course or Station of Life to adopt to Support ourselves and Families." Nor was that all. The militia had been "Caluminated [*sic*] and despised" and "treated . . . with Indignity and Contempt."

While the militia suffered, the rich and the "disaffected" were escaping military service. The new law authorizing heavy fines for "Delinquents not forming in Militia" would not rectify this abuse, for "Men in these Exorbitant Times can acquire more by Monopolizing, or by an under Trade, in one Day, than will defray all their Expences of Fines or Penalties in a whole year." Thus "the Midling and poor will still bear the Burden, and either be totally ruin'd by heavy Fines, or Risque the starving of their Families, whilst themselves are fighting the Battles of those who are Avariciously intent on Amassing Wealth by the Destruction of the more virtuous part of the Community."

Describing the abuses they had endured during 1777, the militia noted: "We had Arms in our hands, and knew the use of them; but instead of avenging ourselves, or retaliating on our Innate and Worse of Enemies, we patiently waited the Interference of the Legislative Authority." This point was probably not lost on the Council when the militia "humbly" asked it to use its influence to bring the Assembly to remedy the existing evils. The memorial urged that any able-bodied citizen who would not serve in the militia be fined "in proportion to his Estate" or that, alternatively, the Assembly drop all fines and "leave it to the Militia who obey the Call to Compell every able Bodied Man to join them." Such action had to be taken "lest when the Militia are call'd forth, by leaving such numbers of Disaffected in their Rear, they, by pursuing their usual Methods render our Situation worse than making us prisoners of War."[21] In short, it was a poor man's war.[22] And because of the disaffected monopolizers, the poor were getting poorer—and insulted for their trouble. An equitable solution *had* to be found.

The memorial's implication of possible violence is significant. The members of the militia, as individuals, lacked power. If their memorial was at all correct, they lacked economic power. Many of them could vote, but having the vote was hardly equivalent to having effective political power.[23] Certainly the Assembly for which they could vote

[21] Samuel Hazard *et al.*, eds., *Pennsylvania Archives,* 1st Ser., VII (Philadelphia, 1853), 392-394.

[22] Complaints that the regular militia was composed of the poor were of long standing. See J. Paul Selsam, *The Pennsylvania Constitution of 1776: A Study in Revolutionary Democracy* (Philadelphia, 1936), 74-89.

[23] Freemen who had taken the Oath of Allegiance and were taxpayers could vote.

had not been able, or possibly not willing, to punish monopolizers or militia dodgers. The only effective power the militia possessed was the threat or use of physical force. It should not surprise us that the militia raised the specter of violence. If the legislature could not or would not control artificially high prices and the "disaffected," the militia could either take it—or take to the streets. The actions of the militia in the Fort Wilson incident must be seen in this context of mental anguish economic distress, and political impotency.

Militiamen were not alone in feeling that something had to be done about prices and disaffection. Ten days after the memorial was presented, a number of Philadelphians, headed by Christopher Marshall, a fervent believer in price control, issued a call for a general town meeting to regulate prices.[24] It was not mere chance that this call occurred in late May. On April 20 the ship *Victorious* had arrived in Philadelphia. When the cargo, including dry goods which soon rose dramatically in price, remained on board for a long period, the suspicion spread that forestalling was afoot. Because Robert Morris had contracted to dispose of the cargo, indignation focused on him.[25] More important, prices had taken an especially high jump in the middle of May. Sarah Bache, writing to her husband, observed that "as soon as the bad news came from Virginia [invaded by the British on May 10], they raised the prices of everything. . . . You can't think how much worse the money is since you left this [city] . . . Many families yesterday went without bread; not a bit to be bought."[26] It seemed that many merchants, especially Morris, had gone too far.

Some Philadelphians were disturbed by the prospect of a general town meeting. Elizabeth Drinker said that "many are apprehensive of a mob rising on second day next—with a view of discovering monopolizers etc." On May 24, the day before the meeting, what Drinker called "Threatening Handbills . . . with a view to lower the prices of provisions

---

Since all white males who were at least 18 were eligible for militia service, some would have been too young to vote. See Chilton Williamson, *American Suffrage from Property to Democracy, 1760-1860* (Princeton, N. J., 1960), 82-83.

[24] William Duane, ed., *Extracts from the Diary of Christopher Marshall, kept in Philadelphia and Lancaster, during the American Revolution, 1774-1781* (Albany, N. Y., 1877), 231.

[25] For an analysis of Morris's role in the events of the summer, which finds him innocent of the various charges brought against him, see Hubertis Cummings, "Robert Morris and the Episode of the Polacre 'Victorious,'" *PMHB*, LXX (1946), 239-257. For Morris's defense of his actions see *Pa. Packet*, July 8, Aug. 5, 1779.

[26] Quoted in Frederick D. Stone, "Philadelphia Society One Hundred Years Ago, or the Reign of Continental Money," *PMHB*, III (1879), 384.

etc," were posted.[27] Sarah Bache described what happened when a man, generally believed to be "a great speculator," tried to pull down one of the posters. "The mob (I should not call them by that name), the militia seized him, and after taking him about on a horse, bareheaded, lodged him in the Old Gaol. They took up several others and put them in the same place."[28] That night members of the militia, who had been reviewed that afternoon, stood guard. On the morning of the 25th the German-town militia came into the city to attend the town meeting scheduled for five o'clock.[29] During the day persons described only as "men with clubs" went to several stores and "obliged" sellers to lower their prices.[30] By the time the meeting convened an attempt at price regulation seemed inevitable.

When the meeting opened, Daniel Roberdeau, a merchant and militia officer who was associated with the "radical" element in state politics, was unanimously elected chairman. He thereupon denounced those who were "getting rich by sucking the blood of this county." Perhaps remembering his Locke, he also offered a philosophical defense of action by the people: "There is at present no law for regulating the prices in the shops and markets, neither is there any law to prevent such regulations being made, and therefore the whole rests upon the virtue and common consent of the community. I have no doubt but combinations have been formed for raising the prices of goods and provisions, and therefore the community, in their own defence, have a natural right to counteract such combinations, and to set limits to evils, which affect themselves."[31]

Several resolves were then adopted, "after some amendments," proclaiming that "the public have a right to inquire into the causes of . . . extraordinary abuses, and prevent them," and the meeting elected two committees to carry out its directives. One committee, whose members were also to serve on a larger general committee, was authorized to in-

[27] Henry D. Biddle, ed., *Extracts from the Journal of Elizabeth Drinker, from 1759 to 1807 A.D.* (Philadelphia, 1889), 116.

[28] Quoted in Stone, "Philadelphia Society," *PMHB*, III (1879), 383.

[29] *Ibid.;* Biddle, ed., *Drinker Jour.*, 116; Duane, ed., *Marshall Diary*, 217; *Pa. Packet*, May 25, 1779.

[30] Biddle, ed., *Drinker Jour.*, 116. Although it is possible that these actions occurred after the general town meeting, the late starting time of the meeting makes it probable that they occurred before the meeting.

[31] *The Pennsylvania Evening Post* (Philadelphia), May 29, 1779. Roberdeau probably did not prepare his address by himself, for Marshall said on May 22 that "six persons were appointed to draw an address to be delivered" at the general town meeting. Duane, ed., *Marshall Diary*, 217. For Roberdeau's past activities see Brunhouse, *Counter-Revolution*, 24-25, 56, and Warner, *Private City*, 27.

vestigate Morris's role in the case of the *Victorious*. The general committee was ordered to see that prices were systematically lowered on a month-by-month basis until they reached the level at which they had stood on January 1, 1779. The committee was also empowered to "collect" charges "made against persons intrusted by congress, with the expenditure of public money, or the execution of public commissions." Having done this, the committee was to ask Pennsylvania's Continental delegates what steps were being taken to punish those guilty of such impropriety. Finally, the general committee was directed to "take measures" to insure that anyone "who by sufficient testimony can be proved inimical to the interest and independence of the United States" not be allowed "to remain among us."[32] The militia, many of whom were at the meeting, must have been pleased.

Not all Philadelphians shared the militia's joy. Sarah Bache probably reflected the view of numerous Philadelphians when she said, "I hope the regulation will have a good effect, but cannot help feeling a little frightened about it; for, since I have begun to write, there is nothing but Huzza constantly at the Gaol" as people believed guilty of crimes against the populace were clamped into jail.[33] Possibly animated by such anxieties, on May 28 the Executive Council issued a carefully worded resolve designed to short-circuit the power of the general committee. The Council noted that persons suspected of abuses ranging from "inimical practices" to forestalling had been put in jail by other than "the ordinary course of justice." In order that "Justice be done, . . . and also that reasonable and proper satisfaction be given to a people long injured and insulted by the abettors of the tyranny of Great-Britain," the sheriff was to compile a list of those jailed. City magistrates were to make a "strict enquiry" into the charges against such people and, if there was "reasonable ground," they were to appear at the next court of quarter session. If those accused could not post bond, they would have to remain in jail. The citizens were urged to accept this measure and to support the "honour and safety of Government" lest "common enemies" have "grounds to rejoice."[34] What the resolve did not say, of course, was that actions against the town meeting resolves were not necessarily actions against the law. And magistrates could bind people over for trial only if they had apparently broken the law.[35]

---

[32] *Pa. Evening Post*, May 29, 1779. The term general committee has been used for clarity; the town meeting did not give its elected committees special designations.
[33] Quoted in Stone, "Philadelphia Society," *PMHB*, III (1879), 384.
[34] Broadside, "In Council . . . May 28th, 1779" (Philadelphia, 1779).
[35] This point was made in a vigorous defense of committee action and attack on

There is no evidence that the committees appointed by the town meeting had been responsible for putting people in jail.[36] But, probably in part to placate the Council, the general committee published a detailed description of their intentions on June 1. Members of the general committee would be present at the courthouse every day save Sunday to receive evidence of violations of the town meeting's resolves. They pledged that "in the present time of general suffering and resentment" they would see that no "innocent persons" shall "by mistake . . . [be] exposed to the unmerited censure of their fellow citizens." Anyone believed to have violated the town meeting's resolves would be so notified in writing. The committee would only "ascertain the facts; they would not punish offenders." Those found guilty would be left "to make their peace with the public the best way they can."[37] Although that "peace" might be hard bought, the committee's statement seemed to imply a basic acceptance of the Council resolve of May 28.

On June 10 support for one of the resolves of the town meeting was offered by the Philadelphia grand jury. Observing that "the wives of . . . many of the most notorious of the British emissaries [i.e., those who defected to the British] remain among us," the grand jury asserted that these women were giving intelligence to the enemy as well as spreading "poisonous, erroneous, wicked falsehoods" in the city. This "pernicious practice" demanded immediate inquiry and remedy. No action was taken on this proposal—at that time.[38]

On June 28 the same militia company that had memorialized the Council in May issued a public statement in support of the general committee. This address, like the May memorial, reveals the militia's bitterness and their willingness to use physical force if need be. Applauding the vigorous action of the committee to lower prices and pledging their wholehearted support, they asserted: "We have arms in our hands and know the use of them,—and are ready and willing to support your Honorable Board in fully executing the righteous and equitable measures

the Council resolve by "A Pennsylvanian," who argued that "Society as a system have certain rights upon individuals, to demand of them such conduct as is conducive to the common good. This power devolving on the Committee easily distinguishes their [power], from the usual power of law." Pa. Packet, June 8, 1779.
[36] On people being put in jail see Stone, "Philadelphia Society," PMHB, III (1879), 383-384; Duane, ed., Marshall Diary, 218; Biddle, Drinker Jour., 116, 117. These sources say nothing about the committee ordering arrests. Still, they do not record people being put in jail after May 30. It is possible that the committee did order the arrests and then on May 31 decided against that course of action.
[37] Pa. Packet, June 1, 1779.
[38] Pa. Evening Post, June 12, 1779.

for which you were appointed; nor will we lay them down till this is accomplished. We wish not to have the preeminence; but we will no longer be trampled upon." The militia closed their "unanimous" statement with the warning that "if by reason of the obstinacy and perverseness of individuals, your Committee find themselves inadequate to the task, *our drum shall beat to arms.*"[39]

That the militia were in no mood to compromise is indicated by their behavior at a second town meeting held on July 27. John Cadwalader, an opponent of price control by the populace, reported later that he was prevented from speaking at the meeting "by a body of about 100 men, armed with clubs, who had marched in array, under their officers, with fife and drum, and placed themselves near the stage." Because of this action, a number of people at the meeting retired to the College Yard and held their own gathering which refused to be bound by any resolutions passed by the original meeting. Although the rump session denounced the silencing of Cadwalader as "a violation of the LIBERTY OF SPEECH," it did agree to accept the original meeting's plan to elect a new committee composed of 120 persons to reduce prices and stop the devaluation of the currency.[40] It is evident, however, that leaders of the rump meeting remained opposed to price regulation as well as to attempts to ferret out the "inimical."[41] This is demonstrated by the fact that two slates for the Committee of 120—which offered a clear choice for or against the directives of the May town meeting—were rushed into print.[42] The election, according to the report of the Committee of 120, drew out "the greatest number of voters ever known on such an occasion," and the slate of men most

[39] *Pa. Packet,* July 1, 1779.

[40] The quotations and the account of the rump session are from the *Pa. Gaz.,* July 28, 1779. See the same issue of the newspaper for Roberdeau's account which gives no indication that Cadwalader was prevented from speaking or that a group of people left the original meeting in protest.

[41] Cadwalader (whose name is, in various sources, also spelled Cadwallader) had wanted to speak against the type of regulation the committee was attempting. Morris surely did not support the committee's idea of searching out the "inimical" and "disaffected." Rush, Sharp Delaney, Whitehead Humphreys, and Wilson all opposed price regulation. Andrew Caldwell was "a well known conservative." David Lenox was vigorously opposed to popular action. This list of men at the rump session *ibid.* On the attitudes of these men see Brunhouse, *Counter-Revolution,* 23, 72, and John F. Watson, *Annals of Philadelphia, and Pennsylvania . . . ,* III (Philadelphia, 1884), 286.

[42] For example, the antiprice regulation slate was numbered from 1 to 120, and number 1 was Morris. See broadside, "Committee for the City and Liberties of Philadelphia" (Philadelphia, 1779), and cf. broadside, "The Independent and Constitutional Ticket . . ." (Philadelphia, 1779); *Pa. Packet,* Aug. 5, 1779, and Brunhouse, *Counter-Revolution,* 72.

strongly for committee action overwhelmed their opposition, 2,115 to 281.[43]

This resounding vote of confidence for a vigorous assault on high prices and the disaffected turned out to be a hollow victory. A group of cordwainers, tanners, and curriers, who had already challenged the price regulations, continued to resist them. On August 18 eighty merchants sent a long memorial to the Committee attacking the idea of price control by committee.[44] As opposition mounted, the Committee of 120 became less and less effective: its numbers were "too numerous to execute with dispatch, and too various in their ideas to concur in all measures expected from them." Faced with these difficulties, the Committee asked the Assembly to take responsibility for economic control and on September 24 suspended "further proceedings, except in very particular cases, until the determination of the Assembly be made known." In so doing, the Committee bitterly noted that price abuses had greatly multiplied and that the currency had depreciated "more within these few days past, than in the four preceding months." After four months of town meeting resolves and committee action the merchants remained as "impolitic" and prices as oppressive as ever.[45] If the militia wished to prove the sincerity of their earlier pronouncements, they would now have to take to the streets with their drum beating.

Shortly after the Committee of 120 admitted defeat, probably on September 27, members of the militia held a meeting at Burn's Tavern on the city commons and resolved to "send away the wives and children of those men who had gone with the British, or were within the British lines." The meeting sent for militia captain Peale to be their "commander" in this action. Although Peale had been a member of the general committee appointed by the May town meeting, he tried to dissuade the militia. The militiamen were not impressed. They said they would implement their resolution or "sacrifice their lives" in the effort. Seeing that the militia could not be moved, Peale refused to lead them and left the meeting.[46] Thus rebuffed but perhaps still hoping to secure Peale's support, the militia sat tight, elected a Committee of Privates, and scheduled an-

[43] Pa. Packet, Aug. 5, 1779.

[44] See ibid., July 15, 1779, for a statement signed by James Roney, a statement of 10 cordwainers, "A Whig Shoemaker," and "Justice"; ibid., July 20, 1779, for a statement of Roney; ibid., July 31, 1779, for a statement of Cadwalader and "an honest Shoemaker"; ibid., Sept. 10, 1779, for an address of merchants.

[45] The quotations are ibid., Sept. 25, 1779. For examples of the opposition to the Committee of 120 see ibid., Sept. 9, 10, 1779.

[46] The quotations are from "Statement of Peale," in Reed, ed., Joseph Reed, II, 423-424. See also Morris, comp., "Fisher Jour.," PMHB, XLI (1917), 169; Pa. Evening Post, May 29, 1779; Sellers, Peale, I, 193.

other meeting for Monday, October 4. Peale was asked to attend, as were militia officers Dr. James Hutchinson, John Bull, and Alexander Boyd. These four men, usually viewed as "radicals," quickly consulted together and, fearing "the violent proceedings of the militia," agreed to attend the meeting to "use their best endeavours to restrain, as far as they might be able, any violent and improper proceedings."[47]

On October 2 the Committee of Privates published a newspaper notice "earnestly" requesting all militiamen to come to the mass meeting of the militia, set for October 4 at Burn's Tavern at nine o'clock in the morning.[48] On October 4 itself, a handbill, its source unknown, called the militia to meet on the commons. According to one reporter, this handbill urged the militia "to fall on a plan, to drive from the city, all disaffected persons, and those who supported them." The handbill listed a number of persons worthy of being "seise[d] and put on board the prison ship to be sent to New York." Included in the list were Buckridge Sims, Thomas Story, Jonathan Drinker, and others.[49]

When the militia met at Burn's Tavern, it apparently set about deciding who should be rounded up. Peale and his friends "represented the difficulty of selecting such characters as all could agree to be obnoxious amongst such a body of the people; that in such an attempt they must infallibly differ as to the object,—[and] of course no good purpose could be answered." The militia were unbending, and Peale, joined probably by the others in his group, left the meeting believing that "to reason with a multitude of devoted patriots assembled on such an occasion was in vain."[50] By noon on October 4 the militia were ready to act, although

[47] The quotation is from "Statement of Peale," in Reed, ed., *Joseph Reed*, II, 424. See also Morris, comp., "Fisher Jour.," *PMHB*, XLI (1917), 168-169.

[48] *Pa. Packet*, Oct. 2, 1779.

[49] No copy of this handbill is known to have been preserved. The only primary source that lists names on the handbill mentions just the three names noted above. See Patterson to Rodney, Oct. 6, 1779, in Ryden, ed., *Rodney Letters*, 323. Since Wilson gathered his friends at his home and "said that he had good information he was intended to be taken up," he may have been listed on the handbill. See "Attack on Fort Wilson," *PMHB*, V (1881), 475. On the difficulty of determining who issued the handbill see Alexander, "Philadelphia's 'Other Half,'" 314n.

[50] Attributing this in large measure to the many Germans among the militiamen, Peale remarked that the Germans' "attachment to the American cause was such that they disregarded every danger," and that their "resentment at this time was most violently inveterate against all Tories." Indeed, "they only looked straight forward, regardless of consequences." All of this discussion and planning had taken place before noon. All quotations are from "Statement of Peale," in Reed, ed., *Joseph Reed*, II, 424. See also Biddle, ed., *Drinker Diary*, 121, and Morris, comp., "Fisher Jour.," *PMHB*, XLI (1917), 169.

407

it is not clear whether they intended to do more than take up some "disaffected" persons and parade them through the city.

Drinker, who was not a member of the Republican Society but who had been accused by the general committee of opposing price regulation, was the first to be taken.[51] When he walked out of the Friends' Yearly Meeting, which concluded at noon, a group of militia was waiting for him. For some reason, perhaps because Drinker had been sitting in the meeting for six hours, the militiamen allowed him to go home to eat dinner. Story, Sims, and Mathew Johns were also arrested.[52] (None of the three were members of the Republican Society, and Story, like Drinker, had been accused by the general committee of opposing price regulation.[53]) The four captives were marched to Burn's Tavern,[54] and the whole militia group, one hundred fifty to two hundred strong, then proceeded down Arch Street toward the Delaware. The prisoners were led along "with the Drum after them, beating the Rogue's March." It was now about three o'clock—six hours after the militia meeting opened and three hours after Drinker had been taken up. James Gibson went to meet the crowd and found that it had "halted somewhere about 5th Street." "After some time" the militia began to march again. General Thomas Mifflin soon joined Captain Ephraim Faulkner, the militia's leader, and according to Gibson, "while he seemed to be in Conversation" with Faulkner, "one of the men in the ranks struck or pushed him with his Musquet." Gibson apparently did not think this incident important; he

[51] I believe that Drinker was not a member of the Republican Society because he was not one of the 82 men who were listed as members when the society was formed in March 1779. See *Pa. Gaz.*, Mar. 24, 1779. Nor does Brunhouse, whose *Counter-Revolution* is the standard political history of the period, list Drinker as a member of the society. On the general committee and Drinker see Biddle, ed., *Drinker Diary*, 117, 119.

[52] Biddle, ed., *Drinker Diary*, 121, and Morris, comp., "Fisher Jour.," *PMHB*, XLI (1917), 169. The militia had also attempted to arrest Joseph Wirt, but could not find him. Samuel Fisher, who was not at Wirt's house, says that the militia "ransacked" the house. Fisher may have meant that the militia merely searched the house very carefully rather than that they tore it apart. Since no one mentions the search of Wirt's house, I have no way of knowing if any damage was done to it. But, given the other actions of the militia as they "arrested" their prisoners, there seems to be little reason to think that the house was torn apart. Wirt, who was also not a member of the Republican Society, had been tried and acquitted by the state for treason. See Morris, comp., "Fisher Jour.," *PMHB*, XLI (1917), 168-169, and n. 51 above.

[53] None of the three men are listed as members of the Republican Society. *Pa. Gaz.*, Mar. 24, 1779. On Story and the general committee see Duane, ed., *Marshall Diary*, 218, and Biddle, ed., *Drinker Diary*, 116. I do not know why Sims and Johns, who are rather obscure figures, were anathema to the militia.

[54] Morris, comp., "Fisher Jour.," *PMHB*, XLI (1917), 169-170, 171.

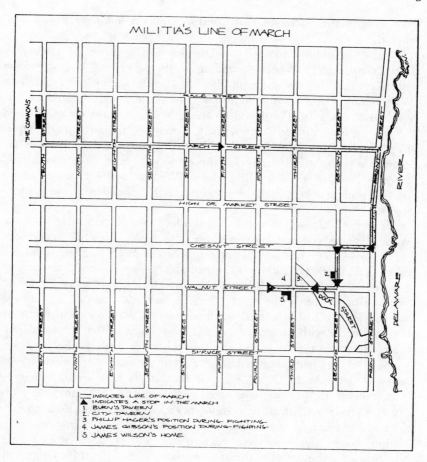

left the march when it passed Third, "not satisfied that they really meant to attack any House, and I was inclined to think that they from their Course did not mean Mr. Wilsons in Particular."[55] Mifflin apparently disagreed. He went to Wilson's home and was inside during the fighting. The militia continued down Arch, turned south on Front, marched to the corner of Chestnut, and turned up Chestnut away from the river. When

[55] All the quotations are from Biddle, ed., *Drinker Diary*, 121, and "Attack on Fort Wilson," *PMHB*, V (1881), 475. See also Shaw to Winthrop, Oct. 10, 1779, in Wainwright, ed., "Shaw's Letters," *ibid.*, LXX (1946), 300, and "Philip Hagner's Narrative," in Reed, ed., *Joseph Reed*, II, 426.

they reached the intersection of Chestnut and Second, they paused and gave three cheers.[56]

While the militia moved through the city, a group of twenty to forty "gentlemen" had been "parading on the pavement" in front of the City Tavern. When they saw and heard the militia, they "retreated" into Walnut Street and entered Wilson's house, which was located on the southwest corner of Third and Walnut. With fife and drum playing, the militia, according to an eyewitness, "followed" the retreating "gentlemen" by turning down Second and moving toward the City Tavern. When they reached the Tavern, they stopped, gave three cheers, and proceeded to the corner of Second and Walnut where they turned up Walnut and marched, as Gibson described it, "in order" toward Third Street.[57]

As the militia was about to cross Dock Street, a half block from Wilson's house, their march was again interrupted. This halt was caused by Colonel Grayson, a member of the Board of War. Grayson, who had persuaded Allen McLane, a Continental captain, to introduce him to Faulkner, wanted the militia to turn up Dock Street, thus bypassing Wilson's house. He spoke of "his fears as to the consequence of attacking Mr. Wilson in his house." Faulkner replied that "they had no intention to meddle with Mr. Wilson or his house, their object was to support the constitution, the laws, and the Committee of Trade. The labouring part of the City had become desperate from the high price of the necessaries of life." As McLane described it, this "halt in front brought a great press from the rear; two men, Pickering and [William] Bonham, ran up to the front, armed with muskets and bayonets fixed, and inquired the cause of the halt, at the same moment ordered Faulkner to move up Walnut Street. Grayson addressed Bonham, and I addressed Pickering, who answered me with the threat of a bayonet, sometimes bringing himself in the attitude of a charge from trailed arms. Captain Faulkner and Mr. John Haverstadt interfered, to pacify Pickering and Bonham." According to McLane, "then word was given to pass up Walnut."[58]

If the militia deserves the label "mob," they should have been the ones to initiate the fighting. But the evidence of the eyewitnesses and contemporaries is mixed. Philip Hagner, a Continental army officer, reported that "the mob marched up Walnut, and as they passed Mr. Wilson's

[56] "Hagner's Narrative," in Reed, ed., *Joseph Reed*, II, 426.
[57] The quotations are *ibid*. and "Attack on Fort Wilson," *PMHB*, V (1881), 475. See also "Narrative of M'Lane," in Reed, ed., *Joseph Reed*, II, 151.
[58] "Narrative of M'Lane," in Reed, ed., *Joseph Reed*, II, 151.

house gave three cheers; the rear of them had passed the house, when Captain Campbell . . . shook his pistol, and discharged it from the third story window; the party in the street immediately faced about, and opened a brisk fire into the house." McLane stated, "I saw Captain Campbell . . . at one of the upper windows . . . heard him distinctly call out to those in arms to pass on. Musketry was immediately discharged from the street and from the house." Peale, who was not an eyewitness, reported that when the militia were "opposite" the house, Campbell "hoisted a window with pistol in his hand, and some conversation having passed between him and the passing militia, a firing began." Gibson saw something quite different:

They [the militia] marched on very slowly until the Rear came nearly abreast of me [two doors past Wilson's house.] I was happy for the Moment to think they intended not to halt as they [had] passed the House so far [;] about this Time some of the sashes of the 2nd or 3d story and I think but am not certain some of the Shutters of the Lower Windows were thrown open. This Circumstance drew the Attention of the Militia and I immagin occasioned them to Halt and give some Language. . . . It appeared to me after some Words the Militia were disposed to put themselves in motion agen when I observed one of them without any Command and not more than thirty feet from me lift his Gun, standing with his face to the eastward, and fired his Gun, whether the shot struck the House or not I cannot say.

Gibson recalled that a second shot and possibly a third were fired from the house.[59] Given the differences in these accounts, it is not surprising that a writer on October 9 noted that "some say that one began [the firing] first, and the others contradict it."[60] The available evidence sug-

[59] The quotations in order of appearance are from "Hagner's Narrative," *ibid.*, 426; "Narrative of M'Lane," *ibid.*, 151; "Statement of Peale," *ibid.*, 425; "Attack on Fort Wilson," *PMHB*, V (1881), 475-476. Wilson adamantly claimed that the Fort Wilson group had called out to the "mob" "not to fire" and that the militia had fired first "without any previous demand or complaint." Wilson to Robert Morris, undated, as quoted by Smith, *Wilson*, 138. (I have not been able to examine the letter myself.) Wilson's testimony is, of course, hardly that of a disinterested observer. And, although this point should be noted rather than emphasized, Wilson may not have been an eyewitness to what happened since the house was large and the people were in various parts of it. See "Narrative of M'Lane," in Reed, ed., *Joseph Reed*, II, 151-152.

[60] Patterson to Rodney, Oct. 6, 1779, in Ryden, ed., *Rodney Letters*, 323. Watson, *Philadelphia Annals*, III, 286, whose work is primarily based on the recollections of

gests that the most judicious course is to conclude that we cannot be sure who fired first. Still, if the Fort Wilson crowd did assault the militia, who was the "mob," who the injured party?[61] Whether or not Campbell fired the first shot, he paid a price. He was the only man in Fort Wilson to be killed. Once shots were exchanged, the firing "became smart on both sides." The battle raged for about ten minutes until, acting on orders from Joseph Reed, the president of Pennsylvania, members of "the aristocratic 'silk-stocking'" City Troop of Cavalry and some Continental cavalrymen came to the Fort Wilsoners' rescue. With the cry "Charge all armed men," Reed led the cavalry "cuting and slashing" into the crowd of militia. Those militiamen who were not arrested on the spot were "soon . . . put to rout."[62]

Wilson and his friends then "sallied out" of the house and "paraded through the streets and were insulted everywhere, especially about Vine Street."[63] Meanwhile the cavalry attempted to round up and jail the offending militiamen. In the afternoon when twenty-seven of the militia were in jail, "a collection of people in the Street" tried to break into the jail to free the militia, but failed. Guards were posted at the jail, and, that night, cavalry patrolled the city. Philadelphians rested uneasily awaiting the morning.[64]

On the morning of October 5 the officers of the Philadelphia militia along with "numbers of the people" gathered at the courthouse to decide upon a course of action. "The officers were," according to Peale, "exceed-

---

people long after the event, said, "As the mob were passing [Wilson's home] and hurrahing Captain Campbell threw up a window and brandished or fired a pistol, while he addressed them in an excited manner. The mob turned, fired upon the people in the house and broke open the door with a sledge."

[61] I am *not* saying that one or the other of these groups should be labeled a "mob." This wording is for stylistic purposes only.

[62] The quotations of eyewitnesses in order of their appearance are from "Attack on Fort Wilson," *PMHB*, V (1881), 475; Hayden, ed., "Reminiscences of Conyngham," Wyo. Hist. and Geo. Soc., *Procs. and Colls.*, VIII (1904), 212, and Shaw to Winthrop, Oct. 10, 1779, in Wainwright, ed., "Shaw's Letters," *PMHB*, LXX (1946), 300. The description of the City Troop is from Brunhouse, *Counter-Revolution*, 75. See also "Narrative of M'Lane," in Reed, ed., *Joseph Reed*, II, 151-152; Hayden, ed., "Reminiscences of Conyngham," Wyo. Hist. and Geo. Soc., *Procs. and Colls.*, VIII (1904), 208-211; n. 1 above.

[63] The quotations in order of appearance are from "Narrative of M'Lane," in Reed, ed., *Joseph Reed*, II, 152, and Hayden, ed., "Reminiscences of Conyngham," Wyo. Hist. and Geo. Soc., *Procs. and Colls.*, VIII (1904), 212.

[64] The quotation is from Morris, comp., "Fisher Jour.," *PMHB*, XLI (1917), 171. See also *ibid.*, 172; Hayden, ed., "Reminiscences of Conyngham," Wyo. Hist. and Geo. Soc., *Procs. and Colls.*, VIII (1904), 214-215; Biddle, ed., *Drinker Diary*, 122; "Statement of Peale," in Reed, ed., *Joseph Reed*, II, 425.

ingly warm, and full of resentment that any of the militia should be kept in the jail." Indeed, Hagner noted, "a majority . . . were in favour of discharging the prisoners." Seeing this, Timothy Matlack, secretary of the Executive Council, deemed it prudent to offer to let the prisoners out on bail. The militia officers agreed and gave security for the appearance of the militiamen then in jail at any future trial. A "large majority" of the officers also "insisted" that the people in Fort Wilson go to jail for a period of twenty-four hours "as a kind of retaliation." No action was taken on this demand, but about noon the twenty-seven militiamen were released.[65] In the afternoon a meeting of "both parties" called by Reed led to an accord designed to avoid further violence. It was agreed that all participants in the incident who had been arrested were to go free on a high bond and that the militia were to choose representatives to "lay their grievances before the Assembly."[66] These judicious steps did not quell the fears of everyone. As one Philadelphian noted, "it is not over. They [the militiamen] will have blood for blood."[67]

The Council and the Assembly may have shared this fear. At any rate, they took out riot insurance. On the ninth the Council sent a message to the Assembly. It spoke of Reed's "apprehensions of great distress among poor house-keepers in this city, from the high price of Flour," and asked the Assembly to authorize the distribution of one hundred barrels of flour with a "preference" being given "to such Families as have performed Militia duty."[68] The Assembly, on the same day, agreed but added a note that preference should go "to the Families of such Militia Men as shall serve on the present expedition." (George Washington had just requested that additional militia be called up.)[69] On the tenth the Assembly enacted a law which dealt with two of the

[65] The quotations are from "Statement of Peale," in Reed, ed., *Joseph Reed,* II, 425, and "Hagner's Narrative," *ibid.,* 427. See also Morris, comp., "Fisher Jour.," *PMHB,* XLI (1917), 172.

[66] The quotations in order of appearance are from "Hagner's Narrative," in Reed, ed., *Joseph Reed,* II, 428, and Patterson to Rodney, Oct. 6, 1779, in Ryden, ed., *Rodney Letters,* 323-324. On Oct. 6, the Council issued a proclamation that required all the principals, including those in Fort Wilson, to surrender themselves. See broadside, "By his excellency Joseph Reed, esq. . . ." (Philadelphia, 1779). For people giving themselves up and being released on bond see *Pa. Col. Recs.,* XII, 128, 130, 137, 138, 139, 141, 144, 152. All of these men were in Fort Wilson. Thus, it appears that after Oct. 4 none of the principals in the incident were jailed.

[67] Patterson to Rodney, Oct. 6, 1779, in Ryden, ed., *Rodney Letters,* 324.

[68] Reed also wanted wood distribution although he did not ask that a preference be given to militiamen in that distribution. See *Pa. Col. Recs.,* XII, 125.

[69] The quotation is from Hazard *et al.,* eds., *Pa. Archives,* 1st Ser., VII, 740, and see also 738, 741, 745, 747-749.

militia's chief grievances. Henceforth officers of the law would be required to arrest upon complaint any person whose "general conduct . . . is such that there is just reason to suspect he is an enemy to the American cause, or that he hath manifested a general disaffection thereunto." If upon examination the person appeared to be guilty, he was to be held without bail until the Assembly could consider his case. Alternatively, at the discretion of these officials he could be sent out of the state. The second part of this law dealt with another of the grievances set forth in the militia memorial of May 12: henceforth fines for not serving in the militia would be levied with "a due regard to the value of such delinquent's estate and circumstances."[70]

Pennsylvania's officials obviously recognized that the way to avoid further violence was to eliminate the militia's legitimate grievances. The Council and Assembly also showed wise restraint when they refused to assign guilt in the incident. Reed dismissed it as "the casual overflowings of liberty," although he expressed the hope that individuals would never again "take the Vindication of their Zeal, or apprehended injuries, into their own hands." It was proposed that an act of oblivion and indemnity would serve better "than a rigorous pursuit of legal measures," and such an act was later passed.[71]

As this narrative suggests, the Fort Wilson incident was a complex affair. Assessing it fairly is no simple task. But from the complexities certain points do clearly emerge.

First, the militia did have a number of genuine ideological and economic grievances. Indeed, the legitimacy of their grievances was recognized at various times by the Supreme Executive Council, the Assembly, and the Philadelphia grand jury.

Second, the militia, like the town meetings which favored committee action, had a philosophical belief in their right as citizens to redress

---

[70] A copy of the law was published in *Pa. Evening Post*, Oct. 12, 1779. It appears that the Council did not relay the May 12 memorial of the militia to the Assembly. This law was the result of another petition from militiamen presented to the Assembly on Oct. 8. This memorial complained about the "disaffected" who remained in the city and about the difficulty of the poor in obtaining salt and flour due to high prices. On the next day the Assembly appointed a committee which wrote the bill enacted into law just one day later. See *Journal of the House of Representatives of the Commonwealth of Pennsylvania. Beginning the twenty-eighth Day of November, 1776, and Ending the Second Day of October, 1781 . . .* , I (Philadelphia, 1782), 363-364, 386-388.

[71] The quotations are from *Pa. Col. Recs.*, XII, 168. See also J. Thomas Scharf and Thompson Westcott, *History of Philadelphia, 1609-1884*, I (Philadelphia, 1884), 402.

the long-standing grievances that the government could not or would not correct, This theory, at least in America, was hardly extraordinary: it was used by many to justify the American Revolution itself.

Third, because the militia lacked economic and political power, the only effective form of power left to them was the use of physical coercion. The militiamen had used physical coercion before the Fort Wilson incident. They had put in jail people who opposed price regulation; they had attempted at the second town meeting to intimidate speakers who opposed price regulation.

Fourth, the militia who marched on October 4 felt that they were supporting the efforts of the town meetings and they did not take to the streets en masse until months of committee attempts to regulate prices and "disaffected" persons had resulted in failure.

Fifth, the events of October 4 did not happen on the spur of the moment. The militia planned their action over time and established committees to organize and implement their operation.

Sixth, the militia did not go on a rampage of destruction on the fourth. In fact, they showed surprising kindness toward Drinker by allowing him to go home to eat dinner before he was marched to the commons.

Seventh, the course of the militia's march does not seem to indicate that they were heading for Wilson's home. It is quite possible that they went up Walnut Street only because the "gentlemen" parading on Second Street went that way.

Eighth, during the orderly march through the city, the militia leader listened to two separate attempts to dissuade the militia from attacking Wilson's home. Furthermore, when just a half a block from Wilson's house, he declared that the crowd had no intention of bothering Wilson or of attacking his home. Given Faulkner's statement, it is possible that the militia may have intended to do nothing more than hold their prisoners up to public ridicule.

Ninth, the exchange of fire between the militia and the Fort Wilsoners began only after most of the militia had marched past the house. This would indicate that there was, in fact, no plan to attack the house.

Tenth, some individual in the militia group may have, on his own, fired the first shot. But it is just as likely, perhaps even more likely, that Campbell fired the first shot. And if a militiaman did fire first, he did so only after the windows in the house had been opened. If a militiaman fired first, could he have done so believing that the people in the house were about to fire?

Finally, it seems clear that the militia did not need to be propagandized to act. In fact, the militia memorial of May 12 was the first major threat of action by the city's populace, and the militia actively supported price regulation by arresting people even before the first town meeting was held. Nor do the actions of the militia on October 4 indicate that the militia were agents of the Constitutional "radicals" in their political feud with the "conservative" Republicans. Peale and other leading "radicals" vigorously attempted to stop the militia from acting. And the militia did not arrest leading Republicans; indeed, the men arrested were not even members of the Republican Society. As much as the sources will tell us, the militia did arrest people who had been charged by the general committee with attempting to subvert price regulation. Most of the militia who marched probably did oppose the Republican Society, but as Brunhouse noted, "the core of the trouble was economic."[72]

Examined in the broader contest of the meaning of the actions of Revolutionary "mobs," the Fort Wilson incident offers both support and challenge to current generalizations about the Revolutionary crowd. It strongly suggests that the term *mob* has too often been incorrectly used with a pejorative implication and should be replaced by "the more neutral term" *crowd*.[73] It also suggests that we must reassess Gordon S. Wood's claim that in early America there were "no bread riots, no uprisings of the destitute."[74] For although the Fort Wilson incident was not a bread riot on the European model, it was—at least in the eyes of the leader of the militia—an act of "desperation."[75] The militia who marched on October 4 did not stage an "uprising" in the sense of revolting, but they did act because, in Faulkner's words, "the labouring part of the City had become desperate from the high price of the necessaries of life." The militia may not have been "destitute," but they thought they were and acted accordingly.

[72] Brunhouse, *Counter-Revolution*, 68.

[73] The quotation is from Pauline Maier, "Revolutionary Violence and the Relevance of History," *Journal of Interdisciplinary History*, II (1971), 130. Maier argues for the retention of the term mob—without quotation marks—and continues to use it in that fashion. However, because "mob" does carry a negative connotation, at least today, the dangers in continuing to use it seem to outweigh any possible advantages.

[74] "A Note on Mobs in the American Revolution," *WMQ*, 3d Ser., XXIII (1966), 639. Richard Hofstadter and Michael Wallace, *American Violence: A Documentary History* (New York, 1970), 109-110, have challenged Wood's claim by presenting what they call a "Bread Riot in Boston, 1713."

[75] On European bread riots see George Rudé, *The Crowd in History: A Study of Popular Disturbances in France and England, 1730-1848* (New York, 1964).

The actions of the militia and of the town meetings also offer strong support for Pauline Maier's claim that Revolutionary Americans attempted to avoid "mob" violence.[76] The militia, having petitioned the Assembly for redress, waited from late May to late September while the town meeting's committees attempted to regulate prices and the "inimical." Moreover, although the militia did use physical coercion before the Fort Wilson incident, they certainly did not display a penchant for violence. The militia and town meetings were willing, however, to use coercion, including physical coercion, to achieve their ends. Their concept of acceptable levels of citizen action does not appear to have been the same as the concept held by those who formed the constituted state government. Indeed, the militia's idea of its right to act was more radical than that of the so-called political radicals—the Constitutional Society leaders.

This different view of acceptable levels of citizen action is not negated by Maier's argument that eighteenth-century American crowds at times "used extralegal means to implement official demands or to enforce laws not otherwise enforceable" and that since at times local magistrates "participate[d] or openly sympathized with the insurgents," the crowd could well be taking "on the defense of the public welfare, which was, after all, the stated purpose of government."[77] But if the October 4 crowd was merely enforcing and extending the government's law, why did the government—represented by the cavalry under the direction of President Reed—go "cuting and slashing" into the crowd without going "cuting and slashing" into the Fort Wilsoners? Why were the only people rounded up and arrested members of the crowd? Why were the Fort Wilsoners allowed to "sally out" onto the streets to "parade" their victory? Unless the governmental officials were predisposed to believe that the Fort Wilsoners' actions were justified and that the crowd's were not, it seems odd that members of both groups were not immediately arrested. The government seemed very concerned about the safety of the Fort Wilsoners; it seemed much less concerned about the safety of the crowd. The government seemed to believe that the Fort Wilsoners had acted properly and that the crowd had acted improperly. At least in this one instance, the concerns and beliefs of the government appear to have been quite different from those of the crowd.

The Fort Wilson incident raises more questions than it answers. Were the concerns and beliefs of the people Maier has called "the new conservatives" really essentially the same as those of the people who

[76] See Maier, "Popular Uprisings," WMQ, 3d Ser., XXVII (1970), 29, 33-34.
[77] Ibid., 4, 8.

formed the crowd after 1776?[78] If, as both Wood and Maier maintain, the threat of crowd action helped create law after 1776, what does that say about how representative and open the "republican" process was?[79] When crowd confrontations, such as the one at Fort Wilson, forced the creation of laws, was it a concern for the needs of the people or a fear of further violence that prompted the legislation? Did the new American governments willingly respond to the needs of the people or did they grudgingly yield to the threat of violence?[80] How much more of a voice did the average person have after 1776? In short, did the creation of an independent America really unify the American people, or was the new nation filled with as much conflict as consensus? I do not claim to be able to answer these questions. Nor do I think it is the duty of others who have studied the crowd to offer definitive answers. Until, however, we examine the crowd in Revolutionary America far more closely than we have, these questions can be answered in only the most tentative way.

[78] Maier, "Charleston Mob," *Perspectives in Am. Hist.*, IV (1970), 188.

[79] *Ibid.*, 181-182, but cf. 194, and Wood, "Note on Mobs," *WMQ*, 3d Ser., XXIII (1966), 641-642.

[80] For suggestive examples from the period before the Revolutionary War see Lemisch, "New York's Petitions," *N.-Y. Hist. Soc. Qtly.*, XLIX (1965), 313-326.

Private Indebtedness and the Revolution
in Virginia, 1776 to 1796

Emory G. Evans[*]

IN January 1775 merchant William Lee of London, the brother of Richard Henry and Arthur of Virginia, wrote merchant John Lidderdale of Liverpool that the colonies were going to stand firmly behind their nonimportation, nonexportation resolves unless Parliament revoked the Intolerable Acts. The effect, he continued, that this would have on British merchants and manufacturers was obvious. The situation was explosive; fighting might commence at any moment. And "nothing can be more clear than that the first blow struck completely cancels every debt due to G. Britain."[1]

The amount of debt Virginians had accumulated by 1776 is on first view astounding. It was over £2,000,000 and represented approximately half of the total American private indebtedness. It was distributed throughout Virginia society, though large planters were most heavily obligated. The involvement of smaller planters and yeomen was a relatively recent development. The consignment method of marketing tobacco that had prevailed before 1750 had primarily involved the larger producers, but during the twenty-five years prior to the Revolution Scottish firms sent resident factors to buy tobacco and sell goods to all classes of growers through an elaborate system of stores. The result was not only the predominance of Scots in the tobacco trade, but also the increasing indebtedness of all elements of Virginia society.[2] How many debtors there were in Virginia cannot be accurately determined, but

[*] Mr. Evans is a member of the Department of History, Northern Illinois University. The research for this article was made possible by grants from the Colonial Williamsburg Foundation and the American Philosophical Society. Mr. Warren Billings, now of Louisiana State University at New Orleans, helped with the statistical information. A version of this paper was delivered at the annual meeting of the Organization of American Historians in Kansas City, Missouri, in April 1965.
[1] William Lee to John Lidderdale, Jan. 2, 1775, William Lee Letterbook, 1774-1775, Virginia Historical Society, Richmond.
[2] Emory G. Evans, "Planter Indebtedness and the Coming of the Revolution in Virginia," *William and Mary Quarterly*, 3d Ser., XIX (1962), 511, 518.

Richard Sheridan in a study of the British credit crisis of 1772 found that 37 Glasgow firms had "31,000 debts owing to 112 stores in Virginia." If we add to this figure the debts owed the consignment merchants, we would probably arrive at a total of 35,000—a conservative estimate. The great majority of these debts were under £100 and were owed to the Scots. The larger debts, on the other hand, tended to be owed to English consignment firms.[3]

Historians such as Charles A. Beard, Isaac Harrell, and Lawrence Henry Gipson, convinced of the paramount importance of economic forces in explaining man's behavior, have been led by the mere size of this debt to conclude that Virginians must have welcomed the Revolution as an opportunity to cancel it.[4] But I have argued elsewhere that the evidence for this interpretation rests largely upon the state's actions during and after the war and cannot explain Virginian motives before passions were aroused.[5] My essential points were: that indebtedness was an expected and accepted consequence of an agrarian economy; that it occurred in colonial Virginia under circumstances that did not result in oppressive control by British merchants and was not acutely resented by planters before the imperial struggle broke out; that the Virginians' closure of the courts in 1774, seemingly prime evidence of their desire to escape their debts, was principally motivated by the hope of forcing the British mercantile community to pressure Parliament into repealing the Intolerable Acts; and finally, that more than a few heavily indebted Virginians opposed independence. British threats to constitutional rights loomed much larger than indebtedness in prewar Virginia consciousness. In this article I will argue further that, although hope of avoiding payment of the debts did indeed develop among Virginians as the war progressed, it was under circumstances that again cast doubt upon the Beard-Harrell thesis.

[3] Richard B. Sheridan, "The British Credit Crisis of 1772 and the American Colonies," *Journal of Economic History*, XX (1960), 161-186, esp. 175ff.

[4] Charles A. Beard, *Economic Origins of Jeffersonian Democracy* (New York, 1915), 270; Isaac S. Harrell, *Loyalism in Virginia* (Durham, N. C., 1926), 26-28; Lawrence Henry Gipson, "Virginia Planter Debts Before the American Revolution," *Virginia Magazine of History and Biography*, LXIX (1961), 259-277. See also Prof. Gipson's *The British Empire Before the American Revolution*. Vol. X: *The Triumphant Empire: Thunder-Clouds Gather in the West, 1763-1766* (New York, 1961), Chap. 8, and *The Coming of the Revolution, 1763-1775* (New York, 1954), Chap. 4.

[5] Evans, "Planter Indebtedness," *Wm. and Mary Qtly.*, 3d Ser., XIX (1962), 511-533.

For two years prior to the Declaration of Independence few British debts were repaid in Virginia. The courts were closed since 1774.[6] Representatives of British firms tried desperately to collect unpaid debts before events progressed too far, but as one remarked, "tho' the People may pretend to be willing they are not [as] ready to pay as when the compulsive Power of the Law can be exerted against them."[7]

Before long things were to be even worse for British merchants and factors resident in Virginia. As early as the spring of 1776 many of them, foreseeing future events, petitioned the Convention in Williamsburg to be permitted to leave the state. The Convention allowed them to depart provided they did not take more than £50 with them and did not secret, carry off, or destroy "any books of accounts or papers belonging to any person in *Great Britain*." This latter provision has been interpreted to mean that the Convention did not want British merchants to retain evidence necessary for the collection of Virginia accounts. Yet the state did nothing subsequently to destroy or seize the records, leaving open the possibility at least that the Convention wanted to insure that accounts were not falsified. Certainly, in this crucial period, delegates did not want substantial amounts of hard money removed from the colony. And, to say the least, their action was hardly severe considering that Governor Dunmore was still waging war in Virginia during the spring and summer of 1776.[8]

[6] On the closure of the courts see Statement of William Hay, No. 2, Feb. 19, 1798, Claims of John Hay & Co., Treasury Group, Class 79, Piece 27, Public Record Office (Virginia Colonial Records Project microfilm, Colonial Williamsburg Foundation, Williamsburg, Va.). Hereafter cited as T. 79/27 and as Va. Col. Rec. Proj. microfilm; Council to Lord Dunmore, June 10, 1774, Colonial Office Group, Class 5, Piece 1352 (Va. Col. Rec. Proj. microfilm, Williamsburg). Hereafter cited as C. O. 5/1352; Dunmore to Secretary of State, Dec. 24, 1774, C. O. 5/1353 (Va. Col. Rec. Proj. microfilm, Williamsburg); William Allason to Walter Peter, July 1, 1774, Allason Letterbook, 1770-1789, Virginia State Library, Richmond; William Carr to James Russell, Oct. 23, 1774, Russell Papers, No. 2, Coutts & Co., Bankers, London (Va. Col. Rec. Proj. microfilm, Williamsburg); David John Mays, *Edmund Pendleton, 1721-1803, A Biography* (Cambridge, Mass., 1952), I, 245-248; Robert P. Thomson, "The Tobacco Export of the Upper James River Naval District, 1773-75," *Wm. and Mary Qtly.*, 3d Ser., XVIII (1961), 383-407.

[7] James Gilchrist to Isaac Robley, Oct. 12, 1775, Original Correspondence of the Secretary of State, C. O. 5/134 (Va. Col. Rec. Proj. microfilm, Williamsburg).

[8] *The Proceedings of the Convention of Delegates, Held at the Capitol, in the City of Williamsburg, in the Colony of Virginia, on Monday the 6th of May, 1776* (Williamsburg, 1776), 165; Gipson, "Virginia Planter Debts," *Va. Mag. Hist. Biog.*, LXIX (1961), 276.

Soon the state got tougher. In January 1777, after independence, the new government ordered "all the natives of Great Britain who were partners with, factors, agents, storekeepers, assistant storekeepers, or clerks here, for any merchant or merchants in Great Britain" as of January 1, 1776, to leave the state within forty days. The legislature feared that while these persons remained they would have "frequent opportunities of seducing and corrupting the minds of the people" and of corresponding with and giving "intelligence to the enemy." The only exception was for those British citizens who "uniformly manifested a friendly disposition to the American cause or are attached to this country by having wives or children here." By early spring 1777 most of the several hundred people in the proscribed categories had left the state. But hardly had they departed when citizens of Mecklenburg County petitioned the legislature, which reconvened in May 1777, to extend the order to married as well as single factors. The complaint was that most of those who had been allowed to remain were showing a lack of friendship to the American cause by refusing to accept the paper currency of Virginia in payment of British debts, thereby encouraging depreciation and undermining the state's financial position.[9] This patriotic argument, of course, does not obviate the possibility that many Virginians just wanted to pay their debts in paper money, but clearly the motivation was not crudely simple. The legislature considered the Mecklenburg petition during the May session, but did not enact the necessary legislation until the following fall. The fiscal problems brought up in the petition could not be resolved simply by removing the remaining representatives of British firms from Virginia.

By the winter of 1777-1778 a novel program had been worked out, largely a product of Thomas Jefferson's fertile mind. Impetus for the plan probably came from Congress's call in November for the confiscation of loyalist estates. A bill was introduced to the legislature on January 17, 1778, which provided that all debts due British subjects from citizens of Virginia could be paid into the recently established loan office

---

[9] Purdie's *Virginia Gazette* (Williamsburg), Jan. 3, 1777; H. R. McIlwaine, ed., *Official Letters of the Governors of the State of Virginia*, I (Richmond, 1926), 80, 87; George McCall to Archibald McCall, Apr. 26, 1777, *McCall* v. *McCall*, Chancery Records, 1779-1785, Essex County Court; *Journal of the House of Delegates of Virginia, 1776-1790* (Richmond, 1827-1828), May 1777 session, 10, 15, 34, 72. Hereafter cited as *Journal of Delegates;* Petition of Mecklenburg County Inhabitants, May 4, 1777, Legislative Petitions, 1776-1791, Virginia State Library.

of the state. This office would give the debtor a certificate of payment which would discharge him from further obligation to the creditor for the amount he paid in. Virginia's heavily indebted citizens could thus pay their debts in depreciated paper currency. The plan benefited not only the debtor, but the state as well, by increasing the stability of paper money and transforming the liabilities of its citizens into public assets. The responsibility of the state to the creditor, if any, was not mentioned in the bill, and the intent of the legislature cannot be determined from the existing evidence. Another section of the bill provided for the sequestration of all real and personal property in Virginia belonging to British subjects. The owner retained title to the property but all profits from a sequestered estate would go into the state treasury while hostilities continued. Jefferson and his colleagues hoped that such measures would stabilize the finances of the state and check inflation. The act for sequestering British property passed with very little difficulty on January 22, 1778. Just prior to its passage the state courts were reopened for all except British debt cases.[10]

From the very first the Sequestration Act failed to accomplish what it was designed to do. The provision for debt payment raised only about £42,000 during the first year, and by May 1780, the date of its repeal, the total payments amounted to only £273,544, of which £119,000 had come in during the last two months of the act's life. By that time the sterling value of the payments amounted to only £12,035. Surprisingly only 307 individuals or firms took the opportunity to pay their debts in this fashion.[11] Some undoubtedly did so for patriotic, and some for other,

[10] Dumas Malone, *Jefferson and His Time.* Vol. I: *Jefferson the Virginian* (Boston, 1948), 259-260; *Journal of Delegates,* May 1777 session, 95, 102, 106, Oct. 1777 session, 113, 125, 126; William W. Hening, ed., *The Statutes at Large; being a Collection of All the Laws of Virginia* . . . (Richmond, 1809-1823), IX, 368-369, 377-380, I, 227. Hereafter cited as *Statutes at Large;* Harrell, *Loyalism,* 80-81, 85-89; Julian P. Boyd, ed., *The Papers of Thomas Jefferson* (Princeton, 1950-), II, 170n-171n; Edmund Pendleton to William Woodford, Jan. 31, 1778, David John Mays, ed., *The Letters and Papers of Edmund Pendleton, 1734-1803* (Charlottesville, 1967), I, 246-248.

[11] British Debts Paid in Virginia Currency During the War, C. O. 5/1334 (Va. Col. Rec. Proj. microfilm, Williamsburg); *Virginia Gazette, or, the American Advertiser* (Richmond), July 12, 1786; Harrell, *Loyalism,* 83; Treasurer's Office Records, Journal of Receipts, Jan. 15, 1777-Apr. 2, 1782, Virginia State Library. Hereafter cited as Journal of Receipts. Harrell says that the sterling value of the payments amounted to £15,044 and cites Library of Congress Transcripts of Colonial Office Records and Auditors Books, 1778-1781, Virginia State Library. I have accepted the figure in C. O. 5/1334 (Va. Col. Rec. Proj. microfilm, Williamsburg) which is cor-

reasons. There were both knaves and heroes in Virginia. But the fact remains that out of an estimated 35,000 debtors, only 307 came forward to pay their money into the loan office.

The portion of the act which provided for the sequestration of British owned estates was amended in 1779 to allow for outright confiscation and sale. Sales continued to the end of the war, but the property of only about one hundred persons (most of them British merchants) was sold, and as in the case of debt payment the amount of money raised proved insignificant. Neither provision of the Sequestration Act helped answer the problems it was designed to solve, and in the years to come each was to produce much difficulty.[12]

The Sequestration Act of 1778 is often cited as proof that repudiation was a strong force pushing the colony towards revolution. Yet it, and other Virginia legislation respecting debts and British property, were not enacted until the British were Virginia's enemies and the financial needs of the state were pressing. In this framework the Sequestration Act cannot be treated simply as a mask for ulterior motives, but emerges, at least in part, as an attempt to bolster the state's currency and stabilize its finances at the expense of the enemy.

Although Isaac Harrell, in his provocative study *Loyalism in Virginia*, suggests that among those who took advantage of the Sequestration Act were the cream of the patriot leadership, the number of patriot leaders among this group of 307 was not great. Only 25 appear on either

---

roborated by the *Va. Gaz., or, Amer. Adv.* cited above. Harrell also implies that over 500 persons made payments, but I can find only 474 recorded payments representing 307 individuals and firms.

[12] Harrell, *Loyalism*, 92-93, 96, 98, 103, 111-112; *Journal of Delegates*, Oct. 1779 session, 9, 13, 26, 36, 40, 43, 52, 58, 60, 75, 78, 79, 87, 108; *Statutes at Large*, X, 153-157, 366-371; G. McCall to A. McCall, July 3, Nov. 28, 1779 (letters must actually be 1780 since he refers to events happening after these dates), *McCall* v. *McCall*, Chancery Records, Essex County Court; Escheated Lands, 1780-1817, Auditors Papers, No. 128, Virginia State Library. Records of Inquisitions against British Subjects, 1775-1787, T. 79/72 (Va. Col. Rec. Proj. microfilm, Williamsburg); List of Names of All the Persons against Whose Estates Inquisitions of Escheats and Forfeitures have been recorded in the General Court of Virginia, Mar. 22, 1787, Audit Office, Class 13, Piece 102, Public Record Office (Va. Col. Rec. Proj. microfilm, Williamsburg). Hereafter cited as A. O. 13/102; Virginia Loyalist Claims, Aug. 10, 1784, T. 79/124a (Va. Col. Rec. Proj. microfilm, Williamsburg). It is difficult to determine how many individuals and firms had property sold. The only Virginia records that I can find list under 100 through 1787. British records vary. The Loyalist Claims show 129 in 1784, but by 1787 this list had swollen to over 250. I feel certain that this is an inflated figure.

Jack P. Greene's list of 110 political leaders from the period 1720 to 1776 or Jackson T. Main's 100 largest property owners of the 1780s.[13] Strike from these 25 those who were either dead or had fled to England (Lewis Burwell, John Blair, and John Randolph); those who cannot be considered political leaders (Roger Atkinson, William Digges, John Robinson, and Francis Willis); and those who were bill collectors for British firms and who either willingly or under pressure accepted paper currency for the debts they were collecting and paid it into the loan office (Benjamin Waller, Paul Carrington, and Edmund Pendleton), and 15 remain. Waller, who paid in £14,705 of collected money, explained in 1783, for example, that he was forced by law to accept the paper currency in payment of debts and "besides at the time there was the danger of being accounted a Tory and treated accordingly in Case of refusing Currency."[14] Of those left the most notable are Thomas Jefferson, who paid £2,666 of debts he inherited as a result of his marriage to Martha Wayles Skelton, Carter Braxton (£260), Archibald Cary (£8,391), Benjamin Harrison (£2,140), and George Wythe (£20). It is true that 10 of the 15 paid debts that were over £1,000 and the total for the group was £40,208—a substantial sum. But £29,000 of this amount was paid by Richard Adams, William Brent, Archibald Cary, and Mann Page. Aside from Cary these four cannot be considered to have been in the upper echelons of patriot leadership. Patrick Henry, George Washington, Richard Henry Lee, George Mason, Thomas Nelson, and John Page, among others, do not appear on the list. And among the luminaries who do appear, Jefferson, who was most responsible for the framing of the Sequestration Act, Wythe, and perhaps Harrison, favored the opening of the courts to British creditors after the war and an equitable arrangement for the payment of debts.[15] It seems reasonable

[13] Harrell, *Loyalism*, 84; Jack P. Greene, "Foundations of Political Power in the Virginia House of Burgesses, 1720-1776," *Wm. and Mary Qtly.*, 3d Ser., XVI (1959), 485-506; Jackson T. Main, "The One Hundred," *ibid.*, 3d Ser., XI (1954), 354-384; Journal of Receipts, 1777-1782.

[14] See items concerning Waller, Carrington, and Pendleton in Journal of Receipts; Benjamin Waller to Davison and Newman, July 28, 1783, T. 79/32 (Va. Col. Rec. Proj. microfilm, Williamsburg); Pendleton to James Madison, Mar. 31, 1783, in Mays, ed., *Pendleton Papers*, II, 440-441.

[15] Journal of Receipts; on Jefferson and Lee see n. 31 below; *Page v. Pendleton and Lyons*, Wythe (Va.) 127-132 (1793); "Conservator Pacis" in the *Va. Gaz., or, Amer. Adv.* (Richmond), Oct. 25, 1783; Benjamin Harrison to [governor of another state], Oct. 17, 1783, *The History of America in Documents: Original Autograph Letters, Manuscripts and Source Materials* (New York, 1950), Pt. II, 12-13; *Journal*

to conclude that for them the debt payment portion of the Sequestration Act was primarily an attempt to stabilize the state's finances and not to provide an easy way out for individual debtors.

The idea that money might be raised by the payment of British debts into the state treasury did not die easily. In July 1782, with the state's finances in desperate straits, the portion of the "act for sequestering British debts" was revived. In the previous fall, as a hedge against inflation, military certificates had been issued for "arrears in pay" due the state's soldiers. These certificates bore interest and were to be redeemed periodically. The revenue provided for this purpose proved inadequate, however, and it was thought that a revival of the Sequestration Act would help solve the problem. Payment of "one tenth part or more" of British debts could be made annually in May in specie, tobacco, or hemp. It was also hoped that additional money could be raised by a provision in the law expediting the sale of escheated estates.[16]

The new act failed to fulfill its purpose. As early as August 1782 Tappahannock merchant George McCall commented that he "would not give the Treasurer £100 for his ten years collection out of the many hundred thousands [which] by this law he ought to receive." The prediction proved true, for no payment of British debts into the treasury under this law was ever made since the first payment was not possible until May 1783 and by then the signing of the preliminary articles of peace had been announced in Virginia. The debt payment provisions of the law clearly conflicted with article four of both the preliminary agreement and the final treaty signed in September. Although the state was to keep its courts closed to suits for British debts for a long time, it was not prepared to continue such a law in time of peace. Evidently both the state and its citizens felt that the treaty of peace abrogated the debt payment provisions, for the act was never formally repealed, nor is any reference to it to be found after 1782. In May 1783 the legislature declared that "funds formerly appropriated . . . for redemption of

---

of Delegates, Oct. 1787 session, 79-80. Harrison was probably for debt payment although it cannot be definitely proved. Joseph Jones seems to be the one important person in this group who opposed the opening of the courts. He said that he was for payment, but consistently voted against the removal of impediments. Joseph Jones to Thomas Jefferson, Dec. 29, 1783, Feb. 28, 1784, Boyd, ed., Jefferson Papers, VI, 428-430, 565-567; Journal of Delegates, May 1784 session, 41, 72, 75, Oct. 1787 session, 51-52, 79-80.

[16] Statutes at Large, X, 462-468, XI, 82; Minute Book, House of Delegates, May 1782 session, 84, 85, Virginia State Library.

the certificates granted . . . to officers and soldiers of the Virginia line"
had "proved inadequate" and levied a variety of new taxes for the
redemption of the military certificates.[17]

The inability of the legislature to decide upon a firm policy regarding
British debts during the last years of the war reflected the wide differences of opinion on the question in Virginia. In the fall of 1781 a law
was passed which stopped executions for most debts until December
1783, but in May 1782 the date on which executions for debts other than
British could begin was advanced to March 1783. More interesting was a
related provision which allowed executions for British debts to begin at
the same time if the debt had been assigned to a citizen of Virginia prior
to May 1, 1777—an interesting concession considering that less than a
year earlier a hostile British army had been in the state.[18] Many Virginians
who saw nothing wrong with the payment of prewar British debts into
the treasury as long as hostilities continued still viewed them as an obligation that would ultimately have to be met. Edmund Randolph's
conflicting feelings mirrored those of a number of his countrymen.
He wrote to James Madison in June 1782 regarding the portion of the
military certificates bill affecting debt payment that its merits were "great,"
but "I cannot forbea[r] fearing, lest we should precipitate the U. S. into
difficulties upon a negotiation [for peace], which we might possibly
avoid by stoppin[g] at the point, at which we now are." Randolph continued concerning the opening of the courts to British debt cases:

I, whose interest speaks so strongly in favor of the act, do really contem-
plate it with apprehension. Ravaged as our country has been, the little
surplus over domestic want, must be drawn into the public coffers. With
what are we to pay our old debts? Mr. Morris's notes, which are receiv-
able in taxes will banish specie pro tanto: and if executions are to be satisfied by specie alone, the poor man, who has disdained to avail himself
of the tender law, must part from his freehold at 1/4 of its value to some
tory, whose debt remains unextinguished because he obstinately refused
paper currency.[19]

[17] G. McCall to A. McCall, Aug. 3, 1782, *McCall* v. *McCall*, Chancery Records,
Essex County Court; *Statutes at Large*, XI, 196-197. A thorough check of the Journal
of Receipts for the 1780s has revealed no payments under the revived debt payment
portion of the Sequestration Act.

[18] *Statutes at Large*, X, 471-474, XI, 75-76.

[19] Edmund Randolph to Madison, June 20, 1782, William T. Hutchinson and
William M. E. Rachal, eds., *The Papers of James Madison* (Chicago, 1962-), IV, 357.

Later in the fall of 1782 Randolph advised Madison that a group in the House of Delegates were going to "attack . . . those debtors to british subjects," [including Governor Harrison] who had "lodged depreciated money in the treasury for the discharge of their british debts" on the grounds that these persons were "not strongly fortified by ideas of propriety and justice." But subsequently he reported that the session was marked by "a firm and unremitted hatred to Great Britain" which resulted in repeal of the legislation reopening the courts to cases involving British debts assigned to Virginia citizens before it became operative. The repeal stated that "great and ruinous inconveniences and hardships" would result unless a "remedy" was "applied" and therefore "no debt or demand whatsoever contracted with, or due to any British subject . . . shall be recoverable in any court of record within this commonwealth" if it had been assigned after April 19, 1775. Interestingly enough, the provisions of this repeal were to remain in force only until December 1783. Clearly Virginians in 1782 did not think that the war had totally abrogated their British debts.[20]

Peace, however, brought no easing of the situation respecting the debts. In the fall of 1783 a proposal to liberalize citizenship requirements and provide for the easier admission of aliens into the state was initially defeated with the region south of the James River voting solidly against it, but was subsequently divided into two separate bills and passed. The only persons excluded were "citizens or natives" of any of the United States who after April 1775 had served in the British army or navy or who had been the owners or part owners of a "privateer or other armed vessel, cruizing against the United States. . . ." It was also stated that nothing in the legislation "shall be construed to contravene the treaty of peace with Great Britain . . . ," but this provision was not of much benefit to British creditors since the act prohibiting executions for British debts was continued for another year. This latter action was a clear breach of the Treaty of Paris, and there were some who were perturbed by "this base act of [the] Assembly." In fact, Peyton Skipwith felt that "the House is already ashamed of such an act of injustice and I do not myself entertain a doubt of repeal taking place ere long. . . ."[21]

[20] Randolph to Madison, Nov. 8, Dec. 27, 1782, *ibid.*, V, 262, 453; *Statutes at Large*, XI, 176-180.
[21] *Va. Gaz., or, Amer. Adv.* (Richmond), July 5, Dec. 6, 1783; Statement of William Hay, T. 79/27 (Va. Col. Rec. Proj. microfilm, Williamsburg); *Journal of Delegates*, Oct. 1783 session, 42, 60; *Statutes at Large*, XI, 322-325, 349; Peyton Skip-

Skipwith represented one of three schools of opinion on the question of debts in Virginia at the close of the war. There were those, like him, who felt that the debts should be paid, but that the payment should be spread over a long period because of the general economic situation; there were others who opposed any payment at all; and lastly, there were those, probably constituting a majority, who owed few or no British debts themselves and fluctuated in opinion according to the relative persuasiveness of the others.

The group favoring nonpayment argued, in the words of one, that "the debts . . . of the British subjects [are] equally forfeited with their right to property amongst us, and [we] can never consent that the good citizens of this State shall lay *at the mercy of British creditors on account of such debts;* neither do we think there should be any authority in the *laws* to *compel* the payment of such debts to British subjects, after our citizens have sustained such hardships and injuries within our own country by a mode of warfare unwarrantable, and by attempts upon their liberty unjustifiable." "Would it be just," asked another, "to take from the worthy citizens of our country, who have fought and bled in this unequal conflict" and give "to a set of men, who of all others are least deserving."[22]

The rebuttal to this view was perhaps best expressed by George Mason in a letter to Patrick Henry in 1783.

Had it been in the Power of the American Commissioners (which it certainly was not) to have abolished the British Debts here, it wou'd have been but short sighted Policy to have done so. The far-fetch'd Arguments, which have been used to shew the Distinction between this and other Wars, wou'd not have been approved, or comprehended, by the Bulk of Mankind; and with what Degree of Confidence cou'd foreign Merchants have ventured their Effects here, if upon any national Quarrel, they were liable to Confiscation? I cou'd have wished indeed that some reasonable time had been allowed for the Payment of British Debts, and that the Interest on them had been relinquished. As to the first, the Desire of the British Merchants to reinstate themselves in their Trade here, will prob-

---

with to William Jones, Jan. 30, 1784, *Skipwith* v. *Farrell and Jones* (1799), Ended Cases, U. S. Circuit Court, Richmond. The geographical vote on the liberalized migration and citizenship proposal is seen subsequently in all other votes concerning British debts or related questions.

[22] *Va. Gaz., or, Amer. Adv.* (Richmond), June 7, 1783, Jan. 3, 1784.

ably prevent their pressing their Debtors; and as to the last, their Bond-Debts only will carry Interest.

Mason then observed in a passage that has invariably been quoted out of context that in "Conversation upon this Subject, we sometimes hear a very absurd Question 'If we are now to pay the Debts due to British Merchants, what have we been fighting for all this while?'" But he replied for himself:

Surely not to avoid our just Debts, or cheat our Creditors; but to rescue our Country from the Oppression and Tyranny of the British Government, and to secure the Rights and Liberty of ourselves, and our Posterity; which we have happily accomplished. The Ministry in Great Britain, and the Torys here, have indeed constantly accused us of engaging in the War to avoid the Payment of our Debts; but every honest Man has denyed so injurious a Charge with Indignation. Upon the Whole, we have certainly obtained better Terms of Peace than America had Cause to expect; all the great Points are ceded to us; and I can not but think it wou'd be highly dangerous and imprudent to risque a Breach of it.[23]

Arguments representing both sides of the debate appeared with equal frequency in the newspapers, and by late 1783 and early 1784 representatives of British firms began to feel that a majority of Virginians at least accepted the idea that British creditors should be treated fairly.[24] One wrote home that the people "are disposed to pay as soon as they are able," and another, that by "the best information the general disposition of the people, arising from an unequivocal belief that all legal obstruction to the collection would be removed, was to pay, their debts, as fast as they possibly ... [can] from the annual produce of their estate...."[25]

At the same time Virginians remained outraged at the "depredations and plunder Committed by the British Army" and were especially angered in the spring of 1783 by the refusal of its commander, Sir Guy Carleton, to return slaves who had been carried away during the war.

[23] George Mason to Patrick Henry, May 6, 1783, Robert A Rutland, ed., *The Papers of George Mason, 1725-1792* (Chapel Hill, 1970), II, 771-772.

[24] For examples of the opposition see *Va. Gaz., or, Amer. Adv.* (Richmond), June 7, 14, Oct. 25, Nov. 1, 8, Dec. 20, 1783, Jan. 3, 1784; for those in favor of payment see *ibid.*, June 7, 14, July 5, Oct. 25, Nov. 29, Dec. 27, 1783, July 17, 1784.

[25] William Hay to James Baird, Dec. 12, 1783, T. 79/27 (Va. Col. Rec. Proj. microfilm, Williamsburg); Alexander Horsburgh to William Cuninghame, Aug. 21, 1784, T. 79/1 (Va. Col. Rec. Proj. microfilm, Williamsburg).

Carleton's decision proved to be crucial in the subsequent development of Virginia attitudes on the debt question. This violation of the preliminary peace treaty made it easy to argue that, if the British were not going to abide by its provisions, neither would Virginians. Prior to the news of Carleton's action Henry Tazewell wrote John Francis Mercer that the part of "the Treaty which stipulates for the payment of British Debts is objectionable in the Eyes of some . . . but the Treaty I suppose must be held sacred." Later, in August 1783, Ralph Wormeley said that before "this affair [Carleton's refusal] our Legislature was disposed to give effacy to the article [Article 4 of the treaty] . . . , it may now be doubted, what will be their resolution next meeting. I have my apprehensions of the issue. . . ." Of course, Carleton's action gave some Virginians the excuse they had been waiting for. Nonetheless, it is clear that it was a turning point in public opinion, the more so when the British also refused to move from the military posts in the Northwest Territory.[26]

In addition, the general economic situation in Virginia after the war worsened. Although the reopening of ports to British commerce in 1783 brought a resurgence of prosperity, in the fall of 1785 the bottom fell out of the tobacco market, and the remainder of the decade was depressed. Moreover, even the two-year period of relative prosperity was deceptive. Tobacco prices rose to unprecedented heights and there was a vast influx of manufactured goods, but these facts masked the disarrangement wrought by the war. Prosperity did not return equally to all regions of the state or to all persons. Norfolk and its hinterland, dependent as they were on the West Indian trade, remained depressed throughout the decade. Individuals' circumstances also changed. As merchant William Allason put it, "we have not only had a revolution in Political government but also in many peoples private circumstances. . . ." Many who before the war had no credit or property "are now most opulent" while others who "were in good credit" and were large property owners

---

[26] William Anderson to Samuel Gist, Feb. 1, 1783, A. O. 13/30 (Va. Col. Rec. Proj. microfilm, Williamsburg); Henry Tazewell to John Francis Mercer, Apr. 19, 1783, Mercer Papers, Virginia Historical Society; Ralph Wormeley, Jr., to Edward Montague, Aug. 10, 1783, Wormeley to [?] Corbin, June 13, 1786, Ralph Wormeley Letterbook, 1783-1802, Alderman Library, University of Virginia, Charlottesville; Pendleton to Madison, June 10, 1783, Mays, ed., *Pendleton Papers*, II, 452. Pendleton told Madison that gentlemen "rejoiced at the slaves having been sent away from New-York, as an infraction of the treaty which would justify the non-payment of British debts; however this was only private conversation."

had lost both credit and wealth. As always war had had its effect, and many people were not in position to take advantage of the economic upswing in 1783 and 1784.[27]

Also, hard money was extremely scarce in the state throughout the decade. In July 1781 paper currency ceased to be legal tender. Holders of this paper were allowed to redeem it the next year for certificates valued at 1000 to 1 and carrying 6 per cent interest. This action was accompanied by heavy taxation as the state attempted to repay its war debt. The inrush of long awaited manufactured goods in 1783 and 1784 combined with the above factors to deprive the country of almost any circulating medium. With little or no money, hard or otherwise, Virginians were justifiably concerned about the effect of opening the courts to British creditors. Jefferson summarized the problem when he wrote British merchant Alexander McCaul that there "are two circumstances of difficulty in the paiment of these debts. To speak of the particular state with which you and I are best acquainted, we know that it's debt is ten times the amount of it's circulating cash. To pay that debt at once then is a physical impossibility. Time is requisite. Were all the creditors to rush to judgement together, a mass of two millions of property would be brought to market where there is but the tenth of that sum of money in circulation to purchase it. Both debtor and creditor would be ruined, as debts would be thus rendered desperate which are in themselves good."[28]

---

[27] Alan Schaffer, "Virginia's 'Critical Period,'" in Darrett B. Rutman, ed., *The Old Dominion: Essays for Thomas Perkins Abernethy* (Charlottesville, 1964), 152-170; Robert Beverley to William Beverley, June, 1783, Robert Beverley Letterbook, 1761-1793, Library of Congress; John Hyndman to Robert Carter, Nov. 29, 1783, Carter Papers, Virginia Historical Society; Peter Lyons to Gist, Nov. 7, 1783, May 10, 1784, A. O. 13/30 (Va. Col. Rec. Proj. microfilm, Williamsburg); John Syme to Archibald Hamilton, Mar. 31, 1785, A. O. 13/85 (Va. Col. Rec. Proj. microfilm, Williamsburg); Madison to Richard Henry Lee, July 7, 1785, Gaillard Hunt, ed., *The Writings of James Madison* (New York, 1900-1910), II, 149-152; *Va. Gaz., or, Amer. Adv.* (Richmond), Oct. 15, 1785; *Journal of Delegates,* Oct. 1785 session, 22, 24, 54; David Ross to Hercules Ross, Aug. 22, 1783, *Ross v. Ross* (1806), Ended Cases, U. S. Circuit Court, Richmond; W. Lee to Luke Staveley, Aug. 10, 1784, Lee to Edward Browne, Apr. 26, 1785, May 11, 1785, Lee Letterbook, 1783-1787, Virginia Historical Society; W. Allason to Henry Ritchie, Dec. 22, 1784, Allason to Robert Allason, May 18, 1785, Allason Letterbook.

[28] Jefferson to Alexander McCaul, Apr. 19, 1786, Boyd, ed., *Jefferson Papers,* IX, 388-390; Harrell, *Loyalism,* 114-119; John Sutton to Carter, Apr. 3, 1782, Carter

All of these factors—the scars of war fresh in Virginia minds, Carleton's refusal to return the slaves, the general economic situation, and the scarcity of money—operated against the early acceptance of a settlement favorable to the British creditor. From the summer of 1784 until the close of 1787 a number of efforts were made to have the state abide by the Treaty of Paris, but all were unsuccessful. In June 1784, James Madison presented a plan in the House of Delegates which provided for the opening of the courts to suits for British debts and the installment payment of these debts. As a preliminary move he proposed a resolution that all acts of Virginia which prevented compliance with the Treaty of Paris be repealed. This was defeated by a substantial margin, as was an alternate plan which would have opened the courts after the British had paid reparations for slaves seized during the war. The vote was similar to the one of the previous December on the proposal to liberalize citizenship requirements. The region south of the James River was almost solidly opposed to any easing of the restrictions on the payment of British debts.[29]

It was in this May 1784 session of the assembly that Madison and Patrick Henry began to debate issues that involved much more than the state of Virginia. Madison, the nationalist, and Henry, the localist, were consistently on opposite sides of almost every major issue including British debts. Henry had allegedly said in the debate on the Sequestration Act that "wars between . . . nations [should] cancel every contract betwixt their citizens" and in June 1784 proved himself extremely sensitive on the issue. The region south of the James River was Henry country, and the votes of this area on issues involving British debts paralleled Henry's position.[30]

Papers; Randolph to Madison, May 21-24, 1782, Hutchinson and Rachal, eds., *Madison Papers*, IV, 263-265; G. McCall to A. McCall, Aug. 3, 1782, *McCall v. McCall*, Chancery Records, Essex County Court; Petition from Northampton County, June 12, 1784, Legislative Petitions, 1776-1791; Madison to James Monroe, June 4, 1786, Hunt, ed., *Madison Writings*, II, 244-246; *Virginia Independent Chronicle* (Richmond), Sept. 5, 1787; D. Ross to James Carmichael, Dec. 6, 1786, *Ross v. Ross;* Henry Skipwith to William Short, Aug. 7, 1787, *Short v. Skipwith* (1806), Ended Cases, U. S. Circuit Court, Richmond.

[29] *Letters and Writings of James Madison*, Congressional edition, I (Philadelphia, 1865), 83-85; *Journal of Delegates,* May 1784 session, 41, 54, 72-75.

[30] See "Philo Decius" [James Montgomery?], *Decius's Letters on the Opposition to the New Constitution in Virginia, 1789* (Richmond, 1789), 92. Henry's sensitivity

By the fall of 1784 Madison's chances of success improved. Feeling was developing against the assembly's failure to accept his moderate plan in June, and Henry would shortly be out of the legislature. It was time to pick a successor to Benjamin Harrison as governor, and as Madison noted, "Mr. H. I understand does not refuse and it certainly depends on his option." Henry took the option, presenting an opportunity which Madison promised "will be embraced to renew the subject in the Assembly."[31]

With Henry out of the way those in the assembly who favored abiding by the treaty moved quickly. A bill was introduced on December 18, 1784, which opened the courts to suits for British debts but which provided that payment for these debts could be made annually over seven years with no interest for the period of the war. The bill passed rapidly through the House of Delegates and, on December 30, was sent to the Senate where there was some delay. But by January 5, after a conference ironed out disagreements between the two houses, it was clear that the bill would pass the next day, which also happened to be the day scheduled for adjournment. Unfortunately, on the night of January 5 the weather turned severely cold, and the James River became clogged with ice. Eight members of the House of Delegates who were staying in Manchester

---

can be seen in the case of John Warden who, after the Madison resolve had been voted down, said publicly that the legislature "had voted against paying for the coats on their backs." Henry moved that Warden be seized and forced to apologize. The motion was carried, and Warden, under the threat of a prison sentence, acknowledged his error before the house. See "Decius" in *Va. Ind. Chron.* (Richmond), Mar. 11, 1789; *Journal of Delegates,* May 1784 session, 57.

[31] Madison to R. H. Lee, Nov. 14, 1784, Lee-Ludwell Papers, Virginia Historical Society. It is interesting to note that, with the exception of Henry, most of the Virginia notables associated with the coming of the Revolution were in favor of opening the courts to British creditors after the war and arriving at some sort of equitable means of payment. Madison, though of a somewhat younger generation, represents the ideas of this group best, but such disparate types as George Washington, George Mason, Thomas Jefferson, and Richard Henry Lee felt the same way. See Jefferson to Madison, Apr. 25, 1786, Boyd, ed., *Jefferson Papers,* IX, 433-435; Mason to Henry, May 6, 1783, Rutland, ed., *Mason Papers,* II, 769-773; Mason to George Washington, Nov. 27, 1787, *ibid.,* III, 1019-1022; Washington to David Stewart, Nov. 5, 1787, and to Bushrod Washington, Nov. 10, 1787, John C. Fitzpatrick, ed., *The Writings of George Washington,* XXIX (Washington, 1939), 302, 312; R. H. Lee to John Adams, Aug. 1, 1785, Lee to Richard Bland Lee, Feb. 5, 1794, James C. Ballagh, ed., *The Letters of Richard Henry Lee,* II (New York, 1914), 378-381, 563-575; *Journal of Delegates,* May 1784 session, 41.

were unable to get back across the river, preventing a quorum in the house. After waiting two days the assembly adjourned until March and, as it turned out, ended the chance of opening Virginia courts to British debt cases for another eight years.[32]

There were two more attempts prior to the ratification of the federal Constitution to do away with legal impediments to debt collection. But Madison's bill in the fall of 1785 was so crippled with amendments that he did not bring it to a vote and let it die on the table. Two years later, another attempt was engineered by George Mason and George Nicholas. Over the vigorous opposition of Henry's constituency (Henry himself was temporarily absent) they were able to pass a resolution, by a vote of seventy-two to forty-two, that all acts repugnant to the Treaty of Paris be repealed, but that the operation of such a law be suspended until all other states took similar action. When a bill was presented to carry out the intent of this resolution, however, Henry was able to have it amended so that it would not go into effect until the British gave up the posts in the northwest and recompensed Virginians for the slaves seized during the war. The amended bill passed by a majority of forty-nine, positive proof of Henry's tremendous influence. Soon afterward, the legislature also acknowledged the state's liability for the money paid into the treasury under the Sequestration Act of 1778 according to a scale of depreciation reducing the amount to the actual sterling value at the time of payment, plus 6 per cent interest. At the same time no judgment was made as to the validity of such a payment; that decision was left to the courts. The law was made operative simultaneously with the opening of the courts to British debt cases, for many feared that, if the state

[32] *Journal of Delegates,* Oct. 1784 session, 48, 76, 77, 92, 94, 95, 105, 106, 107, 110; Madison to Monroe, Dec. 4, 1784, Madison to R. H. Lee, Dec. 25, 1784, Hunt, ed., *Madison Writings,* II, 96-97, 99-100; Henry to R. H. Lee, Jan. 9, 1785, William Wirt Henry, ed., *Patrick Henry: Life, Correspondence and Speeches,* III (New York, 1891), 265-267; Madison to Jefferson, Jan. 9, 1785, Boyd, ed., *Jefferson Papers,* VII, 588-598. One wonders if the eight delegates truly could not get back across the river, and one's suspicions are heightened by a letter of Henry to Richard Henry Lee in which he seems to protest too strongly the severity of the weather and the attachment of the stranded gentlemen to the bill. But Madison in a detailed letter to Jefferson (above) made no accusations. There was substantial feeling that the act had in fact passed and was law since both houses of the legislature had approved it. But nothing came of this. See Pendleton to R. H. Lee, Mar. 7, 1785, Mays, ed., *Pendleton Papers,* II, 475-476.

rendered itself liable for the sterling value of the debts, the bulk of the citizenry would be taxed to pay the debts of a minority. This act settled that question. And there the matter stood, as far as the state was concerned, until 1793.[33]

It is clear that throughout the period of the Confederation the attitude of the public gradually hardened as the legislature killed one attempt after another to open the courts. Alexander Horsburgh wrote to his employer, the Scottish merchant William Cuninghame, after the resolution calling for the opening of the courts had been defeated in June 1784, that the public's "language is greatly changed. . . ." The "bulk of the people begin to harbour an opinion they may get clear of them [British debts] altogether without making payment." He went on to say that it would depend on the action of the assembly in the fall of

[33] *Journal of Delegates*, Oct. 1785 session, 99, 100, 113, 115, Oct. 1787 session, 51-52, 57, 77, 79-80; Madison to Jefferson, Jan. 22, 1786, Feb. 19, 1788, Boyd, ed., *Jefferson Papers*, XIX, 194-202, XII, 607-610; Madison to Monroe, Dec. 24, 30, 1785, Hunt, ed., *Madison Writings*, II, 205-207, 210-212; *Statutes at Large*, XII, 528, 529-530; Mason to Washington, Nov. 6, 27, 1787, Rutland, ed., *Mason Papers*, III, 1011-1012, 1019-1022; Monroe to Madison, Dec. 6, 1787, Stanislaus M. Hamilton, ed., *The Writings of James Monroe*, I (New York, 1898), 178-180. Forrest McDonald in his *We the People: The Economic Origins of the Constitution* (Chicago, 1958), 266-267, evidently unaware of the passage of the bill, argues that an aye vote on the initial resolution to comply with the treaty only after other states had also removed impediments to debt collection was "in effect" a refusal "to abide by the treaty," since such action by the states would be "virtually impossible" to attain. I disagree with this interpretation. On Nov. 17, 1787, after the initial resolution was offered, an attempt was made to amend it so that the operation of such a law would be suspended "until the Treaty of Peace is complied with" by Great Britain. The amendment was defeated 75 to 42. A final amendment was then attempted which would "compel payment of all debts due to British subjects, in such time and manner as shall consist with the exhausted situation of this Commonwealth." This was defeated 69 to 48. The vote was then taken on the original resolution, and it was passed 72 to 42 (*Journal of Delegates*, Oct. 1787 session, 51-52). The men in favor of this successful resolution represented those who had been in favor of removing legal obstacles to the collection of British debts throughout the 1780s. Henry, though not present on Nov. 17, was opposed to the resolution. And those who did vote against it had also voted against, or represented areas that had been opposed to, the only other clear-cut vote on the removal of impediments to the collection of British debts on June 7, 1784 (*ibid.*, May 1784 session, 41; see also vote on June 23, 1784, *ibid.*, 74-75). Finally Prof. McDonald does not explain that a bill was prepared pursuant to the resolution that was passed on Nov. 17, and this bill came before the whole house on Dec. 3. It was then that Henry, who was again present, was able to have the bill amended pursuant to his own views.

1784 whether the public would recover a disposition to pay. If no action were taken, "the people will be confirmed in a belief that they shall never be obliged to pay...."[34]

When the assembly did not act positively in the fall of either 1784, 1785, or 1787, the public's attitude continued to change, as Horsburgh predicted. In May 1784 Richard Hanson wrote to his employers, the British merchants Farrell and Jones, that the people were much divided. Some "are not for paying, others are for it at different periods without interest but it is supposed the majority [of the assembly] will be for complying with the treaty in the fullest extent and pay everyone with interest...." But in August 1784, after the legislature had decided not to open the courts, he wrote that "debtors ... are determined not to pay if they can possibly avoid it"; in August 1785, that "there is little hope of doing anything with them till the court is open"; in October 1785, that "there is no prospect of receiving payment here ... the Assembly have been setting six weeks and not a word said"; and in January 1786, that "none of them will pay anything." The conduct of the assembly, he said, encouraged the people to believe that they "never shall be obliged to pay their just debts."[35]

Much of the responsibility for the shift in public opinion lies with Patrick Henry. He was a localist by conviction and strongly opposed compromising any interest of Virginia. But his violent opposition to the payment of British debts needs more explanation than that. A study of the 307 persons and firms who took advantage of the Sequestration Act suggests deeper motives behind his stand.

Of the 307, I have been able to locate the residence of 214 and establish the occupation of 99. Approximately half of the 214 lived south of the James River or in the tier of counties bordering on its north bank. Another 65 lived in counties located on the headwaters of the York River, that is, on the Pamunkey and the Mattaponi Rivers, including Hanover, Spotsylvania, Caroline, and King William Counties. Of those remaining, 33 lived in the Northern Neck or in counties bordering on

[34] Horsburgh to Cuninghame, Aug. 21, 1784, T. 79/1 (Va. Col. Rec. Proj. microfilm, Williamsburg).
[35] Hanson's letters to Farrell and Jones, May 19, 1784-Dec. 30, 1800, T. 79/30 (Va. Col. Rec. Proj. microfilm, Williamsburg).

the south bank of the Rappahannock River. Another 6 lived west of the Blue Ridge Mountains. With respect to occupation, of the 99 identified, 47 were planters, 36 were merchants, 7 were lawyers, 6 were physicians, 2 were printers, and 1 was a ferryboat operator.[36]

The distribution of the debts paid into the loan office, in terms of amount, compares favorably with the best available estimates of the distribution of all debts owed by Virginians. Two hundred twenty-one of the debts paid into the loan office were under £400, and 141 of these were under £100. Only 25 were in the range of £400 to £999. Of the remainder, 29 were between £1,000 and £1,999, and 32 were £2,000 or over. In the range of debts under £400, 60 of the debtors lived south of the James River or in counties on its north bank. Another 51 in this range lived in the counties on the headwaters of the York River. It should also be noted that 17 of the debtors who owed over £1,000 lived south of the James River or on its northern bank. The counties on the headwaters of the York River had only six of this group, and the Northern Neck nine. Of the remaining five that I have located, four were in Gloucester County and one in Augusta County. The geographic distribution of these debts is probably typical of the distribution of the total Virginia debt since the greater portion was owed to Scots merchants whose stores were largely in the areas where most of the 307 were concentrated. For example, of the 14 stores which William Cuninghame and Co. had in Virginia, 8 were in the upper James River valley or south of the James. Two others were in Spotsylvania and Caroline, which were also counties having a heavy concentration of debtors.[37]

What emerges from these statistics is that most of the debtors, large and small, who took advantage of the Sequestration Act, lived south of the James or on its northern bank and in that group of counties located on the headwaters of the York River. A majority of all Virginia's debtors

[36] In searching for the place of residence and occupation of the 307 persons I have relied primarily on Earl G. Swem, comp., *Virginia Historical Index* (Roanoke, 1934-1936) which indexes the major Virginia historical and genealogical magazines. The use of this index does not, of course, represent a definitive search, but it certainly is a substantial start.

[37] The amount and range of debts has been computed from Journal of Receipts. For estimates on total debt distribution see Sheridan, "British Credit Crisis of 1772," *Journal Econ. Hist.*, XX (1960), esp. 180-186. The location of the Cuninghame stores can be found in the Claim of William Cuninghame, Mar. 15, 1784, A. O. 13/29 (Va. Col. Rec. Proj. microfilm, Williamsburg).

may also have lived in these regions. When the roll call votes on the issue of debt payment and related issues are examined, it is found that support for Patrick Henry's position came primarily from these regions. I do not wish to make excessive claims on the basis of an estimated 1 per cent of Virginia debtors, but there does seem reason to believe that Henry's position on the debt question derived, at least in part, from the indebted character of the regions from which he drew support.[38]

Of the ninety-nine persons I have been able to identify in terms of occupation, thirty-six were merchants. Of all the economic groups in Virginia none had more to gain from the Revolution. Prior to the war Scots or English merchants had dominated the mercantile scene in the Old Dominion. With the outbreak of hostilities they were forced out of Virginia, affording the Virginia merchant a great opportunity which he quickly took advantage of. William Lee, who before the war had known the Virginia economic scene perfectly, commented on his return after the war that he found himself "as much at loss and perhaps moreso than I should at Constantinople so much has the late accursed war altered both men and things."[39]

Times had changed, and the Virginia merchant who had been of little consequence before the war did not want his old competition back again. In 1786 Petersburg merchants petitioned the assembly not to allow certain persons to return to the Commonwealth "who had formerly deserted it in the hour of danger and joined our enemies, or had been expelled for their inimical sentiments. . . ." Both Petersburg and Richmond merchants in 1784 and 1787 strongly opposed an arrangement which would provide for installment payment of British debts. They did not want the position of the British merchant strengthened in any way.[40]

Of the thirty-six merchants who took advantage of the Sequestration Act, twenty-three lived in the geographical regions that supported Patrick Henry. Eleven served in the legislature at one time or another be-

[38] I have relied on four roll call votes to plot regional support for and opposition to the opening of the courts to British creditors. They are June 7, 1784, June 23, 1784, Nov. 17, 1787, Dec. 3, 1787, *Journal of Delegates*, May 1784 session, 41, 72-73, 74-75, Oct. 1787 session, 51-52, 79-80.

[39] W. Lee to Staveley, Aug. 10, 1784, Lee Letterbook, 1783-1787.

[40] Petersburg, Legislative Petitions, Nov. 13, 1787; *Journal of Delegates*, Oct. 1785 session, 54, Oct. 1786 session, 20, Oct. 1787 session, 45; Madison to R. H. Lee, Dec. 25, 1784, Hunt, ed., *Madison Writings*, II, 99-100; Madison to Jefferson, Jan. 9, 1785, Boyd, ed., *Jefferson Papers*, VII, 588-598.

tween 1776 and 1788. John Syme of Hanover County, who was Henry's half brother, served in the House of Delegates from 1776 to 1778 and 1781 to 1782, and in the Senate from 1784 to 1788. Syme paid £10,584 in British debts into the loan office. Others who also had long tenure in the assembly were Parke Goodall from Hanover County and Richard Adams from New Kent County.[41] The influence of these merchants was another potent factor in Henry's fight against the payment of British debts.

Finally, a look at the Virginia ratifying Convention of 1788 is instructive with respect to the behavior of Patrick Henry and his followers. In the conflict over the ratification of the Constitution the question of British debt payment was one among a variety of issues used by opponents in an attempt to block ratification. As Madison remarked, "every advantage is taken . . . to work on the local prejudices of particular sets of members. British debts, the Indiana claim, and the Mississippi are the principal topics of private discussion and intrigue, as well as of public declamation." In the actual debates the question of British debts was seldom discussed, presumably because Henry chose not to speak to the issue if he could avoid it. Edmund Randolph, Henry Lee, and others tried to "smoke him out" but with little success. All that was necessary was for him to ask, as he did, what would happen "when congressional laws are declared paramount to the laws of your state, and the judges are sworn to support them." But neither "public declamation" nor "intrigue" on matters such as this was successful in blocking ratification, and Patrick Henry lost the greatest political battle of his career. It is paradoxical that heavily indebted Virginia ratified the Constitution. But the debt issue was only one of many in a complex situation, and the votes on debt payment in the 1780s indicate that the state's citizens were of a divided mind on the question. Suffice it to say that in their losing battle opponents of the Constitution drew support from roughly the same areas that opposed the opening of the courts.[42] A comparison of the votes of

[41] For John Syme's debts, which were incidentally paid into the treasury by Patrick Henry, see Journal of Receipts, Apr. 5, 1779. Syme is an interesting fellow who had a long history of debt evasion. Eventually in 1797 he was ordered by the Circuit Court to pay the executors of the British firm of Farrell and Jones $53,954. See *Jones Executors* v. *Syme* (1797), Ended Cases, U. S. Circuit Court, Richmond. See also derogatory remarks in *Decius's Letters*, esp. 73-77. Earl G. Swem and John W. Williams, comps., *A Register of the General Assembly of Virginia, 1776-1918* (Richmond, 1918), has been used to check membership in the legislature.

[42] Madison to Washington, June 13, 1788, Hunt, ed., *Madison Writings*, III, 179;

those persons who favored opening the courts to suits for British debts during the 1780s with their votes in the ratifying Convention indicates that they also favored the Constitution. For example, seventy-three men who were in the House of Delegates during the fall session of 1787 were also elected to the ratifying Convention. Of these fifty-five had voted that fall on the resolution to remove impediments to debt collection: twenty-three who were in favor of opening the courts voted for ratification, and twenty-two who were against opening the courts opposed ratification. Four were for the Constitution but against removing impediments while in the case of six the reverse was true. If there was a debtor faction in Virginia, as I think there was, it was also an antiratificationist group.[43]

The establishment of a new national government was followed by the creation of a federal court system which in turn opened its doors to British debt cases. The United States Circuit Court, Virginia District, began operation in 1790, and immediately British creditors started legal action against Virginia debtors. The main problem was that creditors could not bring a suit in federal court involving less than $500, and the majority of debts were below this figure. State courts were still closed to British debt cases. Even in federal courts litigation was slow, and very few cases were won between 1790 and 1792.[44]

1793 was a better year for the creditor, partly because suits begun earlier were finally concluded. Out of sixty-eight cases, fifty-two were decided in his favor. That year also saw the beginning of the destruction

---

Jonathan Elliot, ed., *The Debates in the Several State Conventions, on the Adoption of the Federal Constitution,* . . . (Washington, 1836), III, 27, 28, 80, 174, 177, 191, 543; McDonald, *We the People,* 266-267, 269-281; *Journal of Delegates,* Oct. 1787 session, 51-52, 57, 79-80.

[43] *Journal of Delegates,* Oct. 1787 session, 51-52; McDonald, *We the People,* 269-281; Swem and Williams, comps., *Register of the General Assembly,* 26-27, 243, 244.

[44] Statement of William Hay, T. 79/27 (Va. Col. Rec. Proj. microfilm, Williamsburg); Samuel Flagg Bemis, *Jay's Treaty: A Study in Commerce and Diplomacy* (New Haven, 1962 [orig. publ. New York, 1923]), 436; Extract from a Virginia letter, June 20, 1794, C. O. 30/8, 344 (Va. Col. Rec. Proj. microfilm, Williamsburg); *Dunlop and Cross* v. *Hawes,* Feb. 21, 1788, *Drummond* v. *Cater,* Nov. 16, 1792, *Gilchrist Executors* v. *Buckner Executors,* May 14, 1794, Caroline County Appeals and Land Causes, 1777-1807, Virginia State Library.

of the legal defenses used by debtors. The usual arguments had been that payment into the loan office fulfilled their obligations; that Great Britain had violated the Treaty of Paris by failing to return slaves and move out of military posts in the Northwest Territory; that the law of 1782 preventing the recovery of British debts in state courts was still in force; and that independence annulled debts. In May 1793 George Wythe in the Virginia High Court of Chancery ruled that payments into the state loan office did not discharge debts due British creditors. The following year the United States Circuit Court temporarily negated this decision by ruling in the case of *Ware* v. *Hylton* that, though bona fide debts were collectable, credit should be given for money paid into the loan office under the Sequestration Act. But the plaintiff appealed on error to the Supreme Court, which ruled in 1796 that the Treaty of Paris under the Constitution was the supreme law of the land and annulled all acts contrary to its provisions. This decision coupled with Jay's Treaty of 1795, which restored the posts in the northwest and provided for settlement of the slave question through arbitration, eliminated the main defenses Virginians had been using to avoid payment.[45]

Even before the Supreme Court's decision, British creditors were increasingly successful in the federal courts. In 1794, 65 out of 91 cases were decided in favor of the plaintiff; in 1795, 98 out of 118; and successive years brought similar results. In 1795, too, advertisements for the sale of land because of federal decisions favorable to British creditors began to appear in Virginia newspapers.[46]

In the state courts which had jurisdiction over a majority of debt cases the progress was slower. Debts under $100 were tried in county courts and from $100 to $500 in the district courts. One debt collector, retained by a British firm, reported that as late as 1798 Virginia's district courts were filled with judges having "violent prejudices against

[45] Record Books, 1790-Nov. 1794, Ended Cases, U. S. Circuit Court, Richmond. Concerning arguments by defendants see, for example, *Dobson and Daltera* v. *Crump and Bates* (1794), and *Donald Scot & Co.* v. *George Gray* (1796), Ended Cases, U. S. Circuit Court, Richmond; *Page* v. *Pendleton and Lyons*, Wythe (Va.) 127-132 (1793); John Bassett Moore, ed., *International Adjudications, Ancient and Modern, History and Documents*, III (New York, 1931), 192-212; *Ware* v. *Hylton*, 3 Dallas (U. S.), 199-285 (1796).

[46] Record Books, Nov. 1793-Sept. 1796, Ended Cases, U. S. Circuit Court, Richmond. On the sale of land see, for example, *Virginia Gazette and General Advertiser* (Richmond), Mar. 11, 1795.

the payment of British Debts." He also reported that the county courts were worse, for despite the fact that the conditions of the suspending clause of the 1787 act were being met as a result of Jay's Treaty, "at this Day, in some of them, a Recovery cannot be had at all." By 1797, however, British creditors were winning most of their suits even in the state courts.[47]

The previous year Virginia enacted legislation which made effective the law of 1788 establishing the liability of the state for British debts paid into the treasury. Persons who had taken advantage of the Sequestration Act now received certificates which recorded the actual sterling value of the money they had paid. These certificates bore 6 per cent interest. Furthermore, persons whose estates had been sequestered (not confiscated) during the war could receive similar certificates for the amount paid into the treasury from the profits of their estates. These acts represented the final legislative statement of the Old Dominion on British debts. After twenty-two years the question of repayment was resolved. No legal impediments stood in the way of the British creditor, and he or his executors did very well in the vast majority of suits against Virginia debtors.[48]

Once hostilities had commenced, the question of British debts assumed an increasingly important role in Virginia politics and remained a major issue for a decade and a half after peace returned. Wartime

[47] Statement of John Hay, T. 79/27 (Va. Col. Rec. Proj. microfilm, Williamsburg). For an example of a case won in a county court see *Glassford and Henderson* v. *Thomas Hackett, Executor of Robert Mickleburrough*, June 13, 1797, Caroline County Appeals and Land Causes, 1777-1803; Harrell, *Loyalism*, Chap. 5.

[48] Samuel Shepherd, ed., *The Statutes at Large of Virginia, 1792-1806* ... (Richmond, 1835-1836), II, 17. Examples of the state paying creditors of those who had paid money into the treasury can be found in Escheated Lands, Auditor's Papers, No. 128. Harrell, *Loyalism*, 173-178. British creditors were eventually to have an additional recourse. The Convention of 1802 provided that the United States would pay Great Britain £600,000 ($2,654,000) and a commission was formed to adjudicate claims. By May 20, 1811, this commission had awarded £415,921 to British creditors. See Moore, *International Adjudications*, III, 8-10, 356, 359-422. William Branch Giles reported that by 1792 he had been involved in at least 100 debt cases for the creditor and that "in all cases within my recollection in which the debts were established by competent testimony, judgments were rendered for the plaintiff." See Dice R. Anderson, *William Branch Giles: A Study in the Politics of Virginia and the Nation from 1790 to 1830* (Menasha, Wis., 1914), 6.

legislation designed to injure the enemy and strengthen the state's financial position also served the private interests of the individual debtor. Some may have had this end in mind since before the war, but the possibility of permanently repudiating prewar obligations does not seem to have gained majority support until around 1784. Even in areas where economic motives appear to have been strongest and from which Patrick Henry gained the greatest backing in his opposition to reopening the courts, those involved were for the most part not those who had led Virginia to revolt a decade before.

The Virginia Magazine
OF HISTORY AND BIOGRAPHY

VOL. 92   JULY 1984   No. 3

CONSCRIPTION IN REVOLUTIONARY VIRGINIA

The Case of Culpeper County, 1780-1781

by JOHN R. VAN ATTA*

THOUGH military drafts seldom occur without controversy in democratic countries, the early American option allowing draftees to produce substitutes in their places often made conscription workable, even under the least auspicious conditions. During the Revolutionary War, with states forced to enact conscription in order to fill troop quotas set by Congress, the draft and substitution system, for all its imperfections, helped in providing soldiers for the Continental army. Why this system worked between 1775 and 1781 has been something of a historical riddle, the answers to which are bound to throw additional light not only on military practice, but also on the structure and dynamics of late eighteenth-century societies in the maelstrom of revolution.

With the answers to this question most likely to be found in the states individually, Virginia happens to offer an interesting case for study. Late in 1780 the Virginia assembly moved to raise three thousand men to fill the state's 1781 quota of Continental soldiers. Leaders in every county were to split their local militia into the number of divisions, or "classes," equal to the county quota of recruits. Each of these county militia classes would in turn supply a single recruit, who could be a volunteer, a draftee, or a substitute for a draftee. The assembly demanded that counties draft militiamen if too few volunteers came forward, and law required that county militia

---

*Mr. Van Atta is an assistant professor of history at Hiram College.

commanders assure the raising of capable troops, not physically unfit or incompetent men.[1]

Researchers have accumulated only a small amount of information on the actual working of pre-Civil War drafts.[2] Often the records needed for such studies are scarce and fragmentary. The sources available generally call for tedious and time-consuming research techniques. While the Virginia militia and Continental line have been studied nonquantitatively, there is a shortage of statistical analyses of conscription in Revolutionary Virginia counties.[3] How and why did this draft and substitution system operate? Who actually entered the Continental service, and who managed not to? What, if anything, can be gleaned of the motives behind individual service in the Continental army during the latter years of the war?

In Culpeper County, part of Virginia's northern Piedmont, the 1781 draft functioned substantially as lawmakers intended. For reasons closely linked to the social and economic characteristics of the county and its surrounding region, Culpeper filled a large part of its Continental quota in 1781. The survival of a rare combination of local documents makes it possible to examine this Culpeper draft in detail. A look at draftees and substitutes in Culpeper offers insight that not only helps to confirm conclusions of previous studies, but also illuminates sociological factors that bore significantly on conscription practice in Virginia.

---

[1] "An act for recruiting this state's quota of troops to serve in the continental army" (William Waller Hening, ed., *The Statutes at Large . . . of Virginia* [13 vols.; Richmond, Philadelphia, and New York, 1809-23], X, 326-37).

[2] For recent discussions of recruiting policies during the Revolutionary War, see Edward G. Papenfuse and Gregory A. Stiverson, "General Smallwood's Recruits: The Peacetime Career of the Revolutionary War Private," *William and Mary Quarterly*, 3d ser., XXX (1973), 117-32; Mark E. Lender, "The Enlisted Line: The Continental Soldiers of New Jersey" (Ph.D. diss., Rutgers University, 1975); Robert A. Gross, *The Minutemen and Their World* (New York, 1976), pp. 146-53; Charles Royster, *A Revolutionary People at War: The Continental Army and American Character, 1775-1783* (Chapel Hill, 1979), pp. 131-36, 266-70, 295-308, 320-27, 373-78. Useful older studies include Arthur J. Alexander, "Pennsylvania's Revolutionary Militia," *Pennsylvania Magazine of History and Biography*, LXIX (1945), 15-25; Alexander, "Service by Substitute in the Militia of Lancaster and Northampton Counties (Pennsylvania) During the War of the Revolution," *Military Affairs*, IX (1945), 278-82; Alexander, "How Maryland Tried to Raise her Continental Quotas," *Maryland Historical Magazine*, XLII (1947), 184-96; Orville T. Murphy, "The American Revolutionary Army and the Concept of *Levee en Masse*," *Military Affairs*, XXIII (1959), 13-20. For a detailed account of Revolutionary War military policies in general, see Don Higginbotham, *The War of American Independence: Military Attitudes, Policies, and Practice, 1763-1789* (New York and London, 1971).

[3] See John R. Sellers, "The Virginia Continental Line, 1775-1780" (Ph.D. diss., Tulane University, 1968) and John D. McBride, "The Virginia War Effort, 1775-1783: Manpower Policies and Practices" (Ph.D. diss., University of Virginia, 1977). The latter work in particular draws inspiration from John W. Shy's stimulating essay, "A New Look at Colonial Militia," *WMQ*, 3d ser., XX (1963), 175-85. Several of Shy's essays, urging a study of military history in its social, economic, political, and intellectual contexts, are gathered in his *A People Numerous and Armed: Reflections on the Military Struggle for American Independence* (New York, 1976).

Beginning in 1776, Congress fixed annual quotas of men to be raised from each state for Continental army service, but the states had difficulty in raising volunteers to fill these quotas. Virginia sent only 5,744 recruits to the army in 1777, even though its quota for that year was 10,200 men. In 1778, with the first use of a state draft to raise soldiers, Virginia provided 5,230 of the requested 7,830 regulars. The Old Dominion contributed 3,973 troops in 1779, though the quota was 5,742.[4] Thousands of Virginia militiamen served in the field during these years, but this cannot fully explain the shortage of regulars. The problem was that constant political uncertainty and worsening inflation made a shambles of the bounty system for attracting volunteers.[5] By the latter years of the war, then, only conscription remained as a feasible recruiting device.

The structure of any contemplated draft was critically important. Though militia drafts were common in the colonies, a conscription policy in Revolutionary Virginia was not likely to succeed unless designed to win general popular acceptance. Even during this time of military crises, many Virginians stood ideologically opposed to a Continental draft and preferred to serve in local and state militia. In May 1777, a month after Congress urged states to institute drafts from their militia, Thomas Jefferson wrote that such compulsion "ever was the most unpopular and impracticable thing that could be attempted. Our people even under the monarchial government had learnt to consider it as the last of all oppressions."[6] In November 1780, in reference to the assembly's effort to enact the last of its several state drafts during the war, James Madison cautioned that "the principles of liberty . . . ought never to be lost sight of in a contest for liberty."[7]

According to Edmund Pendleton in 1777, the assembly debated three approaches to conscription: to draft indiscriminately from among the whole adult white male population, to select only from among the unmarried men, or to take only "Vagabonds and those who approach nearest to them." Pendleton himself preferred the second approach, believing younger men most suitable for service. He, for one, dreaded taking married men because it seemed "cruel to force men from their Families to a distant Countrey for two or three years." Even more unfair would be "to point out any men and con-

---

[4] William Wirt Henry, *Patrick Henry: Life, Correspondence and Speeches* (3 vols.; New York, 1891), II, 9.

[5] Royster, *A Revolutionary People at War*, pp. 296-98, 308-11.

[6] Jefferson to John Adams, 16 May 1777 (Julian P. Boyd et al., eds., *The Papers of Thomas Jefferson* [Princeton, 1950-   ], II, 18).

[7] Madison to Joseph Jones, 28 Nov. 1780 (William T. Hutchinson and William M. E. Rachal, eds., *The Papers of James Madison*, II [Chicago, 1962], 209).

demn t[hem] as Vagabonds or worthless without a Regular trial." [8] Most legislators understood that single men who were poor or too young to own much property and who did not serve in the militia were the most expendable socially and militarily. Yet many assumed that if a draft had to be instituted, it should be based on egalitarian principle or pretense.

On 2 June 1777 the House of Delegates agreed to several resolutions giving substance to the first of two draft laws the General Assembly would pass that year. These resolutions, while requiring service of draftees or their substitutes, offered well-established Virginians every chance to avoid the draft. One possibility offered to militiamen was exemption from being drafted in return for producing any recruit, other than an apprentice or servant, who agreed to stay in the army at least three years. Another provision offered a choice to "every bachelor above the age of thirty years, worth an estate... of 500£ currency," of entering the army, procuring a substitute, or paying an annual fee for his freedom of choice. The amount of the fee was to increase proportionally for bachelors having larger estates. The House approved a resolution permitting separate enlistment of apprentices and servants and forbidding Virginia creditors from "imprisoning, or otherwise restraining" new recruits for any debt not exceeding fifty dollars. [9]

Virginia's first two Revolutionary War draft laws incorporated these provisions and provided that militia commanders failing to enforce drafts would forfeit their offices and pay five hundred pounds in state currency. Draftees could free slaves and send them as substitutes, but law prohibited accepting any blacks or mulattoes lacking certificates of freedom. [10] Married militiamen were not to be included in the 1777-78 drafts. Each draftee was to serve for one year and receive fifteen dollars, unless he opted for a substitute. Single men would draw lots with the words "service" or "clear" written inside. Those drawing service notices had to appear at appointed locations or had to get others to go in their places to avoid being classified as deserters. Counties could receive a deduction from the draft for each Continental deserter

[8] Pendleton to William Woodford, 29 Nov. 1777 (David John Mays, ed., *The Letters and Papers of Edmund Pendleton, 1734-1803* [2 vols.; Charlottesville, 1967], I, 238-39).

[9] 2 June 1777 (*Journal of the House of Delegates of the Commonwealth of Virginia* ... [May 1779 session] [Richmond, 1827], pp. 51-52). For an examination of exemptions from Continental service offered in Virginia during the Revolutionary War, see Arthur J. Alexander, "Exemption from Military Service in the Old Dominion During the War of the Revolution," *Virginia Magazine of History and Biography*, LIII (1945), 163-71.

[10] "An act for the more speedily completing the Quota of Troops to be raised in this commonwealth for the continental army, and for other purposes" (Hening, *Statutes*, IX, 275-80).

apprehended. Quakers and Mennonites drawing service lots could escape service, providing they secured proper substitutes.[11]

In October 1780 the assembly retained the structure specified in these earlier laws. Again legislators assigned draft quotas for each of Virginia's seventy-two counties. The quotas varied in size according to the extent of a county's militia. Loudoun County had the largest quota of 117 men, Warwick County the smallest charge of only 7 men. County militia units were to be divided into enough classes to accommodate these quotas, this time without regard to marital status. Each militia class would deliver one recruit —a volunteer, draftee, or substitute. Increased bounties for volunteers reflected the impact of wartime inflation. With the ratio of Continental notes to specie dollars at 77 to 1,[12] Congress would provide $12,000 in paper currency to men agreeing to serve for the duration and $8,000 to any three-year recruit. In addition, any man who served to the end of the war could expect a land bounty of three hundred acres and either a "healthy sound negro, between the ages of ten and thirty years" or £60 in specie. The assembly tried to lessen the problem of desertion from the ranks by withholding full compensation until after the war.

If too few volunteers responded to these offers, drafts would occur again. Draftees were to serve a period of eighteen months, but any draftee was free "to procure a substitute to serve for the said term of eighteen months, at any time within ten days after such draft." The draftee or his substitute had to be a man between the ages of eighteen and fifty years of able body and sound mind. He could not be a prisoner of war or a deserter from the enemy, nor could he be required to serve longer than eighteen months. Draftees would receive $4,000 in paper currency and nothing else. A substitute could expect the same amount in addition to whatever he received from his employer. Presumably, draftees or their agents had to make it materially worthwhile for men to substitute rather than to enlist as volunteers.[13]

The 1780 statute, like previous draft laws in Virginia, proved accommodating for draftees with the means to find and to hire substitutes. Poor men without connections had less chance to escape service if drafted. Conscription in Virginia put less emphasis on compulsion than on the freedom to avoid service by securing a substitute. Since many substitutes were not members of county militia, Continental ranks could be reinforced without

---

[11] "An act for speedily recruiting the Virginia Regiments on the continental establishment, and for raising additional troops of Volunteers" (ibid., pp. 337-49).

[12] E. James Ferguson, *The Power of the Purse: A History of American Public Finance, 1776-1790* (Chapel Hill, 1961), p. 32.

[13] "An act for recruiting this state's quota of troops" (Hening, *Statutes*, X, 326-37).

proportionally weakening the state's ability to defend itself. Hiring substitutes evidently carried no stigma; indeed, to pay the cost of a replacement would have been regarded a patriotic act in itself.[14]

Most of Virginia's quota of Continental troops for 1781 were to be drafted and then sent against British forces to the south. But Sir Henry Clinton's invasion of the Chesapeake made the 1780 draft law difficult to enact. In counties whose militia was in service elsewhere, drawing lots was impossible. Even in counties where local units remained, militiamen were anxious to protect their property and families against invading British troops. Some Virginia units had just returned home exhausted and horrified after extensive service and brutal treatment under Continental commanders.[15] In Northumberland County only three men enlisted for the duration of the war; draftees comprised the rest of Northumberland's quota.[16] Pendleton's Caroline County likewise found conscription inevitable.[17] An official account of the 1781 recruits revealed that only thirty-eight of Virginia's seventy-two counties produced men for the army, and only thirteen came close to meeting their quotas. There were 198 enlistees for the war, 50 volunteers for three years, and 775 draftees or substitutes—a grand total of 1,023 men. Of these, only 773 reported to camp, 58 were unfit for service, 140 deserted, and 52 simply stayed at home.[18]

What is most interesting, however, is not that Virginia raised so few recruits in 1781, but that a few counties still produced as many as they did. Whether the 1781 draft could succeed at all depended on responses at the county level. As designed, the conscription system had a good chance to work in counties where available manpower provided not only a group of potential draftees but also a pool of ready and willing substitutes.

Culpeper was one such county. Covering nearly a thousand square miles, it was enormous in size and well-endowed in high-quality farmland. Though no major engagements were fought there during the war, the county had made military sacrifices for the Revolutionary cause well before 1781. In 1775, Virginia's Third Revolutionary Convention ordered Culpeper, in

---

[14] See Royster, *A Revolutionary People at War*, pp. 66-69.

[15] Edmund Pendleton thought recruiting in Caroline County would be hurt because the county militia had returned from service "sickly & murmuring at the treatment they met with below, from forced Marches & too Strict Attention to Order" (Pendleton to James Madison, 4 Dec. 1780 [Hutchinson and Rachal, *Papers of Madison*, II, 222]).

[16] Report of the Northumberland County results (Thomas Gaskins to Jefferson, 13 Apr. 1781 [Boyd et al., *Papers of Jefferson*, V, 430]).

[17] Pendleton to George Washington, 16 Feb. 1781 (Mays, *Papers of Pendleton*, I, 339).

[18] General Return of the Recruits Raised for the Continental Army Under the Act of October 1780 (Report of Col. William Davies, 29 Nov. 1781, Executive Communications, Box 2, 8 June 1780-24 Dec. 1782, Virginia State Library, Richmond [hereafter cited as Vi]).

combination with neighboring Orange and Fauquier counties, to raise a battalion of minutemen to be joined with forces from other districts for service near Norfolk against Lord Dunmore. At that time, about 300 men were recruited from the Culpeper district. Though most of the battalion marched home in the spring of 1776, members of that group led by Col. Edward Stevens took part in the war later at Valley Forge, Brandywine, Camden, and Guilford Courthouse.[19]

Even without this tradition of service, Culpeper still would merit distinction in the eyes of historians because it is the only county where a 1781 militia class list is known to have survived. This class list, a twenty-eight-page booklet with 106 numbered columns of militiamen, features the names of Culpeper's draftees and their substitutes. County personal property and land tax records from 1782-83 make possible an economic profile of Culpeper men involved in the draft. A Revolutionary War army roll of Virginia recruits entering the Continental service between 1777 and 1783 supplements these tax records by providing the names, ages, occupations, birthplaces, places of residence, and other personal information for most Culpeper County recruits of 1781. This collection of materials is well suited to expose the actual working of a Revolutionary War draft.

The tax records leave little doubt that military organization in Culpeper directly mirrored county social structure.[20] Tables I and II demonstrate how average levels of land and personal property ownership corresponded with descending levels of rank.[21] Among the largest holders of Culpeper property in 1782-83 were colonels James Pendleton, William Thornton, and John Thornton. Pendleton had 2,040 acres of land valued at £612, as well as 53 slaves, 16 horses, and 65 head of cattle; William Thornton, 2,939 acres at £1,512, 27 slaves, 13 horses, and 32 head of cattle; and John Thornton, 2,204 acres at £1,122, 41 slaves, 6 horses, and 38 head of cattle. Ephram Rucker, who owned the least personal property among the colonels, had only 13 slaves, 7 horses, and 13 head of cattle. Col. James Slaughter had only 203 acres in Culpeper County at a valuation of £102. Like other

---

[19] Leo S. Mason, "To Have Lived Then—the 1700's," in *An 18th Century Perspective: Culpeper County*, ed. Mary Stevens Jones (Culpeper, Va., 1976), pp. 115-37; E. M. Sanchez-Saavedra, " 'All Fine Fellows and Well Armed,' " in ibid., pp. 15-21, esp. 15, 16, 21; John T. S. Kearns, "The Importance of the Battle of Great Bridge," in ibid., pp. 23-24.

[20] Culpeper County Land Tax Book, 1782; Culpeper County Personal Property Tax List, 1783, Vi. On the social hierarchy of Virginia militia, see Rhys Isaac, *The Transformation of Virginia, 1740-1790* (Chapel Hill, 1982), pp. 104-10, 344.

[21] It was impossible to verify the identities of some Culpeper militiamen because of the frequency of certain names. One cannot determine, for example, which of ten John Browns is the John Brown who served as a substitute for William Henry, the draftee from Culpeper class number 80. Cases presenting this sort of difficulty had to be eliminated.

TABLE I

Average Personal Property Holdings for Culpeper County
Militia Officers, Draftees, and Substitutes

RANK	SLAVES	HORSES	CATTLE
ALL OFFICERS (39)	12.5	6.5	20.0
COLONELS (7)	31.0	10.3	33.6
MAJORS (3)	15.0	6.0	21.3
CAPTAINS (19)	8.4	6.2	18.2
LIEUTENANTS (8)	6.6	4.0	9.6
ENSIGNS (2)	1.5	4.5	9.5
DRAFTEES (52)	3.0	3.1	7.1
SUBSTITUTES (14)	1.3	1.9	3.6

SOURCE: Culpeper County Personal Property Tax List, 1783, Vi.

prominent Virginians, these leaders probably owned land in other counties as well.[22]

Among the majors, Henry Hill held the most slaves, with 17, but James Green had the most livestock, 7 horses and 35 head of cattle, as well as the most land—1,216 acres valued at £273. William Stauton's personal property holding of 29 slaves, 3 horses, and 35 head of cattle topped the militia captains. Benjamin Lillard owned only 3 slaves, 3 horses, and 8 head of cattle. Capt. Henry Towles had 1,230 acres of land valued at £308. Lillard held only 64 acres of land at £27. Among the militia lieutenants, Joseph Early's holdings were so atypical—23 slaves, 10 horses, and 52 head of cattle—that to have included him in the averages for lieutenants would have distorted the totals. Early also owned 736 acres valued at £442. Lt. James Murray had only 1 slave, 4 horses, and 8 head of cattle. James Finney had the least land for a lieutenant—163 acres at £49. The wealthiest ensign was George Crister, who owned 3 slaves, 4 horses, 11 head of cattle, and 177 acres of land at £62. Ensign John Hume held no slaves, 5 horses, 8 head of cattle, and apparently no land of his own. Four of the captains, five of the lieutenants, and one of the ensigns do not appear in the land tax book for 1782,

---

[22] The property tax for 1783 consisted of a head tax of ten shillings per tithe to be applied to whites and blacks alike, plus additional charges for cattle, horses, and carriages. Tax officials were reasonably thorough in assessing county residents. The tax records show that officials assessed at least some of the poorest inhabitants—men owning no personal property at all—at the minimum possible charge of ten shillings. For some idea of the holdings of the most prominent Virginians, see Jackson T. Main, "The One Hundred," *WMQ*, 3d ser., XI (1954), 354–84.

TABLE II

Average Land Holdings for Culpeper County Militia Officers,
Draftees, and Substitutes

RANK	NUMBER OF ACRES	VALUATION
ALL OFFICERS (41)	579.4	£248.0
COLONELS (7)	1344.4	620.4
MAJORS (3)	607.3	188.3
CAPTAINS (23)	447.3	184.6
LIEUTENANTS (6)	310.0	147.2
ENSIGNS (2)	188.5	66.0
DRAFTEES (32)	253.7	116.0
SUBSTITUTES (9)	172.1	62.8

SOURCE: Culpeper County Land Tax Book, 1782 (microfilm), Vi.

leaving possibilities that they had no land, that their land was taxed under another's name, that they had moved or died.[23]

Obeying the 1780 law, Culpeper turned to the draft upon failing to recruit more than a few volunteers.[24] Of 106 recruits, the "Culpeper Classes" lists ninety-nine draftees. Forty-six of these draftees secured substitutes. The 1777-83 army roll reveals that fourteen substitutes whose names did not appear on the "Culpeper Classes" entered the army on behalf of Culpeper County in March 1781. But it also shows a total of only forty-two substitutes actually reporting in March, four less than the total presumed in the "Culpeper Classes." This means that some of the men who had agreed to be substitutes either changed their minds about the agreements or disappeared without returning compensation already received from draftees.[25] The army

[23] Jackson T. Main found that a majority of the adult white males in Virginia during the 1780s were not landholders. Although most of the landless were very poor, some owned enough personal property to indicate that they must have had access to land (Main, "The Distribution of Property in Post-Revolutionary Virginia," *Mississippi Valley Historical Review*, XLI [1954-55], 241-58).

[24] See "A List of the Classes in Culpeper County for January 1781, for Recruiting this State's Quota of Troops to Serve in the Continental Army, drafted 19 March," Vi. Under the provisions of the 1780 law, militia divisions able to furnish a volunteer prior to the draft were not required to select a draftee. This apparently occurred in the cases of five Culpeper divisions. It also appears that such volunteers were randomly called "substitutes." The lack of the name of any draftee from the same division distinguished these volunteers from the other type of substitute listed in the "Culpeper Classes."

[25] William Davies of Chesterfield County knew firsthand the frustration of handling unreliable volunteers and substitutes. He observed, "From the open toleration, I might justly say, protection which is afforded to deserters, and from the ruinous fondness the Assembly have always shewn for short enlistments, enlisting and deserting have become the professed employment of numbers of men in this state. I have received nine recruits under the late law, two of them deserted before

roll indicates that ten draftees whose names also did not appear as draftees on the "Culpeper Classes" entered the service in March 1781. These ten replaced earlier draftees who for reasons unclear could neither serve nor hire substitutes. After recent militia duty, some of the original draftees may have been physically or psychologically incapable of Continental service.

Most of Culpeper's substitutes were men of low social status. Tables I and II demonstrate the differences between average property holdings of the draftees and substitutes, but perhaps the most striking point is that seventy-eight draftees (68 percent of the total) owned no Culpeper land at all in 1782.[26] Cadwallader Slaughter, Thomas Graves, Sr., and William Duncan, Sr., were among the wealthiest draftees. Slaughter held 25 slaves, 10 horses, 20 head of cattle, and 600 acres of land valued at £450; Graves, 11 slaves, 6 horses, 13 head of cattle, and 1,202 acres at £418; and Duncan, 5 slaves, 6 horses, 22 head of cattle, and 99 acres at £255. Among the twenty-five leading slaveholding draftees, seventeen (68 percent) arranged to have substitutes in 1781. Eight of the twelve leading landholders among draftees (67 percent) had substitutes. The poorest draftee found in the 1782-83 records was Benjamin Colvin, who owned no personal property whatsoever and held no land. Twenty-six of the draftees in the tax records had no slaves. Four of these twenty-six owned no cattle, three had only a single cow, thirteen owned only a horse, and seventeen were landless. Only ten (38 percent) of these twenty-six had substitutes in 1781.

The average property and landholdings of draftees with and those without substitutes confirms what might be expected: Draftees without substitutes were poorer than those who engaged proxies. Twenty-six of the forty-one draftees who acquired substitutes in 1781 held an average of 4 or 5 slaves, 4 horses, and 9 head of cattle in 1783. Sixteen of these forty-one found in the 1782 land tax book had an average landholding of 267.9 acres at an average value of £136.4. The personal property average for twenty-eight draftees who did not acquire substitutes in 1781 was a single slave, 2 horses, and 5 head of cattle, while the average landholding for thirteen such draftees was 244.5 acres at £83.5.

Knowing which draftees actually reported to the army in 1781 opens the

dark, and three others were preparing, but I was beforehand with them as I suspected it; they will soon, however, forget their punishment and take themselves off, I have no doubt." Davies reported that Littleton Adams "was enlisted by a division in his county; they paid him part of the money, but he refused to come till he had the whole." When the division refused to pay immediately the rest of the bounty, Adams disappeared with the portion he had (Davies to Jefferson, 18 Mar. 1781 [Boyd et al., *Papers of Jefferson*, V, 173-74]).

[26] By all indications, the land tax books were a dependable record of land ownership in Culpeper County for 1782 and did provide the names of most if not all of the county's landholders.

way to additional insight. Of the twenty-eight draftees without substitutes found in the personal property records, the army roll gives no account for twenty (71 percent). These twenty had an average personal property holding of 1 or 2 slaves, 2 or 3 horses, and 6 head of cattle. Seven of the twenty owned land, an average of 327.8 acres valued at £109.1. Four of the remaining eight draftees who did enter the army in 1781 owned a single slave, and the eight had an average of 2 horses and 4 head of cattle. Six of these eight had an average of 147.7 acres of land valued at £53.5. The point is that some of the wealthier draftees who at first chose not to hire substitutes later did acquire them or managed some other way to avoid army service. On the other hand, some of the poorest draftees and many of the substitutes perceived their civic duty, material advantage, or both in proceeding with Continental service.

Having established the economic status differences between militia officers, draftees, and substitutes, a more complicated problem remains in determining who the substitutes were and how draftees acquired them. A few clues to personal identities appear in the "Culpeper Classes." Five of the classes produced no draftee because in these cases volunteers had agreed to serve. For three of these volunteers the class list gives brief descriptions. Enoch Cox, both a member of and a volunteer serving for class number 8, was "by trade a Shoemaker, 19 yrs. of age, 5 feet 9 in. high." William Wedgroof, one of only two Culpeper men to offer service for the duration of the war, was "5½ feet high, a Free Mulatto, 19 yrs. of age," and a resident of the town of Culpeper. John Tim, the other recruit for the duration and a member of class number 29, was six feet tall, a carpenter by trade, and also a resident of the town of Culpeper. None of these appears in the personal property tax records for 1783, and none owned Culpeper land in 1782. Because these volunteers were called "substitutes" for the classes they represented, it is likely that class members joined in hiring proxies to avoid drafting anyone.

Benjamin Cave, a substitute for his apparent relative John Cave of class number 66, owned the most personal property and the most good land of all the proxies—10 slaves, 3 horses, 14 head of cattle, and 259 acres at £247. But most of the substitutes appearing in the tax records were much poorer and probably were not relatives of draftees for whom they served. Nine of the fourteen substitutes included in the 1783 records owned no slaves. The poorest of these nine was William Brady, who possessed only a horse and no land. None of the nine had more than 2 horses, and three of the nine owned no cattle. Why did these substitutes not simply volunteer to serve for three years or for the war, thus becoming eligible for the large bounties? The most likely answer is that they saw greater advantage in making private arrangements with draftees and in serving for the shorter term of eighteen months, as opposed to serving for longer and risking not being paid from doubtful public funds.

In a few cases the surnames of draftees and their proxies suggest family relationships. There were considerable differences between average holdings of substitutes having the same surnames as the draftees they replaced and those of substitutes having different surnames. Personal property tax records existing for three of the nine substitutes whose surnames matched those of the men they replaced show an average holding of 4 slaves, 3 horses, and 11 head of cattle. Records for nine of the thirty-two substitutes not having the same last names as their corresponding draftees give an average of no slaves, 2 horses, and 2 head of cattle. Insufficient data here precludes comparison of landholdings. Still it is clear that proxies appearing to be family members of draftees they replaced were wealthier than most Culpeper substitutes in 1781.

There are only scattered clues as to how Virginia draftees found substitutes during the Revolutionary War. One method attempted in the 1777-78 draft was to send servants to the army in return for a draft exemption, a procedure that favored wealthier draftees. Lawmakers took action, however, to prevent this sort of draft evasion. An 18 June 1779 report of a Committee of Propositions and Grievances in the House of Delegates recommended that county militia commanders block draft eligibles from hiring apprentices and servants to serve as substitutes on their behalf.[27] Servants probably would have welcomed any chance to end their indentures. This and other forms of draft evasion had not ended by 1781. A December 1780 petition from a group of Winchester borough mechanics prayed for "exemption of mechanics' apprentices from being enlisted by recruiting officers, or hired as substitutes without the consent of their masters or parents."[28]

Escaped slaves also tried to enlist or perhaps to serve as cheap substitutes in the army. Indeed, three Culpeper substitutes, Philip Phillips (aged twenty-two), Thomas Shaw (aged forty), and Joseph Hughes (aged thirty-one), were black. Virginia newspapers, while providing little detail about

---

[27] 18 June 1779 (*Journal of the House of Delegates* [May 1779 session], p. 55).
[28] 5 Dec. 1780 (ibid. [Nov. 1780 session], p. 36).

draftee-substitute relationships, did note movements of runaway slaves. The *Virginia Gazette* of 24 March 1781 ran the following advertisement:

> Run away from the subscribers in Brunswick county, two very likely slaves, viz. George and Tull. George, about 23 years old, 5 feet 9 or 10 inches high, a crafty sensible fellow, and once before run away and enlisted during the war under Colonel Buford, and went southwardly as far as Hillsborough, from whence he was brought home.... Tull, is a large mulatto fellow, about 27 years old, 6 feet high, well dressed, was seen near Richmond, and said he was going to Fredericksburg to enlist in the service, or join a regiment.[29]

Aware that escaped slaves entered the army with unsettling frequency, the assembly earlier had attempted to halt the easy recruitment of blacks:

> Whereas several negro slaves have deserted from their masters, and, under pretence of being freemen, have enlisted as soldiers: for prevention whereof: *Be it enacted,* that it shall not be lawful for any recruiting officer within this Commonwealth to enlist any negro or mulatto into the service of this, or either of the United States, until such negro or mulatto shall produce a certificate, from some justice of the peace for the county wherein he resides, that he is a freeman.[30]

Another forbidden practice was for draftees to hire deserters as substitutes. The prohibition was, of course, hard to enforce. Court martial records show cases of substitutes who had been disloyal to one side or the other. An October 1780 court martial held in the town of Staunton disclosed that John Massey, a substitute for John Blaire, was in fact a British deserter. Instead of punishing Blaire or rejecting Massey, the court honored the deserter's wish to get away from the British and permitted him to serve instead as a substitute for James Buchanan, a draftee in Augusta County, who had been marked for Continental service in the West.[31]

Unfortunately, the payment of substitutes is as difficult to uncover as the manner of acquiring them. Payment may have come in a variety of forms. Anything of value from currency to personal effects could have changed hands. Possibly some substitutes gave service as a favor not only to relatives but to close friends. Patriotic motives could have played a role here, too. However subtle or complex the motivations were, at least a few substitutes

---

[29] (Richmond) *Virginia Gazette* (Dixon & Nicholson), 24 Mar. 1781.

[30] House committee amendments to the bill entitled "an act for the speedily completing the Quota of Troops to be raised in this commonwealth for the continental army, and for other purposes," 26 June 1777 (*Journal of the House of Delegates* [May 1777 session], p. 102).

[31] Augusta County Court Martial Records, 1756-1812, p. 201, Vi.

received massive payment for their agreements. In 1777 General Washington expected men who consented to serve as substitutes for the war's duration to demand a price that "would in all probability amount to an enormous Sum." [42] David Jameson thought militia units would make considerable monetary sacrifices just to prevent another draft in 1781. He told James Madison that some divisions had raised £5,000 in state paper currency for volunteers prior to the county drafts, and he thought that amount might even double, "for who will run the risk of being drafted if he can by taxing his Neighbours procure a Man?" [33]

Compared to Jameson's estimate, some Culpeper proxies may seem quite expensive, but inflation must be accounted for in that judgment. The "Culpeper Classes" provided no detail on compensation arrangements between draftees and their substitutes, but Culpeper County deed books contain scattered fragments of agreements between militia members and substitutes. Militia classes sometimes pooled their resources in order to attract a substitute to serve on behalf of one member. In other cases, men from various classes combined to lure a volunteer. A deed book entry of 23 August 1780 shows fourteen Culpeper men, members of different classes, acknowledging themselves indebted to William Cannaday for "£50,000 current money" in return for Cannaday's consent "to enter into the Continental service as a substitute for the above bound persons." [34] The "current money" referred to here was the greatly depreciated state currency that Virginia tried to redeem in 1780-82 at the rate of £1,000 in paper to £1 in coin. [35] Despite its dubious value, however, the £50,000, in addition to the Continental bounty, obviously struck Cannaday as an attractive sum.

It is fair, then, to conclude that some substitutes were poor men looking for lucrative deals, but financial criteria alone cannot provide a complete picture of the Culpeper recruits of 1781. Luckily, the 1777-83 army roll picks up where tax records leave off. Forty-two substitutes and thirty-two draftees from Culpeper actually entered the Continental army in the spring of 1781. Tables III, IV, and V show the ages, occupations, and birthplaces for 95 percent of these recruits. Substitutes tended to be younger than draftees, to represent a wider range of occupations, and to have been born in a greater variety of locations. The document shows that sixty-seven of the

---

[32] Washington to Patrick Henry, 13 Nov. 1777, George Washington Papers, Library of Congress (microfilm reel 45, ser. 4: 26 Oct.-3 Dec. 1777).

[33] Jameson to Madison, 13 Aug. 1780 (Hutchinson and Rachal, *Papers of Madison*, II, 57-58).

[34] Culpeper County Deed Book K, pp. 284-85, Vi.

[35] Curtis P. Nettels, *The Emergence of a National Economy, 1775-1815* (New York, 1962), p. 30.

TABLE III

Ages of Culpeper County Recruits of March 1781

AGE	DRAFTEES		SUBSTITUTES	
	NUMBER	PERCENT	NUMBER	PERCENT
16-19	5	16.1	20	47.5
20-24	12	38.7	9	21.4
25-29	7	22.6	6	14.3
30-34	3	9.7	1	2.4
35-39	1	3.2	2	4.8
40-44	1	3.2	2	4.8
45-50	2	6.5	2	4.8
TOTAL	31	100.0	42	100.0

SOURCE: Revolutionary Army Book, vol. 1 (Register), Vi.

TABLE IV

Occupations of Culpeper County Recruits of March 1781

DRAFTEES	NUMBER	PERCENT	SUBSTITUTES	NUMBER	PERCENT
PLANTER	24	75.0	PLANTER	27	65.8
FARMER	2	6.2	FARMER	4	9.7
CARPENTER	2	6.2	CARPENTER	2	4.8
SHOEMAKER	2	6.2	SHOEMAKER	1	2.4
COOPER	1	3.1	COOPER	2	4.8
MILLWRIGHT	1	3.1	WEAVER	1	2.4
			JOINER	1	2.4
			BRICKLAYER	1	2.4
			MILLER	1	2.4
			BUTCHER	1	2.4
TOTAL	32	99.8	TOTAL	41	99.5

SOURCE: Revolutionary Army Book, vol. 1 (Register), Vi.

total seventy-four men resided in Culpeper County in 1781, but length of residence is impossible to determine. Because most substitutes owned no land or personal property in Culpeper in 1782-83, many could have been either recent settlers or temporary residents of the county in 1781. That so many proxies originated in places other than Culpeper implies some degree of regional geographical mobility as well as economic instability.

TABLE V

Places of Birth of Culpeper County Recruits of March 1781

| | DRAFTEES | | | SUBSTITUTES | | |
PLACE	NUMBER	PERCENT	PLACE	NUMBER	PERCENT
CULPEPER CO.	21	67.7	CULPEPER CO.	17	41.5
OTHER COUNTIES	7	22.6	OTHER COUNTIES	15	36.6
ENGLAND	2	6.5	ENGLAND	3	7.3
MARYLAND	1	3.2	PENNSYLVANIA	2	4.9
			NEW JERSEY	2	4.9
			SOUTH CAROLINA	1	2.4
			SWEDEN	1	2.4
TOTAL	31	100.0	TOTAL	41	100.0

SOURCE: Revolutionary Army Book, vol. 1 (Register), Vi.

Substitutes who had been skilled tradesmen, often seven or eight years older than those claiming farming occupations, were most likely former indentured servants.[36] The average age of these workmen was twenty-nine years, whereas proxies formerly engaged in agricultural work were twenty-one or twenty-two years of age. Free laborers found no bonanza in war-torn Virginia, and for some, military bounties or payments from draftees represented a means of survival as well as a service to their country.

The impulses and problems of youth explain the readiness of many substitutes. Almost half of the Culpeper proxies who reported to the Continental army were under twenty years of age. One fifteen-year-old Culpeper boy enlisted in the service. Perhaps the army attracted youngsters eager to prove their mettle against the British and show an ideological attachment for the Revolutionary cause. If so, then some youthful militiamen and others too young for militia duty found substitution a way of simultaneously showing patriotism, seeking adventure, and obtaining compensation sufficient to offer hope of higher status in years to come.[37]

Indeed, the odds are that many young men saw payment for military duty in 1781 as a possible antidote to a grim future of economic dependence. At

[36] On indentured servitude in colonial America, see Abbot Emerson Smith, *Colonists in Bondage: White Servitude and Convict Labor in America, 1607-1776* (Chapel Hill, 1947).

[37] The relative youth of the Culpeper recruits compares with the findings of other studies of the Continental rank and file. For the best critical discussion of scholarly work regarding various motives for Continental service, see Royster, "A Note on Statistics and Continental Soldiers' Motivation," in *A Revolutionary People at War*, pp. 373-78.

least twenty of the forty-two substitutes and sixteen of the thirty-three draftees from Culpeper who entered the army in 1781 were "farmers" and "planters" who owned no Culpeper land. These young, landless men had to choose between the risks of war and a life of cultivating land belonging to relatives or economic superiors.[38] There is evidence to suggest that for young men who did not stand to profit much by inheritance, Virginia's Tidewater and Piedmont regions did not promise a bright economic picture for the 1780s. By that time, most good land in Virginia proper had been taken, and a growing majority of adult white males owned none.[39] Instead of leaving parts of their estates vacant, large planters often rented them to needy small farmers. The growth of tenancy marked a trend toward greater economic inequality in Virginia society. As land concentrated in fewer and fewer planter hands, the tenant class grew proportionally. Eighteenth-century Virginia lacked urban centers capable of absorbing this growing reservoir of poor rural inhabitants. Fast responses to newspaper or poster advertisements offering the rental of land plots to desperate farmers indicated the supply of would-be tenants.[40] Unless lured by military alternatives during the Revolution, increasing numbers of young Virginians turned to landlords or other agents for an agricultural living.

The option of substitution therefore offered certain men an enticing range of opportunities that otherwise would not have existed. Payment for proxy service provided poor men a chance to supplement meager landholdings or to own land for the first time. It offered financial possibilities of migrating to Kentucky or Ohio where land was both plentiful and available. For others, substitution probably represented an escape from oppressive obligations to fathers, creditors, or landlords. Depressed tradesmen, tenant farmers, and restless youths found possible answers to their problems in military service. For such people, participation in the Revolutionary War was something more than a commitment to the cause. Fighting in the army represented, in fact, an opportunity to achieve personal independence, a chance for self-sufficiency and increased self-esteem. It was a risk of life in pursuit of a more encouraging future.

---

[38] It is possible that some of these landless young farmers were using land belonging to their fathers or other relatives. However, one can identify at least twenty-one cases (seven substitutes and fourteen draftees) of Continental recruits who were over twenty-one years of age and did not hold land of their own in 1782. Also, the records provide several instances of men under twenty-one who did apparently have land of their own that year.

[39] Main, "Distribution of Property in Virginia," *MVHR*, XLI (1954-55), 243. See also Main's *The Social Structure of Revolutionary America* (Princeton, 1965).

[40] See Willard F. Bliss, "The Rise of Tenancy in Virginia," *VMHB*, LVIII (1950), 427-41; Isaac, *Transformation of Virginia*, pp. 133, 136.

Perhaps military rolls and tax records tell us more about how Revolutionary War drafts worked than about the motives of soldiers for serving. The motivations of ordinary men are no less complex and often tougher to unravel than those of prominent people. Here, to be sure, any body of evidence brought to bear is limited. When property and status records are the main sources at hand, one is inclined to assume that economic considerations alone guided men's thinking. But such a conclusion is inadequate, particularly when the economic records themselves point to a wider array of influences, as in the case of Culpeper County. Though most Culpeper substitutes were poor men with an eye for the main chance, there were some who agreed to serve on behalf of family members; and all forty-two who actually reported for Continental service in March of 1781 did so instead of deserting. What is more, thirty-two Culpeper draftees, men who likewise could have turned their backs on the Continental effort, also went forward to reinforce the army's ranks and to risk life and limb.

As Virginia's pragmatic lawmakers recognized, self-interest and patriotic allegiance were not mutually exclusive and could work in complementary ways. Virginia draft laws, with the traditional option for draftees to acquire substitutes, made allowance for the diversity of motives that inspired men to service. Such laws had the effect of attracting a large proportion of soldiers who had been economically disadvantaged in civilian life, but this does not mean that selfless devotion to family, county, state, or nation must have paled among the reasons for Continental service. Indeed, the discovery that any part of Virginia's beleaguered militia could come as close to filling a county quota in 1781 as Culpeper did is testimony to the continuing persuasiveness of Revolutionary ideals.

In any war, the raising of soldiers is a matter of tapping an available surplus of population.[41] Armies must be composed of men who can be spared, at least temporarily, from civilian pursuits. For Revolutionary Virginia, as for other states, success in war required the maintenance of local agriculture, commerce, and defense, as well as the willingness to take up arms for the general cause. The decision as to how best to fight the British in 1780-81 was not, and could not have been, easy for many Virginia militiamen. The opportunity for draftees to seek substitutes to serve in their places suggests a legislative respect for individual judgment in times of military need that the emergence of modern industrial society has left no longer practicable.

---

[41] For some valuable observations on the composition of eighteenth-century American armies, see Fred Anderson, "A People's Army: Provincial Military Service in Massachusetts during the Seven Years' War," *WMQ*, 3d ser., XL (1983), 499-527.

It also suggests an awareness of political and social realities that made a draft and substitution system feasible in Virginia. The number of available poor in Culpeper County, the accessibility of its militia for a draft, and that militia's self-conscious tradition of patriotic service combine to explain the county's ability to raise much of its Continental quota.

THE VIRGINIA PORT BILL OF 1784

by DREW R. McCOY[*]

As the military struggle for political independence drew to a close in the early 1780s, the Commonwealth of Virginia still faced the formidable task of achieving economic independence as well. Economic life in pre-Revolutionary Virginia had been influenced greatly by external agents—in particular, the years between 1750 and 1775 had witnessed the phenomenal rise of Scottish mercantile influence in the river valleys of the Piedmont.[1] The life of a Virginia tobacco planter was often marked by indebtedness and dependence upon the Scotch factor or English merchant who marketed his tobacco and provided foreign manufactures in return. Because of the absence of any major commercial entrepôts in Virginia, the marketing system was highly decentralized. British merchants or their agents had penetrated most of the major inland waterways by the time of the Revolution, as wharves and retail stores were to be found scattered throughout the river valleys. Many planters resented their dependence on these merchants, who exerted such an inordinate influence on their economic destiny.[2] Among prominent Virginians, James Madison in particular saw the permanent elimination of the pre-Revolutionary commercial system as a pressing need in the early 1780s. While essentially a confirmed advocate of a stronger central government as early as 1780, Madison nevertheless recognized in 1783 that the commercial interests of the different states varied considerably, and that any forthcoming commercial treaty with Great Britain might well have to reserve to Virginia the right to regulate its foreign commerce. He noted that all the southern states, unlike their eastern brethren, needed the means to encourage the growth of their own

---

[*] Mr. McCoy is a graduate student in history at the University of Virginia.

[1] Jacob M. Price, "The Rise of Glasgow in the Chesapeake Tobacco Trade, 1707-1775," *William and Mary Quarterly*, 3rd ser., II (1954), 179-199.

[2] As Price and others have noted, there were two sides to this story. Planters made liberal use of credit to their own advantage, and it can cogently be argued that Glasgow financed the economic development of the Piedmont frontier. Price asserts that the individual planter usually did not run up an irredeemable debt, and further points out that Scottish creditors experienced great difficulty in recouping what was owed to them, which for some firms was a fantastic aggregate sum (*ibid.*, pp. 196-198). Nevertheless, hostility to the Scots on the part of Virginia planters was rampant, and in the eyes of many historians this resentment directly fueled a revolutionary consciousness among influential planters in the tobacco colonies. See, for example, the recent article by Marc Egnal and Joseph A. Ernst, "An Economic Interpretation of the American Revolution," *William and Mary Quarterly*, 3rd ser., XXIX (1972), especially pp. 24-28.

shipping and seamen in order to prevent a relapse into the Scottish and English monopoly.[3]

As the negotiations in Europe ended, however, Virginians, like most Americans, hungered for a return to normality and a release from wartime austerity. By May 1783 Virginia ports were once again fully open to British ships, and several of Madison's correspondents looked with anxiety at the throngs of Virginians who rushed to purchase foreign commodities. Governor Benjamin Harrison wrote to the Virginia delegates in Congress that he looked upon the newly-arrived merchants as "locusts that are crouding here as so many emissaries sent to sound our inclinations and to poison the minds of our people and if possible bring them back to their old and destructive paths." [4] The British government, meanwhile, had begun to reassert some of its familiar prewar arrogance. A royal proclamation of July 2, 1783, announced that American vessels were to be excluded from the British West Indies, prompting the Virginia House of Delegates to adopt unanimously a resolution in December urging that the American Congress be granted power to impose nationwide retaliatory measures.[5] Prosperity was slowly returning to Virginia, but for Madison and many other Virginians it was a superficial and precarious prosperity, for it was accompanied by a return to the prewar pattern of indebtedness and dependence upon British mercantile influence.[6]

It is in this context that the so-called Port Bill of June 1784 must be viewed.[7] As chairman of the Committee of Commerce in the House of Delegates, Madison moved in the spring of 1784 to develop a bill which would restrict Virginia's foreign trade to a few enumerated ports.[8] Initially, he seems to have

---

[3] Madison to Jefferson, May 13, 1783, and Madison to Edmund Randolph, May 20, 1783, *The Papers of James Madison*, edited by William T. Hutchinson and William M. E. Rachal (Chicago, 1962-   ), VII, 39, 61-62.

[4] Harrison to Virginia Delegates, September 26, 1783, *ibid.*, VII, 359. See also Edmund Randolph to Madison, May 24, 1783, *ibid.*, VII, 73.

[5] *Ibid.*, VII, 385.

[6] Writing to Jefferson on December 10, 1783, Madison fumed that "the situation of the commerce of this country [Virginia] as far as I can learn is even more deplorable than I had conceived" (*ibid.*, VII, 401).

[7] The only extended scholarly treatments of this legislation are in two unpublished doctoral dissertations: Myra L. Rich, "The Experimental Years: Virginia, 1781-1789" (Yale University, 1966) and W. Augustus Low, "Virginia in the Critical Period, 1783-1789" (University of Iowa, 1941). Low's discussion is sketchy and incomplete, while Rich's able treatment is marred by a misreading of the provisions of the original law and an overly strong reliance on Madison's correspondence for contemporary attitudes towards the measure. For an interpretive overview of the Virginia economy in the 1780s, see Allan Schaffer, "Virginia's 'Critical Period'" in *The Old Dominion: Essays for Thomas Perkins Abernethy*, edited by Darrett B. Rutman (Charlottesville, 1964), pp. 152-170.

[8] The attempt to create towns and commercial centers in Virginia through legislative means

preferred having Norfolk as the sole port of entry and clearance.[9] The potential advantages of restricting trade to a single or a few ports were obvious. Restriction would encourage the growth of major commercial centers in Virginia which could rival Baltimore and Philadelphia, two cities which denied Virginia much commerce that was rightfully hers. It would keep the British (and particularly the Scots) out of the inland river valleys where their experience gave them an insuperable advantage over potential competitors; forcing all foreign trade to take place in large coastal ports would offer merchants of all countries the opportunity to compete on equal terms. Indeed, Madison's main purpose in sponsoring the Port Bill seems to have been "to reduce the trade of G[reat] B[ritain] to an equality with that of other nations."[10] The pre-Revolutionary organization of Virginia's commerce had also effectively hindered the rise of native middlemen who might purchase from wholesale merchants and sell to individual consumers. In this connection, Madison wrote to Thomas Jefferson in August 1785 that one function of the Port Bill would be to separate retailing from importing and wholesaling, giving native Virginians control of retailing throughout the inland river valleys. This division of labor would logically result from the operation of the restriction law, and Madison considered it "the only radical cure for credit to the consumer which continues to be given to a degree which if not checked will turn the [advantage of a] diffusive retail of merchandize into a nuisance." He reasoned that if a retail shopkeeper bought the goods of a wholesale merchant on short credit he would be unable to extend any credit to the consumer.[11]

A further objection to continuing the old system of decentralized river

---

had a long history, dating well back into the seventeenth century (Edward M. Riley, "The Town Acts of Colonial Virginia," *Journal of Southern History*, XVI [August 1950], 306-323; John C. Rainbolt, "The Absence of Towns in Seventeenth Century Virginia," *ibid.*, XXXV [August 1969], 343-360). During the 1760s disgruntled Virginia planters had considered schemes similar to Madison's also directed toward undercutting economic dependence on Britain (Egnal and Ernst, "Economic Interpretation," *William and Mary Quarterly*, 3rd ser., XXIX, 27).

[9] Randolph to Jefferson, May 15, 1784, *The Papers of Thomas Jefferson*, edited by Julian P. Boyd (Princeton, 1950-   ), VII, 260-261. Joseph Jones of King George County, who was a member of both the Committee of Commerce and the ad hoc committee assigned to develop the bill, wrote to his nephew James Monroe on May 29 that "the true policy" of the proponents of the bill was to limit foreign trade to one or at most two ports (James Monroe Papers, Manuscripts Division, Library of Congress).

[10] Madison to Jefferson, August 20, 1784, *Papers of James Madison*, VIII, 103.

[11] Madison to Jefferson, August 20, 1785, *ibid.*, VIII, 345. In a communication to Hogendorp sometime in May 1784, Jefferson discussed how native merchants of small capital would find it to their advantage to deal with wholesale merchants at Norfolk, should foreign trade be restricted to that port (Boyd, *Papers of Thomas Jefferson*, VII, 215-216).

commerce involved revenue considerations. Presumably, restricting trade to a few ports would facilitate the collection of impost duties and discourage smuggling. While Madison was certainly aware of the need to curtail illicit trade, this aspect of the Port Bill was undoubtedly secondary to his basic desire to crack the British monopoly of Virginia's commerce.[12] Jefferson, who wholeheartedly supported the restrictions, offered a further reason why the new commercial system might encourage more efficacious revenue procedures. He wrote to Madison that "One of my reasons for wishing to center our commerce at Norfolk was that it might bring to a point the proper subjects of taxation & reduce the army of taxgatherers almost to a single hand." This would avoid undue expense for the state and, more importantly, ease the burden of direct taxation on the farmer.[13] Lessening this burden was of secondary importance to Madison; in this regard, Jefferson's comment further reveals that support for restriction might be grounded in considerations other than those stressed by the leading advocate of the policy.

The bill which finally became law in June 1784 deviated from Madison's guidelines in several respects. Its preamble stressed the dual functions of placing "the trade and commerce carried on between the citizens of this commonwealth and foreign merchants . . . upon a more equal foundation" and of assuring that "the revenue arising from commerce . . . be more certainly collected."[14] Five ports were enumerated, however; Madison wrote to Jefferson that "We made a warm struggle for the establishmt. of Norfolk & Alexandria as our only ports; but were obliged to add York, Tappahannock, & Bermuda hundred."[15] The law stated that ships and other vessels trading to Virginia from foreign parts which were owned either completely or partially by non-Virginians were "to enter, clear out, lade and unlade" at these five ports. The penalty for violation was to be payment of double the amount

---

[12] During a journey along the Potomac in March 1784, Madison was informed of "several flagrant evasions" by foreign vessels loading at Alexandria (Madison to Jefferson, March 16, 1784, *Papers of James Madison*, VIII, 10). A perusal of Madison's letters during the 1780s, however, makes his priorities clear.

[13] Jefferson to Madison, December 8, 1784, *Papers of James Madison*, VIII, 177-178.

[14] William Waller Hening, editor, *The Statutes at Large, Being a Collection of the Laws of Virginia from the First Session of the Legislature in the Year 1619* (Richmond, Philadelphia, and New York, 1809-1823), XI, 402-403.

[15] Madison to Jefferson, July 3, 1784, *Papers of James Madison*, VIII, 93. Joseph Jones had reported to Monroe back in May that "there appears a general disposition to confine commerce to a few ports, the prevailing opinion I think to a port on each river" (Jones to Monroe, May 29, 1784, Monroe Papers). When Jefferson (in Europe) discovered that more than one port had been named, he was disappointed but added that "I trust that York & Hobbs' hole [Tappahannock] will do so little that Norfolk & Alexandria will get possession of the whole" (Jefferson to Madison, November 11, 1784, *Papers of James Madison*, VIII, 127).

of normal duties.[16] Both Madison and Jefferson objected to the exemption given citizens of Virginia. The latter feared that "by the contrivance of merchants" the basic function of the bill would be subverted, since it would be easy for British merchants to hire natives to transact their business.[17] Madison assured Jefferson that "The warmest friends to the law were averse to this discrimination which not only departs from its principle, but gives it an illiberal aspect to foreigners." He added, however, that the discrimination, which placed the citizens of other American states on the same footing with foreigners, was "a necessary concession to prevailing sentiments." [18]

This would not be the last time Madison would have to grapple with "prevailing sentiments" in Virginia, which supported the adoption of a rigorous, state-centered mercantilistic system. While he supported, in general, the development of Virginia shipping and seamen, it seems clear that Madison sponsored the Port Bill more with the intention of luring non-British foreign merchants to trade in Virginia's coastal ports than with putting the Commonwealth's trade entirely in the hands of native ships and citizens. As he wrote to Jefferson, in a sentence which he chose at some time or other to delete, "I still fear that many of them [i.e., foreigners] may mistake the object of the law to be a sacrifice of their conveniency to the encouragement of our mercantile citizens, whereas in reality it was as far as foreign trade came in question only meant to reduce the trade of G[reat] B[ritain] to an equality with that of other nations." [19] To this extent, Madison's outlook embodied a restrained and limited mercantilism, especially compared to the vision of those virulently anti-foreign Virginians who conceived of anything or anyone outside the state as foreign.[20]

---

[16] Hening, *Statutes*, XI, 402-405. In her dissertation "The Experimental Years" (p. 153), Myra Rich mistakenly reports that the exemption extended to all United States citizens, rather than just Virginians.

[17] Jefferson to Madison, November 11, 1784, *Papers of James Madison*, VIII, 127.

[18] Madison to Jefferson, August 20, 1784, *Papers of Thomas Jefferson*, VII, 402. At this time, Madison apparently believed that the distinction between Virginians and other Americans was merely "an erratum" that would "no doubt be rectified." He would soon be disillusioned.

[19] *Ibid.*, VII, 402, 409.

[20] Forrest McDonald, in *E Pluribus Unum: The Creation of the American Republic, 1776-1790* (Boston, 1965), describes an economic program conceived by Virginians in the 1780s which included a significant increase in Virginia shipping in the trans-Atlantic trade. Strangely enough, McDonald ignores the Port Bill in his discussion of the new Virginia system of the 1780s (pp. 72-76). Most of the sentiment for a narrow mercantilistic system surfaced in the form of petitions to the October 1785 and October 1786 sessions of the General Assembly, as will be discussed below.

The Port Bill of June 1784 was a classic mercantilist measure in that it specifically encouraged the development of native (i.e., Virginian) seamen. A second part of the bill dealt with "the bay or river craft" which would be employed by Virginians to carry goods and produce between the enumerated ports and inland areas. Noting that "whereas the navigating small country craft by slaves, the property of the owners of such craft, tends to discourage free white seamen, and to encrease the number of such free white seamen would produce public good," the bill stipulated that "not more than one-third part of the persons employed in the navigation of any bay or river craft, below the falls of the rivers, shall consist of slaves." [21] Madison never mentioned this aspect of the Port Bill in any of his correspondence, thus indicating that it was tangential to his basic concerns. What seems clear, in short, is that support for the Port Bill undoubtedly came from individuals or groups whose priorities and interests differed from those of its chief sponsor.

The legislature deferred implementation of the Port Bill until June 10, 1786. James Monroe, who was basically sympathetic to the cause of restriction, wrote to Jefferson that this postponement stemmed from "the expectation that the craft necessary for the river carriage will be prepar'd by that time, so that from the commencement it may effect no injury to the people." He feared, however, that such a hope was visionary, that "Those who otherwise would turn their attention to the subject will think it too uncertain an event to calculate on, and the operation of the law will not find a single vessel prepar'd to supply the exigency it will require." Monroe further worried that the object of the law would be defeated unless only one large port town were erected at a time; as the bill then stood, each of the enumerated ports' operations would be confined to the river on which it stood, which might permit a large commercial center like Baltimore to continue dominating the bulk of Virginia's trade. Monroe feared that these imperfections and the two-year delay in implementation would encourage efforts to repeal the bill before it took effect. He hoped such efforts would fail, and that the existing bill would prove to be "only a step to a more wise and mature system of policy." [22] But his suspicions were correct. The bill had passed in the House of Delegates by a very slim margin, 64 to 58, and the opposition soon organized efforts for repeal. [23]

---

[21] Hening, *Statutes*, XI, 402-404.

[22] Monroe to Jefferson, July 20, 1784, *Papers of Thomas Jefferson*, VII, 380.

[23] When the vote is plotted geographically, it becomes apparent that the sections favoring the measure fell chiefly in the trading orbits of the designated ports. The area around Norfolk and Portsmouth, in particular, formed a solid bloc of support. Several vital trading centers,

Writing to Jefferson in August 1784, Madison noted that "the act which produces most agitation and discussion" among the people at large was indeed the Port Bill. In one lengthy sentence he characterized, from his point of view, the nature of this opposition:

Those who are devoted from either interest or prejudice, to the British trade and meditate a revival of the old plan of monopoly and credit, with those whose local situations give them or are thought to give them an advantage in large ships coming up and lying at their usual stations in the Rivers, are busy in decoying the people into a belief that trade ought in all cases to be left to regulate itself, that confining it to particular ports is renouncing the favour which nature intended in diffusing navigation throughout our country; and that if one sett of men are to be exporters and importers, another set to be carryers between the mouths & heads of the rivers, and a third retailers thro' the country; trade, as it must pass thro' so many hands all taking a profit from it, must in the end come dearer to the people, than if the simple plan s[houl]d be continued which unites these several branches in the same hands.[24]

Like Monroe, Madison feared repeal; these objections to the bill, "tho' unsound, are not altogether unplausible; and being propagated with more zeal & pains by those who have a particular interest to serve, than proper answers are by those who regard the general interest only, make it very possible that the measure may be reversed before it is to take effect."[25] Opposition mounted in 1785 while a nationwide commercial depression, which was to be especially severe in Virginia, began. By June, Boston, New York, and Philadelphia manifested considerable mercantile unrest, but Madison doubted that simliar unrest would spread to Virginia, since most Virginia merchants, unlike their northern counterparts, were subservient to British interests, and Virginia planters knew too little about commercial matters to recognize the cause of their distress and combine in defense of their interests. After comparing relative price levels in Virginia and Philadelphia, Madison concluded that although planters suffered severe losses as a result of Virginia's marketing system, they seemed unable to recognize and support the obvious measures necessary to remedy the situation:

It is difficult notwithstanding to make them sensible of the utility of establishing a Philad[elphi]a, or a Baltimore among ourselves, as one indispensable step towards

---

particularly Petersburg and Richmond, were not included in the bill and the surrounding areas tended to oppose it. The area around another such center, Fredericksburg, ironically did not solidly oppose the bill, although this area was soon to petition for its repeal (W. Augustus Low, "Virginia in the Critical Period," p. 146, and map VI on p. 215).

[24] Madison to Jefferson, August 20, 1784, *Papers of James Madison*, VIII, 102-103.
[25] *Ibid.*, VIII, 103.

relief: and the difficulty is not a little increased by the pains taken by the Merchants to prevent such a reformation, and by the opposition arising from local views. .I have been told that A[rthur] L[ee] paved the way to his election in Prince William by promising Dumfries that among other things he would overset the Port Bill. Mr. Jefferson writes me that the Port Bill has been published in all the gazettes in Europe with the highest approbation every where except in G[reat] B[ritain]. It would indeed be as surprising if she should be in favor of it as it is that any among ourselves should be against it. I see no possibility of engaging other nations in a rivalship with her without some such regulation of our commerce.[26]

Madison accurately predicted that the Port Bill would undergo "a fiery trial" at the October 1785 session of the General Assembly, at which several petitions urging modification or repeal were presented.[27] Two petitions arrived in late November from "sundry inhabitants of the counties of Lancaster, Northumberland, and several other counties" urging that a new location be selected for the port on the Rappahannock; the petitioners suggested that a town be created on some part of the Cocotoman River (a tributary of the Rappahannock) to take advantage of a fine natural harbor.[28] All the ensuing petitions, however, called for outright repeal—one from the corporation of Fredericksburg, two from Prince William County, and one from Culpeper County. Arguments against the bill usually proceeded on two separate levels, one practical and one more theoretical. The Prince William petitioners denounced the bill as "unjust and unequal" and "greatly injurious to the state in general." It was unjust and unequal because it would deprive "a very great number of citizens of the principal advantages of navigation which they before the Revolution enjoyed, and still do enjoy" and also because "those citizens who have built and improved in other towns on navigation under the faith of laws, should the act take place, will lose, by the depreciation in the price of their houses, the greater part of their property." The bill would be injurious to the state "because the enormous expences attending the conveying to and shipping the different commodities from the five ports . . . must come out of the pockets of the planters and farmers; and of course greatly diminish the value of lands." The Prince William petitioners also strongly doubted whether the bill could achieve its purported end of an "equality among foreign merchants." "The British merchants and their agents," they argued, "are so

---

[26] Madison to Monroe, June 21, 1785, *ibid.*, VIII, 307-308. See also Madison to Jefferson, August 20, 1785, *ibid.*, VIII, 344-346.

[27] Madison to Jefferson, April 27, 1785, *ibid.*, VIII, 268.

[28] Lancaster County Legislative Petitions, November 25, 1785, Virginia State Library. All petitions are in the Virginia State Library in Richmond.

well acquainted with the proper places for fixing retail stores that by carrying on that business from the five ports they would perhaps engross a much greater share of the trade than they at present have." [29]

On a more theoretical level, the petitioners noted that they "conceive that the security and happiness of a republick consists in its wealth and power being divided as well among the several districts and towns as among the individuals," for "otherwise equality and with that security will be lost." In view of all these objections, then, and considering Virginia's unstable condition following a long and expensive war, the Prince William petitioners insisted that should the Port Bill be allowed to go into effect "the consequences will be distressing indeed and the risk greater than . . . prudent to hazard." [30] The wording of the Culpeper and Fredericksburg petitions was virtually identical to that of Prince William, with the interesting difference that they referred to the wealth and power of a republic needing to be *equally* divided among its towns and individuals.[31] All the petitions received during the 1785-1787 period advocating repeal of the Port Bill repeated two or three basic forms. This might indicate some degree of inter-county organization and a desire to impress the legislators with a uniformity of opposition sentiment.[32] Extensive and painstaking research into the signers of these petitions might indicate to what degree Madison's assessment of the nature of the opposition to the Port Bill was accurate. For the case of Fredericksburg, convenient evidence exists which undermines Madison's implication that the merchants who opposed it were those who were tied to British interests, anticipating a revival of commerce under the old system. In June 1784 merchants and traders in Fredericksburg and nearby Falmouth petitioned the legislature against repeal of a law passed during the war to restrain extensive credits, arguing that its repeal would be particularly injurious to "the American purchasers and importers" by "giving a preference to an Establishment which hath heretofore been found injurious to this state." [33] Almost half (nineteen of forty) of the names attached to this petition reappeared the following year on the anti-Port Bill petition. Similarly, in December 1784, a memorial to the legislature sponsored by a meeting of merchants in Fredericksburg blasted British re-

---

[29] Prince William County Petitions, December 9, 1785.

[30] *Ibid.*

[31] Culpeper County Petitions, December 9, 1785, and Fredericksburg Petitions, November 28, 1785.

[32] For an indication that such motives and organizations existed for petitions relating to a different matter, see the letter of G. Nicholas to James Madison, April 22, 1785, *Papers of James Madison*, VIII, 264-265.

[33] Fredericksburg Petitions, June 8, 1784.

strictions on American commerce and urged the General Assembly to "pass such resolutions as may effectually tend to remove the grievances complained of"; once again, slightly less than half (twenty-four out of fifty) of the signers of this anti-British petition also opposed the Port Bill.[34] What this might indicate, in short, is that a significant number of native merchants who actively opposed British control of Virginia's commerce failed to support a measure designed in part to terminate that control.[35]

The bill was strongly attacked in the October 1785 session and nearly defeated. Amendments passed the House of Delegates but failed in the Senate; the bill's adversaries then unsuccessfully attempted to suspend its operation until the end of the next session. Although it was left intact, Madison pessimistically predicted that its repeal would undoubtedly come at the next session, adding that its opponents would already have succeeded if they "had known their strength in time and exerted it with Judgment."[36] By this time, Madison's interest in the Port Bill had waned considerably, and he was now focusing his efforts to remedy Virginia's declining situation on plans for commercial reform at the national level. The important question had been raised at this session of the Assembly as to "whether relief shall be attempted by a reference to Cong[ress], or by measures within our own Compass," and Madison had castigated "the mercantile interest of most of our towns except Alexandria" which, due to narrow ideas and an illiberal animosity toward northern shipping, had endeavored to devise some sort of navigation act for the state of Virginia alone.[37] Petitions poured in from Norfolk, Suffolk (and Nansemond County), Portsmouth, and Petersburg lamenting the deplorable state of Virginia's commerce and uging the Assembly to retaliate against the British Acts of Navigation, which, the petitioners argued, were destroying the Commonwealth's shipbuilding industry and hindering the rise of native mer-

---

[34] Fredericksburg Petitions, December 2, 1784.

[35] A perusal of several manuscript collections also suggests that large planters in the Tidewater area who marketed their tobacco with British merchants under the old consignment system were indifferent to the Port Bill. See, for example, the Robert Beverley Letterbook (Manuscripts Division, Library of Congress) and the Ralph Wormeley Letterbook (Alderman Library, University of Virginia). Both men frequently discussed commercial matters in their correspondence, yet never mentioned the Port Bill. This silence also characterizes the business and personal correspondence of William and David Allason, who were independent retail merchants operating out of Falmouth (Allason Letterbook and Correspondence in the Virginia State Library).

[36] Madison to Jefferson, January 22, 1786, *Papers of James Madison,* VIII, 477. See also Madison to Monroe, January 22, 1786, *ibid.,* VIII, 483.

[37] Madison to George Washington, November 11, 1785, *ibid.,* VIII, 403-404, and Madison to Washington, December 9, 1785, *ibid.,* VIII, 439.

chants, vessels, and seamen.[38] Madison was decidedly hostile to this burgeoning mercantilist movement in Virginia, for it was only a further reflection of
the parochial mentality which had persisted "in putting Citizens of other
States on the footing of foreigners" in the Port Bill.[39]

This session of the Assembly was further marked by an increased concern
with the problem of better securing the revenue arising from customs. A
statute was enacted which authorized any citizen to seize a vessel that failed
to enter legally and pay duties—the informer was entitled to one half of the
proceeds following prosecution and condemnation before a court of ad-
miralty.[40] There can be little doubt that many Virginians now viewed the
Port Bill as a necessary remedy for the evil of smuggling and the evasion of
duties.[41]

By early 1786, in short, the Port Bill as Madison had initially conceived it
was virtually dead. If it were to survive as a program of commercial legislation, clearly it would be for reasons other than those Madison had cherished.
Those groups or individuals who might have supported the bill in June 1784
as part of a mercantilist program for the state were now more interested in
other matters, but those who had been primarily concerned with the Port Bill
as a revenue measure had even more reason to champion it or like legislation.
Even Joseph Jones, one of the architects of the bill who had shared Madison's
sympathies, now seemed to support it primarily for the revenue it would bring
in. Writing to Jefferson, he expressed his confidence that, if given a fair
trial, "the measure would prove beneficial and establish itself from its fruits,"
adding that "doubtless it would greatly aid the collection of impost revenue,
and suppress these evasions which are now too generally practiced by the sub-
tile and interested trader." [42] Madison retained only a fatherly interest in the
Port Bill, for by May 1786 he saw the problem of Virginia's commercial
plight to be too great for palliatives on the state level, where the situation was

---

[38] Norfolk (City) Petitions, November 4, 1785; Nansemond County Petitions, November
4, 1785; Portsmouth Petitions, November 5, 1785; and Petersburg Petitions, November 24, 1785.
[39] Madison to Monroe, January 22, 1786, *Papers of James Madison*, VIII, 483.
[40] Hening, *Statutes*, XII, 46-47.
[41] The customs collector at Norfolk, Josiah Parker, wrote to the governor in February 1786
and discussed the problem of vessels running up the different rivers without entering at all.
"The Port Bill will take place in June," he noted, "and I conceive then that every Foreign
vessell for Elizabeth, Nancemond or James River must enter here." He added optimistically
that only one good armed pilot boat and a barge under the direction of the naval officer at
Norfolk would then be needed for efficient supervision (William P. Palmer, editor, *Calendar
of Virginia State Papers and Other Manuscripts Preserved in the Capitol at Richmond* [Rich-
mond, 1875], IV, 92).
[42] Jones to Jefferson, February 21, 1786, Boyd, *Papers of Thomas Jefferson*, IX, 297.

too chaotic and unstable to allow any comprehensive, constructive program. He saw the bill's repeal as inevitable, particularly since adequate preparations for its implementation had not been and would never be made—"To force trade to Norfolk and Alexandria, without preparations for it at those places, will be considered as injurious. And so little ground is there for confidence in the stability of the Legislature that no preparations will ever be made in consequence of a preceding law. The transition must of necessity therefore be at any time abrupt and inconvenient." [43] Madison realized by now that the unpopularity of the Port Bill made its intended operation infeasible and its success impossible.

The law went into effect as scheduled, however, on June 10, 1786.[44] Immediate repercussions are unclear; Charles Yates, a Fredericksburg merchant, wrote to James Hunter in July that "we are here dead as doornails—trade not only dull but dead indeed," without, however, mentioning any specific effects of the Port Bill.[45] The elections for the October 1786 session of the General Assembly did not bode well for the measure, as Madison was reelected only after overcoming considerable opposition and George Mason, recognized by Madison as the leader of the anti-Port Bill forces, decided to reenter active politics.[46] More petitions urging repeal were presented, the longest and most interesting being an individual protest by "a private citizen" —who turned out to be Mason, by far the most articulate opponent of the law. Mason's memorial consisted of a battery of rhetorical questions, each designed to highlight the impracticality, unjustifiability, and general foolishness of an act to restrict foreign trade to certain ports. It reflected an intense agrarian-mindedness, and in laissez-faire, anti-urban rhetoric repeatedly warned against the deleterious effects of unnecessary and unjustified interference by government in the natural operation of Virginia's economy. Virginia's inland waterways were a natural blessing, Mason argued, not to be tampered with by partial and unsound legislative policies; he similarly stressed that the extensive trade and large population of Philadelphia and other great

---

[43] Madison to Monroe, May 13, 1786, Madison Papers.

[44] In the June 8 issue of the *Virginia Journal and Alexandria Advertiser*, Charles Lee, the naval officer at Alexandria, gave notice that "the Port Law" would soon commence and be in force, warning that "all persons trading in Potomack River with this Commonwealth are hereby required to conform their conduct to the aforesaid law."

[45] Charles Yates to James Hunter, July 13, 1786, Hunter Papers, Alderman Library, University of Virginia. James McRae, the searcher at Alexandria, informed the governor on August 22 that he had seized a vessel from North Carolina for violation of the Port Bill, but advised her release on the grounds of the ignorance and poverty of the master and owner (Palmer, *Calendar*, IV, 165).

[46] James Currie to Jefferson, July 9, 1786, Boyd, *Papers of Thomas Jefferson*, X, 109.

cities were due to natural rather than artificially contrived causes. Large populous cities in Virginia would be a liability rather than a boon, anyway, since they would be vulnerable to foreign attack and would require garrisons and a navy for protection. Mason climaxed his anti-urban appeal by reminding the General Assembly that the morality and manners of great commercial cities were inimical to republican virtue, as the history of ancient civilizations amply demonstrated. Virginia, Mason concluded, should be grateful for its natural advantages and the benefits of infancy. "Are not a people more miserable and contemptible in the last," he asked, "than in the early and middle stages of society? And is it not safer and wiser to leave things to the natural progress of time, than to hasten them, prematurely, by violence; and to bring in the community all the evils, before it is capable of receiving any of the advantages of populous countries?" If they sincerely hoped to escape their current distress, Virginians would do better, Mason concluded, to practice honesty and frugality than to rely on any artificial legislative ploys.[47] Mason's protest reflects well how elements of a Virginia brand of republican ideology might provide fuel for opposition to the Port Bill.

A petition from Fredericksburg citizens reminded the Assembly of their earlier anti-Port Bill petition and reported that "this act they have since seen carried into execution to their great loss and damage, and they are sorry to find from its operation, their fears were but too well founded." [48] A petition from Madison's county, Orange, signed by over fifty persons, similarly complained that "they find themselves greatly hurt and aggrieved" by the operation of the Port Bill and likewise called for its repeal.[49] Three petitions from Fauquier County, with over 250 signatures, echoed these general sentiments.[50] And a further petition from Prince William followed both the rhetorical question form and many of the arguments of Mason's personal protest. The petitioners declined to take up the Assembly's time by repeating "manifold" and "evident" objections. Instead, "they will only remind you of the situation of the country, and the principles of your constitution; and then ask if such a law can be reconciled to them."

Is that equality preserved among your citizens, they have a right to expect? Is it probable such an institution will tend to the promulgation of virtue? Is it reasonable that the interest of at least forty nine of your citizens out of fifty should

[47] The protest is printed in Robert A. Rutland, editor, *The Papers of George Mason, 1725-1792* (Chapel Hill, 1970), II, 859-863.
[48] Fredericksburg Petitions, November 17, 1786.
[49] Orange County Petitions, December 6, 1786.
[50] Fauquier County Petitions, December 6, 1786.

be sacrificed to the remaining fiftieth? Will it secure the property of your citizens against the invasions of foreign enemies? Or can the additional carriage of bulky and heavy articles, render them more valuable? Trusting to your wisdom and justice they hope the law will be repealed, and pray for the prosperity of the Common Wealth.[51]

Much to Madison's surprise, and in spite of these appeals, repeal of the Port Bill failed by a vote of 69 to 35 on December 11. In fact, five delegates who had voted against the bill in 1784 now switched and voted against repeal.[52] It seems clear, however, that much of this support arose strictly from revenue considerations. Reporting the vote on repeal to his father, Madison added that "amendments however are necessary and will probably take place." [53] He later admitted that the measure "owes its success less to its principal merits, than to collateral and casual considerations," one of which was the popular idea "that by favoring the collection of duties on imports it saves the solid property from direct taxes." [54] There had been strong pressure in the Assembly at this session for enormously high duties on imports—partly for the purpose of revenue and partly to stimulate manufactures—which Madison described as potentially "a dreadful blow" to Virginia's commerce.[55] While this effort failed, Madison had predicted correctly that the session would not end without substantial amendments to the Port Bill. The preamble to the amended bill reflected the priority now placed on purposes which Madison viewed as "collateral and casual":

For the better securing the revenue, arising from duties on imports and exports, whereby the burthen of taxes upon the people may not be encreased, and for regulating the trade of this commonwealth, whereby foreigners may be placed on a more equal footing, and the increase of seamen in this state be promoted by a due attention to internal navigation, for the extension of the commerce thereof; *Be it enacted* . . . .[56]

The amended bill was to take effect on April 1, 1787. It provided for an expanded number of ports under two categories—eight ports of entry and

[51] Prince William County Petitions, December 6, 1786.

[52] *Journal of the House of Delegates, 1776-1790* (Richmond, 1827-1828), October 1786 Session, p. 98.

[53] Madison to James Madison Sr., December 12, 1786, Madison Papers.

[54] Madison to Jefferson, December 9, 1787, Boyd, *Papers of Thomas Jefferson*, XII, 411. In his letter to Madison of December 8, 1784, Jefferson had indicated that this aspect of the Port Bill had contributed to his support of it. See footnote 13.

[55] Madison to Edmund Pendleton, January 9, 1787, Madison Papers.

[56] Hening, *Statutes*, XII, 320-323.

clearance and nine ports of delivery for loading and unloading—and stipulated that "any vessel built within the United States, and wholly owned by any of the citizens thereof" was permitted to load "at any port or place within this commonwealth, with any article or articles for exportation." Madison could thus at least be pleased that the original discrimination between citizens of Virginia and those of other American states which he found so loathsome had been rescinded. The new law provided for much stiffer penalties for violation—forfeiture of vessel or goods, as the case required—and incorporated a provision of the anti-smuggling law passed a year earlier, in that one half of the confiscated proceeds would go to the Commonwealth and the other half to the informer. It also contained provisions which would please mercantilist-minded Virginians interested in encouraging native shipping and seamen—all river and bay craft had to be registered, crews could not be more than half slave, and any such craft found to be owned or partly owned by foreigners (non-Americans, once again) was subject to confiscation.[57]

Despite these amendments, the continuing push for repeal of the Port Bill finally succeeded at the October 1787 session of the General Assembly. Petitions against the measure continued to come in, with one from Spotsylvania County making the standard argument for repeal.[58] Another from New Kent County urged that for practical reasons a new port be selected for the York River should the verdict of the legislature go against repeal.[59] And one from Caroline County, echoing Mason's appeal to natural law and laissez-faire principles, deemed the law "repugnant to the interest and principles of free commerce, counteracting the gracious dispensations of Providence in defusing [sic] trade and navigation through the great part of the state by our several rivers (particularly adapted to the nature of our staple commoditys)." These petitioners further pointed to the situation of the freeholders below the port of Fredericksburg who had to bear the added cost of transporting imports and exports eighty miles up the Rappahannock to that town. Considering that these freeholders' lands were taxed according to their supposed advantage of living near a navigable river, this situation seemed especially unjust. The petitioners urged, therefore, that the Port Bill be repealed or amended by adding a port at Port Royal or Fredericksburg, or that the land tax be appropri-

---

[57] Hening, *Statutes*, XII, 320-323.

[58] Spotsylvania County Petitions, October 26, 1787.

[59] New Kent County Petitions, October 31, 1787. A year earlier, a petition from Petersburg similarly complained of inconvenience due to a port not being designated at a proper location, and also requested either an adjustment on the grounds of practicality or repeal (Petersburg Petitions, November 4, 1786).

ately adjusted.[60] Following repeal of the amended act, Alexander Donald, a Richmond merchant, drew up a plan for a new bill at George Mason's request. He reported to Jefferson that the new measure was designed to "more effectually secure the Revenue than the former, and . . . remove the many objections the Merchantile People had to the Last." [61] This final "Port Bill," passed on January 5, 1788, drastically expanded the number of ports under three categories: six of entry and clearance, fifteen of delivery for foreign vessels, and twenty for delivery for vessels of the United States.[62] In most of its other provisions it was similar to the amended act of a year earlier, but the resemblance between this final act and the original bill of 1784, in both provisions and basic purposes, was superficial to say the least.

Above all, the final anti-Port Bill petitions gave evidence of the immense difficulty in insuring equity and justice when attempting to implement the radical regulatory program embodied in the Port Bill of 1784. Opponents of the measure always appealed to principle—that it was "unjust and unequal," or "repugnant to the interest and principles of free commerce"—but these appeals were always grounded on the valid assertion that the bill, as structured, was impracticable. The effective and reasonably impartial implementation of the Port Bill, especially in its original form (not to mention the form which Madison would have preferred), would have required a spate of supplementary legislation to provide for enforcement and any necessary compensations, a revolutionary degree of economic centralization in the state, and a radical reorganization of the state's geo-political economy, necessitating construction of new river craft and wharves and alterations in the basic pattern of economic activity for many Virginians. Too many Virginians, some imbued with an agrarian-minded defense of a "natural" economic order and the local liberty it engendered, were unwilling to make such drastic changes in order to promote the economic independence of the Commonwealth. Madison's struggle to convince his state of the need for reform at the federal level, begun in earnest by at least 1785, ultimately resulted in victory, and he would go on to New York in 1789 to continue his efforts to break the British hold on Virginia's commerce, this time within the broader context of achieving national economic independence. With the adoption of the new United States Constitution by Virginia in June 1788, the final "Port Bill" passed at the beginning of that year became both irrelevant and unconstitutional.

---

[60] Caroline County Petitions, November 15, 1787.
[61] Donald to Jefferson, November 12, 1787, Boyd, *Papers of Thomas Jefferson*, XII, 346.
[62] Hening, *Statutes*, XII, 434-438.

Civilian-Military Conflict and the Restoration of the Royal Province of Georgia, 1778–1782

By Patrick J. Furlong

Battered, scattered, and delayed by a late autumn gale, a small British squadron sailed from Sandy Hook in November 1778. Embarked with Commodore Hyde Parker in H.M.S. *Phoenix* was Lieutenant Colonel Archibald Campbell, with his own Highlanders of the 71st Foot, four battalions of Loyalists and two of Hessians, a small force indeed to recapture Georgia from the rebels. Archibald Campbell of Inverneill, at the age of thirty-nine, was an experienced officer of distinguished Highland ancestry, a member of Parliament, and more recently a prisoner of war in Massachusetts. This was his first independent command, and he was naturally pleased by the honor but disappointed that it did not bring him a promotion.[1] Campbell's general orders, issued at sea on December 22, listed the reduction of Georgia and the relief of southern Loyalists as the chief objectives of the expedition, and he warned his troops not to injure the inhabitants, for he intended to return the province to its due obedience to the crown.[2]

Tybee, at the mouth of the Savannah River, was sighted the next day. Campbell and Parker knew nothing of the rebel de-

[1] Sir Henry Clinton to Lord George Germain, November 8, 24, 1778; Campbell to Clinton, November 8, 15–16, 1778; Campbell to Lord Rawdon, November 23, 1778, Sir Henry Clinton Papers (William L. Clements Library, University of Michigan, Ann Arbor, Mich.). Another copy of Clinton's dispatches can be found in the Colonial Office Papers in the Public Record Office, London, hereafter cited in the following form: CO 5/236/277–79. For a sketch of Campbell's career see Henry M. Stephens, "Sir Archibald Campbell," in *The Dictionary of National Biography . . . from the Earliest Times to 1900* (22 vols., London, 1949–1950), III, 794–95; and also Charles H. Walcott, *Sir Archibald Campbell of Inverneill* (Boston, [1898]).

[2] Clinton to Campbell, November 8, 1778, British Headquarters Papers, PRO 30/55/1535 (Public Record Office).

Mr. Furlong is associate professor of history at Indiana University at South Bend. Research for the article was supported by an Indiana University summer faculty fellowship.

fenses, but after questioning several prisoners they moved up-river past undefended swamps and landed their troops within two miles of the city. The rebels under Major General Robert Howe held a strong position: one flank was protected by the river, with the other and most of their front as well covered by a swamp. Campbell feinted in front and sent a strong flank attack through the swamp along an obscure and unguarded path pointed out by a slave. The outnumbered and outgeneraled rebels broke, with about five hundred falling prisoner to the British. The rebels left eighty-three dead on the field of battle, while the British lost only three killed and eleven wounded. The city itself fell without a shot, and Georgia's disgruntled delegates in Congress demanded a court-martial for the incompetent Howe.[3]

Colonel Campbell moved quickly to exploit his brilliant success. The settlement at Ebenezer was taken on January 2, 1779, and a few mounted troops moved fifty miles up-country on the banks of the Savannah River without meeting resistance. Campbell and Parker jointly issued a proclamation which brought forward a number of Georgians willing to accept royal authority, while another offered ten guineas reward for the capture of any officer of the rebel government. The next military objective was Augusta, the principal settlement of the back-country, more than a hundred miles upriver from Savannah, where Campbell hoped to rally large numbers of loyal frontiersmen. Meanwhile Brigadier General Augustine Prevost advanced from Florida, and when he joined Campbell at Savannah on January 17 all of low-country Georgia was firmly under British control.[4] The immediate military objectives had been accomplished with relative ease, but this victory had to be fitted into the grand strategy for the suppression of the American rebellion. The political problem, not surprisingly, was a good deal more complex.

The expedition against Georgia had been long considered but hastily organized. Throughout the summer of 1778 Clinton had hesitated in planning his winter operations. From Florida, General Prevost suggested that the rebels in Georgia were so

[3] Campbell to Clinton, January 16, 1779, Clinton Papers, and also CO 5/97/112–18; Alexander A. Lawrence, "General Robert Howe and the British Capture of Savannah in 1778," *Georgia Historical Quarterly*, XXXVI (December 1952), 303–27. Howe was tried and acquitted.

[4] Campbell to Clinton, January 16, 1779, Clinton Papers; Augustine Prevost to Clinton, January 19, 1779, CO 5/97/110–11.

weak that the province might be taken with ease, but Clinton was not convinced. Then, in mid-October Clinton received a strong suggestion from Lord George Germain that "the recovery of South Carolina and Georgia in the Winter . . . is an object of much Importance . . . ." Germain, the secretary of state for the colonies, had said much the same thing months earlier, but Clinton had to be prodded. Always anxious to please his superiors, he soon replied that he was sending three thousand men against Georgia, though he typically complained that he could not spare so many. Moving with unusual dispatch, Clinton had the Georgia invasion force ready to sail within three weeks.[5]

Archibald Campbell, experienced in politics as well as in war, understood well the difficulties of his position in Georgia. In addition to his military orders he acted under instructions from the frustrated peace commissioners at New York, Frederick Lord Carlisle, William Eden, and General Clinton himself. They directed him to prepare for the reestablishment of civil government in Georgia and gave him a provisional appointment as governor, which he was to publish whenever he might have "a reasonable Expectation of being able thereby to encourage & maintain any considerable proportion of the Inhabitants in a Return of Loyalty . . . ." As soon as a temporary government could be established and the frontiers of the province secured, Campbell intended to return to Britain. His personal report to Clinton concluded with a respectful but very firm suggestion that a civil governor be ordered to Georgia at once. Restoration of the usual forms of government "would be a model to future Conquests, and from the happiness of its form, may at this Juncture, conquer more Provinces than Twenty Thousand Troops."[6]

The imperial authorities at Whitehall approved all Clinton's arrangements for Georgia and entertained great hopes of success. Before word of success reached England, Germain confirmed Campbell's appointment as temporary governor and

[5] Clinton to Germain, March 8, July 27, October 8, 1778; Prevost to Clinton, September 16, 1778; Germain to Clinton, August 5, 1778 (received October 18); Moses Kirkland to Clinton, October 13, 1778; Kirkland to Peace Commissioners, October 21, 1778; Clinton to Germain, October 25, 1778; Campbell to Clinton, November 15-16, 1778, Clinton Papers.

[6] Peace Commissioners (Carlisle, Clinton, Eden) to Campbell, November 3, 1778, Thomas Addis Emmet Collection (New York Public Library, New York City); Campbell to Clinton, January 16, 1779 (second letter of this date), Clinton Papers.

ordered the lieutenant governor, the chief justice, and the attorney general to return and assist the military rulers of Georgia.[7] Despite his disclaimers, Campbell was clearly an able governor. Public order was maintained with little difficulty, and he persuaded many Georgians to join his forces. "I have got the Country in arms against the Congress," he told William Eden. "In short, Sir, I think I may venture to pledge myself, that I have taken a stripe and star from the Rebel flag of America." This was not boasting, for the purpose of his letter was to urge Eden to use every exertion to secure "a Proper Governour for this Province; with every necessary arrangement for the Reestablishment of Legal Government." There was no one at Savannah capable of filling the office. "As to myself," Campbell said, "I am by no means calculated for it. I only profess myself a soldier, and mean as soon as I have given a handsome proof of Gratitude to my Sovereign for the unmerited distinction I have already been honoured with, to retire from the Bustle of Publick employ." In New York, General Clinton showed no concern for Campbell's problems, either civil or military, though he was of course greatly pleased by this success, which reflected credit upon himself as commander-in-chief.[8]

In Georgia, Colonel Campbell concerned himself not only with expelling the remaining rebel troops and encouraging loyalism but also of necessity with all the details of civil administration. He appointed a superintendent of the port, issued price regulations, licensed imports, and ordered stiff fines for any merchant found trading with a person who had not sworn allegiance. A Board of Police, which met almost daily, was the chief instrument of military government. It concerned itself with the administration of property, heard minor civil and criminal cases, issued at least ten tavern licenses, and named overseers for vacant plantations. Early in March, Campbell appointed commissioners of claims to manage vacant estates and provide for the relief of needy Loyalists, while a "civil" government under military officers assumed the general supervision of the province. His arrangements settled, Campbell sailed for England on March 12, leaving Lieutenant Colonel James M.

---

[7] Germain to Clinton, December 3, 1778 (received February 20, 1779), Clinton Papers; Germain to Campbell, January 16, 1779, PRO 30/55/1680.

[8] Campbell to Eden, January 19, 1779; Clinton to Eden, February 5, 14, 1779, Auckland Papers, Additional Mss. 34,416, ff. 246–47, 261–62, 271–73 (British Museum, London).

Prevost, a younger brother of the general, to govern Georgia with the title of lieutenant governor.[9]

The one person most deeply concerned with the province of Georgia was in London, but he had great hopes that he would soon be able to return to Savannah. Sir James Wright had been an able, honest, and popular governor, but he had not been able to withstand the revolutionary movement sweeping the colonies.[10] After the patriots forced him to leave in 1776 he took up residence in London and from time to time submitted proposals for the recovery of his province. His emphasis was always on a permanent settlement of imperial problems; military victory alone could never restore the old empire. Taxation was the basic colonial grievance, but Wright still believed that American representation in the House of Commons was a practical solution. He explained what should have been obvious to the ministry, "that there will be no Harmony or Cordiality, unless the Point of Taxation is fully and Clearly Settled." Military occupation would lead only to further insurrection, and in Wright's mind "the only True Way to Conciliate and restore Harmony and affection, and to Hold the Colonies to *advantage,* will be by Granting a Generous Plan or Constitution for America . . . ."

The rush of events had made reconciliation an improbable dream, but Wright was thinking of the only practical solution from the imperial point of view. If independence was to be rejected, as of course it had to be by every loyal servant of George III, then some alteration in the imperial system of government was plainly required. The failure of the existing arrangements could no longer be denied by reasonable men; Wright knew America far better than the American secretary did, and he pressed on to explain the necessity of accepting virtual autonomy for the thirteen provinces. The imperial legislature

[9] Orders issued by Parker and Campbell, January 15, 1779, copy in CO 5/97/197; Campbell's instructions to Commissioners of Claims, March 5, 1779, copy in Lord George Germain Papers (Clements Library); Clinton to Germain, March 30, April 3, 1779, CO 5/97/195, 205–206; James M. Prevost to Clinton, March 15, 1779, PRO 30/55/1830; Lilla M. Hawes, ed., "Minute Book, Savannah Board of Police, 1779," *Georgia Historical Quarterly,* XLV (September 1961), 245–47.

[10] Wright to Germain, April 26, 1776, CO 5/665/82–84. A good account of Wright's earlier career is Kenneth Coleman, "James Wright," in Horace Montgomery, ed., *Georgians in Profile: Historical Essays in Honor of Ellis Merton Coulter* (Athens, Ga., 1958), 40–60; see also William W. Abbot, *The Royal Governors of Georgia, 1754–1775* (Chapel Hill, 1959).

at Westminster would retain power to regulate commerce, and royal commissioners would assess the wealth of the various colonies so that the burden of taxation might be distributed equitably. The chief rebels would naturally suffer some disabilities, though Wright carefully avoided proposing any criminal penalties, and with equal caution he repeatedly insisted that loyal subjects must be compensated by Parliament for their losses. In closing, Wright looked to Ireland and reminded Germain that America could never be ruled "as a Conquered Country." The attempt would be too expensive, of no benefit to the empire, and doomed to failure with the coming of the next war.[11]

These views, outlined in February 1777, formed the basis of Wright's policy for as long as he could hope for Georgia to remain within the British empire. His reforms would have satisfied few rebels in this second year of the war, but no responsible British politician dared go further. That summer Wright was joined by Lord William Campbell, the exiled governor of South Carolina, and together with their lieutenant governors they submitted a scheme for the recapture of their provinces. In common with many British officials, both civil and military, these colonial administrators argued that a small force landing in the South would bring many Loyalists out of hiding if sufficient protection could be offered. The war to the northward, they emphasized, was not going well; submission did not follow the victories of the army. "We Humbly Conceive the Case would be very different in South Carolina and Georgia . . . ." Reestablishment of royal authority in the two southernmost colonies seemed "an absolute Certainty" to the governors, but they warned that the attack should come during the next winter before loyalism was totally suppressed by the growing strength of the rebels and while the Indians still favored the British.[12]

Governor Wright individually urged a similar plan in October. The rebel government of Georgia was divided and distracted, and the occasion seemed to be "most favorable" for recovery of the province. Lieutenant Governor John Graham had volunteered to return by way of Florida and do what he could with troops and Indian allies available there. Wright professed his willingness to cooperate, but he prudently warned that ships,

[11] Wright's Notes on Considering the State of Affairs in America, dated February 12, 1777, were sent with a covering letter to Germain on February 13, 1777, Germain Papers.

[12] William Campbell, Wright, William Bull, and John Graham to Germain, August 29, 1777, CO 5/116/80–81.

artillery, and supplies would be required if a recaptured colony was to be held against counterattack. Nothing was attempted during that season, but Wright and Graham remained hopeful. In July 1778 they again proposed the recovery of Georgia, with South Carolina if possible, by itself if necessary. If Lord Carlisle's peace mission led to the separation of the northern colonies, they suggested that it would be advantageous for Britain to keep Georgia, not only to protect Florida but also because its plentiful unsettled lands would provide refuge for Loyalists expelled from the northern colonies as well as timber and provisions for the West Indies.[13]

By 1778 British war policy was forced into new channels by John Burgoyne's surrender at Saratoga and by the French alliance with the rebels. Loyalist military assistance became more important as the ministry struggled to mobilize every possible resource. In March of that year Germain sent his first dispatch to Sir Henry Clinton, newly appointed commander-in-chief for North America. Among the many objectives called to Clinton's attention as matters of "great importance" were Georgia and South Carolina with their many presumed Loyalists. Clinton had more important concerns at the time, and in August Germain reminded him to do something about Georgia during the next winter campaign. It was this dispatch which Clinton received in October, a few days before he began to organize Campbell's expedition.[14]

Colonel Alexander Innes sailed from Tybee on January 23, 1779, carrying the first news of Campbell's success. After a swift passage he landed at Falmouth in the west of England and rode post to London in forty-six hours, reaching Pall Mall at midnight on February 22–23. The news of victory came at a moment of ministerial desperation, and the moneyed men of the City were elated with the report, which the ministry published

[13] Wright to Germain, October 8, 1777, *ibid.*, 5/665/99–100; Wright and Graham to Germain, July 17, 1778, *ibid.*, 5/116/82–83. What effect these proposals may have had is unknown; there is no known reply. A typescript of the first letter may also be found in the unpublished continuation of *The Colonial Records of the State of Georgia* at the Georgia Historical Society, Savannah. This series is unfortunately far from complete and not entirely accurate.

[14] Paul H. Smith, *Loyalists and Redcoats: A Study in British Revolutionary Policy* (Chapel Hill, 1964), 78–79, 83–84; Germain to Clinton, March 8, August 5, 1778, Clinton Papers. The second letter was received on October 18. The confusion of British policy and Clinton's personal difficulties as commander are skillfully analyzed in William B. Willcox, *Portrait of a General: Sir Henry Clinton in the War of Independence* (New York, 1964), especially 211–26.

immediately. Innes was honored with a long royal audience and conferred at length with several ministers.[15] The sequence of events at this decisive juncture is by no means clear. Innes was a staff officer in Campbell's confidence as well as Clinton's, and doubtless he discussed civil as well as military affairs during his meetings with Germain. As secretary of state for the colonies Germain had full direction of the efforts to suppress the rebellion in America by both military and political means. One might assume that Governor Wright, then living in London, would be summoned for consultation, but he seems to have been ignored. At the end of February, in a letter to Thomas Hutchinson, a former governor of Massachusetts, Wright described the capture of Savannah and went into a lengthy discussion of military affairs, but he said not a word about civil matters or the possibility of his own return. There is no reason to suspect that Wright would have concealed such a matter from Hutchinson, and all evidence indicates that Governor Wright was entirely in the dark.[16]

Little more than a week passed, and without warning Wright received orders to return to Georgia immediately to reestablish the civil government. Germain gave no explanation for this major shift in policy. If the purpose of the British military effort was indeed what it appeared to be, the suppression of insurrection and the restoration of the old form of colonial government, then Wright's orders were reasonable enough. But why Georgia? New York had been under British control for three years, yet nothing was attempted there. If Germain had any consistent policy, the secret was well kept. He considered each case in isolation without regard for unity of effort or for the effect one action might have on affairs elsewhere. Georgia had been captured; no one objected strongly to civil government there as Clinton did object in New York; the governor was willing to return; the plan offered some very important potential advantages; and little could be lost by trying. Governor Wright was accordingly directed to resume his office and to sail from Portsmouth in the appropriately named frigate *Experiment*. A few days later Wright told his friend John Robinson

[15] Innes to Clinton, March 3–4, 1779, Clinton Papers; *Gentleman's Magazine*, XLIX (February 1779), 100; Campbell's report was printed at length in the April issue, *ibid.*, 177–80.

[16] Wright to Hutchinson, February 27, 1779, Hardwicke Papers, Add. Mss. 35,427, f. 173 (British Museum).

that before receiving the king's command to return he had had only private hints of his new orders and that the suddenness of his departure surprised him greatly.[17]

Wright's instructions arrived at the end of March, the first in a fresh series of dispatches to the governor of Georgia. Germain gave official voice to his hope that active military operations would have advanced into South Carolina by the time Wright arrived, so that "nothing will be wanting to compleat the public Tranquility but the Declaration of His Majesty's Commissioners putting it [Georgia] at the Peace of the King." This proclamation was the final legal requirement for the restoration of civil jurisdiction, and once this was accomplished Wright was instructed to proceed to the appointment of a new Council of undoubted loyalty. The election of an Assembly was given high priority, so that all the people of British America might "see it is not the Intention of His Majesty & Parliament to govern America by Military Law; but, on the contrary, to allow them all the Benefits of a local Legislature, & their former Civil Constitution."

Germain's instructions wisely allowed Wright broad discretion, particularly in the matters to be brought before the revived Assembly. The secretary hoped for measures increasing the powers of the governor and indemnifying loyal subjects for their losses, and he held out a half promise that if Georgia took the lead in making a permanent provision for imperial revenue the province might receive special favor from king and Parliament. Germain closed by asking suggestions for alterations to the old provincial constitution, "tending more firmly to unite the Province with Great Britain; & render that Union indissoluble . . . ." The unfortunate peace commissioners, recently returned from New York after the total failure of their mission, were not consulted. Germain ignored their proffered recommendations and curtly directed them to prepare a proclamation putting Georgia at the peace of the king and to deliver the document to Governor Wright at once.[18]

---

[17] Germain to Wright, March 8, 1779, CO 5/677/67–68. For a discussion of policy regarding civil government in occupied colonies see Carlisle and Eden to Germain, November 27, 1778, Clinton Papers; for Clinton's objections to civilian rule of New York see Willcox, *Portrait of a General*, 379–80. Wright to Robinson, March 11, 1779, Audit Office Papers, AO 13/37/494 (Public Record Office).

[18] Germain to Wright, March 31, 1779, CO 5/677/68–72; Carlisle and Eden to Germain, March 8, 1779; Germain to Carlisle and Eden, March 16, 1779,

All was in readiness for Wright's return except for one detail which Lord George Germain overlooked for several weeks. The colonial secretary exercised both military and civil authority over the American colonies, but there were important distinctions among the officers who received orders from him. Wright was given legal power to return Georgia to civil jurisdiction, thereby excluding the province from Sir Henry Clinton's jurisdiction insofar as his nonmilitary powers were concerned, but Clinton's opinion in this important matter was not solicited. Germain delayed more than a month before telling him of the new policy, and then he made no effort to clarify the tangled problem of civil-military relationships.[19]

Thus a state was destroyed and a province reborn. An experienced and able colonial administrator was ordered to a difficult post with wonderfully ambitious instructions to unmake a revolution. If the governor was to succeed, he would require great help from the general. The governor was no soldier, and he knew it; the general was not equally self-denying in his political role.

Governor Wright reached Savannah on July 14, 1779, and found the military lieutenant governor out of town. He waited politely until Lieutenant Colonel Prevost returned before officially resuming the exercise of his office. He was disappointed to find his province less secure than he had been led to expect, but Campbell had established an administration so close to the old familiar forms that Wright felt his only choice was to proclaim Georgia at the peace of the king. The uncertain military situation made an early election impossible, and Wright feared all efforts "to reestablish Solid Government and good order" would be feeble until the Assembly could be revived. The Council, however, was reactivated immediately. About the military weakness of the province there was no dispute; General Augustine Prevost was emphatic on this point. His command

---

ibid., 5/230/186–91, 194. A signed and sealed copy of the proclamation, dated March 24, 1779, may be found *ibid.*, 5/230/213, and another copy, unsealed, *ibid.*, 5/665/126–27.

[19] Germain to Clinton, March 3, 31, April 22, 1779, *ibid.*, 5/97/88–92, 144–45, 183; Germain to Campbell, April 1, 1779, *ibid.*, 5/97/146–49. Only in the April letter, received August 24, did the secretary tell the general of the restoration of civil government in Georgia, Clinton Papers. Frederick B. Wiener, *Civilians Under Military Justice: The British Practice Since 1689, Especially in North America* (Chicago and London, 1967), provides an excellent analysis of the complex legal aspects of military government during the American war.

was scattered, and many of his men debilitated by the July heat, while the rebels were so active that it became dangerous for royalist forces to move beyond their camps.[20]

The change in authority at Savannah did not bring any great alteration in the administration of the town. The temporary civil officers appointed by Campbell were continued in office by Governor Wright and submitted their final reports through his office many months later. So long as Campbell had remained in command the work of these officials received the cooperation of the army, but with his departure the claims commissioners found themselves in difficulty with Lieutenant Colonel Prevost, the acting governor. He refused to uphold their authority and did nothing to halt plundering by the troops. As chief magistrate Prevost "openly and warmly" supported the most notorious offenders, and the commissioners were threatened with punishment under military law if they continued to obstruct the army. Governor Wright established a revised board of claims, but it too confessed general failure, although it no longer suffered quite so much from the army. Housing in Savannah was a major problem, for the army arrived first and naturally took the best for itself. The commissioners found few of the remaining vacant houses fit for rental and retreated in order to avoid "an open rupture with the army." Only legislative sanction would give them the necessary power, they reported gloomily; many army officers openly defied them, particularly by keeping captured slaves as personal servants.[21]

Such were some of the initial problems of the restored provincial government, and the governor discovered little to cheer him. "The more I am able to see into the true State of affairs here," Wright reported a fortnight after his return, "the more I am convinced of the wretched Situation the Province is in, & how nearly it was being totally lost, while the army was carrying on their operations in South Carolina." Nevertheless, Wright

20 Wright to Germain, July 31, 1779, CO 5/665/141; Council minutes for July 22, ibid., 5/665/143–44; Prevost to Clinton, March 15, July 30, 1779, PRO 30/55/1829, 2151; Henry Sheridan to General John Vaughan, July 24, 1779, Egerton Mss. 2,135, ff. 73–78 (British Museum).

21 Wright to Germain, May 20, 1780, forwarding reports from Board of Police (Lewis Johnston, James Mossman, William Telfair) and Commissioners of Claims (Martin Jollie and G. Kensall, appointed by the military administration in March 1779, and Jollie, Kensau, and Johnston, named by Wright in July), CO 5/665/259–69.

remained confident of eventual success. When Germain eventually replied to these dismal reports, he conceded that the distress of Georgia was unexpected at Whitehall, but his high hopes remained unshaken.[22]

Wright's administration functioned as much as possible as it had in the days before the rebellion. The new Council cooperated in the appointment of justices of the peace, ordered prosecution of stubborn rebels, set forth rules for swearing the oath of allegiance, and directed posting of quarantine notices as prescribed by the Small Pox Act. But repeated pleas for more effective protection from maurauding rebels could be answered only by referring petitions to "the General."[23] With the approach of winter Wright was increasingly discouraged, even though a strong French and rebel attack was driven off after a hard siege. The premature transfer of troops to South Carolina, he repeatedly observed, left Georgia "Naked and Defenceless." As it was, he faced a resurgence of rebellion against which the civil government would remain feeble until he could call elections and convene the Assembly. He pleaded also for a small force of provincial cavalry to combat the fast-moving rebels.[24]

Germain's high hopes were frequently disappointed, and it could hardly have been otherwise with communications as they were. The secretary's first hopeful letter to Georgia was seven months in reaching the governor. In reply, Wright once again explained his problems and the need for better support from the army. No British colonial governor could ever afford to neglect patronage, and Wright was far too experienced to forget this, regardless of the troublesome work involved. After further difficulties, Wright finally achieved his great ambition and issued writs of election for a new Assembly. The voting in April 1780 generally went well, particularly in Savannah. He

[22] Wright to Germain, August 9, 1779, *ibid.*, 5/665/163–64; Germain to Wright, October 27, 1779, *ibid.*, 5/677/76–77.

[23] Wright's last years of service as governor are surveyed by Kenneth Coleman, "Restored Colonial Georgia, 1779–1782," *Georgia Historical Quarterly*, XL (March 1956), 1–20. Council minutes for July and October 1779 may be found in CO 5/665/153–58, 184–89; a printed proclamation giving price regulations, *ibid.*, 5/665/241. Many of these Council minutes are printed in Allen D. Candler, comp., *The Colonial Records of the State of Georgia* (26 vols., Atlanta, 1904–1916), XII; other minutes are in Lilla M. Hawes, ed., "Some Papers of the Governor and Council of Georgia, 1780–1781," *Georgia Historical Quarterly*, XLVI (September, December 1962), 280–96, 395–417.

[24] Wright to Germain, November 6, 1779; January 20, 1780, CO 5/665/180–81, 205–206.

was "*very hopeful* to be able to accomplish several things" and remained firm in his opinion that an active Assembly was essential for the full return of the province to its former prosperity.[25]

Germain belatedly approved Wright's summons for the election. Restoration of the Assembly would, he hoped, more than anything else the British authorities could do, reconcile all Georgians "to the Blessing of a Civil Government." As the Assembly convened, a group of loyal subjects spoke in the same vein, sending the king a formal message of thanks for returning the province to such blessings "whilst the other colonies in rebellion . . . groan under tyranny and oppression." Salutes and an entertainment marked the king's birthday celebration, and Governor Wright played host to the Council and Commons as well as to officers of the army and the militia. That same day both houses passed a formal vote of thanks, telling the king of their hatred for rebellion and their gratitude for "the early re-establishment of Civil Government" and more particularly for Parliament's remission of internal taxation. The existing distress of the province was carefully noted, however, even on this happy occasion.[26]

The Assembly busied itself with measures to meet the wartime emergency, disqualify individuals of doubtful loyalty, and relieve distressed Loyalists. Summer heat soon weakened their diligence, and Wright reluctantly agreed to an adjournment. Parts of the backcountry were still not under British control because the inhabitants feared to show their "true loyalty" while rumors that the royal troops were about to abandon Augusta were widely circulated. Wright was never foolish enough

[25] Wright to Germain, February 10, 1780, and for patronage concerns, April 6, 1780, *ibid.*, 5/665/207–208, 255–56; Clinton to Germain, March 24, 1782, forwarding letters from Wright and the Council, William Petty, 2d Earl of Shelburne Papers (Clements Library). For the election see Lilla M. Hawes, ed., *The Proceedings and Minutes of the Governor and Council of Georgia, October 4, 1774, Through November 7, 1775, and September 6, 1779, Through September 20, 1780* (Savannah, 1952; Vol. X of the Georgia Historical Society, *Collections*), 61–62, 74–75; Wright to Germain, February 18, April 6, May 20, 1780, CO 5/665/211, 245–46, 272.

[26] Germain to Wright, June 7, 1780, CO 5/677/83–84; address from the judges, grand jurors, and citizens, *ibid.*, 5/665/250–53; Hawes, ed., *Proceedings and Minutes*, 100–104; Savannah *Royal Georgia Gazette*, June 8, 1780, copy in CO 5/665/292–93; address of the Council and Commons House of Assembly of Georgia, June 8, 1780, *ibid.*, 5/665/296–97.

to think that Georgia could be held without a strong military force, and he knew that without such protection the work of the Assembly would lose all meaning.[27]

Revival of the Assembly was successful as a symbol, but the great benefits so confidently predicted were never realized. The Commons of Georgia could pass laws, but it was never able to raise sufficient revenue to meet the minimum needs of the province. The rich low-country plantations had been devastated, and there was no money to assist the many needy loyal subjects or even to pay the militia. Parliament provided an annual subsidy of about £3,000, but this paid only some essential salaries and left a contingency fund calculated for peacetime requirements. Governor Wright achieved one great success in the Assembly, although it represented a solution to a burning issue of 1765 not to those of 1781. This was the act levying a duty of 2½ percent on all exports, "as the Contribution of Georgia, to the General Charge of the British Empire" —in other words, the revenue which George Grenville had unsuccessfully sought from the colonial assemblies before proposing the fateful Stamp Act.[28] Wright had hoped for 5 percent, but most members thought 2½ percent all the ravaged province could afford. After some objections the Commons voted unanimously for the duty, "And as the *Foundation* is now Laid, I presume it will be no difficult matter to raise the duty, when the Province is at *Full Peace* & begins to People again, & recover its Produce & Trade."[29] Germain praised Wright for this great achievement and assured him that his long efforts reflected "the greatest Honor upon You, and raises You in the Regard and Esteem of Your Sovereign . . . ." The

[27] Wright to Germain, July 17, 19, 1780, *ibid.*, 5/665/298-300, 302-303. The Commons worked in the familiar colonial pattern of numerous select committees; the most active member was Attorney General James Robertson, who loyally supported the governor.

[28] The incomplete Assembly minutes, from May 9, 1780, to January 15, 1781, make up CO 5/708. After repeated delays, Wright sent thirty-three statutes to the Board of Trade in January 1782; several others were lost. Of those submitted, thirty-one were eventually approved, but only after Georgia had again been lost to the rebels; see Wright to Board of Trade, January 23, 1782, *ibid.*, 5/652/42, enclosing statutes filed as *ibid.*, 5/685; for approval see William Selwyn to Thomas Townshend, December 7, 1782, *ibid.*, 5/652/44-47. For Wright's comments see his reports to Germain, May 17, September 18, December 20, 1780; March 9, 1781, *ibid.*, 5/665/247, 332; *ibid.*, 5/176/129-30, 158-59; and also William Knox to Wright, August 19, 1781; and Evan Nepean to Wright, June 27, 1782, *ibid.*, 5/677/101, 106; for estimates for 1780-1781, totaling £ 2,986, see *ibid.*, 5/176/118.

[29] Wright to Germain, April 9, 1781, *ibid.*, 5/176/168-69.

always optimistic Germain expected the example of Georgia to be followed by the other colonies as they were recaptured, and he flattered Wright "that You have led the Way in Measures, which have the fairest Tendency to heal the unhappy Breach between Great Britain and America . . . ."[30]

Adequate military protection for Georgia was a problem less easily solved, and Germain's fair words were of no use in fighting the rebels. From the first days of his return Wright pleaded for more troops, and particularly for cavalry. Despite the confidence of the local army commanders he remained doubtful: "I am no Soldier," he told General Clinton, "but I don't like many things I hear and see." Early in September 1779 Wright's greatest fears were proved well founded when the Comte d'Estaing arrived off Tybee with some five thousand troops and advanced upon Savannah to open a formal siege. Wright feared that the military might give in against such overwhelming odds, but the resistance was spirited and effective. After five days of bombardment the French and American invaders assaulted the British lines and were repelled with heavy casualties, d'Estaing among them. The defenders' losses were relatively light, but the countryside was once again devastated.[31]

The repulse of the allied attack against Savannah was a stirring victory for British arms, but it did nothing to ease Wright's problem of protecting Georgia against rebel irregulars. The king's thanks for the successful defense of Savannah pleased Wright, but in the same dispatch Germain encouraged him to punish stubborn rebels but denied his request for money to pay the militia because such payments would set an expensive precedent. Wright was expected to defend his impoverished province with local forces, but he lacked the money to keep them in the field. According to the governor's careful estimates, prepared in cooperation with the military, the effective defense of Georgia required five hundred men at the capital, a similar force up-country at Augusta, smaller detachments at Ebenezer

[30] Germain to Wright, June 4, 1781, *ibid.*, 5/176/160–62. The secretary's dispatch of August 2 conveyed the king's thanks to the Assembly for the Export Duty Act. *Ibid.*, 5/176/176–78.

[31] Wright to Clinton, July 30, 1779; Wright to Patrick Tonyn, August 7, September 11, 1779, extracts in Clinton's Secretary of State Letterbook, II, Clinton Papers; Wright to Germain, November 5, 1779, CO 5/665/172–79, gives a full account of the siege. See also Alexander A. Lawrence, *Storm over Savannah: The Story of Count d'Estaing and the Siege of the Town* (Athens, Ga., 1951).

and on the river below Savannah, and several galleys at Tybee to patrol the coast.[32]

British authority had little success in protecting Georgians who announced their adherence to the king. Wright himself suffered losses totaling £8,000 from an attack against two of his plantations within twenty miles of the capital. "The only thing that can give us peace and security," Wright argued, was at least 150 mounted troops specifically assigned to service within Georgia. At his own expense he established three small patrols of about twenty-four men each, but some of them were compelled to operate as infantry because of a lack of suitable horses.[33]

When General Clinton shifted his major offensive effort to Carolina during the spring of 1780 he provided only temporary relief. The army, despite Clinton's brilliant capture of Charleston, failed to break the spirit of rebellion, and from the back-country it was the military which appealed for help during the summer of 1780, asking that Lieutenant Governor Graham be sent westward to reduce the spirit of disaffection. Meanwhile the Georgia militia was busy disarming suspected rebels under a disqualifying law passed by the revived Assembly. Those who promised faithful obedience would—if accepted by the local magistrates and militia officers—be restored to good standing and their arms returned on condition that they enroll in the militia.[34] As the British main force under the command of Charles, second Earl Cornwallis, marched into the interior Wright renewed his request for a few cavalry, but Cornwallis refused to detach even fifty horse, politely telling the civilian governor that they would not be needed now that his troops controlled most of South Carolina. The General was supremely confident, but he had not yet heard from Colonel Thomas Brown, who was forced into a small stockade at Augusta by heavy rebel attacks originating largely from the Carolina back-country.[35]

[32] Wright to Germain, November 9, 1779, CO 5/665/193; Germain to Wright, January 19, 1780, ibid., 5/677/77–83; Wright to Brig. Gen. James Paterson, February 14, 1780, ibid., 5/665/224.

[33] Wright to Germain, April 4, May 25, 1780, ibid., 5/665/242–43, 284; Wright asked Clinton to reimburse his expenses, June 2, 1780, PRO 30/55/2798.

[34] Wright to Germain, June 9, 1780; Wright to Cornwallis, July 28, 1780, CO 5/665/290, 324–25; Col. Nisbet Balfour to Wright, July 27, 1780; and Wright to Balfour, August 19, 1780, ibid., 5/665/328–29.

[35] Cornwallis to Wright, July 18, 1780, ibid., 5/665/324; Wright to Germain, August 20, September 18, 1780, ibid., 5/665/320–21, 326.

Seven hundred rebels were reported attacking Augusta, and with all of Georgia open to their raids there were only 300 regulars fit for duty at Savannah plus a mere 150 militia. Wright urged Colonel Nisbet Balfour to advance into the backcountry to ravage the rebel strongholds and relieve Augusta, and at the same time he complained bitterly to Whitehall that Georgia had been "too soon & too much weaken'd" as the army shifted its attention elsewhere. With the help of faithful Indians, Brown did manage to hold out until relieved by a rescue column from Carolina. Thirteen rebels who had professed allegiance to the king and thereafter resumed their treason were among the prisoners, and they were executed as a warning to other potential turncoats. "We are doing every thing Possible to Root out Rebellion in this Province," Wright reported, but he lacked the necessary strength, though the Assembly dutifully voted him greater powers over the militia and increased his authority to call out slaves for labor on the fortifications.[36]

The rebels took advantage of every opportunity during the closing months of 1780, although the loyal militia was repeatedly summoned for active service. The Council recommended that pay and subsistence be allowed the militiamen and again urged that a troop of horse be raised, at local expense if no other way appeared possible. If such measures were not taken, the Council warned, the faithful and hard-pressed Loyalists would be ruined and the province lost once again. From his vantage point in England, however, Lord George Germain found much to encourage his high hopes. Clinton's capture of Charleston, he told Wright, "must have removed all your anxiety for the safety of Georgia & placed that province in such a state of security & tranquility as to leave you at full liberty to pursue your purpose of . . . restoring civil Government in all its legal Forms."[37] Victory at Charleston provided little relief for the harried Loyalists of Georgia, but Wright sent report after report before he began to penetrate the dream world the colonial secretary had created for himself. Germain perused Wright's dispatches, approved his every action, and assured him from across the

[36] Wright to Balfour, September 18, 1780, *ibid.*, 5/665/330–31; Wright to Germain, September 18, 22, October 29, 1780, *ibid.*, 5/665/334, 342; *ibid.*, 5/176/116.

[37] Council to Wright, November 21, 1780, *ibid.*, 5/176/125–27; Wright to Germain, December 1, 1780, *ibid.*, 5/176/123; Germain to Wright, July 7, 1780, *ibid.*, 5/677/84–85. The secretary reiterated his high hopes and approved Wright's stern policy against traitors in a dispatch of November 9, 1780, *ibid.*, 5/677/89–90.

ocean that Cornwallis by his operations in Carolina would relieve all pressure of rebel attacks on Georgia. British victories were frequent, "but I am sorry to say the consequences have fallen far short of the just expectations of your lordship . . . ," Wright calmly replied.[38]

The rebels lacked the strength to take Georgia, but they continually harassed the province. During February 1781 they roamed freely near Augusta, murdering eleven active Loyalists, several of them in their own beds. The rebels moved rapidly on horseback, and the loyal militia, still operating as infantry, was helpless against them. Both houses of the Assembly again urged the governor to raise a troop of cavalry at the expense of the British government, and Wright did manage to persuade sixty of the better militiamen to serve on their own mounts. He appealed once more to Germain for funds to pay them, since the army still did nothing.[39]

Nothing Wright could say seemed strong enough to destroy Germain's confidence. The colonial secretary repeatedly praised the governor, but he did nothing to answer his requests for more effective protection except assure him that Cornwallis's successes would surely bring relief. As the campaign of 1781 opened the secretary reminded Wright that the restoration of the Assembly was earning Georgia Loyalists the gratitude of both king and Parliament. "We have done all that we could," Wright wrote in a dispatch which crossed Germain's in mid-Atlantic, but the Assembly could accomplish only so much, while the unpaid militia was "worn out by Continued Alarms." Augusta was again in grave danger, and the governor and his Council appealed once more to the army commander at Savannah. Repeatedly warned that inaction might lead to the loss of the greater part of the province, Colonel Frederick von Porbeck insisted that he had too few men and refused to take any action. Augusta fell to the rebels on June 5, 1781, and became the seat of their revived state government.[40]

[38] Wright to Germain, December 20, 1780; January 25, 1781; Germain to Wright, February 7, 1781, *ibid.*, 5/176/129–30, 134–40, 120–22. The governor's reply to Germain's repeated empty assurances appears in his letter of January 25, 1781, *ibid.*, 5/680/11–12; another copy, *ibid.*, 5/176/142–43.

[39] Wright to Germain, March 5, 1781, enclosing reports from militia officers and extracts from his correspondence with Cornwallis, *ibid.*, 5/176/150–55.

[40] Germain to Wright, April 4, 1781; Wright to Germain, May 1, 1781, *ibid.*, 5/176/144–47, 184. Extracts from Council minutes were included in Wright's reports of May 25 and June 12, *ibid.*, 5/176/190–92, 196–99; see also Candler, comp., *Colonial Records*, XII, 499–506.

"The People are Ruined, & can pay no Taxes," Wright confessed in the spring of 1781. He had been forced to purchase food in the amount of £2,562 to feed Loyalist refugees and to provide subsistence for militiamen on active duty. Meanwhile Wright estimated the annual expenses for the two troops of horse he sought at the impossible sum of £7,816 7s. 10d., far more than the total annual peacetime revenue of the province. Cornwallis's glorious victories did nothing to secure Georgia against attack, either in the backcountry or in the coastal swamplands. His once prosperous province, Wright explained, was greatly reduced in both population and wealth, though there were still many good and faithful subjects "who have & will do every thing in their power to Support His Majesty's Government." Moved almost to anger, Wright said, "I am no Soldier my Lord, but I always thought & still do, that it would have been more for His Majesty's Service to have Secured *Effectually* what was *Reduced*, & to have made these Provinces usefull & serviceable . . . ."[41]

Sir James Wright had his dreams, but he had few courses of action open to him. If the counterrevolution was to succeed, Wright's policies gave the best hope of lasting success. If his dream was an impossible one, then the entire British war effort in America was without purpose. Germain was perhaps dimly aware of these considerations, but he was never willing to supplement his repeated verbal encouragement with significant material support. Cornwallis won battle after battle and eventually found himself at Yorktown. Behind him in the "conquered" provinces rebel irregulars raided almost at will. "My Lord it gives me great Pain, that I have it not in my Power to write any thing pleasant," Wright reported in May 1781, "and I know it must hurt your Lordship to receive Continual disagreeable Accounts, and I assure you, it hurts me much more."[42]

From Charleston Colonel Nisbet Balfour could offer no encouragement; South Carolina too needed reinforcement. There was nothing to spare for Georgia. One of the few private civilian accounts of this period gives an even more dismal view than the official reports. Thomas Taylor set out for Augusta early in 1781, when Cornwallis's victory at Guilford Courthouse had given every expectation of some security, but before he reached

---

[41] Wright to Lords of the Treasury, May 15, 1781; Wright to Germain, June 14, May 5, 1781, *ibid.*, 5/176/204–206, 208, 186–87.
[42] Wright to Germain, May 25, 1781, *ibid.*, 5/176/188.

his destination he encountered disturbing news of rebel activity. Augusta soon fell, and the Loyalist commander, a Colonel Grierson, was murdered after his parole had been accepted. The American authorities expressed their regrets but did nothing to arrest the murderers. Taylor thought this nothing unusual, for such murders were commonly spoken of as "Georgia paroles." In the end Governor Wright was satisfied that he had done his best, that the Georgia Loyalists had been faithful, and that it was the army which had failed to give the support which was clearly within its means, had it ever thought Georgia sufficiently important.[43]

Lack of military support was one aspect of Wright's troubles with the army, but he faced also a continuing problem of upholding civil authority. The problem of reviving civil administration in an active theater of military operations was at bottom insoluble, but British policy called for restoring provincial government not permanent military occupation. Restored Georgia was to be the chief example of the mildness of British measures, to show the way toward peace, to undermine rebel resistance elsewhere. As an experienced colonial administrator Wright was entirely familiar with the problem of balancing military and civil authority in time of war. He anticipated the difficulties he would find in Georgia and asked before leaving England "What is the Proper Line between the Civil and Military Departments, as I would by no means Encroach on the Military or have the least . . . Misunderstanding with the General . . . ." He was equally determined that the general should not "Encroach upon or interfere in the Civil Government." Under an old regulation which Wright wished reaffirmed a governor commanded all of the king's troops within his colony unless superseded by a general officer actually within its boundaries. "I wish to avoid all disputes," said Wright in concluding his long memorandum.[44]

General Sir Henry Clinton received his orders from Germain, as did Governor Wright, and there was no doubt in the

[43] Balfour to Wright, May 4, 21, August 1, 24, 1781, Emmet Collection; Taylor to John Wesley, February 28, 1782, Shelburne Papers; Wright to Shelburne, A Concise View of the Situation of the Province of Georgia for 3 Years Past, probably late 1782, *ibid*. Georgia's defense problem was familiar to Wright; he had felt himself inadequately supported during the French and Indian War. Trevor R. Reese, *Colonial Georgia: A Study in British Imperial Policy in the Eighteenth Century* (Athens, Ga., 1963), 90–94.

[44] Points on Matters Which It Seems Necessary to Have Some Directions About, undated memorandum, probably March 1779, Germain Papers.

minister's mind about the theoretical limits of civil and military jurisdictions. The secretary explained his policy in an explicit instruction to Clinton arising fr~m a conflict between the governor of the Bahamas and the commander of a small detachment there. "Captain Grant mistakes his Situation," Germain ruled, "and acts inconsistent with his Duty, in refusing to obey the Orders of the Governor, who is at all times Commander in Chief of the King's Troops within his Government, when no General Officer is present." Clinton was also under standing instructions to promote the restoration of civil government everywhere in America. "The great end of all His Majesty's Measures," Germain reminded him, was "the re-establishment of Legal Government in the Revolted Provinces."[45]

As Governor Wright resumed his office he was very careful to avoid conflict with General Prevost, and when the reestablished Council at its first session expressed the need for more effective protection, the governor replied that he had no force under his own command and that it would be necessary to apply to the general for assistance. Within a week the Council and the governor agreed without dissenting vote "that they should not interfere or Attempt to Meddle with any of the Negroes Captured by the Army, but leave that Matter to be conducted by General Prevost . . . ." During the siege of Savannah there was the finest cooperation, and the Council concurred with the governor that there was no need to declare martial law because the general already exercised such extensive authority that he could use no additional powers. Most of the dwellings in Savannah had been taken for the use of the army, and when the provincial courthouse was seized the chief judge simply asked Wright to apply to Prevost for suitable accommodations.[46] If there was no conflict during the first months of the revived civil government, it is clear that the principal reason was civilian deference to the military. The army made no complaints.

The absence of sharp disagreement, however, cannot be taken as evidence of general concord between Wright's admin-

---

[45] Germain to Clinton, June 2, January 23, 1779, Clinton Papers; for a general view of command structure and problems see Piers Mackesy's excellent and interpretative *The War for America, 1775–1783* (Cambridge, Mass., 1964), especially 55–56, 156–59, 233–34.

[46] Clinton to Wright, September 9, 1779, PRO 30/55/2273; for Council minutes, see Candler, comp., *Colonial Records,* XII, especially 437–41, 445; Hawes, ed., *Proceedings and Minutes,* 50–51, 70, 84–86.

istration and the army. The governor was obviously dissatisfied with the military's understanding of his mission and of the policy of early reestablishment of civilian rule. This was the theme of a long letter to the commander-in-chief after some six months of the experiment in Georgia. Wright took great pains to reemphasize for Clinton "that one principal object of the Kings Ministers in ordering the Civil Government to be Re Established in this Province, is to shew the other Provinces, that if they are reduced, or return to their allegiance, they will enjoy their former just and mild government . . . ." With Clinton's failure or unwillingness to understand Wright's position, conflict could not be long averted. The general's decision to concentrate his forces against Charleston while leaving backcountry Georgia in the hands of the rebels moved the governor to strong protest. Georgia was left virtually defenseless, and the royal and ministerial expectations for the civil government would be "totally frustrated."[47]

Strong protests were also directed toward Germain, who had the power to alter Clinton's plans if he could be persuaded to issue appropriate orders. Wright was especially disturbed by Clinton's policy of generous pardon for rebels of doubtful repentance. Under an order issued some months after Wright's return Sir Henry Clinton was a commissioner for restoring peace and granting pardons, and by accident or otherwise Georgia was included within his jurisdiction. Wright had earlier warned Clinton against indiscriminate pardons for rebels who remained "traitors in their hearts," and he suggested that all pardons be conditional upon enlistment in the British service or a property bond as security for good behavior. Clinton was not impressed by these arguments, and in March 1780 he issued a proclamation offering pardons without condition or exception. There was nothing to prevent rebels from accepting pardons and returning to disrupt the elections planned in Georgia. Pardoned rebels could claim all the protection of the laws, serve on juries, and if they dared, even stand for election to the Assembly, all of which distressed true Loyalists.[48] As Wright had feared, some of the pardoned rebels did engage in new treason, and the civil power, both executive and judicial, found

[47] Wright to Clinton, February 3, March 3, 1780, CO 5/665/219–23, 226.
[48] Wright to Clinton, February 3, March 24, 28, 1780, ibid., 5/665/219–23, 230–31, 233–34; a copy of Clinton's commission for restoring peace, ibid., 5/178/33–34.

itself involved in complex legal disputes when the accused pleaded immunity under military law.[49]

John Houstoun, lately governor of the state of Georgia, claimed that he had been induced to join the rebellion without any intention of seeking separation from the empire, adding that he feared for his safety if he returned to Georgia. By this time Clinton and his fellow commissioner Admiral Marriott Arbuthnot had come to doubt the scope of their jurisdiction, and they asked Germain for instructions. They took the opportunity to criticize Wright for the severity of his policy, suggesting that his actions and the measures of his Loyalist Assembly would in fact discourage war-weary rebels from seeking British protection. Two years after he had made his decision to restore the provincial government in Georgia, Lord George Germain still had no policy. He could only advise the commissioners to avoid doing anything which might seem to alter the former provincial constitutions. The Loyalists of South Carolina eagerly sought the restoration of the old constitution, but Clinton showed no inclination to accede to their wishes, though the military government found itself in serious difficulties as the occupation continued. Several former provincial officials helped administer the captured parts of the colony under military appointments, arranging for the probate of wills and other strictly civil matters. Clinton's disagreement with Wright remained unresolved.[50]

One might suspect that Wright had personal difficulties with the commanders at Savannah, but the contrary seems to have been the case. Troubles came on matters of policy, not personality or prestige. Colonel Alured Clarke, who assumed command in the summer of 1780 and remained until the following spring, got on particularly well with the governor. What Wright wanted was better protection, and Clarke was desperately short of men, having only 211 fit for duty in January 1781. Colonel Clarke hoped to leave Savannah, but his second in command

[49] One such dispute may be traced through the following letters: Attorney General James Robertson to Wright, June 22, 1780; Col. James Simpson to Wright, July 6, 1780; Simpson to Clinton, July 16, 1780, Clinton Papers; Germain to Wright, August 3, 1780, *ibid.*, 5/677/86–88; Wright to Germain, August 17, 1780, *ibid.*, 5/665/306–307. A Georgian accused of treason had appealed to Col. Alured Clarke, the Savannah commandant, alleging that he was immune from civil prosecution because he was a prisoner of war free on parole.

[50] Clinton and Arbuthnot to Germain, April 30, 1781; Germain to Clinton and Arbuthnot, March 7, 1781, *ibid.*, 5/178/121–22, 108–109. James Simpson gave Clinton a detailed account of affairs in Charleston in his letter of August 30, 1780, Clinton Papers.

was a German officer "who seems totally unacquainted with the Laws of the Province." Relations between civilian and military authorities were difficult enough when the "Principal officers on both sides, know the Line of Authority, & are on the best Terms, & desirous, & take Pains to avoid altercation." Some of the German officers, so Wright had heard, thought themselves "totally Exempt from all Civil Power or Authority whatever." The governor was "perfectly happy" with Clarke, but with the change in command he feared that "disagreeable things may happen . . . ."[51]

Aside from his clashes with Clinton over civil jurisdiction Wright's greatest problem was the ineffective protection provided by the outnumbered and immobile force at Savannah, which even under the best commanders was plainly inadequate for the security of the province. But in the eyes of the generals Georgia had been captured, and as long as the royal troops remained safe in town the troubles of Loyalist planters and aged civilian governors mattered little. "The Military," as Wright told Germain in a moment of complete disgust, "give little attention to any thing but what is their own department." This was the essence of the problem of Georgia and of the entire counterrevolutionary effort. The army could see only the war, while Wright, with a lifetime of political experience, saw further, but he was never able to convince Germain, the minister responsible for providing the indispensable coordination.[52]

After the surrender of Cornwallis at Yorktown, Continental forces under Generals Nathanael Greene and Anthony Wayne advanced on Savannah, while the Indians were rumored to be readying an attack in support of the rebels. "God knows what will become of us," Wright lamented in an official letter begging once again for reinforcements, sending his message in a vessel sailing especially for New York to seek help from Clinton. By mid-January the enemy's forward units were within ten miles of Savannah, the only remaining British post in Georgia. Wright seemed about to give up hope, but he did not. His situation was truly desperate, and still he was politician enough to have patronage on his mind. The surveyor general of the province

[51] Clarke to Nisbet Balfour, January 2, 24, 1781, Cornwallis Papers, PRO 30/11/62/14–16, 24–25; Wright to Germain, April 2, 1781; Wright to Cornwallis, April 2, 1781, CO 5/176/164–66.
[52] Wright to Germain, September 18, 1780, ibid., 5/665/334; for strategic and political considerations see Mackesy, War for America, 474–75.

had been dead only three days when Wright wrote asking the appointment of a brother of the deceased in order to aid a distressed loyal family.[53]

The Assembly convened again in February 1782, and acting on instructions from Whitehall, Wright prepared to ask them for a quitrent statute. Most of the province was under enemy control, but the forms of colonial government were maintained until the end. The Commons formally told the governor on February 23 what he knew all too well, that the province was distressed beyond belief, that four hundred rebels were advancing on the capital, and that the regulars refused to do garrison duty, forcing the militia to assume this burden. Helpless, Wright could only reply that he had no means of providing assistance, though Clinton had 20,000 idle soldiers at New York. The civil administration of Georgia was so depleted that Wright himself copied out Clinton's message for enclosure with a dispatch to Germain. Clinton assured Wright of his high regard for the importance of Georgia and then passed the buck to General Alexander Leslie at Charleston. Wright also copied for Germain another letter from Clinton, which spoke of Georgia as already lost and hinted that it should be evacuated, although Clinton characteristically avoided taking such responsibility upon himself.[54]

In a private letter to William Knox, undersecretary for the colonies, Wright complained bitterly of the army's duplicity. "This Province will be totally lost," he warned bluntly, unless relief came quickly. "The generals &c. &c. have always set their Jaws against this Province," Wright complained. "I can't tell why, unless it is because the King has thought proper to Reestablish his Civil government here, which the military cannot bear." The Continental troops were closing in, but General Leslie refused all help, as night raiders approached almost within musket shot of the British lines, burning barns with impunity. From New York, meanwhile, Clinton reported to Whitehall that Savannah was in "a very respectable State of

[53] Clinton to Alexander Leslie, December 20, 1781, Shelburne Papers; Wright to Germain, December 18, 1781; January 18, 1782, CO 5/176/216, 230. For patronage matters see Wright to Germain, January 22, 1782; and John Graham to Germain, January 31, February 25, 1782, ibid., 5/176/232, 234–37, 263–66.

[54] Wright to Germain, February 12, 1782; Address of the Commons and Wright's reply, February 23, 1782, CO 5/176/239–40, 261–62; Wright to Clinton, March 3, 1782, PRO 30/55/4179; Wright to Germain, February 16, 1782, including copies of Clinton to Wright, January 6, 1782, and Clinton to Leslie, December 20, 1781, CO 5/176/244–50.

Defence." The lines at Savannah did hold somehow, and despite his apparent loss of hope, Wright continued his efforts.[55]

The news of the disaster at Yorktown shattered North's tired ministry, and Lord George Germain was the first to leave. Early in March the new American secretary, Welbore Ellis, addressed his first dispatch to the governor of Georgia. In all probability it never reached Savannah, and had he seen it Wright could scarcely have wondered at the enclosed copies of parliamentary debates which would within a few days bring down North's government. The king was still adamant that the loss of any of his colonies could not be considered, but a majority of the Commons had tired of the American war. The new ministry drafted a dispatch in June, which may never have been sent and was certainly never received, telling Wright to address all reports to Sir Guy Carleton, the new commander-in-chief at New York. All his orders would henceforth come from General Carleton.[56] The military had at last prevailed.

News of Carleton's arrival reached Savannah much earlier, although Wright had no way of knowing about his broad discretion over all British affairs in North America. Wright told the new commander-in-chief what he had so often told Clinton, that Georgia was desperately in need of assistance. "I presume the King having possession of this Province, or not will make a very material difference on a treaty of peace &c." Wright was never more mistaken. Carleton on May 24 sent a routine announcement of his assumption of command, adding only that he was sending General Leslie some orders regarding the troops at Savannah. Leslie's orders, *dated a day earlier*, carried a very different burden. The governor's greatest fears were surpassed, for Carleton ordered Leslie to evacuate Savannah, and Florida as well. Vessels were already sailing southward to carry off the garrisons. "Proper attention," Carleton politely added, "must

---

[55] Wright to Knox, February 12, 16, 23 (completed March 5), 1782, CO 5/176/241, 253, 255–56; Clinton to Germain, March 1, 1782, Miscellaneous Papers (New-York Historical Society, New York City); Wright to Leslie, May 15, 1782, Emmet Collection.

[56] Ellis to Wright, March 6, 1782; unsigned draft, dated June 5, 1782, CO 5/176/220–21, 251–52; a good brief account of the decision to abandon the American colonies is given by Mackesy, *War for America*, 467–77. The best account of Carleton as commander-in-chief is Paul H. Smith, "Sir Guy Carleton, Peace Negotiations, and the Evacuation of New York," *Canadian Historical Review*, L (September 1969), 245–64, especially 255. Carleton's instructions directed the withdrawal of all British forces, and he delayed only in the case of New York.

. . . be extended to the Governors, their followers, and Inhabitants, whom they may recommend." Thus did the army put an end to the experiment of restoring civilian administration in the midst of a counterrevolutionary war. Wright received from Carleton not even the courtesy of direct notice of his removal.[57]

General Leslie informed Wright as soon as Carleton's order reached Charleston and, perhaps to forestall the inevitable protests, warned that the order left him no discretion whatever. Management of the evacuation was confided to Alured Clarke, once again commanding at Savannah, and he was instructed to consult with the governor and to prepare for immediate withdrawal. Wright, of course, did protest vigorously, and Leslie naturally answered that he had no choice except to obey Carleton. "I cannot more sincerely regret," he added, "the necessity of so distressing a measure."[58] The final arrangements for the evacuation of the British province of Georgia were made by Governor Wright and General Anthony Wayne, who on July 11 dated his orders from the American headquarters at Savannah.[59]

From Tybee, where he was for a second time sailing away from his lost province, Wright acknowledged his one routine dispatch from General Carleton. Of the orders he had received through Leslie he said only, "Necessity obliges me to Comply." Carleton was surely not aware, he added sadly, of the sufferings of the Loyalists of Georgia, and he repeated for the last time his belief that with five hundred men the province might have been held for the empire. When he arrived in England, Wright told Lord Shelburne that he was utterly astonished at receiving orders to surrender his province to the enemy.[60]

Georgia had been captured by the British army, but at ministerial initiative and for civil purposes, not for any clearly

[57] Carleton to Wright, May 24, 1782; Wright to Carleton, May 30, June 1, 1782, PRO 30/55/4645, 4697, 4716; Carleton to Leslie, May 23, 1782, Emmet Collection, and in draft form also in PRO 30/55/4636.

[58] Leslie to Clarke, June 4, 1782; Leslie to Wright, June 4, 21, 1782, Emmet Collection; Address of Governor and Upper and Common Houses of Assembly to General Leslie, June 16, 1782, PRO 30/55/9987.

[59] The negotiations may be followed in Greene to Wayne, May 21, 1782; Greene to Leslie, May 25, 1782; Clarke to Wayne, May 29, 1782; Wright to Wayne, May 29, 1782; Wayne to Clarke, May 30, 1782; Wayne to Wright, May 30, June 7, 14, 1782; Leslie to Greene, August 13, 1782; Wayne to the merchants of Savannah, June 17, 1782; Wayne's orders of July 11, 1782, Anthony Wayne Papers (Clements Library); Wright to Wayne, May 29, 1782, appears in draft form also in PRO 30/55/4687.

[60] Wright to Carleton, July 6, 1782, PRO 30/55/5025; Wright to Shelburne, November 21, 1782, AO 13/37/492.

perceived military advantage. The experiment of restoring civilian administration while active military operations continued was clearly a failure, although not an ignoble one. Colonel Archibald Campbell, Governor Sir James Wright, and Brigadier General Alured Clarke all served honorably. They gave their best efforts to revive the province of Georgia. Blame for the failure, insofar as the responsibility may be laid to individuals, rests upon General Sir Henry Clinton, who never supported the defense of the province, and upon Lord George Germain. The colonial secretary possessed the authority, the information, the means, and the duty, but he failed to provide the essential coordination and support. He failed because he never looked beyond the affair of the moment. He had no plan for Georgia, only occasional schemes. He simply presupposed a policy of restoring the *status quo ante bellum,* and nowhere in his extensive correspondence with Wright over a period of more than two years is there any evidence that the colonial secretary ever seriously considered the implications of the policy to which he committed Lord North's ministry. His inept role in the collapse of the restored royal government of Georgia was not among Germain's most serious shortcomings, but it is symptomatic of his approach to the duties of his office and of his lack of strategic vision. He was neither evil nor stupid; neither was he a success in anything he undertook. Wright's diligence could not overcome this handicap.

Might Wright's dream have succeeded? The Savannah River was a suitable "natural boundary"; and supported by British Florida, it is not unreasonable to imagine that Georgia and the Gulf coastal plain might have attracted as many Loyalist émigrés as Nova Scotia and Upper Canada. Certainly, the peace negotiators at Paris considered this possibility.[61]

[61] Richard B. Morris, *The Peacemakers: The Great Powers and American Independence* (New York, 1965), 345–46, 370–71, 428.

The Structure of Politics in Georgia: 1782-1789

William W. Abbot[*]

IN any generalizations about the Southern colonies, Georgia persistently pops up as the inconvenient exception, the special case. Not that Georgia was ever radically or fundamentally different from its sister colonies; it just seems always to have been more so or less so something-or-other than they. Happily, colonial Georgia is unimportant enough, except strategically, for the general historian often to ignore it, or at most to note its peculiarities in an aside. But despite the relative unimportance of Georgia in eighteenth-century America, much of its story is worth the telling. Between 1775 and 1789 Georgia underwent a revolution, and a successful revolution at that—a rather rare and wonderful thing. And the insignificant colony and state of those years became in time a powerful principality in the Cotton Kingdom.

On the eve of the American Revolution, Georgia, the youngest, the smallest, the poorest, and the most exposed of the thirteen colonies, was peculiarly dependent upon Britain for support. Nowhere else were the influence of the royal governor and the relative strength of the loyalists so great. But, by the same token, Georgia's perilous weakness drew the colony close to its more powerful Carolina neighbors. When in 1775-1776 the focus of power in America shifted from London to these shores, Georgia was irresistibly and by hard necessity drawn toward the new power center and into the orbit of revolution. Weakness kept Georgia loyal as long as Britain's strength remained unimpaired, and weakness pushed the colony into revolt when Britain faltered and South Carolina grew militant and bold. Granted it was not quite so simple as that, the fact remains that Georgia entered the Revolution by its own private back door.

Georgia's youthfulness in particular helped to set it apart. Appearing late on the scene, it reaped the crop of a century's hard-won colonial and imperial development. Its institutions took shape after colonial govern-

* Mr. Abbot, book review editor of the *Quarterly,* is a member of the Department of History at the College of William and Mary.

ment had reached maturity, and they were more often than not managed by men who had learned the workings of them in Carolina or Virginia. Almost from the beginning, Georgia's frontier experience had been less the Old World adapting itself to the New than the upper South adapting itself to the backwoods of the lower South: her frontiersmen were native Virginians or Carolinians, not Englishmen. When the Revolution came, this youthfulness increased the dangers and widened the possible range of political and social experiment. Georgia, with borrowed institutions, lacked the time-tested experience of the older colonies to give its social fabric the toughness and resilience necessary to withstand revolution intensified by civil war and invasion. There was no deeply rooted and near-autonomous local government, as in Virginia, to help bridge the gap between dependent colony and independent state. Yet the revolutionists did make the transition successfully, and in their own way. The political structure which these men created and manipulated is worth examining.

As the radicals edged Georgia toward the final break with Britain, James Wright, the royal governor, issued a passionate warning that touched the heart of the dangers inherent in revolution: "You may be advocates for Liberty," he said, "so am I; but in a constitutional and legal way. You, gentlemen, are legislators, and let me entreat you to take care how you give a sanction to trample on law and government; and be assured it is an indispensable truth, that where there is no law there can be no liberty. It is the due course of law. It is the due course of law and support of government which only can ensure to you the enjoyment of your lives, and your liberty, and your estates; and do not catch at the shadow and lose the substance."[1]

In their first move to overcome the disadvantages of spurning the "constitutional and legal way," the leaders of the Revolution in Georgia gave a constitution to the state in 1777.[2] They were seeking to "ensure" liberty with law, to make the shadow of revolution the substance of government under which men might enjoy their lives, their liberty, and their estates.

[1] George White, *Historical Collections of Georgia: Containing the Most Interesting Facts, Traditions, Biographical Sketches, Anecdotes, Etc. Relating to its History and Antiquities, From its First Settlement to the Present Time* (New York, 1855), pp. 50-51.
[2] *The Federal and State Constitutions, Colonial Charters, and Other Organic Laws of the States, Territories, and Colonies Now or Heretofore Forming the United States of America*, ed. Francis Newton Thorpe (Washington, 1909), II, 777-785. All references to the Georgia constitutions of 1777 and 1789 are to the texts in this volume.

The wiser of the revolutionists saw that there had to be a legitimate basis for the re-establishment of "the due course of law" and for the reassertion of governmental authority to replace the old sanctions which they had repudiated when in 1776 they took up arms against their king.

Hardly had constitutional government been established in Georgia than it began to come apart at the seams as civil war and foreign invasion swept over this frontier community. Between 1778 and 1782 state government in Georgia was perforce haphazard and irregular, but after the British troops had withdrawn from Georgia in 1782, men once again turned their attention to politics and government. The political leaders of the state then set out to make the intentions of the constitution of 1777 a reality. Working within that framework of government, they began the task of shaping the institutions, practices, and policies of government to meet the everyday needs of a frontier society, newly independent. Their ultimate success assured the accomplishment of the crucial transition from colonial status in the British Empire to statehood in a federal union.

When Georgia emerged from the chaos of war, the state was still little more than a string of settlements along the coast and up the Savannah river opposite Carolina. The little town of Savannah perched on the bluff above its river a few miles from the sea was, as it had always been, the hub and heart of the state. Although a sprinkling of Jews, Italians, Germans, and West Indians gave the tiny capital a certain cosmopolitan flavor, the town and the county of Chatham were predominantly English. To the south of Savannah, down the coast, a community of Congregationalists from South Carolina had settled and there for thirty years had prospered and multiplied. After Georgia threw in its lot with the other states in 1776, this hotbed of rebellion became Liberty County. The region embracing Chatham and Liberty counties, the center of provincial wealth and culture in the booming days before the Revolution, immediately resumed its former importance in 1782. Below Liberty, on down toward Georgia's old Spanish frontier, were two more coastal counties, Glynn and Camden. Both were sparsely settled, a band of hardy Scottish Highlanders being the most valuable inhabitants there at the southernmost tip of the new United States.

The settled land of the interior lay along the Savannah river and its tributary creeks. The Savannah flowed between Georgia and South Carolina in a southeasterly direction past the upcounty metropolis of Augusta, just below the falls, and on down for some 150 miles past Savannah

and into the Atlantic. A congregation of German Protestants, the Salz-
burgers, led a rather communal and self-co. ined existence in the mud
bottoms of the Savannah river and Ebenezer creek immediately to the
north of tidewater Chatham. The Salzburger county was called Effingham. Above it were two upcountry river counties, Burke and Richmond,
both of which had long been settled, mostly by Carolinians. To the north
and west of Richmond lay the fertile land of Wilkes County which had
been opened to settlement shortly before the Revolution. The trickle of
settlers from the Carolinas and Virginia into this area before 1782 was
now to become a flood. The architects of Georgia's political structure in
the 1780's were working in the context of an elongated frontier that was
rapidly, almost explosively, thrusting itself into the wilderness in three
directions, to the west, the north, and to the south.

The men who led frontier Georgia from colonial dependence in the
1770's to equality in a federation of states in the 1790's were those who
held certain key offices in the government and who knew how to use the
powers of their offices to make their influence felt, not only in directing
the policy of government but also in forming the very institutions of
government themselves. In the 1780's, ambitious men in Georgia who
desired a strong voice in public affairs—whether to further their private
interests or to promote the general welfare—did well to give their attention to the House of Assembly. Noble Wimberly Jones, the acknowledged
leader of the radicals who led Georgia into revolution in 1775-1776, and
Jonathan Bryan, the doughty and aged rebel, immediately took seats there.
James Jackson, the English immigrant who had become a general in the
Georgia Revolutionary forces at an incredibly early age and was in 1782
at the threshold of a brilliant political career, hardly missed a session in
the 1780's. Also usually present and active in the business of the legislature
were such men as the respected planter-lawyer William Gibbons, Sr.; John
Habersham, the former leader of the Liberty Boys, and his brothers
William and John—three sons of a distinguished father; Edward Telfair,
merchant and planter; and the leader of the upcountry, William Few—all
ambitious men and men of standing in the state.

For the politically minded men of the Revolutionary generation in
America, the state legislatures generally gave ambition its greatest scope.
Unpleasant memories of troublesome royal governors made the various
Revolutionary constitutional conventions reluctant to bestow upon the
state governors full executive powers. The framers of Georgia's constitu-

tion of 1777 gave a passing nod to the developing principle of the separation of powers: "The legislative, executive, and judiciary departments shall be separate and distinct . . ."; and then proceeded to hamstring the governor completely and leave the judiciary ill-defined and awkwardly constituted. The whole document with its impractical and even radical overtones makes it clear that the framers intended the unicameral legislature to overshadow every other part of government;[3] the history of the House of Assembly in the 1780's reveals that this was the case in actual fact. The Assembly dominated the whole structure of government; it controlled both men and measures. Its members asserted the supremacy of the legislature so consistently and so completely that the executive and judiciary remained without real power and almost without function. Geography, the temper of the people, the organization of society, the strength of tradition, and the good sense and common virtue of the ordinary lawmaker limited the power of government, it is true; but within the government itself the dominance of the legislature was virtually complete.

Before 1789, when a new state constitution was adopted, the Georgia executive was never more than an appendage of the House of Assembly. The Assembly elected the governor[4] and, except in one instance, chose him from its own numbers;[5] and it paid his salary.[6] He had little power except what the Assembly saw fit to allow him and few functions except those which the Assembly chose to assign.[7] Obviously a prospective governor had to have strong support in the Assembly in order to be elected, and, if he wished to do more than sign his name—and that "with the advice of the executive council"[8]—he had to be, in effect, a leader of

[3] In 1777 the Chatham County grand jury complained that there was "no Check on the Assembly." Joseph Clay to Henry Laurens, Oct. 21, 1777, *Letters of Joseph Clay Merchant of Savannah 1776-1793 and a List of Ships and Vessels Entered at the Port of Savannah for May 1765, 1766 and 1767*, in *Collections of the Georgia Historical Society*, VIII (Savannah, 1913), p. 55.

[4] *Constitution of 1777*, Article II.

[5] Samuel Elbert, who became governor in Jan. 1785 was the only one of the ten governors elected between 1781 and 1789 who had not been returned as a member of the House of Assembly at the time of his election.

[6] "Journal of the House of Assembly," Aug. 21, 1781; Jan. 12, 1782; Jan. 15, 1784. The microfilm copy of the journals from 1781 to 1789 in the University of North Carolina Library, Chapel Hill, was used in preparing this article except in rare instances when "Journal of the House of Assembly from August 17, 1781, to February 26, 1784," *The Revolutionary Records of the State of Georgia*, ed. Allen D. Candler, Vol. III (Atlanta, 1908) was used. Because of the confused pagination of the manuscript, all citations are made by date rather than by page. Hereafter cited as "Journal."

[7] *Constitution of 1777*, Articles XIX-XXII, XXX, XXXIII.

[8] *Ibid.*, Article XIX.

the Assembly while in office. Governor Edward Telfair, who retained his strong following, exerted considerable influence in political matters as Georgia's chief executive;[9] Governor Lyman Hall, who was so foolish as to alienate the most powerful men in the Assembly, was unable to prevent the abrupt termination of his long political career at the hands of this hostile group. [10]

The legislature so successfully avoided any threat of rivalry from the executive that the government was crippled when the Assembly was not in session. The governor often found himself in the unpleasant predicament of having an emergency on his hands with neither the authority nor the money to do anything about it.[11] He could call the legislature into special session—that was all. James Jackson, an ambitious man and a leading politician from the time of the Revolution, was probably less than honest when he refused the governorship in 1788 with the excuse that it was "an office which he did not think his age or experience entitled him to."[12]

The judiciary was even less independent of the legislature than was the executive. War and independence had raised legal questions which existing laws did not answer. At times the judges could not even know what the existing laws were or which ones were in effect, because the text of many had disappeared somewhere to "the Northward"; and many local records, which might have provided bases for decisions, had been lost or destroyed during the Revolution.[13] The courts were further handicapped by the constitutional provision that the chief justice should attend every meeting of every court except the petty Courts of Conscience.[14] The result of this confusion was that the House was forced to spend much of its time performing the duties of the courts in settling personal affairs and private disputes. Of the two hundred petitions heard in the January session of 1783, almost all had to do with private problems, many of which would ordinarily have been left to the courts.

The legislature, however, was not always bowing to necessity when it usurped the functions of the judiciary. Some of the legislators were more

[9] "Journal," Jan. 2–Feb. 14, 1786.
[10] *Ibid.*, Jan. 9–Feb. 25, 1784.
[11] *Ibid.*, May 1–26, July 1–8, 1783, for example.
[12] Thomas U. P. Charlton, *The Life of Major General James Jackson* (Augusta, Ga., 1809), p. 178. The copy used here was "reprinted from type" in Atlanta, n.d.
[13] "Journal," July 12, 1783; Feb. 3, 1785.
[14] *Constitution of 1777*, Articles XL, XLVI.

than willing to by-pass the courts in order to get a favorable decision on legal questions.[15] At times, the Assembly actually weakened the judiciary. It frequently changed the local judges—seven times in five years it appointed new ones for Wilkes County, for instance.[16] In 1782-1783 Georgia was for many months without a chief justice because the Assembly refused to elect one, and, when the office was filled, the legislature persisted in attempts to suspend the occupant and to withhold his salary.[17] Thus the judge, like the governor, was a functionary of the legislature. He, too, held office at the pleasure of the legislature and performed the duties it gave him.

The true measure of the legislature's domination of politics and government is to be seen in the relation of the House of Assembly to county government. Local administration was largely in the hands of the justices of the peace. It is true that the Assembly seldom encroached on the magistrates' prerogatives of overseeing local courts, elections, and tax collecting, but what it did do was to make certain that the justices had no existence independent of the legislature. The magistracy in Georgia was not in any sense self-perpetuating or permanent. In the early 1780's the House canceled all old commissions and issued new ones at least once a year.[18] Most of the justices were reappointed, but enough names were dropped or added each time to make it clear that the justice held office at the pleasure of the Assembly.

The justice of the peace in the county and the representative in the Assembly were often, of course, one and the same man. Of the assemblymen from six of the original counties between 1781 and 1789, well over half were at one time or another justices of the peace,[19] which is not sur-

[15] An indication of this is that on July 23, 1782, the House considered five personal petitions from its own members.

[16] "Journal," Aug. 8, 1781; Jan. 12, Apr. 30, 1782; Feb. 4, 1783; Feb. 14, 1785; Jan. 17, Feb. 6, 1786.

[17] Ibid., Aug. 8, 1781; Jan. 8, 12, Apr. 30, Aug. 5, 1782; Jan. 31, Feb. 4, July 17, 28, 1783; Feb. 14, 1785; Jan. 17, Feb. 6, 1786.

[18] Ibid., Jan. 12, Apr. 30, May 1, 1782; Jan. 31, Feb. 4, 8, 17, Aug. 1, 1783; Jan. 15, 16, Feb. 24-26, 1784; Jan. 10, 19, Feb. 11, 14-15, 19, 1785; Jan. 17, Feb. 3, 6, 8-9, 11, 13-14, Aug. 5, 14-15, 1786; Feb. 8-10, Oct. 26, 31, 1787; Jan. 31, Feb. 1, 1788; Feb. 4, 1789.

[19] To be more exact, out of 170 who acted both as representative and justice for the same county, 134 were serving in the legislature in 1781-82 when the first post-Revolutionary commissions of the peace were issued; or, after 1782, they were in the Assembly prior to or during the year of their selection as justices. All tabulations which include the year 1783 are not completely accurate because some of the names listed in the "Journal" for that year are illegible.

prising. It is suggestive, however, that nearly 80 per cent of these legislator-justices had been members of the legislature *before* they were justices of the peace. The priority or relative importance of the two offices need not concern us at the moment; the significant thing is that clearly the House of Assembly had the final word on the character and make-up of local administration. As a result, the local magistracy was the product of the legislature, not its foundation and not its source of power, as it was, for instance, in Virginia.

The structure of government in Georgia offered the legislator the opportunity to exercise power, but the thing that led three hundred and more men for months at a time to leave off clearing land and raising crops on the frontier and to abandon the hard-hit businesses and plantations on the coast was not the lure of naked political power alone. The uses to which the Assembly put its power were of intense and intimate concern to every man of substance, regardless of his personal political ambitions. Indians, loyalists, and bad money raised serious problems in the 1780's, problems which had to be met with legislation; but the crux of men's interest in government was land, and land lay at the heart of most of the important legislation.

Land was the source of income for the state: land was taxed, and the sale of land gave the government funds for operation when taxes did not suffice. Land was the basis of the new currency. The confiscation and sale of land belonging to the loyalists prolonged and heightened the Tory problem, complicating and delaying their absorption into the new body politic. The great influx of immigrants in search of land intensified the Indian problem. Land was what the Indian was defending; land was what the settler coveted. Whenever a new area was added to the state, the Assembly had to provide for its disposal and for its political organization. In all of its ramifications, public land policy affected, personally and directly, nearly every man in Georgia during this decade. The frontiersman, the planter, and the land speculator, even the merchant, had a stake in the government's actions touching land. The supremacy of the legislature in the structure of government made it necessary for the aspiring politician to seek a seat in the House of Assembly if he wished to make his weight felt in public affairs; the importance of the Assembly's activities in the everyday life of a citizen made it wise for the provident man to have political aspirations.

To gain a seat a man had first to be elected at the polls. Few of the men who came to the hamlet of Augusta to set up a new House of Assembly in the summer of 1781—and not many more of the representatives who were elected in December of that year—won their seats in the sort of election which the constitution of 1777 provided.[20] No elections could be held in the counties still overrun by British troops. After 1782, however, the justices seem to have followed the prescribed procedure of holding a general election in each county on the first Tuesday in December, when they collected written ballots from the voters, kept a list of those voting, counted the ballots cast, notified the winning candidates of their election, and sent to the House of Assembly a list of those elected.[21]

The men who voted in elections were supposed to be resident adults, "liable to pay tax," or worth ten pounds, or mechanics by trade.[22] In an agrarian society where two hundred acres of unimproved land could be had almost for the asking[23] and where few white men were hired laborers, nearly every family must have had one man who met these requirements. Yet in the first congressional election of 1790, less than one in six white adult males cast a vote in six of the original counties.[24] Unless this election differed greatly from preceding ones, which is not likely, the candidate for the state legislature had to gain the approval of only a tiny fraction of the people. But be it said that the smallness of the vote did not come from any conspiracy on the part of the lawmakers to restrict the electorate. Of

[20] *Constitution of 1777,* Article II. See the "Journals" for 1781-82 and "Minutes of the Executive Council, from January 14, 1778, to January 6, 1785, and Journal of the Land Court, from April 6 to May 26, 1784," *The Revolutionary Records of the State of Georgia,* ed. Allen D. Candler, Vol. II (Atlanta, 1908), p. 283. At best, the justices from the southern counties did no more than take an informal poll of the refugees from their county who happened to be in Augusta at the time. On Nov. 16, 1781, the Executive Council ordered: "That notice be given to the Electors for the Counties in Alarm, that they meet at Augusta in order to elect members to represent them in General Assembly of the State." In 1782, elections were held in Augusta to fill the vacancies in the House for the southern counties. Elections for seats held by the unoccupied counties were also apparently sometimes held in Augusta in 1782.

[21] See "Journal," Jan. 8, 14, 1784; Jan. 9, 1787.

[22] *Constitution of 1777,* Article IX.

[23] *A Digest of the Laws of the State of Georgia,* ed. Robert and George Watkins (Philadelphia, 1800), p. 258. With certain restrictions, after 1783 any head of a family could obtain 200 acres of land by paying the usual fees.

[24] MS "Minutes of the Executive Council Commencing 8th January 1789 Ending May 14, 1789," Department of Archives and History of Georgia, Atlanta; *Return of the Whole Number of Persons within the Several Districts of the United States According to an Act Providing for the Enumeration of the Inhabitants of the United States* (Philadelphia, 1791), p. 55.

the five hundred-odd white men who lived in Effingham County in 1790, many more than the eleven who voted were certainly eligible under the law: they just didn't vote. The compulsory voting provision of the constitution of 1777, obviously, was generally ignored.[25] A good guess would be that the voters were a fair cross section of the men who had the will to vote, irrespective of any legal spur or hindrance.

The basic representation in the Assembly was by counties. In accordance with the constitution, Chatham, Effingham, Burke, Richmond, and Wilkes, had ten seats apiece, and Liberty had fourteen. The five smaller counties had between one and ten seats each. Two seats were assigned to the port of Sunbury and four to the port of Savannah. In addition, the men chosen by the House to serve as Continental delegates automatically became members of the Assembly.[26] The six seats allotted to the Savannah and Sunbury merchants to "represent their trade"[27] dispel any notion that the principle of representation of numbers had entirely supplanted the principle of representation of interest. The sixteen seats for wealthy Liberty County as opposed to only ten for more populous Wilkes were a proper recognition of the greater stake in government of the Liberty merchant and planter.[28] On the other hand, the apportionment of members roughly on the basis of population among the five smaller counties was in a way recognition of the right of every freeholder to representation in the legislature.

Georgia was not yet wholly committed to the theory of geographical representation any more than she was wholly committed to representation by numbers. The newness of the state and the mobility of its population undoubtedly had retarded the development of local attachment and pride among the voters. Certainly they paid little attention to the length of time a man had lived in the state. Many Carolinians and Virginians went to the Assembly as soon as they had fulfilled the minimum legal requirement of a year's residence in Georgia. Moreover, county boundaries were sometimes ignored altogether. Between 1782 and 1789 at least thirty men represented, at separate times, two or more counties in the Assembly, and

[25] *Constitution of 1777*, Article XII. No record of prosecution has been found.
[26] *Ibid.*, Articles IV, V, XVI.
[27] *Ibid.*, Article V.
[28] The two seats given to Sunbury made the total for Liberty County 16. Whether the new territory of Wilkes was more populous than Liberty in 1777 or not, no provision was made to adjust the representation when the population of Wilkes should be six times that of Liberty, as it was by 1790.

often a justice of the peace in one county represented another county in the legislature.[29] Although the voters seldom looked beyond the neighboring counties for representatives, this was a time when a John Wereat could sit for tidewater Chatham in January and for upcountry Richmond in July.[30] Even so, the general scheme of representation *was* by counties and the voters *did* usually elect men who lived in their own county.

The candidate, once elected, had to satisfy the constitutional requirements for membership in the Assembly, as they were interpreted by the House. Besides specifying that a member be Protestant, male, white, and over twenty-one, he was required to be the owner of 250 acres of land or the possessor of £250. He was supposed to have lived in his county for three months immediately prior to election and in the state for at least one year.[31] And he could not be on the public pay roll when elected.

The Assembly never challenged any member's economic qualifications, but it consistently upheld the ban against state officials in the legislature. Less scrupulous in enforcing the residence requirements, the legislators were prone to view a member's residence in the light of his standing with the House leadership. In 1783 the Assembly barred four men returned from Chatham County because they had been living behind the British lines and therefore had not lived in the *state* of Georgia for the preceding twelve months. The seating of four replacements who supported the dominant clique in the powerful Chatham delegation does more than suggest that the greatest fault of the disqualified men was that they were unacceptable to the Chatham leaders.[32] This is the only instance of the Assembly invoking the requirements for state residence; but a number of representatives ran afoul of the county-residence rule. In a time when many owned land in more than one county, it is not surprising that the voters occasionally chose men who did not actually live in their county.[33] Nor is it too surprising that the Assembly challenged some of these and let others by without a word. In 1783 William Gibbons, Sr., an important figure in the group which controlled the House, arrived to represent the

[29] Nine of the 43 men who were justices of the peace in Chatham, 1781-89, were elected to the legislature in one of the other counties.

[30] "Journal," Apr. 20-24, July 13, 1782.

[31] *Constitution of 1777,* Articles VI, XVII.

[32] "Journal," Jan. 11, 20, 1783; Joseph Clay to Cornelius Coppinger, Feb. 8, 1783, in *Letters of Joseph Clay,* p. 172

[33] Between 1781 and 1783, nine men were returned from two or more different counties in different years.

third of three different counties in as many years.[34] No one troubled to ask whether Gibbons had moved from county to county three months or more before each election. In the next year, Dr. Lyman Hall, who as governor had offended the powerful members from Chatham the year before, was promptly ejected from the House by a strict application of the county-residence rule. Dr. Hall had obtained a seat midway in the session to answer charges that he had deliberately prevented the attendance of Georgia's delegates at the Continental Congress in 1783. By almost the identical vote which approved these charges against Hall, the House adopted the report of the Committee of Privileges and Elections recommending that Hall be disqualified because he had voted in a special election in Chatham County two days before he was elected in Liberty, where he had lived for nearly thirty years. With complete inconsistency, a few days later the House allowed him to sit for Glynn County.[35]

Candidates who noted the contrasting fortunes of such men as Gibbons and Hall could be excused if they drew the conclusion that it was more important to stand in with the powers-that-be in the House than it was to comply with the strict letter of the law. As a matter of fact, the record shows that one had little reason to fear disqualification unless he were *persona non grata* with the House leadership. The only real hurdle to be cleared came on election day, and even this was not too difficult. Proper gentlemen kept a façade of indifference before elections, and most of the candidates probably refrained from crass electioneering.[36] They really did not have to bestir themselves. There was a chronic surplus of seats and a chronic dearth of candidates. In proportion to population, the House was exceedingly large (in 1787, for instance, ninety-eight seats for a white population of possibly 40,000), and the stringencies of life on a frontier scarcely recovered from the effects of war drastically limited the number of men available for office. Through the decade, Effingham County, which usually

[34] Gibbons was qualified to sit for Liberty on Aug. 17, 1781; for Camden, Jan. 1, 1782; and for Chatham, Jan. 13, 1783.
[35] "Journal," Jan. 9–Feb. 25, 1784. Before the session was over, the Assembly got rid of Hall for good after accusing him of fraudulent action as governor.
[36] The evidence for this is mostly negative but convincing. There is no record of such men as Clay and Gibbons seeking office. It was apparently illegal to do so. There were always a number of men who refused to take their seats in each Assembly. Men who were outside the state at the time of election were sometimes chosen. And Clay's scornful use of the terms "Demagogues" and "Democratical" (*Letters of Joseph Clay*, pp. 35, 54) perhaps reflected something of the gentleman's attitude toward such things as electioneering.

sent no more than half the representatives it was entitled to, was in search of candidates, not the candidates in search of votes. Politics was not so much the story of men seeking office as of the officeholders competing for power; the center of political conflict was not at the polling place but within the House of Assembly.

If it can be said that the men who controlled the important committees —those dealing with the general matters of land and fiscal policy, the disposal of the loyalists and their property, Indian affairs, and the regulation of government—dominated the legislature, then nineteen men can be identified as the real leaders between 1782 and 1789.[37] Their names, and the number of years between 1782 and 1789 that they were leaders in the House of Assembly, are as follows: James Jackson (7); William Gibbons, Sr. (5); Joseph (4), James (3), and John Habersham (2); Joseph Clay (3); and John Houstoun (3), all of Chatham County; Benjamin Andrew (4), Nathan Brownson (4), and Richard Howly (2) of Liberty County; Edward Telfair (7) of Burke County; William Few (6) and Seaborn Jones (2) of Richmond County; and John King (4), Abraham Baldwin (3), Arthur Fort (3), Stephen Heard (2), Florence Sullivan (2), and Benjamin Talliaferro (2) of Wilkes County. These nineteen men held two out of three of all significant committee positions and together they held 404 seats on the 193 committees (usually only three men served on a committee). One or another of the nineteen was speaker in twelve of the thirteen sessions. Three of the nineteen were elected governor, and eight of the group were chosen a total of twenty-four times to be delegates to the Continental Congress.

An inquiry into why these particular nineteen men reached the top of the political ladder in Georgia raises fundamental questions about the elements of political power in eighteenth-century Georgia and about the qualities of leadership necessary in the House of Assembly. One element of the political picture to be considered is sectionalism, the basis for the alliances in the House which most nearly approached the status of political factions or parties. An understanding of the whole problem of sectional-

[37] A minimum of 366 men were elected to the Assembly, 1782-89, but only 98 of these were both present an average of one day a year and members of one committee a year. Of these 98, 52 never took a leading part in any session of the legislature. The remaining 46 dominated the Assembly. One or more of the 46 was on every one of the 193 important committees, 1782-89; they were a majority almost without exception, and they filled every place in well over half of the committees. Only 19 of the 46 were leaders during at least two of the eight years, 1782-89.

ism in the 1780's is absolutely essential for unraveling the still uncompleted story of political developments in early Georgia, but for the present survey of the bases of political power and leadership it proves, in the end, surprisingly unimportant.

The most persistent sectional split in the House of Assembly arose from the alignment of the upcountry against the low country, the frontier against the coast. The counties of Chatham and Liberty, with their satellites Glynn and Camden—the land of sea islands, salt marshes, great live oaks, and Spanish moss—made up the low country or tidewater. The planters on the land along the banks of the tidal rivers and streams raised all of the rice, the staple crop of the state; and the merchants of the bustling little ports of Savannah and Sunbury were in a position to monopolize the export-import trade. The break between the tidewater region and the upcountry of the small farmer was sharp. Effingham County, with its German inhabitants engaged in subsistence farming of the fertile pockets of the great pine barren, provided a distinct racial, cultural, economic, and geographic contrast with the adjacent low country. The country above Effingham had been largely the home of trappers, Indian traders, cowherds, and bands of roving outlaws which terrorized the Carolina back country. Only since the 1760's had families been coming across the river in any numbers to farm the land, giving this area a semblance of order and respectability; but during the 1780's tens of thousands of Virginians and Carolinians flocked into the Georgia upcountry (mostly to Wilkes County on the northern frontier), tripling the population of the state in eight years.

Until 1785 the political domination of the tidewater planter and merchant was virtually complete and unchallenged.[38] Then, rather suddenly, the upcountry made its move to wrest a share of power for itself, and succeeded brilliantly.[39] Although continuing to have a strong voice in public affairs, the old leaders of the Assembly after 1785-1786 never regained undisputed control of the Assembly, and their monopoly of state offices was forever lost.[40] This striking shift of power and leadership from one section to another makes well-nigh irresistible the temptation to see in the embryo

[38] The members from Chatham County alone held well over one third of all committee positions. Every governor, every speaker of the house, every chief justice, every attorney general, every treasurer excepting one, and every Continental delegate excepting three was either from Chatham or Liberty County.

[39] "Journal," Feb. 1785; Jan.-Feb., Aug. 1786.

[40] Three of the last four governors and two of four speakers, 1786-89, lived beyond the tidewater. There was a similar shift in committee positions.

sectionalism the appearance of real political parties, with all that that implies.[41] It would then logically follow that the shift in Assembly leadership simply reflected the increase in number of "Country Members"[42] as settlers poured into the frontier. But this will not do. The upcountry members had a majority in the Assembly from the start, both on paper and in fact.[43] Furthermore, the nineteen powerful leaders were dominant figures in the Assembly whenever they were present, regardless of sectional alignments. Almost without exception, each became a leader as soon as he arrived in the Assembly and remained a leader as long as he was a member of it. The legislative careers of upcountryman William Few and tidewater's James Jackson are particularly striking examples of this.[44] It is only slightly overstating the case to say that the upcountry assumed a greater share of leadership in 1785-1786 because men with the necessary qualifications of leadership had come to settle the Georgia frontier.[45]

Although there is no very satisfactory biography of any of the nineteen leaders of the Georgia Assembly, and none is possible for most, the available information suggests two or three of the more obvious factors that helped to boost them to the top of the ladder. All, of course, were on the "right" side in the Revolution; most had been leaders of some sort in either a military or civil capacity. That there was also a connection between a man's family and his success as a politician even in so new a place as Georgia seems certain. Through the scanty personal records of these men runs the persistent thread of the familiar eighteenth-century consciousness of family bonds and of family responsibilities. Anyone who runs his eye down the roll of the House must be struck with the recurrence of such names as Gibbons, Houstoun, Habersham, and Heard. The long list of assemblymen who were in some way or another closely related to the royal

[41] The shift is illustrated by the changing ratio of the number of Assembly leaders from the tidewater to the number of Assembly leaders from the upcountry: 1783, 8 to 3; 1784, 9 to 2; 1785, 5 to 5; 1786, 6 to 7; 1787, 6 to 5; 1788, 3 to 4; 1789, 2 to 7.

[42] Joseph Clay to Ralph Izzard, Mar. 12, 1778, in *Letters of Joseph Clay*, p. 68.

[43] The four counties up the river were entitled to 40-43 seats; the four on the coast to 32, and the upcountry members outnumbered those from the coast in actual attendance by an average of 7 men a day.

[44] In 1782 Jackson was a member of 16 committees; in 1783, 31; in 1784, 22; in 1785, 12; in 1786, 33; in 1787, 12; in 1789, 18. Few was appointed to 17 committees in 1782; 50 in 1783; 38 in 1784; 30 in 1785; 38 in 1786; 6 in 1788; and 23 in 1789.

[45] Five of the six upcountrymen from Wilkes among the 19 leaders did not become leaders until after 1785, it is true, but they were not members before that time, and four of the five did not come to Georgia until after 1780.

governor, James Habersham, to Sir Patrick Houstoun, or to the old rebel Jonathan Bryan,[46] bears out the importance of family ties and of family status in raising men to places of political eminence in eighteenth-century Georgia.

The "Gentleman of Family"[47] was also a man of means. All nineteen of the leaders under discussion were well-to-do, and some were rich. However, what is more arresting if not more important is that most of them were doctors, lawyers—men of education. The three upcountry leaders, Edward Telfair, William Few, and Stephen Heard, were men of knowledge and of experience; they were perhaps the only really qualified upcountrymen prior to 1785. And the leaders of the Assembly from the tidewater were all men of some learning. Unfortunately there is no record of the level of education in Georgia in 1785, but it is likely that an educated man was a great deal rarer than a man with "family" or with wealth. Abraham Baldwin, who came to the Georgia frontier directly from Yale College, was elected to the legislature as soon as he satisfied residence requirements, and he became an important member of the House on the day of his arrival there. Besides his natural gifts he had nothing to offer but a superior education.[48]

The model young politician would have courted planter Gibbons's daughter, got himself a big rice plantation near Savannah, and studied law up East. And if he had had to choose between the three, he perhaps would have been wise to go East. Joseph Clay, one of the leaders from Savannah, got to the essence of political success in his day when he spoke of public officials as "Men of Abilities & Capacity and Fortune."[49] The Houstouns, the Gibbonses, the Habershams had family, wealth, and education; Telfair had family and wealth; Baldwin had education; and James Jackson and William Few started out with none of these. But what they all had in common was ability and the capacity for leadership.

These nineteen men who had a commanding voice in the affairs of Georgia's House of Assembly must take a large share of the credit, or the blame, for whatever the government did or did not do to cope with the problems which pressed in upon the people of the state in the 1780's. The

[46] Fifteen, many of whom were leaders, can be immediately listed.

[47] William Pierce's "Notes in the Convention of 1787," in *Documents Illustrative of the Formation of the Union of the American States* (Washington, 1927).

[48] Henry C. White, *Abraham Baldwin: One of the Founders of the Republic and Father of the University of Georgia, the First of American State Universities* (Athens, Ga., 1926).

[49] Joseph Clay to Henry Laurens, Oct. 16, 1777, in *Letters of Joseph Clay*, p. 49.

development of suitable institutions of government and the reorganization of a society turned topsy-turvy by war, independence, and prodigious growth claimed much of the time and talent of the leaders of the House of Assembly. Like all good revolutionists they learned early the value of law and of respect for law in establishing their new regime,[50] but as practitioners of republicanism they were not so quick to see that adherence to the principle of the supremacy of the legislature did not mean that the legislature should in fact monopolize all the functions of government. That they finally did see it, however, is borne out by the radical changes made in the relation of the legislature to other parts of government shortly before and after 1790. The governor became a real executive, unfettered by the council and vested with the power of veto.[51] In a reformed judicial system, the judges were allowed to operate the courts with greater independence and efficiency. County courts manned by local justices with a longer tenure of office and state courts with two or more circuit judges replaced the old courts under a single justice.[52] Local government gained new strength when the legislature turned county administration over to the new inferior (county) courts and left most local matters to be attended to by them.[53] Georgia, like some of the other states, had found its initial experiment with state government unsatisfactory.

Many of the above changes were made in the new constitution of 1789, the year that the Federal Constitution was first tried. In drawing up a new frame of government for the state, the men in the constitutional convention at Augusta certainly benefited from their knowledge of the Federal document and undoubtedly from the experiences of other states; but without their own experience as leaders in the House of Assembly they might well have failed to recognize the need for changes or the efficacy

[50] One of the main characteristics of this post-Revolutionary period is the constant attempt of the legislators to justify and enforce their actions by claiming for them the sanction of the state constitution and of English law and custom. When the Chatham leaders entered the secretary's office in 1786 and carried off some of the public papers, they argued that they had acted properly because the governor had exceeded his authority under the law which authorized the transference of the papers and because the law itself was unconstitutional. John Houstoun, et al., to Mr. Johnston, printed in the *Georgia Gazette,* Savannah, Apr. 17, 1786, and reproduced in the *Georgia Historical Quarterly,* II (1918), 214.

[51] *Constitution of 1789,* Article II, Sections 6-10.

[52] Watkins, *Digest,* pp. 389-407. This is the basic judiciary act from its passage Dec. 23, 1789, until the adoption of the constitution of 1798. In practice, the local judges were usually given life tenure.

[53] *Ibid.,* pp. 305, 405, 424, 425, 434, 443, 451, 453-454.

of these particular changes, for Georgia or for the federal government.[54] Even though many of the drawbacks to the system of government under Georgia's constitution of 1777 were as evident and their correction as obvious as those in the United States government under the Articles of Confederation, evident weaknesses are not always recognized, obvious changes are not always made. The leaders of Georgia were showing signs of political maturity, and even of statecraft.

The tactics of the leaders on the floor of the House of Assembly in the 1780's provide the plainest signs of their growing mastery of the art of government. The basic organization and procedure of the Assembly were not, of course, invented by the Georgia planter and frontiersman; but the minor variations which these leaders worked out to increase the efficiency of the House and to make it more easily manipulated attest to their ever-increasing political sophistication. One sign of this was their tendency through the years to place more and more business in the hands of standing committees, another was the timing of elections for state and local offices by the legislature; but for our purposes the growing political dexterity of the Assembly leaders is best illustrated by their changing attitude toward the election of the Executive Council. At the beginning of the January session the House chose two members from each of the counties entitled to ten or more seats to sit with the governor in an advisory capacity. At first the leading men of the Assembly were chosen;[55] but after the more astute politicians came to see that, with all its impressive title, sitting watchdog over a toothless governor was poor sport, they usually refused to serve. When the House turned to the less important men in the county delegations for councilors, it found that the delegations had become reluctant to part even with their less active assemblymen. Of the sixteen men elected on January 9, 1786, ten were absent and four of the remaining six were from counties which had no absentees to elect.[56] With the nose of a practical politician for the location of power, the Assemblyman shunned the hollow honor and thereby sealed the doom of a useless institution, clearing the way for the creation of an effective executive branch of government in 1789.

[54] For the leader's part in ratifying the constitution, see "Minutes of the Georgia Convention Ratifying the Federal Constitution," ed. E. M. Coulter, *Georgia Historical Quarterly*, X (1926), 223-237.
[55] *Constitution of 1777*, Article V; "Journal," Aug. 17, 1781; Jan. 2, Feb. 1, 1782. These included such men as Jonathan Bryan, Charles Odingsells, William Gibbons, Sr., Benjamin Andrew, and Stephen Heard.
[56] "Journal."

The House of Assembly succeeded in bringing the government outlined by the constitution of 1777 more nearly in line with the actual requirements of the state after the Revolution. The men who led the way had the ability to perceive both the need and the means of adapting political institutions and practices to the demands of the time. This political sense also made for success in devising measures for solving the immediate and pressing economic problems confronting the citizens of the state. The acquisition and distribution of land by the House of Assembly, it is true, brought forth in its leaders a fair share of greed, selfishness, dishonesty, and plain stupidity. The loyalists and the Indians certainly felt the arbitrariness and injustice of some of the Assembly's actions. The settlers occasionally suffered from the discrimination and ineptness of the laws. And the politician often enough showed his dishonesty and satisfied his greed by using his position in the Assembly to gobble up large tracts of land.[57] But the problems centering around land also brought into play a fair measure of self-denial, imagination, integrity, and intelligence in the make-up of the leading men in the legislature. The loyalists were harshly treated, but the policy was mild enough so that by 1789 one pardoned Tory and the young son of another had become influential assemblymen.[58] Land was taken from the Indian, but it was done by purchase and freely negotiated treaty as well as by coercion. The land laws, while not perfect, were sufficient to distribute land in the space of five years, in an orderly and efficient manner, to perhaps twice as many people as were living in the state when the land office opened in 1784. With all of its shortcomings, the House of Assembly succeeded in laying the groundwork for a society in Georgia which grew rich and powerful when cotton became king.

Whether related to matters of policy or of government, the questions which the leaders of the Assembly had to answer and the problems which they had to solve were practical ones and their answers and solutions were what they conceived to be practical answers and practical solutions. Under the pressure of events in a strenuous time, the leaders sought the workable and the effective. By this common-sense approach to their task the men in the House of Assembly brought order and stability out of violence and confusion; they prepared Georgia for statehood in a federal union.

[57] A hint of the scandals to come in the gigantic land frauds of the 1790's is discernible in the tax returns for Wilkes County as early as 1785. *Early Records of Georgia: Wilkes County*, ed. Grace G. Davidson (Macon, Ga., 1932), II, 13-70.
[58] Thomas Gibbons and Josiah Tatnall.